THE CARDS WILL TELL THE STORY

THE POSTCARD CENTURY

2000 CARDS AND THEIR MESSAGES

TOM PHILLIPS

Thames & Hudson

Rima started opening, one after another, the drawers of an oak filing cabinet, 'You seem to surround yourself only with the past. Furniture, vases, first editions I can understand. But postcards! why postcards?'

'No you've misunderstood. It's newness that I collect', said Vellinger, 'objects that were when they were made or issued bang up to date, the latest novelty. Postcards always celebrate topicality, events and things of the moment, and that's why they whisk you back in time so perfectly. Nothing is more nostalgic than the modernity of the past.'

HWK Collam
(from Come Autumn Hand, Chapter XI)

To Hansjörg Mayer for over thirty years of support & encouragement & ever more valued friendship.

First published in the United Kingdom in 2000 by
Thames & Hudson Ltd, 181A High Holborn, London WC1V 7QX

First published in the United States of America in 2000 by
Thames & Hudson Inc., 500 Fifth Avenue, New York 10110

British Library Cataloguing-in-Publication Data
A catalogue record for this book is available from the British Library

Library of Congress Catalog Card Number 00-101171

ISBN 0-500-97590-6

Designed by Tom Phillips
Production Supervision by Narisa Chakrabongse, Hansjörg Mayer,
Paisarn Piammattawat and Suparat Sudcharoen

Printed and bound in Thailand by Amarin Printing and Publishing (Plc) Co., Ltd.

Frontispiece : Rarlor Series 16 Des.

November 28th 1918. Glamrhyd in Venice to Miss Liza Davy in Newquay,
Hope you are having a good time at New Quay now. It's grand out here. You
will miss the Flying men now the war is over. No more walks.   Fig. 1

PREFACE

The Postcard Century is not a random title. Firstly this book celebrates a century throughout whose entire length the postcard has been in popular and current use. It may well happen the twentieth will be the last as well as the first century of which that might be said. It is hard to imagine that anyone will be sending (let alone collecting and delivering) so physical an object in 2099.

Secondly it tells a story (not of course the only story) of those hundred years both in pictures and in the words that, in so many different hands, accompany them.

It can be seen as a composite illustrated diary in which nearly two thousand people have made their entries. Each card and each message is both a captive and a witness of its time and, as with any true diarist has no benefit of hindsight.

Any other hunter gatherer of cards with different preferences and interests (not to speak of prejudices) and different luck in his or her quest would have assembled quite another sort of journal.

The cards I have searched for are those that have in their pictures or messages (and ideally in both) some special flavour of their time. High history vies with everyday pleasures and griefs and there are glimpses of all kinds of lives and situations.

The book is more an account of people than of events. It bumps into history as a ball on a pin-table hits or misses, by hazard. The march of the great moments of the century is sometimes heard far off and at others is documented by eye witnesses. There is no equivalence of occasion and person; great happenings are often recounted by humble bystanders and trivial occurrences related by the privileged.

This is a selection made from over ten thousand cards I have collected for the purpose: those ten thousand were selected from what must be going on for a million I have searched through.

The part played by chance in such an enterprise is both annoying and beneficial. As an example, a long sought-after postcard relating to the Gulf War arrived after I had finished the body of the work. Prefaces and Introductions are invariably written last and therefore it appears here as Fig. 50.

November 27th 1944. Mrs Herman Kemer in NY to Miss Elizabeth Curnan in Saratoga Springs, *Thanks for your card. Would be interested in 15 new cards from you, for the same number from me. Or - could you send me 1 used foreign card for 2 new cards (though not foreign). Either exchange would be acceptable. Thanks! Rose H Kemer.* Does this card indicate Mrs Kemer's advanced tastes or is it just a free hotel card used to inaugurate the real business? Card collecting from its boomtime at the start of the century was now very much a minority sport. It took art quite a long time to catch up with the classic purity of this view of the Hotel Phillips. The uniquely American alchemy by which a black & white photograph becomes this crystalline abstraction has no British counterpart.

Fig. 2

October 10th 1973. Adrian Henri in Los Angeles to TP in London SE5, *an example of infinite regression - a man buying a postcard of a man buying a postcard of a man etc. etc. Thanks for the catalogue & the invites. I'm just here for a week. love Adrian.* I'm not sure this really is a man, but the small child seems to have already found a card to his (or her) taste.

Fig. 3

INTRODUCTION

Like many artists I have always collected, or rather amassed, postcards. For quite a lot of my career I have used them as source material for painting. Those I did not use grew into piles and found their way into boxes and drawers, waiting a turn that would never come. About twenty years ago I looked at this accumulation and played with the idea of making a diary with a postcard representing every day of the century. A quick look through the first box or two convinced me of the folly of this since, as I should have guessed, most cards are sent in the holiday months which would have made November or February quite a struggle.

Ten years later the millennium started beckoning on the horizon. It seemed to ask the practitioner in every field 'What is your millennium project?' and straight the answer came: to revive my initial scheme (it seems to have been called at one time, in Churchillian fashion, A Postcard History of the English Speaking Peoples in the Twentieth Century) in some more practicable form. I looked again through the cards I had, and was surprised by how far they left me even from the starting line. They had been acquired with no regard to their messages, and many were unused.

Yet the project haunted me and sometime in 1996 I set about the task in earnest. Like so many enterprises lightly undertaken it turned into an obsession; what had been escapade turned into quest, leading me into a nether territory that I had scarcely imagined.

I have spent the last three years or so in one of the most eccentric worlds I have encountered. It would take a Dickens both to describe its locations and to characterise its denizens.

Most of the cards shown in these pages were bought at Postcard Fairs (an excellent cameo of such an event is given by a correspondent in 73r). These occur weekly in various municipal centres, sports facilities, church halls, stadia and racecourses. This alone gives one a rigorous course of study in civic architecture of the fifties and sixties, as well as an intimate acquaintance with their car parking arrangements and the characteristically ethnic nature of their refreshment.

At monthly intervals a substantial fair takes place in London in the brutalist interior of the Royal National Hotel and larger fairs are organised throughout the year, some lasting two or three days, in Leeds or Nottingham or York and among the neo-fascist stands of Twickenham Rugby Ground. Every pursuit has its Lower Depths and in the world of postcard collecting the bottommost circle is found every Saturday in the dank concrete bunker called Charing Cross Collector's Market (also inhabited by coin and stamp dealers as well as the pushers of that latest of collectibles the phone card). This is strictly for recidivists.

It would be inaccurate to say that all postcard fairs take place in bleak wasteland, far from real life and ordinary amenities: there are of course exceptions. The Bexhill event is held in the famous De La Warr Pavilion (see 76e), one of England's few Modernist architectural masterpieces, and London's chief annual mart (The Picture Postcard Show) has as its venue the well-proportioned, and centrally situated, Horticultural Hall.

Such fairs take the form of any other market with rows of stalls (referred to as tables) on either side of gangways inviting a snake-like progress through the lines. Each dealer's table is laden with long coffin-like boxes in which are filed, under various headings, his stock. Some dealers keep their better cards in unwieldy albums with multipocketed plastic leaves. Since new material of any quality is hard to come by (and tends to disappear before ever reaching the filing boxes) a regular visitor who lacks a plan of action might easily find himself ploughing through the identical cards he looked at a month before.

Although I tend to use 'he' and 'him' as a convention to avoid 'he or she' etc. there are women dealers and women collectors, though they are vastly outnumbered by men just as the young are outnumbered by the elderly. It is a hobby that, like all hobbies, desperately tries to attract the young. One suspects however that, as with bowls, it is eternally serviced and sustained by the over sixties who come to it after retirement.

The majority of those who attend postcard fairs are collectors of topographical cards, usually of their own locality. Others search out a particular subject. These can be broad categories like Advertising or fields so narrow as to make it unlikely that any new acquisition could be made. One collector might ask for postcards featuring corkscrews, another goats. Once his obsession has become known to the traders he only has to be seen approaching to be told whether they have a newly acquired card, put aside for him, featuring Teddy Bears or Wurlitzers or Snowmen. If not he is hailed with words along the lines of 'Nothing for you today, Ron'.

There is certainly no category so obscure that it has no collector nor any topic which, once hunted for, does not yield in the end a surprising quantity of related items. The man who collects goat cards for example has over seven thousand of them and, looking through his collection, one soon comes to believe that few cards are produced which do not include some appearance, however oblique, of a goat... one peers at a picture of a stolid alderman and yes, there on a badge on his regalia, in a small quartering, is a goat. But obsessions are obsessions and the specialist in question does indeed have a tuft of white beard. He tours the world with his wife who collects postcards relating to tea. Cards representing goats drinking tea pose a problem.

All human activities soon develop their own hierarchies and the runners, who comb street markets and charity shops for postcards and bring their finds to recognised dealers, represent the lower ranks. The marshals of the field are those who only have gleaming albums with acid free mounts and whose very demeanour freezes away the more humble punter (who is unlikely to find a postcard in their immaculately ordered stock under £20 or $30). They produce glossy catalogues illustrated in colour in which each card is described with an expertise comparable to that of a dealer in antiquarian books. By and large these fine and rarefied wares were not for me since almost all their chosen items were pristine and unsullied by the degradation of postal use. Only once, from a sumptuous American catalogue worthy of a dealer in Fabergé eggs, did I buy such a card for this book (58a) which, being modern and used and having a 'small bruise at one corner', was priced at a modest $30. Its rarity and relevance and charm won the day.

These are the final arbiters of value and the words Postcard Collecting do not belong in their literature, for they are Deltiologists. This term was invented in America to hoist a hobby from the junkshop dust into a vocation and a science. It is an innocent enough invention confected from the Greek and as legitimate in the end as philately, since the ancient Greeks had neither stamps nor postcards. But it has stayed resolutely on the US side of the Atlantic. I use it in this book to designate to what one might call heavy-duty experts and expertise: there are as yet no English enthusiasts who refer to their pastime as deltiology. The more obviously derived French term cartophilie (a bastard etymology) has failed even to cross the channel.

May 25th 1905. GL to Pearl Agnew in Durban, Natal (a punctilious girl who writes its date of receipt, 16th June), *so glad to have your letter & cards. Playing here this week. Hope you are well & everything going straight.* This is the type of card (even if not a Real Photo) that most of the throng at a Postcard Fair are seeking, i.e. their own locality in days gone by. Here, a stone's throw from where I write is the Grand Theatre, Peckham, a casualty no doubt of the cinema's growth. Two people are just entering for the matinée of the Grand Christmas Pantomime, presumably late in 1904. Much though I was pleased to find this card I would have been more excited to find one of the Odeon and the Labour Exchange that replaced it; or the huge Job Centre that replaced both (to celebrate British Film Year) in 1985.　　　　Fig. 4

August 23rd 1915. Anon in Angola, Kansas (still a mighty small place on the map) to Luke Williams in Baltimore, *Yesterday I went to Oklahoma. It was a delightful drive... Today is the first time it has rained since I am away from home.* The fabled goat collector would have no trouble filing this, but there are probably onion collectors and farmhand collectors too. Kansas collectors however should beware. The card was published in Waupun, Wisconsin by the enterprising Stanley Johnston to be overprinted with the name in red of any place that would buy it. This kind of card, called in the trade an Exaggeration card, is peculiar to the USA.　　　　Fig. 5

BEFORE THE LAST MAN DIES
AND ALL THE TREASURE IS SPENT

With acknowledgment to St. Louis Post-Despatch, U.S.A.

August 22nd 1950. Agnes in London to NJ Hart Esq., W.S.F. Congress c/o Town Hall, Folkestone, *Dear Norman. Not knowing O'Leary's address I have written asking Keith to send it to you (O'Leary is not an F.U. member) Thompson was in yesterday He is coming to your Conference & will pay you the lot when he arrives. Best success to you.* This card issued by the Federal Union used a cartoon from the St Louis Post Despatch proposing a United Europe. On the back a quotation from Victor Hugo says he represents 'a party which does not yet exist. This party will make the twentieth century. There will issue from it first the United States of Europe...'. 1950 was early days to be reviving Hugo's idea though, in the month this was posted, Churchill had called for a European Army. The Common Market was still four years away and Britain's entry in to the EEC was in 1973. Such a card could be any price from 5p to £5. I found it in a 20p box at the Annual PTA Fair. Fig. 6

Maison Natale de V.HUGO   Maison Natale d'Auguste et Louis LUMIÈRE
1802   1862   1864

July 7th 1992. *Dear Mum & Dad,* write Pete & Tom from Besançon, *Thanks for the phone call. It was nice to hear from you. Glad... you're enjoying the summer weather over in Britain. This morning it seems that the lorry drivers have won and maybe they'll start going back to work. Tom finishes today for the school holidays... Take care.* Victor Hugo would have loved the epic possibilities of the film as first demonstrated long after his death by his neighbours the Lumière Brothers (who were to Cinema what the Wright Brothers were to Aviation). The card came from a box marked 'Moderns: all 5p' at the same annual Fair at the Horticultural Hall. Fig. 7

Whatever name it cares to give itself it is an amiable world and full of characters some larger and some smaller than life. It has its buccaneers and mountebanks and rogues, its badgers, moles and Mr Toads. There is enough of a Mafia to make it intriguing and a degree of honesty, trust and fair dealing that recalls some earlier age of innocence. There is a sense of camaraderie that is infectious, perhaps born from its character as a travelling circus. No matter how distant the fair you attend a core of the usual suspects, both of dealers and collectors, will be there as if some caravanserai of estate cars moves eternally through the night to pitch up with their piles of narrow boxes among the local traders of Penzance or Galashiels.

It would be quite wrong to imagine the punters to be a mere gathering of anoraks. Nerds there are of course, as may be found on the fringes of any pursuit, yet, amid the leaning searchers panhandling in the ranks, one spots the immaculately coiffured grey head of a famous operatic conductor, or the ascetically shaven skull of one of the world's leading modern art entrepreneurs.

Some traders are not by inclination part of this shifting circus but can only be found in their shops, or (visitors by appointment only) in some upstairs room in a dingy house in a road off a road that is itself difficult to find. Once again Dickens or Balzac would have to be invoked to provide the full flavour. However there are few kinds of shopping that bring forth more conversation and hospitality, for most who deal privately are themselves addicts supporting a habit via a little commerce. They invariably have their own specialised personal collections of unpurchasable treasures, as well as a fund of information always given freely.

Shops entirely dedicated to postcards are a rarity. Philately tends to be the subsidising merchandise that allows postcards to be indulged in. Here, as one can never do at fairs, one may sit down and go through a stock at leisure. One shop I have visited regularly has provided not only the characteristically congenial atmosphere but cups of tea and an ashtray and, over a period of two years or so I have been through that dealer's entire stock, from Advertising and Ayrshire to Zanzibar and Zoology, a whole wallful of mysteriously numbered boxes.

I have pursued these same trails through American fairs from a baking marquee in Orlando to a somewhat sinister hotel in New York, and have walked the long gauntlet of street markets in Paris, Milan and Berlin. Wherever my proper profession has taken me I have sought out the local representative of this far flung freemasonry, and been guided to the haunts of by now familiar transaction. Indeed I have made it a condition of giving a lecture or participating in a conference that there would be some possibility of following the postcard trail. I volunteered for instance to speak at my exhibition in San Marcos, Texas, knowing that I was armed with the address of a nearby dealer.

To my dismay he said he would be unavailable that evening. His stock was all packed up, he explained, for he was the guest dealer at the deltiological society in another part of town. Yet, immediately, he rang back to suggest that I be his guest at their soirée. This involved me and my own long suffering host in a backstreet adventure trying to find the local Veterans' and Ex Servicemen's Club (a venue that had an English enough ring to it) and, thereafter, a very odd three hours which included an immensely specialised lecture on vending machine returns at the World Columbian Exposition. The talk was illustrated with slides of cards virtually indistinguishable from one another (to the uninitiated). Yet I got to see the dealer's stock and found the Private Breger card I had been looking for (44s).

Such intriguing forays lead one into parts of towns that are authentically about their own business where one might still receive that welcome to a stranger that is denied to tourists. How else would I have got to see a whole street in St Louis whose trees were inhabited by dozens of pale home-made Halloween ghosts. The postcard is the alibi; the quest is all. Where else might one expect to find the earliest known card sent from Eastbourne (to Vienna, in 1895, see Fig 23) than in an austere private dealer's apartment in Milan? That I was there at all and had pounced on the card with glee (even though it was highly and correctly priced by a knowledgeable expert) meant that I had become, if only for a while, a postcard twitcher.

The other route to sought-after cards was via the auction house. By and large this is more precarious since, unless one actually attends the auction, one does not see the goods in question. What was an intriguingly murky reproduction in a catalogue can spring to disappointing and expensive life when it arrives on the mat. British auctions take place in inconvenient places like Bournemouth, Nottingham, Croydon and Cirencester. Auctioneers' catalogues, even those of the most diligent, do not feel it part of a card's description to indicate whether it has a message of any interest, unless it had been sent from the Titanic as the ship went down (a use which would for once increase rather than diminish its value). Nonetheless I have made one or two good guesses and got rich returns, as in the case of a large carton classified as 'Saucy postcards, postally used, mostly 60's & 70's', which turned out to contain a sequence running from 1951 to 1977 from (and occasionally to) Fred & Jean who year by undaunted year savour the dubious delights of various holiday camps (Fig. 8). Actually attending auctions and their viewings involves an acquaintance with a whole new set of all too likely locations (disused church, theatre bar etc.) but there, peering through the boxes and albums, or bidding in the room, are all the faces you have come to know.

Having, by getting my numbers confused, travelled all the way to Cirencester to buy the wrong card of the Titanic (later swapped for a better one, see 12a) I decided to stick to the postal end of bidding. Some postal auctions are so tiny that there are scarcely fifty lots. A regular treat is the arrival from America of Barr's Postcard News, a newspaper-style gathering of mini-auctions accompanied by coarse-screened black and white (mostly black) illustrations. Although the pages are enlivened with excellent articles from the likes of Lewis Baer and Roy Nuhn, the meat of the matter is the listings of the largely part-time dealers. The style of the paper retains a homespun American look so unreconstructedly old-fashioned that you could mistake it for a catalogue of agricultural machinery from the twenties.

Ringing up people in remote parts of America after midnight English time and suddenly to be in part of a room with children, a distant ballgame on the TV and the noise of dinner plates being put away was a never failing delight. Telephoning from so far away gave me a sort of status in itself as I heard Elmer or Chuck say, 'Doris, it's a guy from London, England!' to his wife. It was by this means I got hold of a batch of cards sent home from Europe by Max Church in World War II. The sequence gives a unique perspective on that experience, followed by a moving peacetime coda, a card whose short message could be expanded into a novel (47r). They were offered to me (as a result of attempting to buy something of the same type) by one who styled himself, very much in the character of that periodical, Old Mr Postcard.

I am too unpractised a cybernaut to take full advantage of the internet's various buying stations and as yet have only successfully managed a single purchase (albeit from Australia). Perhaps I have been

"WHEN I PUT A JIVE RECORD ON, SHE MILKS HERSELF —ALL I HAVE TO DO IS—HANG ON!"

A 'BAMFORTH' COMIC

June 22nd 1960. Fred & Jean in Weymouth to Mr E Crook in Sunbury on Thames. One of their cheerier bulletins from a Holiday Camp, *Dear Dad, Just to say we are having a much better time now. We have made friends with a couple of Londoners & they are real cards. Lots of love.* The image comes from the late fifties. The disc on the Dansette (?) portable record player is, judging from the sleeve shown, a skiffle number performed by Lonnie Donegan who played and sang with Chris Barber's band, to whose music I also jived in a Greenwich dance hall in 1956.   Fig. 8

July 1st 1945. Max Church on service in Weimar has appropriated some German propaganda cards (see 45a) and sends one to his father in Detroit. This is no 264 of the daily cards he has sent home. The War is over, but not his duties, *Hi Dad, I went on our trash truck to the dump today. I saw something I won't forget for some time. There were crowds of people there & when the truck stopped they would all rush aboard & grab the bread out of the garbage, then they go through the trash & pick out the cigarette buts & other things, Max.* The picture by favoured war artist Schnürpel shows an infantry grouping at Sebastopol.   Fig. 9

25th March 1984. Janet & John in Peking to Lady SH in Pulborough, *A good start to the holiday by being hi-jacked! In your papers perhaps? terrific excitement at our end of the world because of tricky political situation - Red China - Free China HK. Off we went to Taiwan, where we were surrounded by soldiers, police, ambulances, arc-lights, the lot. for 8 hours - not entirely pleasant but the chap who wanted to blow us up was arrested so all was well... we missed over a day of our Peking tour as we had to return to HK. Then all passengers sitting near the chap had to give statements (that included us) - what a palaver. Now we are enjoying the tour & hope to see the terracotta warriors of Xian. Do hope your barking nephew is giving you no trouble...* Did the Wright Brothers dream of a flight to Peking or imagine a hi-jack? A card from a box marked 'Foreign, used, 5p'. Fig. 10

June 9th 1909. Mr & Mrs A in Dayton, Ohio to Harold P Sloeman in Chicago, *How would this do instead of a pony?* Wilbur Wright was back in America by the time this was posted from the brothers' home town. In a month Bleriot would fly the Channel. It needed their triumph in France (see 08a) for the Wright Brothers to become news in their own country. J B Miller & Sons published this card sometime after that event but still described the Wright Flyer as an air ship. Sketchy though it was the Wrights' first plane was built with aesthetics very much in mind. Fig. 11

spoilt by all the added intrigue and interest that various human encounters have given me.

Luckily journals like Barr's make less of a distinction between old cards and those produced since World War II. The paucity of material from recent days made me more reliant on friends as time marched towards the present. The most recent years of all had of course hardly come on to the market except in lots found at Oxfam and various charities. Only a few categories have seeped through the dyke that protects the worshipful old from the flood of the modern. Royalty, Holiday Camps, Aviation and 'TV related', now feature in the selections of some quite staid dealers. The low value (5p - 20p) put on modern cards of most types, especially when used, still tends to make them unprofitable to deal in.

Two or three friends helped me enormously by letting me have all the cards they had ever received. Many others either supplied odd cards they had found lying around, or persuaded friends of theirs to surrender their accumulations. One or two scoured boot sales and market stalls for me wherever they were. The list of such enablers, supporters, scouts and foragers is long and they are incompletely listed and inadequately thanked as a legion d'honneur under Acknowledgements. For myself it became a no-holds-barred campaign of vigilance. When visiting the homes of friends, or their places of employment, no pinned up card in works canteen or bar was safe from my predatory gaze.

THE MYTH OF THE GOLDEN AGE

There is a generally held belief in postcard circles that cards ceased to be of interest sometime around 1940 or even earlier. This of course is a slowly moving frontier and has crept begrudgingly towards the fifties even during the period of my search.

The mythical Golden Age has stayed where it is, finishing around 1920. A Silver Age of adjustable length now can be discerned trailing after it like a comet's tail.

American collectors are more elastic, perhaps because their sense of history is more compressed. US publishers kept to the original size for a longer period (into the seventies and beyond) than their British counterparts, who moved to the larger and now universal continental size (the 4" x 6" card that you now see in most racks). British postcard traders, however, are more reluctant to accommodate in their conveniently sized filing boxes any intruders, however interesting, even though some of such cards are by now half a century old.

This is what, in part, led to the difficulty of finding later material, a dilemma that put the canons of deltiology in question. In one sense, and not unwittingly, this book is an attack on the tenets of a faith, a polemic against the way the postcard is seen and understood by those who claim to have its welfare most at heart.

What I hope these pages prove is that the postcard is seamlessly interesting from the beginning of the century to its end. In all its history it has defined life rather than merely mirrored it, giving a more human picture of the world than any other medium. Postcards are crammed with random people, dressed as they really were at the time and behaving with that authentic inconsequentiality that makes everyday life so difficult to fake.

If one were seeking the vernacular aesthetic of a period the postcard is where you will find it. Here world documents itself in terms of the way it wishes to be seen. Because people vote for it with their small change its vision dare not risk losing the endorsement of the public in general. It is the least elitist form of artefact.

Somewhere along the line nostalgia conditions the market, though it is a dying generation whose memories now reach back to the so called Golden Age. Nostalgia, while seeming to be a virtue of postcards, is in fact their worst enemy. Postcards have always, as one of their main functions, celebrated the new. What we look at and think quaint, be it car or shop-front or skyscraper was at its appearance on a card the very latest thing. What you see in these pages is to a great extent a series of Latest Things, from Bleriot to the first moonwalker and from the original Paris Metro to Eurostar. The people on cards are wearing what is newly fashionable. In their homes, at leisure among modern furniture, they are using, or listening to or watching the latest device.

This much of postcard collecting is governed by the Nostalgic Fallacy so well described by Collam in the quotation that heads this introduction, 'Nothing is more nostalgic than the modernity of the past'. Collam's hero, the arch aesthete Vellinger, goes on to describe how, in looking at postcards, one 'must perform the continuous feat of seeing this urgent newness in the older pictures whilst imagining the future quaintness of present scenes. In this balancing act is the rich experience of a perpetual present and an eternal time gone by. Every card we look at can be in the same instant new and old'.

Though written in the forties this suggests a way of seeing that would give equal value to cards of all periods. It is an act of the imagination to see the views of modern Bromley (in Fig 13) as part of the remembrance of things past. It is also a way of keeping young in one's mind. Curiously enough the card, posted in 1988, already shows in the old-style parked taxi the first signs of maturity.

A visual conundrum is presented by retrospective cards, i.e. reprints in modern format of old images. They are almost entirely banished from this book. Paradoxically, by negating their original texture and characteristic feel, their publishers have by making them new, robbed them of their original modernity. From this dilemma came one of the agonising problems of assembling this book, for it is ridiculously easy to get a new image of Marilyn Monroe or Elvis Presley and extremely difficult to find one posted when they were still alive. Old photos of the Beatles are reprinted by the million yet the flavour of their up to dateness is only captured by a card like 63a with its message that would now be impossible to write except to someone on Mars, 'Have you heard their records?'.

A similar problem hovers over current views which so often try to capture an unspoilt corner of a village or a landscape uninvaded by present day machinery. This is the quest of the picturesque, another enemy of the postcard. Worship of it (the error of the Heritage industry) encourages a failure of nerve, the assumption that we can no longer do things well. The picturesque assassinates the present with the past.

Printing techniques date very quickly. One by one they fall out of use and it is thereby relatively easy to identify a period. This fact can add layers of absurdity to Olde Worlde images in which people dress in past costume and walk about (in Williamsburg etc., see 83h). In no card does the postcard technique look so much at odds with the subject, announcing it as doubly fake. It cannot be long (and there are already intimations) before colour printing achieves the resolution of those black and white photographic cards which can be examined for further detail under a magnifying glass. This will establish a new realism to replace the succession of realisms that have already been

Beach Studies (The Pier), Eastbourne

October 3rd 1904. *Dear Mother* writes L.E. to Mrs Morton, also in Eastbourne, *Please will you send me my knife in the case as soon as you can. I am just going out for a walk. With best love.* We must assume the knife and the walk are not related. The performance of photography was now less complicated and these paddlers, candidly snapped, seem oblivious of the camera. An eternity of seaside photos is born.   Fig. 12

BROMLEY

March 23rd 1988. To David (a charity figure who tried in the eighties to get into the Guinness Book of Records for the largest collection of postcards) in Luton, *Dear David. This is where I live (Bromley). It's a very nice place. Love again from the Old Granny.* If the granny really is old then she has some flexibility of mind, for she sees Bromley's latest additions as part of its being a nice place. The entrance top right to the Civic Centre reminds me of the windswept path to many a postcard fair.   Fig. 13

Filey Edwardian Festival - 28th June to 6th July.

Photograph by Max Payne ©

July 10th 1997. Anita Gwynne in Sheffield enters the Evian competition affixing the necessary coupons and giving her answer to the quiz question, Water. She chooses a card sold in aid of a hospice, one of a series, and sends it to Plymouth. There is no fakery here but the pitfalls of the new revisiting the old are well illustrated since the attempt to look Edwardian is thwarted by the newer technology used. A real Edwardian of course, after the initial shock of the printing method, would soon point out anomalies of style in dress and deportment, as in the man in this group. One glance at the cut of his jacket, the hang of his trousers, the wearing of a sleeveless pullover with a blazer, the knot of the tie and its clashing colour would have him arrested as an alien time traveller. Ironically the card was printed by ETW Dennis in Scarborough who were printing postcards a hundred years before and whose heyday was in the era being here genially but unrigorously imitated.   Fig. 14

2859   LYNEHAM R.A.F. STATION

September 8th 1953. Les & Hilda in Chippenham to Kate Sinfield in Sleyning, *Just a card until we get home to let you know that we arrived safely in Eric's car & quite a good journey down. Weather is mixed here it is fine this morning & we are going into Calne as we have not been there before. Last night we went to Bingo at the village hall & Barbara won a prize a set of baking tins our turn on Saturday we hope. John & I went to football at S on Wednesday & enjoyed the game. Eric went to see a friend of his at Melksham. Well all the best for now...*   Fig. 15

accepted. Just as we can learn to see the newness of the objects and prospects in old cards we can stretch the mind to see as 'realistic' the antiquated printing of previous decades. Realism can then be appreciated for what it is, an aspect of fashion and style.

The postcard world owes a special debt to those in the early years of the century who collected modern cards and kept them in good condition for another generation to enjoy. The assertive modernity and the realism of their images as well as the advanced design of their graphics was precisely what seemed to make them most worth preserving. Thousands of messages on the backs of such cards ('another one for your collection' or 'here's the latest card for you album') testify to the early collecting craze. The best way of repaying this debt is to value the cards of today with the same zeal.

BORING POSTCARDS

A book entitled Boring Postcards (Martin Parr/Phaidon Press) recently revisited (perhaps unknowingly) a territory explored in the seventies in an exhibition, Wish You Were Here. The catalogue of this show included Richard Morphet's magisterial essay on the postcard aesthetic to which I later replied with a further text called The Postcard Vision. Parr's book might just as well have been called Gripping Postcards in that it reproduced many of the seminal images that so influenced artists at the time and which contained many of the seeds of minimalism, installation and performance art. Pop art had similarly used many of the characteristics of postcards in the previous decade (Richard Hamilton and Peter Blake being obvious examples).

There are of course cards which seem to be competing in some obscure contest to attain absolute featurelessness as if there were an esoteric plot on the part of publishers to equal Samuel Beckett in spareness and Andy Warhol in dumb absence of event. My own contender (Fig 15) for the Challenge Cup of Dullness has as its most lively point of interest the lettering of its caption. Over ninety percent of the rest of the image is taken up by either an almost undifferentiated grey sky or land unvisited by incident. The small band of action towards the bottom of the picture is itself dominated by long low buildings of impressive monotony. Yet there is a state of visual inertia that is nonetheless imposing. Each time I come across this card I find myself admiring more and more its truth to experience and pictorial daring.

The message on the back has something of the same character, a perfect cameo of life's lesser dealings in 1953. No uprising is mentioned nor national festivity, nor is anything of special interest alluded to; but again absorption in its nuances and minutiae brings a moment and its actors to life.

In that respect it is typical of many of the two thousand or so messages transcribed in this book. The mere action of copying them out yields more information than at first sight appears to be there. Ripples of disquiet beneath the surface, hints of the larger life of which they are mere shards, combine with telltale signs of character and mood.

THE MESSAGES

The postcard was the phone call of the early part of the century, the mode of making arrangements, placing orders or just keeping in touch. With up to five deliveries a day local cards were amazingly fast ways of communicating: it is not uncommon to find messages written at lunchtime to say the writer will be late home for tea.

Even when the phone existed as a reliable appliance it was mainly installed in offices, as more recently fax machines and computers have been. As late as the fifties it was largely a middle class phenomenon. International calls were quite a performance involving booking in advance and fairly punitive charges.

At the very dawn of the century the postcard was still a novelty and one senses that it was considered quite sophisticated. Its use spread very quickly, especially below stairs. Indeed, one of the most common functions of cards after 1902 was the exchange of news between members of a scattered family, each in service at different places. Almost as common are the greetings from old colleagues of domestics who had left their posts. Strong emotional bonds are found in the sisterhood of girls in service.

One reason for the growing popularity of the postcard was the small demand it placed on the writer in an age when schooling, for most people, was over at the age of fourteen. A letter seemed to require a rigmarole of formality and correct layout that daunted the untrained, but almost everyone could manage a few words on a card. It was also cheaper and carried the bonus of a pleasant or interesting picture.

The postcard message while being informal developed its own prescription and tacit rules and, rather like haiku, contained necessary elements. The greeting, the weather, health of writer, enquiry as to health of correspondent, signing off; such was the standard pattern, either enough itself or forming a safe basis for permutation and variation. It can be seen to be the skeleton of almost all cards to this day whether they were posted on holiday or from friend to friend, relation to relation or neighbour to neighbour (cards are often sent from just a couple of streets away).

The example of Max Church, the American serviceman, has already been mentioned. His sequence of daily cards deals with these conventional topics, yet also recounts the growing up of a callow youth into a man who, in the space of a single and singular year, was exposed to the privations of a battered and impoverished Europe, the glimpsed horrors of Buchenwald, the culture of Paris and, it seems, the confrontation of his own sexuality.

Another sequence from World War II had already been widely scattered throughout the postcard trade before I came across it. Card by card I acquired (by enquiry and legwork) a fair sampling of the regular postcards sent to Kath, an evacuee, from her father in London. He describes the blitz at first hand and, in the restrained fashion of the time, conveys the pain of separation (Fig 17).

Each would deserve a book to itself since I can only afford a glimpse of a glimpse. Other voices in these pages are heard more than once (especially those of Fred & Jean the inveterate campers) but largely the messages are isolated and their context of incident and relationship has to be inferred. A whole hinterland of tragedy can be discerned behind a few words, or the curtain can briefly rise on a scene of joy and celebration.

Before the telephone comprehensively took over the territory, courtship was a natural province of the postcard. What now is breathed down the phone, left on machines or e-mailed, had for half a century to be committed to the card, often sent to the lover's home where the prying eyes of parents or siblings or servants might see it. Couples of course developed their own private languages but the final mode of obtaining privacy was a code. Some of these were primitive,

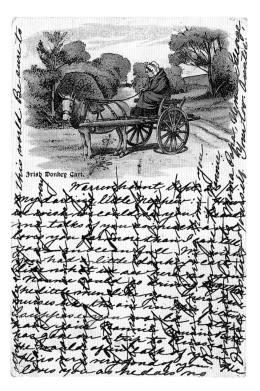

September 21st 1901. Master Willis Wilmot's Auntie is visiting Ireland and sends him a card to New Orleans. Her use of cross writing is typical of early American writers of cards and is not at all difficult to read if the script is well schooled (though little Willis may have a bit of trouble). The message is as inconsequential and rambling as any phone call might be from doting adult to small relative, *Warrenpoint. My darling little Nephew:- How we wish we could see you. Grandma talks of you so much and loves you more than I can tell you - an ocean full. We wish you had a little donkey cart like what we see here as you and Nannie could go driving together. The little men like you here have nurses like this one in the picture. I suppose you would rather have your Nannie. Cousin Bert has gone on a trip to Russia. He would often talk of you. He loves you as he does no other boy in all the world. Be sure to say your prayers every morning and every evening till Auntie gets back. Be sure to write me right away what little thing you want me to bring home to you. Remember me to Nannie. Fondest love to Mama, Papa, Henry, George, Dollie, Sister and yourself your lov. Auntie.* Willis's eyes may have glazed over somewhat at the bit about saying his prayers but he would have perked up at the idea of a present (noting the cautionary word 'little'). Fig. 16

"LONDON UNDER FIRE" CORNER OF KING STREET, ST. JAMES. 86873

September 25th 1944. Mr West writes from London to his evacuee daughter Kath in Harrogate, *Dear Kath - Hope you are well - we have had nothing to worry about but still have an alert now and again. It rained all yesterday and is cold this morning. E [her older sister Elsie] had a loverly time at the dance. Lots of love, Dad xxxx.* Typically, Mr West plays down the dangers of the War even though their own house, it would seem, had been bombed. Fig. 17

March 9th 1909. Jenny writes in code to Sapper D Taylor on a card depicting policemen helping a soldier to reach the top of a wall to give his sweetheart a kiss. Translating the simple cypher is here only slightly delayed by Jenny's incomplete mastery of it, *Dear Dennis, Does anything like this happen at C or G? I have got a touch of fleu. I shouldn't want a copper to help me should you? How do you like G now. The slush is awful here. Fond Loves to the best o boys.*

Fig. 18

October 6th 1916. From Somewhere in France and on the back of a French village view whose name has been obliterated by the censor G writes to Lance Corporal Flint of the Artists' Rifles in Romford, *Many thanks for your interesting letter and also for your ripping snap of the Zepp. Congrates for getting one up. Best of luck in your new stunt. Will certainly write to both mentioned in letter. Leslie appears to be rather unfortunate after all, being medically unfit for a Com. in any case for the Infty... Write again soon. Cheers. I am in the pink.* Zeppelin raids began in 1915 and concentrated on the South East of England.

Fig. 19

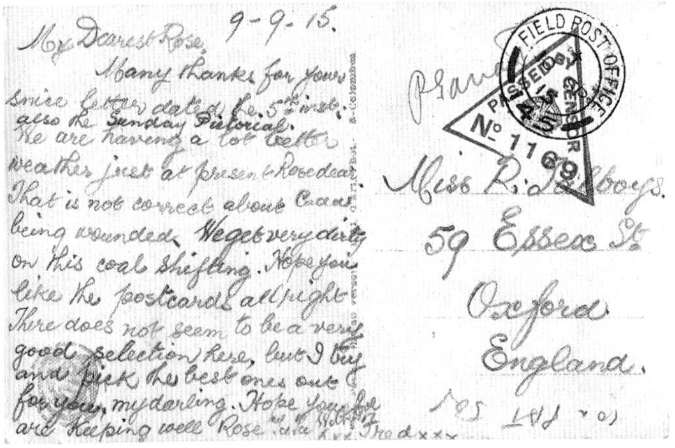

September 10th 1915. Also from Somewhere in France to Miss Talboys in Oxford. *My Dearest Rose. Many thanks for your snice letter dated the 5th inst. also the Sunday Pictorial. We are having a lot better weather just at present Rose dear. That is not correct about Cudds (?)being wounded. We get very dirty on this coal shifting. Hope you like the postcard all right There does not seem to be a very good selection here, but I try and pick the best ones out for you, my darling. Hope you are keeping well Rose Ta Ta with love xxx Fred xxx.* The card is of the tinted French romantic type similar to 16n. Written in the usual indelible pencil.

Fig. 20

like backslang or mirror writing, but more elaborate cryptic devices were frequently published in magazines and were eagerly adopted (also wisely in the case of 03p). Once women took their place in business shorthand could fuel an office romance. Even when codes were not used (or the simple strategy of signalling endearments by the position and angle of the stamp) one sees time and again the old method of writing the message upside down in relation to the address. This was meant to avoid the gaze of all but the nosiest of postmen.

To retain the full flavour of messages they are, throughout the captions of this book, transcribed as they appear with all their disjointedness, eccentric spellings and wayward grammar. No expletives are deleted in later cards nor any political incorrectness adjusted in the communications of any period. What always seems remarkable in older messages is that they often carry on without any help from commas or full stops (my mother used to write virtually without punctuation which I thought eccentric until I started reading the backs of postcards). Some messages whose words are purely conventional are paraphrased. Many, however, are given in full, though routine greetings and signings off are largely omitted. Where the text is shortened the omissions are indicated by dots. In all other respects the texts are merely copied out, often after long staring at impenetrable handwriting. The pleasure of suddenly being able to read a word that at first sight looked like a string of m's followed by an unattached loop is almost as great as the moment of suddenly overhearing a real voice or being party to a revealed fragment of someone else's existence.

As with domestics, absence is a constant theme and no separations were more brutal than those occasioned by war. These are among the most touching notes, especially in those cases where the chirpy words of a World War I soldier are darkened for us by the knowledge of his imminent death. Sometimes the tension can be electrically felt as the weary serviceman wets once more the point of his indelible pencil and confines himself to the few phrases allowed by the censor. From *Somewhere in France*, he gives his formulaic reassurances from a rat-infested trench that, *all is A1,* and he is *in the pink.*

In an ideal (though infinitely more cumbersome) world all the written sides of cards would be reproduced since much of the flavour of a message lies in its script and layout, but some sense of that variety can be tasted in the earliest years when messages were restricted to the picture side of the card.

The range of messages apart from the obvious themes already mentioned only gradually reveals itself to give a panorama of human activities and emotions dealing with everything from a lost glove to the explosion of the atom bomb. What is just as absorbing is the steady change in usage and language as twentieth century shifts in English unfold. Even though later technologies affect the number of postcards sent (after their heyday as the world's most efficient and popular mode of communication) the messages, allowing for new freedoms in language, do not in essence differ all that much. Eerily, as the changes are rung on standard phrases, the novelists and poets of the time are evoked (by what after all is their source material) and we hear voices from Hardy, Wharton, Bennett, Wells, Runyon, Chandler, Beckett, Murdoch, Pinter and an Amis or two. All these and others are echoed as the more stilted early cards are gradually transformed into the letting-it-all-hang-out manner of younger cardsenders at the end of the century.

This is not the place for analysis of such matter, but one example tells the tale well enough. If one takes the current words for expressing enthusiasm about someone, somewhere or something they replace themselves at fairly regular intervals. Old terms vanish never to reappear. Roughly in order of appearance they are *Capital, First Class, Topping, Ripping, Excellent, A1, Grand, Top Hole, Spiffing, Smashing, Marvellous, Super, Stupendous, Fabulous, Terrific, Fab, Ace, Sensational, Brilliant, Brill, Awesome, Wicked;* all of which can be reinforced by *awfully, absolutely, jolly, really, pretty, utterly, bloody, dead etc.* and permutations such as *pretty bloody terrific.* Similarly endearments undergo fashions over the years though my favourite will always be *Yours to a cinder xxx* (frequently found in the twenties). Cryptic expressions of affection or desire occur in acronyms whose meaning can only be guessed at but one assumes might occasionally be hotter than the most often used favourite S.W.A.L.K. (Sealed With A Loving Kiss).

In the spirit of structuralism one could reduce this volume merely to the list of the names of the senders and recipients. Put in chronological order these would tell a story in themselves, a random core sample of habits of naming over the last hundred years. As the century proceeds into living memory I have suppressed identities to offer privacy to those whose cards have drifted my way or have been offered to me to use. Nonetheless the christian names of individuals and couples seem to date the message with almost as much certainty as the postmark. Could there ever have been a couple circa 1900 who signed themselves *Nikki and Elvis* or might there be one in 1999 who could end with *loving greetings from Horace and Madge*? Fred & Jean seem completely at home in the middle of the century where we in fact find them. Some individual names are particularly relishable but of all the girls I would like to have met I must choose Philately Holtgreve, who appears in 1934.

THE HISTORY OF THE POSTCARD

It is hard to imagine an earlier mention in literature of the postcard, than that by Francis Kilvert who in his diary for Tuesday October 4th 1870 writes, 'Today I sent my first post cards, to my mother, Thersie, Emmie and Perch. They are capital things, simple, useful and handy. A happy invention'. The Post Office Act of 1870 permitted the first Post Cards to go on sale on Oct 1st. Kilvert, a thirty year old country curate living in Wales, was very quick off the mark. Coincidentally it is only the day before that he makes one of the first references to the dawn of air mail. 'Oct 3rd. How odd, all the news and letters we get from Paris now coming by balloons and carrier pigeons'.

It was this beginning that was celebrated in 1970 (see 70p). However, these Post Cards, handsome though they were (and indeed more elegant than their Austrian counterparts issued a year earlier) lacked any pictorial matter. The USA followed suit in 1873 with their own official postal cards. This set the precedent of unwrapped mail and represented the first milestone in the evolution of the picture postcard. Virtually a quarter of a century of debate and dithering lay ahead in both England and America while European countries quietly established the pictorial card as a genre. Germany led the way with illustrated greeting cards depicting resorts and tourist sites. These almost invariably feature the words Gruss aus (Greetings from) and allow space for writing on the picture side. They were the models on which most early cards were based.

In 1893 The World's Columbian Exposition took place in Chicago and America's first official picture postcards were sold there (largely from vending machines). Luckily Chicago was rich in immigrant German printing expertise and the results were impressively produced by chromolithography, a high quality colour process.

Chips in Sofia is clearly at the end of his tether. He even puts the date when he is going to be back (December 26th) rather than the actual date, clear on the Bulgarian postmark as 13th December 1906. His message seems to rain down angrily on the theatre whose facade he has defaced with hanged figures and the slogan HOME SWEET HOME, *Dear Nell* he writes to Elsie Nobel in Charlton, SE London, *This is the last of my cards now, so will be the last from this hole, thank G. Will of course send you one or two en route but I may get home before them, that doesn't matter does it. Cannot tell you the day yet, patience my dear and it will come along in a letter. How did the (?) go off, all right rotten or nicely thank you? Will make the best of this card being the last would write inside the theatre only ??? not open yet. The town would not accept the Electric light instalation, serves them right if they can't stand a joke, what do you say? Come home! Oh, alright, give me a chance to pack my things up and say goodbye to my sweethearts and (?) does not matter which. Have just done 5 mins work and I am tired so I sit down to write this now I find it is dinner time so will just finish it as I go to the grub shop. Here I am calling it names. Grub don't know what it is these last 3 months am as thin as a match and cannot get fat no matter how much I try will try harder this next two week you bet. What ho, my time is drawing near now 13 days from now at the very outside. So good bye dear letter - tomorrow best love to all yours ever. Chips. P.S. This is a Chinese Puzzel.* Fig. 21

May 2nd 1995. Janet & Tony to Mr & Mrs B in Horsham. *On our hols in Weymouth. Weather up to today been good but it has rained all to-day. Have been to Monkey World (for rescued chimps) and Abbotsbury Swannery.* In order to chime with the picture postcard's centenary the card takes some liberties with dates. The girls on the left look much more like early twentieth century bathers, and daring for their day (see Fig 12). Remarkably enough the publishers, Bamforth & Co., who entered the postcard business in 1902 could have produced both images from stock. Fig. 22

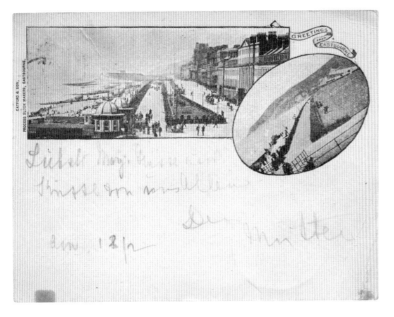

February 12th 1895. To Fräulein Mizi von Gasleiger from her mother in Eastbourne wishing her *Grüsse und Küsse from us all*. One of the earliest picture postcards produced in England, printed by Catford & Sons, soon after the picture card was officially allowed. Fig. 23

September 19th 1900. From Dot in London E.C. to Mrs A M Raphael, South Tottenham, *My Dearest Et. I do hope you are getting on all right, how is little 'Coo' Love from your affec. sister Dot.* Posted at breakfast time, Et could have been reading this over her lunch at 1.30pm, admiring the new range of colour postcards by Raphael Tuck & Sons. This, printed in Saxony, is the first standard size colour picture postcard issued in Britain. The view of the Tower of London is one that has changed very little. Fig. 24

A year later the picture postcard in Britain became legitimised. Unlike the Chicago Fair examples these, which started emerging towards the end of 1894, were dingy affairs. They were not helped by the strange squarish format insisted upon by the Post Office. The example here of such a Court Card (as they were referred to) is typical. It can hardly have lured many to the delights of Eastbourne though it shows views that are still current, especially the famous Carpet Gardens (see 55s). It also adopts the German formula 'Greetings from Eastbourne'. Significantly it was bought and sent by a continental visitor no doubt already used to finding view cards wherever she travelled. She must have been disappointed by the smudgy printing even as she consigned it to the post box on February 12th 1895. It reached its no doubt equally unimpressed recipient in Vienna on the 15th.

The excellent Picture Postcard Annual has for a number of years been collating earliest posting dates from all over Britain and this is one of only a handful of surviving cards sent in those first few months. With such lacklustre production it is little wonder that the picture postcard was not an instant success.

Popularity had to wait (as evidenced by the same tables) for the real coming of age of the British Postcard in 1899 when the Post Office finally capitulated to the standard format allowed by the Universal Postal Union. Raphael Tuck & Sons immediately issued a full colour set of London views. The first of these, and in a sense the first true British postcard, was a view of the Tower of London (fig 24) complete with Beefeater.

Thus the beginning of the century virtually coincides in Britain with the advent of the regular shaped postcard, and, as can be seen, the postcard cliché was born with the medium: one can still buy a current card at the Tower of London featuring a general view with inset Beefeater.

Only one restriction remained that separated the century's earliest cards from the standard versions used today. This was lifted in 1902 when senders of postcards in the UK were at last permitted to write on the same side as the address, thus liberating the whole front surface for pictorial use. America followed suit in 1907.

The rest of the postcard's history can easily be traced in this book. The format of Tuck's London views remained standard until well after the World War II. A second, larger but squarer type gained currency in Europe which the USA was slower to adopt. Towards the end of the century all regulations seemed to relax and outsize cards appeared. Gargantuan cut-outs sprang up in the 1990's spelling nightmares for the neat storage systems of collectors. Fortunately these still have only a novelty status and the basic postcard size has held its own thanks in no small degree to its adoption by Freecard publishers. These marvellous receptacles of memory, bearers of image and carriers of news still seem what Kilvert called their ancestor in 1870, 'a happy invention'.

DATING THE CARDS

In the upper reaches of the deltiological world where collectors put the highest value on cards virtually untouched by human hands, dating an item is problematic. With the photographic variety a great deal of expertise has grown up about types of sensitised paper and their identifying signs. Unused cards are often dated by collating them with examples that have lost their virginity in the post.

For the purposes of this work the date given is that of a card's postal use There are many clues available to support conjecture when postmarks are unclear. The best of these of course is a handwritten date in the message from more diligent correspondents. Sometimes a postmark slogan may place the date within an Exposition or around some key event like a Coronation. The content of the message may help with the mention of some specific occasion ('we saw Apollo 2 lift off') and even talk of deep snow in London might (usually) help decide whether a faintly indicated month is September of December.

Postmarks are wayward things that can emboss their way right through to the other side of the card or give its surface a diffident kiss of ink. They can usually be deciphered, though one has to remember which way round they put the month and the day in different countries. Alarmingly, in Thailand what seems a pleasant sixties view of a street or temple turns out to have been sent, according to the postmark, in the year 2519.

Stamps can be of great assistance though not so much in the years before inflation was invented when both design and the rate of postage might remain static for decades. Modern life has seen to that. The ever accelerating cost of postage gives a useful bracket of time. The odd sedate commemorative stamp was quite an event in earlier years but towards the latter half of the century the hitherto unexploited philatelist was singled out as fair game, and stamps on both sides of the Atlantic now succeed each other at intervals of sometimes less than a month. The smaller the country (and there are some states like San Marino that only seem to have a philatelic identity) the more frequent, larger, and more lurid the stamps.

On the assumption therefore that most people use a not too obsolete stamp this can give a good lead. In the very first years of the century, however, even a change of monarchy did not disturb the sender. In distant British colonies stamps depicting a young Queen Victoria were still in use five or six years after her death.

A real Sherlock Holmes would have consulted weather records to correlate 'terrific downpour between Ipswich and Colchester this lunchtime' with a fuzzy postmark to deliberate between the 13th and 18th April, but I confess that having weighed all reasonable evidence I made in many cases an educated guess. Over 95% of the cards are of an unequivocal date.

THEMES AND SUBJECTS

Postcards provide the world's most complete visual inventory. Few things, people or places have not at some time or other ended up as the subject, or an unwitting or unintentional component, of a postcard.

In the fairs already described dealers have settled on a group of categories which enable them to impose some order on this plenitude. The litany of subjects is repeated in their trays and boxes all over Europe and America. Since there is a consensus I have usually referred to topics under these headings.

Almost all these categories are represented somewhere in the following pages. My own interests and predilections (not to speak of prejudices) play a part in my choice yet I have also tried to keep a special watch on certain themes as much as the chance nature of the availability of material has allowed. These are the role of women, the development of the aeroplane and the automobile, and the rise of cinema. Also an eye has been kept open for architecture and fashion.

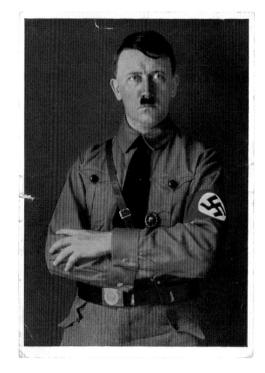

ST in Germany to Mrs WF Turner in Honeywell Road, London SW11, *We had a glorious hot day yesterday - to-day is freezing cold & likely to rain & real English weather Helga is off at the last minute what a blow I shall never recover Elsa cannot explain very well in English something about his wife cannot come - shall ask waiter at café to find out for me. H.H. is here for a week - stay with Frau Wagner. love. ST.* The photo is a classic Hoffman image of circa 1932/33. The message written in pencil had been erased but was decipherable in raking light. The 15pf Bismarck stamp was partially removed and unfortunately took with it the date and place of posting (BE remains on the fragmentary postmark, which could well be Berlin, and an 'a' at the bottom). The slogan part of the cancel is complete, enjoining the recipient to support the Hitler Youth (with a picture of a hut). A clear pencil date 1937 seems a later addition in another hand, though nothing is incompatible with that as a year of sending. I would have guessed a date of 1935/6. What is of course completely unrecapturable is Mrs Turner's reaction to this image two or three years before the War. And what its fate was in the years up to April 2000 when I bought it at a London fair from a Worthing dealer?   Fig. 25

Mr Chas Albert Kays in Cumberland, Maryland receives from Vera in Miami this highly datable card on which the American Post Office have confirmed back and front that it was sent on the correct day, as already implied in the inscription, and received in Washington the day after. Ambiguity is further removed by a special Air Cancellation and the presence of the 5c Air Mail commemorative stamp. Vera writes, just in case Chas hasn't got the point, *Thought you might like this as a souvenir.*   Fig. 26

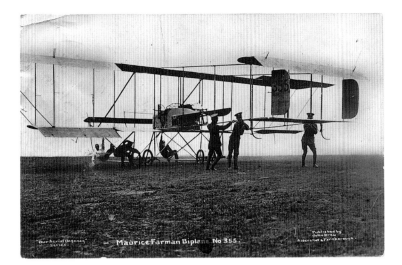

July 4th 1914. Aunt Daddles to Master W J Baker, The Beacon School, Crowborough, Essex, *I am sending you this post-card of a biplane. I saw 12 aeroplanes flying at Aldershot on the King's Birthday...* Aunts and Uncles, as will emerge in these pages, are good at choosing the right cards for the growing boy and girl. The skeletal elegance of the Wright Flyer still characterises Farman's plane. But war is only a month away and by December less fragile-looking German planes would be dropping bombs on Dover and aerial warfare will have begun in earnest. Fig. 27

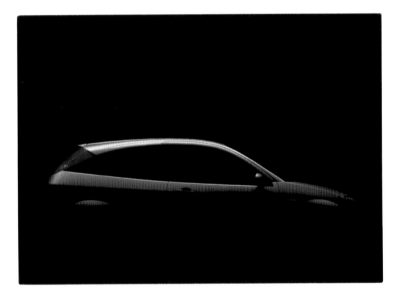

December 30th 1998. David Johnson responds to the Star Trek Quiz in the Radio Times. The question would pose no problem for a Trekkie since the answer is Captain James Tiberius Kirk. Though less graphically artful than 10a, this advertisement follows the same format that has served Ford Motors for ninety years; i.e., show the car clearly without any distracting elements. What would a Model T owner, or even Henry Ford himself, think if given a sudden future glimpse of this Ford Focus. Fig. 28

FEMINISM

Women were of course invented before the beginning of the century but the realisation of their proper role in society and their acquisition of rights has been perhaps its most important single development. From a voteless, socially subjugated and legally disadvantaged condition in 1900 to the ambiguities of the post-feminist state in the 1990's it has been an epic tale that here, inevitably, has to be conjured from a sequence of telling fragments. Needless to say it is not only the images that tell the story but the content and style of the messages which speak, in sum, so eloquently of the relations between women. In some small way the easiness of communication via the postcard (as well as its use as a propaganda vehicle) has played a part in the long process of emancipation.

AVIATION

The stirring story of flight is coterminous with a century which began with empty skies and ended with ailing satellite stations and talk of litter in space. Concorde as it streaks overhead still looks new but was built only sixty years after the Wright brothers convincingly demonstrated to the outside world the possibility of controlled powered flight (08a). There is as yet, amazingly enough, no really substantial study of aviation postcards. Collectors however have long known that with respect to the early years of flight the postcard provides the most comprehensive pictorial coverage. Aviation was initially regarded as a sport and early aviators were more photographed than any other kind of sporting hero. Every flying machine and every wrecked aircraft became a postcard and in the messages on such cards are hidden eye witness accounts of many feats and tragedies.

OTHER TRANSPORT

The automobile was also born with the century speeding from 3 to 300 miles per hour in 3 decades. Singly, in groups and in jams it is seen in every urban card. The postcard was and is one of the primary methods of promotion for the motor industry, from the advent of the Model T Ford (see 10a) to its distant successor the Ford Focus which in 1998 is advertised in a graphic mode as stylistically distant as the vehicles themselves. No better social indicator could be found than the two saloons advertised in 33p & 33q.

The comic card gleefully covers the rise of the automobile, its uses, abuses and related snobberies and itself provides a sociological history of succeeding models and their drivers.

The train, and truck, the boat and hovercraft all make their appearances and the London bus becomes a familiar sight around Eros as type succeeds type from the horsedrawn Tilling to the conductorless buses of today. I confess to not being a maritime enthusiast and in this book ships most often tend to sail into view when they bear messages that reinforce their interest.

THE CINEMA

Also born with the century was the cinema whose first (often almost furtive) appearances, mixed in with other entertainments as a sideshow (Fig 29), gave no intimation of its future as the dominant artistic and entertainment medium of the century. Motion Picture stars replaced stage actresses as collectable faces and in their wake came a seemingly endless series of the Hollywood homes of film celebrities, as well as a succession of pictures of stars signing their footprints on the Pavement of Fame outside Grauman's (later Mann's) Chinese Theatre (an essential rite of passage into superstardom).

In random fashion the cards in this book also collide with the cinema via the films being shown at the London Pavilion in Piccadilly Circus. These include, as well as run of the mill cinema fodder, such landmark features as Blow Up, Nanook of the North, A Hard Day's Night, The Graduate and Quatermass (as well as the odd James Bond). However, it is the sudden view of a suburban Picture Palace that stirs my memories of a thousand and one nights of youthful movie-going, especially in those years when Granadas and Majestics had ceased to be the lit-up magnets of their district (Fig 30). For the cinema was always modern, and films were the safe currency of conversation, as they are in those messages which speak of arrangements to see this or that picture or merely 'going to the flicks'. For a very long period the latest film was the most vitally contemporary experience available to the average man, woman and child.

ARCHITECTURE

The local Odeon was also likely in any High Street to be the most advanced building to be met with until well after World War II. For the British at least, architecture was something that happened somewhere else. What we had was buildings, invariably anonymous. Luckily bad and good buildings carry equal rations of the story of their time. Each urban card if massively researched would reveal a tale of blighted careers, forgotten awards, local government scams etc. Every skyscraper on the New York skyline must hide a similar saga.

In singling out some of the century's most influential buildings it is no accident that the book begins with a major new exhibition space, the Grand Palais in Paris, built with all the stylistic rhetoric of its own day, and that it approaches its end with the equivalent construction of the 1990's, The Guggenheim Bilbao, the finest song of structure and surface of that decade. At intervals throughout the century it is the Exhibition/Exposition that has given architects a special license to make radical constructions with innovation as part of the brief. Unluckily the century ends with the least attractive of them, London's Millennium Dome (or technically speaking, tent). This fails to recapitulate the excitement of what London offered exactly halfway through the century in the Festival of Britain, or indeed any of the other signature buildings of International Expositions.

FASHION

Fashion, like architecture, is everywhere present and also divides into specific and accidental encounters. Even though there are cards that feature individual fashions, almost all inhabited views show what is the prevailing dress for different climates or occasions from ball-gown to beachwear. The latter makes the full cycle from total cover up in 1900 to almost nothing at all in 2000. Fashion is also a perennial theme of comic cards which usually show the latest outrage in women's outfits and, very occasionally, an outburst of male peacockry. Year by year rebellion is signalled in the way women dress or do their hair. Shock is registered by apoplectic fathers, and dazzled approval by young men.

Fashion advertisements show the vertical journey from haute couture, via the big store to the rag trade equivalent of Tupperware which promises that for a few dollars you will walk out of the clothes party looking like a million.

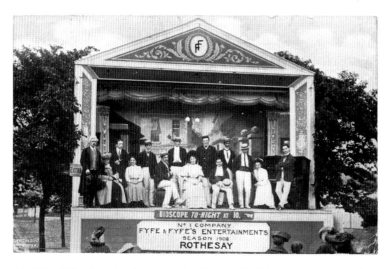

July 13th 1908. FR playing the season in Rothesay with Fyfe & Fyfes writes to Sam Ventura (who has a name redolent of the Halls and the Pier) in Holloway, *So glad to hear that things are looking up although the weather has again turned against us. Hope it gets fine next week as the Glasgow Fair commences then - its the time to make money, at least 'clear something' off the bad weeks. Have no more news so must conclude...* The novelty of the cinema (Bioscope To-night at 10) seems not to have entirely eased the fortunes of this troupe.
Fig. 29

July 22nd 1967. Andrew Tack writes to John Keatly in Mindford, Norfolk, *I thought I would have heard from you when you were coming up here... so drop me a line won't you... job is great with plenty of women about so I am enjoying it.* The scene dates from 1955, still good times for the cinema though television is an ever increasing threat. Quite a routine bill at the Gant's Hill Odeon however, with Playgirl, starring Shelley Winters, and Taza Son Of Cochise, starring Rock Hudson. The design of all the Odeons in Britain was under the direction of Harry Weedon, sometimes referred to as the Lutyens of the High street.
Fig. 30

This Fashion Conscious Group
Featured in *Glamour* and *Woman's Day*
For BEELINE FASHIONS

March 9th 1965. Janet McKibbin sends a Beeline invitation to Miss Ruby Martin in Goshen, Indiana for 7.30 on March the 16th with the usual printed message, 'It will be a lot of fun seeing and perhaps even modelling the latest fashions. I think it is a terrific way for a few of us to get together.' She adds her own exhortation (Did she do this for everyone in order to personalise the messages?), *Come early so we can visit!* This is the archetypal sixties room. One knows the chairs, the carpet, even the picture, perfectly. See 66a to observe that little was to change in a year. Fig. 31

June 19th 1904. Aunt C writes to Master Randolph Maitland in Fife from Albany, Western Australia, *How Wd. you like to see people like this. We arrived here all well... had letters from Warwick all well. Much love to you all.* Master Maitland had probably never seen a face quite like this and the card was in all likelihood not meant to give the best impression of the Aborigine. Ninety years later the same face could serve to embody primeval wisdom and spiritual wealth. Fig. 32

Anyone who has designed the costumes for a play is only too aware of how difficult it is to dress a crowd convincingly: no one would mistake a stage crowd for the real thing. Any postcard of a largish group of people will show why. Even in those eras when fashion is at its most distinctive people contrive to look particular rather than generalised. Though you might put a date on a card as a whole, many individuals will be dressed as if for ten or even twenty years earlier (just as not everyone in a street crowded with cars is driving this year's model).

ETHNIC

What we do know about a crowd in a Western street is that they are not by the postcard trader's definition, Ethnic. Although I have had many dealings with ethnography (as found in museums) it is a term I have always had trouble with since it seems merely to mean 'people we find peculiar'. This does not appear to include ourselves, even if I, a Welshman, am talking to a Jewish trader. The assumption is that all those human beings so bizarrely dressed that one sees in Piccadilly Circus or on the beaches of Blackpool or Miami are, in some special degree, normal, whereas people of different colour and customs in faraway places are distinctly odd. My own response is to view all the people in this book as anthropological curiosities and all their activities as manifestly ethnic. The pure human being at uncomplicated ease in his environment, where all freakishness falls away, occurs rarely. The Australian in 66k is an example. Picture of his ancestors were, however, produced and sent in quite a different spirit, as in fig 32 where the message endorses the intention of the card. Certainly it would need pages of ethnographic detail (analysis of bonds of kinship, expertise in exotic dress, explanation of regalia etc.) to elucidate, even for me, the esoteric panoply of 69d & 69e. If it ever reached a postcard dealer's box in the Congo it would surely go straight in the section marked Ethnic.

There is a subsection that crops up in most stocks called Ethnic Glamour which seems to mean black women without their clothes on. This tempts one to question which are the greater anthropological curiosities, the subjects or their collectors.

For ultimate confusion in this realm one would have to go where the wires of race, design, ritual and location are tangled beyond any ethnographer's powers of analysis (see 75k).

ADVERTISING

Right from the beginning of its history those with something to sell or something to promote soon discovered the efficacy of the postcard. In America, as has been mentioned, the first real picture postcards were promotional and the total number sent afforded the Columbia Exposition not only a profit but an advertising mail shot with all the work done for free by those who put them in the post.

Almost every card advertises something if only the good taste of its sender. Resorts and beauty spots often add their self glorifying details on the backs of cards or, as in the case of Skegness, develop a marketing logo and a slogan (one of the first of such devices?) to tell you that Skegness Is So Bracing.

By the beginning of World War I almost every firm had its own postcard and many local traders sent out photographic cards of their shopfronts dressed all over for the occasion. Successful poster campaigns often had a lucky second life as postcards.

One of the smartest moves in advertising was to invest in a hoarding at a much photographed site. Consider the extra publicity gained by companies whose named products appear bright and large in Piccadilly Circus. Bovril led the way with their huge electric sign in 1910. Millions who had never been to Piccadilly Circus learned the name and soon were told, with equally illuminated firmness, that Guinness was Good for Them etc.

Services that involved correspondence to remind their clients of deliveries or appointments were quick to see the benefits of combining publicity with the necessary to & fro of mail. The hairdresser for example who thought to nudge a customer's memory could simultaneously tempt them with new stylistic inventions (72m). Restaurants and hotels, even theatres, offered complimentary cards to their patrons in tacit return for free dissemination. Some merchandising operations became postcard-based as in the case of home-selling ventures like Tupperware Parties. However nightmarish the prospect would seem of shelves full of yellow and azure plastic, the campaign has been a global success.

By the sixties and seventies promotional habits had changed. The new brand of advertising manager would hardly stoop to use a common postcard. In the nineties all was transformed again by the ubiquitous rack cards with their smart graphics and cryptic, ironic or oblique pictorial strategies (compare the Boomerang card for Selfridges, 99f, with 32a and 35d).

The two booksellers' advertisements below indicate the wide possibilities now open. Both Shipley's and Waterstone's issue their own cards. Shipley in the Charing Cross Road revisits the traditional shopfront card, which emphasises his individuality as a specialist seller of fine books on the arts. The giant chain of Waterstone's characteristically grasps the modern nettle in a card, that pointedly uses their website as their address.

COMIC CARDS

PC may be the standard abbreviation for postcard but it hardly suits the comic sort. They are there in effect to subvert correctness of any kind. Their job would seem to be to deflate pomposity, to undermine orthodoxy and to push against convention and taboo. The other, paradoxical, side of their coin is that by trading in ready-made prejudice they actually endorse its attitudes. In sexual matters, by verbal wink and pictorial nudge, they may even reinforce the taboo they mean to attack. Even so they have sometimes served to embolden the faint hearted to embolden the timid.

There are more comic cards in this book than I would have originally expected. Partly this is because of the frequently high level of their artistry. More often it is because in terms of the preoccupations and trends of the time the comic postcard gets there first. Whether it be the latest in fashion, television, pop music or even political change, the comic is always up to date.

In early years the photographic card responds to disaster and records it with astonishing speed. The cartoon artist, however, does not actually have to wait for anything to happen. He merely makes it up. It would be hard to find a picture of a television in any other form earlier than 35a.

Being the author of everything in his images he has to get things absolutely right; and of the moment. One false move with regard to dress, furniture, coiffure or car style and his work has no currency. No one's job is more literally on the line.

November 16th 1982. Linda Moentmann does not give Debbie Miller in St Louis, Mo. much notice for her Tupperware Party on the 18th but urges her to *Bring a friend and receive a special gift.* Still going strong (see 56n). Tupperware Home Parties no longer offer 'A work of art for 39 cents' (as Earl Silas Tupper described his original bowl) but, more importantly, some sort of social life for isolated wives.   Fig. 33

November 19th 1995. DS to TP in London, *Not an RP but very much in the high style, like the shop & you were right, it* **was** *here & not too expensive.*   Fig. 34

January 25th 1999. Jack Feldman in Watford enters the Radio Times 'Win a Health Farm Break/Weight Watchers', and uses Waterstone's free card.   Fig. 35

A dilemma for the book buyer. Do we have to forgo the one in order to have the benefits of the other? All the dot.coms of the world do not quite equal the learning and experience of a specialist bookseller, yet convenience, coffee and all the extras, are quite a lure. Something for Jack Feldman to think about at the Weight Watchers' farm (where, if he has won, he will, if he is lucky, lose).

The local cider seems very innocuous at frist but then it begins t...

August 23rd 1993. Michael in Taunton to Mr & Mrs F in New Malden, *sunny so far - forecast was wrong - cloudy, outbreaks of rain. There are several camp chores to do. So far I've done the cooks wash up. Tomorrow I'll be doing the shopping...* Besley is the last inheritor of a populist style of cartoon card and has an unerring eye for detail. (as in the determined rusticity of the table and converted barrel chair). Fig. 36

HE IS THE EGGMAN
goo goo goo joob

Greetings from ~~Liverpool~~ NEWCASTLE! ~~Beatle City~~?

February 25th 1989. D sends this card from Newcastle upon Tyne to Michael P in Wandsworth and only adds the words, *Gooble Wooble doo?* Mr Heseltine held many a tricky portfolio and the egg throwing incident of August 2nd 1982 (in Kirby when he was, thanklessly, Minister for Inner Cities) was only a prelude to other attacks. A few months after this card was sent he was sprayed with red paint by students supporting the Greenham Common Women. A colourful career. Fig. 37

This is achieved as much by what is left out as by what is put in. The photographer is at the mercy of what is there. Pity John Hinde's representative who had to make photos to prove that holiday camp life is one long round of smiling delight (72n etc.). He only has to enter a lounge and set up his equipment for at least one of its occupants to lapse into a stupor. The comic artist on the other hand draws his juke box, dresses his crowd in the latest gear and writes on a notice board the top bands of the hour (65r) with not a dowdy aunt or comatose adolescent to be seen.

For the same reason the comic card quickly goes out of date yet if it is a recyclable gag it can, like an ageing song, be reissued with all its elements revived. I am sure I met the splendid joke 'Bach's Organ Works' (69q) in a 1930's version with a more bashful couple passing a rustic church but have not been able to trace it. McGill certainly revised his bread and butter winners many times in a long career.

Least durable of comic drawings (though, as time capsules, often valuable for a book such as this) are those dealing with once burning political issues. Nothing is more opaque than an old political joke. The stalest bread on the table of humour is an unrecognisable politician dealing with a forgotten controversy accompanied by a topical caption which now reads like a verbal cobweb.

The universal figures of little man, nagging wife, nosy do-gooder, obtuse policeman, pompous official, querulous cleric are all still with us and were there among Chaucer's pilgrims seven hundred years ago. The poor evanescent politician, be he red or blue, fades to nothing as the years pass. Who in the next generation will remember Mr Heseltine and who even now could say when and where and why he had an egg thrown at him? Certainly more people will know the source of the caption (I am the Eggman) than its target. Heseltine (who even as we speak is stepping out of the limelight) will join Balfour and his Education Bill (see 03q) in the attic of historical obscurity.

Some cartoon cards rely on catchphrases from long jettisoned television shows or from radio programmes that boomed out of the giant sets of the past, or even from the music hall stage. Perhaps a gnarled hand belonging to one who remembers everyone saying, 'Bow Wow' (see 16s) is now turning these very pages. I myself vividly recall the now completely unfunny catchphrases of Tommy Handley's ITMA that in wartime made even my father laugh. Yet, despite the unrecoverable reference of the humour, Tempest's drawing is magnificently sure and Mrs X's message is of a frankness that puts most comic cards to shame.

It is the saucy seaside postcard that for many people still defines the genre. Early in the century the risqué joke matched the heightened spirits and lowered morals of a Wakes Week (when industrial towns especially in the North of England shut down in turn and their workers migrated en bloc to the nearest seaside resort) or, somewhat later, the statutory fortnight by the sea, or even a charabanc jaunt for the day. By the 1980's their time had essentially passed and the endless racks of ribaldry had started to disappear. The last posted card that I have in the classic small format (Fig 38) is appropriately a piece of broad bottomed humour in every sense and comes from the House of Bamforth (purveyors of sauce to the multitude throughout the century). The style makes it attributable to Arnold Taylor who first makes his appearance in these pages in 1929 and seventy years later in 1999 was hale enough to attend the opening celebrations of the Bamforth Museum in Holmfirth. The message symptomatically is brassier than the card itself. None of the successors of the lineage (Taylor himself was apprenticed to Doug Tempest) had brought new life to the comic PC and by 1990 its artists cast around in vain for any remaining taboo (91o), for life had by now left everything hanging out.

Newcomers had to find a different slant on the world as did Besley who emerged in the 1970's with his own brand of lugubrious humour. His cartoons tend to capture the blight of weather, traffic jams and a sense of alienation from things rural and coastal that reflected the decline of traditional holidaymaking. Perhaps the seaside postcard should have migrated, with its purchasers, to Torremolinos and Benidorm in the seventies.

The undisputed King of the genre is of course Donald McGill who first appears here one year after his postcard debut (06o) and bows out in the year of his death, in 1963, aged 87 (having completed his batch of cards for the following year). Not surprisingly his cards had started to look a little old-fashioned by the sixties but for half a century he kept his style flexible, even managing to accommodate to the poor paper, limited colour and ragged printing of World War II (I have not seen a single example of these austerity cards where the colours were in register; see 43m). The sheer application and quality of draughtsmanship that underlay his output can best be seen in what could be called his White Period around World War I.

He lived a quiet bourgeois family life in South East London and maintained an ingeniously innocent front with regard to his world of archetypes and their playlets of sexual innuendo. When on trial for obscenity in Lincoln in 1954 he claimed ignorance of the obvious hidden meanings behind his drawings, thereby putting the onus of impropriety on his questioners. Even with the notorious Stick of Rock, Cock (a self evidently outrageous piece of ithyphallic gigantism) he claimed it was merely one of a series of figures carrying large sticks of rock in various ways (see 14p).

What was more surprising than this last litigious stand of provincial puritanism is that, for the fifty years before, his work had not seriously been called into question. Indeed, a cartoon by Harry Partlett (who signed himself Comicus) issued sometime around 1910 makes McGill seem quite restrained (Fig 40).

So prodigious was McGill's output that George Orwell, in his famous essay, assumed the signature hid a whole cottage industry of comic draughtsmen. This lofty publicity only increased McGill's notoriety and his celebrity came to overshadow the skills and achievements of Tempest and Taylor and the gentler humour of Reg Maurice who were his equals.

The infrequency of competitive examples confirms the absence of a parallel tradition in the United States or any other English speaking country. Most comic cards in America are adapted from cartoon characters established outside the world of the postcard. Light hearted greetings cards abound and political cartoons can be both blunt and pointed, yet American postcard humour tends to be more purely visual. This can be seen from the running joke (which has been running for most of the century) of Exaggeration, where vast single fruit weigh down waggons and huge rabbits are hunted. Often these are local boasts (as to which State's apples etc. are the biggest). Variations on the theme exists in their thousands (see Fig 5).

Although no professional artists in the US seem to have made a lifetime's career with comic cards there was, during World War II, a group of largely anonymous servicemen artists, some extremely expert and stylistically individual (e.g. 42a), who produced cartoons of life in the forces. Private Breger who served in Europe and drew many of his cards in Britain (44r & 44s) is the outstanding case. He also

June 23rd 1989. From Lyme Regis to Miss W in Romford, *Bonjour Bots, How's it hanging weather here is good - I'm on the beach admiring some horny talent at the moment. Loadsablokes (I get off with a scouser called Adam) and we've met lots of talent. Is Jason still brain of Britain? Got to go got some talent looking at us luv ex-Wedge (Maddy) PS Work next Friday ok?* This is more or less the end of the line for the standard saucy seaside card. What was once thought to be corruption, and debasement of morals, turns out to have been innocence itself. Fig. 38

A Stick of Rock, Cock?

September 4th 1961. Fred & Jean are in Weymouth and write home to Jean's Dad in Sunbury-on-Thames, *Everything O.K. Still very hot. Saw a table-tennis demonstration last night with Bergman and the Jap World Cham.* This is the card that raised the blood pressure of watch committees and became material evidence at McGill's trial for obscenity. Fig. 39

January 11th 1911. From Leicester to J Marnott in Leamington Spa, *Dear Jim, Just a few lines hoping you are having a good time and plenty of money. Boxer is out of training for about a fortnight owing to an attack of Measles he took bad last Monday (certainly) is going strong. I see by the News of the World you made a draw last but you will have to do better to get the championships we managed to get into 2nd place from the bottom but the bottom club resigned so we are again at the bottom. The L's managed to win last Sat but it was a very poor game... I don't think the L's will win next week at Chelsea for they are getting worse... are you looking out for a fresh job its no use to you looking here for one there's too many out of work but you are not done yet there's many a slip you know. from your pal Ern.* The card's double entendre is outrageous as the two nurses discuss how they get by. At the extreme left a small part of another card appears showing how they were all butted up on the sheet for maximum economy of production. Fig. 40

August 6th 1912. GR in Streatham to Miss Rosie George in Winchester, *What miserable weather you are getting for your holidays I expect to go on home on the 19th but I hope it will be finer than it is now or else I shall have to stay in bed for a week for a change. You will see this is a photo of the big ship that went down I don't know if you have seen it before...* The last sentence sums up a world before newsreels, television and fully illustrated newspapers: an equivalent disaster vessel would now have been shown from every angle inside and out. Publishers of postcards reprinted their Titanic cards (and, with slight modifications, their cards of her sister ship the Olympic which this may well be) with the relevant details within hours of the news breaking. Fig. 41

produced comic cards while serving later in Korea but I have never been able to track down a used example.

Apart from occasional eccentrics like Glen Baxter (85r) whose cunning appropriation of a boys' story illustration style is coupled with subverting captions, the drawn cartoon has largely given way to various montage techniques. These which involve drawing, photography and graphic elements have become a universal genre for satirical cards practised in Britain the USA and elsewhere. Generally they are less merciful than mere caricature and recent American Presidents have proved easy targets. The advent of the computer as image laboratory has begun to create a new generation of artists and a new set of comic possibilities.

THE POSTCARD AS PHOTOGRAPH

Although photography provides the starting point for the majority of cards a clear line is drawn by collectors between the Real Photo and its printed equivalent, whose image breaks down under magnification into a maze of dots or squiggles.

Amongst those who specialise in topographical areas or the serious aficionados of film stars or trains the Real Photo (RP in postcard literature) is king.

Cards that bear witness to this or that disaster or celebration are mostly of such a type, as are those that portray the parts of towns unknown to tourism.

From early in the century images could be mass produced on photographic paper with the appropriate postcard back, hence the thousands of photo postcards of music hall performers and actresses. Personalities such as the Dare Sisters (see 07p) spent more time and earned more money posing for picture postcards than on the stage. Such cards are usually classified as Real Photographs yet are not the subjects of the true enthusiast's quest.

What the obsessive collector is on the look out for are the cards which were made only by the handful, of specific events, people and places. In these cases the photographer himself is the publisher and is more than likely to be a purely local figure.

Such practitioners would have a studio to which people in the neighbourhood could come and have their (almost statutory) photo taken in postcard form against a suitable backdrop. What more searching image could have been produced of this Salvationist couple (Fig 42) against a painted cloth of vaguely pastoral elements than by the jobbing photographer who no doubt presented them with their likenesses when they returned the next day.

Outside his studio would be the rows of local houses which quietly supplied another living for him, since there is scarcely a street in Britain that has not been made into a postcard. Talfourd Road, Peckham, where I am writing, exists as a postcard which I have seen only once, unpurchasably lodged in the collection of a South London dealer. Had I not set eyes on that example I would not have known of the card's existence - there are surely others, for the photographer, having snapped the street (possibly from either end) would have sold them from door to door, or put them with similar views of neighbouring streets in his shop window.

Thus there exists in collectors' albums and dealers' boxes a virtual doomsday book of Britain, its people and their habitat, as matters stood in the first quarter or so of the twentieth century. Here neglected places are celebrated and unsung people memorialised.

At the seaside other opportunities presented themselves and the beach photographer was a common sight until the sixties (when too many people had cameras of their own). If he was lucky he would photograph a whole charabanc load of trippers, each of whom would buy a postcard print .

In London's Regent Street a photographic business offered a series of fantasy backdrops and a wardrobe of appropriate clothes so that the client could become a milkmaid or a ship's captain or a Viking hero. On a smaller scale the local photographer might have one such installation, an insecure looking aeroplane or a real motorbike in front of a painting of the open road (Fig 43).

On both sides of the Atlantic postcard-backed black & white film was available until well after World War II, allowing anyone to make their own card of their house or family or celebratory get together. These often give the frankest glimpses of daily life and daily dress. It is from the American equivalent of such possibilities that Andreas Brown and Hal Morgan made their haunting book Prairie Fires and Paper Moons.

These humble examples are among history's unique documents and the RP postcard is still the repository of untold details of life which are to be found nowhere else ranging from a picture of a child with a new bicycle to the Titanic steering out towards its doom.

THE POSTCARD ARTISTS

Of the three broad categories into which postcards are lumped by traders, Topography, Subject and Artists, the cards by named artists are, as a group, the highest flyers and the most costly to buy.

In the context of real art these are all at best secondary figures but deltiology has its own pantheon. At its top are artists like Alphonse Mucha and Raphael Kirchner. Mucha was a seminal figure in the history of graphic art (one of the inventors of Art Nouveau). He hardly made any postcard designs as such but various decorative works of his transfer admirably, with the help of fine printing, to the format. Kirchner, a true postcard artist, hovered in his Viennese way on the witty margins of soft porn and was thus extremely popular with soldiers (especially the British) in the First World War (see18m).

Both are represented here but in a dog-eared and scrawled-on condition that would not recommend them to the collector. There are more rarefied artist designs that seem to have been targeted from the beginning by the cartophile and have seldom seen the inside of a post office or suffered the indignity of landing on a mat. These therefore (not really being postcards in anything but shape and name) need not concern us.

More democratic as purveyors of glamour were commercial artists like the Canadian-born Boileau and the creator of one kind of archetypal American girl, Harrison Fisher. So curious is the sphere of postcard dealing that the only card by Boileau (17a) that I could have been tempted to buy at the going rate was knocked down to me for a pound since it had inconsiderately been posted and had writing on both sides. The dealer was oblivious of the fact that the message was virtually a suffragette manifesto.

A middle ground is held by curiosities such as Louis Wain (03k) whose haunted cats stayed popular until the late twenties. These typify a whole menagerie of animals by various artists who enact human roles. This area was taken over later in the century by Disney (see 30e etc.) and the thespian creatures that are cooked up for TV series (avidly collected by those that saw them when young).

November 18th 1908. SH writes from Ipswich (where this postcard was taken by H Walters) to Mrs Cathorpe 16th Coy. R.G.A. *Dear L. Thanks for your p.c. hope you & both well, as it leaves me at present. Do you know who this is. I am sorry to say they are gone, fresh People have come. Sorry you & going still further away hoping I shall see you before you go with much love xxxx.* The card is evidently not written by either one of this intense couple who seem to gaze out beyond the photographer as if to Salvation itself.   Fig. 42

October ?th 1910. Jenny in Southport has been to W Findley the photographer in Shakespeare St. and sends the result to someone special. *Dear Joe, I enjoyed this flight splendid I don't think - The girl next to me is my companion & our workmate don't you think it would make a fine picture for Chips yours with love Sweetheart Jennie.* This, bought for 50p, is the type of card I most enjoy, whether the subjects are soaring through imaginary clouds, speeding in cars or on motorbikes along fictitious roads, or rowing on dry water. The combination of the pictorial and photographic where vehicles are sketched in with all the confidence of a Picasso makes most surrealism look tame. This and the above represent the only kind of cards I actively collect.   Fig. 43

August 6th 1915. Lena in Nottingham to Miss D Bestwick in Long Eaton. *Dear Dolly, Thanks so much for card. I was disappointed when Stan told me at dinner time that you could not get. but am looking forward to seeing you at the same time tomorrow. Hope you will be able to get. Bye Bye. Lots of love to all xx.* Harrison Fisher cards were not commonly used in England. Their world of reference is to an All American Girl whose robust beauty chaps like Art here would moon over. No fin de siecle limpness or decadence survives in these near amazons who are ready to run the world, with their sisters, the Gibson girls. There is no parallel English tradition nor comparable skill in virtuoso colour illustration. Fig. 44

August 29th 1904. AB is caught up in the Russo-Japanese War as indicated by his brief message to Mrs Tahourdin in Filey, *Thanks for your letter. Just off to front, Tokio.* Perhaps he is heading for Port Arthur itself (see 04a etc.). This Japanese image represents quite another postcard tradition deriving from the woodcut, one of many Japanese styles of card in which routine postcard techniques were used, but to quite independent ends. Japan produced some of the most inventive and richly printed cards, almost all by anonymous designers (see 20k). Fig. 45

Half way between the cards that have artistic pretensions and the straightforwardly comic card are the hosts of toddlers who (like the animals, but more meaningfully) play out adult roles. At first I overlooked their merits even though, in the putti of renaissance and baroque art, they have their historical lineage. More and more I came to see how they could express situations that representations of adults could not quite cope with. This of course is a trope carried over by McGill, Taylor and others into the true comic card.

Rural views and urban scenes also have their sketchers and painters who work to the classic format. One only has to think how conveniently the paintings in museums fit on the postcards in their shops to realise that such a shape evolved over centuries as the ideal vehicle (horizontally for landscapes and vertically for portraits). Few of these figure in this book since the principal English practitioners represent me academicism plodding in the wake of the picturesque. The most famous of them, A R Quinton seems (even though he was born in Peckham) a jobbing dullard when compared with a continental equivalent like Emanuel Wielandt (01r) who has both flair and imagination and the wit not to finish his work to death. But mainly as is the case with cute, but much collected, American artists like Clapsaddle, their work passes me by.

There are of course isolated examples of fine artists being involved in postcard production (rather than merely having their work reproduced in that form) like Kokoschka and some of the members of the Wiener Werkstätte. It is fortunate that the greatest artist of modern times, Picasso (who was of course involved in every possible medium) generated some postcards both in his role as a promoter of Peace (see 49a) and as an advertiser of his own pottery exhibitions at Vallauris.

It is only at the end of the century that fine artists have responded to a fascination with the postcard by producing cards of their own. In the work of painters like Richard Hamilton (73p) and Dieter Rot (87t) is found the true confluence of art and card and a valuable aesthetic commentary.

My own taste in postcard artists veers, as with photographs, towards the anonymous artisan. We know many biographical details of many a dreary dauber of animal studies, flowers, pretty scenes etc. but usually know nothing of the unnamed designers whose various abstractions and arrangements convey their matter in hand dramatically or sensually. Always there have been graphic artists whose touch could transform a diner into the place that embodies all modernity, or make an advertisement for a hotel into a poem of wish fulfilment.

The cards produced between 1905-20 that go under the general heading of their publisher, Bamforth, are in a dream world of their own. They are nearer to cinema than photography. These illustrations to various songs of love, religious sentiment and patriotic fervour convey their message through surrealistically coloured montages. Immensely popular in their day they are found in great numbers still in postcard fairs. Their profusion has made them undervalued as art and they have yet to be recognised for their beauty and imagination.

OMISSIONS

There are a few categories missing from these pages which yet appear in postcard catalogues and yet others that are distinctly underrepresented in terms of collectors' enthusiasms.

Since the nature of this book dictates that cards should be postally used, it has to omit the largest group of cards that postmen never see i.e. that lurking under the heading of Erotic. This is a subsection of the general category Glamour and degrees of eroticism are indicated by titles like Deshabille borrowed from the French (a naughtier race than ourselves in English mythology). These were never intended for posting and would not in any case have reached their destination. Most are innocent enough, being of a kind once advertised as 'studies for artists; sent under plain cover'. Especially outrageous would have been those showing pubic hair. I have not explored the lower depths of this branch of collecting though I guess there must be some scandalous and scary items hidden from the normal gaze.

Nudity was permissible however if the subject (female) was black or a reproduction of a statue or a painting. In the first case the picture would come under the heading Ethnographic and in the second, Art. Being black or being art in some strange way did not count as real. Such mysteries would need another book to explain. Yet, even when the taboos started to fall away the process of increased permissiveness was gradual. Special license seemed to be given to girls on beaches throughout the century who were somehow allowed to be more scantily clad than those in any other context. This held true until at least the mid-eighties. Male nudity (frontal) still manages to raise an eyebrow.

Although there are many kinds of novelty cards made of different materials (leather, cork, wood) or featuring things that squeak, or surfaces on which matches can be struck, I have no taste for them. They rarely relate to anything or have messages of interest. Silk cards either woven or printed, a great favourite in the First World War, are avidly collected. Needless to say such delicate things were invariably posted in envelopes.

Only two types of novelty are present here neither of which can be shown to its full advantage. The Hold To Light card of the Royal Academy (02a) does indeed, when held up against the light, spring to life as a night time scene with blazing windows, and the views seen through the Zeppelin's porthole (31p) change as one turns the still functioning wheel.

There are of course in this volume none of the new reprints of nostalgic postcards (many of which however reproduce spectacularly fine images). To include these would merely confuse the issue. When as in the case of the Victory Anniversary (95r) an old image becomes part of an entirely new design this can lead to a moving combination of styles.

Some cards are not here merely because I have not been able to find any used examples of the period, most notably the anarchic cards by John Stalin (whose real name is John Churchill) produced in the late seventies which predate the ironic satires of the mid eighties. The early issues based on Private Eye covers would also have been welcome but this is precisely the kind of material which, though out there somewhere, is extremely difficult to find.

I fear I have rather unjustly omitted properly to represent the rich American tradition of greeting cards (for Thanksgiving, Halloween etc.) yet the examples I have looked through have either been posted in envelopes or bear scant messages (usually repeating the words on the front). Fig 49 was a recent lucky find. As well as having a touching message it exemplifies the characteristic vigour of this uniquely American genre.

These are but a sample of the sort of omission that this book is guilty of: there are countless other 'ones that got away'. Sins of commission, of which there are no doubt an equal number, I take full responsibility for. The card I would most liked to have found complete with message and sent from the spot in 1936 is that showing Jesse Owens winning his gold medal (much to the annoyance of Adolf Hitler) at the Munich Olympics. There is a

January 27th 1999. From Mrs Price entering a Radio Times competition and hoping to win a set of 'Mardi Gras Mosaic Tableware' for which (if she is lucky) one hopes Mr Prices shares a taste. Strictly speaking this is not a Picasso postcard: it is a reproduction of work done in 1957 making fun of his secretary Jaime Sabartes. The 76 year old master is completely at home with standard postcard imagery (a pin up of Leslie Caron) as well as the mixture of drawing and photograph that became one of the postcard's comic strategies. This is the first and last straightforward art reproduction in the book.   Fig. 46

January 26th 1904. Amy in Gloucester sends this sultry pair of amorous girls to Miss Clift in Wycliffe, *How are you getting on, Please write me. With love from Amy* and sends her another one in the same series on June 16th. What these two affectionate friends are enjoying would now be, unambiguously, a Lesbian embrace. But attitudes to sentimental liasons between women were different in 1904. Nonetheless the erotic temperature is quite high and by 1954 it would be inconceivable to send such a card through the post. I have never seen a card of this type sent by a man.   Fig. 47

Not surprisingly an unposted card, later than Fig. 47 and quite a few steps beyond in explicitness. This is no innocent example of torrid affection but a frank and sophisticated portrayal of Lesbian intimacy. Yet it is a chaste image vis-a-vis the world of fleshly taboo. It is no.6 of a series, perhaps describing an aftermath. The composition is beautiful and the tray makes an excellent foreground still-life as well as being a telling element in the narrative. Even the Francis Bacon curtain plays its enigmatic part. Though bought at a street market in Berlin it still cost £6.   Fig. 48

July 3rd 1909. Helen, of Troy, NY (which must itself have given rise to a few jokes), to Master Blair Goslin in Wilkesbarne, Pa., *Your postal received and we were all glad to hear from you. I was wishing Tuesday that I could see you to let you know I get a little homesick to, to see you Blair. But we know we can't see each other so it isn't any use to cry. I have a little girl to come and play with me every day and we have such good time in our back yard. My papa is going to Alwo (?) in Aug. and then mother and I will go to the lake. I wanted mother to paste me on here for stamps.*   Fig. 49

postcard of Martin Luther King as well quoting his famous speech 'I have a dream...' but I suspect it was made long after the event since it appears in auction catalogues fairly regularly, always unused (see front cover).

Reproductions of actual works of art are also excluded (except for Fig 46 and one or two of my own) although these are one of the most frequently utilised genres. It seemed to me they were somehow outside the pale yet the early chromolithographic versions of old masters have a fidelity to the feel of paintings that many modern museum reproductions lack. Pictures of sculpture in situ are another story and appear quite regularly.

HOW THIS BOOK IS ARRANGED

Each annual section starts with a dated page. This features a card reproduced full size plus a view of Piccadilly Circus and another of the New York Skyline, all posted in that year.

The first card is chosen to give the flavour of the time. It does not always refer to key events of the year for this would only have led, so rich has the century been in grisly warfare and staring demagogues, to a succession of bigwigs and battles. Other things may chronicle the changing face of the age just as significantly. Science, humour, fashion, architecture etc. are all part of the world's wild parade. Transient glories like the rise of London's Carnaby Street can provide as rich a symbol as yet another military coup. Chance of course plays a part since often I found the right card but posted in a year that did not give it special resonance (Elvis Presley and Marilyn Monroe proved elusive in that way). The years of the two World Wars are an exception. Not only did their events dominate the consciousness of the Western world but scarcely any cards were produced in them (especially in Britain) that did not relate in some way to their pursuit.

The preliminary cards, being (with only two or three exceptions) the proper size, also help to offset the problem of seeing the others in such reduction that one is not aware of shifts in scale and format. Even these generous pages however could not cope with some of the giant cards that emerged in the eighties or the sprawling shapes of the recent cut-out novelties.

Acting both as a clock and a stylistic barometer, as well as underlining the predominantly Anglo-American nature of my selection, the views of Piccadilly Circus and the New York Skyline got to be like old friends. The fact that one relates to the Thames and the other to the Hudson, thus seeming to refer in tandem to the publisher of this book, is purely (though pleasantly) coincidental.

In reality they make for very erratic timepieces since people do not always find or send the current card of either place. My own effort to do so on the 31st December 1999 ended in failure. Thinking to buy the very latest view of Piccadilly Circus I spent an hour there looking and could find no card even showing it at any time in 1998 much less in 1999. Many cards on sale dated back over twenty years.

There are inevitably for both locations periods when few cards were produced. The two World Wars were not the only gaps in the case of Piccadilly Circus. Eros, its focal point, had a habit of being removed while building works went on (constructing the underground station etc.) though publishers were not above a cut and paste job to slip it back in (see 24b). The early years of the New York panorama had their fallow architectural times when producers of cards were more than content to recycle old views in different tints or even, for variety's sake, to swap night for day. Each major building was a blow to such easy profits. After 1932 it was hard to get away with a view lacking the

Empire State building and after 1974 the absence of the World Trade Center would be even more noticeable. Even so the odd skyscraper seems to rise only to fall within a year, then rise again for the duration.

The shortest time lag between a card's use and the moment it represents can be a matter of weeks, though this is rare. With Piccadilly Circus the average gap is about five years though the longest is a startling 47 years (42b). The Circus has, of course, many more features by which it can be dated, even in some instances by the very hour and day, thanks to clocks and specific events. Prevailing fashions, modes of transport, changes in traffic arrangement all help, but particular assistance is given by what is on at the theatre and cinema. Often in the caption it is not my own erudition that is being displayed but that of David Oxford whose admirable postcard-based book on Piccadilly Circus points out many things that I would have missed. I only take issue with him once or twice, mostly over his reliance on Halliwell for dating films. Any keen cinemagoer in England has known the frustration of waiting (often over a year) for a new American movie to reach London.

I have no such expertise to lean on with regard to New York and the aspect I chose (rather than Times Square or a place equivalent to Piccadilly) leaves me without people or traffic or signs that give any helpful clue. Therefore the commentary concentrates, except in obvious instances, on atmosphere and graphic diversity.

Assembling a century's worth of each of these places has been a diverting agony. Since the subject and the posting date was what I sought, the messages that appear on the backs have a useful randomness, a corrective to the more selected texts on other cards in the book as a whole.

What strikes me, seeing them all now assembled in order, is the consistency of both places. Piccadilly Circus is in essence much the same and the New York Skyline seems like a single planned structure erected over a long period.

In each annual four page section the second and third pages exhibit further cards posted in that year. These are arranged with no particular regard to chronology of day or month. Any ordering by date would have imposed a scheme so rigid as to preclude aesthetic consideration or thematic links. The fourth and last page continues this process and ends with notes that are for the most part the kind of dry information about publishers, photographers , serial numbers etc. that delight only the specialist. This last column also either features details of some individual card (to compensate for the small scale of original reproduction) or supplementary cards together with remaining fragments of messages etc.

A NOTE ON POSTCARD PUBLISHERS

A list of publishers' credits appears at the end of each year and a general listing after the index. Twice is not quite enough to thank the many producers of cards who have enriched this volume with their skill. The durability of some postcard publishers is impressive. Both Valentine's and ETW Dennis, names often found on recent cards, were producing postcards well before 1900 and carried on through the century adapting to all the changes in size and taste and printing methods.

Others come and go or merge together or reappear under different names. The other great survivor is Bamforth & Co a pioneer in many genres and a staunch champion of the seaside comic. Raphael Tuck issued the first true coloured English postcard and similarly changed chameleon-like with the times.

April 4th (?) 1991 (month and day are indistinct in the Air Force Postal Service franking). This would have been the introductory card for 1991 had I got hold of it in time. Received via Richard Minsky from Barbara Slate it finds an equally appropriate place here. Mike writes to Barbara S in New York, *Hi, well you haven't sent me a lot of your work but that's alright you have given me a lot of support wile I have been hear and I really do wish to thank you. I probably will not be leaving until around Sept. but at least no more war. Well bye and God Bless.* The outline of Kuwait surrounds a Valentine verse to the various forces 'But then YOU came and brought hope to us all/That Kuwait would be free and Saddam would fall/We'd like to thank you for your courageous stand/To expel the Iraquis and free our land' etc. Published by the Kuwaiti Information Center in Cairo one wonders how it was distributed. Did every serviceman fighting under all these flags receive one?   Fig. 50

PICCADILLY CIRCUS. 19th CENTURY

PICCADILLY CIRCUS TODAY

July 27th 1997. On this oversize card BH writes to TP in Peckham, *Here's two for the price of one, or one card and a half to be more accurate - might be useful or might be a spanner in the works. Off to see some no doubt tedious cricket at the Other Place.* Presuming this card was published in the nineties the captions are somewhat cavalier in their boast that the two views span a century (nor of course do they even present the same aspect). The modern view dates from 1979 and the nineteenth century is well ahead of its time with two motor-buses in view. 1906/7 would be a safe date. Thus barely three quarters of a century separate the two.   Fig. 51

126 - Lower New York, Through Brooklyn Bridge Arch.

November 27th 1942. Gil in New York to Mr A J Petrie in Glendale, Cal., *Your card was a mighty relief. Not hearing from you-all after the Princeton Yale game, I was right worried. Nearly froze to death at that game. We should have got those Yankees down younder in Jungletown. Old Devil North Wind came up between the Halves and blew it until it was blue all over the place. Let's hear what you-all's doing way down yonder in L.A. I'm mighty curious.* This dramatic viewpoint is a favourite among photographers of New York and occurs repeatedly in the superb photos of Wm. Frange. Here Huberman, another self-publisher takes advantage of the dark diagonal of the Brooklyn Bridge. Fig. 52

In America the equivalent to these giants is Curt Teich & Co who seem to define the so called Linen Card and then move on to Chrome cards with the same assurance. John Hinde whose name merges with that of Teich in some recent cards was the photographer/publisher who injected a sense of showbusiness into the British topographical card.

I hope that publishers will see the frequency with which their images are borrowed as an indicator of praise, and think kindly of a book that celebrates their craft. Also highlighted in the commentary is the often recurring phenomenon of the postcard beating art by a short head.

If I have a favourite among publishers it is Frith & Co whose cards inhabit an invented world of space, composition and colour that evokes a paralle world. Their aesthetic arrives unannounced and haunts the middle years of the century. The inhabitants of a Frith landscape are also themselves changed utterly as if in an enactment of Pelleas et Melisande. It is a special case of the argument that each publisher is the creator of a unique world, consistent unto itself and tangential to reality (whatever that, on the latter day, may turn out to be).

Perhaps most of all one would wish to thank (since one cannot credit them) the legion of anonymous producers of cards who in the earlier years are often in the majority. This book with pleasurable reverence lays a wreath on the tombs of the unknown photographer, the unnamed artist and the unacknowledgeable publisher.

June 1st 1964. Valentine's, still in Dundee, send out a card to launch their 'new Real-Photographic Advertising Service for YOU'. Despite the promise of 'Small Editions! Low Costs! Seven Days Delivery!' GA Dunn & Co. Ltd. of Murraygate who receive it may have thought this kind of card was becoming a little old-fashioned. Style watchers would not immediately guess that this was the mid-sixties card from a publisher that once led the field. Fig. 53

February 1st 1992. L Darch goes for the Radio Times Shakespeare Competition and his answer to the no doubt browfurrowing question is Ralph Fiennes. This is a CPC Freecard and actually advertises Pot Mash, an instant food in a tub. The prize is a Sony Playstation with Tomb Raider thrown in. The image itself cunningly uses the graphic language of another kind of advertising card, i.e. those that luridly festoon London phone kiosks to serve as unofficial Yellow Pages for prostitutes. Fig. 54

July 27th 1906. Evelyn finds a Rotary card bearing her own name to send to Miss Fagg in Sidcup, *My dearest H... of course I will come like a shot ... will it be permissible to walk about in the day without a hat? as then I need only bring down one? I shan't say anything to Bert about coming ... Won't it be jolly to have a picnic on the Saturday. I do hope it will be fine.*   fig. 55

January 5th 1971. RM in Stockwell to TP in Camberwell, *Ian Tyson showed some of us the fascinating first fascicle of <u>A Humument</u> at the Tate yesterday... I meant to ask in Dec. how the Compartmented Bench picture & others - are proceeding?* This fine example of the Frith manner shows how the publisher controls the sky and colours of the world to create his own parallel universe of pink cars and caravans with the village left in black & white. All the incidents and features are beautifully poised in a daring composition.   Fig. 56

July 28th 1962. Philip in Deal writes to his mother in Peterborough, *Dear Mum We arrived at Kingsdown after taking the wrong turning once - It is a very extensive camp here and there are some foreign scouts camping near. Today it is lovely and fine and we hope to go swimming.* Though neither this or the card above are acknowledged Frith publications they each catch the elegiac mood of that publisher. It's hard to believe that this one though said to be by P B Nevill is not printed by Frith so exactly does it match that otherwordly palette of blue, green and siennas.   Fig. 57

October 2nd.   Three figures seem to step out of a Manet painting in the nineteenth century and head towards the Grand Palais (newly built for the Paris Exposition Universelle) from which they will emerge into the twentieth. Mr Storm's brother at the Broad St Station pharmacy in Philadelphia will receive the card on the 11th and may perhaps admire the progressive mixture of Impressionism and Art Nouveau elegance achieved by its 24 year old designer Jack Abeillé.   00a

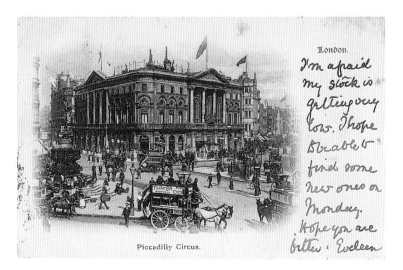

November 24th.   There is usually a time lag of a few years between the image on the card and its posting. A bus here advertising The Girl I Left Behind Me dates the card to 1895. Eveleen writes to Mrs Damon in Bath, *I'm afraid my stock* [i.e. of cards] *is getting very low. I hope to be able to find some new ones on Monday.*   00b

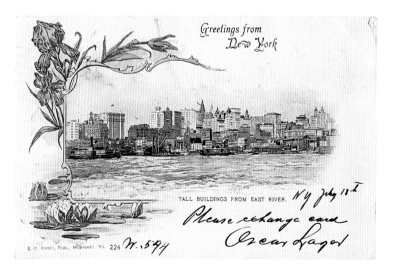

June 18th.   As on the Thames so on the Hudson. Oscar Lager gives his club membership number (W.594) asking Mr Neberlein of 606 E 156th St to swap cards with him. The buildings from East River may now be dwarfed by their present counterparts but at the time they were just as worthy of comment.   00c

October 1st.   LG writes from Moseley Park to T T Greer appearing on tour at the The Hansa Theatre in Hamburg, wishing him success. Döcker, despite the disdain with which the writer treats the card's design, is now one of the most keenly collected of Art Nouveau postcard artists.   00d

March 15th.   Louise M Davy in Clapham sends her neighbour Miss Ethel Gaines a cheery message wishing her the triumph of Ladysmith rather than the desperation of Majuba. Harry Payne, the prolific military artist, makes his debut on this classic Boer War image.   00e

December 21st.   Georgia in Philadelphia writes to Mrs Woodall in Euclid Ave, St Louis, Mo. The Electric Flyer of the Washington Alexandria and Mt Vernon Railway looks ahead of its time and the price of 20 cents for the round trip sounds reasonable. A vignette simulating the style of a steel engraving.   00f

July 9th.   Nothing has equalled chromolithography for precision of colour and tone. This is a vivid example, here used by Mr Karoly in Portsmouth to tell his son in London of his crowded program of musical toil with operas by Wallace, Balfe, Donizetti and Verdi, all tackled in quick succession.   00g

October 25th.   From the hotel depicted WGG, on what seems like a successful painting trip, writes to W Collingwood in Bristol. His final remark is of special interest indicating as it does how novel and unfamiliar the postcard habit still was for the English, *I am well and enjoying myself and follow the fashion, you see, in sending Ansichtskarte.* [literally 'view cards'].   00h

July 16th.   *Look well at Kitchener*, writes grandpa in Margate to Masters Jack and Lionel Harris in Maidstone, *and both try to be as good & as brave as he has proved.* Kitchener (see 14a) was then chief of staff to Lord Roberts (whom he soon succeeded) in the Boer Campaign. He became Minister for War but died in 1916 when the ship taking him to Russia struck a mine.   00i

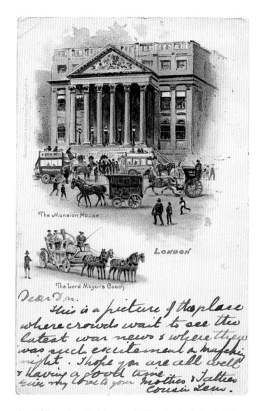

Postmark indistinct. *Aren't these cards lovely, they are the best we can buy,* writes Beattie Lyons' aunt to her in Edgbaston from the Paris Exhibition. This de luxe tinted card has added spangles. *The exhibition is too wonderful... just returned dead beat* she adds, the inevitable chorus of World Fair visitors.   00j

August 21st.   Rehearsing a soldier's farewell that we shall see on future cards (e.g. 15a) but here with a stiff Victorian decorum. PE writes to Elizabeth Homstead (they are both in Eastbourne) in evident distress, *Doctor just left measles in the worst form in despair for the little dears.*   00k

June 9th.   Len to his cousin Don in Belfast, *This is... where crowds wait to see the latest war news & where there was such excitement Mafeking night...* Tuck the publisher was the British pioneer of coloured cards. This from their first series was chromolithographed in Saxony.   00l

October 29th.   Mr Riggs-Miller is in Rome during Holy Year and has seen Pope Leo XIII, heard Mass in St Peter's etc. He tells Miss Cambier in Sunderland, *Have never seen anything like the churches here - inside at least* . The proprietor of the Hotel Giannelli has (like the owners of the inns on 00h and 00n) taken advantage of the postcard craze to produce this combination of hotel publicity and desirable souvenir of a pilgrimage.   00m

September 19th.   'Gruss aus' (greetings from), the formula that heads so many of the early German cards, has become the name for the whole genre of viewcards with undivided backs, the only legal form in Britain until 1902 (or in the US until 1907). PH sends this from what seems to be a pleasure garden with a glum message to Signor Bergers at Lake Maggiore, *My luck again - going back to London - am afraid now no good hoping.*   00n

GENERAL NOTE. Each year takes up four pages. The first shows a card of special relevance in that year plus a view of Piccadilly Circus and of the New York skyline posted in that year. The second and third pages form a double spread of cards sent in that year with comments and excerpts from their written messages. The fourth page gives notes, supplementary illustrations, details of publishers etc. together with the remaining messages. An index lists topics and place names together with artists, photographers and publishers. Except in very rare instances where noted all cards are in English and postally used, the date of posting heading each caption. The erratic spellings and punctuation (or lack of it) in the original messages are retained. All cards are from the author's collection.

September 7th. Before the postcard settled into a regular format this squarer shape (now referred to as Court Cards) was much in use. This view of the Old Curiosity Shop was sent from London to a Miss Euclides, University Street, Athens, *The above is one of the houses dear to the hearts of Londoners and indeed everybody who has read Dickens works. Very shortly this has to be pulled down for new street improvements. all old landmarks are vanishing before the stern hand of improvements. I bought this for you in 'Little Nell's' bedroom. The offside still has a few curios in the window but mainly photos and cards of the house. Thousands of visitors, Americans etc. visit the old place yearly. thought you would like this before it passes away.* As it happens the Old Curiosity Shop, unlike little Nell, was reprieved. 'Americans etc' still visit the shrine. For a progress report turn to 1999.   00o

November 6th.   On this peaceful view of Loch Katrine Elizabeth, freshly arrived from the USA, gives Mrs Knollenberg in Richmond, Ind. her first impressions of England, *...oh so glad to be on land once more! Landed at Tilbury yesterday about 2a.m. and passed numerous little farms and villages on the 22 miles up to London. We found a delightful place to stay - Foreign Mission Club, 149 Highbury New Park. Today we are resting but expect to start out tomorrow. Everything seems queer and 'out of date' - houses, trains, people and all. Will write again soon. Love to you & all.*   00p

00a. Editeur P.S. à D.Erika 640 H. Design by Jack Abeillé.

00b. Publisher unknown.

00c. E.C.Kropp. Milwaukee. No.224, Flag PM Station L.

00d. 'Modern' Serie 29. Kunstverlag Rafael Neuber, Vienna. Artist E.T.Döcker.

00e. *May your future be free from Majubas and full of Ladysmiths.* Paardeberg was a British victory which together with the relief of Ladysmith brought revenge for their defeat at Majuba in 1881. The relief of Mafeking completed the process.
Harry Payne, the artist, was born in 1858 and was the finest of military artists for the postcard trade, producing about 700 cards before his death in 1927.

Raphael Tuck & Sons Empire Postcard No280.

00f. *Fletcher leaves tomorrow and will be out to the house about 7pm Friday. He says not to wait supper for him you can fix something after he gets there. feel 1st rate today. The Dr & everyone says I'm looking better. 6 letters today. will miss F when he's gone, much love. Georgia.*

Private Mailing Card. Publisher unknown.

00g. *Dear Dayso, I only want to tell you that I have to play tonight the whole Maritana, then tomorrow Trovatore, Daughter of the Regiment and Bohemian girl, (Such is my fate) hope you are well. your Father.*

Publisher unknown.

00h. *Sunday. I had a very fine day up at this place yesterday snow mountains among clouds all round the horizon. Also I got a few sketches. Tomorrow I hope to get on to Innsbruck and home by about the end of the week. There has been very little but the finest weather and I have been busy all the time, doing a lot of work. Whether it will turn out any good I don't know...*

Verlag von C.Haschke. Schmittenhohe. Printed in Leipzig by Louis Glaser.

00i. The message begins, *I was much pleased with both of your nice letters all well meet now at the London Chatham Station on Wednesday next 18th with train 11.40am....*

Publisher unknown.

00j. *Dr B. You see I have kept my promise... Paris is too glorious, there is no place like it, but I wish I had one of you to see the shops they are indescribable - the exhibition is too wonderful, we have just returned dead beat. yr. loving aunt.*

C.N.& Cie No.107 (Palais Lumineux with gold applique and coloured spangles and silver frost).

00k. 'On Duty's Call'. Publisher unknown. series 24B.

00l. Raphael Tuck View Postcard No.9. Chromolithographed in Saxony.

00m. The writer continues, *Unfortunately we have only three weeks for Rome when three years would not be too much... We think of going to Naples tomorrow...*

Published for J.Lengyel by Lit.L.Salomone. Rome.

00n. Published for A.Horn by Kunstanstalt E.Winkler. Dresden.4540.

00o. Publisher unknown

00p. Publisher unknown

00q. Post Office. Germany

This pre-stamped card was dutifully posted on the 31st December 1899 and efficiently received on January 1st 1900. Specially produced by the German Post Office for the purpose of New Century's Greetings, these were referred to as Sonnenaufgangskarte (Sunrise Cards). This written largely in English was sent by members of the Paradies family to Miss Babetta Kahn who seems to have married into the family and to be living with grandparents, *To Babetta. To the diamond wedding the dear Grandparents and also to the approaching New Year we all send our hearty congratulations with a many of good wishes from your loving aunt Emmy.* (plus various other family signatures in old and new style german handwriting). We shall in due course find out what will happen to a card posted on the 31st December 1999.   00q

July 29th.   This eminently Victorian card of Victoria reminds one that a little old lady reigned over an empire at the start of the twentieth century as her now elderly great great granddaughter rules its scattered remnants at the end. Rudolf, practising his fluent but quaint English (*I am glad your holy days are much amusing*) writes to Hans Meyer of Carlsfeld in Erzgebirge. Miss B at the Berlitz Language School is evidently much on his mind. Queen Victoria died on the 22nd January.   01a

July 30th.   Addressed to Winnie (as in 01i) Butler, Hohenlinden, Westgate on Sea this view of circa 1899 shows a peaceful Piccadilly. The writer bought the card the day before at the Women's Exhibition at *the Earl's Court, where I passed a long and happy day.*   01b

December 31st.   Unusually for the time, since writing on the back was not as yet allowed, this crisp cartoon-like graphic of New York at twilight left no room for a message to Ralph Bettman in Edgewater, Chicago. But it would only have taken a few words to animate the rather slapdash sky.   01c

July 31st.   This was a card received by those who subscribed two shillings to 'Links of the Empire' for a set of four posted from relevant points in Scott's first Antarctic Expedition. It was mailed when Discovery set sail. Scott failed to reach the pole on this voyage and set out on his second fateful expedition in 1910. (see 13j)   01d

April 29th.   The new King is sixty years old and his notoriously long-suffering wife not much younger. They will be crowned next year. Edith writes to Ethel Exton of Sydenham Hill, London, *How is the Gondolier?....Is Ernie still as silly as he was? Write budget soon.*   01e

June 3rd.   Ask a silly question ...Filippo Leoni in Milan has evidently enquired of John Dunlop in Bradford as to what the local costume is, imagining the sort of quaint folk outfit one might find in regional Italy. *This is the best I can do for you by way of costumes in connection with Bradford,* is John's reply.   01f

April 18th.   The graphic sophistication of this cromolitho multi-view (albeit printed in London) shows that New Zealand did not lag behind in postcard production, though ARP tells Harold Paget in Tunbridge Wells that *Auckland of course after Sydney and Melbourne seems very small indeed.*   01g

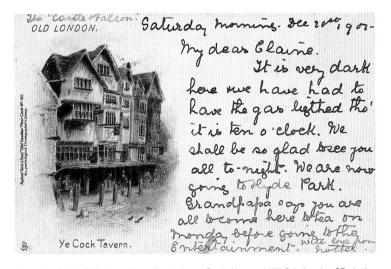

December 21st.   Elaine's mother writes to her at South Norwood Hill Rd., London SE., in the decorous style of the time, though one would like to know what the 'Entertainment' was. Raphael Tuck's ever popular London series has reached No161 with this view of the now much transformed Cock Tavern.   01h

August 24th.   Miss Butler in Westgate-on-Sea receives a card from Gatchina, *Today we saw the Empress Dowager leave for Copenhagen. Stood at the Entrance to which she drove up and afterwards saw her enter the train.* The curious naturalism of the tinted photographic card from Russia is uncharacteristic of the period.   01i

December 27th.   Polly is still sending cards of the Universal Exhibition which continued well into 1901. Writing to Mrs Fisher in Blackpool she reminds her of the moving platform, *wasn't it funny ?* In fact it looks rather sedate and, with its advanced lamps and functional balustrade, a spartan contrast to the showy Italian Pavilion.   01j

January 25th.   M.de Gratz in Bern picks a fashionable card to post to Mme. Cumior at the Hotel Beau Lite, Lausanne and finds a tortuous rationale for sending a March card in January. Alphonse Mucha, one of the inventors of the Art Nouveau style, was the most distinguished artist whose work was seen regularly in postcard form.   01k

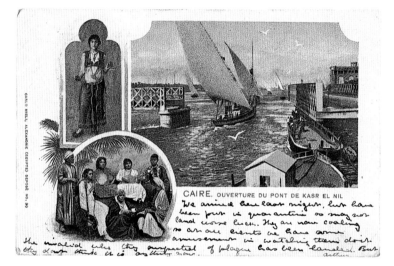

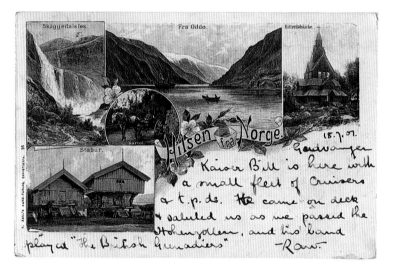

December 22nd.   Arthur to GB Paget in Tunbridge Wells, *We arrived here last night but have been put in quarantine so may not land worse luck.* Still there was the coaling to watch and the plague scare soon subsided. The card was delivered via the ship purveyors Vella & Portelli dei Port Said, as announced by a bold red rubber stamp.   01l

July 22nd.   RAW writing from Gadvanger in Norway tells Mr Hannan in Leeds, *Kaiser Bill is here....He came on deck & saluted us as we passed the Hohenzollern, and his band played The British Grenadiers.* Wilhelm II was then viewed affectionately, as grandson of Victoria, though he would become the bogeyman of World War I.   01m

June 2nd.   A classic Gruss Aus sent from Belle in Dresden to Mrs Andriessen in Beaver, Penn. The great composer/virtuoso Paderewski is staying at Belle's hotel. She has been to his opera Manru which had its world première in Dresden that week. Paderewski would later become prime minister of Poland.   01n

April 21st.   For Mr Turnbull at University College, Oxford, finals are fast approaching but his friends all seem to be in Cannstadt admiring the Vienna Ladies Orchestra. In student style they join in wishing him success, *May the Tabs be sat upon, Write you worm!* etc. College records show that Turnbull got a second.   01o

A LADY PAVEMENT ARTIST.—From "Living London." Edited by G. R. Sims, and published Fortnightly, 7d. net, by Cassell and Co., Limited.

10.XII.01.

I was coming round Tomorrow, but perhaps I had better not, for we have a case of S.F at

December 10th.   Watched by it seems an almost entirely male audience the lady pavement artist rehearses her vignetted views. Now herself vignetted the stylish presentation hides a lowly if skilled profession. Sent within Thames Ditton to Mrs Scatliff it is evidently No1 of a sequence of cards. Perhaps the others were also in this London Life series.   01p

June 21st.   YLB (Your loving Brother) George writes to his sister in N.London from St.Petersburg, *I shall be so glad to leave Russia as I am eaten alive by mosquitoes....last night we worked before the cousin to the Czar of Russia....How would you like to put your leg up like that ?* The erect limb in front of a priapic statue is unmistakably suggestive.   01q

December 21st.   MMM sends Christmas greetings from Rapallo to Mrs Hitchcock in Egremont, Cheshire. The choice of cards is impeccable. The vivid paintings of Manuel Wielandt are matched as ever by the fine printing of Nister. Compared with these the efforts of earnest British topographical artists seem somewhat pedestrian.   01r

May 5th.   Franz asks Mrs Ethel Hall of The Chase, Clapham whether she has any photos in stock and sends this Lieutenant's Fantasy, very much in the erotic German taste of the time. *Do you like these smart girls? Something to fight the Boers.* Perhaps Franz and Ethel Hall really do share the same taste since he signs off *much love.*   01s

01a. *My dear friend. your card caused me indescribable joy you may be sure. It was also a great surprise to me, then I never thought you were fond of writing English letters. I am glad that your holy days are much amusing and I think they are much more interesting than mine are. Since your departure I have not taken some remarkable excursions, as you have done and I have also not had any pleasure. But nearly I had forgotten to say you that I visited the 'International Exhibition of Fine Arts' at Fryday. It was very nice there. next time I will write you still more about it. Now, I will describe you a little of what has happened in the Berlitz Schools in the last time. At Fryday when I buried [?] the school money there, I met Miss B. and had the pleasure to talk with her for a long time. Yesterday I saw Miss B. when I was at Allmarkt. There played the band of the 'Schützen - Regiment'. But I think I have written quite enough and I will finish now.*
Giving my best regards to your family I am yours for ever. Rudolf. your card from Wildenhall I received this morning and tell you my last thanks.

Osnabrucker Papierwaren Fabrik, Berlin.

01b. Publisher unknown.

01c. Franz Huld NY. 173. Private Mailing Card (vignette of lady with umbrella).

01d. Wrench 'Links of Empire' Postcards Series 3 No.1

01e. C W Faulkner & Co., London

01f. H Graham Glen. Wortley, Leeds.

01g. Printed by Waterlow & Sons Ltd. London

01h. Raphael Tuck. 'Old London' Postcard No 161. Designed in England. Chromographed in Saxony.

01i. G.K.A.

01j. A.Taride, Paris.

01k. Publisher unknown. Artist Alphonse Mucha.

01l. *The invalid whom they suspected of plague has been landed. But they don't think it is anything now.*

Carlo Mieli. Alexandria. Deposé No.30

01m. *Kaiser Bill is here with a small fleet of cruisers and t.p.ds* [torpedo destroyers].

H.Abel. Kunstforlag. Christiania. No.16

01n. *Dear Mama - came here yesterday - spent a long time in the museum - saw the beautiful 'Sistine Madonna' and couldn't look at it enough. Had a pleasant call on Herr Knothe - Paderewski is at out hotel - we heard his opera 'Manru' at the Kgl. Theatre last eve. Very warm here. Will return to B [Berlin?] this eve.*

Louis Klemick Verlag, Dresden No 104.

01o. Dr.Trenkler Co. Leipzig.

01p. 'Living London' series. Cassell & Co.

01q. Phot. Blum. Frankfurt. Phototypie Knackstadt & Näther, Hamburg.

01r. S.Velten, Karlsruhe. Chromolithography by Nister, Nuremberg. Artist Manuel Wielandt.

01s. Bruno Büger Verlag. Lith Hnst. Leipzig. Artist A.F.

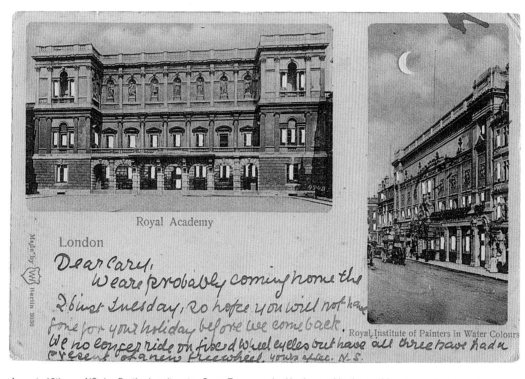

02

Royal Academy

London

Royal Institute of Painters in Water Colours

August 19th.   NS in Dartford writes to Cary Tuppeney in Hastings with the exciting news that they have now *all three had a present of a new free wheel* to replace their fixed wheel cycles. Miss Tuppeney will no doubt be pleased to receive such a grand card which, when held to the light, shows a night time scene with windows and moon brilliantly lit. The Royal Academy still stands and thrives in Piccadilly, whereas the premises of the Royal Institute of Painters in Water Colour, with its imposing busts of famous practitioners, is now only a facade above shops. In 1902 the RA's Professor of Sculpture was Alfred Gilbert, the artist responsible for the statue of Eros featured below with its aluminium still shining.   02a

London. — Piccadilly Circus.

November 14th.   APW writing to Mrs Glover in Eastbourne takes advantage of the new freedom (as of Jan. 02) to continue the message on the back *...could not write to you last week but my cold was wicked*. The view is in the summer of 1893 when the Eros monument was surrounded by a low wall.   02b

October 21st.   In the United States the message was still restricted (until 1907) to the picture side. Ray heartily congratulates Mrs Nathan in Lenox Ave NY City, though we do not know what for. The tall buildings seem to predict New York's future rather than reflect its present.   02c

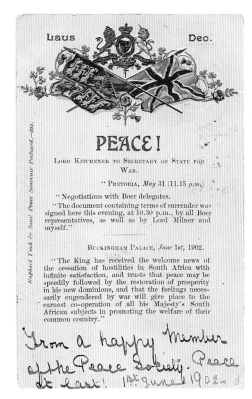

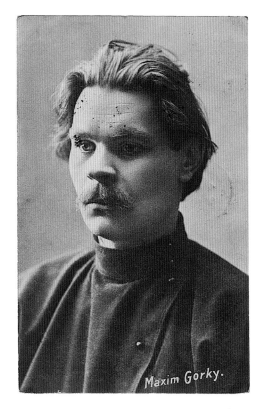

June 6th. From Holloway to Miss Minnie Crusland in Glasgow. A happy card whose joy will not last long if it relies solely on peace, only fitful glimmers of which will be seen this century. *All his Majesty's South African Subjects* refers of course to the white ones, though the King's message contains curious pre-echoes of a much later accord in South Africa. 02d

December 9th. Mr McFarlane in Dumbarton Rd, Glasgow uses a free advertising card for his order to Mr Tulloch in Argyle St, *Please send 1 1/2 st. Black Pudding 1 1/2 st. White Pudding & oblige*. The use of famous faces to promote goods was already part of marketing strategy (see 02k). The space above, designed for messages, is now redundant. 02e

September 13th. Miss A L Jones in Battersea Park, London, receives this card from a correspondent in Dresden who offers neither comment nor signature. In an age of vignetting & decoration such a powerful and uncomplicated presence seems all the more striking. This is the year in which the Russian writer triumphed with his challenging play, The Lower Depths. 02f

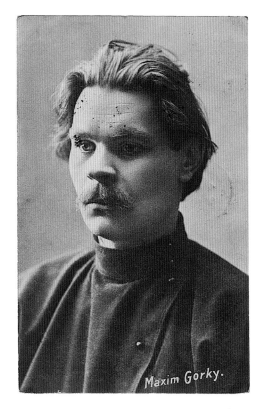

September 1st. Bertha, though unimpressed by the rather ponderous arch erected by Canada for the August 9th coronation route, sends a card of it to Miss Bimbele Hulton in Venice. Postcards were still used mainly by the middle and upper classes, familiar with them through travel; but the habit soon spread. 02g

January 17th. Postcard humour had not yet come into its own and with a few exceptions it was locked into political intricacies or juvenile puns as in this joke (already one presumes old by 1902) which FHP in New York duly and dully reinforces for the benefit of Miss Hope in Lowell, Massachusetts. 02h

November 6th. Gruss aus Chicago seem at first sight strange words to read, as is the German caption in old script. The message to Miss Helen N Blackman, 303 W 77th St New York re President McKinley (who had been shot by an assassin in 1901 at the Temple of Music in Buffalo) is itself enigmatic. 02i

December 11th.   Surrounded by a thicket of heraldic paraphernalia including at least twenty-one eagles all rendered in continuous-tone chromolithography and meticulously embossed, Kaiser Wilhelm II looks the complete emperor: Mr Fairwell Jones, was surely impressed with the iconographic splendour of the image if not the man. MFJ wishes him the season's greetings from Dresden.   02j

October 24th.   Nothing could prove a greater contrast than this coarse-screened offset litho 'Coronation Souvenir' in which the new King and Queen are somehow caught up with an advert for Bird's Custard Powder (still going strong). From MP in Southport it is addressed to Mrs Palin in St Briavels, Glos., ...*I will see after the Prayer Book. What about the cups and saucers....*   02k

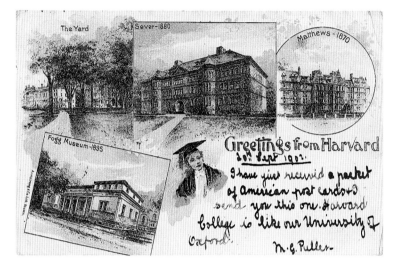

September 20th.   Harvard is a fine and privileged place yet these almost brand new buildings can hardly have reminded Mr Lewin of *our University of Oxford* when he first looked at this 1895 card from Mr Pullen in Battersea. A chromolitho in four colours, it has a sketchy look and the Boston publisher has not mastered the multi-view format enough to save the Fogg Museum from tumbling out of the ensemble.   02l

October 23rd.   Mr Bernstein in Cheltenham is the lucky recipient of this fine Parisian card from the evidently broadminded Walter & Bess. Ample flesh with expert photography and tasteful tinting declare its French origins, *My very dear man. Delighted with your letter, and with the news that the very necessary goods are to hand. Saw l'Aiglon at Sarah Bernhardt's theatre. Folies Bergères last night....*   02m

December 6th.   Details of the Royal progress through Egypt reach Mr Veitch in Peebles. He has subscribed to Royal Chain Postcards one of which is sent from each stop complete with printed bulletins in a neat hand. Today's describes the beginning of a momentous event, the opening by the Duke of the Aswan dam. These were more relaxed times (for the less regal tourist) when one could stand on top of the Sphinx's head. 02n

October 29th.   Elsie Messent in Brixton Rd receives a sun drenched card from Naples finely drawn and printed with abundant local colour (why is it that in the Mediterranean sun even washing looks picturesque?). Her correspondent is not the last this century to resent the fact that postcards deceitfully inhabit their own eternal summer. *Beastly wet days - not a bit like <u>this.</u>*   02o

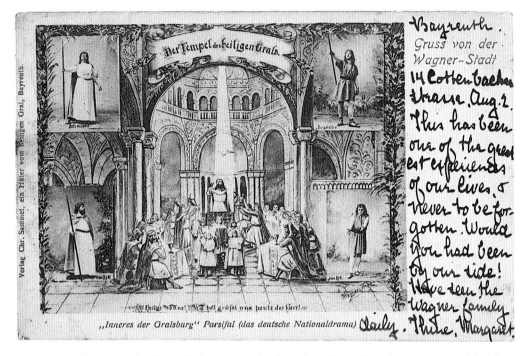

02a. WH. Berlin. 3036 (Burlington House 4949).

02b. Publisher unknown. No.5777

02c. American Souvenir Card Co, 'Patriographic'. NY.7

02d. Tuck Peace Souvenir Postcard 662. Embossed

02e. Publisher unknown. Photo: W.Davey

02f. K.& B.D. (Germany)

02g. Hartmann. 1085. Printed in Saxony

02h. International Art Publ. Co. No.774. Artist C.G.F.

02i. Koelling & Klappenlach, Chicago. No.27

02j. Kunstantalt, Heinr. & Aug. Bruning, Hanau Dep. 11055

02k. Publisher unknown

02l. Armstrong & Co. Lith. Boston. American Souvenir Co.
Copyright 1895

02m. Editions du Panorama de Paris. Les Saisons: Sous les
Armes.

02n. Royal Chain Postcards. London

02o. Ediz. Artistica Richter & Co. Naples. 398

02p. Verlag Chr. Sammet, Bayreuth.

August 2nd.   Gruss von der Wagner-Stadt announces that Bayreuth as far as Wagnerites were concerned had been subsumed into the identity of its greatest citizen. A busy card celebrating a current production would have been all that was available at the shrine itself, a situation that remains pretty much the same today. Although many publishers (including Tuck, as in 02r) were already bringing out sumptuously coloured series based on the music dramas, anything smacking of superficial pleasure was deemed to betray the master's vision. This card depicts the climactic moment of eucharistic light in Parsifal, Wagner's last masterpiece of mythological fusion. A drawing based on the Bayreuth staging is surrounded in turn by photographs of some of the principals including the great Belgian heldentenor Ernest van Dyk whose Lohengrin and Parsifal were so admired. The whole card was a labour of love on the part of the proprietor of the Künstlerheim Café Sammet, one of the two artistic meeting places approved by the inner circle. Christian Sammet signed each card in a way appropriate to the opera shown (or sometimes merely as Chr. Sammet, Wagner-Apostell). Here he designates himself 'ein Hüter vom Heiligen Graal' (guardian of the Holy Grail). Miss Anne Norris at 401 Penn St, Huntingdon, Pennsylvania receives an enthusiastic message, *This has been one of the greatest experiences of our lives & never to be forgotten. Would that you had been by our side! Have seen the Wagner family daily. Thine. Margaret.* The composer's widow, Cosima (Liszt's daughter) was still at the helm. She would soon retire in favour of the son, Siegfried. They would be in attendance at most performances and much seen in the intimate little town. Cosima might not have been amused by the present wranglings amongst her descendants in their unseemly tug of war to gain control of the Festival. What Margaret had seen and been moved by was Wagner's authentic versions of his work guarded in a spirit of pious conservation by his wife.   02p

July 10th.   In quest of a grail no less elusive the International Socialist League hold their fortieth congress in Stockholm. They are grouped in similar fashion. The event seems sparsely attended, although (unlike its Wagnerian counterpart) one or two women boost the numbers. The card was published by the ISL itself.   02q

May 24th.   From Tuck's Wagner series (printed appropriately enough in Bavaria) comes the moment when Wotan 'shews Siegfried the Burning Rock'. It's not quite what happens in the opera (which would explain purist objections). At a less heroic level May in Taffs Hill asks Edna in Cardiff when their next game of tennis is to be.   02r

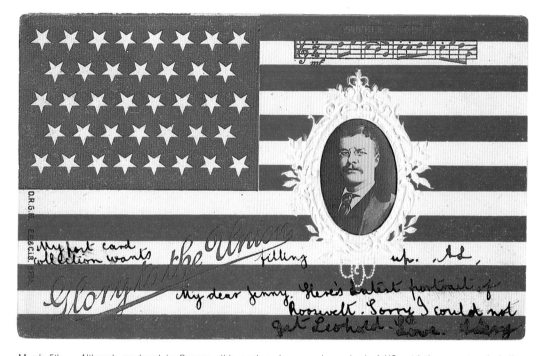

03

March 5th.   Although produced in Germany this card carries a maximum load of US patriotic apparatus, including a vignette portrait in an embossed frame of Teddy Roosevelt. 1903 was the year in which he established the first American wild life sanctuary and in which the Teddy Bear was born. It was named after the President as the result of a shooting (or rather non-shooting) incident in which Roosevelt had spared the life of a bear cub in 1902. Lucy sends this to Jenny Gillon M.O.C.B. a fellow exile in Frankfurt, regretting that she could not find a postcard of Leopold, the Belgian King.   03a

October 30th.   Animated night scenes were still outside the postcard photographer's range but this anonymous artist's impression seems to have the right feel. EHBG writes to Miss Heard, Church Lodge, Avondale Rd, Peckham of his local election chances, *Over 500 promises....enough to put us at the top of the poll.*   03b

September 2nd.   Posted from NY City at 12.30pm this river panorama carries no word from its sender to Anton Flasch at 16 First Avenue, Nyack NY (who receives it the following morning), except for the printed 'Greetings from Picturesque America' on the heraldic device.   03c

November 6th.   Sent within Thetford, Norfolk to Mr Rivert. We shall never know the story behind the enigmatic message *Sorry it was wet last Sunday*. These are the days before registration plates. In 1903 the speed limit was raised to a heady 20mph though the highway code according to this picture was still rather lenient.   03d

April 24th.   *Paris looks so funny* writes LL to Jacob Nigg. One wonders whether he specifically means the new Metro Stations by Guimard and their extravagant Art Nouveau style, or perhaps his wretched journey has merely taken its toll. Such stations are to Art Nouveau what Odeon Cinemas are to Art Deco.   03e

PASSIVE RESISTANCE DAY, 29TH OCT., 1903.—AFTERNOON CONFERENCE, CITY TEMPLE.

December 23rd.   Not perhaps the cheeriest choice of cards for A & A in Romford to send as a Christmas Greeting, yet solidarity is all and Miss Pape in Beverley, Yorks, may well have joined in this opposition to Balfour's policies which chained education to religion.   03f

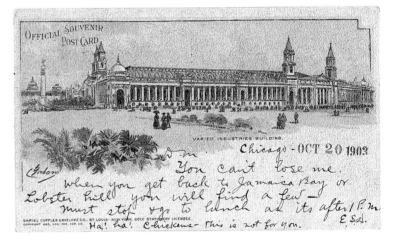

October 23rd.   I suspect ESD is writing to his wife Mrs Daniells who is staying in Rutherford, N.J. and that the chickens are their children. Both Jamaica Bay and Lobster Hill sound enticing. Mr Daniells is well ahead of the game in sending a view of the fabulous 1904 St Louis World's Fair.   03g

October 1st.   Ettie writes from Eastbourne to Mabel Lines in London SE, *I have one like Cissie's PC. How many PPC's have you now. I have 220.* Thematic cards were largely issued in series, most often of six: good marketing was thus matched by printing convenience and efficiency.   03h

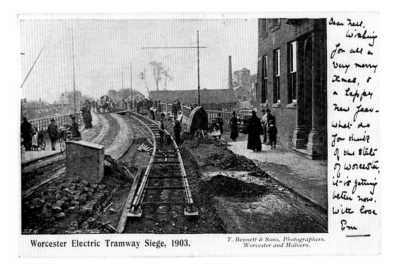

Worcester Electric Tramway Siege, 1903.   *T. Bennett & Sons, Photographers,
                                                Worcester and Malvern.*

December 24th. Also not quite in the robin and holly mode for Christmas Greetings yet it brings pictorial news from EM in Worcester to Nellie Davis in Tenbury. Laying a tramway caused this kind of havoc in other towns and cards with similar captions are found with their Boer War echoes. According to EM relief seems to be near.   03i

July 16th.   On this elegant Art Nouveau card with its fine enamel colours Enid in Bournemouth writes to a friend in New Brighton using a learned latinism to baffle servants who might wish to pry. *Did you osculate Ernest goodbye*, she asks.   03j

September 9th.   The cats of Louis Wain (who seldom drew anything else) were, and still are, the rage among card collectors. At least this smug feline does not stare with those ever-widening eyes that seemed to presage the artist's final madness.   03k

September 16th.   The French set the trend for making postcards of popular posters before the turn of the century. Gypsy who lives in a house called Mysora in Bexhill sends this to Miss Badbrook whose home is Inglenook in East Sheen. Nestlé is still with us.   03l

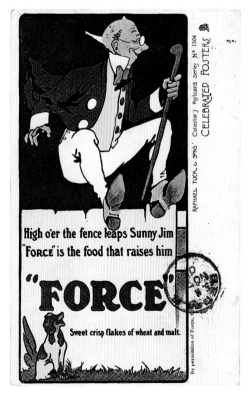

September 19th.   In the small world of the postcard a minor artist can be king. Raphael Kirchner at the age of 24 draws Nina his wife and muse as a liberated woman. This is the soft porn of the era and JS sends it boldly to Mrs Creswick in Kingston-On-Thames, adding as an unconvincing disclaimer the words *Tut. Tut.* 03m

November 6th.   *Yes by dam* writes Binny from Northallerton to Nurse Shackleton in Aiskews, *I'll take care of the little darlings for you. Will feed it on "Force" & you too when I see you.* Sunny Jim became a catch-phrase that my father was still using 50 years later. Unlike Nestlé, Force, and Sunny Jim, still linger on the supermarket shelves.   03n

November 6th.   High over an invisible Crystal Palace sails Stanley Spencer's pioneer airship. Meanwhile in other places Count Zeppelin's more ambitious prototypes are well advanced and a few weeks after this card is sent the Wright Brothers will have inaugurated the age of the aeroplane.   03o

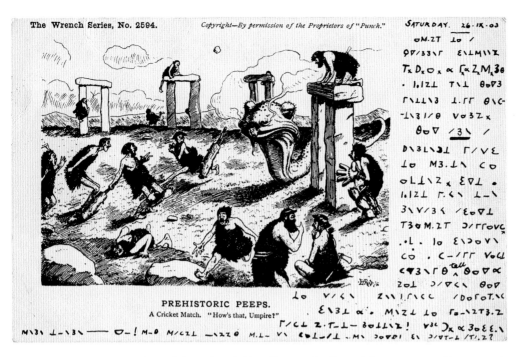

The Wrench Series, No. 2594. Copyright—By permission of the Proprietors of "Punch."

PREHISTORIC PEEPS.
A Cricket Match. "How's that, Umpire!"

September 26th.   In the days of large households with servants the coded message was the answer to postcard privacy. Shorthand, mirror writing and other strategies were common and the odd foreign or obscure word (as in 03j) could come in useful. Usually the encrypted matter was no more gripping than the general run of postcard messages but here is a hot one well worth the half hour or so it takes to crack the simple cypher. Sent from Liverpool to Miss Hitchcock at 40 Churchill St, Sprugfield, Mass., it reads *Owing to a quarrel between GPO and LNWR* [Post Office and Railway respectively] *I didn't get your letter till yesterday morn and you are a perfect lamb to write so often. But I didn't like the remark about growing callous. If I do become so I shall tell you and not cause you to make needless apologies. Bert and I went to Lohengrin last night. Rotten! Mrs R and Robbie were there - Oh! Why wasn't Henry with me so we could be caught again?* The humour of the Punch cartoon, as so often, eluded me though the bearded figure in the foreground appears to be a caricature of the great cricketer W G Grace (see 11j). Wagner's music drama seems to have been the loser that evening.

03p

WESTMINSTER CARTOON SERIES No. 2.   "Equivocal Company."

September 7th.   Even more unalluringly obscure than antique Punch jokes are those old political cartoons in which dead issues are rehearsed by forgotten protagonists. Here at least the matter is enlivened by the novelty of a motor car with a beer barrel engine and pumps for steering handles. Luckily Mr Gills words to Miss Trix (Miss Beatrice Reeve Bray) in Okehampton, Devon, clarify the issue somewhat and provide a link with 03f. He seems to be helping with a speech. *Balfour may do, & think what he likes but we won't have compensation to publicans out of the rates neither will we have the Education Bill for we are not only Passive Resisters but, I believe we must be Active Resisters. How will that do for you?*

03q

03a. Published D.R.G.M./E.B&C.i.B No 9794

03b. *Over 500 promises. If all are true, enough to put us at top of poll.* Two more sheets *returned last night. I take oath of secrecy at Town Hall at 12.00 today.*

Raphael Tuck. London Series 770 artist anonymous.

03c. Arthur Livingstone, Publisher, New York.4.

03d. Anonymous (apparently German origin) serie 1158.

03e. *My dear Mr Jacques. I have travelled very well. I am now in Paris. We had a very pleasant sea voyage , but getting near Dieppe I was very sick. I was quite alone in my carriage till I got on the boat 'Tamise'. A young girl & her father were my companions. I feel rather tired. Paris looks so funny. My best greetings.*

KF (Kunzli Frères) Paris. 2467 57257

03f. Publisher unknown.

03g. The St Louis World's Fair was opened in April 1904 but the card is more on time than the fair itself since the original scheduled opening was to have commemorated the centenary of the Louisiana Purchase in 1803.

Cupples, the publisher had the official concession on postcards and grossed over $100,000.

Samuel Cupples Envelope Co. St Louis/New York. Artist C Graham.

03h. I am not sure that 'very slow' is a useful translation of 'adagio' . It leaves no room for 'largo' which would have to be 'very slow indeed'.

Signed PVB (i.e. Percy Bradshaw, who after a career in postcards and journals, ran a succesful art school in London).

Henri Moss & Co. London Series 4415. Printed in Germany.

03i. T.Bennettt & Sons, Photographers. Worcester & Malvern. Signed S.T.H. on photo.

03j. Publisher anonymous. Signed by artist H.E. (prob. Helmut Eichrodt, born 1872, worked in Karlstruhe).

03k. *We hope you arrived home quite safe and were able to sleep we are still under the Tammy from Oxford & Cambridge.* (to Mr Musto in Tufnell Park, from Southend)

03l. *Many thanks for your letter. it came while I was in hospital where I was for nearly 5 weeks with Diptheria.*

H.M & Co's Famous Posters in Miniature Series. 4421.

03m. Kirchner's cards were hugely popular & became the pin-ups of World War I towards the end of which he died aged 41.

E.Storch, Vienna (printed Reisser, Vienna) c.1900.

03n. Raphael Tuck. Celebrated Posters Series 1504.

03o. From J.S. to C.E.Parnell Esq. in Streatham Hill saying, *I shall be coming to see you tomorrow evening. Hope...it will be convenience - just for 1/2 an hours chat & to give apologies this time.*

Anonymous. Printed in Saxony No1325.

03p. The Wrench Series No.2594 (via 'Punch')

03q. Westminster Cartoon Series No2. Artist F.C.Gould.

Port Arthur   Tent near foundation stone

"Ecclesbourne" 24-11-04. My dear "darlint"! Don't be cross, will you? How would you like to go the a nuss (sometimes called a nurse)

November 24th.   This Russian treaty port in NE China was the first focus of the Russo-Japanese war which flared up earlier in the year. Britain allied itself with the eventually victorious Japan. The Red Cross was strongly present complete with its women nurses to whom the card refers. Despite the baby talk the message to Miss Field in Selwyn Rd, Eastbourne may have a serious intent and even *Don't be cross, will you?* could be a warning pun. Britain had been shocked the month before this card was sent by an attack on Hull trawlers by the Russian fleet (see 04d).   04a

London   *Newspaper Boys waiting for the "Special Edition", Piccadilly Circus*

May 2nd.   A swarm of newsboys guarantees publicity for the Football Echo's launch. Sent to Mrs Kruyt in Amsterdam with a message in franglais hinting at naughty things to come, *Je vous envoie 2 nouveautés très <u>shocking</u> quand on comprend l'anglais surtout le language 'very special'.*   04b

4686
Tall Buildings
of lower
New York.

October 1st.   A preoccupied Aunt Minne breaks the US Post Office rules and writes her flustered message on the back of the card (perhaps thinking pencil doesn't count). An indulgent official lets her get away with it and it is delivered to Mrs Herbert Herring, Foxcroft, Maine, without surcharge on her one cent stamp.   04c

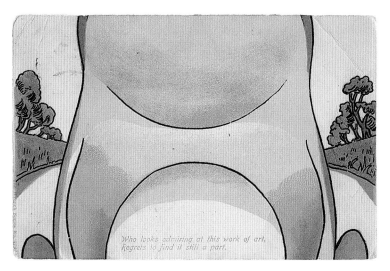

October 31st.   Speedy reactions, both in the mass production of this card and in its sending to Mr Kirby in Lincoln. The message is typical, *Shall we sit down and cross our hands to a game like this. no.* On Oct 10th the Hull fishing fleet was attacked by forty Russian warships ineptly heading for Admiral Togo and their nemesis off Korea.   04d

June 27th.   The middle of a three card trick. Sent to Miss Davies in Durham it no doubt baffled her as it did me until I found the other two to complete the picture (see note). The cryptic writer says, *If I could only disguise myself I would take advantage of the Leap Year. You would no longer be like this picture.*   04e

January 4th.   Thackeray perfected the Write Away which provided a start to the message. His wit kept them in use beyond the age of writing-on-front-only. Gertrude Butler in Lincoln receives this nicely misused example, *Oh my boots do hurt me I bought them from Dunns sharnt go there again Don't like the girls in the shop neither.* 04f

August 20th.   Wilfred Orange soberly reminds Ernest Coleman in Stroud Green of an appointment, then lets rip on the front, *I worship at the shrine of the beautiful Clara.* This forthright photo captures Clara (later Dame Clara) Butt's majestic good looks. With matching voice she was the contralto for whom Elgar wrote his Sea Pictures.   04g

January 23rd.   *Note the cake,* writes JWM from Baltimore to Mr Draper in London. Now (even without the historically distorting lens of Political Correctness) we would note that there is something creepy in the spectacle of whites blacking up to mimic the dances of their imagined inferiors.   04h

April 27th.   Darby & Joan, born in an 18thC ballad, have been inseparable ever since. Here Ethel as Joan writes to Claire her Darby longing for a time when they can be together. Passionate messages were common between women, but Ethel emphatically repeats *piles of love* on the back. Perhaps 04j is the kind of *Baby PC* referred to. 04i

DR. ELGAR.
2544. Rotary Photo. E.C.

A Fair Catch. JWS 2421

November 7th.   Mary Green in Loughborough sends this card with seventeen nestling babies on it (by no means a record) to Gert in Leicester, *will you come over to the fair on Thursday after work as I perhaps shall not be abble to go out on Sunday.* There were many series of such Multiple Baby cards.   04j

April 9th.   HSL tells Arthur Deakin in Gravesend *I have been staying in E'bourne for Easter.* Elgar was by now Sir Edward: a festival of his music had just taken place at Covent Garden. Here is the epitome and exemplar of the Edwardian country gentleman: no nuance is missing, right down to the pipe in kid-gloved hands.   04k

November 5th.   The fixed-wheel bike with single brake increased the social scope of ordinary people in rural areas, with the occasional surprise bonus. S in Ryde, IOW makes an assignation with Molly Davidson, *If you are not doing anything this evening meet me at six, am off duty then and not going home. Love.*   04l

The Last of " DAN LENO " the King's Jester.
November 8th. 1904.

The Cigarette girl

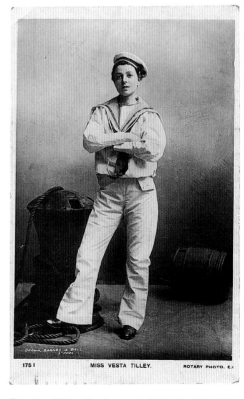

1751   MISS VESTA TILLEY.   ROTARY PHOTO. E.

November 17th.   The long cortège of the King's Jester (he gave a Royal Command performance in 1903) heads for Tooting from which Tom writes to Wm Clark in Billericay, *What price the other side your humble was there also unfortunately in the other affair I marked in paper otherwise all well.* Dan Leno was 44.   04m

August 3rd.   IM in Johannesburg writes to Mr Hogg at the chemists in Station Road, Capetown, *Yours to hand. I thought you had got washed away by the floods...* It is inconceivable of course that such an image of a white girl could have been sent so openly: who knows but that this situation may one day be reversed.   04n

December 11th.   Jim drops a wistful hint to Miss White in Belgravia, *Dear Druce. just one more to add to your collection. I should like to see you in this dress. With love xx.* Vesta Tilley, The London Idol, a cheeky male impersonator was also a woman of fashion married to an MP. She died (as Lady de Freece) in 1952.   04o

July 20th.   One who signs himself Wilson writes to John Steven, Fernlea, West Kilbride, Ayrshire. *Just been round these works which are really worth seeing but ignorance has spoiled the effect, The visits have been very successful but heat has been awful 105° in shade on Sunday. Hope to have a day sightseeing tomorrow. Leave here on Saturday for Sinnovitz? en route to Copenhagen.* This beautifully composed view of the AEG works (so tempting to have made such a circle the centre of the picture) complete with members of the workforce gives some idea of the huge scale of these components and of the factory itself. The printed caption tells us that we are looking at 6000 P.S. three-phase dynamo engine (all one glorious word in German) of which the firm has produced six examples in the present year of business. Such pride in the poetry of engineering is a special province of the German postcard.   04p

November 8th.   JCG in Chinnampo (Nampo), the port of Pyongyang in the west of North Korea sends a card of the battle of Nanshan, another theatre of the Russo-Japanese War. His message to Miss Bland at the Steamer Hotel in Fleetwood, Lancs, is terse, *Well. Hoping you are the same.* Perhaps time is short, and in any case the card within a card format of the design leaves little space. The layout and embellishment of the card could be described as Art Nouveau with a Japanese accent. Its vignetted views show scenes of devastation in Nanshan whose defoliated and shattered landscapes prefigure the Korean War of fifty years later when Pyongyang experienced successive occupations, (captured by the UN troops in 1950, by the Chinese in 1951 and recaptured in 1951). Not for the last time (see 73a) one is reminded of the words of Tacitus, 'Having made a wasteland, they call it peace'.   04q

04a. (posted Willesden) *My dear darlint! Don't be cross will you? How would you like to go and be a nuss (sometimes called a nurse) in this picture (I mean the one on the other side)? Had any snow your way yet? You might let us snow if you haven't. Good-bye. Be good. Sleep well Best love. All well. You too? Yours ever, Quite mad!*

Publisher unknown.

04b. *I thank you madam for your cards...I send you 2 up to the minute ones of a 'very shocking' kind if you understand English, at least its 'very special' jargon.*

The Wrench Series. No 2258. photo W.P.Dando

04c. *Dear Gertie I guess you think I am never going to answer your post card. I have just got done in the garden. I have had lots to do. Good Bye. write soon.*

Souvenir Post Card Co. A Loeffler. 4686

04d. Russian Outrage on Hull Fishing Fleet. 22.10.04. Another copy of the same card from Elsie Whichells posted (Nov 4th) to her father says *Dear Dad. Thought you would like a B Eye View how the R.Warships fired on our poor English trawlers.*

Valentines Series. Artist unknown

04e. The doggerel caption for this central section reads:-
Who looks admiring on this work of art
Regrets to find it still a part.
Evidently this was the one of the series to send first since either top or bottom of the picture would give the game away. Many such puzzle sets exist depicting snakes, alligators, King Edward VII etc.

Wrench Series4797. Printed in Saxony.

04f. Raphael Tuck. 'Write Away' Post Card Series 645 IV. Designed in England. Chromographed in Saxony. Artist Lance Thackeray.

04g. Rotary Photographic Series. 3860. Photo by Fellows Wilson.

04h. National Art Views Co. NY.City. No 412.

04i. Raphael Tuck 'Art' Postcard. Series 1152. Artist anonymous.

04j. Publisher unknown. Series 303.

04k. Rotary Photographic Series 2544.

04l. JWS (J.Welsh & Sons) 2421.

04m. Publisher unknown.

04n. Sallo Epstein & Co, Durban.

04o. This card like many produced by Rotary exists in tinted and untinted versions.

Rotary Photographic Series 1751.

04p. AEG.Berlin. P.K.26.

04q. Printed and published in Japan.

September 15th.   Hop picking in Kent was the traditional working holiday for London's east-enders and scenes like this of a crowded cart in front of the now naked hop poles have a pastoral charm. Tony, writing from near the hop fields in Sevenoaks to William Murray in Edinburgh, gives a darker side of the picture, *It is a happier sight to see the 'Hoppers' on their road to the Hop plantations. They are overflowing with joy as they drive along... alas! They often return to their homes without one of their number. He may have died, been locked up in prison or is too ill to remove. Lots of sickness amongst the pickers always. It makes me sad to see humanity on so low a scale & also makes me realise what I have to be thankful for. am coming home soon Willie.*   05a

January 4th.   HC merely remarks to Miss Smith in Bronkhurst, Hants *I am in London at the place you see on the card will write soon.* The inconspicuous vehicle in the foreground centre left might be an early appearance of a motor car amongst the horse traffic.   05b

February 3rd.   This unremarkable view of the North river skyline is considerably enhanced by the exhortation in red to Vote Soon (for your candidate to be a delegate to the International Congress of Insurance Writers) as well as the flurry of wavy postmarks in the sky. Sent to Allen D Ball in Ludlow, Vermont.   05c

July 13th.   FH sends a Write-Away card to Miss G.Payne in Brighton and continues on the other side *I've just come home. been on the lying system. Poor darkie wants to know if he might hang his hat up to me now....They all got the sack at the Hippodrome fresh stock this week.* See note for more of the unravellable plot.   05d

August 27th.   MDP in Moscow to Miss Williams in Haverfordwest, *A view of the Palace Square, St Petersburgh where the people were shot down on that terrible Sunday. Have just completed my pilgrimage to Holy Moscow.* A fragment of the prehistory of the revolution. Bloody Sunday, the massacre of petitioning workers, was on Jan 22nd.   05e

December 13th.   CS in Auckland tells Miss Stead in Montreal *It is a common sight here to see the Maoris rubbing noses though it might strike you as being rather funny...* Denton's photographs of Maori life were sympathetic (compared with the average Australian view of their own Aborigines) and the props were authentic.   05f

February 18th.   Lottie to Miss Hollands in Higham, Kent from Rochester. *hope you will like this one of course dear you know the history of this place...* The Jezreelites' temple had no rooms but formed a huge ladder from which on the Latter Day they would be drawn up to heaven by their hair (which like their nails they never cut).   05g

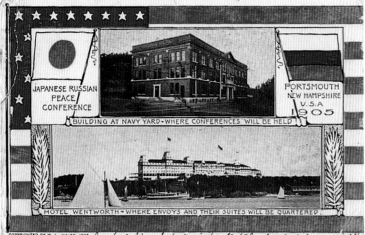

August 13th.   After the defeat at Tsushima and the Potemkin mutiny (immortalised by Eisenstein) the Russians had little option but to settle terms in Portsmouth, NH. This card was sent to Mrs Tobelman, Jamaica Plain, Mass. by JEU who is to leave Portsmouth just before the Peace conference gets under way,   05h

October 15th.   American publishers were just as quick on the draw as their English counterparts when it came to a spectacular accident. Sterling Baer's laconic message to Mrs Mabel Clark of Laurel Hill, Norwich, Conn., hardly matches up to the dramatic situation.   05i

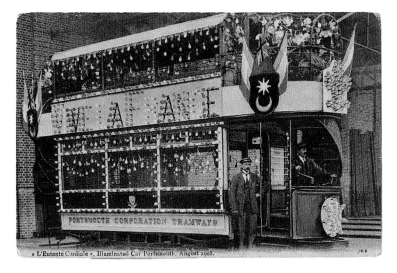

September 25th.   Grace, with many kisses, writes to Mrs George Martin in Bristol, *Dear Grandmother we took the Royal Maryann to Southsea on Monday but the sea was so rough we could not sail her*. Vive la France was a novel sentiment to express in lights but a new understanding had grown, furthered by royal visits etc.   05j

April 19th.   MT to Miss Penlington in Malpas, Cheshire. *I am instead of the teacher on the right hand side. The other young man, being a pupil teacher, Teachers have not come yet*. This largely solemn study of Brynsiengyn Council School was posted in the legendary Llanfairpwllgwngyllgogerychwyndrobwllllantysiliogogogoch.   05k

August 25th.   This group of Batwa from the Ituri forest brought to London by Harrison, explorer and big game hunter, visited Parliament in sailor suits and performed (in a programme including polar bears and a Rob Roy show) their 'native dances wearing only girdles of grass, against a scenic background', at the Hippodrome.   05l

Precise date unclear.   Flo writes to Mrs Johns in Bohemia, Newport, Mons., *Just in time to meet the train have had tea now going to enjoy the show*. One person panicking behind a bar might now be more typical of the Coliseum, home of English National Opera and still the most congenial of grand theatres.   05m

January 23rd.   Will tells Nell in Cheltenham that he will write tonight and is off to Peterchurch. Anthony Ludovici made illustrations of Dickens, whose world, as can be seen in this fully characterised rather than caricatured study of a fish and chip shop, persisted well into the 20th century.   05n

October 21st.   *What does this remind you of Eva*, writes Nell in Warwick to Miss Smith in Oxford, *Do you ever see the boy. I often think about it don't you. I wonder if he does*. A magic episode remembered but Nell is a pragmatic girl of the present as the rest of her robust message confirms.   05o

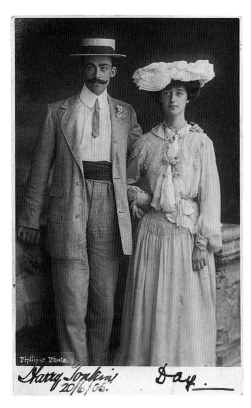

05a. Y&C (Young & Cooper, Maidstone). No 8 in the series.

05b. Publisher unknown. No 77982

05c. Photoelectrotype Eng.Co.NY. Irving Underhill. Overprinted for Diamond Jubilee of NY Life Insurance Co.

05d. The Message continues *I said good evening to Charlie for first time. Been along Terminus with the big man good thing his girl wasn't anywhere about. They all got the sack at the Hippodrome fresh stock this week. Just had a p card from EM cheek I told him I wouldn't write love from FH.*

S.Hildesheimer & Co. London & Manchester. Printed in Austria. artist Sydney Carter.

05e. St Petersburg No 162

05f. S.M&Co.Series. Photo Denton (F.J.Denton)

05g. Publisher anonymous. No 440

05h. Copyrighted by W.L.Julian 1905.

05i. Wreck of the 9th Ave 'L' at 53rd St & 9th Ave., NY September 11, 1905. publ R.Weigel, Jersey City.

05j. Trichromatic PC by J.Welch & Sons Portsmouth. 'Printed at our works in Belgium'.

05k. Roberts, Blaemaris, 1905. Detail below

05l. *Dear K. Your card and letter to hand, also I saw the carriage on the top of the van as I came on duty stomp for time. Nance will be writing soon....have you this one before.*

Scott Russell & Co. Birmingham. The 'Scott' series No 747

05m. Raphael Tuck & Sons. London Coliseum Series

05n. Davidson Bros. Pictorial cards from originals by A.Ludovici. Series 6102

05o. Publisher unknown. Series No 925

05p. Phillips, photographer unknown (presumably Liverpool)

05q. Rotary photographic series. 101A

05r. Publisher unknown

05s. G.W.Faulkner & Co. London. No 503F. Photo Elliot & Fry.

June 20th.   Harry Tonkin and Day have had their photo taken by Phillips in their summer leisure finery, a young married couple. They send it from Rice Lane to Miss V Saunders in Brainton, N Devon. Day writes *am sending through post as am afraid cannot send them the other way. writing tonight.*   05p

October 21st.   Gerrie Jones sends a photo card of England's greatest actor (the first to be knighted) who died on October 13th, to Miss Annie Ramsden in New Plymouth, New Zealand. Irving's wife maintained that repeated performances, by public demand, of the melodrama The Bells hastened his end at 67.   05q

November 16th.   Miss Harwood in Stratford on Avon receives this card, *Hope you will not fall in love with this gentleman, because he will be going far away perhaps the MS would be rather jealous what say you? Don't you think he is rather nice?* Who Oluwole Bankole was remains a mystery.   05r

March 15th.   From Finsbury Park Edith sends Jennie Ball in Hornsey a picture of Paderewski (see 01n) and invites her to tea *on Saturday. I will hurry from business. Hope you will like the card. I could not get Tschkowsky (?). Don't forget the canvas. Isn't it fine Dad having bought the house...*   05s

Looking up California street, San Francisco, Cal., after the earthquake and fire, April 18, 1906.

August 2nd.   Sent to Miss Annie P Bundy, Topeka, Kansas (the entire address) to thank her for a gift. This scene of devastation after the double catastrophe of the San Francisco earthquake and fire matches anything in the apocalyptic visions of later cinema. It pre-echoes the epic movie style of central view with deep perspective. Miss Bundy left her postcard collection to the Topeka library whose deaccession stamp this shamelessly bears.   06a

Piccadilly Circus,   London.

RIVER FRONT BY NIGHT, NEW YORK

August 5th.   Hetty Kinsey writes to Miss Lily Hundall in Cliftonville (at Doves Nest) with the sort of confused messages reminiscent of those now left on answering machines. Thomas Tilling's horse bus is headed for his depot in Peckham. This was the first route to be fully motorised (in 1906/7).   06b

January 16th.   This romantic night view of the river front is probably based on a daylight photograph. Until 1907 the US charged an extra cent for writing on the address side of the card. EUB's mild rebuke to the uncommunicative Mr Carey in Clapham Junction is therefore restricted to the small space provided.   06c

March 23rd.   From *Flo & Co* in Paddington to Beatie Brown in Wiveliscombe, Som. ....*We see by the paper Mr Dennis intends to leave the circuit if Mr Green stops. We went to see the Japanese sailors yesterday the heroes of Port Arthur. Love to all.* The typewriter was still a formidable engine.   06d

May 26th.   Miss Willsher in Cliftonville gets a card from Australia but via Peckham where her friend must have been given it the day before, *I spent an hour with Mrs Richardson yesterday & did enjoy it hearing all about her adventures in Australia.* On the front MJM writes *This is not very pretty but it comes from Australia.*   06e

December 11th.   Quite a lot of leg to be showing in 1906. Jim Pipe sends this German card from Bulford Camp, Salisbury to his wife Clara in Bower Hinton, Somerset, with a nicely suggestive message. *She will have to be careful, otherwise her seaweed will get slightly damp. Hoping you are all well at home.*   06f

February 26th.   Emmie from St Gabriel's Hostel, Camberwell to Emmie Luscombe in Brentford, *We had groups taken because our Lady President, Miss Wild, has just left us. Her successor is a fussy, wiry parchment-like old soul. Have been busy writing out application forms. Am trying B'ford or Acton. Sounds like freedom soon doesn't it.*   06g

July 14th.   *Dear Sir. Sorry unable to send chicken & rabbits today, chicken are rather scarce this week. Will send beginning of next week if any. Yours truly Pople & P.* Mr Jones the fishmerchant in Clevedon might have thought this ironic in view of the spectacular display (complete with proprietors, staff and, upstairs, womenfolk).   06h

June 15th.   Moon, Spoon and June those handy rhyming words for songwriters are brought together here. SEM writes to Miss Toombs in Brandon, Suffolk, *Just a line to ask if the "Moon" revealed anything this time where you & "A" were at Whitsun hope you had a very enjoyable time, "we did but had no moonlight"...*   06i

March 2nd.   Lawrence writes at length (and somewhat archly) to Mrs Whitehead in Glasgow, *I seem to spend quite a lot of my time looking out for cards that I think will interest you. Does this?* He describes his writing place in the British Museum Reading Room (which now forms the centre of the BM's Great Court).   06j

August 29th.   A sends Mrs Percy, Married Apts, Ross Barracks, Shorncliffe this saucy card on the theme of photography, the alchemy of the period. *The apples up here are simply lovely looking like wax - my mouth is watering whilst writing. have you started to learn that song yet viz. Hush! don't wake etc. ?*   06k

August 29th.   W C Butler is in Geneva for another Esperanto Conference and writes to William Wall in *Bristol, Anglolando*, describing the ease of communication via Esperanto *the most wonderful ...invention of the 19th Century*. This card of the 1905 Kongreso Esperantista in Boulogne must contain the record number of named people.   06l

July 26th.   *...you see I have got you a P.C. like you wanted* writes EC in Faygate to Mrs Vine in Newdigate, places local to Britain's first major road accident. On the Kent firemens' outing everyone wanted to sit on the open top of the double decker. When the brakes failed the bus lurched out of control. Ten were killed.   06m

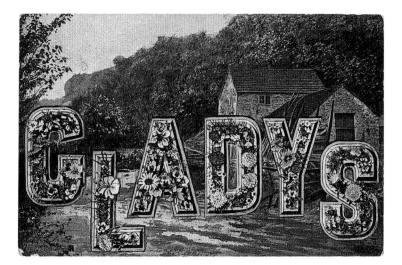

October 5th.   Em in Dunedin, New Zealand writes to Gladys Brooke, a vicar's daughter in New Plymouth, Taranaki, *...How do you like this PC Gladdie? I have been hunting all over town to get a 'Gladys' for you.* These lovely cards interestingly do not just repeat the same letters but have many variant designs.   06n

December 13th.   *Dear old bessie just a PC to you hoping this will find you doing your work better than the Slavey in this Picture. Don't her Master Dress her nice...* Writes Daisy to Miss B Hall in Dursley. This is Donald McGill at the outset of his almost sixty year career as a comic postcard artist, probably published in 1904/5.   06o

While you are drinking beer and wine
I eat the grapes so sweet and fine;
And when you kill the little birds
They sing for me their latest flirts.

Genesis i. 27.

Mr JOSEPH SALOMONSON
of Amsterdam
(ex-Consul),

MEVA,

The apostle of natural life.

September 20th. *Dear Lily: You will see I am sending you the photo of my latest mash. Miss B will be awfully jealous. I shall have to be dressed the same will let you know when we are coming to sunny Southsea for the honeymoon.* Brighton was evidently the place to see Meva since on an identical card Tot reports a sighting (Oct 14th) to Nance in Clapham Common. 06p

No. 13. *Published for Newcastle Socialist Society, by permission of H. M. Hyndman.*

H. M. HYNDMAN.

Wage-slaves under better conditions remain wage-slaves still. No improvements of the capitalist system of production can change or seriously modify the bitter struggle which must go on so long as the system endures in any shape. It is for the rising generation of Englishmen to decide whether in this country the substitution of organised co-operation for anarchical competition shall be brought about consciously and peacefully, or unconsciously and forcibly.

Hyndman's "Commercial Crises."

February 10th. Robb greets Mr Lewis of Leigh in Lanark with slogans, *The defeated Candidate for Burnley, Father of English Socialism, The Rebel of England. Would that he were in the House.* The Labour Party became a political reality in 1906, yet Hyndman quit to form the National Socialist Party in 1916. 06q

06a. M.Rielder. Pub.Los Angeles

06b. *37 Coin St. Blackfriars. Dear Lily I have only just heard by what train we shall be coming by tomorrow (Saturday) Mr Marshall says we are to go by the 8.30 train tomorrow morning from Charing Cross. I daresay we shall be down almost before you have time to get this card. The only thing would be for us to find the house & then come back for you at the station with love from Hetty.*

Publisher unknown

06c. Ill.Post.Card Co. NY.1934

06d. *I think Beat likes children so I am sending her a pair...did Edie Wilse go to Dunball Saturday? If they did they had rather a rough journey the weather has been very cold in London lately...*

Publisher unknown.

06e. *....Mr W & I are going to the Garrick this afternoon. Did I tell you we heard Vivien Charter I never was more charmed with anyone. I'm afraid this estate business will be a very expensive affair difficult to get money from mortgages.*

Published by Daisy M.Bates.

06f. German card with heraldic lion device. Serie No 1593

06g. Publisher and photographer unknown.

06h. Vearncombe Photo. Bridgewater

06i. Trichromatic PC by J.Welch & Sons Portsmouth. 'Printed at our works in Belgium'.

06j. *I said I'd send you another card by the end of the week so here it is. You'll be able to cover... your walls with them soon & make a regular portrait gallery! Hardly any work to do so went home in the middle of the day again. Not going to the smoking-concert tonight; don't feel like it; so shall stay at home and be quiet - write to Arthur probably....I really think I shall have to start my autobiography. You must be getting mixed with my 'PAST'! But it's really not so horrible or mysterious as you possibly imagine! Also when I send you some Edwards' letters perhaps you would find marginal notes useful! Anyway I don't want any mystery as far as you are concerned, as you say you are interested (& of course I know you are!) but it would be a long job & you'd have to have it in penny numbers. Yours Lawrence.*
[on picture side] *I generally sit at the desk next but one on this side to the brass rail place. The black books with white labels in the circular cases are the catalogue. There's another room thro' the glass doors under the clock & others & miles & miles of book-cases besides what you see.*

Lawrence sounds a bit self important to me, like someone to be mistrusted in an Iris Murdoch novel. If I were Mrs Anderson I'd steer well clear.

E.T.B & Co.London 782/621. (66438)
(Taylor. E.,Beverley).

06k. Davidson Bros. Drawing by Tom Browne. Serie 2585.

06l. *This is a picture of some of the members of our last Esperantist Congress (1905). Here in Geneva I met several thousands of persons of all nations & I can understand them by means of Esperanto (& be understood by them) as easily as if we both spoke English. I believe Esperanto to be the most wonderful discovery or invention of the 19th Century - certainly it is the one which will have the most beneficent influence on mankind. yours ever.*

Esperanto and optimism go together. Reaching a peak in the thirties it is now almost disappearing in face of the relentless progress of English as a world language.

The numbers and names are just as difficult to decipher in the original

Publisher anonymous (presumably the Esperanto Soc.)

06m. Ironically the Kent firemen had decided for the first time to go by omnibus rather than train (a decision carried by one vote) on their annual outing. It is difficult to imagine from the wreckage that this was one of those solid open top double-deckers seen for example in Piccadilly Circus on 10b.

Publisher unknown.

06n. *Dear Gladys. Of course it is <u>my</u> turn for a letter from you I have been wondering what has come over you. Fancy you forgetting me like that <u>I am</u> greatly offended. Tell Bert I'll give him a punch next time I see him. He will know what for. His letter to A.A....*

E.F.A. (Excelsior Fine Arts Co.) Christian Names Series.

06o. *....how was you on Sunday night I was talking to that boy from Swanwell you know Frances Dennys?*
Donald McGill was born in 1875 and died in 1962 in Blackheath where he lived most of his life (his house in Bennett Park sports the only blue plaque dedicated to a comic postcard artist). He had already prepared his 1963 cards when he died.
This particular image seems to belong to a group that uses a Write Away style message. They are undated but may well have been drawn in 1904.

E.S.London (Empire Series. pictorial P.C.Co Ltd) 2009

06p. Publisher unknown (presumably 'Meva' himself)

06q. Newcastle Socialist Society.

06r. G.L.Co. 1025/4 (France)

February 27th. Auntie Adela in Rye hopes Dorothy Noakes in Robertsbridge will add this to her album, *Are you & Frank really trading bicycles?* Cabaret acts like La Loie Fuller (of Moulin Rouge fame) with her whirling veils provided an alternative tradition that allowed modern dance to emerge as an art form. 06r

A BUSY SPOT ON HAMPSTEAD HEATH.

October 30th. All the Fun of the Fair in 1907 often included a cinematographic booth. What was to be the dominant art form of the Twentieth Century was still a side show though already here quite elaborate. Ironically enough the success of the cinema was to be a major factor in the decline of the postcard as a source of image, of reportage, of romance and entertainment. Small money makes hard choices. Here on offer at the Queens Cinematograph run by Mittocks Circus among the 'Empire Varieties' are 'Stirring Stories and Incidents of our Army & Navy'. BD writes to Mrs Shemming in Wanstead, Essex, *Sorry I didn't come to see you on Sunday I was in the country shooting...* 07a

January 19th. LL (Lucien Levy a leading French Postcard Producer) came to London in 1905 and, despite wayward spelling, captured with his usual lively refinement the genius loci. Jess writes to Mrs Maber in Bournemouth. 07b

May 13th. Though we are now blasé about aerial views they were a considerable novelty in 1907 when Mr Coats sent this spectacular panorama based on a photograph taken from an airship, to his son Martin in Manchester, Md. 07c

July 8th. Leila is at the Jamestown Exposition in Norfolk Virginia and buys a card of the two submarines on show (here populated by cheerful marines) to send to Minnie Thomas in Urbana, III., *What do you think of these for warfare. My it is hot today but the exposition is fine.* 07d

May 23rd. Minnie in Canada writes to her sister Melinda Ahearne in Lawrence, Mass., *this is you and little tommie in your autto, ahah.* Such giant highway speedsters must be what turned the head of Mr Toad. Motoring was new and lacked protocols: women drivers (in the postcard world) were almost as numerous as men. 07e

February 7th. Alice in St Leonards exchanges news with Miss Trowell in Bexhill *...Had a card from A.T. asking us to tea on Sunday but you know W. won't go. Cross is still expecting to come isn't it funny can't understand her.* Few cards are inhabited with such vibrant actuality as this scene, a moment in several lives caught forever. 07f

September 8th. AM in Liverpool to Miss Trockell in Stonehouse, Glos. *Have four rooms let.... had an American for 2 nights and saw her off on the boat.* The brand new Lusitania was soon to break the transatlantic record, crossing in under five days. German submarines sank the ship in 1915 with a loss of 1400 lives. 07g

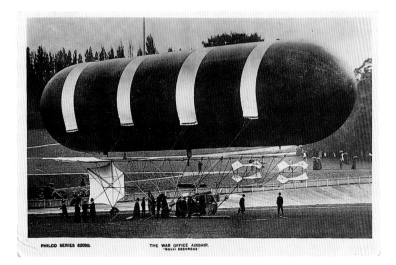

November 8th. Miss Holford in Sidmouth from J in Brixton. *Thought you would like to have this.* J may have seen Nulli Secundus fly over London a month before. She would not see it again since its fabric made from the intestines of 200,000 cattle perished in the rain. Cody recycled the engine for other flying experiments. 07h

June 18th. There had only been a sprinkling of suffrage cards before this year. Suddenly the campaign had caught fire. The idea of Votes for Women typically evoked for men a world turned upside down. Mother is reading 'How We Got the Vote - by Mrs Spankhurst'. Sent by SK to Jennie Potterton in Belfast arranging a visit. 07i

May 30th. A couple of classes up. The same reaction but with more irony. CB writes from St Hugh's to Miss Gostelow, Kingston, Oxford, *Let me give you a friendly word of advice and don't leave your poor fellow to such torture. I say by the way is the happy day fixed?* Women smoking in this period always signals danger. 07j

March 2nd. Jack in Birmingham not only *saw this man....and talked to him*, but purchased one of his postcards to send to Miss Sagley in Worthing. Among the many feats of walking, rolling, pushing etc. in these years (see 08d) this must have been one of the most pointlessly eccentric. 07k

September 30th. Mr Sykes, in Guinness Buildings, Fulham Palace Rd hears from E Spikins Sec. DDR, *Dear Sir & Bro. Can you manage to attend opening of new tent at Ingrams Coffee House, Fulham Cross, Tuesday next at 8.* The Rechabites were named after Rechab a biblical teetotaller. 07l

April 16th. H in Reading sends a dull message of thanks to Lil Grey in Folkestone *for her last p.c.* She should have been pleased to have found this no doubt free but rather spectacular card to send in exchange. Schweppes, one of the great Piccadilly Circus advertisers, is now a Coca Cola subsidiary. 07m

December 23rd. Fanny has visited Victor Beadell's New Time Studios (The Largest in the East End) and sends the result to her friend Kitty Friedelberg in Stoke Newington as a birthday-cum-Christmas card. The paper moon set-up was a staple of photographic studios on both sides of the Atlantic. 07n

September 13th. Addressed to J M Caso, Motor Engineer, Droitwich. This barrel organ/motor car gag is a suitable exchange. His correspondent praises the card of Bewley he has received, *What do you think of this and the ones I sent yesterday- What would you say if anyone ask you a ridiculous question like this one pip-pip.* 07o

February 25th.   *Dearest Evelyn. At last send PC. Hope you have enjoyed yourself this evening with B. Have just seen F with 2 girls what do you think of that. I will be his no more, see you soon,.* Ena writes from Chiswick on one of the endless series of cards showing the Dare sisters, Phyllis and Zena (see note).   07p

September 20th.   After shore leave from H.M.S Jupiter R Ferguson sends this new photo (on which he cuts a fine figure) to his sister in Sailley, Birmingham, *Hope you are all quite well at home. All quite well home here. just returned to ship from 4 days leave. This is my Photo just had a few done.*   07q

August 22nd. *Dear Nellie. I am sending a PC at last. We have taken another shop so I have not much time. Zena Dare was here last week she was nice I went to see her write back Elsie.* Zena and her younger sister made their stage debut in 1899 in 'Babes In The Wood' (when she was twelve and Phyllis was nine). Zena had the longer stage career retiring only in 1965 after she had played the last role she created, that of Mrs Higgins in My Fair Lady, for six years on end. When Elsie saw Zena Dare in 1907 she was at the height of her fame and one of the most photographed artistes of all time.

August 27th.   G.Cox would earn his place here as a cricketer but it is Charlie's message from London to Ruby Weeks in Brighton, that has always intrigued me. *Dear Ruby will you please meet me at the corner of Holbeck Row on Sunday morning and I will give you a suck of my toffee apple.*   07r

March 6th.   Robertson's the maker of this mystic bulb ply Mr Miller in Birmingham with their advertisement complete with fake hand-written message, *...We find they give a much better light than any other make...I forget the price but know I have saved money by using them. write soon. Kind Regards, Jack.*   07s

December 5th.   America conquers Europe in this defining image of the public history of aviation. In August 1908 Wilbur Wright flies past the grandstand at Harandières racecourse to give the first demonstration of sustained and controlled powered flight. The machine is seen heading towards the camera with the propellers behind the wings. The brothers had made few flights since the 1903 triumphs at Kitty Hawk. While this display had a commercial motive it inspired a whole generation of heroic aviators, especially in France. Wilbur died young but Orville lived to hear of the Hiroshima bomb being dropped from an aeroplane. Mr Munro in London receives this card from J T Morgan in P.O. Seine, and, probably, his first glimpse of a wonder of the age. Wright was showing the paces of the 'Flyer' in the most advanced country in the arena of aeronautics at the time.   08a

July 27th.   Millie in Fulham writes to Miss T Pearson in Hastings, *We are just off to Ravenscourt Park to see the Peacocks.* The motor bus on the far right advertises The Dairymaids which dates the view to 1906. It ran for nearly 250 performances and was in fact revived in 1908 itself (see 08g).   08b

February 8th.   Sent from Harrisburg, NY to Miss Emma Coffman in Fort Spring, West Virginia, *Well Emma, how dos this to fire winter and tell you that it is cold up this way. This leaves us all well...as ever L.C.C.* The address is in a surer hand than the message.   08c

WITH . .
MISS ADA RUSSELL'S COMPLIMENTS.

MARIEDL, The Tyrolean Giantess.
Age 27.   Weight 360 lbs.
Daily Diet—Cereals & Vegetables, 14 lbs., 2 quarts OXO & I quart of Milk.

January 25th.   *The 'Gentleman' went through here last Saturday walking for a wager & is to find a wife as well.* Harry Bensley, the Man in the Iron Mask, in fact had 200 offers of marriage as he travelled through 12 countries (inc. the USA). Reaching Geneva in 1914 on the home stretch he decided he must join up. He died in a lonely bedsitter in Brighton in 1965.   08d

August 30th.   Albert in Oldham is very free in writing to his aunt in Popeswood. *I suppose we shall see you coming back about this size you blooming great squash. This is the girl I was telling you about she is 27st. and 19 years of age we went to Blackpool Sat and had a ripping time don't get to saucy when the coom back or else the'll get theyead punching.*   08e

February 3rd.   The thing you want to know about giantesses is how tall they are, a fact not given either here or in Ve's message from Hollerton to Nellie Wellings in Kidderminster. She claims not to have *any news about our year* but goes into rare detail. Is Mariedl stealing an advantage by wearing a very tall hat and standing next to someone rather small?   08f

THE FRANCO-BRITISH EXHIBITION.
V384-10   THE FLIP-FLAP.   RAPID PHOTO. E.C

October 23rd.   Robert Courtneidge's revival of the 1906 success, The Dairymaids was evidently a lavish production and this scene looks like a show-stopper. It is the play advertised on a bus in 08b. Lil in Cambridge writes to Gert in Hackney, *Left out the stamps in my hurry to post letter.*   08g

September 3rd.   Difficult now to imagine that the London's White City really was once a forest of gleaming stucco Pavilions. The Flip Flap was a major attraction. *Went to the White City on Monday. We went up in the Flip Flap. I did not care very much for it. But we did like the scenic railway it was some fun....*   08h

November ?th.   From Santa Margarita, Cal., Esther sends her sunny class photo to Miss Kathleen Pope in Lewisham, probably a pen friend, *As our school had our pictures taken I thought I would send you one....it is only one class. The one with a cross on is me.* Did Kathleen send back a grey SE London equivalent?   08i

MRS. PANKHURST.

The National Women's Social and Political Union,
4, Clements Inn, W.C.

THE SUFFRAGETTE: *Pouting in Prison.*

THE MINERS' LAST MESSAGE.

March 16th.   Jess in Birmingham sends Josie in Bath a stark document of the mine disaster at Hamstead Colliery a fortnight before, *for your album....This is the message one of the miners wrote before they died.* Produced by Warner Gothard it is perhaps more telling than their usual elaborate photomontages.   08j

August 29th.   Nobility of purpose is exemplified in this fine study of Mrs. Pankhurst wearing her Votes For Women badge. The Suffragette movement was now nationwide. Pollie in York sends this to Mrs Newlove in Scarborough reciting domestic news, *E arrived safe this morning very glad to have her back.*   08k

August 22nd.   Comic cards on the Suffragettes abounded, both for and against (mostly the latter at the outset). 'Pouting in Prison' strikes a more equivocal note. It was sent by Rob in Folkestone to Mr Carter in Hampstead Garden Suburb, *a nice storm last night, back today.*   08l

WINSTON SPENCER CHURCHILL, ESQ, M.P.   ROTARY PHOTO, E.C.

James B. McGregor in his 108th year after voting Nov. 3, 1908, at the Town Hall, Newport, N. H. *108-nov 6.*
Published by J. W. Johnson & Son

May 21st.   Becky in Grantham is eager for Miss Torkington in Ilford to see her new photo, *My dear T. Do you recognise anyone. Will write you dear with love & kisses.* On the dirt road in front of dingy buildings Becky with her brand new bicycle looks proud, determined and independent.   08m

October 12th.   *Winston Spencer Churchill forever I hope your leg is better,* writes Muriel from Manchester to Mr Tutie in Clapham. Churchill was now a member of Asquith's cabinet and had just become engaged to Clementine his Society bride. A man of destiny, he will appear many times in this book.   08n

December 1st.   Edith in Newport NH, writes to M E Truworthy in Scituate, Mass., having added the fact that James B MacGregor reached his 108th birthday, *Our 'Grand Old Man'. Oldest 'Free Mason' in the world has been one nearly ninety years. Fine picture of him. Have not seen you this way yet.*   08o

September 7th.   D Whalley writes from Great Halwood to Miss E D Whalley at 119 Sunny Hill Road, Streatham, London SW, *Dear Tiny, Feel champion A1 in health - just making ready for a walk over Hills before dinner and then to Whalley at Clitheroe. So' tata for the present. hope you have a fine day for washing, Drying etc. yours aff*. Not by the sound of it (or the sureness of its script) a letter from one of the mill employees who from the early morning, when with clattering clogs they head for work, laboured until early evening in the pandemonium of noise that came from a thousand wheels, belts, gears and engines. The poor lighting is evidenced here by the infrequent spacing of gas lamps. Most striking of all, however, is the extreme youth of so many of the millhands only one of whom looks over twenty five and most of whom are barely (or not even yet) teenagers.   08p

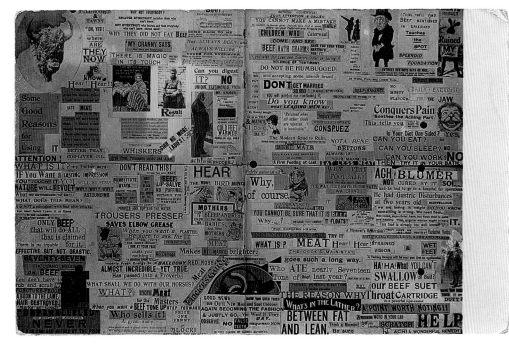

December 22nd.   W N Nicholls in Cheltenham greets C C Mountford of Hill House, Wormley, Herts towards Christmas with the message, *Best wishes to you Charles from us. This is a relic of our bully beef times. Your ever etc.* This chance survival from what was no doubt an extremely small number of copies is a fine amateur example of concrete poetry in the form of a collage cut-up. Many avant garde artists would later think they were doing this sort of work for the first time. This, with its fine title (given in the message) Bully Beef Times, is of a standard of ambition, invention and anarchic word-play that make it worthy of a place in the well known Sackner Archive of Miami Beach, the world's leading collection of concrete and visual poetry.   09q

08a. *Dear Sir. I have been to Mr Galopin this morning....I gave the packet to Mrs. All is done with the child but we are very miserable as the wether is...I will be back at work Tuesday.*

Etoile. rue d'Amsterdam. Paris. No 108

08b. Davidson Brothers, London. Series 5035 - 3

08c. Publisher unknown. No 698

08d. He set off from Trafalgar Square on January 1st. The card was posted from Canterbury.

Leparc Croydon. For the Man in the Iron Mask.

08e. Publisher unknown. photo Willson's

08f. *How are you getting on after the holidays? Alas! I've quite forgotten that we ever had any. I haven't any news to tell you about our year. Miss Hogg has left SKC to go to Chichester. They like the new superintendent. D.Finch is at W'hampton P.T.Centre & has boys of 18 & 19!!! May Lee is at an Upper Grade Schl Islington as Science Mistress Daisy is at Rotherham & I'm going to see Fan this week: she is very well. Evelyn and Dorothy are awfully keen on Hockey. Mattie Clyde is at St Katherine's practising school; what choice!! Hope you are well.35*

Publisher unknown.

08g.for Robert Courtneidge by Mills & Co Printers, Wardour St.

Detail of bus from 08b advertising The Dairymaids.

08h. Rapid Photo Printing Co.London V384-10

08i. Publisher unknown

08k. Sandle Brothers. London. No 108. Photo: Schmidt

08l. Tuck 'Rapholette' series 8090. Processed in Saxony

08m. Publisher unknown

08n. Rotary Photographic Series 96A. Photo: Thomson

08o. J.W.Johnson & Son

08p. Publisher unknown

08q. Publisher unknown

August 23rd.   *See the conquering hero come*, quotes the writer of this card before going on to domestic greetings. The arrest and imprisonment of Mrs Pankhurst was perhaps the turning point in the annals of Women's Suffrage. This particular postcard has made a long journey from its London publisher to the Orange River Colony whence, from Bloemfontein, FM sends it to Mr Miller in Scotland. By the time it reaches him in Glasgow the strategy of hunger strike and the horrors of forcible feeding had darkened the agenda.   09a

April 27th.   EM writes to Mrs Bowler in Holloway, Bath. *Dear Alice All right up here talk about traffic it is one continual whirr! am in pretty comfortable digs and should be glad of a line if you have the time.* Solid wheels on uneven stone setts must have added to the fun.   09b

September 28th.   To Mrs O'Harris in Providence RI, *This part of the city looks just like Fairy land now. Each and every one of the high buildings is outlined with electric lights & the towers loom up like palaces. The illumination of the warships & fire works Saturday night made a sight I'll never forget. Marion.*   09c

July 24th. One unwitting seed of an Empire's downfall is ironically carried in the poor Native joke (see note) related by Connie to Mrs Prideaux in New Port, Essex on this card. Among the improbably collaged figures around a non-existent table we recognise many of the cast of this book (Chamberlain, Kitchener, Churchill etc). 09d

May 1st. The Fisk Jubilee Trio are about to arrive in York as they tour England. The chairman Mr Goldthorpe asks Mr Brunnskinn if he will *support them on the platform? Your presence would be much appreciated, and the trio are worthy of all the support we can give them.* Their programme advertised modern and traditional songs. 09e

October 9th. Gladys Lord in Godalming receives a topical card from New York. *How do you like this of the two explorers? Not quite so fond of each other in real life!* At the time this was posted the fantasist Cook was claiming to have reached the pole a year before Peary. He was eventually proved a liar and disgraced. 09f

October 20th. *Olsens whole thrashing crew except one - from your friend H.Naize.* F H Proel in nearby Glencoe receives this card from Plato, Minn. Perhaps he is the missing member, gone off to town. Those remaining make a formidable group, one of whom, his hat at a rakish angle, neglects to smoke either cigar or pipe. 09g

May 22nd. GP writes to Miss Rhodes in Derby. *Just arrived here after long & most tiresome ride....beautiful scenery. How's the garden?* Workington sounds like the made up name of an industrial town in Dickens but this night scene of the Moss Bay works proves it all too real and Bosch's apocalyptic visions all too accurate. 09h

June 16th. *I wonder if you can find Tony on this card you will be like this one day being drilled at school, your loving friend Tony.* Master Carl Klaaren in Highbury may look on this with pleasure or despair. These boys are doubly lucky: they might just be too young to serve in the First World War and just too old to serve in the second. 09i

July 30th.   *What do you think of the other side?* writes Ethel in Dover to Daisy in Stoke Newington, *great excitement here last Sunday when M.Bleriot came over in his Flying Machine.* More than any other event this 36 minute channel crossing made flight a reality to the public, the political and the military imagination.   09j

July 27th.   Lou, also in Dover and writing only 48 hours after Bleriot's landing, only remarks to A in Eastbourne, *It is nice to be some folks...They look rather please with themselves.* Mme Bleriot who had sensibly travelled by boat does indeed look 'please' and has evidently brought Louis his best overcoat to change into.   09k

68   Hubert Latham crossing the Channel in his Aeroplane. —LL.

CODY IN FLIGHT.

August 1st.   Here from Lucien Levy is the high poetry of flight. But it is entirely cooked (ready for Latham's inevitable victory in the cross channel race). Latham had to ditch his machine in the channel. The stationary propeller gives the game away. Daddy writes to Master Guy D in Bristol, *wouldn't you like to be up in the air.*   09l

October 20th.   GLE staying at the Queen's Hotel, Blackpool writes to Sarah Buckle in Forest Hill, *We are having a very interesting time* [at the aviation display] *here. you can see all in the newspapers better than I can describe.* Cody was the first person to fly in Britain but since he was a US citizen this somehow did not count.   09m

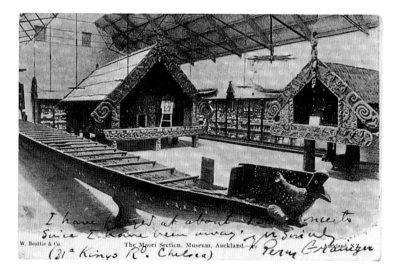

W. Beattie & Co.   The Maori Section. Museum, Auckland.

A £150 SNAPSHOT.

June 20th.   Composer/pianist/eccentric the Australian Percy Grainger writes from *off Italian coast* to Miss Cornwallis in Maidstone, *I have played in about 150 concerts since I have been away...It will be a delight to be back in London.* A card of ethnographic artefacts reflects his pioneering interest in the roots of art.   09n

February 3rd.   Jane Walman is saying something to Jack Ball, farmer, Hesketh Bank nr Preston. *Just a few lines to tell you here we are - look at the back Dear Jack you must come on Wednesday to me and I will look out for you.* £150 is a lot of money: the kind of photographer who snoops for gain here begins his long career.   09o

At the skating rink.

Some funny sights are seen here

"It's nice to have something soft to fall on."

April 14th.   Eliza in Harrogate to Mrs Plowman in Leicester, *Sorry its nearly time for us to come home but still we shall have to make the best of it. You ought to see Elsie on the skating rink, she had to see what the floor was like a time or two.* Roller skating, or Rinking as a craze had just reached its height in 1909. 09p

August 17th.   Lily Driver in Dewsbury is asked *How will this suit you at the new rink? are you going?* Rinks had sprung up everywhere and championships were held in the Crystal Palace. There were as many spectators as rinkers, many of them men in the hope of seeing something more than an ankle. 09q

Mode 1909!!!

Le Sourire Nº 133

La Mode in 1909

October 5th.   *Is this anything like your new hat? I am better again today but rather busy. Yrs.* M.T.E. *T.* Lehar's operetta 'The Merry Widow' swept Europe after its Vienna preview in 1905 and with it the fashions it inspired, notably the headgear described here as Mode 1909 which was more an event than a hat. 09r

August 3rd.   Daphne Foley in Liscard receives from Trouville the sort of card that makes a girl green with envy. *This is quite a small hat to some of the merrie widows! & oh! the frocks, you would be so interested in it all the french talk all around hundreds of bathers - the place packed - it is Race-week. B.P.* 09s

1909 MESSAGES·NOTES·PARTICULARS

09a. ....*Hope you had a good time in Thirso. K.R. [Kind Regards] to self & Mrs M. Shall write in detail later. F.M.*

Photochrom Co Ltd.

09b. Tuck 'Silverette' . London Series I. 1560

09c. Hudson Fulton 1609/1807. Manhattan series Churchman Co./Irving Underhill

09d. *Do you feel any better for your change. Why is a Kaffir girl like a prophet? Because she has very little on her (honour) in her own country.*

Rotary Photographic Series 7121A.

Detail showing ratio of drawing to photography. Note the tiny hands of the Prince of Wales.

09e. Publisher unknown

09f. ....*Many thanks for the enclosure - yes it is at Sandringham. I remember the piece, am pleased to have a copy. Every 'shooter' might take it to heart.*

The Cook Pub. Co. NY

09g. Publisher unknown

09h. The Derwent Series 01G. photographer J.R.T.

09i. Publisher unknown

09j. Daily Mirror

09k. Whorwell Photo, Dover

09l. LL (Lucien Levy). 68

09m. National Series No 958 (Millar & Lang)

09n. New Zealand. W.Beattie & Co., Auckland

09o. The Star Series. GD&D. (Gottschalk, Dreyfus & Davies)

09p. Davidson Bros. London 4865

09q. Bamforth Series no 1462

09r. I do not know what M.T.E. stands for - Many Tender Embraces?

G.L.&Co. 2746/6

09s. The verse in a free translation says:-
    Alas with hats like this life's far too chancy
    You kiss the Aunt instead of your fiancée.

Artist F.Roberty. Most Roberty cards are coloured in by hand.

FORD MODEL-T-TOURING CAR, $950.00, EQUIPPED.

Ford Motor Co., 1723 Bway., N. Y.

May 27th. J H Stark the proprietor of Model Ford Garage, Park Ridge NJ hopes that Mrs S S Bogert of Pearl River NY has $950 to invest in a Model T. She would perhaps do better to wait until after 1913 when assembly-line production gets underway and the price will drop by half. Although the Model T was the subject of many jokes and provided the Keystone Cops with all their car chase hilarity it had sold 15 million by 1927 (when production ceased) and had democratised motoring. 10a

March 7th. From Ethel to Mrs Hamley in Plymouth, *Thought you would like a peep at pet shop*. Circa 1907 a solitary horse-bus mingles with motorised rivals carrying an advert for Nestlés, one of whose products is being consumed as I write, in a road which the Peckham bus advertising Tatcho will pass in half an hour or so. 10b

September 14th. Mr Rich in Rockland ME writes a scrawled note to Nellie in West Trumont, *Dear Wife We left fast point this morning anchored here at 5pm. From your Husband W.Rich X*. The Singer building is dead centre of the view as it will tend to be until the Woolworth building starts appearing after 1913. 10c

15793   STACK OF CASKS. BASS'S BREWERY, BURTON-ON-TRENT.

Mr Grahame-White.   Illustrations Bureau

July 22nd.   Ancient architecture is reflected and modern sculpture predicted in this magnificent arrangement of beer-barrels. Jim writes to the Greens in Newcastle under Lyme *Thanks for PC bit a swank to day you know I am sweet 22. my word if you are not off what do you think of Burton trade mark on the other side xxx.*   10d

August 1st.   The Boltons living in Blackpool write to their son and daughter in Keighley of Grahame-White who dominated British aviation after 1910. *We all was getting tea when he passed over our House. We saw him in the air. he was going beautifull. I am in shirt sleeves on Beach writing to you. grand whether here. sun powerfull.*   10e

We are having an awfully jolly holiday at
BROADSTAIRS.

"Our Coast Defences"   ATS

The Mappin Art Gallery, Sheffield   "Scott" Series No 9

July 25th.   Eva writes to Mrs Crouch at no.23 Woodside, Wimbledon, *I am glad no.30 & the cat are alright. We shall be home sometime Friday aft. Would you mind getting me 1 stale loaf 1/2 pint milk & 1/2 best butter from the dairy & put them in the larder for me. The weather is not a bit good. so little sun.*   10f

October 5th.   To Miss Daisy Clifford in Leicester from a friend in Sheffield, *thought this would be nice to add to your collection; as I know Art Galleries are a bit in your line when your thoughts are not too much occupied with Bertie and Gymnastics.* The central portrait is of the gallery's founder, Mr Mappin, the stainless steel magnate.   10g

BOY SCOUTS.
THE AMBULANCE AT WORK.

"LEST WE FORGET"   PC.231
EMERGENCY EXIT   SOUTH AFRICA
BIRMINGHAM TOWN HALL DECEMBER 18 1901 BACK DOOR
MARQUIS OF WINCHESTER   EARL OF AVA   EARL OF AIRLIE
WHILE Mr LLOYD GEORGE (DISGUISED AS A POLICEMAN) WAS RUNNING AWAY FROM HIS COUNTRYMEN —   THE LORDS WERE LAYING DOWN THEIR LIVES FOR THEIR COUNTRY

July 16th. Baden Powell (see 10p) founded the Boy Scouts in 1907 and its American movement in 1910. Boer War hats have now given way to baseball-caps. Aunt Edith to Master Coombes in Worthing, *when are you going to join the Boy Scouts? I shouldn't like to see you looking like this poor boy on the ambulance though. My own scouting days were brief but I remember being the stretcher case.*   10h

December 10th.   Lords Reform was in the news at the start of the century as at its end. This card reminds Lloyd Gorge of his cowardice in 1901 and of the bravery of the Lords in the Boer War. OB in Wimbledon to Miss H in Weston-Super-Mare, *why don't the radicals like the word 'Referendum'. I suppose it is too clear for the Working man to understand. They like dangling 5 or 6 important matters before him so as to confuse him.*   10i

OH, WHAT A DIFFERENCE !
"Tha need'nt swank so much; tha's this to come back to, owd lass"

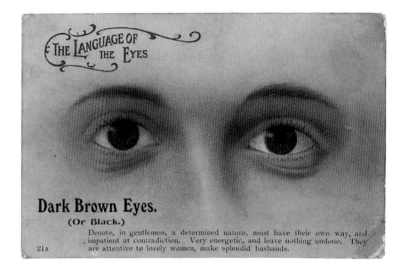

THE LANGUAGE OF THE EYES

Dark Brown Eyes.
(Or Black.)
Denote, in gentlemen, a determined nature, must have their own way, and impatient at contradiction. Very energetic, and leave nothing undone. They are attentive to lovely women, make splendid husbands.

August 3rd. The mills are empty and Nance with the others is in Blackpool. She writes to Eliza Officer in Wirksworth, *We are having fine times. We have seen a lot of flying machines Dad as gone back today.* Blackpool was the scene of a great aviation display. Nance would return to a troubled mill in a year of disputes and lock-outs. 10j

February 14th. Posted to Will Wright on Valentine's Day, *I hope you will like this PC. It is the nearest colour I could get out of your description. Now you see your character, & you can't get away from it. Give my best love to George...with love from Reg McKay.* One of many 'Language of' (flowers, stamps etc.) series. 10k

OETZMANN'S COTTAGES
JAPAN BRITISH EXHIBITION

August 16th. Using this card given away at the Japan-British Exhibition Edith covers the blurb on the back with her pencil message to Miss Everard Row in Bexhill on Sea, *These little houses are so pretty, the windows are so nice also fireplaces...* £230 pounds would buy the bungalow and £450 the mock-tudor, both familiar sights in England today. 10l

March 12th. *Have sent you one of those photos I promised you while at Brum. Had it wet Sat. afternoon and Sunday so could not go anywhere this week.* So writes Jack to Miss Blackmore in Birmingham after his return to Montacute, eager that she should appreciate the full gleaming glory of his new Motorcycle, an Enerjetik. 10m

WHEN AT THE SEASIDE DON'T FORGET THE WIFE & KIDS!

F.S.

81 The Bleriot Aeroplane. — LL.

February 28th. EDD sends a rhyming message to Mr A Starr in East Hatly, Sandy, Beds. *The hills are high the waters are deep / of thinking of you I cannot sleep / my thoughts are always of you and the time / when I shall be yours & you will be mine.* The sentiment is clear but the choice of card puzzling though it is typical of the lively style of Fred Spurgin (whose real name was Izydor Spungin). 10n

July 12th. NA writes from Bournemouth to Mabel Richards in Stoke under Ham, *We saw Hon. Rolls in this airship. It is such a funny looking thing and makes a noise just like a motor. I am sorry my holiday is over.* There is a tragic PS, *Since writing this card have just heard Rolls has been killed. Isn't it awful?* More than 20 aviators died in 1910. The name of Rolls lives on through his partnership with Royce. 10o

THE BOY SCOUTS.
Lieut.-General Baden Powell reads the King's Message.

August 8th.   King Edward VII died before he was to
address the Scout's gathering and George V sent a
message here read out by the founder Baden-Powell.
Though Royal sanction was a great lift to the movement
it was the new King's son, George VI, who was to
prove the champion of scouting. Susie writes to thank
Mrs Lister in Saffron Walden for hospitality.   10p

ᚦHE ᚲOMEᚦ.
AND THE PLANET VENUS.
As seen at Oxford, Jan 29, 1910.
Copyright. Taunt & Co, 2838.

March 13th.   Halley's Comet was a spectacular sight in
January. Taunt of Oxford helps the negative with
some judicious scratching. The comet's return in 1986
was a flop proving, to my mother at least, that even
comets weren't what they used to be. LH to Eve
Sherwood in Oxford, *My love... the wind is horrid.
The Jews secretary has been today.*   10q

1910 MESSAGES·NOTES·PARTICULARS

10a. Published Ford Motor Co. NY.

10b. Kingsway Real Photo Series.

10c. Theocrome serie 78. George P Hall & Son NY

10d. Kingsway Real Photo Series for Messr Bass etc. W.H.Smith

10e. The message begins *We had a fine day yesterday at army
when getting tea. Graham White came flying over our House
& came round Tower & stop on sands & then commenced
flying again back to the Field....* (Grahame-White died in
1959)

National Series 1265. (Millar & Lang) photo: Illustrations Bureau.

10f. Tuck Oilette. 'Fun on the Sands' Series I. 9466

10g.   This card, chanced upon in the early seventies
provided me with a store of haunting images.

Scott series no.2

10h. National Series (Millar & Lang). 845

10i. National Union of Conservative and Constitutional Associations.
printed by David Allen & Sons.

10j. Valentine's Series

10k. H.G.L (H.Garner Leicester)

10l.   The message indecipherable in places as the writer
acknowledges, *Went to Regents Park & Zoo yesterday. we are
walking everywhere. This street is as long as Cranford to the
town. If you do not read all this it won't much matter its all
about distances.*

Oetzmann & Co Ltd. Hampstead Road

10m. Published by correspondent.

10n. F.S.Comic Series. (Fred Spurgin)

10o. LL (Lucien Levy) Eltlinger's Aero Series

10p. Davidson Bros.

10q. Taunt & Co. Oxford

10r.   The message continues, *I and May are still together but
when we get orders tomorrow we shall no doubt have to
part....*
The rhyme in loose translation reads.

> Working man it's time to wake
> Know the powers that you can take
> Every wheel will stand quite still
> if <u>your</u> strong arm exerts its will.

10s. Burns & Oates for The Tablet.

Mann der Arbeit, aufgewacht!
Und erkenne deine Macht!
Alle Räder stehen still,
Wenn Dein starker Arm es will.

October 10th.   Unrest in Romania was not new and
this is a socialist call to arms or rather to down tools.
(see note). Edgar writes to his mother Mrs Smith in
Gloucester. *I have left Vasini & am now in Bucharest
awaiting orders from F & PS what to do next....I hope
I have got to come back to England as I have had
enough of this country...*   10r

THE ONLY PORTRAIT OF KING EDWARD VII
TAKEN IN THE COMPANY OF AN ENGLISH
PRIEST (FATHER BERNARD VAUGHAN).
"Tablet" Copyright)   *(Burns & Oates, London, W.*

May 31st.   The gullible catholic JPC writes to Bro
Mulgrew at St.Benedicts in Fort Augustus, *This unique
snapshot will probably interest you. Undoubtably two
of the greatest men of the century and another triumph
for photography.* More like a triumph for cutting two
figures out of a crowd and making them seem alone in
intimate conversation.   10s

March 25th.   Shell's blazing dawn of the age of aviation seems to predict the end of all surface transport. Even the poor chap on the bike will have to get airborne and the horsedrawn bus carries its Shell advertisement like a sentence of death. Strangely absent from the scene is that mainstay of the petrol industry, the motor car. Luckily such prophecies are only partially realised. WW from Leigh, Lancs writes to his cousin Mr Danby of Newport, Salop with a less apocalyptic message, *Many thanks for 'Sweet Peas' to hand this mng. We are all very well etc.*   11a

July 27th.   *No one has run away with us yet,* writes Esther to Mrs Elley in Aungier St, Dublin, as George V in his coronation year presides over sedate cabs with the newly fashionable white-walled tyres and a smart pony and trap whose occupants are sporting their summer boaters.   11b

April 15th.   *Dear Father* writes James to Mr Henry Severson in Eastman St., Stoughton, Wisconsin *just received mamma's card. I hope you will have a most pleasant Easter.* This standard view shows the Central Building partly masking the tall Singer Building.   11c

September 13th.   Bert posts a first British airmail card to Mrs Hannah Woodridge in Wallington, *I am sending this to commemorate a great event, the first Aerial Post. As you see this, carried high through the air, may it serve to lift your thoughts high above the heavens to him who has allowed man to solve this problem of flight.*   11d

May 30th.   Harriet Cooke in Leicester receives this topical joke (one of scores featuring cheerful injured servants) about the new Compensation Acts, *I hope it is fine this Holiday I shall put my best clothes in a parcel on the back of my byke well Dear I will now close with Fondest love from yours forever Jim P.W.A.K.x [x7].*   11e

March 23rd.   HVS in Oxford writes to Miss Nellie Shaw using a promotional card for G B Shaw's, You Can Never Tell which ran at the NY Garrick for 128 performances in 1905 and looks, typically, like more talk than action. *Have been very ill... I saw articles in papers. believe we have sold another copy. Good luck to Sedlok.*   11f

November 30th.   Jack from El Oro has nothing to say to Mrs Prees in Cheltenham about the turbulent events in Mexico, *Love to yourself Stella. please ask Will to write.* After the overthrow of Diaz rebels continued their struggle under Pancho Villa and Zapata. Southern separatists in Mexico today still call themselves Zapatistas.   11g

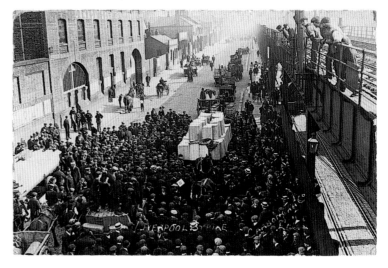

January 20th.   Anarchist was the sort of trigger word that Terrorist is today. Churchill as Home Secretary puts on his top hat and rushes to Sidney Street where the police and Scots Guards are laying siege to the anarchist hideout. A fortnight later Bert in W.Hartlepool writes to Lil Briggs in Perry Hill, *PPC & letter to hand thanks for same. Havnt got any W. Will soon be with you just about frozen Love XX.*   11h

September 3rd.   From Liverpool to Miss Barn in Newcastle on Tyne, *Am back again quite safely. Had a glorious time.* Liverpool was the first focus of the industrial unrest. The violence and riots at the docks turned into strikes involving railwaymen and the miners in quest of a minimum wage. With Labour's new voice in parliament and an ever strengthening Trade Union movement, something had to give.   11i

July 31st. J in Weston-Super-Mare reminds Mr Gallop in Bristol, *Please do not forget I leave 3.18 tomorrow.* The new Prince of Wales (later Edward VIII/Duke of Windsor) meets the incomparable W G Grace who retired from first class cricket in 1908 after scoring 54,211 runs and taking 2,808 wickets.   11j

October 6th.   JH in Constance to Jean McMichael in Seaforth Ontario, *a whole bunch of things to tell you ... remember the time I caught them on the fence say the pockets arrant in the right place. I wonder if she feels like we did ha ha.* Dungarees as an emphatic fashion will make their comeback eighty years later.   11k

June 13th.   From *Guess who* in Pontiac, Mich., to Miss Mabel Carter in Caldwell, Ohio a simple *Ha Ha, Ho Ho* (repeated 27 times). 'Has anyone (here) seen Kelly' was a music hall song. With these images men should have seen the writing on the wall. Women workers would soon be real enough in the coming war.   11l

November 13th.   Ernie Brooks writes home to his parents in Peckham. Having just arrived in Capetown he buys this card to send. They might think it 'a bit strong'. But it is difficult to tell in this period when the naked female form was completely taboo unless the model was black, as here, or appeared as art. For some reason being black or being art did not count.   11m

May 25th.   Sent from Camp Hill D.O. Birmingham and addressed to Mdlle Doris in London SW, *My dear little Doddy when shall we three meet again. What do you think of the funny donkey on the other side just like me don't you think so xxx ?.* Fantasy faces made from nude females also took the form of exotic characters or, mysteriously, composers like Wagner.   11n

April 17th.   Let's hope Miss Hammond in East Molesey was not having breakfast when this arrived from E C Phillips in Auburn, NY. *This is the Electric Chair that they use in the Prison here instead of hanging people....I hope you had a good time at Brighton. I have been gardening all this week. What was the relationship between Mr (?) P & Miss H?*   11o

Telephone 9420 Gerrard

Maison Lewis de Paris
210, Regent Street, W.

11a. Published by Shell. no.188

11b. Davidson Bros Ltd. 'All British'

11c. Detroit Publishing Co. 'Phostint' card 12082

11d. Gustav Hamel was the pilot, on a plane provided by Grahame-White's company. The illustration features a biplane whereas in the event a monoplane was used.

The General Post Office.

11e The message begins, *thanks for PPC Sunday morn....Dear I think I shall be able to get work in Leamington when I like to go and look for it. I sharn't trouble before the holiday.*

Davidson Bros. Artist: Tom Browne. series 2637-4

11f. David Allen & Sons for Vedrenne-Barker.

11g. Aztec Curio Store. Ciudad Juarez. Mexico. 544.

11h. Valentine's Series.

11i. Carbonora Co. Liverpool

11j. Beagles Postcards 123T. Photo Ernest Brooks.

11k. *Swell time on Friday night. I had company. it will be allright for the 31 don't fail to come back. special spelling this week as crazy as you and me ha ha. say don't wear your best dress and don't say anything but be sure to come back.*

Ounston Weller lithograph Co. Suffragette Series No2.

11l. SB Series 391

11m. *Dear Father & Mother. Arrived at 6.00am. Just been ashore. A merry Christmas from me and the Graces. Ernie*

John G.Bain. Capetown.

11n. G.G. & Co. 5132.

11o. Hamiltons Drug Store. Auburn N.Y. Made in Germany 7827.

11p. Maison Lewis de Paris, London.

11q. Valentine's Series. Artist: Chas Coolin.

11r. Inter Art Co. Harem Series no.861. Artist: P.S.(?)

11s. Publisher unknown. Photo. Central News.

September 3rd.   Mabel writes to Maud Avery in Grays, Essex, *Now you must be a good girl I never see you now Maud where do you get to?* Here we see the excesses of the Merry Widow hat refined to stylish simplicity complete with a dyed ostrich feather, all artistically composed in an oval frame.   11p

August 30th.   Beat Ludlam from Grimsby writes to her mother in Sheffield, *...we was on here last night I shant be sorry when its Friday because all they will do is walk on the front or stop in one place.* The centrifuge is tricky in any skirt. Hobble skirts seem somehow at odds with the growing mood of women's emancipation.   11q

INSIDE A HAREM.

June 6th.   Mabel in Bournemouth writes to Flo Watford in Forest Gate, *I did not know Alic was going into Hospitall. I hope he will soon get well again. Flo look out next week for me like this in my harem that one let me tell you old sport Love to all.* In an era of radical fashion the harem skirt showing trouser legs was the ultimate shock outfit. Mabel will make a hit and cause a gratifying scandal.   11r

August 11th.   Post coronation gloom. FFP to Mrs Muzzell in Burnes Green, Sussex, *By this time all the decorations and stands have been taken down, but, with all the workmen refusing to work until they get better pay ...it is feared our food will go up in price, as it cannot be got to the Markets in the usual carts... It is a pity these things cannot be settled without so much suffering, especially to the poor.*   11s

September 19th.   Message on the back of card depicting Maurice Levi & his Orchestra at Churchill's, B'way at 49th St NY. addressed to Mr Louis Guinayer, lawyer, Cormain & Elison, Paterson NJ. No signature but Mr Guinayer might have known its source.   11t

984.T.
THE ILL-FATED AMERICAN LINER "TITANIC," THE LARGEST SHIP IN THE WORLD, WHICH FOUNDERED
WITH GREAT LOSS OF·LIFE. 15th OF APRIL 1912, OFF NEWFOUNDLAND ON HER MAIDEN VOYAGE.
BEAGLES' POSTCARDS.

April 22nd.   F from Crewkerne writes to E E Gale of the Civil Police in Tarquah, Gold Coast (which it reaches on May 9th) - *I thought you might be interested in this. What an awful disaster. It is the only topic of conversation.* Many publishers brought out cards of the Titanic (or a hurriedly disguised Olympic, its sister ship) within a day or two. This almost certainly is the Titanic. No card however goes undoctored. Smoke has been added to all four funnels to give animation to the image (at the expense of veracity, since only three of the funnels were actually smoke-stacks).   12a

July 12th.   A sober view typical of Judge's whose cards always have thick light and atmosphere. LM in Balham writes to Gertie Reeks in Hastings *I was very pleased with your pretty card I have had a letter from Twickel and have not to go back yet....Hoping to see you again, one day.*   12b

November 12th.   This view, with the river void of shipping, is probably based on the identical photograph to 10C. Sent to Stroudsbury PA, it is from Lizzie to Mrs Vliet. *Nan & Mr Phelps were here Sunday and we went up the river she & I. Write to Davison about potatoes.*   12c

April 28th. *My dear mater.... As you say in your letter the Titanic is the most terrible affair. I think I must have known some of the crew. Will write again soon...* Fred in Marseilles writes to his mother, Mrs Rowling, in the Old Kent Road. The quality of French mass produced litho cards is almost the equal of British photographic types and here PB is on a level with LL (Lucien Levy). 12d

January 1st. (posted at 3am) *Dear Jack. Am I never to hear from you again. This is a souvenir of Xmas eve in 'Frisco'. A 100,000 people gathered to hear Kubelik play on the main St. This flashlight was taken at 7 o'clock and shows up fine... Happy New Year to you & yours.* R P Scoter sends this to his friend Mr Brixey in London but seems to be more interested in his photographic technique than the great violin virtuoso. 12e

July 4th. Betty Scott in Chiswick gets a sharp reminder from Alice, *What do you mean by being absent, I didn't say you would be, what is the matter with you now, I hope you haven't got whooping cough again.... you must come tomorrow for the League Cricket Match and also for Algebra...* Art was evidently well provided for and the music master was Gustav Holst, busy writing the St.Paul's Suite when this card was sent. 12f

August 14th. Miss Smith in Brighton receives this rather gloomy card from Bostard Camp, *I thought you would like a PC of this accident it happened quite close here they are like birds here 5 & 6 at a time flying over the camp I should like a trip in one.* The writer is undeterred by this proof of the fragility of early aircraft which seem essentially to have been made of a few broomsticks and the wheels of a pram. 12g

March 1st. SK in Cannes to Miss Weatherhead in Scunthorpe Hall, Bingley, *We are so much enjoying our holiday. Cannes is so nice having tea at the Golf Links. Balfour has just started on a round.* SK not only shows off with her picture of their chauffeured car outside the very grand Albion Hotel, but drops names: Balfour was the Tory leader. Cannes at the time was 'select' and much frequented by the English rich. 12h

March 5th. Mrs Saxby in Meadows, Notts. from Standard Hill, *You did not manage all the gipsy told you it seems. I did smile, our people could not make out the meaning of the PC....The men are all out on strike now. Hope you have got plenty of coal your way. Best love to all in the yard & heaps for yourself. Jo.* D H Lawrence (in Sons & Lovers) was immortalising Nottingham miners at the very time when this was sent. 12i

October 22nd. A writes to Miss Savage c/o Holdron's (a smart store in Balham) ...*so my letter was opened by another Miss Savage, she must have rubbed her nose against some of the stuff as pictured over.* Coal strikes hit hard at a time when everything relied on it. The label on the piece of coal here is addressed to 'The Museum, London. Curio Section'. 12j

February 12th. 'Fluffy' writes in cringing mode to H.R.H. Princess Gerta von Sachsen-Weimar *It is very good & kind of Your Highness to send me even a card when so full of engagements - & I deeply value & fully appreciate such thoughts.*...This card shows German printing once again in the lead with a finely reproduced colour photograph. 12k

February 22nd. EMS in Bonn writes to Mr Sandell in Southampton *I thought you might like to see the German students in duelling 'rig-out'. Personally I think them hideous.* Ceremonial outfits and ritual scarification (as on these faces) were part of university tribalism. Mühlberg's Student Life series is full of atmosphere and character. 12l

July 15th. Rose Todd in Moorhead, Minn. writes to Borgie Danielson in Detroit, *Are you going back to the T.B.I next Fall. I think I may.* Irving Berlin's song needed no further caption even when only a few months old: the title already sang itself. Berlin lived to be a hundred and was still writing songs when the Beatles made their debut. 12m

September 2nd. From her daughter Laura in Plymouth to Mrs Maria Boundy in Perranporth. *I hope you will like this card of General Booth who has just died... tell my darling Millie I will writes soon.* On the base of the Booth monument outside the Salvation Army HQ in Camberwell death is not mentioned. The founder was 'promoted to glory in 1912'. 12n

Date unclear. SJ in Canada to Mr Sam Johnson in Newtown Butler, Co. Fermanagh, *just a line hopeing to find yous well as this leaves us at present no surrender.* Carson's picture appears on the banner over his motto. The regalia of Orangemen has not changed. King Billy appears on one drum, Victoria on the other. Bowler hats are worn to this day. 12o

July 3rd. This memorial card with its mourning edge of black was amongst the most popular and helped to fix the idea that the ship's band played the hymn Nearer my God to Thee as the ship went down. The recent Hollywood film shows a small string ensemble playing on deck though we have (such is the wild discontinuity of the movie) already seen the ship at a sickening angle that would cause a tumbling cascade of men, instruments and music stands. At some time or other it seems the tune was played. One feature of this card that endorses the film's fitful attempts at realism is the look and bearing of the luckless Captain Smith. L in Dublin sends the card to her aunt Mrs Laughrin in Southampton, *tell Louis I am seeing about the Lodging today.*   12p

12a. Such memorial cards are not too difficult to find. The ones that fetch high prices are those posted before the actual sailing or (even more sought after) sent by passengers or crew from the ship itself at the beginning of its voyage, especially if from identifiable victims.

Beagles postcard 946T. Photograph: Central News.

12b. Printed on blueish card. PM. Balham. Judges Ltd. is still an active postcard publisher.

Judges Ltd.

12c. Success Post Card Publ. New York. No.1022 copyright 1909 by Irving Underhill. New York.

12d. Publishers PB

12e. Privately published. Slogan postmark of World's Panama - Pacific Exhibition 1915.

12f. The message continues, *but you must come tomorrow for the League Cricket Match & also Algebra, I am going to be good so it will be a record lesson.*

Photo. Tourists Association. Turnham Green.

12g. M.Barnet, Bulford Camp Studio, Salisbury Plain.

12h. Photographie Lückefeltt - Ostende- Albazia. Cannes

12i. J.Starr & Sons. Wigan 'CBB' series. Photo: Tailor.

12j. The message concludes, *It did not matter who read that letter as far as I was concerned for it would perhaps do good. I can't promise for tonight but I shall come if possible perhaps by train unless foggy. The A noted with thanks.*

J.Salmon, Sevenoaks No.414

12k. The message proceeds in similarly glutinous fashion *I do not expect a letter till some of the parties are over & then tell me about Merry & Löbbecks visit to you. I will tell you directly my lovely Ex-Libris book arrives - to assure you of its safety, With all love, gratitude, & devotion - Fluffy.*

T.S.N. Serie 1257 (6 Dess).

12l. The message continues, *The carnival was quite fun. We enjoyed ourselves at the dance here.....tell Dad it is mean of him to write in German!! I had to have it translated - he need never write in German characters as it appears they are very seldom used now.*
[Old german handwriting is particularly impenetrable to the modern eye]

Verlag der Hofkunsthandlung Edm. von König Heidelberg. Studentenleben. Nr 14.

12m. The Fairman Co. NY. HE of Pink Perfection

12n. The Rapid Photo Printing Co. Ltd. London 5836.

12o. Flap under banner with photographs of other notables, Bonar Law etc. In the battered copy seen here these have been ripped out except for the top of Bonar Law's head.

Mailing Novelty, Valentine's Series.

12p. National Series

12q. Except for the year the date is unclear but certainly, from the tone of its message before the disaster.

Rotary Photographic Plate Sunk Gem Series

12r. Valentine's Series.

Date unclear. To Miss Swingler, Cottingham, Yorks, *Dear Kate, That was a very jolly card of the Titanic. Though it does not give one quite the right idea of its immensity You want to be in a little rowing boat beside it to feel insignificant....we are enjoying heavy rain showers all this week.* Any collector of postcards would prefer to have the card Kate sent to her friend, even though Madame Esty in 1897 created the role of Mimi in La Bohème for the English stage. Kate's card was probably of the ship on its trial sailings.   12q

February 14th. HSG in Kandy sends an 'ethnic' card to Miss Green in Clifton Bristol. The typical message reads *would you like to be ornamented like this?* a question which of course begs a negative answer. Many Miss Greens however in 1999 would be quite likely to answer yes. However some would think double nose piercing and multiple piercing of the ear a very moderate allotment since pierced lips, eyebrows and nipples are now commonplace and studded tongues not unknown.   12r

July 28th. From Brixton Miss Toombs in Brandon, Suffolk, receives this torrid card, *Isn't this saucy. Do you like the position? If so, we can try and see, if we can do likewise. Roll on Sunday and home eh? That's the place for sp ----- g eh what! Toodle oo. Derrick.* There's spooning and spooning and this may have brought a blush to E's cheek. This is as far as you could go on a sendable postcard in 1913 and one hopes that E got to the post that morning ahead of her parents. But the days of firelight and spooning are not long and Derrick may soon be marching to oblivion.   13a

October 7th.   Other versions of this view show the central No.12 bus with a poster for the Coronation Exhibition at the Great White City (1911) here masked with a Dewars Whisky advertisement by the publishers. From Paddington to Miss Simpson in Castle Cary, Londonderry, Edward Dickson writes, *very fine out here. How is Miss Thompson ? Mrs Webb?*
13b

June 3rd.   The Manhattan Bridge was completed in 1909 at what still seems a high cost of $13,400 000. Combining with the smart new boat to emphasise the image's modernity, a distant relation of the Wright Flyer is introduced. An overawed Mrs Hasmond writes to Ida Dunsmore, of Emma St, Syracuse, NY, *Never expect to see anything equal to this again.*
13c

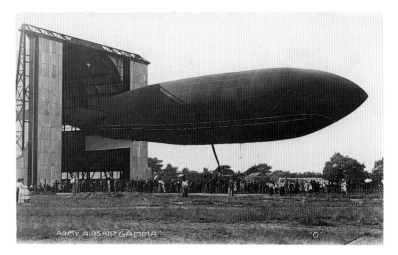

January 30th.   Alice in Nyack writes to Mr Louis T Bailey in Lancaster NY with this striking image of an engineering marvel and explains, *This is a picture of one of the means of transport between Jersey City and Hoboken, and the quickest way too.... I'll keep on sending cards if each one can extract a letter from you. Come on and write me again soon. you have more time than I...* I'm sure Mr Bailey obeyed.   13d

October 6th.   Bob writes to W G Stride Esq. PAC in Wimborne from Aldershot where the army airships with their Greek-letter designations were based, *did you go to dance? Could you send on some of Mr Rowe's own corn plasters. I can't get any like his here. Add it on to the account I now owe you. Henry has sent on some apples....just been for a 14 mile walk past Frimby. Watching football & rugby on Saturday in camp.*   13e

March 27th.   From RJJ to Miss Dorothy Thompson, The Manse, Melrose, *Did you ever hear of Northwich where many of the houses are leaning all sorts of ways nearing the Salt-Pits and much falling in?* Northwich gave a new meaning to the familiar idea of house subsidence. That the foreground building is a solicitor's office no doubt speeded up the business of seeking compensation from the mine companies. 13f

September 5th.   To Mr Leslie Gardner, Ettrick, Wisconsin, *Hi Kid - Rec'd your card OK and will now take the pleasure of answering I was going to the Gale fair but we had the threshers then. See Clint wanted me to rent me adams farm, but don't think he is going to now. as ever. Vera.* This is the generic bottom of the postcard barrel with the village name rubber-stamped. The caption is eccentric and the children look challenged.   13g

October 15th.   *Dear Kitty* writes Maud to Miss Applegate in Hornsey, *can you come out on Friday 7.30? Do come if you can as I want to talk to you. don't be late. This is my other young man's photo, nice boy, only he drinks. I'm going flying with him on Saturday (don't think).* Before the advent of film stars young aviators were the heart throbs. Gustav Hamel (see 11d) looks as if he knows it. Hendon was London's theatre of flight and Hamel one of its stars. In under a year he too would meet his death.   13h

July 15th.   Are these straightforward blocks of ice? L Fronall's mock-tetchy note from Hammersmith to Miss Jackson in Cirencester gives us no information although he knows that Louis is the boss, *Louis told me to send you this also his love only he was too busy to write it. He said 'What do I keep a clerk for' I said I did not engage to be a cupid.* The three objects visible out of the four have an enigmatic and individual form of interior shapes and fault-lines.   13i

March 6th. News came to England in February that Scott had been dead a year, having reached the pole in January 1912 only to find Amundsen had preceded him. Scott's last words plus a poem (And glory guards with solemn round the bivouac of the dead) accompany heroic imagery. Elsie in Bournemouth makes Easter arrangements with Dora Yeates.   13j

June 24th. JW, from officers training camp, writes to Mrs Brown at Embsay Vicarage, Yorks, *we have just come back tired from our long field day & bivouack. Tomorrow, the last day, we dig trenches.* This is the generation soon to be lost and it is hard to look at such a cheery sextet without thinking how many would be sacrificed in the earnest trenches to come.   13k

May 22nd. Alice Dixon in Eastbourne to William Hutchinson in York. *George Henry of to camp on Thursday morning me and Julia are coming to Alne on Saturday night......we are going to cycle and then gone to Easingwold.* This venerable piano joke comes from the slogan that appeared on sheet music (the equivalent of today's recording industry).   13l

March 6th. Mr Hawthorne in Kettering, Northants gets a postcard from his son of the new American president, an image of calculated sobriety, *Dear Dad, wonderful day here, March 4th. the inauguration of the president... Fond love. Charles x.* Wilson was reluctant to enter the First World War yet won the Nobel Peace Prize for dealing with its aftermath.   13m

July 13th. Millie in Baldock writes to relatives in Letchworth, Herts. *Dear aunt mother & J & Rose will be to see you on Wednesday all being well. 10 train from here. your niece.* The spread of literacy down the class structure led to a huge growth of popular magazines. Tit-Bits outlasted many rivals but gained a rather sleazy reputation in later years.   13n

June 14th. Its a good gag and Reg Carter makes it into a generic card recyclable for any seaside town. BB replies to W Bertram Esq. in Addis-Combe, *Yes, by the 2.26.... lovely sitting on the downs - really 'the pure breath' etc.* The suffragettes here are wearing mourning today. [as a tribute to their martyr Emily Davison who was buried that day.]   13o

13a. PH529

13b. W.M.B.& Co.London 'Majestic Series'. No 750

13c. H.F.& Son. American Art Publishing Co. Photo Irving Underhill

13d. Success PostCard Co. NY. No.1010

13e. Gale & Polden

13f. Llew. Evans, Northwich

13g. AA. No 421-16

13h. Flying at Hendon Series. No 53

13i. Publisher unknown

13j. Tuck Oilette. 8626

13k. Gale & Polden 63

13l. Bamforth & Co. Series 1235

13m. B.S.Reynolds Co. Washington

13n. Publisher unknown. (Tit-Bits presumably)

13o. J.Salmon

13p. Julian Bendix. Charterhouse series no 302

13q. SB Series 2. USA

13r. Marcuse Day & Co Ltd. London. Printed in Prussia 290/6

13s. Clock Tower Studios, Margate

May 10th.   A in Bradford to Master F Clark in Hull, *Dear Frank, having very bad weather here hope you can play out at aunties.* The Children's Charter was a series of reforms brought in (with no help as usual from the House of Lords) to ensure that school-children were fed and had medical facilities, and were shielded from such things as strong drink and tobacco.   13p

April 17th.   In the sleepy South-Eastern corner of Minnesota WP sends from Lacrescent to Richard Alfright in Hokah (which still only boasts 700 inhabitants) this raunchy card of a girl who as they say is no better than she should be, *Hello old sport How are you coming i am fine and dandy What are you doing to keep yourself busy i will be out your way this summer From your friend.* He has plenty of time to make the trip from the banks of the Mississippi since Hokah is only five miles or so from Lacrescent.   13r

February 18th.   From Hilda F Lancaster in Sileby to Mrs Walter Poltman in Loughborough, *am writing this Leicester Station. Just off to the Palace. Have just been to Granville School Bazaar.* Marcuse, Day & Co were specialists in romantic images and this tobacco fantasy is immaculately conceived. There is much artistic cunning in such photographic concoctions.   13q

July 24th.   From F & N in Ramsgate to Mrs A Head in Rochester, Kent, *Dear Grannie Head just a card to let you see we are having a pabble Nellie enjoying herself wanting cornet just now.* Clock Tower Studios of Margate obviously had a photographer stationed at Ramsgate to take snaps and process them quickly; all too quickly in this case for the right hand side was not fixed. Yet this fragment of three lives is touchingly caught. They all look straight at the camera. Beyond it somewhere on a deckchair their shoes and socks lie and the large hat for which her hair is designed. He is not alone in being dressed more or less for the office with only a boater to indicate some momentary liberation from drudgery. He is young enough to go to war when after the initial draft Kitchener (see 14a) will be pointing at married men also. Nellie here with the obligatory bucket and spade could be in her nineties now.   13s

October 7th.   The most enduring ikon of the First World War is certainly this Kitchener recruiting poster based on a photograph by Bassano. The hand is evidently drawn as is the simplified uniform. To judge from Mr Eade's message on this postcard version to his mother in Weeley Heath, Essex, Kitchener had already claimed one of the family. *I have been up to the War Office this afternoon and he says that they would have heard long before now if he had been dead but they can't bring all the wounded over here, as we haven't heard he says he thinks he must be better again they know at the War Office directly.*   14a

July 16th.   *My word, I am seeing life*, writes Lucy from Acton to her cousin Mrs Espin in Barton-on-Humber. The Peckham-bound No 12 bus advertises the Coronation Exhibition (of 1911) at the Great White City. Wilkie Bard a comedian who died in 1944 is topping the Pavilion bill.   14b

August 15th.   *Hello Frank*, writes Mabel to Mr Frank Connors in Pittsburgh, Pa., *Some class to these sky-scrapers don't you think so? Be good.* A name guide to the various buildings is helpful but is hardly needed to assert that the Singer building, which has dominated views so far, is now itself dwarfed by the Woolworth building.   14c

October 14th. 'There must be punishment' says the blackboard in the 'War School' as England bends over a desk with Montenegro, Serbia, Belgium etc. *It looks as if this very punishment is to be administered to all enemies of Germany. Hope everything is well in New York* writes AE Sitting in Frankfurt to Mr BA Ludwig in Front St, New York City, in fluent English on this German propaganda card.   14d

September 12th. From WHC in Eccles to Mrs Oliver in Ashford, Kent, *Dear M - just a card to reach you on Sunday morning hope all are well. What a fearful thing this war is - I thought we were all too civilised & too Christian for such carnage.* With the war only a month old worse is to come and this Wellsian vision of the Apocalypse must have had the same impact as images of nuclear terror on a later generation.   14e

December 22nd. Gordon at training camp in Folkestone writes to René Partridge in Lewisham, *Dear Babe, Feeling jolly & putting on weight. Hope you will have a good Xmas. amitiés.* Gallons of blue and red went into the patriotic fantasy cards the French produced in the war, a genre in its own right. We see the same actor/soldiers over and over again with stirring captions in verse (see note).   14f

October 16th. John S Sellar in Haylake receives a card from a schoolfriend written in careful capitals, *Marion has passed first aid as well as nursing so she hopes to be in the detachment. I have painted two boats. Do you like being a scout. love. Charlie.* The allies look an odd assortment to the later eye with Serbia, Russia and Japan; and the USA (as yet) a notable absentee.   14g

June 13th. From Kathleen Hipwell in Kobe to Miss Nora O'C Fisher in Portarlington, Queens Co., Ireland. *We are going to Japan to print the Bible in Chinese roman letters. 3 mths of hard work - remember us in prayers - 17 lepers were baptised just before we left Pakhoi...* Faith will no doubt work its wonders amongst the benighted savages on this charming card (a studio production with garden backdrop).   14h

September 14th. Dad writes from Paris to Denis Browne in Felstead, *Searchlights are almost the only illumination here at night. The city is very quiet. All the places of amusement are closed & many of the shops also.* The Lucien Levy card shows an early experiment in aerial armament with the machine gunner shooting above the propeller in a position that doesn't recommend itself for comfort or safety.   14i

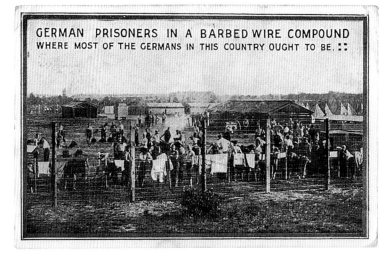

August 19th.   *Dear Ma*, writes Frank to Mrs Walters in York, *Another mug of me and part of campers. The Terriers have collared 30 tents so we are rather short-handed. On Monday we walked to Forge Valley. We are the terrors of Scarbro - I am very glad I came.* Holiday Camps had started in the previous decade. Two weeks into the war this is now being used to break these young men in.   14j

October 7th.   Lewis from Aldershot to Daisy Miles in Milton-under-Wychwood, *You would just like to see these Germans and they can't half laugh and play football they are better than Milton we see some fine fun and their is a big fair not far from us and we have been down and got caught and march back.* Visual pre-echo makes one think of concentration camps (albeit a British Boer War invention).   14k

December 1st.   *Frascati's - Kindest regards to you & yours... Elliot W   Thisheute. Tony wishes you were here with us at your old favourite place - however when you come down it's lock stock and barrel, you will see.* Not too severe inroads yet into the Frascati set though perhaps the absent Mrs Oehme in Chorlton-cum-Hardy knows more than the others can guess.   14l

August 14th.   Jack writes from Swindon to Mrs Adams and the children in Bristol, *Glad to say am alright we have been put up for a few days in a Ladys house and they are very kind to us But we are leaving this is that photo am sending again we are going to March to Oxford 30 miles away...sending on money.* Three good nurses Jack will always remember from his strike or hunger or protest march.   14m

June 19th.   Effie Miethe in Georgetown, Ill. gets a card from another theatre of war. *Don't write me till I write again*, the unnamed soldier says, *I will send you a card from Mexico I am in Maramoras now this is the way they burry an office in Mexico I was in town when this soldier was killed Juarez I will leave Mexico soon.* An uneasy peace was declared July 9th. Censorship forbade cards like this of the war in Europe.   14n

April 30th.   Vi writes to Master David Williams in Bristol from the Savoy Hotel, Dresden, *This is the great big airship which I have seen flying over the houses twice since we came here. I have taken a photograph of it so I hope to show it to you when we come back.* Soon these airships would be fitted with bombs and heading for England. The word 'Sachsen' (Saxony) on the side has been added by the printer.   14o

I'M BRINGING YOU HOME A PIECE OF ROCK FROM RHYL

I WANT TO BE IN DIXIE !!

"HERE MISSIS ! YOUR NEW CANARY'S BEEN AN' EATEN THE GRAMOPHONE !!"

August 5th.   On a card covered in over sixty pencil kisses Sidney in Rhyl writes to Messrs Bailey in Stafford...*a wonderful time of it here and it would do you good. Love from your Brother and love to my nephew Sidney.* Comic artists change and develop (compare the confidence of this with 060n). A generic card with an early mention of seaside rock.   14p

March 14th.   To Mrs Riley in Horsham from a schoolmaster in Eastbourne who writes at length on the ups and downs of the sports teams etc. This might be designated McGill's White Period. The parrot must have heard an early recording of Dixie (written 1859) rather than Dixieland Jazz which coincidentally surfaced in Chicago this same year.   14q

10513-15   LONDON LIFE. BOOTBLACK.   ROTARY PHOTO. E.C.

WHAT EVERYONE SHOULD KNOW
CANAL STATISTICS.

Meeting of the Atlantic & Pacific
THE KISS
OF THE OCEANS 1915

May 18th.   Fred writes to Miss M Storey in Bridgewater, Somerset, from Paddington, *I have a place at John Lewis & Co Oxford St Start tomorrow at 9oc Live out Print Dresses not bad.* Rotary's London Life Series is prized for its reticence and accuracy compared with others, avoiding as it does the obviously picturesque or sentimental.   14r

February 23rd.   From (anon) in Los Angeles to (name obliterated) in Rockville, Conn., a simple message, *Some kiss.* One of the most inventive cards of the era. Designed by C A de Lisle Howard it was copyrighted in 1910 by a San Francisco novelty company to promote the Panama canal which, though scheduled for completion in 1915, was opened on August 15th.   14s

1914 MESSAGES·NOTES·PARTICULARS

14a. Regent publishing Co. The War Series no 1851

14b. Stein & Russell Real Photographic London Views, 121

14c. Tauman Co. New York. Luclay Buck 5161

14d. G Gabrillowitsch. Frankfurt. a. Main.

14e. Naval and Aerial Warfare. G.P. (Gale and Polden)

14f. The rhyme translates as:

> Soldiers, sleep on, enjoy the sleep of kings
> While our brave birds protect you with their wings

Tailhades-Levallois-Parret. Gloria 62.
Photomontage: M.Boulanger

14g. 'Classic' All British Series, W.N.Sharpe, Bradford.

14h. The message starts
Have never thanked you for Xmas parcel & socks especially... (and continues)...*They wish us to go on furlough next summer so may see you then. One of our schoolboys has been chosen for ordination in view of taking charge of the church at Pakhoi...*

Made in Japan.

14i. The message starts,
Dear old chap, I had a grand crossing and am having a pleasant time here. As yet I have not got any work to do but hope to get fixed up tomorrow. Perhaps we may be sent near to Bordeaux by the French Red Cross people...(and continues)...*It is perfect weather. I saw an aeroplane today over the city. We have heard no guns of course as the fighting is far from here.*

Edia. Paris LL (Lucien Levy)

14j. Publisher unknown

14k. The War Series No 1866. Regent Publishing Co.

14l. Restaurant 'Frascati', London

14m. Publisher unknown

14n. Publisher unknown. Photo: R.Runyon. (Azo square)

14o. 6425. Kunstverlag Rudolf Brauneis, Dresden

14p. Publisher (J.Asher). No A1420 printed in Bavaria.

14q. *The Avenue, E'bourne. Many thanks for the usual. Re Punch - one of the boys here has it sent when it happens to be a specially good number (he did not have one last week) and I will let you know when he does get it. So sorry to hear about K...Yesterday St Peter's (6) beat Brighton Banks(5) although at one time they were leading by 4 to 1. Some of us went to the 90's performance at the Hippodrome & 9 of us came back by the 11.15 from B'ton arriving here 12.10 Mrs H came back last Tues. & Lionel today - also a couple (Mr & Mrs Price) whom they picked up at Matlock. Lots of the boys & Ratcliffe have had a sort of mild 'flu. Do you like this card? Hope you are both fit. Love from A.I.J.R.*

The beautiful pedantry of how many boys went to Brighton and how many came back etc. is phrased exactly like an exam question.

Joseph Asher & Co. London. Funny Parrots A1197

14r. Rotary Photographic Series. 10513 - 15

14s. DPE Novelty Series. San Francisco.

TO MY DEAR ONE.

Whate'er you are doing
Wherever you roam
My thoughts are ever of you
Always just thinking
Of those left at home
And the one who always is true.

June 16th.   A husband writes from camp to his wife, Mrs Shields, in Marshall St, Edinburgh. *Aldershot, Friday. time 3.45. My Own Dearest Darling Wife Minnie the weather here is something awful a wet shirt every day with sweat well dear we had a march this forenoon with full packs on everything you require was on your pack it was lovely walking in a scorching sun & dusty roads heap of love all's well Hubby. [15 kisses].* Soon no doubt he would be writing from 'Somewhere in France' (all the censor would allow a soldier to say) and might be regretting the swap of dusty roads for a wilderness of mud. This type of dramatised card made popular by Bamforth often featured a hoped for or remembered moment as an inset. Here the kiss (more passionate than contemporary taste would usually allow) as well as the model posed before a backdrop painted as a hut, captured the writer's mood.   15a

May 7th.   This card is in fact an advert for Mellins Food. Their name occurs on a building and on a van outside the Pavilion. The printed caption on the back recommends it for babies and aged persons. HM writes to Miss Recor in Stowmarket, *Have a nice house here. Will writes you after Whit if I don't have time before.*   15b

September 20th.   From M to Dr St Denis, New Bedford, Mass., *Parcel post bundle rec'd this a.m it went to Southport. axe is a fine one, sponges we did not need. What is the other tool intended for? Beautiful day, we are bustling to go tomorrow.* Another rather indeterminate aeroplane is introduced into the sky.   15c

THE MILITARY MISS

Prepared to 'Face Powder.'

WHICH IS THE QUICKEST WAY TO THE HOSPITAL MY BOY?

STAND IN THE ROAD AND SHOUT "THREE CHEERS FOR THE KAISER", SIR.

En Avant!

Pour la Victoire

·155·

April 22nd.   T G Garrard hears from Alice in Kingston-on-Thames, *My dear Tom, Ern went up to Stockton again to-day & he has passed for the R.A.M.C.* [the Medical Corps]. *He's jolly pleased. He will be billeted at home until they get the right number & then he will be down at Egham.* A good pun and a pretty woman (in a greatcoat vastly too large) makes its point.   15d

January 19th.   Its amenability to so many variations has made this joke virtually indestructible, though more likely to be used now of football teams. TSE somewhere in Hampshire writes to Miss G Willard in Usk, *I shall be home today Sat. & will see you as usual. I thought I was never going to have my leave but better late than never.*   15e

April 23rd.   It sounds as if Private Wilkins' En Avant days are over as he writes on a card, probably bought in France, to his sister Alice in Brettenham, Norfolk, *The Germans have winged me again, this time I have got a bullet through my right knee, it is going on alright...your loving Brother.* In gesture and style these actor/soldiers are pure silent film.   15f

CONTINUOUS PERFORMANCE

IT'S EVER SO NICE IN THE CINEMA

"IT" Naturally Follows.

May 19th.   S F Streatfield working for the Red Cross at a Belgian Field Hospital writes to Lord Leigh in Kindworth, *we had a share in the last battle 60, 50, 40, 35 being brought in on consecutive days.* Postcards of ruins and war damage abound but few are more eloquent than this blasted interior with its lonely figure surveying a tumbled cross and fallen saints.   15g

November 26th.   From GE in Milton Abbas to Miss G Miller in Shillingstone, *Have you got Earn home yet I am going home tomorrow.* The idea of the back row of the cinema being the haunt of lovers evidently sprang up even before plush seats. Darkness gave privacy (elsewhere difficult to find) and the continuous performance offered uninterrupted delight.   15h

June 25th.   Edie Adams writes to Private Sidney Sharland at Worgret Camp in Dorset, *Don't you dare say she is not pretty - I do hope you three won't go out yet we all three send our best to you all.* Spirited Edie sounds like an 'It' girl. 'It', Elinor Glyn's novel described a special magnetic vivacity some women possess. The meaning of the word spread generously.   15i

October 12th.   To Master Denis Elgan in Hammersmith, W London from Merlow, *Dear Denis, I have been listening to a concert in this tent and thought I would send a p.c. to you old chap before I turned in for the night I hope you will be a good boy and not give mummy any trouble, God bless you yr loving father.* A strained looking group and a sense in the message of imminent departure.   15j

July 8th.   'Somewhere in France' soon became the serviceman's code for 'writing home from the front'. Walter, an officer is still in England and has been *finding suitable places for our company to move to...I don't know how many miles we went, about 150 I should think. I hear they're working 3 Sundays out of four at the aeroplane works.* He is writing to Dot, Miss L Dent, in Bristol.   15k

August 5th.   EML writes to the Rev Hobday in Wellington, NZ. The card takes five weeks to get there and the Rev Hobday had meanwhile moved to Paraparaumu, *we also saw another aeroplane captured at the Battle of the Marne...The place is full of troops, les blessés & Women in black.* The Taube (ironically 'Dove') was the premier German fighter plane as the war began.   15l

October 15th.   H W Whithy must be an officer since he countersigns his own card and stamps it with the censor's stamp. He is also meant to obliterate the name of the place so as to give no clue to his whereabouts: this he duly does but does not spot the name Saint Omer repeated on the right... *as you see I'm back again at the front or rather somewhere in France* he writes to A A Berrin in Putney.   15m

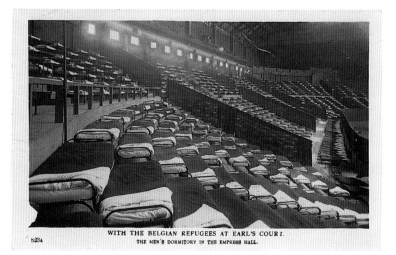

November 18th.   A Belgian refugee M Havel Peeters uses this card to learn how to express his new whereabouts, *War Refugees Camp Earl's SW* and sends it to a benefactor Mr Eric Lowly in Farnham, Surrey with a few words in Flemglais *nieuw work naast week I moeton hebben.* The array of beds indicates the extent of the problem in dramatic fashion.   15n

January 21st.   It takes two to play footsie and all four feet here in their fine buttoned shoes are well engaged. The miniature ballet is directed with all the flair of a great film-maker with only one touch of colour. Such an image exalts the postcard form: it is hard to imagine it existing in another medium. Naughty Boy was a chorus of a music hall song. From Grace in Weybridge to her sister Hilda Wilson in Woking.   15o

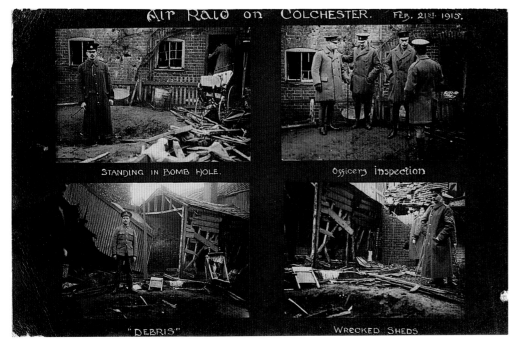

Air Raid on COLCHESTER. Feb. 21st 1915.

STANDING IN BOMB HOLE.   Officers Inspection

"DEBRIS"   WRECKED SHEDS

15a. C.P.C. (City Postcard Co) Our Lads series

15b. The Photocrom Co Ltd. Tunbridge Wells

15c. Finkelstein Art Series No 24. American Art Publishing Co.

15d. Publisher unknown

15e. E.Mack, Hampstead, London. 652. artist: Reg Carter

15f. Gloria. 155

15g. Publisher and photographer unknown. Red Cross PM.

15h. Printed in Great Britain. W.681. artist: W.Stocker Shaw

15i. The message begins, *Dear Idney - I - know, We were so glad to get your long newsy letter. Remember us all to Mr Jennings...It is a terrible wet day - enough to give one the blues. You asked me to send you on one so I am doing my little best...*

W & K (Wildt & Kray) London Series no3497

15j. Publisher unknown

15k. Publisher unknown

15l. Neurdin Frères, Paris

15m. He continues, *I'm in a town far away from the strafing... sorry not to see you while I was in Richmond but...I left in somewhat of a hurry.* (FPO 'G'. Censor 537)

15n. Davey & Hackney, London. Actual Photo Series. 823A

15o. *...What a miserable day it has been today hope it will be a bit better for Sunday so Ta Ta Dearest with fondest love. hope you will like this P.C. from your loving Sister Grace.*

It is rare at this time to see as publisher such a palpably Teutonic name plus the almost inflammatory information that the card was printed in Berlin. Grace evidently gives it no thought but many publishers have overprinted their 'Printed in Saxony', 'lithographed in Prussia' etc with decorative borders, and words like British Manufacture are proudly shown. The company of Schwerdtfeger is a case in point. Based in Berlin they were represented in Britain by Giesen Brothers. Karl Giesen was in fact the president of the Postcard Publishers' Association at the outbreak of war. He ceased trading at that point and sold out his stock to Thridgould and company whose name was as English as Schwerdtfeger was German.

E.A.Schwerdtger & Co, London. printed at their works in Berlin.

15p. Publisher unknown (presumably a local photographer)

15q. Red Letter Photocard in association with Essanay Films.

March 9th.   A new horror and an instant reaction from an anonymous local photographer. Two effects of the Zeppelin raids at the beginning of 1915 were quick to sink in. That Britain's island identity had changed forever was a shock, but even more threatening was the sudden involvement of women and children, hundreds of whom would be killed or injured before the last Zeppelin raid in August 1918. The Colchester photographer's gathered views are hardly apocalyptic nor does the caption 'Wrecked Sheds' chill the blood yet the censor moved in quickly to protect the public from much grimmer scenes. Promoted instead were artists' impressions of Zeppelin attacks and photographs of wrecked airships with pictures of the heroes who brought them down. The east coast provided the first targets swiftly followed by Colchester and nearby towns as war from the air headed towards London. It was the Kaiser's own reluctance that delayed attacks on the capital especially its historic monuments, including Buckingham Palace (the home of close relatives). Miss G Hassal at 34 Stanley St Bedford, receives this card from Colchester itself, *Dear Gertie, How will this suit your Highness Splosh? Did you manage it. Feeling funny myself now, Best love, Herbert.*   15p

RED LETTER PHOTOCARD.

(Charlie Chaplin.)   **Second Thoughts.**   (Charlie the Tramp.)

August 16th.   In training at Doncaster race-course Private Dale of the Royal Scots receives a card from Manchester, *Mr Dale, I hope you are quiet well and that you like Doncaster with love and I hope you will be coming home from your loving little friend Connie* [24 kisses]. The formal address to Mr Dale suggests that Connie is not properly (or yet) 'his girl'. Perhaps she used the card she had found in the current issue of Red Letter to make her feelings known. The postcard shows Chaplin's new 20 minute film The Tramp, the first film which features the trademark walk of the little man into the distant sunset. Chaplin's comedies made a timely appearance and it was in 1914 that he first adopted the tramp outfit with hat and stick. No doubt his films were shown at the camp and Connie might well have been pleased to have something so topical to send. Yet all this speculation is made idle by the fact that 17866, Lance Corporal (as he had become) W A Dale was killed in action on the 1st July 1916 at Ovillers on the Somme, near which he now lies buried, at Gordon Dump Cemetery in what is known as Sausage Valley.   15q

Characteristic configuration of censor's stamp, Army Post Office date stamp, censor's initials and 'On Active Service'.

SINN FEIN REBELLION

D.B.C. SACKVILLE STREET, DUBLIN.   BEFORE AND AFTER

May 24th.   L K Horan, a Dubliner, writes to Mrs Deanes in Newcastle on Tyne, *We arrived home quite safe We had a fine night crossing and did not meet with any submarines. This is a view of Dublin hope you will like it. If you look close you will see me amongst the ruins.* A fine irony graces the message just a month after the Easter Uprising and one of England's worst political blunders.   16a

Precise date unclear.   Alice writes to Mrs Peck in Wisbech, *I am glad I made the bonnet the right shape hope you are going on alright tell Mendle to cast on 80 stitches and do 200 rows and there you are what is the little dear little mite name to be....* This is an early photographic night-time view taken in 1913.   16b

July 16th.   Leah writes to her Aunt Celia in North Java NY, *Well I suppose you were surprized to here that I am down here but was so busy in the P.O. & everything I did not have time to write. Having a fine time. WUYO.Co.R.F.D.* Roebling's great bridge, completed 1883, is photogenic from any angle.   16c

July 10th. *France. Dear Eunice, many thanks for letter and photograph. I think it is awfully good...we are up to our eyes in work again.* Mrs Flowers in Abbots Langley receives a card illustrating the most famous marching song of the war, composed in 1912 by Judge and Williams; an odd choice since it deals with the homesickness of an Irishman in England. I've struggled in vain to fit the French words to the tune. 16d

June 1st. Someone signing himself 'a' writes to H Trollope in Palmers Green from County Cork, *Two of our prisoners being brought into Fermoy. The little chap minus the hat was the ringleader of the local trouble & we think it was him who murdered the police inspector which caused all the trouble locally.* The style of this message is still recognisably characteristic of Irish political utterance (who is 'we'?). 16e

May 12th. Tom to Mr and Mrs Church in Bursley, *Dear Gerta & Norman...we are just behind the line at the moment making to [censored]. This is a view of the front line of trenches [censored] having taken them over from the French. I am in the best of health...* Despite the censor's pencil the place name Bonvillers aux Bois can be deciphered as the site of this touching image of Mass being said in the trenches. 16f

September 11th. Jim tries out his French on the front, *Us après la guere*, as he writes to Miss Whiteman in Bedford, *Dear Kit...could do with a swim in the river we have such a weedy stream here. Your old blinds don't keep Zepps off Eh. Try a mouse trap & some of that toasted cheese you believe in. Hope you are not dumpy. I am quite festive...* Another LL card from 'Somewhere in France'. 16g

November 22nd. Somewhere in America, within Iowa to be precise. Mrs Jones writes from Cascade to Miss Lida Elliot in Preston, *Dear friend I am glad I went to Preston, am glad I met the Preston ladies...will you please fill out the name of Mrs Lockard. I had a 1hr 20min stay in Sabula, visited Mrs Dyer & Miss Rogers till 10 min before train time. Hope it did some good.* Somehow we know these ladies who are urging America towards the worst excesses of prohibition, and will succeed before the decade is out. 16h

October 3rd. Sent to Mrs Aplin in Tunbridge Wells from a Field Post Office and written in the inevitable purple of an indelible pencil this French propaganda card sums up the growing mythology of the martyrdom of Edith Cavell. The officer has fired a point blank shot having failed to command his squad to execute her after she had fainted. Execution (she acknowledged herself to be guilty under German law) turned into assassination and assassination into a symbol of German brutality. 16i

September 23rd.   As Tipperary was the archetypal song of the war this Bairnsfather line was the archetypal joke. We do not hear the rest of the dialogue but it shows the ancestry of the fatalistic humour in Waiting for Godot. Gertrude Blendell in Ticehurst to her parents in Romford, *Weather fine. HP over on Monday too many creepers for my liking otherwise alright more tired than empty.*   16j

January 17th.   Private Longbottom sends a card from the front to his parents in Harrogate and has a pretty good stab at translating the ingredients of Pig's Head à la Wilhelm (though he ducks the rhyme at the end) *Dear Ma & Pa... a few lines to let you know I'm feeling in the pink again. hope to pay you a short visit shortly... your ever loving son.* Jack Longbottom was killed in action at Neuville-Vitasse on April 19th 1917.   16k

June 16th.   RWS in Paris to G Leatham in Poona, *There's no need to ask if you remember this. Oh! the good old days! was at the Grand Guignol last night & much thrilled by things épouvantables!...* Risqué acts in a Monmartre review must seem a long way away to a colonial official in Poona and not exactly prime news from France, yet he no doubt enjoyed Neurdin's beautifully tinted Moulin Rouge.   16l

January 22nd.   Jack is in Rothesay writing to Nellie Kegg in Gretna Green *...very heavy snow here and I suppose there was plenty snow where you are...will write when we get up to Glasgow. We are lying down the Clyde.* Women had found the secret. It was not just the work that gave independence but the earnings (sometimes equal pay for equal output).   16m

August 30th.   To Miss M G Pierce in Eastbourne on this typical French romantic card bought at the front, *I am allright but weather is awful. we are smothered in mud. I was out all day yesterday & didn't know it was Sunday until 4 o'clock, what a life, watch going fine M.L.* [much love] *Fred.* The hand-tinted image seems to combine flower, eye and a daydream.   16n

July 13th.   From Harwich to Keighley, *Dear Edie. just a line to remind you that (Jack) will be home alright on Monday night & that he is getting quite excited about it. I keep saying hurry up Monday...I am ashore again for a change...just beginning to rain so I think I will turn into the pictures... your affectionate boy.* Bamforth's photomontage at its most brilliant.   16o

THE RAIDER
PUBLICATION SANCTIONED BY OFFICIAL PRESS BUREAU.
PUBLISHING OFFICE
39, ST. ANDREW'S HILL, E.C.   Copyright

GOING!
GOING!!
GONE!!!
The man behind the Gun.
LT. W.L. ROBINSON. V.C.
3787 F
"STRAFED" BY LIEUT. WILLIAM LEEFE ROBINSON V.C.
CUFFLEY, 3RD SEPT. 1916.
ROTARY PHOTO, F.C.

March 23rd. This frequently reproduced photograph was taken by H Scott Orr from his studio window in Woodford Green, London and readily sanctioned by the censors. Miss Doris Castleton in Englefield Green receives it from her father in Greenwich with news of lodgings, *Tell Mother Auntie Rose is quite willing to let us have the rooms...just opposite us at seven and sixpence per week.* 16p

October 1st. A C Cook in Enfield to Mrs Adams in Worthing confirming his date of arrival at her boarding house. The shooting down of a Zeppelin (or in this case a Schutte-Lanz airship) was watched by thousands in E London as Leefe Robinson in his B.E.2C attacked the searchlit goliath and brought it down in flames. No pictures could have pleased the censor more. Robinson died in captivity in 1918. 16q

Miss Edith CAVELL
lâchement assassinée
par un officier allemand

Condamnée à mort par un tribunal militaire en Belgique, pour avoir favorisé l'évasion de soldats anglais et belges, miss Edith Cavell, de Norwich, infirmière volontaire, est amenée au poteau d'exécution le 12 octobre au lever du jour. Elle tombe évanouie. L'officier allemand donne à ses soldats l'ordre de faire feu; ils hésitent à tirer sur le corps pantelant d'une femme. Le monstre galonné tire son revolver et penché sur la victime lui brûle froidement la cervelle.
(REMEMBER!) SOUVENEZ-VOUS !

Never mind it will soon be Easter then I can have you to myself again. I went to bed by 9 o'clock on Sunday. I was in by myself after tea till 7.30. I wish you had been there d....t to keep me company...with my very best love to you chicken I am yours forever Kathy xxxx.

Bamforth & Co. Witty Series No 239. Artist: Tempest

BAKER 171
THE NOTED PLACE FOR TARTS
CONFECTIONER
O.K SAUCE
BOW-WOW.

Have I punched your ticket, Sir?
—— Bow-wow!
TRAMWAY Co

April 16th. Sarah writes from Morpeth to Cissie Kidd in Newcastle-on-Tyne, *...shall be delighted to see you. And with the greatest of pleasure I shall do as you ask anything to oblige a lady...your loving friend etc.* Before TV, or even radio, catch phrases could sweep the country in days. 'Bow Wow' seems to be somewhere between 'Oh! Boy!' and 'Hot Stuff!'. 16r

March 21st. *Dear Albert*, writes Kathy in Binsley to her man in Birmingham, *well d....g I have been dreadfully downhearted again today so I am going with Annie to the pictures to see if it will cheer me up a bit. But I fancy my mind will be with you...* then adds, *The old chap on the p.c. has a 'Thumby Erection'.* The conductress is a sign of the times. 16s

THIS.IS.HOW.WE.OUGHT.TO.HAVE.BEEN.
OUR BEST.DAYS.GONE.IN.BUSINESS.
NOW.ITS.WAR.AND WORK
WHILE.MEN.FIGHT
PRAY.GOD.SEND.VOTES.TO.BRITISH WOMEN
TO GIVE.OUR.CHILDREN SENSE
TO SETTLE.DIFFERANCES WITHOUT.A FIGHT
AS.WOMEN.BORN.WE.ARE
THE MONOPOLY
OF.THE.STATE

February 16th.   Ezra Pound would have been proud of the combative style of this battlecry for women's suffrage. Belasco's play of 1905 (made five years later into an opera by Puccini) gives a title to the card and the fine archetype of independent womanhood here romanticised by the Canadian born artist Philip Boileau. Boileau who died in this same year was a prolific producer of glamour pictures, all a far cry from Sheffield where Elisa writes, or Stockport where her sister Tettie (to whom she communicates with kindly vehemence) lives. The reverse of the card (see notes) shows clearly how such a spirited intelligence felt itself wasted by the injustices of the time.   17a

July 23rd.   E Wallis in Clementina Rd, Leyton writes to Mrs Lee a mile away in Sedgwick Rd about a minor transaction, *if you should be coming this way Wednesday you can have the money....* A despatch boy and a street cleaner feature in this fine 1909 view of Swan & Edgar's Corner.   17b

January 2nd.   CCE is back in New York and talks to Dorothy Allison of Sellisgrove, Snyder Co., Penna. of going *to Connecticut in a few days to see the Fochts. New York does a lot of hustling as well as building of skyscrapers.* Already the pointed tower of the Bankers' Trust building is being hidden.   17c

Kamarade !
Kamarade !

February 10th.   Here be stereotypes. Mr Robb Smith writes from France to his son Alistair in Chislehurst, *This rather good I think, what do you say. I have seen a good few Boche prisoners & they do not strike me as being beauties. Personally I have no time for them & hate to see them going about. I should like to see them doing the Kamerad tricks. Daddy.* No squarer jaw was ever seen, nor pipe more firmly gripped.   17d

February 5th.   To Miss Dugden in Burslem, *This magnificent building is the new Town Hall of Colchester...I went to a sale of Zeppelin relics here on Saturday (from the Zeppelin shot down a few mile from here, L33) I am bringing a few pieces home for you. The sale was held in the gorgeous room with 2 big painted windows...the Garrison band played magnificently during the sale.*   17e

HE HAS GONE TO THE COLOURS, TOO.

May 15th.   To Miss E Pobjoy in Cardiff from Barry, *I say Nursey I bet you'll be like this in the next war. (What Oh.) Poor kid something to keep the home fires burning for! Oh Swish Sport. I say Nursey do hurry up and Drop a Line.* If even the artists have gone to war things must be bad seems to be the purport of the card. The little girl is not inventing abstract art; she had been beaten to it by Kandinsky ten years before.   17f

I CAN'T GET OFF AS I USED TO DO
BUT THE KHAKI BOYS ARE QUITE IN CLOVER
SO I THINK I'LL JOIN THE ARMY TOO —
WHEN THE NASTY HORRID WAR IS OVER!

July 4th.   Gwen in Burton-on-Trent writes to Miss Goodgaunt in Nottingham, *Dearest Edie, Having a top-hole time. Have you heard God Send You Back To Me* (see 18o) *its ripping, beats all the others. I'm bringing a copy back so don't get one.* A constant theme of comic cards in World War I was disapproval of non volunteers. Conscription saw to that, but there were still dodgers. Is this perhaps a gay caricature?   17g

I hope to catch the next train home

July 31st.   To Miss E Holden, Touch Wood, Bunch Lane, Haslemere, *Miss. This is what I have to do when I stop and cuddle you at Touchwood But never mind the next will come along Dear and have a spoon nine.30 sharp and don't be late in the morning your ever good for nothing sure. yep. goodnight.* McGill like the soldier is well in his stride. Everything is keenly observed, and made to work (including telegraph wires).   17h

MISS MARY PICKFORD
THE FAMOUS FILM ACTRESS.

February 10th.   Vi in Kettering sends this to Eunice Goodman in nearby Geddington as a birthday card. Rotary have now added this Famous Film Actress to their immense gallery of stage personalities. Mary Pickford was the first international screen star (see 20a). Samuel Goldwyn said of the world's sweetheart 'It took longer to make one of Mary's contracts than it did to make one of Mary's pictures'.   17i

THE CINEMA, PARTRINGTON, E. YORKS

The
Earl Roberts
Rest House
for
Sailors &
Soldiers,
289/291,
Pentonville Rd.
King's Cross,
N.

66 Beds.

Open Day
and
Night.

March 1st.   *Dear Eve, This is the hall where we gave a concert at about a month ago. We got 5/- each* [25p]. *So that kept us in cigs for a day or two...Best love George.* A village of a thousand souls or so would hardly boast a cinema as such and as the message shows, it was an all purpose hall. Yet here they would see Mary Pickford and Charlie Chaplin and thrill to the Perils of Pauline.   17j

July 27th. To the same Eve as 17j in Newcastle on Tyne, *Am here @ 4am. Had a nice bath 4am now waiting for bacon and eggs. I will give them stick. This is an lovely place to stay. I don't think I will see all London this time. The cockneys are just getting out of bed. Best love George.* Dazed minds and tired limbs needed such refuges where they could drink meat tea, albeit beneath a portrait of Kitchener.   17k

Si vous aimez les Fleurs
Vous m'aimerez moi-même,
Car elles sont mes sœurs
De par leur tendre emblème!

FURIA
1740/4

"We Have no Quarrel with the German People. We Have no Feeling Toward them but one of Sympathy and Friendship." (Woodrow Wilson.)   2181

November 4th.   Fred is still *Somewhere in France* and still sending romantic cards to Miss Pierce (see 16n) who is now at Cave's Oriental Café in Western Road, Brighton, *Many thanks for welcome Sunday letter. I am A1. Well in the mud again. that is old news in your last letter but do not believe it. I take no notice of it. I hear Mac is fed up already. M.L.Fred.*   17l

September 6th.   America had declared war on Germany in April. Perhaps Maud and Willie in Minnesota were somewhat out of touch. Nonetheless this is the sentiment they choose to send to Laura Sprague in Sioux Falls, S Dakota, *...I got the towel. It sure is nice. When I write a letter I will tell you what presents we got, dishes, knives, forks, a clock, spoon and other thing. Folk went to Dakota to see Mary.*   17m

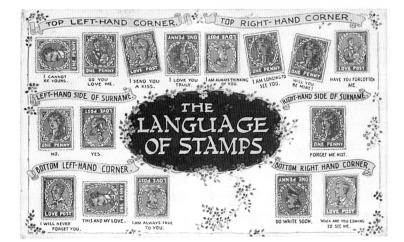

August 22nd.   From Annie to Miss Bell in Kilmarnock, *...are you very busy. This is the language of stamps, if I come across the Flowers I will send it on. Enjoying myself immence. Best love.* She rounds off her message with a distinctly placed stamp saying 'longing to see you'. There were conflicting stamp codes and I have hesitated to interpret any except this, even when messages were probably intended.   17n

October 23rd.   Ern writes from Manchester Military Hospital to his sister Nell Edyvean in Holsworthy, N Devon, *This is a photo of the ward that I am in at the hospital of course it was taken before I arrived here so it is no good looking for me.* A fine ward in a modern light airy hospital with electric light was fit for heroes. Ern does not complain of his wounds.   17o

"Tu as été exempté? . . . Pas par moi!"

**Who's the old Tribunal anyway
— I haven't exempted you !!**

November 15th. From Valletta, Malta, to Miss Windredge in Bermondsey, *My dearest Amy. Just a card from shore. I am scribing this before supping... been doing a bit of shopping this evening all on my own - quite enjoyed myself too... going to stop ashore all night so that I can buy some gear for the mess at the early morning market. Ta-Ta. all love xx Fred.* 17p

TO DRESS
EXTRAVAGANTLY
IN WAR TIME
IS WORSE THAN
BAD FORM
IT IS
UNPATRIOTIC

"WELL / THEY CAN'T SAY
I'M UNPATRIOTIC !!"

December 21st. To Mrs Downes in Fordingbridge, Hants with the brief message *Save up it's war time.* Surrounded by the work of Donald McGill and Reg Maurice poor Stocker Shaw looks an artist of exceedingly modest gifts. He invariably tries to put his principal figures in profile to make things a little easier for himself. (see 16r). 17q

**I WONDER IF YOU'LL
MISS ME SOMETIMES ??**

April 17th. To Pte D E Folkes RAMC in Blackpool from Daisy, *Dear David; Did you say you were hungry well, here's a potato to get on with: yes, in war time. you don't know how generous I am. When are you coming home? I'm nearly pegging out. When you come bring 'Vic' with you.* The potato shortage was the result of a very poor harvest in 1916. 17r

THERE'S A LONG LONG
TRAIL AWINDING.

POTATOES
TO-DAY.

April 13th. From Alice in Herne Hill to Mrs Corny in South Queensferry, Scotland. *Dr: At: G: This is some of the real thing. I expect you will be seeing Mother on a P.C. one of these days. Have you experienced anything like this up there yet?.* The stall advertises Potatoes To-Day and a typical orderly British queue develops as the word gets around. 17s

17a. *My dear Tettie & Tottie, Thank you dearie...I note you are keeping free from colds and the babies too. I have heard that if you have an income of £26 a year you have no need to pay Health Insurance and the State will do much for mothers. New Laws they say we have been kept in the Dark your Daughters must not Employers as to let children have time to finish their education. I wish I was a baby now. We were born when babies was cheap. God ever bless and guide you & yours dearie. Your ever loving sister Elisa xxx* (to Mrs Mapplebeck, Newmills, Stockport).

Reinhold & Newman NY No 755. artist: Philip Boileau

17b. Publisher unknown. (tinted version of a commonly used photograph). No 22.

17c. Success Postal Card Co. NY. No 1188

17d. Lafayette Série No 07. Artist: Mac

17e. Publisher unknown

17f. Inter-Art Co. London Artistique Series 1905 British Manufacture throughout.

17g. H.B.Series (Hutson Bros) No 61. Entire British Production.

17h. Inter Art Co. London. Comique Series. No 1541 British Manufacture Throughout

17i. Rotary Photographic Series 11873A

17j. J.Stockdale, Patrington (though he mis-spells the name of his own village in the caption)

17k. Publisher unknown (The Earl Roberts Rest House)

17l. The 'poem' translates roughly

> If you hold flowers dear. Your love for me is true
> They are my emblems clear. my sisters of the dew

Furia 1740/4 FPO 150 Censor 2157

17m. Publisher unknown. USA. 2181

17n. Central Publishing Co. Glasgow

17o. Publisher unknown

17p. Inter-Art Co. London. Artistique Series. No 1428 British Manufacture Throughout. Artist: Donald McGill

17q. Publisher unknown. W908 Artist: Stocker Shaw

17r. Regent Publishing Co. London No 2646 Artist: Reg Maurice

17s. Evidently these two potato cartoons were done in the same batch judging by the adjacent series numbers and by the postmarks. Topicality and speed were of the essence.

Regent Publishing Co. London. No 2645 Artist: Reg Maurice

November 12th.   *Dear All. What glorious news*, writes Maude to the Clarkes in Upton Park, Essex on the day after the Armistice, *seems too good to be true. Great excitement up here. Oh how I wanted to join in it all but we were open until six. I too felt we ought to be all together yesterday but never mind. Looking forward to seeing you all on Sunday. Three cheers for the boys who have fought for dear old England.* The long awaited presence of the Stars and Stripes helps balance the image as it helped the balance of power, one of the major factors that moved the Great War towards its end.   18a

June 15th.   The view was taken a fortnight after the sinking of the Titanic. A news placard announces strikes aboard the Olympic, her sister ship. Aunt Mary writing to Master Black is a mine of misinformation about Eros. It is one of 24 cards she is sending him. One hopes the others are not so misleading (see note).   18b

May 12th.   Mrs Paul Jereczek in Dodge, Wisconsin, receives an almost telegraphic message from her son, *Exceptional Medical Replace. Unit 24. Overseas Casuals, Camp Merritt. N.J. Dear Moth:- Will sail in a few days. E.D.* We will see the identical view again as 20c heavily disguised as a night scene.   18c

Entrée triomphale à METZ, du Maréchal Pétain, le 19 Novembre 1918

February 8th.   Ted, somewhere in Italy, sends this celebratory card to Maud in Brighton still couched in the circumspect words of censored mail, *just a few lines hoping you are in the pink to say this leaves me in the pink*. How many men in fetid clothes, exhausted and bruised, had licked the purple lead of indelible pencils to write that they were *feeling A1* or that they were *in the pink* ?.   18d

December 3rd.   Ethel Dollew in Whimple, Devon receives a card from France with an injunction to look after it (which she seems duly to have done), *Another PC for you will send you some more tomorrow keep them as there is an history attached to them with love your affect Bro Walter*. With ten million dead, the armistice signed and the Kaiser in flight Marshal Petain seems to amble towards Germany.   18e

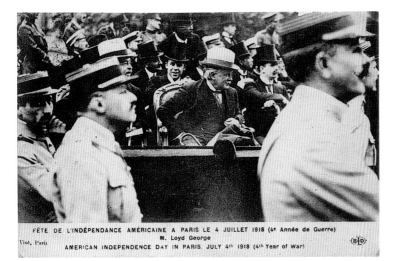

FÊTE DE L'INDÉPENDANCE AMÉRICAINE A PARIS LE 4 JUILLET 1918 (4ᵉ Année de Guerre)
M. Loyd George
AMERICAN INDEPENDENCE DAY IN PARIS. JULY 4ᵗʰ 1918 (4ᵗʰ Year of War)

National War Bond Tank (Trafalgar Square 1917) Copyright Nº1.

July 22nd.   Lucien reaching le Havre writes to Olive Malneux his wife, *Had a very good crossing. Hope you had a safe journey home and met Miss.M at the station...I am off by the afternoon train*. With the enemy temporarily repulsed from the environs of Paris there was some cause to celebrate Independence Day and, finely in focus between French soldiers, the British Prime Minister seems in good spirits.   18f

February 21st.   To Miss Lidyard in Brockley from Poole, *Dear Pitt, I got a letter about the 1914 star I shall get it from this lot but I did not get the ribbon never mind any more. Well Pitt we are at work all day till late at night it does not matter as there is no place to go to*. The war effort takes its toll. Here in a clever campaign of 1917, tanks toured England to raise funds, looking themselves like huge money-boxes.   18g

Precise date unclear.   Ma in Bournemouth writes to Mr Bates in Wood Green, London, *Gee whis and he means it to by the look of things are you coming back I have got the rats here fair and honest beef again this week and not much of that no jam or matches*. Though not quite on top of American slang Ma, like the card, tells it as it is. Rationing hit hard with two prescribed meatless days. Everyone had the rats.   18h

January 3rd.   It takes forty days for Private J G Hindle's message from Komand 405 Prisoner of War Camp, Munster, to reach his daughter Alice in St Mary Cray. He is only allowed a few words, *A Happy New Year with love from Daddie* on a card seemingly produced by French prisoners in the cheerless confines of the camp. It was a luxury to have something other than the pictureless official card to send.   18i

I wonder where that chap gets his
marrow seeds!

We girls are all mad on the TANGO,
In this dance we certainly CAN GO,
To get the steps right,
We must be hugged tight—
So we can't (if we would) let the MAN GO.

Diving with engine running.

July 28th.   N writes from Ventnor to J W Salmon at the Market Gardener in Putney, having found the appropriate card combining vegetable and phallic prowess, *Hope the allotment is doing well. Don't eat all the peas.* Allotments spread as rationing began to bite and imports became ever more restricted. Dig for Victory was an early slogan of World War II.   18j

July 8th.   A message to Tommy Jones in Welshpool is obliterated by his own note telling himself to get a copy of How to Read the Bible in the Twentieth Century. The tango was the dance craze of the war made all the more enjoyable perhaps by the knowledge that the Kaiser had strictly forbidden it. Fred Spurgin doesn't attempt the sensuality of Kirchner's ladies.   18k

October 7th.   G T Clarkson produced a series of vivid impressions of the new warplanes in flight though their names were not given for security reasons. BM in Breamore writes to Mrs Downer in Fordingbridge, *Just a card I don't know were you have heard Its trial again young Flos husband is killed there seems no end of it one thing after another for them.*   18l

OD SEND YOU BACK TO ME (3)

Though we are parted—love lives for ever,
When hearts are fond and true;
So, till our meeting—let us remember,
Ever I pray for you.

February 27th.   Did Mrs Keighley in *London NW, Blighty* pin this up or was it from her husband's precious horde? *...this is the stuff to give 'em,...Dear Wife...when you see mother ask her if she sent the fags if not let me know.* Kirchner, an Austrian, ironically seems to have helped the allied effort (though he never knew the outcome, dying aged 41 in 1917). 18m

January 25th.   This printed picture captioned The Black Watch Leaves Aldershot has the informal look of a family photo. Jackie Warner in Glasgow writes to his Mother at Seamill Hydropathic in West Kilbride, *My dearest Mamma, I hope you have arrived safely at the Hydro...writing this on Friday morning at 25 to 9...I must hurry off to school.*   18n

February 18th.   Clare writes to Mabs in Totton near Southampton, *hope you will like it that we have heard so many times...arrived on Saturday just in time for 2nd House Hippo.* This is the song described as 'ripping' by Gwen (17g). Bamforth issued song cards in sets. Members of the Bamforth family and the firm's staff posed for these evocative pictures.   18o

BRITAIN'S MAIDS OF WAR

Phyllis, "the Maid of the Air"

BRITAIN'S WOMEN WORKERS

Painting identification marks on aeroplane wings

18a. Tuck 'Oilette'. For Freedom Postcard no 3149

18b. Aunt Mary writes, *That is a very nice bronze statue* (wrong: it is made of aluminium) *of Mercury* (wrong: it is of course Eros) *over the fountain, he has a wing at his heel to show he is quick - the messenger of the Gods* (all wrong).

W & C Lane, London. A344 1073

18c. H.Finkelstein & Son. American Art.Pub. Co. photo Irving Underhill.

18d. Omaggio delle Officine Ricordi alle Truppe Alleate. Produzione Italiana

18e. Charles Bergeret. 41

18f. E.le Deay, Paris

18g. W.H.J.Holloway, Ealing No 1

18h. The Regent Publishing Co. No 3140. Artist: Reg Maurice

18i. Published by or in Munster II camp. No 39

August 21st.   Tom in Derby to Mrs Gardener in St Margaret's-on-Thames, *I went up as far as Hammersmith with de Becker. Get Mrs Wright for Saturday night and come with me to see your mother*...Her topical postcard is half male fantasy half the new reality. Women over 30 gained the vote in 1918. 'Phyllis' would still have had to wait.   18p

July 15th.   To Master John Richards, from Minnie in Grand Rapids, Michigan *...things are so funny this summer and don't know what to do next. Work is light so many boys going out makes a difference.* These flimsy cards produced as propaganda seem most often to come from America or, like this one, were used internally there.   18q

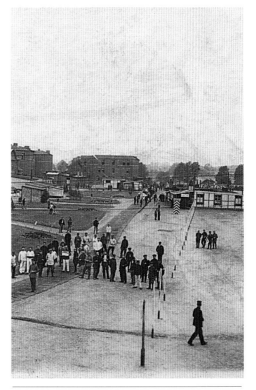

18j Inter-Art-Co. Comique Series. No 2301
British Manufacture throughout. Artist: Dudley Buxton.

18k Inter-Art Co. No 550. Artist: Fred Spurgin.

18l. Tuck 'Oilette' Series. 'In the Air'. No 3101. Artist: G T Clarkson

18m. L-E, Paris (Librarie de l'Estampe). Artist: Raphael Kirchner

18n. F.A.P. A423

18o. Bamforth. Songs Series 4976/1

18p. Series no 371. British manufacture. Artist: ?

18q. No publisher given. S4

18r. Bamforth Witty Series No 605

18s. Regent Publishing Co., London No 3248 Artist: Reg Maurice

What time does the balloon go up, please?

I'M DOING MY BIT FOR THE BOYS AT THE FRONT.

March 7th.   Elsie in Winchester sends a topical card to Miss Dolly Genning in Haslemere. Fuel shortages and notices saying vehicles must not be used for pleasure led to the adaptation of some cars to run on gas. Cars with these grotesque bags never became common, but the postcard, especially the comic card, is an indefatigable chronicler of novelty.   18r

September 14th.   To Lizzie Martin in Skegness from Mary in Nottingham, *hope you have a good time wish I was with you with best of luck from one of Roses pals.* Women's work in munitions factories had a direct bearing on the war. It undeniably forced the government's hand especially as images of women workers were used as propaganda.   18s

VICTORY MARCH OF THE ALLIED TROOPS IN LONDON, JULY 19th. 1919.
GUARDS PASSING THE MEMORIAL TO THE FALLEN.
PHOTO. DAILY MIRROR   169 H BEAGLES' POSTCARDS

October 2nd.   The Armistice of 1918 became Peace in June 1919. The Victory March could at last parade before the Cenotaph; or at least appear to, for Lutyens' memorial was not in fact ready in time. What we see here is a plaster model of that masterpiece in which mass and delicacy are perfectly united as Classicism elides into Constructivism. Nor of course have all the troops returned: many were retained on occupation duties. Minnie writes to Miss Swann in Guildford... *Just a card to tell you that laddie set sail for Home on the 22nd of Sept hope to be with us some time this month we are all delighted.* He has missed the victory festivities but it sounds as if he will get a hero's welcome in Hambledon.   19a

PICCADILLY CIRCUS. LONDON.
COPYRIGHT L. No. 15.

April 19th.   The publisher has masked out the Pavilion announcements to make his reprinted view (of 1911) not so obviously out of date. Bella writes to Mrs Sait in Gosport, Hants. *My dear Amy. Can you picture me walking about in the bustle on the other side am getting more used to it now though...*   19b

Skyline of Lower New York as seen from Jersey City.

June 11th.   Cecil to Miss V Kempicki, Cathedral Hotel, Bristol, England, *I am sending you one more card for your collection. Peace is not sign yet, so am not in position to tell you just when we expect to leave. Hope you are all well Love & kisses from Cecil.* Perhaps Cecil was one who did get back in time for the Victory Parade.   19c

December 23rd.   Ada writes to her Aunt not far away in Hampstead to say she will come tomorrow night instead. She uses a card issued to raise funds for the French Red Cross to support the homeless of villages like this. Together with the paintings of official war artists like Paul Nash such images give a reality to grim statistics (6,000,000 acres of French land laid waste, 2,000,000 refugees etc.).   19d

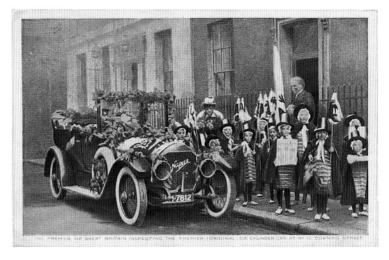

June 7th.   To the Misses Lander in Sheffield from Rotherhithe. *Dearest chicks... Had a letter from Dave. Am meeting him Wed. he goes to France at night. I go to Hampton Ct. on Sunday. What price Bayuda. was it a come off. Going up west for dinner & a walk to see the shops. Lyons Corner House for tea. Love Mums.* Is Lloyd George getting this car as a gift; or just publicising it? Today there would be questions in the House.   19e

July 3rd.   Rifleman Alf Groves sends a card to Miss M Miles in Watford. He has reached Rome but as for so many the wait for demob is long. Yet he is seeing a bit of the world in relative peace. The pansy is a thought (Pensée: Italian borrows the French word) and M its recipient, *Dear M. Just a card to let you know we are a few more miles nearer Blighty Slow but sure. Love xxx Alf.*   19f

January ?th.   Frank is still somewhere in France yet there is a sense of things being relaxed; the censor's mark is perfunctory, with no signature, the Field P.O. stamp is blurred. He can now get his hands on satirical cards like this (which has a gentler flavour than one might expect) to send to Lottie Lovelock in Brighton, *Here is a post-card that will amuse you I think...*   19g

June 2nd.   To Master Alan Wareham at St Edmund's Vicarage, Dudley *...there was such a crowd round King's Cross Station last Monday night when Mr Hawker & Commander Grieve came home... I have had a bad head for a boy threw a big stone which hit me on the head. Love to you all Auntie Chaddick.* Ten years after Bleriot's Channel Crossing the goal was a non-stop Atlantic flight. Hawker and Grieve got £5000 from the Daily Mail for trying. Was the card adaptable to any outcome?   19h

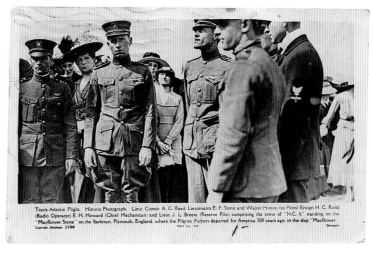

July 14th.   Will in Devonport to E A Atkins in Uffingham, Rutland, *Leave granted from 12 Friday till Monday 6.45am on condition draft does not go before then. Thanks for pen.* Only two weeks after Hawker's failure an NC4 Flying Boat makes the journey from Newfoundland to Plymouth via the Azores with a total flying time of 57 hours 16 minutes. To arrive at the spot from which the Pilgrim Fathers departed for America was poetic, and seems to have been appreciated by many ladies with hats.   19i

October 18th. Nellie writes to Mrs Boyd in Evesham, *So pleased to hear you are better... The weather is a treat now it will help to shorten the winter a little.* The card advertises Pavlova's appearance that week at Birmingham's Prince of Wales Theatre. Even in photographs Pavlova looks special. Now she is 38 years old and still touring the world with her company. Perhaps Nellie has booked to see a legend. 19j

September 19th. New Woman to New Woman. Irene in Eastbourne to Gladys in Lewisham, *have been for some lovely walks. I am not looking forward to going back to the office one scrap. There are heaps of Americans here and they certainly are fine fellows. Have you started business again yet or are you having a lazy week. Hope you like P.C.* (and no doubt the smart bathing suit with matching hat and sash). 19k

November 7th. Dorothy in Southampton to Flo Cowdery in Newport IOW, *...lovely here. I have got some ripping photos am going to see Eddie Polo to-night We went to the Palace last night. I never saw anything like it.* Did Dorothy pick this up after seeing one of Pearl White's silent serials? The Perils of Pauline, with their cliffhanger endings, still featured in Saturday morning children's cinema shows in the 40's. 19l

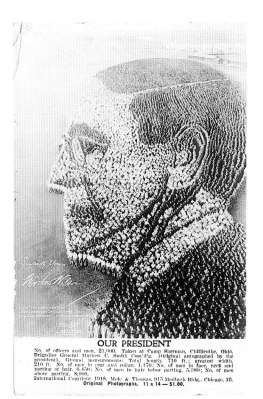

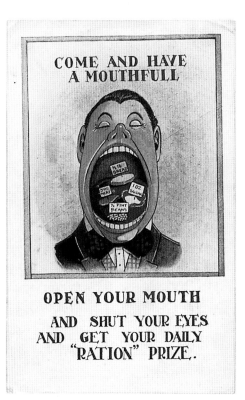

April 11th. From John Dickerson in Delaware to his mother, *State Sentinel received for which I thank you very much. I was going to subscribe for it myself but you beat me to it.* 21,000 officers and men make President Wilson's face at Camp Sherman, Ohio. The result is not pretty but (given perspective problems) impressive. Pity the 8,000 above the parting. 19m

No Postmark. *Dear Ernest and Margaret, I hope you had a very happy Xmas. We all enjoyed ourselves here & everything went off beautifully. This is a photograph of myself taken in the hospital sat: fancy dress with our united love wishing you a happy New Year. Auntie Dot.* The allied flags are not consigned to the attic but re-cycled in celebratory fashion. 19n

February 20th. Violet in Eastbourne to Mrs Smith in London W4, *How did you like the cold weather last week - we were nearly frozen at school & now we have 3 mistresses with influenza. Miss Wright is now the latest victim.* The epidemic of Spanish Flu killed more people world-wide than did the war itself. 19o

"THIS IS A NICE LITTLE CLOCK— IT GOES FOR
EIGHT DAYS WITHOUT WINDING."
"BY GUM! AN' OW LONG WILL IT GO IF YOU WIND IT."

April 17th.   Ted writing from Godalming to Mr Towner in Eastbourne seems resigned to army delays, *You will be surprised to know that I am still around here, also the others. And no one knows when we may go. Had what was supposed to be the last pay yesterday but the moving seems just as far away as ever. anyway keep smiling it isn't for ever, only for life maybe...*   19p

"How can we play 'husbands and wives'
when we're both girls?"
"Women are doing all the men's jobs
nowadays!"

August 21st.   To Miss M Kelly in Hastings, *Dear 'Old Nick'... All A1. I am going away on my Honeymoon with 'Dick' I know what you are saying 'Come Out' Sissie will look over while I am writing... I went to Eltham with the Bhoys (Dancing) We are having the party Sat - of course with my (Hubby) swank - Hope you are using my bathing costume - Ruth.*   19q

1919 MESSAGES·NOTES·PARTICULARS

19a. Beagles 169 H. Photo: Daily Mirror

19b. Lilywhite Photographic Series. L no 15.

19c, NY.205. Irving Underhill

19d. Frances Day in aid of British Committee of the French Red Cross.

19e. James Walker (Dublin).

19f. IPA CT Autocolore. No 346

19g. Published by FH. Artist unknown

19h. Publisher unknown

19i. Abrahams. 1108

19j. Photo: Claude Harris, London

19k. Publisher unknown. 4906. British Manufacture Throughout. Artist unknown

19l. Pathe Frères Cinema Ltd.

19m. No. of officers and men 21,000. Taken at camp Sherman, Chilicothe, Ohio. Brigadier General Mathew C Smith com'd'g (Original autographed by the president). Ground measurements. Total length 710 ft. Greatest width 210 ft. No. of men in coat and collar, 1,170: No. of men in face neck and parting of hair 6,450: No. of men in hair below parting 5,380: No. of men above parting 8,000.

Mole & Thomas, Chicago

19n. Photo by Percy Simmons, Chipping Norton.

19o. C.P.C. (City Postcard Co., London) Series 599. Artist unknown

19p. The Regent Series No 3303. Artist: Reg Maurice

19q. Inter-Art Co. London. Comique Series. 2703. British Manufacture Throughout. Artist: Reg Maurice

19r. Bamforth & Co. Comic Series No 760. Artist: D Tempest

19s. M & L Ltd (Millar & Lang) National Series 823. Artist unknown

Is that you, John? What're you doing?
I was just wondering how that jazz step
goes, dearie!

August 19th.   Charlie in Wakefield replies to Edith & Holland Wilson's card from Blackpool, *if we too were only with you we would have a better time Oh-la-la-Compa.* The music-hall refrain was not exactly Jazz but Britain was only just discovering the word and what it meant from the Original Dixieland Jazz Band, just arrived at the Palladium. Tempest's cartoon jazzes up a venerable comic theme.   19r

THE WATER IS RIGHT
UP TO MY
EXPECTATIONS

July ?th.   From Coalbrookdale to Will Jones in Coventry, *...I will meet you on Saturday at 6 o'clock at your House... from your old Pal, E Wellings.* The style of the drawing is simple and that of the bathing suit up-to-date. The classic pun-at-one-remove was used both by Shakespeare and music hall comedians. Censorship could not touch a double meaning like this without displaying its own prurience.   19s

August 8th. Annie sends this luxury tinted card with embossed borders from Hendon to Florrie Cowdery in Newport, Isle of Wight, *I thought you would like this photo of M.P. & D.F. as you will see it was taken whilst they were here in London.* Mary Pickford and Douglas Fairbanks were the great romantic stars of the silent screen and their marriage was made in heaven and Hollywood. But the dream couple also knew how the business worked. They teamed up with Charlie Chaplin and the director of epics, D W Griffith, to form United Artists, a distribution company which has survived to this day as a major name in cinema. It was responsible in more recent years for the James Bond films. 20a

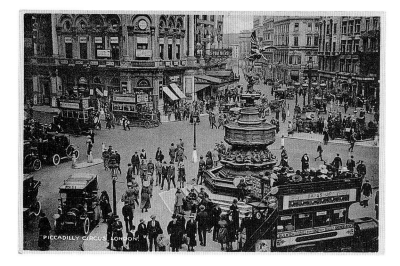

August 15th. Uncle Jack sends Miss O'Cloke in Torcross congratulations (he doesn't say what for) giving his new address as 7th Prov. Field Amb. Tendring, Kent. The inevitable No 12 bus advertises Heinz products as well as Tails Up at the Comedy Theatre which (like As You Were, playing at the Pavilion) ran for over a year. A view from 1919. 20b

October 6th. Louis Silver has joined a correspondence club (he is no 8381) and writes to André Perrain in France, *Dear Friend, I am a new member and would like to x with you C-L-P-S. I hope we get along very well to-gether. Please write soon.* I do not know the code of the club, and C-L-P-S remains a pleasant mystery. 20c

August 19th.   From Wakefield to Morecambe. *Dear Sisters, Please do look sharp & ring for the lost goods we are spending the night in waiting room. Send John down at once with the car. The pickles M & B. (PS Lovely Beds).* The kidding message echoes the card's phone repartee. Reg Maurice as ever is first with the new. This flapper is an early model. Soon she'll be slimmer, her skirts shorter, and her hair bobbed.   20d

March 28th.   From within Alfreton to Edith Heggs, *Who goes to see the Lightning Raider. from. A. Friend.* No doubt a serial of the time: in any case it is good to see that films (before they uttered a word) were already being blamed for violence. Could Tempest's cartoon be the first publication to link the two? The argument has not run out of fuel. Today's screen carnage would shred the pillows and see the husband pulped.   20e

September 1st.   Elsie from Ilfracombe to Mrs Morrey in Harlesdon... *It's gorgeous here. We have been for some fine sea trips & altogether have had such a good time that the thought of coming back to dirty old Pitkins makes me shudder.* Such eloquently tinted views were the taste of the period and often as here have a high sense of abstraction with a grasp of composition and tonality that derives from the English water-colour.   20f

July 29th.   Jack writes from Tooting to Miss Poyne in Stillorgan, Co Dublin, *Dearest Kitty, Thankyou love for your letter & please tell your dad that I have managed to get 2 of what he wanted but couldn't get any more... xxxx.* Between the liquidity of Art Nouveau and the formalism of Art Deco many bold graphic strategies were tried. This striking image is both severe and relaxed.   20g

August 19th.   Sarah Robertson writes to her sister in Bristol to wish her a happy birthday and to say that she could not get off work because *Mrs C is in bed with bad cold see you Sunday all being well.* One wonders what record on the turntable would prove a match for this modern woman's air of calm if slightly melancholy sophistication... Jerome Kern's Look for the Silver Lining perhaps, recorded earlier in the year.   20h

July 8th.   Lida in Guilford, Maine, to Mother ten miles away in Wellington, ...*trying all of this week to get over there but I am going to keep trying you bet, got all ready to go today even got my hat on so you see I come within and inch of it ha ha but I am going to the dance if I have to walk. Wish you was over here for it is g-- awful lonesome.* Andy Warhol grew up with such images: the feet show where he learned to tint.   20i

OLD HOMESTEAD NEAR CALEDONIA, O.

WARREN G. HARDING
REPUBLICAN CANDIDATE FOR
PRESIDENT OF THE UNITED STATES

RESIDENCE MT. VERNON AV.
MARION, OHIO

August 23rd. From the Senator's home base in Marion, Ohio, Minnie King writes to Mr Peterson in St Thomas, North Dakota, *Am sure you are an admirer of Sen Hardings & I send greetings from the administration Bldg, next to his home & we go over in a few minutes to meet him. These cards lying on the table.* Harding/Coolidge was a winning ticket but President Harding died suddenly in 1923 and Coolidge stepped in.   20j

March 13th. Ichiro Ita in Tokyo asks Donald Gould in Southampton if he wants to exchange with a fellow reader of the Children's Paper, *This is our Crown Prince and his residence. Have you any pleasure to see this card? Send yours and get ours!* Donald will be pushed to match such embossed luxury. Hirohito took over from his deranged father in 1921. He died in 1989 having ruled in amazing times.   20k

16176.   Mash Tuns for Malt. Guinness's Brewery, Dublin.

August 27th. Not a usual choice for a woman to woman card. Mildred writes in Leicester to Miss Coles of Humberside Road, *...hope you reseved PC... Pleased to hear from you Dear. I have lots to tell you.* Such mysterious and gleaming machinery has more the air of a set for a science fiction movie than a place which mashes the malt that makes the stygian stout.   20l

August 13st. Harry and Lizzie send their seaside group photo to the Warringtons their relatives in Casterton, *The group was taken on the beach and I am writing this beside the shining sea which looks charming... We have had several Hot Sea Water Baths which are very refreshing.* The beach photographer has a ready-marked board saying 'Having a Good Time in Hastings' plus code number. Which are Harry & Lizzie?   20m

HANDS UP!

You'll get into my bad books if you don't write soon !

August 12th. A whiff of the Raj via this saucy parody of the famous salon picture September Morn. To Harold Ryper in Calcutta, *Brighton somewhere, Bertha & I are down here for the day - no ayahs only nice tarts!!! What?... Don't follow cupid's example.* Censorship's byzantine protocols permitted painted nakedness. Thus many French Salon painters made a tidy living from PC reproductions of semi-erotic photorealist nudes.   20n

March 15th. Mr Bishop at Radstock Station receives a card from MG, *...coming tomorrow Tuesday. I cannot think why I have not heard. I am going away for good will tell you all news.* McGill's bad books seem a quaint index purgatorium with Zola and Balzac still considered 'fast'. Meanwhile James Joyce is publishing Ulysses and censors are hounding D H Lawrence for The Rainbow. (Aristotle's Masterpiece is a fake treatise but <u>almost</u> tells how babies are born).   20o

August 12th.   B Bull in Lisala, Belgian Congo writes to Miss Dobbs in Kentish Town, *How would you like one of these for best boy?... A little black girl beside me wants to know if I am writing all this in Ngombe. What a hope after 2 days here!* Not all cards out of Africa depict half naked women. Some, like this, show normal scenes of every day life. Three men are making the special baskets for carrying rubber.   20p

April 1st.   May sends from Kingston, Jamaica, an intriguing card to Master Waters in Dublin, *I am afraid I will not be able to get the flower from the palm - They are not flowering now - The coker nuts and dates are on them. Will try & get a green coker nut for you. Nick is collecting coins... It is lovely here - awfully hot 'kiss me Auntie' xxx & love to Daddy.* A nice no nonsense locally produced card by Duperly & Sons.   20q

MAJOR TURNER AND MAJOR BERRILL

"Dat girl hab no taste, she always ober dresses!" Just a Luxury Tax Girl! Dat's all!

July 27th.   From Liverpool to Miss Merritt in Brighton, *My dear B. Just a card to thank you for sending the corsets they are fine. Glad to get your letter but I really am so busy. I am taking 60 people to Southport on Thursday for the Outing going by motor. Glad you had a good time at the outing much love in haste. Ensign.* These two Salvation Army officers must be serving in some very exotic outpost.   20r

August 19th.   Not from far away places but from Something-on-Stour to Irene Jones in Sth Yardley, *Having a ripping time, feel so-so this morning, have clicked with a Boy from Bambury. hurry up & write Love Lily.* Generic blackspeak in cartoons is as simplistic as that of Germans in war films. This reprint has added lines (same language, different hand) about Luxury Tax.   20s

40,000 EMPLOYEES AT THE FORD MOTOR COMPANY'S PLANT, DETROIT, MICH.

September 26th.   Mr Ossman writes to Mr Paul Cerack at 192 Main St, White Plains NY, *Am waiting here for the train. You as a mechanic ought to be one of the employees at this plant, Regards*. The Model T is still in production but the factory is also producing eighty tractors a day. The Fordson tractor made up for the sudden loss of men and horses to the first World War. By the time those men had returned the whole face of agriculture had changed. This was the new world of work, with Motown as its Capital.   21a

December 9th.   Swan & Edgar make a personal appearance, having appropriated this Tuck view as their customer reply card. It is beginning to look out of date but S&E is a conservative store who *acknowledge with thanks, Remittance with order* [from Mr Taylor in Dunston-on-Tyne] *which shall have our immediate attention.*   21b

September 10th.   The panorama here is much enlivened by the handsome warship USS Dreadnought attended by its tugs. Mena is on a tour of various states and writes to Mr Jim Clay in 5th Street, Laurel, Michigan outlining her plans for the rest of the trip. *New York is fine*, she says, *can cross B-way for the fun of it.*   21c

"In the Clouds." (waiting for the clouds to roll by !!)

February 8th.   From Gorvin to Mr Wright at the French Gramophone Co in Paris, *Many thanks for chic PC am sorry I cannot answer with an equally interesting one but then London is such a staid old proper place. Oh! to be in Paris! If you meet the lady on the reverse, oblige an old forsaken celibate & do the necessary, then write & tell me what its like.* Barribal's smiling sirens are all based on his wife, Babs.   21d

NOW HE CAN'T SAY I'SE A FLAPPER.

July 21st.   Alf writes to Minnie Liddall in Levenshulme, *20 Regent Rd Blackpool, Note the change of address. The other place was far too dear and there was late dinner in evening dress. Am here with the manager of Winter Gardens. Have taken 6 fairly good orders today. Best Love XX.* Mabel Lucie Attwell's cute kids appeared prolifically from before the First World War till well after the Second.   21e

PHOTO. DAILY MIRROR. LENEARS & GEORGES CARPENTIER. 158.K. BEAGLES POSTCARDS. 'FAMOUS BOXERS' SERIES.

August 13th.   May in London to Bert Samson in Southampton, *How is this. I think that these photos are the best I have ever seen. Do hope you are well.* Carpentier the great French heavyweight had been at the top of the sport since defeating Billy Wells in 1913. Six weeks before this card was written he succumbed, as did everyone else, to Jack Dempsey (in four rounds). As May observes this is a fine action shot.   21f

C.M. 122. MRS. VERNON CASTLE LILYWHITE LTD
SHADOW STAGE PHOTO WELL KNOWN PICTURE PLAYER ALL BRITISH PHOTO PRINTED

August 11th.   Mother in Manchester to Mrs Kenyon in Hadfield, *You will find the skirt wide enough you can't have it wider than the body & then again I put all the stuff in I hadnt a bit more... glad to hear you have good digs.* Fred Astaire and Ginger Rogers re-created the lives of dance duo Irene & Vernon Castle. Vernon was killed in a plane crash but Irene lived until 1969.   21g

"PUSSYFOOT" NOSEY PARKER FROM THE U.S.A.

PROHIBITION

THIS— YANKEE NOODLE HAS COME HERE, FROM ACROSS THE OCEAN ; TO ROB THE BRITON OF HIS BEER— WHAT A "DOTTY" NOTION !

W.F.B.

DOLLARS FOR DIRTY WORK IN ENGLAND

PHILIP REID. PRINTER & PUBLISHER. 47, FLEET STREET, LONDON, E.C.4.

August 16th.   A liberal Auntie in Exeter writes to Miss Lill Delling in Exmouth apologising for absence of letters. The threat of prohibition was real with Pussyfoot Johnson on the warpath. The American evangelical thug, who would kill in the cause of prohibition, was on a world tour after his triumph in the US. He is here demonised with Britain's own Nosey Parker.   21h

PROHIBITION MEETING WILL BE HELD HERE SHALL ENGLAND BE DRY ?

I don't believe England will ever be dry !

June 22nd.   From Cardiff to Harry Thomas in Jersey, *No No Harry not dry yet, but very soon will be, so please bring Something back with you. Poor Bert is still holding on but not with his teeth, they are all out & he is on the Monkey diet.* One guesses the Monkey diet is soft bananas. McGill couples the English weather and a critical issue of the day.   21i

August 20th.   The pictures of punitive looking workplaces are now countered by glimpses of model factories as on this card sent to Mrs Reed, *Dear N, Have Been over Lever's Factory to-day it's very fine, cheerio: Reg.* An all female staff inhabits the light and spacious room where Lux soap is packed. As with Cadbury's at Bournville an ideal workers' village was set up (see 34d).   21j

July 7th.   Evelyn Richmond from Kosice in Czechoslovakia to Mrs Whitlock in London SW7, *We are very busy & very travelled & are coming home in the Autumn. Blouses going strong!... Laura going to the English dentist in Vienna next week for 3 days.* This romantic view of the Tatra Heights of the Carpathian mountains hovers richly between painting and photography.   21k

March 31st.   *Am writing this in the demonstral sitting by Keith & Florrie. We hope to get a letter from you... at any rate pray for us tomorrow from 2.30 onwards & send us plenty of wireless courage,* Edith and Lilian send these Morris Dancers to Bert Morrall in Newcastle, Staffs. Though the ritual had some ancestry as Moorish Dance it was a fruit of the current revival, reinvention and invention of folk traditions.   21l

March 2nd.   Donald Macrory's mother writes to him in Londonderry, *Isn't this a fine big house we are in? So far I have not left anything in the bath room!!... we were at a theatre last night and going to see Chu Chin Chow tonight - just off to the Badminton much love darling... Mummie.* Station hotels were in those days grand not only in size; and Victoria Station's traffic looks to have been distinctly easier to negociate.   21m

February 15th.   Marjorie at Derby Teacher's Training College writes to Dora Wilkins in Kettering, *I have been so busy. Yesterday was Speech Day - it was somewhat cold in white dresses. This afternoon I'm going to be busy & at the wash tub. It is terribly cold here: but the life makes up for deficiencies.* This ensemble typified the keep-fit enlightenment and eerily reminds me of abject hours in my own school's gym.   21n

January 17th.   Margot, writing from Tournai in Belgium to Miss Sara Pipson in Brighton, is in a postcard time warp as she restricts her message to the front of an already antique card, as if writing at the time of Tosca's première in 1900. Riccordi, Puccini's publisher issued a set of chromolithos to go with each opera. They were evidently still available. Replicas can still be bought at Riccordi's shop in Milan.   21o

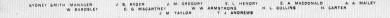

THE AUSTRALIAN CRICKET TEAM, 1921

SYDNEY SMITH MANAGER   J S RYDER   J M GREGORY   E L HENDRY   E A MACDONALD   A A MAILEY
W BARDSLEY   C G MACARTNEY   W W ARMSTRONG   H L COLLINS   H CARTER
J M TAYLOR   T J ANDREWS

June 23rd.   Dad writes to his son Master G Lance at the Leys School, Cambridge from Scarborough, *Dear old Geoff, Here are the Australian Team to cheer you up - wish I could be with you today and tomorrow - Hope you had a good OTC* [officers training corps] *inspection - Cheerio. wonder if May is with you - no letter from her this week - good luck - How good of Gee to ask you to dinner. Drawing Prize. Lance?* Pinholes suggest that Geoff put this up in his locker or his study. School records show him not to have been an active cricketer but he may well have won the art prize in view of his later career as a painter. He would in any case not have been very cheered by England's performance as Australia retained the Ashes without much difficulty. England's only victory (in a pattern often repeated) was in the last Test Match at the Oval once the series had been decided. England was captained on that occasion by the Hon L H Tennyson, a name redolent of the epoch when cricketers were either classed as Gentlemen or Players (each category having a separate entrance and dressing room). No such class division affected Australia whose captain, W W Armstrong, looks to be a giant. Coincidentally I write this on a day in August 1999 when the English team, after losing a Test Match series to New Zealand, has dropped to its lowest level ever in the international ratings.   21p

September 1st.   From Dad & Mother in Ilfracombe to Miss Bineham in Langley, *Starting for Clovelly yesterday morning. I wonder if you will know anybody in the motor coach... We had a lovely day & both think Clovelly the most wonderful place we have ever seen - I have sent a tin of cream to the cottage this morning for you.* What they call a motor coach was more often referred to as a charabanc (and more accurately, since it was no more than a car with benches). The charabanc craze (motoring for the masses; privately owned cars were still for the better off) was well under way before the war whose restrictions put a stop to pleasure trips and whose exigencies caused the commandeering of such vehicles for military use. The name of Victory Cars suggests the post war boom that saw hundreds of charabancs bumping around England on their solid tyres. A photo was taken on setting out which would be processed and purchasable by the trippers' return. Seen somewhere in the back three rows are the Binehams.   21q

1921 MESSAGES·NOTES·PARTICULARS

21a. Publisher unknown. (Ford Motors)

21b. Tuck Oilette. No 8931. Artist: C E Flower. Post Card overprinted *Printed Papers.* Stamp Perfin SE)

21c. Enrique Muller. New York. 7076. Slogan PM: Address Your Mail to Street and Number.

21d. J Salmon, Sevenoaks. Artist: Barribal

21e. Valentine's Attwell Series. No310

21f. Beagles & Co. 158K Famous Boxers Series. Photo: Daily Mirror

21g. Mother goes on some more about the skirt but we have got the drift. Fred Astaire & Ginger Rogers starred in The Story of Irene and Vernon Castle in 1939.

Lilywhite Photographic Series CM122. Photo: Shadow Stage

21h. Philip Reid, London. Poem signed W.F.B (also artist?)

21i. Inter Art Co Comique Series 2959. Artist: Donald McGill

21j. Valentine's Series 62701

21k. Samuel Foldes/Jeno Schlattner 2217

21l. 'Wireless' here would probably be read as 'telepathic' rather than as anything to do with the infant radio. But the language of the card is odd in any case since the word 'demonstral' does not seem to exist.

Publisher unknown

21m. Pulman's, London

21n. Publisher unknown. (Derby Teachers' Training College)

21o. G Riccordi & C. Milano. 068

21p. Philip G Hunt & Co, London/LNA

21q. Publisher unknown. (Knill's Victory Cars)

THE THREE ROYAL PRINCES.

September 5th.   D from Harrogate to Miss Bowling in Hutton le Hole, *We have called to see Miss Bellamys, They have a nice house - & Dr Bellamy has just been nice and invited us out on Friday.... Es gibt etwas unterschied zwischen Ellie & Miss Bellamy but I suppose they'll get on all right! I shall come early on Saturday it gets so busy later - so if you've asked a tennis crowd I shall be back in time!* D breaks into slightly misunderstood German to convey secretly the idea that Ellie and Miss Bellamy are at odds. Here (cut out from a crowded scene) are the three Princes at the races, young men seemingly at large and only just emerged from an almost brutal upbringing. Had they met Macbeth's witches they would be amazed at their prophecy, that two of them would be King but only one crowned, that one would be King and Duke thereafter and another the reverse. On the left and looking more at home than the others in sporty gear is the Prince of Wales (later Edward VIII/Duke of Windsor). In the middle is Prince Henry (later the Duke of Gloucester). On the right, unaware of his task to come, is the future King George VI.   22a

November 10th.   Lillian writes to Phoebe Jones in Cwmgwrach near Neath *My dear Phoebe. Do you recognise this small place. eh. what.* Bob (?) Barrett is at the London Pavilion. Whatever happened to Pink's High Class Jams so tantalisingly advertised on the No 3 bus?   22b

April 25th.   John Baitz endeavouring to write to Mr George Lemann, Port Allegany, Pennsylvania, is having a struggle with his English, *I seand Beast wishish Beafor I leave from NY too yue send good bay,* which suggests that Mr Baitz may be a first generation American.   22c

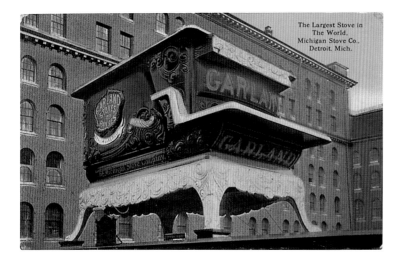

The Largest Stove in The World. Michigan Stove Co., Detroit, Mich.

August 7th.   HCB in Wyandotte, Mich. to Mr Coalin Flink in Columbia, Penna, *The stove on the other side of this picture would keep you warm allright. You ought to see the speedboat on the river here. They can go 35 miles an hour. They have an airplane service between Detroit & Cleveland. It takes them 90 minutes.* If it's the largest something (or the fastest) this must be America.   22d

November 9th.   When Mr Lardent sends his clients a card they receive something more like a tract with quotes from Milton and the Bible, *Dear Bro Carter* he writes to Manchester, *L-43 out of stock. The 10 for this comes in handy... just off to the press - trust friends will like them - they are appreciated! L-93 may be had on same terms as sacred pictures - see price list. Warm Love in the Lord.*   22e

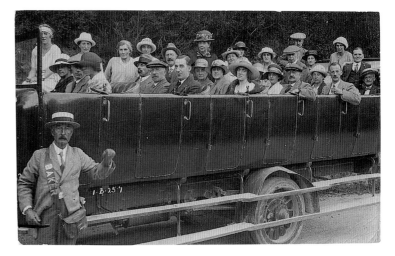

September 4th.   Mr Thrush writes in haste to Mr Harcourt also in Birmingham and omits to put the right stamp on. Perhaps Mr Harcourt thinks it worth the extra penny he has to pay for Postage Due to get some information, *Have examined Weighbridge it is 16 feet. All enquiries should be made to Cyril Blunt.* Sounds like a haulage problem but not concerning this modest lorry with its cargo of local street boys.   22f

My dear Mother writes Glad in Southampton to Mrs Barnes in Cheadle Hulme, *The weather here is rotten. Rain. Percy hopes to sail on the Olympic on the 23rd. I hope to be home when you all arrive. that is if Olympic sails. Do you know anybody on card taken in Jersey.* The standard question. Percy seems to have no qualms about sailing on the sister ship of the Titanic.   22g

JUST FANCY! WHEN WE STARTED AN HOUR AGO, WE WERE ALL PERFECT STRANGERS TO EACH OTHER!

August 31st.   Winnie writes from Cleethorpes to Miss Richards in Woodyeats to let her know they are having a fine time. This vehicle is remarkably similar to that in 22g. Most charabanc cartoons, like this by Archibald English, feature drinking as the main goal of an outing. It also suggests opportunities in other directions which the occupants of 22g's motor coach seem unlikely to indulge in. In later years it was common to see notices saying No Charabancs outside more select highway inns.   22h

November 8th.   R S Postgate at St George's School, Harpenden, receives a card from WP in Cambridge dense with news of Old Boys' teams, *We beat Emanuel 13-10. Keep this card or give it to the MGS for decorations, if you like. 'Bactria' here yesterday.* The locomotive is LNER 1914, Patriot, built as a working war memorial (with sister locos Remembrance and Valour). Until its decommissioning it was garlanded with poppies each Armistice Day in Rugby sheds.   22i

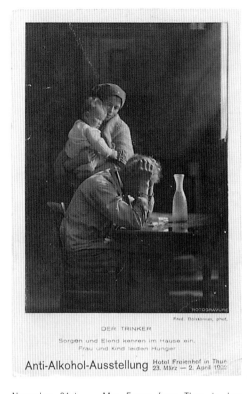

October 28th.   EAB in Hurstpierpoint sends birthday greetings to Mrs Ayling in Hassocks. One presumes this cockerel to be a show bird rather than a fighter that won Mr Fyson the cup for raising £330 for the Red Cross, though he carries it with a hawker's protective glove. Mr Fyson certainly looks proud as indeed does the bird he holds triumphantly aloft.   22j

November 13th. Lettie in Seattle to Mrs Anna Burdy at Xpeku Karis, E Set, Hainag Aget 200 Block, *Many thanks for the papers so kind of you to remember me in that way. This is one of our royal ladies... She isn't beautiful but royal blood is something to compensate for other shortcomings. Is foggy here cant see boat only hear the whistle... I remember you lovingly.*   22k

November 21st.   Mrs Forrer from Thun to her daughter in Birkdale Lancs, *"Tea" received with much Dank exhausted by now through illegal invasions! ...write to ask you to attend lecture by Mr Chapman Cohen next Sunday 26 inst at 'Pembroke Chapel' 7pm discussion & welcome!* The Anti-Alcohol Exhibition looks to have been a sobering experience.   22l

December 25th.   M Bond to Miss James in Gerrard's Cross from Algeria, *All the native women have their faces covered like this one which I think would be rather uncomfortable. I hope you are enjoying your stay at GX. With very best wishes for the New Year.* One of LL's fine studies of indigenous North Africans, this Mauresque is portrayed with dignity in an elegantly composed and finely tinted image.   22m

August 18th.   Uncle Harry in Paignton to Miss Olive Evans in Rhondda, *Dear Niece, Dear, dear! This (see over) is the latest style - white taffeta with flannelette trimmings, straight cut and six inches to allow for bending. It isn't necessary to wear all at the same time - but you must wear the cap and - shoes. No wonder people forget the number of their bathing machines.* I don't think that's quite what the caption hints at.   22n

August 25th.   Ann in Swindon to Hilda Parfill in Highworth, *can't come out tomorrow... going tracking with the Guide & girls are going to Marlborough Mam can't bring all the boys too much worry. Vi & me will cycle out one evening next week.* The photographed clock stuck onto the printed card says 2 o'clock, the official time for changing the hour. At the end of the century the system is still being argued over.   22o

THE SMALLEST HOUSE, CONWAY

22a. Photocrom Co Ltd, Tunbridge Wells

22b. Philco, London. 3226

22c. TB, Cambridge Mass.

22d. C T Photocrom R.27341

22e. Published for Frederick Lardent

22f. Publisher unknown

22g. Baker's Cards, Jersey

April 19th.   Beatrice Hilton to Miss Rhoda Maurice in Failsworth, ...*sorry to hear last week that you were poorly, & do hope you are better. I am just off to the Camp & hope I shall like it. Hope you will be able to come & see us at School...* There are many postcard contenders for Britain's Smallest House though the caption may mean Smallest House in Conway.   22p

August 23rd.   To Miss Hedge in Shortlands, *How do you like our merry group? This is our party you know everyone but Mr & Mrs Jefferson so now you know who they are. Just going for a walk before breakfast. Squirt.* A breezy card from Westgate-on-Sea and a group of attractive people, caught at their merriest for ever.   22q

22h. HB Series (Hulson Bros) No 2389 Artist: Archibald English

22i. The wording on the nameplate is:-
       Patriot: In Memory of the Fallen LNER Employees 1914-1919

If you would like to have more rugger info from the message:- *AS Cohen (OP) is playing regularly for C.U.R.U.F.C. having scored several times... We played Caius II on Sat. 'Jud' (OG) Barendt (OL) & Fleisch (OP) were all playing.*

Publisher unknown

22j. Publisher unknown

22k. Lowman & Hanford. Seattle 3048 R.72791

22l. The image was also available as a poster. Published by the photographer (whose name is ironically Fred Boissonas) Geneva.

22m. LL. Levy Fils & Cie on blue/green stock

22n. Inter Art Artistique Series No 2850 Artist: Barriball

22o. The Campbell Series No 1. RP on printed card

22p. R E Jones Bros. Stationery, Conway 60374

22q. Publisher unknown

22r. Rotary Photo, London M.61-6. Photo: Daily Mirror

22s. M&L (Millar & Lang) National Series 2373 Artist: Reg Carter

MISS G. CECIL STOCK.
DAILY MIRROR BEAUTY 4TH PRIZE WINNER.

MUCH USEFUL KNOWLEDGE MIGHT BE GAINED IF ONLY WE STUDIED THE STARS MORE.

December 28th.   In an ornate hand Cliff writes in Bristol to Miss Cissily Peacock at 16 Park Crescent, *Ma Chère Cissily, How are you. Yes I'll see you usual place Friday 6.20pm. Have booked Hippodrome. Yours as B4.* Miss Cecil Stock may not have got the first prize in the Daily Mirror Beauty Competition but even 4th prize has brought her a small immortality as a tinted card with embossed edges.   22r

August 21st.   Annie to her cousin Mrs Beaumont in Huddersfield, *to Morecombe for our holiday. We only decided in the last week, & we have got very good rooms.* Nothing in the body language of these lovers suggests deceit. Grass, calm sand and well drawn wave make the sparkly stars more effective. But to which one are they speaking, him or her? or both?   22s

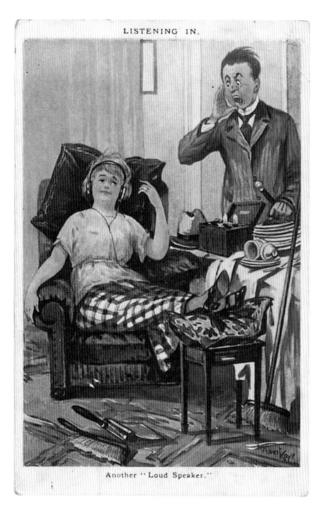

LISTENING IN.

Another "Loud Speaker."

August 31st. Each new medium of entertainment is accused of inducing mindless depravity. The man returns from the office to find his wife transformed into what we would now call a couch potato. The first scheduled programmes had started with a 6pm News from the new Savoy Hill studios at the end of 1922. Perhaps this errant wife has tuned into The Woman's Hour introduced on May 2nd. Radio had ceased to be merely the technological plaything of men, and a license fee of 7/6 had been proposed. Ironically the combination of headphones and a blank stare has once again, with the advent of portable stereos, become a familiar sight. Sarah in Hurstpierpoint tells Mrs Levett in Horsham when she is returning. 23a

PICCADILLY CIRCUS, LONDON.

September 10th. Sent to Miss Bourne in Bargate, Grimsby. J'Accuse (at the Pavilion) is not about Zola or the Dreyfus affair but is a peace propaganda film by the great Abel Gance. Jig-Saw, a revue to which Edgar Wallace contributed, is advertised on a bus which confirms a 1920 date for the view. 23b

Aerial View of Manhattan Island
Showing New York Skyscrapers.   The Heart of the World.

© FAIRCHILD A.C. CORP.

August 10th. Edgar writes to Bill Spridgeon in Long Eaton saying that he is there and will be coming home soon. Fairchild's aerial surveys yielded fine views of New York from various angles. The city is now confident enough to call itself (as Piccadilly Circus is often styled) the Heart of the World. 23c

August 24th.   Mum & Dad in Southend on Sea write to their daughter Agnes Clark in Romford. *I hope you are a very good girl doing all grandma tells you, & knitting my face flannel nicely. I am cutting the pictures of Rupert out of the Daily Express & saving for you...* An admirer of Rupert Bear (as I was to be twenty years later, cutting out the same comic strip) would enjoy these crisp outlines and robust doggerel.   23d

April 8th.   D in Paris finds this war postcard of the wounded cathedral of Rheims and sends it to Miss Bateman in Bramhall, *Saw all the Hindenburg line yesterday - the Chemin des Dames & Hill 100. The restoration is very negligible in this part of the world - we go to Paris again today.* Once the fearful human casualties had been counted and mourned, attention began to turn to other kinds of victim.   23e

July 23rd.   From Cheyenne to Miss Hattie Anderson in Russell, Minn., *Wonder if you would enjoy this Western rough stuff? Lots of cowboys & cowgirls in town. Their Roundup begins tomorrow. We leave this PM. Hilda.* The wonderful spiral composition of this group, completed by the form of the white horse, is worthy of Gericault. The negative shapes are as interesting as the silhouettes. Why didn't Hilda stay for the show?   23f

March 19th.   From New Brighton to Miss Williams in Rhyl, *Dear Don, Dad received his card... Please don't Bob your hair we heard you were going to if you do you must not come home until it grows again glad you are in Pink best love from all Bonny xxx.* Even as a tease this reflects that oldest struggle as the young, striving for identity, challenge the old.   23g

August 13th.   E L Leonard sends this nicely eccentric card from Normandy to Mabel Harper in London SE8, *Thank you very much for the card from Margate. I hope you will keep the rosy cheeks for me to see here, the sea-front is beautiful, miles of fine sand and nobody about except at shrimping time.* Translation:- It's not every day one marries off a daughter.   23h

July 19th.   Mrs King in Walthamstow receives a card from her sister in Margate, a reworking of the well loved theme (10j) of a holiday Cinderella (how gloves must have helped the manual worker: no cosmetic hides worn hands). But there seems no rest for Cis who writes, *been out all day with Dolly she cannot walk had to have 2 nurses. Going to bed. tired.*   23i

September 10th.　H & K send a sophisticated French card from Brighton to Eva Scrase in Horsham, *Returning home tomorrow worse luck. Just off to see The Street Singer. The weather today has turned much warmer now that it is too late. The Belle of New York was rotten.* Apart from the zany shoes and hat this shows the classic one piece swimming costume fully evolved (at least in France).　23j

July 3rd.　The Allens are in Stockbridge Mass. and pick a card from the hotel that will interest Mrs Cleary in Clinton, Iowa. *We are staying overnight in Stockbridge at the Red Lion Inn and this collection of teapots makes me think of you. This however is only a small portion of them.* Collecting, be it of postcards or teapots, is a mystery. Mrs Cleary may even have been a collector of postcards of teapots.　23k

September 14th.　Terry Selby sends a card home to Penge, *Dear Mum & Dad. Had fine weather... not a spot of rain. had a swim 8.0 am this morning in the big pond - it wasn't half hot. Tons of b-berries. be home about 5pm Sat (perhaps) I wonder if I'll feel like C-parade,* Sounds like he's preparing the ground for dodging Church Parade on Sunday. The Silver Queen bounds into a sleepy yet sunny Arundel.　23l

May 7th.　From Whittier, Cal. to Monmouth, Ill., *Dear Sister, glad to get your letter. Come again. Did me a lot of good, Daddie.* The faces and the films of stars were not enough for the growing hordes of cinema fans. Postcards responded by picturing their lavish dwellings. Few were more outlandish or defiant of architectural analysis than Charlie Chaplin's Hollywood home, a long way from Methley St, Kennington.　23m

February 19th.　From Audrey Stoop in Gstaad, Switzerland, to Mrs Rolfe, Hartley Grange, Hartley Witney, *This shows one of the ski-jumpers just before landing. A man here did 42 metres! To them it must be like leaping off into space. No one was hurt the day we watched them.* It would be another year before winter sports featured in the Olympic Games but skiing had become socially smart with Gstaad as prime resort. The Japanese Okabe jumped 137 metres in the 1998 Olympics.　23n

July 30th.　Miss M Miles evidently cannot be on her honeymoon yet (for which Watford would be an unlikely destination) but is near enough to it to receive a teasing card from Ramsgate, *Dear Mable, This card is a little reminder how many will be spying on your first night be an old maid. weve had a good time already plenty of Boys don't forget P.C. Love from Beat.* Even such a mildly suggestive card would be anonymously drawn: seaside Watch Committees were vigilant.　23o

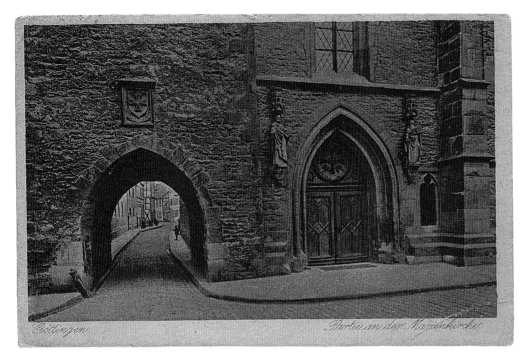

Göttingen   Partie an der Marienkirche

November 1st.   Pallister sends a rather gloomy card to Muriel Barkas in Newcastle. This corner of Göttingen is of architectural note but it is the stamps that catch our attention. The message gives some explanation, *You need not fear of my physical wellbeing - with money one can have anything at all. P.S, Today there was a rather large fall in the exchange - when I drew my cheque - so I have paid my bills & bought some Tauchnitz* [paperback books] *for the seminar and for me at 6 1/2d each.* The Language of Stamps takes on another meaning when a country is in the grip of runaway inflation. As can be seen below (left) the standard post to countries abroad was (in 1913 and through the war) 10 pfennigs. As the twenties dawned the economy started to crumble and by August 1922 (see below right) this had increased to 3 marks 50 pfennigs. By January 1923 the mark stood at 85,000 to the £ (7,000 to the $), twice that in February and six times that in June. In September 600,000,000 marks were needed and by the time this card was sent Pallister's pound would earn him 183,000,000,000 marks and his books would have cost trillions. In this same month Adolf Hitler had staged an attempted coup in Bavaria. Nothing could have been more pleasing to his cause than an unstable economy and a nervous Germany.

23p

JACK HOBBS in BUTTER, in the AUSTRALIAN PAVILION.
The British Empire Exhibition, Wembley.

Photo: Campbell Gray   W & K 63

August 30th.   Among the most talked about novelties in the British Empire Show were the large scale sculptures made of butter. The Canadian Pavilion sported a butter panorama featuring the Prince of Wales with a horse. Australia took a less ingratiating line with their hosts and chose to portray a moment of triumph in Test Match cricket when England's premier batsman Jack Hobbs had just been bowled out. Above him a sign reads 'Australia wins the Test. In Butter' but the British publisher of the card has his revenge by not even mentioning the name of the Australian bowler or keeper (see 21p). The sense of space and a crowded ground is inventively realised. Major art prizes could be won these days by such installations in an esoteric medium. Mrs Bundy posts her card at the Empire Exhibition itself, sending love to Miss Elliot in Farnborough.   24a

September 11th.   John writes home to Keighley, Yorks, after a visit to the Empire Exhibition. Evidently he did not spend too much time looking at the colonial butter sculptures. *Kate took me to Wembley yesterday... went on the Racer, Whip twice and lots of others.*   24b

August 2nd.   Winnie takes time to write to Walter Frost in Hastings, Mich. *I'm waiting in the R.R. station en route to Asbury Park. It's a lovely clear day and I know that 48 hours of ocean breezes will prove refreshing...Isn't the NY City sky line a crazy looking thing. Is 'crazy' already a term of praise?*   24c

August 20th.   Appropriately enough Mrs Harris in Liverpool sends this to an outpost of Empire where her son is Asst. Elec. Engineer to the B.B.&C-I Railway in Ajunere, India, *Got back from Llandudno last night - found your parcel & letters here. Lulu is staying with M so are Simp & Nib!* The jazzy hint in this entrance of Art Deco to come is compromised by the banality of model guardsmen.   24d

August 25th.   Aunt Winnie to Master McFarlane in Middlesborough, *Sometimes on Saturday evening when I am in Leicester I hear all the noise the people and machines are making at this Amusement Park over 90 miles away! Do you know how... by wireless! Have you wireless at your school?* The exhibition's opening broadcast was to radio what the 1953 Coronation would be to television.   24e

May 27th.   From CHY to Mrs Nuttall in Glendale, Cal. *Writing this while having tea in Lyons' Restaurant at the Exhibition... this does not cover more than a quarter of the area.* In the distance, football's romantic mecca, the Twin Towers of Wembley show where the Cup Final and World Cup matches are played. These relics of the show are now themselves doomed in Norman Foster's Olympic Stadium plan.   24f

September 3rd.   EW to Mrs Gott in Gedney Hill, *Having a lovely time, went to Wembley yesterday.* One guesses EW found this card given away at the HMV stand, here shown crowned with its celebrated motif of dog and phonograph. Recording was now a sophisticated business of elegant veneered cabinets without a horn in sight. Sound became big business when radio and gramophone entered into their long marriage.   24g

July 21st.   Will Allen to *Mum & the girls* from the Paris Olympics *Yesterday saw Miss Wills defeat Mrs Vlasco and D Richards defeat Cochet. They were some Tennis matches... Have got the souvenirs postcards of the games.* The US dominated (inc Johnny [Tarzan] Weissmuller's three swimming golds) but it was the feats of Harold Abrahams and Eric Liddell which were immortalised in the 1981 film Chariots of Fire. The British team is shown, complete with Scots pipers.   24h

September 18th.   Charlie Hunter writes from Stoke-on-Trent to his brother in Mablethorpe, *Stoke v Port V at Stoke on Sat. A Great Game. Rivals Meet. Who will win. A Draw I say. So pleased to hear they are repairing sea bank. Find some work wont it. A few ironworkers out of work here. I have plenty of work pleased to say.* In a year of industrial unrest, the worker on the card is glad of what was sometimes referred to as the annual [i.e. bath]. Bathrooms were a middle class prerogative.   24i

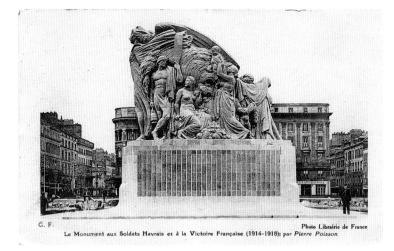

Le Monument aux Soldats Havrais et à la Victoire Française (1914-1918); par *Pierre Poisson*

Edith to Miss Marvel in Bradford, *Havre is half dotty today. The memorial on the other side is being unveiled. you never heard such an excitable din in all your life...* The English viewed the French as lacking in restraint and over fond of gesture. This was also their view of French war memorials of whose rather overblown artistic rhetoric this is a good example. Sculptors had never known such times.   24j

PISTOL PRACTICE, CAMP PERRY, OHIO

September 17th.   From Detroit Police Pistol Team Camp, Port Clinton, Ohio, to Mrs Addie Fisher in Detroit, *Dear Beeby... had a little tire trouble but got here OK just 98 miles down hear Please Dear Baby Put that stuff in a small Backing Powder can and send it to me I am afraid that what I got wont last I did not look in big suitcase nighty nighty Baby from Elmer xx.*   24k

September 14th.   SM sends this postcard of a photo to Miss Mackay in Devizes *with remembrance of a very happy day.* The happy day was September 5th it says and Miss Mackay had added that it was taken by Ernest Filleul. The handsome sports car seems to be parked near one of the Avebury standing stones. In such fine cars on newly made up roads a now lost pleasure called motoring was possible.   24l

August 29th.   This fine and futuristic-looking motor-cycle combination was evidently Mr Easton's irresistible asset as beach photographer at Margate. Nora and her brother (in his cub's cap) are enjoying the imaginary ride having opted for the gender orthodoxy of man on the machine and girl in the sidecar. Nora sends the card to Grandad in Ipswich hoping he is feeling better today.   24m

June 13th.   To Mr Whitney in Handsworth, *Dear Pa our time is getting short now,... Seen nothing of Mr Chatwin. mother and I have won some chocs so you will be alright. love from both. Mabel.* This classic postcard scene is relieved of its potential ordinariness by the strange configuration of people (including the child in the flower border) which seems to have the seeds of a narrative that will involve the man walking towards us with a stick.   24n

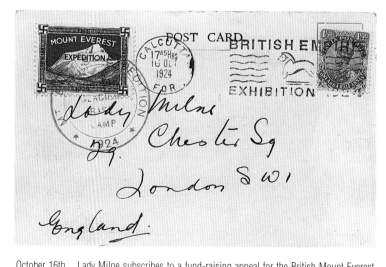

October 16th.   Lady Milne subscribes to a fund-raising appeal for the British Mount Everest Expedition and duly receives her card, *dispatched by Postal Runner to India*, from the base camp (see over for picture side). Franking and stamps include the Expedition's own cancel and the promotional postmark of the British Empire Exhibition, plus a special stamp complete with swastikas as Indian good luck signs (though in Germany their darker history had already begun).   24o

MT. EVEREST EXPEDITION, 1924.
Leader - - Gen. Hon. C. G. Bruce, C.B.

M.t. Everest from the Base Camp in the Rongbuk Valley, T,BET.

Dispatched by Postal Runner to India.

The Film of this great Exploit will be shown throughout the country, commencing at the Scala Theatre, London November, 1924.

SOLE RIGHTS RESERVED.

ENGAGED

24a. Wildt & Kray, London No 63. Photo: Campbell Gray

24b. Publisher unknown

24c. Detroit Pub. Co. Phostint XXII (Huguenot Walloon Tercentenary 1 cent stamp)

24d. Photocrom Co. Celesque Series

24e. A notice to the right of the Rowntrees kiosk points to Tut's Tomb, some hastily arranged sideshow version no doubt, of the tomb of Tutankhamen which had been discovered only weeks before.

Wildt & Kray, London No 27 Photo: Campbell Gray

24f. Wildt & Kray, London No 54 Photo: Campbell Gray

24g. His Master's Voice Ltd

24h. A N Paris 398

24i. Bamforth & Co Seaside Comic Series No 1486 Artist unknown

24j. GF. Photo: Librairie de France

24k. Army & Navy Novelty Co, Columbus, Ohio. (artteich)

24l. Privately published. Photo: Ernest Filleul

24m. J Easton, Clifton Baths, Margate E882

24n. Publisher unknown

24o. Official card of Mount Everest Expedition 1924

24p. Regent Publishing Co No 4413 Artist: Reg Maurice

24q. Beagles & Co 196V

24r. Bamforth & Co based on a drawing by Otto Messmer

O G Bruce though almost sixty led the Expedition (he kept fit by running in the foothills with a Sherpa riding piggyback). Noel was responsible for the epic film which included a shot of the farewell note Mallory wrote when he set off with Irving for the summit never to return. The discovery of Mallory's body in 1999 revived speculation that he may have been the first to scale the topmost point of the roof of the world. 24o

September 24th. Anon, who signs with a kiss, writes from Bridlington to A Wormald in Dewsbury, *I hope you are getting on all right with the whitewashing. I am stopping here to look after the bathing vans, so if you want a job as well let me know. I am bringing some rock back.* Bathing machines (see 22n) were still de rigueur. Maintaining and hauling them in and out of the sea gave work for men, women and horses. 24p

PARAMOUNT STAR. RODOLPH VALENTINO. 196.V. 'FAMOUS CINEMA STAR' SERIES. BEAGLES POSTCARD.

EVERY DOG—I MEAN CAT—HAS HIS DAY. THERE'S **FAIRBANKS, CHAPLIN, VALENTINO,** AND OTHERS, ALL CRYING THEIR EYES OUT 'COS I'M **IT !**

SWANK FELIX!

July 2nd. From Doris in Hackney to Mrs Thomas in Whipps Cross, *Dear Kid, Ear bunged up. I will be down to you tomorrow.* Rudolph Valentino (Rodolpho d'Antonguolla) the great heartthrob of the silent screen, star of The Sheikh, had two more years before his death at the age of 31 would drive admirers to suicide. His funeral was a national event and flowers are still being placed on his grave by the faithful. 24q

November 10th. From K in Abergavenny to Ann Davies in Llanwenarth, *I hope you are not going to forget to come and see us to Day... be like Felix and don't cry.* Felix the cat whose scratchy cartoon films were still being shown at my primary school was a twenties superstar created by Otto Messmer. The mouse rightly tells Felix not to swank: in a few years a greater mouse would largely eclipse his memory. 24r

June 15th.   Tommy in Seaford writes to Miss Nesta V Lord in Crouch End, *Received your PC by the first post this morning. Last night from 6.30 - 8 I practised golf with Mr Sumner & found a new ball. I watered a little of the front then played Bezique with Miss Dodds til 10.15. Then I cleaned Vi's clubs & went to bed. I have just had my lesson & got on a bit better. I asked if I might try another club next time. Now I am going to see what the sea is like for a dip. It is a gorgeous day - so hot, just a little sea breeze. Take care of Fido, see that mother keeps cool tomorrow, with love to all.* Tommy now has the crossword to add to his long list of leisure pursuits. The card from an elegant series shows chauffeur and mistress in the grip of the crossword craze which swept the country after the first newspaper crossword appeared in November 1924 (in the Sunday Express). Though invented by a Liverpudlian it was first introduced in America. Within months every paper carried a crossword puzzle appropriate to its readership. Even the Times succumbed with its own erudite version.   25a

March 22nd.   Mrs Michaelson to her daughter in the kind of big script adults reserve for children, *My precious, Hope your cold is lots better. Heaps of love and kisses, Mother*. Two buses, both advertising the successful revue The Cooptimists, date the picture to 1922.   25b

October 15th.   Cora in Brooklyn doesn't have a lot to say to Miss Laura Cornstack in Ivoryton, Connecticut and uses only a small amount of the allotted space, *Having a good restful time.* This bird's eye view already shows a city which promises anything but a restful time.   25c

January 7th.   Jenny to Maud Seaton, *Sorry not to have written before but you know how time flies when on holiday.* Despite many charms (and Jones & Higgins imposing department store) Peckham seems an unlikely holiday destination. This view is little changed in the 88 years since the photograph. The hairdressers next to which the steam bus and milk cart have stopped is where I had my hair cut a fortnight ago. 25d

November 14th.   From Jess in Miami to John Simon in Worcester Mass., *Did you send me Hanks address. See Carl waits on the young ladies.* These parading Klansmen with their School House float do not crave anonymity. Their resurgence since Griffith's Birth of a Nation (1915) had reached its peak in the mid twenties when they claimed 4,000,000 members and their terrorisation of American blacks was at its height.   25e

May 11th.   From School House, Clifton College, Bristol to Hamilton Bantock in Edgbaston, Back again! Have been down to Margate during hols. *SR!!! Unspeakable! ...Behold the locomotive exchange! How's medicine? I saw LNER 6165 Valour at King's X* [the sister loco of Patriot see 22i] do write... G M Harwood. A fine crisp shot of the greyhound-like Castle Class 94079 (GWR) and the classic LNER 4475 Flying Fox.   25f

November 16th.   L in Olivia, Minn. writes to Mr C in Northfield, *Friday was a very unlucky day here. 2 fires, one a big barn the other a furniture store. Early Sunday morn there was a big wreck near Renville. We went to see that in p.m.... 4 men killed. It was an awful sight a double headed freight & a passenger train. Aunt L is having six ladies for dinner today.* The driver of these frightening civic gents is blacked up.   25g

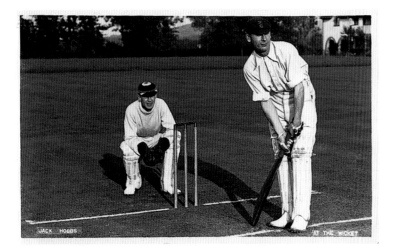

September 3rd.   EE in Brighton to J C B Knight in Reigate *...on our way to Brighton... longing to see the sea, hope we shall get deck chairs and sit on the pier.* This is the real Jack Hobbs rather than his buttery double of 24a. At 44 he is in his prime and in the course of the year scored 16 of his 197 first-class centuries. Next year he was to help England regain the Ashes, finally retiring at the age of 54.   25h

August 28th.   EM in Old Orchard, Maine, to David S Stanton in Yonkers NY. *Greetings from the best beach in the world... Had a shore dinner and nice auto ride today... go home Monday by auto. We are having a Chevrolet Sedan this year...* The spread of the automobile starts a parking problem even in Old Orchard where many Model T's and their like are gathered in three packed lines.   25i

August 14th. B to Mrs Jenkins in Stranraer. He posts the card in Broadstairs after two train journeys taking him the length of Britain, *Arrived safely by previous train to the one that smashed. as daddy used to say - a miss is as good as a mile!* The Wembley Exhibition carried on for a second year. BP had a nervous moment when Persia's Kajar dynasty was overthrown but their oil contract was safely renewed.   25j

August 26th. From A Vance in Isallt, Criccieth to Miss Mary Freeman in Sutton. *We saw this very old lady & she is not Welsh but Irish! She sells these cards herself. It seems a long time since I have seen you, Love.* So the cover of Mary Jones is blown and with it one's trust in ethnic images from the Principality. She is not only a fake Welsh lady in traditional costume but a stooge for Frith & Co, the postcard's publisher.   25k

April 13th. From Lil at the Commercial Hotel in Kippax, Leeds, to Lillie Jaques in Doncaster, *Haveing a good time. Monday, going to Wetherby.* One hopes that the W H Smiths at this station stocks a card which advertises its stall so prominently (complete with postcard carousel). The Times reflects the news from Russia: Stalin's ascendancy is almost complete now that he has ousted Trotsky from the party elite.   25l

March 6th. Mrs L in Stoats Nest to Mr Stanbridge in Kenley, *Do you think you would manage half a ton of Best House Coal for me & ditto for Mrs Horton if so could you manage it for Saturday as we are right out.* Bairnsfather, himself wounded in Ypres in 1916, issued this prediction of an endless war. The World War I babies would not wait, however, for 1950.   25m

March 25th. P & J in Altrincham to Mrs Hill in Crosshouses, *...arrived quite safe sorry to hear about the pets did you have a glass of wine at the f-------l... love to all.* In contrast to the marital disputes of 23a listening to the wireless could be a marvellous alibi for lovers' cheek to cheek proximity, almost better than the piano duets of a previous generation.   25n

May 29th. Mary is not the first to send a message to a friend (Miss Matthews in Oxford) saying *We are at the top of the Eiffel Tower... thought you would like a PC.* The spectacular illuminations are in the high style of the Arts Decoratifs exhibition, which gave its name to Art Deco, an eclectic style that in the event has had a longer currency than Art Nouveau.   25o

"CROSSWORDS."
"Please Mum, what is it a Gent wears beginning with D?"

LISTENIN'!

"I have here an urgent message — "Will the gentleman who took the Ford car from outside Posh Mansions, call to-morrow — there are five more waiting for him!"

25a. Raphael Tuck & Sons. The Crossword Craze. Oilette no 3514 Artist : unknown (Tempest?)

25b. Millar & Lang. National Series. PM: British Goods Are Best.

25c. Manhattan Postcard Co. NY 17040

25d. Valentiny & Co. High St Peckham 73735.
Compare TP 20 Sites n Years, Site 18.

25e. J N Chamberlain, Miami, Fla. 19431

25f. More about railway engines ...saw George Vth Class Queen Mary is LMS 5329. Many Princes have LMS plates ex LYR 4-6-0 no 10455 at Camden sheds, she did look huge.

Loco Pub Co. Photo taken April 16th 1925.

May 31st.   Dear Dais, writes Percy in Norwich to Mrs Partington in Cardiff, *having a topping jaunt round the country with gorgeous weather to enjoy it. Joe & I look a couple of nibs in our +4's - from a man's shop too.* Difficult to know who is what sex and difficult to solve the clue the maid reads out to her mistress. Durex would be premature, which leaves little exclusively male except dickie (false shirt front).   25p

August 20th.   Sal in Lovack to Master Fred Gaunt in Upwood *...I biked to Thrapston with Hilda this morning and we are going to have tea up the park this afternoon. We went up to Drayton yesterday and the gardens looked lovely. The fountain was going. It did look nice. I got Edie's letter this morning tell mum.* An announcer with a microphone like a plant stand makes a typical Model T joke.   25q

25g. Publisher unknown. (Olivia, Maine)

25h. Publisher unknown.

25i. Tichnor Quality Viewcards no 122728

25j. Tuck Oilette. Artist: Charles E Flower

25k. F Frith & Co. Reigate

25l. Inter-Art Comique Series no 3049. Artist: Donald McGill

25m. Bystander. Fragments from France series 4

25n. C W Faulkner & Co. Series 1803. Artist: Albert Kaye

25o. A N Paris 187. AOE. Eiffel Tower PM

25p. Woolstone Bros. Milton Comic Series no 720 Artist unknown

25q. Woolstone Bros. Milton Comic Series no 537 Artist unknown

25r. Publisher unknown?

March 13th.   Ken writes to his friend Master Sid Robinson locally in Dagenham, *Don't forget to be at Liverpool Street as soon after 2 o'clock on Saturday as you can manage it. it is quite all right as I have found that the British Museum is open Saturday afternoons.* The card must verge on the unique in having both real and photographed pin-holes. Did Sid admire the poster on Ken's wall (one can see the floral wallpaper) and ask him to make a postcard copy? He made a pretty good job since the writing is legible, the racy scenes vivid, and there is a heady glimpse of Anna May Wong. Raoul Walsh's Thief of Baghdad, co-written and produced by Fairbanks for United Artists (see 20a), was one of the high points of silent film history. Its camera virtuosity and fast action made it appeal to all levels of cinemagoer. The New York Times described it as 'a feat of motion picture art which has never been equalled'. Fairbanks' fine physique and athleticism was the result of dedicated training. His son, Douglas Fairbanks Jr, had already started out on a rival career. If Ken and Sid had seen the film this shared image would remind them of two hours of cinema magic.   25r

"Me and my Boy Friend, My Boy Friend and me,
There isn't much difference between us, but he
Wears his Hair and his Skirts a bit longer than me."

July 30th. This sent from Bristol without message to Miss S George of Burrows Dairy near Yeovil was meant to speak for itself. Such an extremity of current fashion would probably raise an eyebrow in Bristol, but in deepest Somerset it would cause a commotion. Even the rhyming triplet is on a more sophisticated level than usual for a comic postcard. The girl's shingled hair (bobbing and shingling had brought about a hair-dressing boom) is as severe as it can get. The Fair Isle pullovers are very much à la mode in the mid twenties and the boy sports the latest fashion horror, Oxford Bags (see 26d). Across the Atlantic President Coolidge said he wouldn't be seen dead in them but it was not for his generation that they were intended. Men's clothing tended to change in almost imperceptible stages. It called for such absurdist tactics to express the emancipation of the male from years of timorous conformity. 26a

March 12th. Pearle writes excitedly to Miss Louise Spooner in Kingston, Ontario, *We flew over from Paris & were 4hrs in air and it was thrilling & over 2000ft up, some times above the clouds, but wouldn't have missed it for anything.* The theatre announcements date this view to 1913 when commercial flying was still a dream. 26b

July 5th. This is what the skyscrapers see or rather saw in about 1919/20 in a Rotary view sent by J W Nicholson in Boreham Wood to A Levison in London, *will you dine with me on Thursday evening? 7.30 at the Criterion, Regent St. entrance.* (evidently not the Criterion seen on Piccadilly Circus cards). 26c

"It matters not what you wear in the week - so long as you've OXFORDS for Sunday!"

August 16th. Edie in Cirencester to Miss W Hinton in Frome, *I hope you are having a good time, and nice weather, better than what we have had hear. I am sick of holidays already. We have had to stick indoors.* Oxford Bags were mercifully short lived and finally condemned in Oxford's Isis magazine in January 1927 only to return as Loons in the late 60's. 26d

MISS ESME FITZGIBBON, a charming Musical Comedy actress, writes: "I find Amami Shampoos very excellent. After using them the hair is in perfect condition and looks delightfully glossy. There is also no difficulty in "setting" the hair—as so often happens after using any ordinary shampoo.

May 26th. Miss Mathew's mother in Norwood expected word from her but the General Strike caused a back log of mail. *I will phone you tomorrow morning... just off with Daddy to Streatham. if you were here you could have come... you would see some funny sights lots of people are enjoying the strike especially the boys on motor-bicycles.* Esme Fitzgibbon tries to look like Louise Brooks. 26e

20th September. LO sends from Margate a picture of Cliftonville's perfect cliff arch to J H Baker in Finchley, *What do you think of this picture it is very pretty there - so hot people trying to get into the shade on the front.* The postmark's command, Say It By Telephone, seems to admonish postcard senders. There were as yet only half a million telephones in the country. 26f

"POOR FELLOW, HERE'S A PENNY FOR YOU-NOW PLAY 'HOME SWEET HOME!'"

February 22nd. The old gag of starting handle/organ grinder gets another airing with a commentary from Peg in Tring. She writes to Constance Wright in hospital in Hemel Hempstead, *I am sure it is all for the best. you will feel heaps better and all ready to go flying down the hill when the next snows come!!! Con! don't you just love to think of all our thrills we have had including when you went down on your 'tummy'!!* 26g

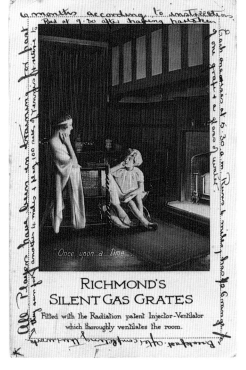

RICHMOND'S SILENT GAS GRATES
Fitted with the Radiation patent Injector-Ventilator which thoroughly ventilates the room.

August 18th. Harry Randall in Blackwater plays games on the back and front of this advertising card in writing to the Hon Sec of the PV (Park View) Club in order to enter the August tournament. One hopes Morris Jenks of the selection committee was amused by this banter. The club seems to have covered all sports including tennis, hockey, and more surprisingly, baseball. 26h

No 137 IVOR NOVELLO
"CELEBRITY" Series

February 13th. From Stratford to Miss H in Dudley, *...we ought to be alright for seats... but, should be glad if one of you could book.* Ivor Novello could do no wrong after his wartime hit, Keep The Home Fires Burning, written when he was only 21. This year he appeared in Hitchcock's first masterpiece, The Lodger. He died in 1951 during his show Gay's The Word. Heavy make up in photo publicity was usual in the 20's. 26i

March 26th.   Vera sends Master Francis Bacon in Barford a card of the burning of the Shakespeare Theatre, *for you to see what the fire was like. I was able to see some of it, as we were not busy. It was dreadful, just like one enormous bonfire, the heat was so intense & every bit of wood was burnt in no time... the men are pulling some of it down now. I have never seen so many cars & people in Stratford.*   26j

June 5th.   D L Hill to Sandy Kinnear in Seaford, *Do you remember crossing this bridge... & hundreds of trams streaming past blocking our way. Wasn't it hasty of Miss True to come & take my place with you at the sea!* County Hall took years to build (as here) and was not complete when opened in 1922. The Council was abolished in 1989. The shamed building is now a hotel/aquarium/McDonalds etc.   26k

July 26th.   To Miss Mansell in Wolverhampton from GB in Somerset, *This is the most thrilling picture of the hunt I can get & you being a huntswoman will appreciate it I know. Had a good round of golf yesterday... just off for a bathe now.* The sight of hounds swimming in pursuit of a stag is not to everyone's taste today, yet with no oddly dressed humans in view it has an elemental drama.   26l

August 9th.   To Mr & Mrs Prosser in Coventry from G in Shanklin, *We came here this morning by bus... we had our lunch in the restaurant on the promenade & have got mother fixed up with dark glasses.* Sunglasses are seldom seen in seaside photos of this period and were still a novelty. One suspects that the view was taken by Mr Pike whose photography shop occupies such a prominent position.   26m

August 26th.   Cordners Ltd. A Real Good Place to Eat runs the blurb on the back of this card sent from Montreal to Miss Dorothy Cathro in Cheshire. J C Hodgson gives his address and writes, *Let me know if you'd like views of Montreal. I'm from Lancashire but I happened to notice your address in My Magazine. I'm a wretched teacher of course.* Did Dorothy reply? Did his cards get less lugubrious?   26n

February 20th.   S in Battersea to Mr B in Kilburn, *Sorry to hear news & shall be glad to see you both... make it Wednesday as I am obliged to have the sweeps on Monday or Tuesday.* Nothing in music is as competitive as brass bands. St Hilda's Colliery won trophy after trophy. These men were now strikers. Though the General Strike soon ended, the miners kept on until starved back to work in November.   26o

PILLION RIDING IS CONSIDERED DANGEROUS --- PEDESTRIANS DON'T LOOK WHERE THEY'RE GOING!

I want one of those caps for motor cycling with the peak at the back!

July 5th. Flo & Dick send this from Lincoln to Miss May Gasson in Caterham, *We are enjoying ourselves alright. No work so we are alright. No Pillion riding now you see the danger.* The motorcycle gained in power and popularity in the twenties. The side-car suited safer couples and pillion riding was the game for the young. The postmark slogan says British Goods Are Best, which at the time was true of motor-bikes.   26p

April 12th. To Mr F K Ennals in Purley from Derek in nearby Croydon. *Many Happy Returns of the day and many good wishes to Gubbins* is the cheery greeting. McGill celebrates the motorcycle craze with a variation on the old comic theme of dim person and shop-keeper. Wearing the obligatory cap back to front was a fashion set by early aviators who imitated the Wright brothers in their trademark style.   26q

August 13th. Maurice is in Philadelphia at the height of the Sesquicentennial Festivities. He writes to James Deary in East Ham, *Hello Friend Jim, Here I am in the city you liked so well. Say by the way where did you live at here. well are you coming over. I like 'Philliy' pretty well.* When Maurice bought this card it was bright and crisp and new with four sharp corners. Three quarters of a century later it is a wreck. The three corners remaining are rounded with handling and the other has graduated from a crease to a tear to final severance. Time and smoky rooms have yellowed its once white edging and generally given it a careworn look. It was found in a dealer's stock bearing the customary caveat A/F meaning 'with all faults, as seen'. Postcard collectors are notorious condition fetishists and such a card unless of amazing rarity (which this is not) would be beyond the pale. It had not been a pretty thing even in its infancy. Indeed it must have been on the edge of unsaleability since the uncentred image and colour registration bears witness to a bad day at the printers (the red half-tone has strayed by almost half a centimetre). It needed someone to take pity on it.   26r

August 27th.   *Dear Bill. This is the Palais of Justice which was burned during the recent revolution,* writes
André to Mr Wright in Sutton, Surrey, *We are leaving Vienna tonight. Please ask Baby to excuse us, we wrote
tails instead of têtes on her card.* With the first talkie to watch and the foxtrot to dance who elsewhere was
going to worry much about riots and strikes in Vienna (or the publication of the Nazi manifesto). This particular
upheaval reflected the usual political polarities and grew out of socialist demonstrations against the acquittal of
Nazis for the murder of communists. Who can now take sides when faced with that dismal pair of ideologies both
of which brought such waste and pain to the century?   27a

May 19th.   *Darling John. Mummy & Daddy are staying quite near the place in this
picture. I hope you are being a very sweet boy & taking care of Nanny & Robert* [ten
kisses] *Mummy.* The view is in 1919 when Messager's operetta Monsieur Beaucaire at
the Palace starred Maggie (later Dame Maggie) Teyte.   27b

May 29th.   The North river view (compare 10c). Ernest Flagg's Singer building still
manages to hold centre stage (it was demolished in 1967). Florence Baldwin writes to
Miss Anna Wharton at the YMCA in Canton, Ohio, *I am having the time of my life visiting
my dear old friends and all look so good to me.*   27c

August 9th.   Bernard in Bournemouth to Cecil Clarke in Nottingham, *Am afraid my correspondence has been neglected, only have had a rather worrying time one way and another. We have this car in our showroom for a week.* Henry Seagrave broke through the 200 mph barrier. Six months later the compulsive record breaker Malcolm Campbell regained his supremacy by 4mph. The duel continued (See 83i).   27d

August 1st.   Mother writes from Lower Edmonton to Mrs E Hodgkinson in Horley, Surrey, on a beach photographer's postcard taken by Gwynne whose premises were opposite the Kinema, Clacton-on-Sea. She asks, *Did Ed have his birthday card & his socks on the 28th June. If I do not hear from you I will know he had it.* Perhaps the sight of these bare feet reminded her there had been no thankyou note   27e

Burning Ghat, Benares.

January 13th.   John writes to Mrs Jones in Whitland, Carmarthenshire, *Thank you so much for loving letter. I am still in bed - the 18th day... Flu is rampant in Davos - there are fifteen cases in this hotel. Buck up, all will be well xxxxx.* If John is in Switzerland for the winter sports he is having a thin time. This curling rink in front of an English Library makes the scene resemble Canadian bonspiels.   27f

June 5th.   To Dorothy Sully in London E12 from George in Karachi, *Dear Dolly, Salaam Memsah'b! It is ages since I heard of you or from you. If I don't come home soon I'll turn Hindu and then when I'm finished with this life my body will be burned on one of these slabs... am still waiting for that call - All Aboard for Blighty. hope you are well and earning heaps of money.*   27g

August 10th.   Both back and front of this card from Skegness are about food and the Gandy family in Leicester obviously take a keen interest in it, *Dear Daddy, We've had duck and green peas, apple sauce and stuffing. Mushroom and bacon is another thing we've had. We are having all kinds of delicious things. Hoping you are doing the same. Been to a tea-dance this afternoon Café Dansant. We are having a peach each. Lots of Love Freda xxxx.*   27h

March 8th.   Lucien Levy (LL) makes a poem of this humble band at the edge of the Algerian Sahara from which Billie writes to Miss Wyld in Eastwood, Notts, *We meet lots of these little caravans when we are on the move. How is Peter - do wish I could have him here - he would enjoy barking at the camels.* One wonders who 'we' are and what Billie is doing there. He is certainly wise to be in the Eastern Sahara since in neighbouring Morocco Marshal Petain has just quelled a violent rebellion.   27i

CUNARD R.M.S. MAURETANIA   TONNAGE 31 000

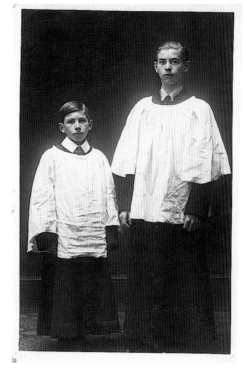

Charlie and Fred

October 7th. *I expect you would be more than surprised at our hurried departure... we are having a delightful time. Much love, Ella.* Mr Ingles in Illesley receives the card and is left to wonder. Although over twenty years old the Mauretania, sister ship of the Lusitania (see 07g), took the Atlantic record in 1924 with a crossing made in 5 days 90 minutes.   27j

Something the 6th. From Saffron Walden to Mrs P Warren in Portsmouth. *Dear Cis, Perc & all, Am sending this photo of Donald and Kenneth to wish you many happy returns... Dons been in choir 5 years Ken 2 years... Your affect Sister.* The two choristers are searchingly seen in this unaffected studio-produced postcard.   27k

February 11th. June Stimson in Wallasey gets a card from her grannie in Birmingham, *Do hope you are all much better & will soon be about. I saw these two little men last Friday night. They acted at the Grand Theatre, Fond love xxxxx.* Human anomalies were staples of the music hall: fairground Midgets were the aristocrats among their kind.   27l

GLAD I BROUGHT THE UMBRELLA — I'VE HAD IT UP EVERY DAY HERE

Cheerio Everybody!

1930

August 24th. E Lekeman writes to York, *Only two fine days so far. Very disappointing but it is a nice rest... It has been a good season for umbrellas I must say.* It was the worst summer since 1879 with 80% more rain than usual. There is no sign that the censor-proof joke has been appreciated. Did Miss Bain get it? I was not aware the phrase existed in 1927.   27m

July 2nd. *Dear Nellie*, writes Ada to her friend also in Tunbridge Wells, *Congratulations on you reaching the age of discretion. Now you are able to think for yourself.* The good-time Prince of Wales says 'Cheerio Everybody!' and has a smoke, or perhaps (for once) not, since the cigarette looks to be added. What then was airbrushed in would now be airbrushed out.   27n

July 18th. Rose A Walter sends this fashion prediction to Mr Cowling in Scunthorpe, intimating that things had already gone this far in Cleethorpes, *How will this suit you better come and see a few for yourself.* Comic artist Arnold Taylor starts his sixty year career here as an apprentice to Doug Tempest with an accomplished piece of work for a sixteen year old.   27o

Comme Douglas Fairbank!

Little Pitche

MISS NORMA TALMADGE.

August 2nd.   A cryptic note from Marlow in Antwerp to Master Joey Oakley in Hove, *I expect you are busy chopping wood & doing the garden. I wonder what you will think of Rita.* The French illustrator evidently thought Fairbanks was plural for Senior and Junior. We are at the end of the most purely international era of a cinema whose universal language was silence.   27p

October 2nd.   Ethel in Manchester tells Mabel Danby in (appropriately) Pickford Lane, she is on her way. It was Norma Talmadge who, visiting Grauman's newly opened Chinese Theatre with Mr & Mrs Fairbanks in 1927, inadvertently stepped into wet concrete and started the Hollywood pavement of stars. Grauman got her celebrated companions to do likewise.   27q

LINDBERGH

June 7th.   From Paris to Mrs Null in Deddington, Oxon, *My dear Nancy. How are you. I helped push this bus across the field when she came down. What about the other Americans. They did well. Having nasty weather wet & Cold. Mrs H is back from America but will have to go back there. very seedy. Hope you are both well. Good bye old dear. Love B.* She may be exaggerating slightly about her role in Charles Lindbergh's triumphant solo crossing of the Atlantic. All reports mention seething crowds breaking through police cordons and tearing at his plane for souvenirs. The story of the flight itself made in 33 ½ hours by an exhausted man guiding an unstable aircraft through storm and fog is the stuff of boys' adventure books (at times The Spirit of St Louis was only 10 feet above the waves). Lindbergh was only sustained by a few home-made sandwiches. He returned to America and a ticker tape welcome. In 1934 the Lindberghs were visited by tragedy when their infant son was abducted and (despite ransom payments) killed. By the time of World War II Lindbergh's advocacy of Nazi ideals made him a tarnished hero.   27r

27a. Iris Kunstverlag. Vienna

27b. To Master John Stead, Bush Hotel, Wokingham, Berks. W&K (Wildt & Kray) London No 190

27c. L Jones & Co. Woolworth Building NY. Rotary Photographic Co 10781 - 52. Photo: Irving Underhill

27d. Sunbeam Ltd. Wolverhampton
Major Seagrave reached 231 mph in 1929 but thereafter it was Malcolm Campbell in his 'Bluebird' series of cars that pushed the record beyond 300 mph in 1935. He died in another attempt on the record in 1949 but his son Donald achieved over 400 mph in July 1964. He too was killed in an effort to break his own water speed record. Thereafter it is largely an American story after Craig Breedlove in October 1964 exceeded 500 miles an hour.

27e. Gwynne. Clacton-on-Sea

27f. Eredi Alfredo Finzi, Lugano

27g. H A Mirra & Sons, Delhi

27h. Woolstone Bros. Milton Series 1122 Artist: Donald McGill

27i. LL (Lévy et Neurdein Réunis) 4
LL is the signature of Lucien Levy, long thought to be Louis Levy. Born Levitsky he was the prince of postcard publishers (éditeurs) in France. The literature about his firm is already tortuous for it has only been in recent years, thanks to the diligence of enthusiasts like Neudin, doyen of French cartophilistes, and Liz McKernan in England that the identity and history of the house of Levy has been unravelled. Notable in Levy's production are the high artistic standards of the photography and the fine printing on superior card stock. The images rival straight photographic reproduction in their detail, which does not break down so readily as that of other printed cards under magnification. Levy also employed the best tinters for the coloured versions of his cards which have an instantly recognisable aesthetic. The other great French publisher was ND, Neurdein, and the history of the two éditeurs is intertwined, involving collaboration, separation and, as in this card, reunification. Hence the announced publisher here is 'Levy et Neurdein Réunis'. In the absence of institutional interest from the academic world primary research into postcards is done by collectors themselves, often at the most scholarly level.

27j. For Cunard / Hotel York, London W1. Artist unknown

27k. Publisher unknown

27l. Publisher unknown. No 254

27m. HB series no 2676. Artist unknown

27n. Photochrom Celesque series No 2038

27o. Bamforth & Co. Comic series 2347.
This may be Arnold Taylor's first published card. The name Bamforth & Co of Holmfirth is still synonymous with the comic postcard which they produced for almost the whole of the century together with the famous series of song cards (see 16o & 18o). The work of Arnold Taylor and his master Douglas Tempest span almost the entire period. Taylor, like many artists, develops throughout his career, adapting his style to current tastes.

27p. A O E Fantaisies Trichromes, Paris No 175. Artist: Little Pitche

27q. Rotary photo S.78.2

27r. AN, Paris

January 11th.   Not waving but saluting. The two elder sons of Mussolini are already adept at the Fascist greeting. Bruno became a pilot and died in action in 1944. His younger brother Vittorio survived the war and went to live as an exile in South America. The third brother, Romano, was their junior. He inherited their father's musical gifts. A popular pianist and bandleader he married the sister of Sophia Loren. Their daughter Alessandra alone continues to serve the fascist cause as an Allianza Nazionale deputy in the Italian parliament. We do not know what Emilie Ascoli means when (writing from Carrara to Mrs Perkins in Durban, Natal) he adds to his conventional message of greeting, *I think this P.C. will interest you.*   28a

July 27th.   A view from 1922 with Johann Strauss's Chauve Souris (die Fledermaus / The Bat) playing at the Pavilion. Alex sends a dull (if not patronising) note to his wife(?) Mrs Johnston at 52 Gordon Street, Aberdeen, *Weather cloudy but still good. This is a famous place.*   28b

May 11th.   On this fine and evocative night view from East River Alex Bernstein writing to Olga in Vienna gives her his next address as Hotel Midland, London (from which, who knows, he may send Olga a card of Piccadilly Circus). Then he is off to Paris to stay at the Grand Hotel du Pavillon.   28c

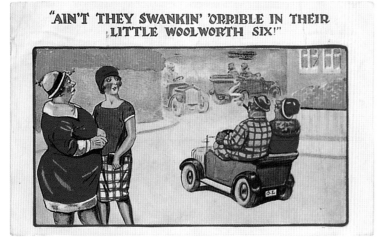

"AIN'T THEY SWANKIN' 'ORRIBLE IN THEIR LITTLE WOOLWORTH SIX!"

229 AMIENS — Caserne Gribeauval. — LL

August 13th.   Bebe in Southend to Bob Nellup in Chiswick *Just a P.C. for now, writing later. It is lovely & warm here this morning, we went to bed before nine last night.* In this month the Morris Minor was launched to compete with the newly popular 7hp Baby Austin. Smaller and smaller low horse-power cars were built with the aim of making the £100 car (achieved by Morris in 1929).   28d

August 7th.   With the resonant postmark Amiens, Somme, to the Misses Whaley in Hitchen, *Have just returned from seeing Fred's grave; an awfully pretty spot about 1500 British buried there. I was able to get a very nice wreath. Weather very good. Love, P.* LL's sombre card of the Gribeauval Barracks fits the mood. The message suggests a first visit though thousands made an annual pilgrimage.   28e

Drighlington. M.Bastow.

EVENING TIDE BLACKPOOL

December 5th.   From Yorkshire D writes to Billy Voce in Liverpool *Here is a view of Drighlington at last. The little shop shown is where I got the P.C. so glad of Mum's and your letters but sorry to hear the Maid's gone. Tell Eric and Alfie I expect them to join you in making things as easy as possible.* M Bastow does his best with Drighlington, cunningly featuring the shop that will sell his cards.   28f

July 9th.   Norman & Minnie sum up their stay in Blackpool to Mr & Mrs Wardleworth & ainky in Manchester, *sun, rain, sun, rain, sun, rain, sun, rain, sun & rain.* They choose a card that reflects a more lyrical aspect of the notoriously brash resort than is usual, a handsomely organised multiple view that shows Blackpool not to be entirely devoted to funny hats, rock and illuminations.   28g

PIER

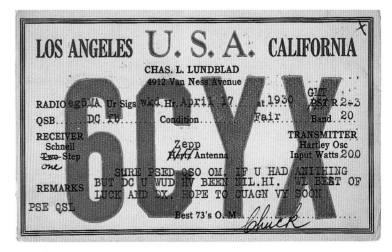

LOS ANGELES U.S.A. CALIFORNIA
CHAS. L. LUNDBLAD
4912 Van Ness Avenue
6CYX

September 18th.   Even more sobre is the view of Hastings chosen by Mother to send to Mrs Bolton in Lincoln, *Bobbie wants me to tell you she has had a lovely time in the Private Swimming Pool where she made good attempts to swim with Norah & June.* Judges, the local publishers still thrive in Hastings though their cards have become less depressing. Rain is best for lamplit night scenes but all we can see is an unpopulated Pier end, where the unheard band plays on.   28h

May 8th.   The standard design of a radio ham's QSL card confirming signal received is instantly recognisable from the clear design and handsome woodblock lettering. More recent versions have pictorial photolithos as their basis but lack the spartan grandeur of what became an international design convention. Here Chuck tells R Munday in New Malden, Surrey that he has picked up his signal in Los Angeles. In the attractive short-hand of the genre he hopes to *CUAGN* [call you again] *VY SOON.*   28i

May 26th.   PM in Marseille tells Miss Crossley in Southampton, *The views here are finer than any p.c. can give.* They must indeed be so to compete with this perfectly composed vision by LL which matches the spectacular bay view with two figures whose eloquent pictorial relationship suggests (abetted by a green cannon and a balustrade) some kind of allegory. 28j

January 30th.   On a promotional card for this train (which also offers a Train Secretary, Maid-Manicure, Barber, Valet etc.) Eddie writes in Brooklyn to Frederick Lange, *This is one of the trains I didn't ride on. after I beat my man in the 115 pound class I went to Washington with another fellow on the train.* It would have been a treat on this stretch to sit in the Observation/Library/Lounge Car. 28k

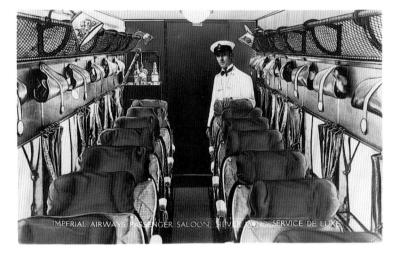

March 29th.   Anne in Paris (to Mrs L C Smart in New York) is very satisfied with her plane trip, *The inside of the plane; steward, buffet lunch 'n everything. Paris is great and we do like this hotel so much Love and a hug for Bruce.* Pan-am will introduce air stewardesses in the coming year but the Imperial Airways steward looks ready to please in this functional interior (see 29a). 28l

July 13th.   Jack at the Henley Regatta (like Wimbledon very much part of the Social Season) writes to Harry Arlott at the Viking Boat Club in Linz, Austria who is no doubt rowing on the Danube. They seem to be a family entirely dedicated (see note) to messing about in boats. *Just a card hoping you are in the Pink! I'm going to Southend on Monday night with P King on his motorbike. We've got Mr Tom at work for us...* 28m

July 28th.   From the SS Borda already in Capetown en route for the antipodes, Violet, a reluctant emigrée no doubt on an assisted passage writes to Winnie Tynan in Sheffield, *Voici a P.C. of the wretched little ship which is carrying me much against my will to Australia with my family... write to me when I can send you a definite address. I hope that you are still happy at your work & working your way to the top of the ladder. You are very lucky & I wish I were still in Surrey St.* 28n

October 1st.   Sophia & Frederica have been to the fair at Danbury, Connecticut and had themselves photographed. They send the result to Ella Tubessing at the Verona Chemical Works, North Newark, NJ, *Here we are at the fair - you don't know what you missed not coming to Kate's yesterday. Will meet you some night soon in N.Y.* Which two of the featured women are the writers strolling through this nice travelling small-town fair in their finery? 28o

"HOW'S THE NEW CAR SUIT YOU?"
"NOT BAD—BUT IT'S A BIT TIGHT UNDER THE ARMPITS!"

1334. "Curley" A Survivor of the Custer Battle.

28a. Ballerini & Fratini. Florence 1229. Photo: Petitti, Rome

28b. Publisher unknown. L176

28c. "Phostint" Detroit Publishing Co. IIIXX. 71587
Photo: NY Edison Co

28d. HB Ltd (Hutson Bros) No 3241. Artist: unknown

28e. Levy et Neurdein Reunis. 229

July 6th.   Amy & Freddie in Blackpool to George Fenten in Manchester, *Just been to the high diving on Central Pier. We are crowded out here. Burnley Wakes. Bought Dispatch see Harold has an advert in. Seen nothing of the Greenwoods. Suppose Harold has spent up. Don't be late on Monday. She is strict now. Just been to the big circus it's a treat.* The new baby cars have replaced the Model T as a source of humour.   28p

October 11th.   From Missoula, Montana to Master Jack Green in St Louis, Mo. *I have seen the battlefields where this Indian fought - there are other Indians around but now they all drive Fords instead of carrying tomahawks. Aunt D.* Alas, Aunt D would not have seen Curley, the Crow scout, who died in 1923 and was buried in the Custer cemetery 'the only Indian thus honoured', says the blurb.   28q

28f. M Bastow No 1 (Drighlington)

28g. Publisher unknown

28h. Judges Ltd, Hastings 7738

28i. QSL card, Generic type

28j. LL Levy Fils & Cie 120

28k. Unico Ltd USA

28l. Imperial Airways Ltd. Croydon. 1A/C/59

28m. Photocrom Ltd, Tunbridge Wells 56922. The message continues *Ghen and myself slept out in Laurie's punt last night. We've been bathing at 6.0 every morning... we cooked our own bacon this morning burnt the rashers. Dad has sold Swaby's Punt for twenty five pounds. We've got the old Queen of Hearts back! I think Collets sculling for England at Amsterdam. Dad has just come back from giving the Jap sculler a lesson.*

28n. Publisher unknown, Danbury

28o. P&O Ltd. Artist unknown

28p. HB Ltd (Hutson Bros) No 3436 Artist unknown

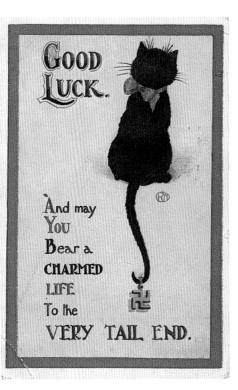

GOOD LUCK.

And may You Bear a CHARMED LIFE To the VERY TAIL END.

June 22nd.   CL to Miss Ross in East Dulwich, *If you are out of employment I can offer you about two weeks work please let me know by return.* The Edison Bell works in Peckham, via the Band of the Irish Guards, have a winner on their hands with The Dawn of Victory whose 78rpm record is surrounded by the entire panoply of victorious allied iconography.   28r

June 10th.   From DH in Henley to Mr Arlett (as in 28m) in Austria. *It was very nice of you to keep your promise of sending me a card... I must now apologise for not believing you, But at first I did think you were kidding me. Well I have not been to a dance yet in Henley so must keep you to your promise.* The innocent Good Luck swastika would have an entirely different meaning when it reached Austria.   28s

28q. JL Robbins Co. Spokane, Washington

28r. Edison Bell Ltd. Artist ? (signature unclear) Thomas Edison was awarded the Congressional Medal in 1928 for his life's work.

28s. Regent Series. Regent Pub. Co. Artist: RH (Raven Hill ?)

IA/C/61 IMPERIAL AIRWAYS PASSENGER AEROPLANE; SILVER WING DE LUXE

June 21st.   Mr Sherwood, a passenger, writes aboard the aeroplane to his wife in Providence, RI. and posts the card when he arrives in Paris. *Great trip! Half way to Paris - eating a bit of lunch!* The London/Paris route became a scheduled service in 1927 (see 28l for another passenger report). Here, presumably at Croydon airport, stands City of Birmingham, one of the Armstrong-Whitworth Argosy fleet, its clean profile enhanced by the functional Art-Deco livery with fine lettering.   29a

August 26th.   Ma writes to Florence Gilmore in Providence, Lynn, Mass., *Will start home tomorrow, Hope you are O.K. Eat!.* Moses King's futuristic fantasy of New York, The City of Skyscrapers, actually dates from 1915 as can be judged from the aeroplanes in the sky which, paradoxically, have become the most old-fashioned looking things to be seen.   29b

September 25th.   From Dolly to Annie in Copnor, *I shall not be around on Thursday as (R Barry) is coming to tea.* This artist's impression of Piccadilly Circus focuses on the new County Fire Office (built in 1927) which is now the Sun Alliance building. The card has the raised impasto surface typical of Tuck's superior 'Oilettes'.   29c

June 3rd.   *Edinbough, Dear Betty. Don't laugh at my typeing... We did not see the bridge quite like this?,%.* Wobbly images occur early on in the history of the postcard starting perhaps with the Eiffel Tower. James writing to Betty Barnard in Sutton is one of the rare senders of such a card who, in his eccentrically typed message, fails to mention drinking.   29d

August 14th.   To Mrs Sutton in Woodbridge, from her son motoring in Scotland, *arrived here yesterday about 6.0pm after a very good run, although it rained all the way.* Much glum information is conveyed, *Carlisle Cathedral... much more interesting on the inside than the outside suggests.* This Scottish floral clock cunningly hides the year's last digit so that it can be used through the decade. (see 49l)   29e

July 3rd. From W F Bewley in Dublin to H H Prince in Pickering ...*just to tell you the good news that I have passed my exam. of course the papers were much easier than the London matric but there were some tricky bits.* Ireland was a soft second chance for those who failed their exams in England. The Ardnacrusha scheme was completed in 1929 and supported almost the entire electricity needs of the Republic.   29f

March 2nd.   To Miss Rooke in East Grinstead, *I can't think what part of Lord St this is. We had a lovely motor ride on Sunday to Rhyl it was bright sunshine there we took our lunch and ate it on the shore. Heaps & heaps of love. D.* An up to date view judging by the women's outfits. Liverpool bustles in the sun. Not too much traffic save the 15 tram. People seem to stroll freely in the road.   29g

October 28th.   D in Burnley to Mr H Fophurn in Stockport, *Have you any chaps like this at your place... Hope work has gone all right and that you did not forget to turn out. 6 hours more pay this week.* The word Tackler does not appear in the dictionary and this genre study of sleeping labour hardly explains what he does. The spanner is also nicely posed.   29h

September 11th.   Doll & Wall in Birmingham send their *Sincere Birthday wishes and congratulations,* on the 21st birthday of Miss Whittaker in Small Heath, choosing the fashionable photomontage kind of greeting card. The colour is crude but effective and even if its application is rather slapdash who can resist a pair of powder-blue collared turtle doves?   29i

R. A. F. MEMORIAL, EMBANKMENT, LONDON.   44

August 18th.   Tops in Kensington to Miss Fox in Witney on a finely composed view of the RAF monument erected in 1923, *Have had lots of bus rides. Haven't I just enjoyed 'em... saw my first talking picture on Fri.* Perhaps Tops saw the first real talkie, The Lights of New York (1928). They were still a novelty with an uncertain future: Chaplin thought them a fad.   29j

Greta Garbo

3531/2   Foreign

September 19th.   Kathy in Leeds to Bess Oldham in Blackpool *Isn't this a beauty? You are having a grand time. I think you are very naughty going out with that young man... I do wish I was with you. Your ever loving friend.* Garbo is now twenty four years old, the star of The Kiss (MGM's last silent picture). This card alone explains what all the fuss was about.   29k

September 13th.   *My dears. In haste. Shall be with you Friday night, trying to catch the 7.30 from W'loo. Can only get a week this year so shall have to hustle a bit to get in some good fishing. xx John.* Is John, who writes to Mrs Hanks in New Milton, one of the gents who stand proprietorially outside this well stocked London tobacconists?   29l

"You vote as I vote or I'll know the reason why!"

July 7th.   RW in Bishop's Castle to Miss Smith in Church Street, *The picture on the other side does not apply to you on polling day but when you are married it will give you an idea how to go on. Have had a topping time.* The 1931 election with its so-called Flapper Vote involved women under 30 for the first time. This helped swing the result towards Labour.   29m

December 27th.   An odd card for WV in Bristol to use for wishing Mr & Mrs Kent a Happy New Year. It shows the moment earlier in the year when Mussolini signed the Lateran treaty giving sovereignty to the Vatican. Mussolini assumed dictatorial powers in Italy in 1925. Here Il Duce gets to keep the golden pen presented for the occasion by Pius XI.   29n

Constable: "What's your name?"
She: "Doris, what's yours?"

September 4th.   Gladys writes to her parents in Gainsborough, *Arrived alright safely. M & I went to Scunthorpe this afternoon it is a nice place. Margaret Aunt & Uncle are ever so nice x.* Both flapper and policeman are beautifully characterised by Reg Maurice against an atmospheric five minute watercolour land and cloudscape.   29o

CIRCULAR TOUR

PROMENADE

S.O. 12-11   ON THE CIRCULAR TOUR, BLACKPOOL.

This with its embossed border surrounding an image produced by Rotary, the expert photographic printers, is a typical upmarket card of around 1909. The presence of only horsedrawn traffic (beside tram No 73) would confirm that, as well as the ample presence of Merry Widow hats among the tram's female passengers. It was sent by Mary on the 31st July 1911 to Mrs Joe Adams, Huddersfield, *Dear Sister, it is now nearly all over and we have had a happy time Alice say yours is the right sort of pies we can join at them when we get back.* One guesses that Mary has come to the end of her Wakes Week. The card was published by the Corona Publishing Co in Blackpool itself, who seem to have gone out of business towards the end of the First World War. The anonymous photographer (rarely credited in such cards) has chosen a moment in a bright day when his scene is animated by the presence of a stylish horse carriage taking two elderly ladies out for a ride. In the distance a milk cart plods in the opposite direction.   29p

On the Circular Tour, Blackpool, by Night.

CIRCULAR TOUR

August 29th 1929.   The circular tour continues: a haunting crepuscular moment when tram overtakes carriage once again and the condemned milkman delivers his nocturnal churns. Sent by Jewitt to Mr & Mrs Baxter in Barnsley, *Dear Friends. Having a Jolly time & good weather, have met Mr & Mrs G.H.P., Proctors family are at the same lodge George Rust also Mr & Mrs Whitwell, Mr & Mrs Smith, The Miss Shepherd. This is really Barnsley atmosphere, wish you were here.* Evidently it is Barnsley's Wakes Week as it was Huddersfield's above. This card is produced in the Advance Series by an unknown publisher who took over the plates from the Corona Company. A lot of handwork has gone into the transformation of day into night. Apart from the different cropping of the photo to lose its original title and gain space above for the new one, the tram has lost its upside down Promenade notice and its number but has gained an immensely powerful front light. The eerie tinting is dominated by the poisonous green of the trees (and the rosy dress given to one privileged passenger). The daylight shadows still remain but the sky, complete with veiled moon, has become more excited. Was this the view's last purchase and last post to bring the infernal circuit to an end?   29q

29a. Imperial Airways Ltd. Croydon Aerodrome

29b. Tuck Oilform Artist: Chesley B ?

29c. Moses King, NY 19603

29d. Davidson's Silver Tone Series

29e. Publisher unknown. Artist unknown. PM: Exhibition Newcastle

29f. Publisher unknown. PM: Buy Irish Goods

29g. Pelham Real Photo Series (Boots) 5291

29h. Publisher unknown

29i. Rotary Photo 734734.T.R.24-12 Poem: Syd

29j. Publisher unknown

29k. Metro Goldwyn Mayer 3531/2

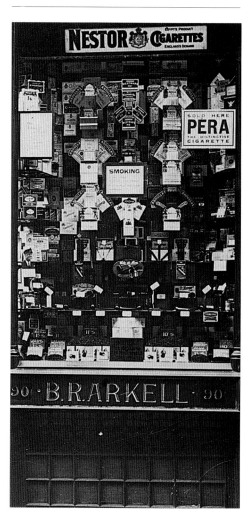

NESTOR CIGARETTES

PERA
SOLD HERE
THE DISTINCTIVE CIGARETTE

SMOKING

B.R.ARKELL

At the far left of the window just below the middle can be seen the postcard met in 1927 of the Prince of Wales enjoying a cigarette. His grandfather appears on packets of King Edward cigars (as he still does). see 27n.

29l. Star photographic Co, London SE1

29m. Inter Art Co. Comique series. Artist: unknown

29n. Polo G Felice, Roma

29o. Regent Publishing Co No 4764. Artist: Reg Maurice

»FEMINA« Das Ballhaus Berlins   HAUPTSAAL

May 16th.   A scene set for any amoral tale of Berlin's Cabaret years. The couple inhabit one of the 'postillons d'amour with curtains' advertised on the back of the card (as is table to table telephone). The mood is sophisticated, liberated, modern, everything that makes Frank write *My dearest Eva, Come to Berlin for a proper holiday. you cannot find the Same in England. Amusement, weather, sights & all are good & I can act as guide.* Was Eva (in Hounslow) tempted? Did she enter the novel whose opening lines this message could so convincingly supply?   30a

June. ? th   Nellie tells Mrs Altham of Langho, Blackburn, *having a good time a terrible storm yesterday I was at the races in Ascot, O. What a sight but the storm came on and made a mess of things feeling A.1.* Eros is absent (see 33B). Cole Porter's Wake up and Dream at the Pavilion tells us we are in 1929.   30b

January 15th.   Aerial views of cities became popular in the twenties and this particular viewpoint continued to be used for the drama of the jutting forest of buildings it affords. Mrs Cutts writes from Grand Central Station to Miss Alice Mitchell in Newmarket NH, Lock Box 29.   She, Elmer & Marion are having a nice time.   30c

R101 THE WORLD'S LARGEST AIRSHIP
OVER LONDON.

"I'm your little Mickey Mouse!"

IMPERIAL AIRWAYS TRIPLE ENGINED AIR LINER OVER
THE LONDON TERMINAL AERODROME.   G 416

April 15th.   Mum to N in Brighton *Auntie has gone off quite peacefully to N.Walsham - Glad you were gone yesterday!!! Now having lunch with Auntie: She has licked your stamps on!* Here is the R101 on her maiden flight in 1919 with 52 passengers on board eating a 4 course meal. In 1939 it crossed the Atlantic in 77 hours but in October crashed and exploded in France ending Britain's airship plans.   30d

March 3rd.   John sends birthday greetings to Master Arthur Legge in Weymouth. A Mickey Mouse card was a novelty in 1930: he had only been in existence since November 1928 when, in Steamboat Willie, he made his cinema debut. As the first cartoon star of the talking film he stayed, with his Silly Symphony friends, at the top for decades. The pianist is Minnie Mouse and the drawing is early Disney at its most vital.   30e

October 2nd.   Boy writes to the rest of the Mason family in Cheltenham, *I am A1. Am just off to Paris with Olly.* He is at Croydon's new aerodrome (the airport of London for years to come) about to catch the Imperial Airways Flight (return fare £8). The newly named Air-Liners with their greater power opened routes to the Empire. There were many stops along the way. A flight to Karachi would take almost a week.   30f

FROM A PORTRAIT BY
MARCUS ADAMS   H.R.H. PRINCESS ELIZABETH

THE FLAPPER VOTE IS ALL THE RAGE.
WE'LL SOON BE VOTING AT MY AGE!

WORK LIKE X
HELL AN   X
BE MERRY IX

November 26th.   From Thornton Heath to S G West in Lisbon *...two weeks at Margate... This photograph was snapped last Saturday morning & I thought you would like and up-to-date one of your godson from your god-father Rodney.* The seaside photographer is glad of a client in October on a windswept prom. A characterful couple to end his season with no one else in sight. 30g

August 22nd.   To Mrs Gweneth Hutchings in Cantal (Auvergne) an unnamed correspondent writes with hot news on a Royal birth. *A little sister arrived on Thursday August 21st the birthday of the youngest son of Princess Mary. Elizabeth is 4 1/2 years.* The sister is Princess Margaret. Elizabeth, captured here in a sturdy pose by Marcus Adams, is the future queen. 30h

August 24th.   Chickie & Roy in Gloucester send love to Auntie Beat & Uncle Reg Crome in Cheddar. *We are having a nice time... Tell Uncle Reg to read the voting card on the other side.* The voting card contains an old chestnut, Work Like Helen B. Merry, slightly misunderstood. Dora Dean's tiny flapper has, like the Princess, the knock-kneed look of all infant girls. 30i

A. Gauthier, phot.
SAINT-CLAUDE - Jura (France)

March 17th.   Bobby to N Levison in London NW. Verguet Frères are evidently major pipe manufacturers with factories in Paris and London. *Things are not too bad. I'm getting on all right with the work & 'the boys'. Both S & P are very nice & jolly & very amusing. I have laughed more here than any other place. Have got another rattletrap to replace the baby something that goes quicker but rattles even more.*   30j

160 GRAUMAN'S CHINESE THEATRE, HOLLYWOOD, CALIFORNIA

June 9th.   To Mrs Gerber in Syracuse NY from Myra in Los Angeles, *Been shopping this a.m. and to see Norma Shearer in the Divorcee. Then to dinner tonite & to see Brothers. Do you wonder I find little time for letters.* Sid Grauman's famous Chinese Theatre on Hollywood Boulevard opened in 1927 (see 27q). The Divorcee was premièred here this year and Norma Shearer signed the famous pavement.   30k

ENSEMBLE, THE HOLLYWOOD RESTAURANT, 1600 BROADWAY AT 48TH ST., NEW YORK CITY

April 9th.   To Frank G Steinitz in Morwich, Conn.   Nelson & Jimmy send *Best Regards to the best baritone in the country.* The caption on the back says of this new restaurant 'At Last American Atmosphere and American Management on Broadway'. Presumably these scantily dressed girls (whose mothers scarcely dared show more than an ankle at their age) provided the American floor-show.   30l

6349 SCENES et TYPES — La Sieste LL

July 1st.   Bobby in Marseilles to Fred Austin in Hammersmith, *How about it. Very hot here Kennels very well served in this town...* Both Picasso and Matisse amassed postcards and used them in their work. Matisse fell in love with this type of odalisque in Morocco and dressed his models in the style, using decorative motifs as LL has done here. Though created for the erotic market this has its own grandeur.   30m

No one in the world
but you..

Who's the one who
shared my sadness?
No one in the world but you.
Who's the one who
brought me gladness?
No one in the world
but you.

RALPH GRAVES & DOLORES COSTELLO
(WARNER BROS. STARS)

May 1st.   To Miss N Power in Walsall from her parents in Rugby, *This is another nice day. Did you say Rabbits?.* Do people still say Rabbits on the first of the month? Here two stars are brought together for a romantic greeting card. Ralph Graves turned to production soon after talkies came in. Dolores Costello's quiet career reached its height as the female lead of Orson Welles' The Magnificent Ambersons. This scene belongs to studio publicity: Dolores Costello married co-star John Barrymore.   30n

September 7th.   Duke writes to Petra Jacobsen in New York, *I just hate this spot. Especially on a sunny autumn afternoon. I now know why they say 'Good Americans when they die go to Paris'. Five more days of this and then London. I detest it all.* Yvon (Pierre Petit) on the other hand loved the city and made his mark as a photographer/publisher with his Paris En Flanant. As LL and ND faded in the thirties Yvon became the preeminent postcard rhapsodist of the French scene.   30o

EDEN HOTEL   PAVILLON

November 21st.   Sydney Scott writes from Berlin SW to his parents in London NW2. *Thanks for your letter of Friday evening. Klein tells me he heard Bruegge has been in bed with the 'flu. If you see him ask him why he has never had the decency to write to me. Went to the cinema last night & am going to a big anti-anti-semitism meeting this evening. Leave for Königsberg to-morrow but will be here again Friday. Fond love etc. New address c/o Eden Hotel.* Had Eva (from 30a) come to Berlin would she have found herself at a Souper mit Tanz (as advertised on the back of the card) at the Eden Hotel and, meeting Sydney, have discovered the other side of Berlin's glittering coin of pleasure at the meeting against anti-Semitism and seen the event perhaps broken up by brownshirted thugs?   30p

30a. Albert Lüdtke for Femina Berlin SW61

30b. Publisher unknown No 88

30c. MP & Co no 59

30d. Wildt & Kray, London

30e. Woolstone Bros. Mickey Mouse Films/Ideal Films. with permission.

With a studio like Disney's which was already employing talented artists to draw the individual frames of his cartoons (every minute of which called for nearly 1500 images) it is impossible to attribute the designs of individual cards. The invention is always his and in such early productions as this one can see the taut vitality of his original creation. Thus Disney is here more the artist than the mere trademark.

30f. Imperial Airways G416

30g. Sunbeam Photos Ltd, Margate

30h. Raphael Tuck Royal Portrait Series No 3969B Photo: Marcus Adams

30i. Kiddies Series No 1056. Artist: Dora Dean

30j. A Gauthier (phot.) France

30k. Western Publishing & Novelty Co. Los Angeles 160/115424

30l. Publisher unknown (Ensemble Restaurant) M 1469

30m. Levy & Neurdein Reunis 6349

30n. Max Kracke. London Talkie Song Series 33

30o. Yvon. Paris en Flanant 58

30p. Eden Hotel Artist: Hans Levi. PM slogan: Werdet Rundfunkteilnehmer (Be a radio listener)

30q. HB, Hutson Bros. No 3289 Artist: Frank Gould

30r. Publisher unknown, Barcelona

IT'S AWFUL HAVING TO DO THIS
TO KEEP MY FAT DOWN.

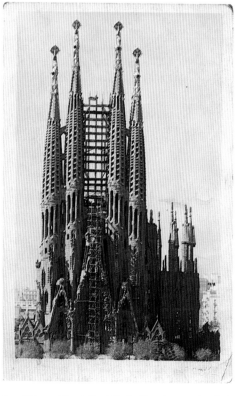

JUST ARRIVED.

July 25th.   Edith in Weston-Super-Mare to Miss Winter in Mangotsfield, *we are having a good time in spite of the wintry weather. I'm sorry that I shall not be able to fix up anything at the office before the holidays. The old B's are quite OK!!! Best love.* Although this little exerciser is tied to the spot with her cumbersome valve radio she is in every other respect pioneering the Musical Aerobics of sixty years later.   30q

Dec 21st.   Miguel Montello in Barcelona sends *Best wishes to you all during the Christmas Season and throughout the New Year.* This view of Gaudi's famous church of the Sagrada Familia shows it still under construction four years after the architect's death in a tram accident in 1936. Work on it has gone on in fits and starts ever since, and even in its never-to-be-completed state it is one of the architectural wonders of the century.   30r

August 22nd.   Sadie Arnowitz writes to her husband Israel from the convalescent home in Clacton *My dear Husband, You haven't done what I told you I am absolute starving for a bit of fruit. I had not fruit all the time I'm expecting you down on Sunday with Eva have a clean shave, put on your grey suit & shine your shoes up & put on a nice tie make yourself tidy dress up Eva smart so don't forget Israel, I suppose you know how to come here won't you you asked by the gate for Mrs Arnowitz. I had a letter from Millie her baby is getting better. You will enjoy yourself here.*   30s

30s. Jinky Series No 9 Artist: H B White

118 MT. RUSHMORE NATIONAL MEMORIAL.

GEORGE WASHINGTON, FIRST OF FOUR FIGURES TO BE CARVED. STATE PARK, BLACK HILLS, S. D.   OA4088

August 22nd.   Flo in Rapid City, S Dakota to Miss Esther Albrecht in Freeport, Illinois, *What did you and Martha decide to do? Did you go East? We surely enjoyed California, Yosemite and Yellowstone... there is only two weeks left for us. It doesn't seem possible does it?* Flo and her husband have made the grand tour of National Parks to arrive at Black Hills where Gutzon Borglum has been busy since 1927 with drills, dynamite and chisels on the epic portraits of Lincoln, Jefferson, Theodore Roosevelt and, here seen emerging from the outcrop, Washington. Not since Rameses II had rulers been so memorialised and none before that had been democratically elected. Borglum did not live to see the monument completed (his son Lincoln took over the task towards the end). It was opened to the public in 1941 (see 41l).   31a

BOVRIL
SMOKE
MURATTIS SCHWEPPES
ARISTON GINGER ALE
MONICO

PICCADILLY CIRCUS LOOKING UP SHAFTESBURY AVENUE. LONDON

August 31st.   Eileen to Arthur Gillingham in Okeford Fitzpaine, Dorset, *Having a good look-round up here arthur lot more people & traffic than Okeford.* Afgar at the Pavilion ran for 300 performances in 1919 starring Alice Delysia. In 1919 there were no systematic rules for traffic, which could proceed in any direction.   31b

MANHATTAN ISLAND. N. Y. C.   © W M. FRANGE

July 3rd.   MHR has joined ship on Staten Island and writes, rather in the style of a 30's detective thriller (see notes) to Jessie Fraser in Roxbury, Massachusetts. Frange, the dedicated photographer of the NY skyline chooses his spot on Governor's Island (see 35c etc.) from which to watch the city grow and grow.   31c

CRYSTAL PALACE. FROM S.E.

March 4th.   Bell in Cranleigh to her aunt in Haslemere, about various illnesses, ending *I seem to have lived through months since a fortnight ago today: it was so dreadful to get ill so suddenly away from home but... it was wonderful how God timed every detail for us & every one was so good & kind...* A late glimpse of the majestic 1851 Crystal Palace (destroyed by fire in 1936) in South London.   31d

September 21st.   Artie to Mrs Velnke in Blue Island, Illinois, *Dear Min & All. We sure had a nice trip here. We got to Elsie & Phil too. They have a nice apt. out 7 mile from the Capitol...* Hoover was an unlucky President. The Wall Street Crash of 1929 and the resulting Great Depression made him the driver of a runaway train. His optimistic words predicting better times began to sound hollow by this his second year.   31e

August 11th.   Florrie to Miss Gardiner in Bristol, *I was so pleased to receive yours & Queenies' cards from Italy... It's perfect here, wonderful scenery, bathing, sunshine Charlie Chaplin & Winston Churchill are both here so you see we are in good company...* Evidently the bread and butter card of Jugand the Biarritz publisher/photographer who does not hesitate to call it an 'etude artistique'.   31f

VICKERS SUPERMARINE S.6.B. (ROLLS ROYCE). BUILT FOR 1931 RACE. "FLIGHT" COPYRIGHT PHOTO

September 11th.   Betty in Gosport sends a fine card to Frank Collins in Woking, *I thought you would like this as it is flying this year. I hope you had a nice time at Switzerland last week. Love.* Not only were the Supermarine Swifts the most graceful of all aircraft but they won the worlds fastest air-race, the Schneider Trophy, more than once. Stanforth exceeded 400 mph in the 1931 race in this plane.   31g

FILLING STATION AT OAK PARK. ROANOKE, IND.

June 4th.   Mildred in Roanoke to Mr & Mrs Walter Jones in Wellsboro, Penna, *Dear Mother & all:- How are you feeling? We are quite tired but having a good time. Our Cottage is right behind the filling station on this card...* This Sinclair gasoline station and its hand pumps was typical of every village with its adverts for Camp and Coca Cola. To have a cottage behind its modern counterpart on Route 24 with bright lights and thundering trucks would not be much fun.   31h

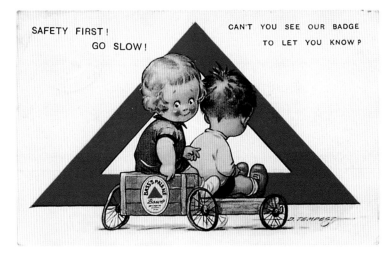

December 18th.   From Dob in Walton-on-Thames to Miss F Elliot in Farnborough, *...not going to London till after Xmas... I am stopping in Kingston in the morning and playing hockey for Walton against Weybridge in the afternoon. Cheerio see you soon...* At the beginning of the thirties crossings, traffic lights, street markings etc were in an experimental stage and the warning red triangle was the beginning of rationalisation. Tempest's children use the Bass label made famous by Manet.   31i

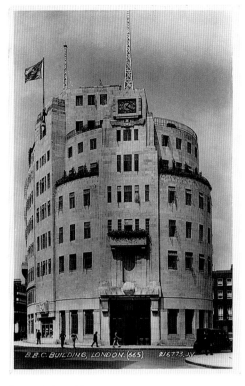

August 2nd.   M in Hampstead to Mrs Beaumont in Liverpool ...*if not convenient tea together... ask Lydia to order the meat to come at 5 o'clock.* Broadcasting house is here not quite finished since it lacks Eric Gill's statues of Prospero and Ariel which were installed by the opening in May 1932. In the war it was painted battleship grey as camouflage.   31j

April 7th.   TWB writes locally in Bowne, Lincs to Mr & Mrs James, *I heard you have just latly get married. I hope you are making marryed life happy from your old pal.* Alum Hughes also designed cards under the name of Alda Hughes. Here she/he depicts a typical interior of the period with an up to the minute dressing table.   31k

March 18th.   To Master William Storer in Measham from Aunts & Uncles in Derry, *Bought at Croydon after Uncle had been in the air. Many Happy Returns. What time is it by the watches.* Amy Johnson in 1930 became the first woman to fly from England to Australia. This year saw her record England/Tokyo flight and a popular song named after her.   31l

August 31st.   A Nannie in Weston-Super-Mare to Edith in Clevedon. *I take Peter & Pat in the park every morn I am in the park now. I went out for a walk Sat night alone. nobody much about. I wanted to go out last night and she said what again she said I will come with I expect you want to see someone I said I don't I don't mind if I don't go out so we did not go out as it began to rain please bring on snaps Wed I want to see you.* 31m

April 16th.   Ona to Miss Ede in Cardiff, *We have just discovered the elections have taken place and that the country is now a Republic. The newspapers were all sold out before we could get one today but otherwise you could not discover that anything had happened at all and the district (Catalonia) was always said to be the most interested in Politics too!* As Ona writes the Spanish King is on his way to exile in London.   31n

December 20th.   From Prague Leslie sends *all best wishes of the season* to George Strouthers in Deal, *this is a portrait of Thomas Masaryk first President of the Czechoslovak Republic.* Masaryk was the architect of Czech independence. While he was a lecturer at London University in 1916 he was sentenced to death. By 1918 he was President and would be reelected until old age forced him to retire in 1934.   31o

**Eine Rheinfahrt
im Luftschiff L Z 127 „Graf Zeppelin"**

1 Burg Rheinfels - St. Goar, 2 Burg Rheinfels, 3 St. Goarshausen,
4 Burg Katz, 5 Loreley - Felsen, 6. Pfalz, 7 Ruine Schönburg

1931 MESSAGES·NOTES·PARTICULARS

31a. Luftverkehr Strähle/A Weber & Co, Stuttgart 79825/5.5.136. DGRM 1077233

31b. Publisher unknown. L180

31c.   10.30am. On board, in _grey_. Not uncomfortable against north wind of 7th Ave canyon - coolish but humidity fairly high. Night on 18th Floor of Gov. Clinton Hotel - (four broadcasts out of a hole in the wall to choose from.) Came across in taxi - first time in Holland Tunnel - much easier. Dock in a jam - 300 in Tourist Class + cabin passengers - Room 31 looks familiar from '23. Murky overhead - May be fog outside.

New York's Best Views. publ. Wm. Frange NY. Made in France

31d. Photochrom Co Celesque Series No 47644

31e. Washington News company. Tichnor 129914

31f. I Jugand éditeur, Biarritz No 64

31g. M & Co (Misch & Co) Flight photo

31h. Wayne Novelty & publ. Co. Ft Wayne, Ind. 123787

31i. Bamforth. Tempest Kiddy Series No 349

31j. Valentine's. 665. 216773JV

31k. Regent Publishing Co. No 1010

31l. Tuck's Real Photographic Postcard No 3867

31m. HB (Hutson Bros) Ltd. No 3460. Artist unknown

31n. Huccograbado. Mumbrié Barcelona No 25

31o. Publisher unknown. Czechoslovakia

31p. A Weber, Stuttgart 79825/55.136

31q. Publisher unknown (E Franch Collection)

31r. Edition Giletta, Nice RC Nice 290

September 9th. _Dear Ma & Pa... It's been a glorious journey through valleys and castles_ writes Rosie at the end of her airship cruise down the Rhine. The Graf Zeppelin LZ127 was a huge success having circumnavigated the world (in 21 days) two years before. Despite the R101 disaster [see 29d] Germany still favoured the airship for international travel. Public confidence was finally ended by the explosion of the Hindenberg in 1937. Meanwhile this novelty card by means of its wheel changes the views of the Rhine from what otherwise looks like a spacious bourgeois interior. 31p

August 4th.   Joan & Eric from Streatham tell their Auntie Miss Coughty in New Cross _Mummy says come to dinner on Monday & stay the night if you like. Thank you for our cards._ The photographer seems to have halted the traffic, including window cleaner and cart, to capture the stately 24 tram somewhere in South East London.   31q

November 9th.   G R Bennett in Sloane Sq. London, receives a card from Melise in Monte Carlo, _These fair ladies are returning with me so I hope you will like them._ Is this a mural in the Thermal Baths? The Joy Of Water may be Gallelli's masterpiece. The figure at bottom right is in a pose of particular abandon. But it's art, so still safe.   31r

July 7th.   From Battersea, London SW, to Miss D Finch in Bridgnorth, *Love my hank & it's just my colour, you got it OK thanks ever so much. Write you more news from France. ever so busy now. Lizzie will have given you the doings & explain about the frock. France address on Mam's card. Best love Aunty.* Perhaps Aunty has been in Selfridges to buy clothes for her French trip and picked up this promotional card which tells its own story on the back:- 'Gloria, the World Famous Mannequin in the Bedroom Scene from Selfridge's "Golden Staircase" Mannequin Parade.' The current spate of hunger marches and riots against mass unemployment does not seem quite to have reached the world of Gloria's silk and satin dream.   32a

March 30th.   Gertrude writes to Nora in Ainsdale, *We are having a lovely time here. We are going to see the play The Desert Song tonight. Have you seen the picture.* This is Piccadilly Circus in 1932 itself. The white lines bottom right are the beginnings of direction markings. The Desert Song was a Romberg/Hammerstein musical.   32b

July 17th.   To Miss J Wilder Gannon in Worcester, Mass., *Ma Ma and I have been down in the big city all day and am a little tired. Well Joan I will say goodbye for now. Dady.* For a few months in 1930 the Chrysler building was the tallest in the world but the Empire State Building soon loomed over it as it does here.   32c

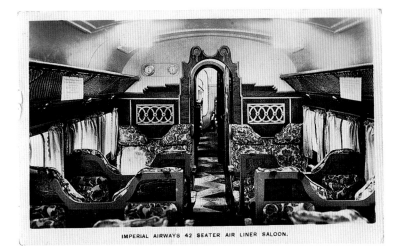

October 25th.   Lizzie in Brighton to Mrs Bloxham in Campden, Glos., *Thank you very much for the nice parcel, the Funeral is on Thursday we shall be able to tell you all about it on Saturday.* The two minutes Armistice Day silence in memory of the fallen, died out as a national ritual but, in the nineties, has been revived though not to the extent seen here in 1931. Is this a contender for the most peopled card?   32d

November 7th.   Aunties could be relied on to send young boys interesting pictures of aeroplanes and John Widdicombe's aunt is no exception. From Cheam she writes to him in Nottingham, *Auntie promised to send you a photo of the inside of an aeroplane... Doesn't it look comfortable.* Indeed it does and nothing like what one now sees on entering a plane. But this is designed for a week of luxury travel.   32e

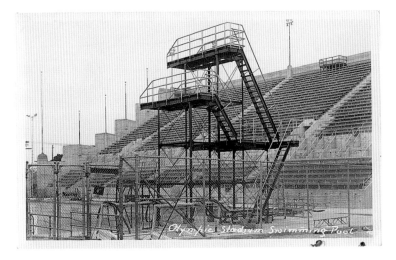

August 13th.   Win in Clapham tells Cliff in Eastbourne that she arrived safely, *The train was only a few minutes late as we stopped at Clapham Junction this time... quite a strong breeze over the common.* This Clapham scene changed little from when I was born there until well into the seventies and is still quite recognisable. Even the people look much as they did in the forties before men stopped wearing hats.   32f

M sends Marie Collins in Seattle a picture of the pool for the 1932 Olympics, the last until 1948 that would not be sullied by political extremism (as in 1936) or merely cancelled like the Tokyo Olympics of 1940. Here, in LA, against the delicate tracery of the diving boards the Japanese dominated the men's swimming events though the host country was finally first in the overall medals.   32g

August 27th.   Rick to Kath in Acton, *Having a great time down here ... Everybody very friendly & all muck in. Cheerio.* Until Billy Butlin expanded the idea later on in the decade into self contained villages the Holiday Camp was little more than a group of chalets, a club-house and a shop. Rick seems to be enjoying himself as is the relaxed group of girls on the right (see note).   32h

March 19th.   Bunnie to Kingsbury Houghton in West Roxbury, Mass, *went to a dance the other night sorry you weren't with us. Stopped at Bol (?) Tower at about one o' clock enjoyed it. We are now at Orlando. Rec'd all nice letters also car decorations.* On many counts this is the last kind of card that would now be posted from Orlando yet its intervals of light and dark have a quiet music.   32i

October 17th.   Master B Leonard in Oxton gets a postcard from Lodz, *This is the chimpanzee I saw yesterday in the zoo at Berlin. He was quite as good as you on your tricycle. He also had a bell which he kept on ringing to make the others get out of the way. Lots of love, Daddy.* At least the chimp is not wearing a funny outfit. The doctored floor makes him look strangely independent of humans.   32j

February 8th.   KVP in Bern to Miss Ursula Radford in Exeter, *Does Wynne Tighe still keep a toothbrush machine? The children's are wearing out and they do like having their name on them; so I wonder if you could send one for each of them... we were able to get the small bears after all, you see.* Like the Tower of London ravens these bears have a protective role in the folklore of Bern and are not in a zoo.   32k

August 26th.   Irene in Diss to Mr Brockman in Ramsgate, *Dear Dolly, The baby rabbit had been touched by the stoat so we let it loose because it was mad. Timmy found it and killed it. We are having chickens for dinner on Sunday. We made 190 egg boxes with Gloria & Rhona.* The wireless now circled the world and a forest of assorted aerials was becoming part of the new townscape.   32l

September 7th.   Mr Holland is on tour trying out his new Riley and writes from here to Mr Pollard at the Coventry works, *My green tourer is taking us around Scotland very well indeed. The high rad & bonnet look very fine but are a great nuisance when topping a steep hill or bridge - I can't see which way the road goes. I find 2nd to 3rd very slow and difficult.* A restrained message and an idyllic view.   32m

June 23rd.   To Margaret Autcliff in Newport IOW from Mansfield, *I thought you might like your maypole so here you are. i should like to be with you to make some sand pies & find lots of shells for the rockery. Grandad & i went a motor-ride on Sunday Night instead of going to Church & we didn't have any wine. just fancey that... Best love from Daddy Billie.* Did anyone ever, except schoolchildren dressed as Thomas Hardy rustics, really dance round a maypole?   32n

May 19th.   Edie in Colwyn Bay to Ethel Dennison in Bradford, *...it is now showery today. I can't say what time I get home but don't wait in if you're going anywhere just leave the key at Mr Taylors shall I try to bring anything from town as I come through let me know...* Science has yet to explain the alchemy of fish and chips and salt and vinegar and paper and seaside night air or why the experiment cannot be reproduced with other ingredients.   32o

July 24th.   Addie in Watford to the Rutherfords in Glasgow *This is a view of my favourite restaurant when in town. I am usually in here once a week. Most comfortable and charges very moderate.* This opened in the twenties, part of the successful Lyons Corner House chain built up since 1907. One was revived in the 1980's in the Strand but has since closed.   32p

August 26th.   Ethel in Rhyll tells Miss Black in Dundee that the weather is glorious, *Having a great time, this place agrees with me A1. Have done some nice sails & walks.* Just as films were blamed for violence so they were for a decline in spoken English, ironically at the very time when the new blood of Americanisms was most enriching the language.   32q

April 18th.   Lilian to Lilian, the one in Diss the other in Exeter, *I went to Morton on Sunday with Bessie and enjoyed myself very much. Mind you & Percy arnt bowled over. with love from your friend xx.* The character who, as ever, is about to destroy harmony is Richmal Crompton's William, a schoolboy anarch brought to life in the drawings of Thomas Henry. He was a useful corrective to middle class pretension.   32r

August 26th.   G in Newquay writes to Mrs Ramsay in Hitchin, *Been to Helston (Floral Dance not on) Then to the Lizard & Kynance Cove lovely spot Still fine & bright & breezy.* The unknown photographer moves to within an inch of total abstraction. Only the titling gives the viewer any reassurance. Strange how near the complete abstract people's taste would take them as long as they had the handrail of the natural world.   32s

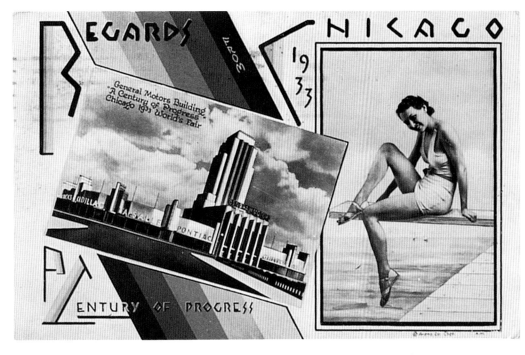

July 20th.   Chicago needed good news. With Roosevelt's 'New Deal' the end of the Great Depression seemed to be in sight and the final death of Prohibition was only months away. With Al Capone in prison & many mobsters dead times were quieter and 22 million people came to this racy fair here announced in suitable style for the world's jazz capital. Even the pose of the bathing belle is as angular as a swastika. Evelyn & Valentine write to the Mellons in Guildford NY., *We went to the stock yards yesterday. You should see them cut ham off & Pork Loins Just 2 cuts for ham and 1 for a loin.*   33a

April 18th. Eros, removed in 1924 for underground works (see 33d), is unconvincingly reinstated on top of a bus by the publisher who, aiming at saleable timelessness, also wipes out the 1930 date from Cochran's Revue. Playbills on two buses for Here Comes The Bride, however, give the game away.   33b

July 23rd.   An evocatively misty quality adds cinematic romance to this standard Jersey view of the Manhattan skyline, now dramatically augmented. Mildred writes a conventional message of greeting to her friend Miss Grace Smith in Altoona, Pennsylvania.   33c

LE GRAND HOTEL — PARIS

September 29th.   LEN in Eltham writes to Miss Brindley in Buxton, *I'm returning on Monday and as usual I shall be pleased to see Derbyshire again.* By 1933 Eros was neither here in its temporary siting surrounded by fellow monuments in the Embankment Gardens nor, as on 33b, on top of a bus. With the completion of works on the underground station it had returned to Piccadilly Circus.   33d

December 9th.   Lillie & Colin McFarlane in Vienna get a postcard from their father, ...*Trusting you are well. CL has arrived with Mrs Lister? and his secretary (my former) of Radius Electric. A complete L——- asylum. Hope to arrive Tuesday.* The Place de l'Opera is replete with swanky cars and the Cafe de la Paix below the Grand Hotel promises all the racy and elegant pleasures of Paris life.   33e

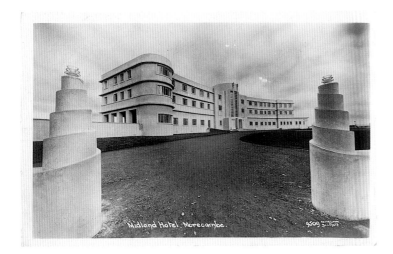

September 13th.   To Miss M R Allinson c/o Mr Smith, The Café, Middleton-in-Teesdale ...*weather is delightful, went to Blackpool by steamer yesterday and it was a treat. Just loafing round Morecambe today and going to see No, No, Nannette tonight. Don't you feel envious. Love AMM.* Oliver Hill's Art Deco fantasy, built in 1930, had probably, three years later, lost this rather bare unfinished look.   33f

November 13th.   A in Morecambe to her mother in Sheffield, *I have read in this morning's paper about Mr Alison killed last night. I did not think he was that age (76). I have been trying to decide on my coat & I've changed it for a blue one, but 5/- more... Tom is putting the difference in... quite plain, fastens up to neck.* Without captions it would look as if one's least favourite weekend guests had arrived.   33g

July 31st.   T Fleet to Ms Baverstock in Basingstoke, *I am haveing a ripping time but the weather is very dull, but I get out all the time I can spare. T Romeo.* Leg Theory and Bodyline refer to the controversy over England's cricket tactics in the Ashes tour of Australia. Fast bowler Larwood intimidated batsmen by bowling at the body (with a leg-side field). The row reached government level.   33h

August 4th.   Mrs Talbot in Bognor to Mr Wright in Didcot, *Hope you are A.1. we are all fine. lovely weather.* Just the message that Billy Butlin did not send home in 1932 from a dismal week in Skegness. This prompted him in 1934 to unite his amusement park to the idea of a holiday camp which would provide A Week's Holiday for a Week's Pay. It looks as if Butlin has also been to see the Cabinet of Dr Caligari.   33i

July 17th.   To Miss Sunny Sandwell in Derby, *You will see where I am posting from. The home of your hero. It's grand here though it's raining hard. Love. Greta.* Sunny's hero had become by now an elder statesman after his loss of the leadership of the Liberals. He lived to see the ending of World War II and the virtual disappearance of his once great party.   33j

August 18th.   Eunice in La Croisie to the Walshaws in Westwood Heath. *This is a delightful spot - The colours are simply marvellous. I think of you each time I go down to the harbour. Brown & blue boats with red orange sails. men in red & blue overalls & blue nets!.* Laurent Nels' photo cannot capture the colour but achieves a generous sweep of action and event.   33k

August 27th.   Betty S to Miss Vivian Brownell on Main Street, Oneonta NY, *I mean what it says on the front you haven't written to me in ages. I am up here for a week with one of my friends from Cohoes (?) We are having a swell time.* American comic cards tend to lack the schooling of their British equivalents but many offer an exuberant zany alternative.   33l

September 2nd.   Gran to Master F Waters in Maidstone, *Many happy returns to my Dear Grandson on his eleventh birthday xxxxx.* Master F is the archetypal middle-class eleven year old in his new secondary school uniform. He would certainly have appreciated the toy, a truck with real lifting mechanism which itself would have appreciated if kept and would be worth more than £100 today.   33m

August 30th.   To Mr & Mrs Phillips in Cheltenham, *am posting this from Port Said but got it in Marseille. Still quite fit & hope you are too. Soon be back to the land & how I hate the idea but never mind... roll on next March.* The Regina bar no longer exists with its jazz (whose coolness is guaranteed by the musician's dark glasses) its champagne and murals 'by such famous Masters as Poggioli and Faust'.   33n

September 5th.   Johnny on holiday in Margate writes in a disciplined schoolboy hand to Mrs Chickley in Bromley, *Thankyou for the cards you sent me. I am having a jolly time down here & I enjoy the Punch & Judy show, also like paddling. there are crowds of people down here.* The slight languor of a couple in which the man always seems dressed for some vague sporting occasion places us firmly in the thirties.   33o

THE NEW CITROEN "TEN"
(THE ONLY LIGHT CAR IN THE WORLD WITH FLOATING POWER)

January 27th. W T Cave Ltd, the authorised agents in Ilford High Road for Citroën cars send their promotional card to Mr Myall Esq. in Coventry Road, Ilford, describing the new 1933 models beginning with this 10hp. (the New Ten) at under two hundred pounds and culminating, via the Big Twelve, in the high powered luxury of the otherwise undescribed Twenty/I.C. the car that zips around in French films full of detectives and could be bought for what seems now a mere £295. Did Mr Myall look in his garage at whatever dusty and now superceded model he owned and ponder on the part-exchange offer of W T Cave Ltd, or that proposal for deferred payments? 33p

December 3rd. Eddie in Bangor to Mr & Mrs Owen in Holyhead, *Shall come on the 12 noon bus from here tomorrow arriving about 1.30pm or I may change my mind and arrive an hour earlier. Shall be able to stay with you till Tuesday morning. Love to all. In Haste.* Perhaps Eddie works at the Ford dealers in Bangor and is using up the unsent cards from earlier in the year that advertised the Ford 8hp Tudor Saloon. It seems, since he is going to come by bus, that he may not yet be the owner of even such a modest vehicle as that. 33q

Only two horsepower and eighty pounds or so separate these cars yet their publicity pitches could not be further apart, exploiting every differential of culture, sophistication and class. The gleaming Citroën is casually parked on a secluded by-road in a shaft of sunlight that makes the river gleam and etches the clean outlines of the car against the soft romantic landscape. A hint of piquancy in the relationship of the two fashionably dressed women gives a narrative that adds to the car's allure and the chic little dog suggests its frisky performance. Without even the benefit of sunlight or shining chrome to relieve its dullness, the Ford 8 looks drably utilitarian even when brand new. It seems to be parked on a suburban common. The nuclear family of Mr & Mrs Average has its picnic tea dressed in their off the peg non-finery. If they have a dog it's a mongrel and probably called Spot rather than Fifi.

1933 MESSAGES·NOTES·PARTICULARS

33a. Arena Photo Post Card Co. Chicago. AM Centenary stamp and PM slogan, A Century Of Progress Station.

33b. Publisher unknown. C131

33c. Art Photo Greeting Co, Elizabeth, NJ

33d. Publisher unknown. No 21

33e. F Robaudy, Cannes. Artist: Plumereau?

33f. Morison? Blackpool? 9509

33g. Excel series 201

33h. Bamforth Comic Series No 3819 Artist unknown

33i. JMJ (Jackson & Son, Grimsby)

33j. Valentine's 209175 JV

33k. Laurent Nel, Rennes 3309

33l. Tourist Comics (6 designs) Series No 327. Artist: E L White

33m. Rotary Photo London Design No 734734

33n. Regina Bar. Artist: DYL (Yan-Bernard Dyl)

33o. Publisher unknown 2370 Artist unknown

33p. Lilywhite Real Photo. For Citroen

33q. Ford Motors

THE "PTERODACTYL".

To Les Allan in S.Woodford SE 18, *Thanks awfully for your card you certainly achieved your objective witness the picture & the 'postal evidence'... & for offering to try and get the air mail stamp... yours Boots.* Thus the hobbyists exchange their news via cards of exciting aircraft like this experimental powered glider designed by Capt GTR Hill. Publisher unknown. 33r

660.

January 30th.   From Berlin NW7 to Reginald Braad in Gordon Street, London WC, *I send this without comment. Don't show it to Derek it might encourage him. love DW.* This short message makes a present day reader bristle with speculation. Few comments are as loaded as 'without comment', and Derek becomes a tantalising figure (perhaps on the fringes of Mosley's British version of fascism). Hitler has been Chancellor for a year and the Third Reich is only six months old, yet the familiar imagery is all in place with a proliferation of swastikas and uniforms and the beginnings of the Hitler Youth. The caption on the reverse reads 'Reichschancellor Hitler greets his young people'. These boys will be ripe & ready for the war when the call eventually comes. The Führer himself (though he will not assume that title publicly until Hindenberg's death in 1934) is iconically complete, the often parodied walk and salute and compelling charm perfected. Was this received with a dismissive chuckle in Gordon Street and did Derek catch an all too exhilarating glimpse of it?   34a

PICCADILLY CIRCUS, LONDON

September 7th.   From WJ to the splendidly named Miss Philately Holtgreve in Washington DC, *This place is sometimes called The Heart of the British Empire - but actually it is cosmopolitan & faintly similar to Broadway in that respect. You must step over later on to see us.* A sunny view circa 1930.   34b

November 27th.   Edmund to Mrs C C Yerkes in Northville, Mich., *Dear Mama. As Rolly wired you I won't be home till the last of the week... we have several projects to work on & we want to get them organised.* The recent giants add to the lustre of New York's nocturnal majesty.   34c

October 26th.   CW in Cambridge to Miss Stubblefield in Melbourn Place, *A P.C. to let you know I may be out tomorrow a.m. It's H's day off. Will meet you at 7 o/c in L unless I hear from you.* George Cadbury of chocolate fame showed that commerce was not incompatible with concern. These choric dancers in Isadora Duncan outfits are factory workers in Bournville's utopian model village. 34d

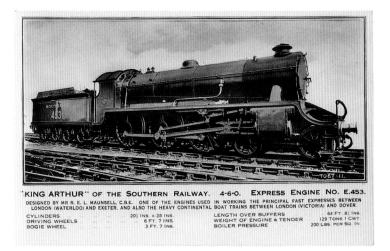

September 7th.   Frida to Alec Freemantle in Reading, *How will this suit, hope it will recompense you for 'Clapham Junc'. Just to remind you to bring your bathing costumes & would you please bring the jelly clock. Come as soon as you can.* The jelly clock is a mystery but I did myself see this engine once hurtle through Clapham Junction and used to know its wheel ratio and even its boiler pressure. 34e

July 30th.   Popsy Redkney writes from Southend to her parents in South Lambeth, *we have been here 4 week got just two more weeks to go lots of people staying at Thorpe Bay this year helps us Bank Holiday week its pack now well bye bye just now.* Southend is the capital of the saucy postcard, the nearest resort to London's East End. Cards all refer to girls 'clicking' with men rather than the other way round. 34f

September 12th.   NVA to Mrs Allender in Heenor, Notts, *Just a line to let you see you are not forgotten even in the London bustle.* This is what was going on during the long absence of Eros from Piccadilly Circus (see 33d). The underground station opened at the end of 1928 but Eros returned in 1932 to a more central site where he had a new octagonal base which gained him over a foot in height. 34g

May 15th.   From Margaret D to Miss Buller in London SW1, *Am still away & afraid I'm too uncertain to promise for May 12th. If I find later that I am going to be at home will let you know if you still need helpers, but I fear - sorry!* In other words, no. The new Memorial Theatre was opened on Shakespeare's birthday in 1932 and was compared to a jam factory. It is in fact a rather more elegant structure than the Gothic original (see 26j) and was the work of a woman architect (Elizabeth Scott). 34h

September 12th.   Jack writing from Boots, Church St, Liverpool to Mrs Wilson in Sheffield, *Got drafted here today for a week end job expect moving again on about Tuesday...* Jack is probably a Boots employee in which case he picked the latest card off their rack. It shows the Mersey Tunnel (which had only been open a few weeks) pictured here with many fine imaginary vehicles flashing past our fearless photographer in both directions. 34i

May 24th.   To Miss Gloag in Chelsea, *I travelled here with K the very day you came back from 'Gloagging'. lovely weather here, no dust, no noise, nothing but beauty & stillness - time, money, almost non-existent! Tots.* The evocative chiaroscuro of this view of Grasse by Yvon is masterly. Its highlighted mini-drama makes it a piece of French cinema one frame long.   34j

July 17th.   Uncle & Auntie in Weymouth to Miss Beryl Norman in Swindon, *These dresses are quite respectable down here: been having a grand time, been bathing every day & the water lovely. We are all like niggers.* The new fad, to go with brief tops and bobbed or shingled hair, is confirmed by this unsigned comic card by McGill.   34k

July 27th.   From Mrs Byrne in Mill Hill to Mrs Brown in London N20. *I shall be so pleased to see you on Saturday...* This presumably is Mrs. Byrne's house, sent with pride. Without this knowledge the concentration on a dwelling of such insistent ordinariness could only accompany an account of some appalling crime or be the mute prelude to a chaotic comic sketch.   34l

August 3rd.   Opal writes to the Throgmortons in Southard, Oklahoma from the Chicago World's Fair (now in its second year) *Going to some stores before going to the fair... This was the most interesting place we visited...* In the Fair's Black Forest Village Red McCarthy (wearing Johnsons All American skates) performs his feat while, beneath the wintry trees, onlookers betray more anxiety than the skater.   34m

November 20th.   To Ewart & Leslie Jarvis in Swindon from Ashford, *Did Dad tell you that a missionary meeting is to be held on Thursday at Lena's house? Our united love. Jessie.* What attitude was intended to be provoked by this card? Perhaps merely a self evident example of heathen folly. Nonetheless it is hard to imagine a Hindu sending a card of a vicar to anyone as an example of anything.   34n

June 23rd.   To Master A Barnard from Coventry, *Dear Alf. Received your card... we're OK down here, remember me to your pa & ma from your friend Ted.* Maurice Chevalier would perhaps at that moment have been filming Folies Bergères (see 36b) in a career that lasted from the silent film era to 1967, his eightieth birthday year. His early autobiography was entitled Man In A Straw Hat.   34o

January 29th.   From Louis Landsberg in Aachen, *Thank you for your kind Christmas wishes... I read in the newspaper that these post-cards are being exhibited today and tomorrow in relation to the past years work of new structure of Germany. I hope this card will be of some use to your collection - there is only a small amount being issued, so I think this card will be a rare specimen of its kind. I am preparing for my second year exam at College... Last year I did fairly in sports coming out 7th with the stone (33 1/2 tons) in Germany whilst I wasn't able to range better than 36th with the shot and 43rd with the disc. These last six months I have hardly trained at all... I was too busy to spend my time with sports. It was pretty hard to paste up these two stamps neatly... the one pfennig stamp was issued in Dec. How are you? Your girl? Everybody?* This anniversary card of Hitler's year-old chancellorship was hot off the press and Hitler makes his first appearance on a stamp. The control exercised over all the semiotics of power, masterminded by Goebbels, already marked Hitler out as in a different league of dictatorship from Mussolini who only made one philatelic appearance in Italy (and then on a stamp which also features Adolf Hitler). The Brandenburg gate in Berlin retains its symbolic importance at the end of the century.   34p

September 14th.   From P to Mrs Robb-Smith in Chelsea *Local costumes are charming, different in every village and the caps are particularly pleasant & most of the girls are better-looking than these!* Only the shoes give a clue to the date of this picture.   34q

July 8th.   Dad sends Ivy Lovegrove his love and best wishes with some kisses. Versatile songstress Gracie Fields, called here a vaudeville and radio star, will in February sign a two year film contract for a record £150,000 with Associated Talking Pictures.   34r

November 18th.   Eddy in Milan sends this emotive card by Bertiglia to Edna Plimmer in Worcester Park, *My own darling... had to work until late. I'll write you on Mon for sure. you know. Are you glad?... Do you love me? How much? xxxoxoxoxoxox.*   34s

You seem so near and yet I miss you
Tho' you are here I cannot kiss you

March 20th.   Miss Ferguson in Norwich receives a card from her father, *Darling Sally, I loved seeing the snaps of you in your kilt with the big 'brooch' showing...* Evidently Vera Paterson had never seen a Televisor, the bulbous washing-machine-like object manufactured from 1930 by Baird, the inventor of television. We still await a set as slim as this. The BBC's first proper scheduled transmissions were in 1936. As so often the comic card was ahead of the game and the cute kids (why is he reading Roman Love?) of Paterson and other postcards artists kept nimble step with the March of Progress   35a

August 20th.   Auntie Catherine chose this up to date (circa 1934) view to send to Mrs Griffiths in Kidwelly, Carmarthenshire, *I am at this place today and I am enjoying time.* The simple hit or miss tinting of this photographic Excel card brings extra space and life to the Circus.   35b

November 5th.   Comparison with 31c will show that Frange kept revising his NY views and must have marked his spot (together with its useful framing tree) carefully. Betty has been to visit her grandfather in Faribault, Minnesota & writes to tell him the bus trip is hard.   35c

JUBILEE
DECORATIONS
AT
SELFRIDGES
1935

CUNARD WHITE STAR LINER, "534"—THE WORLD'S LARGEST LINER.
Launched at Clydebank and Christened by Her Majesty The Queen, 26th. Sept. 1934.

June? To Miss S Dudley at the Midland Hotel, Bournemouth, *My dear Sybill I arrived quite safe here, but what a journey, I met a girl I knew going up to London on the same coach, so we were OK. Then we stopped at Winchester, we nearly lost the bus, you would have laughed to see us running after it... best love, Margaret.* Selfridges (as befits an American store) puts on a fine patriotic display.   35d

March 8th. Nana in Hereford sends a suitable card to Master A F Renwick in Cardiff hoping he is having a nice time. The great liners carry a prosaic serial number until they are christened. It is said that 534 was to be called the Queen Victoria but, when asked if it could be named after England's greatest Queen, King George V replied, 'Yes I'm sure Queen Mary would be very pleased'.   35e

July 23rd. From Bicester to Mrs S Twelvetree in the General Hospital, Northampton, *This is a snap we had taken Jubilee Day from your loving Brother Bill.* Bill, amongst this cheerful band on their way to or from a celebration, is marked with a cross. Many wear party headgear so perhaps their Jubilee lunch or tea is over. The next celebration of a twenty five year reign will be in 1977.   35f

July 20th. To Master Nigel Oakley in Holland Park from Flagstaff, Arizona, *What do you think of these people? They are real red indians & we are living right in the middle of them. Please give that horrible cat of yours a knock on the knose for me. I hope you are behaving properly... Your old Uncle Frankie.* A finely reworked photo becomes like a painting in the hands of the Detroit Publishing Co.   35g

March 22nd. To Hornbys Garage in Sutton-on-Sea, Lincs, sent from Hillman motors to prompt the car dealer with special selling points of their latest model, *Hillman provide an exceptional margin of overhead room - point out how this contributes to absolute lack of fatigue, freedom from any tiredness after long trips.* This couple seem to indicate rather that a certain tension or suspicious unease is induced.   35h

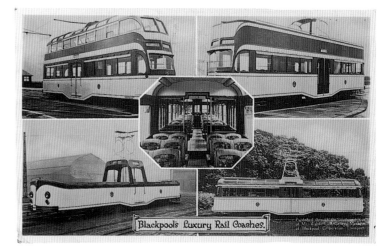

September 4th. From AA to Miss Ashby in Southwick, Sussex, *How do you like the Blackpool luxury coaches We think they are grand & they are ever so comfortable and quite posh as you can see by the centre picture. We have been on each with the exception of the top right, that is open top & it has been a bit too breezy for that.* Local pride seems to be justified by such sleek and streamlined vehicles.   35i

March 31st.   Joy G to Miss Waller in Malvern, *I hear you are not to be trusted with a bike! ...went to an awfully good point-to-point yesterday... been watching a lot of hunting & then following round in the car which is very exciting tearing along trying to keep the hunt in sight.* Carson, outside Stormont (opened in 1932), seems still to gesture No Surrender. He died in October 1935 (see 12o).   35j

February 4th.   Willha in Ardmore, Okla. to Mr & Mrs Walter Sparrow in Flint, Mich., *left Flint 1st day of Feb have made good time staying to nite in Ardmore and I am enjoying every minut.* The flags make these derricks look like fun architecture: with their crowning lights they are reminiscent of Gaudi's church (see 30r). The more necessary lights of night-time industry often have the same magic.   35k

November 19th.   From Grandmother Swett in Honolulu to Miss Sally Skeyton in Elmina, NY, *Isn't this a pretty card? Grandmother is on this boat on her way to see you & Joan. It is a beautiful, hot sunshiny day. I am going to have a nap...* Pictures of ships can be monotonous except from Japanese lines like NYK. Other lines never seemed to have picked up on the idea, or imitated these saturated colours.   35l

August 12th.   Martha and Olive at the Fellowship Holiday Camp, Lowestoft, write to Miss K Chambers in Halifax, *Bathing lovely, This is a view of the Dining room & canteen but it must have been altered, the part in the middle juts out more now.* This might well be some time before, since the boy with the cap and long trousers is playing with a diabolo, a game that had gone out of fashion. It had a muted revival in the 1990's. 35m

June 23rd.   DO in Weymouth writes to Mrs Allan in Hunters Quay, Argyllshire, *I've got the wireless at Wylie Hills. The man who sailed in Lyyra sold it to us. He came over to Hafton one day to see about it. We went over the Courageous yesterday. She is an extraordinary boat.* HMS Courageous was to be the first real casualty of World War II, sunk by a German U Boat on 17th Sept. 1939 with the loss of 500 lives.   35n

August 15th.   From L & B in Nuneaton to Mr & Mrs Knight in Boscombe, *Just a line to say we got your P.C. Mr Pike has written to your digs. We are about the same old lot. Has Rene had a dip yet...* Somehow the typical thirties house as seen in the background here would not be complete without such a path or patio (though coloured crazy paving was taking things a bit far).   35o

35a. J Salmon. Salmon Series No 209 Artist: Vera Paterson

35b. Excel Series No 6122

35c. Wm Frange No 10

35d. Selfridges Ltd.

35e. Valentine's A980 (48)

35f. Publisher unknown

35g. Detroit Publishing Co. Phostint 5698

35h. Hillman Cars

35i. Miller & Co, Blackpool

35j. Valentine's 222497 J.V. (44)

35k. Curt Teich / Oklahoma News Co. 4AH305

35l. NYK Lines. The Sun Never Sets

June 17th.   Mrs Bell in Chelsea to Mrs Bennett in Barrow-in-Furness, *My Dear Friend, arrived alright my son and his daughter meet me at Euston landed 5pm how glad to be among my own dreadful weath i have not time to write as we are of motoring i will write again i heard the wireless sundy for the first time.* An obscure ceremonial moment in the Jubilee procession. Huge crowds thronged the streets of London and a mongrel dog joined the parade.   35p

May 17th.   Earl in Fiji to Geo. & Fern Kitterman in West Toledo, Ohio, *This is the 'head' man down here who makes Head Cheese in Fiji. Got some nice pictures to show when I get home - Grand time.* No more nor less ethnographic an image than 35p. This real headhunter has a similar headdress to the King and is also in formal array: his weapon has however been put to use. But then the King's tribe has, in his reign, killed and been killed by the million.   35q

The Beach Inspectors here are working overtime, since I've been down.

35m. Kessingland Camp

35n. Gieves Ltd

35o. Tuck Oilette No 5023 Artist: Ricardo Brook

35p. Excel Series 3

35q. Publisher unknown

35r. Norman Grut, Photographic Artist, Guernsey

35s. XL Series No 2258 Artist: Donald McGill

July 31st.   From A & N in Guernsey to R de C Peele in Ludlow, *Many thanks for letter and also T.C.P. - very good stuff. I was only introduced to it recently & did not know they put it up in such convenient little bottles. Yes we've seen the little chapel & watched its builder at work in it - It is a gem - How did you hear of it?*   35r

July 12th.   Pyllis in Margate to Miss Townsend in Chinnor, *Have all been in the sea this morning wish you could be down here with us.* This prototype bikini is ahead of its time. McGill's signature is faint as if he had had second thoughts about signing a picture likely to fall foul of the censors.   35s

Eröffnung des Parteikongresses 1936.   51

September 14th from Nuremberg. The opening of the Party Congress 1936 features the visual rhetoric of Nazism in all its numbing symmetry. In his message home (see note) Ken gives an eyewitness account of Hitler and a judgement of his aims as well as a description of a military parade to make this card a real historical document. What did Ken, in amongst these gathered faithful, do when saluting time came round?   36a

November 3rd.   Connie & Rose are off to a show. The picture shows Piccadilly in the previous year when the film Folies Bergeres was featured at the London Pavilion starring Maurice Chevalier (see 34o) and Merle Oberon. A bus advertises The Daily Herald For Peace, whatever that may mean.   36b

March 4th.   Another of Wm Frange's superb skyline views. This one places the Chrysler building plumb on the Golden Section (approx 5/8ths of image width). *Walked down Wall Street* writes DF to Adelia Holtman in Rudolph, Kansas, *but didn't see the money everyone says they got.*   36c

UNIVERSITY OF LONDON.

A drawing by the Architect, Mr. Charles Holden, F.R.I.B.A., of the new buildings which the University propose to erect on a site of 10½ acres to the north of the British Museum. These buildings will provide new headquarters for the University.

MISS AMY JOHNSON. C.B.E.

June 19th.   Steve to Mr & Mrs Roberts in Hull... *nearly finished written exams and the weather seems set for an interesting lazy week-end. Had very brief 'phone call to Dorrie last night - seems all right.* The new Senate building of London University, completed in 1936, was commandeered for wartime use by the Ministry of Information. Steve's lazy weekends might soon be just a golden memory.   36d

May 20th.   Five days after Amy Johnson returned from yet another record-breaking flight (to Capetown and back) John Smith types a note in York to fellow parishioner Mr Eric Jackson, *I forgot to ask whether you could manage to come for the service Thursday 7.30. I hope you will be able.* In 1941 her aircraft was sunk by friendly fire approaching the Thames; a subject of renewed controversy.   36e

DUST STORM APPROACHING AMARILLO, TEXAS, MARCH 31, 1935, TURNING THE TOWN INTO TOTAL DARKNESS

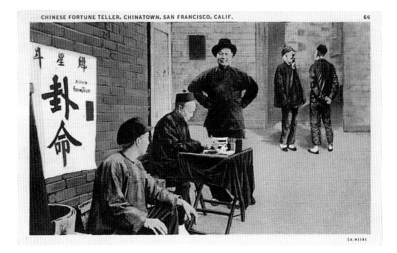

CHINESE FORTUNE TELLER, CHINATOWN, SAN FRANCISCO, CALIF.   66

March 14th.   Irene Rippel's mother in Plainview, Texas writes to her in Secor, Illinois, remote places far distant from each other, *Lena is very low we do not know yet just when we can leave.* The droughts of 1934-40 revealed what greedy husbandry had done to the land as the topsoil disappeared in black winds creating the Dust Bowl. It was the first acknowledged man-made ecological disaster.   36f

March 7th.   Ethel at Terminal Island, Calif. to Miss Barrow in Putney, *got to San Pedro for Los Angeles tonight. Scenery & flowers beautiful. See you have had it very cold. We get the wireless news every day.* More like a stage set than a part of any real place. This fortune teller according to the text on the reverse 'caters to the native and visitor with the occult wisdom of his people brought down thru the years'.   36g

Cunard White Star   'Lancastria'

L'Hôpital Dafoe et Maison de jeu des Quintuplettes Dionne. Dafoe Hospital and Play House of Dionne Quintuplets, Callander, Ontario, Canada. —15.

August 10th.   Elsie on board the Lancastria writes from off the Spanish coast to Mrs Surtees in Lowestoft, *Having a very nice day so far in spite of a heavy bout of seasickness. We get to Gibraltar today. I hear they are doing a lot of bombing. Hope they don't hit us by mistake.* Elsie is in fact approaching a hot spot of the Spanish Civil War where Franco's Fascist troops are surrounded by Republican armies in the South. Though Gibraltar was British its tiny terrain lay between two battle fronts.   36h

August 3rd.   Ernest & Essie write to Ethel & Bob Attwater in Leytonstone from Callander, Ontario, *Here we are up in Northern Canada visiting the home of the Dionne Quints. We... just covered 320 miles. good roads & wonderfull scenery.* The good roads were partly the result of the famous quintuplets attracting such attention to this far flung spot. Their exploitation, removal from their parents and adoption by the state government is a story not yet quite resolved (see 37j).   36i

SMOKING ROOM, REGENT PALACE HOTEL, PICCADILLY, W.1.

January 15th. Elsie to Mrs Crocker in Torquay, *We are up here to interview the bank manager... we have not lost ourselves yet.* The Regent Palace Hotel, now somewhat declined, is often visible on cards of Piccadilly Circus. Targeted at the new middle classes it kept up with every trend in interior design. The smoking room is not opulent but boldly states what is latest in lighting, furniture and floor covering.   36j

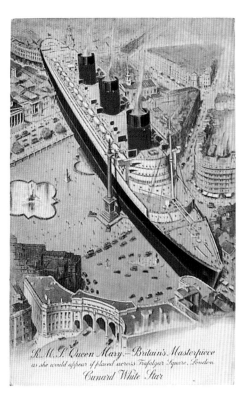

R.M.S. Queen Mary — Britain's Masterpiece as she would appear if placed across Trafalgar Square, London.
Cunard White Star

August 23rd. From on board the Queen Mary (see 35e) AJN writes to Mrs Talbot in S Kensington, *We should reach N.York this evening & are hoping for the record. A thick fog at the moment but we seem to be tearing along as fast as ever!! I suppose it's safe?!* A hint of nervousness mingled with excitement which would soon become proud relief. The ship captured the record and the Blue Riband that same day.   36k

SHIRLEY TEMPLE

August 6th. Dorothy in Weymouth to Mr & Mrs Heard in Bristol, *The sun is grand... we are sitting under the walk not a chair to be had. Spot is quite good and loves the water. Tons of love.* A ray of sunshine during the depression Shirley Temple sang and skipped her way through a host of films inc. this year Captain January (see 38n). Thirty years later she was (as Shirley Temple Black) to stand for Congress.   36l

JOAN CRAWFORD   METRO-GOLDWYN-MAYER PICTURES

September 18th. To Mr & Mrs Ross in Peebles, *Have been in Wigan all day... Walter Ross is coming up to A's tonight. Sheila went off with fever a fortnight tomorrow.* Christine Crawford (in Mommie Dearest) described her mother as more nightmarish than any she had portrayed in 45 years of filming. The cruel lighting of this image, epitomising the shadowy aesthetic of the film noir, makes us believe her.   36m

"IF WE DON'T GET AIR DEFENCE QUICK SOMEBODY'S GOING TO GET IT IN THE NECK!"
"LOOK OUT FOR YOURSELF THEN, MISTER— THERE'S A FLIGHT OF CROWS COMIN' OVER!"

August 20th. Kathy in Boston, Lincs writes to her mother in Dorrington, *we are having a real good time. The weather is so grand for us... two days at the sea Skegness & Mablethorpe. Am writing this at Boston right near the stump. The girls are fine. Arthur is enjoying every day of it.* There seem to be no clouds on the Chapmans' horizon yet others were worrying about the impending danger of another war.   36n

August 13th. Tim writes to Miss Gibbins in Croydon, *Dear Gibby, Having a marvellous time at the Games. came over quite unexpectedly. Have seen a football match, also ice hockey its rather a job to get tickets.* The notorious Berlin Olympics made immortal by Leni Riefenstahl's film was to be a celebration of Aryan supremacy. Hitler walked out after black American Jesse Owens won three gold medals.   36o

36a (verso). Here, with all the appropriate philatelic baggage of the new Party Congress stamp (complete with hands raised in the Nazi salute) and the 1935 issue commemorating the Führer's first Putsch, is the message side of the picture.

Dear Folks. In this grand hall I was given a fine free place near to Hitler. I was at first pleased with the man's serious bearing, but to-day when I was again privileged to occupy a press *seat I was very disappointed in the content and meaning of his speech, because it was one long harangue of hatred against Jews & Russia. Today I attended a display of Germany's new army which I am convinced is being prepared for war with Russia. I am very sorry to be of this opinion because the German people are a very fine folk. I shall be in Berlin Saturday. Cheerio. Ken.*

PORTRAIT BY
BERTRAM PARK **HIS MAJESTY KING EDWARD VIII**

GÖTTERDAMMERUNG
Richard Wagner

THE SUN'S DOING ITS WORK O.K.
(I'M ONLY WAITING TO SEE WHAT
THE MOONLIGHT BRINGS)

AT SHANKLIN

September 1st.   M in London W1 sends this with the new stamp to the Marriott family in Bromley and the traditional, *Long may he reign*. Edward VIII, the once and never King, who, in pursuit of love will abdicate before the year's end without being crowned, here comes fitted out as Colonel in chief of the Seaforth Highlanders and no doubt will have to put on another outrageous outfit before the photography session is over. Bored solemnity is the order of the day.   36p

October 20th.   To Miss Schroder in Brixton from Gussie, *Trademeeting postponed till 23rd so our meeting seems fated... we must book for As You Like It... cheerio my dear till next Monday, on steps between 7.30-8o/c*. Wagner's operas, much performed until the war, became unacceptable, especially since they were Hitler's adopted music. Despite many visits to Bayreuth he never learned that the vanities of Das Rheingold invite the chaos of Götterdämmerung.   36q

July 19th.   Connie and Charles send Mr Bowerstock in Basingstoke this generic card with an almost generic message, *We are having a glorious time... going on the pier soon for the rest of the evening. Both feeling fit. Must ring of in haste*. A new bold poster style showing American influence has come to the seaside postcard with this confidently drawn and airbrushed pin-up in a daring swimsuit; as far as the one piece can go, or as much as it can show.   36r

May 16th. A special Coronation Souvenir card from Tuck in which some dreary old faithfuls from their London stock are vignetted with a composite portrait of the new King and Queen (he by Baron she by Dorothy Wilding). A crown, some browny gold and a Union Jack make the whole thing a bit more lively. It's rather a hasty job for such a grand event from a firm which had produced the earliest chromolithographic cards at the beginning of the century (see 00l). Perhaps the shift of Kings had caught them napping. Florrie C writes from Norwood to Mrs Dickinson in Aintree, Liverpool, *The 'all. My dear M & L. I am in a glorious state of excitement over the Birthday gifts, you may be sure I shall spend them well. I am also most anxious about you...* 37a

June 1st. No publisher acknowledges this cheery card posted a week after I was born. Mrs Arnold writes to her daughter Rachel in Southport, Lancs. There is a pleasing randomness in the colouring with a red pedestal for a green Eros and buses which have unaccountably turned yellow. 37b

June 15th. Writing via SS Columbus to a friend in Finland, Ola seems to be in involved in a posting competition, *I'm quite O.K. sending this for a 'race' described in my letter of the same date... Lots of love & oceans of kisses.* This is the familiar birds-eye view with a distant Empire State Building now breaking the horizon. 37c

THE KING AND QUEEN LEAVING WESTMINSTER ABBEY

HIS MAJESTY KING GEORGE VI. BROADCASTING HIS MESSAGE TO THE EMPIRE, CORONATION DAY, 1937

MARLENE DIETRICH   PARAMOUNT PICTURES

June 6th.   MN in Sutton thanks Mrs Daniel in Bristol for her letter, *I am really writing this to tell you that Miss Bulkey has had to go to Southmead, she is in O Ward. if you go to B.I. fete will you tell Miss Henway & anyone else who is interested in her.* May 12th was the day that had been fixed for the coronation of Edward VIII, but it is his brother who is in the golden coach on the way to Buckingham Palace.   37d

July 27th.   Leslie in Richmond to R S Allan, Royal Squadron, Hotel Ryde IOW. *Dear Bun, Fancy going on the Queen Mary. I wish I could have done, we all enjoyed ourselves last night they gave the Ladies nice Negretti & Zambra opera glasses & the men Onoto pencils. Ashmole girl was not there am having a rotten time at the office.* The King is also having a rotten time battling with his stutter to broadcast to the Empire.   37e

August 9th.   Connie in Chelmsford shares an old joke with Joan Rowe in Tiptree, *Hope you are still alright and not fretting about Jimmy. Well dear... I am going to London Zoo Thurs. Hope they don't keep me there.* The German star became an American citizen in 1941 and entertained the troops, always singing Lili Marlene the song she had recorded both in German and English that was common property of the opposing armies. 37f

ALLES LIEBE UND GUTE

Simpson's-in-the-Strand
The Famous Old English Eating House.

DRAWN BY H. M. BATEMAN.

The gentleman who asked the carver whether the meat was English or Foreign.

ASSIRIAN DRESS

September 5th.   M in Cologne to the Woottons in Leighton-on-Sea, *Just to let you know that I have arrived here quite safely - everything so far has been really 1st class.* This study by Hoffman shows a typical scene of Hitler being kind to children, or rather to blond German ones. This girl's Jewish contemporaries were being daily herded into death camps.   37g

May 14th.   D & N to Helen K Le Favour in Amsterdam NY, *We leave here for Holland - Had dinner in Simpsons last eve with Gerald Hankin. The Coronation was magnificent beyond words.* Bateman almost made a living from this one comic idea, here applied to Simpsons, who still specialise in British beef. The BSE scare of the nineties adds ironic sauce.   37h

January 10th.   Alfred in Iraq to Kate Hartmann in Philadelphia, *Thanks for the stamps and thanks for offering to send me warm under ware which would cause me no end of trouble because it would be hot and I will have to pay duty and besides I have too much with me.* What is Alfred doing in the Middle East, even then a scene of confusion?   37i

The Dionne Quintuplets at Callander, Ontario, Canada. 2.

EMILIE — YVONNE CECILE ANNETTE MARIE

July 1st.   To the Detlars in Pottstown, Pa, from Florence & Guy, *Come up here for inspiration, Ha. Ha. Just saw them playing in the yard and having the morning lunch. They are adorable.* Yvonne, Cecile & Annette still live, though in poor circumstances and ill health. They are trying to claim some of the fortune they generated for the Ontario government when they were its wards of state (see 36i).   37j

OHIO BUILDING — GREAT LAKES EXPOSITION
MAY 29th to SEPTEMBER 6th, 1937   CLEVELAND, OHIO

September 13th.   To Mrs Walter Studerant, Prattsburg, NY, *Dear Cousin Mattie. Tho't maybe you'd like a picture of our Dem. Governor. Say, did you receive the vase we sent? Am feeling fine. About another month. Love to all Jeanette.* While failing to be recognised as an International Exposition the Great Lakes Fair was a huge success, meriting more perhaps than this uniquely pennypinching use of two colours.   37k

THE STATION, WEMYSS BAY.

August 9th.   Sam Lindley in Studdersfield gets a card from his mother, *This is Monday and it rains. We are now on the side of Loch Lomond sat in the car beside the Loch. Your father... likes to go to the top of the mountains & I don't to tell you the truth I like stopping round the bottom... This station was like this card when we went down to the boat from here it is a beautiful station.*   37l

June 12th.   To Philip Kirkpatrick in Cambridge, *I'm terribly sorry to refuse you but Neville will be staying in my only spare room on next Tuesday night, & I have no boy away. The other spare room has a chap in it this half. I can offer all meals.* The eccentric Eton Scoutmaster, A C Beardsley-Robinson, stands by his 1924 Vauxhall ready to leave for Scout Camp in Scarborough.   37m

THE PIG & WHISTLE, BUTLINS HOLIDAY CAMP, SKEGNESS

June 22nd.   Rosie writes to Mr & Mrs Eden in Burton-on-Trent, *Dear Mum, I am very happy at present and I am wearing a big crinoline dress for the dance tonight Mr Butlin gave us these cards to send. Cheerio, Rosie.* Billy Butlin kept his promise and established his camp in Skegness (see 33i). Another sender of this card says *This is a quaint little pub on the premises.* Modern facilities and instant quaintness provided a magic formula. The Pig and Whistle was copied in later camps.   37n

23. COTE D'AZUR — Coucher de Soleil sur l'Estérel

From Peggie in Cannes to M F Robb-Smith in Chelsea, *Glad you and Alastair have escaped the flu. We shall certainly not be coming back before the end of February-especially as the English climate seems worse than usual. We have been to Nice to see the carnival - battle of the Flowers which was very pretty. This is the sort of sunset we see.* The French had cracked the vivid southern sunset with some bold Impressionistic tinter's strokes over a blue & white photograph.   37o

July 28th.   *My darling Chérie!* writes Eric to Mrs Hammer in Sydenham *we have now seen a good deal of the exhibition. Much of the French stuff & a number of pavilions of smaller foreign countries are still quite incomplete... Monday I heard a fine concert of Strauss, Debussy & Beethoven's tremendous Choral Symphony, yesterday frivolity at the Folies Bergeres...* No touch of frivolity mars the Soviet Pavilion.   37p

August (?) 1st.   Peggie to Mrs Robb-Smith in Chelsea, *having a lovely time here in Paris & at exhibition.* National pavilions in the past tried to look impressively lovable. No such sentiment troubles either Jofan's Russian pavilion or Hitler's architect Speer in this rigid exemplar of the high Fascist style. No one could now doubt their aspirations: the ideological cards were on the table in clear aesthetic terms.   37q

GINGER ROGERS   RADIO PICTURES

KATHARINE HEPBURN   7244

July 19th.   Margaret in Blackpool to George Long in Sheffield still using up his Edward VIII stamps, *We've arrived and had a good dinner and we are now off to have tea. Have you let my pigeon die yet or are you feeding it? We are going to Billy Cotton tonight* [a show band]. Ginger Rogers, here in her twenties and in her prime as Fred Astaire's partner, carried on working beyond her dancing years until the sixties on film and TV. 37r

September 4th.   Violet in Wood Green to Elsie Knowles in W Hampstead also using up Edward VIII stamps, *I should like to come over next Tuesday morning. Win is queer.* Ginger Rogers would usually seem like a showgirl in comparison with Hepburn, Hollywood's most sophisticated actress, yet in 1937 they starred together in the award-winning Stage Door and no one could choose between their performances.   37s

July 24th.   From Victor in Berlin to Gerald & Gordon Beck in London NW6 this card features yet another portrait of Hitler by Hoffmann. Victor seems more interested in the philatelic than the political aspect of events, *Dear lads, Next Friday the new three halfpenny stamps come out. Please send me a first day Air Mail letter... how do you like the photo, I have sent my father the stamp hinges...* The tale of Hoffmann is an intriguing one. He first photographed the Führer inadvertently, in a crowd scene in 1914. This discovery cemented the bond between them. Heinrich Hoffmann (party member no 427) thus became Hitler's official photographer, constant companion, and, in that he had no political ambitions, trusted friend. They last met in April 1945 only days before the story's grim ending. This intimate association (Hitler met Eva Braun in Hoffmann's studio) makes it even stranger that in 1908 Hoffmann had a shop in the Uxbridge Road, that he had photographed Edward VII and that his last visit to England was in 1937 to cover the coronation of George VI. This is Hitler in pensive mood by the Chiemsee. 37t

June 9th.   The full extent of Walt Disney's genius was revealed in 1938 when, only ten years after his first Mickey Mouse cartoon, the feature length Snow White went out on general release. One can only marvel at the labour involved in those days of frame by frame, colour by colour, handworked animation. Valentine's gained the concession to produce these cards from Disney studio drawings. They kept them in print until 1941. Auntie Jane writes to Miss Diana Foss in London NW11, *Is this anything like your percussion band? Is it 'Grumpy' conducting do you think? I hope I shall see you on Saturday.*   38a

January 18th.   It is 1933 on this card. Eros has returned and the Guinness clock which was to tell Piccadilly Circus time for forty years is installed. A fine six wheeler bus holds centre stage. Uncle Fred writes to his nephew Freddie in Sandwich Lees, Kent, *Tell Grannie I got back alright. Train punctual, and I didn't get very wet.*   38b

March 22nd.   Wm Frange makes the most of the drama of Brooklyn Bridge. Dave, up late (1.30am), can hardly contain himself to Norma Hardy in Columbus Ohio, *I'm fine. The show is the show of all shows ho ho. It's pretty wonderful. I'm bubbling over to tell you... best ever. It was grand.*   38c

THE PILGRIM OF PEACE
BRAVO! MR. CHAMBERLAIN

Mae West.

if only you could see the colours!

Mount Abu - The Bazaar

October 28th.   NS in Honiton to Miss Parker in Hove, *Just to say dear we managed to get to Bampton Fair yesterday really a wonderful sight... & then on to Exeter for tea & the Chrysanthemum show at Civic Hall which was lovely.* Not everyone said Bravo to Chamberlain in September when he announced, on his return from Munich, Peace for Our Time. Appeasement was not quite the same as peace.   38d

August 27th.   From Los Angeles to Herbert L Willey at the Hotel Manx in San Francisco, *Dear Bert sure was sorry did not see you again before you left. Better luck next time. I forgot to tell you the over eve that Errol called both send best wishes, Mae.* No attempt is made to imitate the signature on this spoof message. Mae West was no dumb blonde. Ten years earlier she had been to prison over her Broadway play, Sex.   38e

October 2nd.   Jean writes from the Rajputana Hotel to Miss Betty Brown in Eaton Bray, *Well here we are among all the panthers. It's a gorgeous spot, and the colours are breath-taking. We go over the desert to Jodhpur... We are both horrified about the Munich Agreement. 'Cold feet' do you think. Anyway it's ghastly.* News went quickly through the Empire: Jean does not see Chamberlain as a Pilgrim of Peace.   38f

"I never worry about the price, I pay for everything with a smile."
"Indeed, and what do you pay the rent with?"

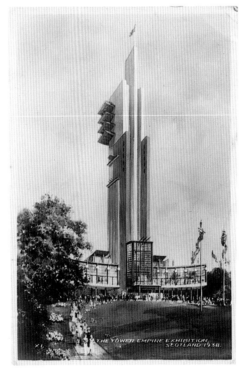

THE TOWER EMPIRE EXHIBITION, SCOTLAND 1938.

Evening Ensemble in Louis Velveteen from British Industries Fair.

July 11th.   Rose in Bognor writes to Irene Lapper in Choumert Road, Peckham, *The weather here is simply grand, wish you were here, I miss Fred though I'm all scorched up like a cinder.* Fashions had undergone a revolution and both they and the ample foodstuffs on the table would be just a nostalgic memory when the table cloth had been dyed for black-out material and the huge tea packet would have to last months.   38g

September 27th.   Betty from the Glasgow Exhibition to Mrs Hand in Putney, *very nice run up here, saw the launch beautifully. Left nice hotel at Manchester at 6am... The launch was very good. The Queen spoke so nicely. but this show is wonderful. haven't seen quarter yet but have yet till 12 midnight. no more now must get in & see more.* Betty evidently took in the launch of the Queen Elizabeth on Clydebank.   38h

February 28th.   From Reading to Miss Barnes in Pakenham, *Just to say we are still in the same old trade. Thanks for cards. Pakenham does look a pretty place... Mother & Theodora send their love. Fondest from Violet & Reg.* Alfred Louis is showing his latest creation at the British Industries Fair. Such clothes would now be seen only in glamorous Hollywood films. Perhaps Violet and Reg are the Reading agents.   38i

April 10th. Josef Vieshofer in Hitler's hometown of Linz writes (in Esperanto) to J Barry in SW London, *Esteemed Comrade! At this time when events of world significance are taking place permit me to greet you and send you this valuable souvenir. It is more or less a farewell souvenir and because of that it is perhaps worth keeping. I am now a member of a great nation and I am happy because I am one of those who after long years of unemployment have found work. Once again comradely greetings.* Hitler made things work and in doing so created work. Despite the comradely greetings (not here a communist salutation) one cannot help reading into a card celebrating the annexation of Austria a kind of provocative arrogance. It virtually puts an end to communication between two friends once linked by the international language of hope. 38j

October 9th. Naomi Polschorsky in Tel Aviv to Miss Lewinson at the Chelsea Polytechnic, *You will probably be surprised to receive any card from Palestine... How did you pass the world crisis. I wonder whether you offered your support to Mr Chamberlain. I enjoy every minute in Palestine but the general situation is very bad.* The fate of Palestine was, as ever, under discussion. Civil disturbances were frequent with Arabs stoning Jews and Jews bombing Arabs. The idea of partitioning the country like some Ireland of the Middle East was about to be dropped. Palestine would become a unified state under British rule, despite the promise that it would be a homeland for the Jews. The mix of cultures is apparent here. 38k

January 12th. Len posts this card in Paris to Mr & Mrs Morris in Battersea, *Glorious journey: Have found a very comfortable room for 2/6d a night. Am alone: Have decided to come on with the party on Sunday. Will write from Chamonix.* Perhaps Len was a supporter of, rather than an activist for, the Republican struggle. The parties and factions with their acronyms not only make the history of the civil war confusing but indicate a profound disunity that was all too ominous. PSU (Partido Socialista Unitado) is here linked with UGT (Union General de Trabajadores), the latter being in direct alliance with the communists. The graphic is typical of revolutionary causes and could come from a later Cuba or Mexico. 38l

May 12th. Anne in New York to Miss B H Benjamin in Akron, Ohio, *Bee dear, sorry but I just rec'd your letter <u>this</u> weekend. I had wanted to write to you today but no minute is my own. So - I'm writing you now from the theatre. The play is marvelous!* Anne's praise of the play may be sincere but it is certainly obligatory since the card is offered by the theatre itself, 'Be your own critic. Let a friend know what you think of 'The Children's Hour'. We will stamp and mail card'. What Anne does not mention is the controversial nature of Lillian Hellman's subject matter, a whispering campaign in a school about a lesbian relationship between two of the teachers. This was pretty strong stuff for the period and helped the show's successful passage into a second year on Broadway. The decorative motif below the image masks the original higher seat prices. Hellman lived with Dashiel Hammett who went to prison in 1951 for refusing to testify at the McCarthy hearings. 38m

August 5th. From nearby Carshalton to Plumpton Green, Sussex, *Arrived safely, having lovely weather and a very happy time here. Shall leave tomorrow for France. with love from R Gilpilla.* This typical multi-view of an outer London suburb outlines the possibilities for the visitor to Sutton. One might admire the straightness of Angel Hill, for example (top left), or stroll into Manor Park and linger before the War Memorial (top right). Shopping always can be relied upon to pass the time though the temptation would be to hop on the 156 bus in Cheam Road to go somewhere, anywhere else. Luckily the Plaza cinema is open and one might join the group of ladies who are preparing to pay their one and sixpence (7 1/2p) to see an old Michael Arlen film, The Virginian, together with, more interestingly, Shirley Temple's new film Captain January (see 36l) in which a little girl is rescued from a shipwreck by a lighthouse keeper. Not a dry eye in the house. 38n

August 24th.   C in Midlothian pointedly uses this Republican propaganda card of the Spanish Civil War to write to the Rev Geoffrey Stott in London W6, *Thought you'd be interested to know that we've just heard from Peter again. He was all right up to August 10th anyhow. He sounds cheery and serene, quite sure that the Governmant will win though it may take a long time yet. He says 'The things we are fighting for* <u>*must*</u> *win and if you could see our bombed villages you'd realise why fascism must be beaten'. Well - best of luck to him! And our best to you and the family. This is a Spanish card. Thought you'd like it.* Peter's optimism is evidently fuelled by his idealism. The Republicans are in ideological and military disarray and with imagined allies like the above, who are, literally, at the moment looking the other way (towards Czechoslovakia and the first rumblings of World War) their days of hope are numbered. The bombed villages, including Guernica (whose fate Picasso immortalised in 1937), were merely target practice for the Luftwaffe and the 'union of the democratic nations' which the card says in three languages 'will end war forever' has already arranged for Peter, if he has survived, and the rest of the International Brigade Volunteers to return home.   38o

March 4th.   The card above, singularly for this book, was neither written in English or sent to an English speaking country. But here art itself is at the front line both in racial and aesthetic terms. HW has visited the Berlin showing of the Degenerate Art (Entartete Kunst) exhibition which had opened in Munich in July 1937. He writes to Herrn Küpper in Duisburg, *Dear Uncle Emil. This exhibition leaves one with the kind of impressions that merely make one shake one's head. sincere Hitlergreetings* [Hitlergrüsse]. Ironically this manifesto against modern art coincided with the presentation in Paris of Picasso's Guernica, a work by the antifascist fiend who, inspired by Negro sculpture had, with the connivance of Jewish art dealers (who must be destroyed) and the deranged German painters in this exhibition (who must be sterilised) caused Holy German Art to be subverted and undermined. However, the Führer, following the model of Soviet Russia in the twenties, would soon bring art to heel.   38p

July 20th.   DW to Mrs A Lowry in Lifford, Co Donegal, *We have just come down from the Tower - a fine clear breezy day & had a great view of the City & Countryside.* Another aspect of the striking de Stijl-like Tower of Empire by Thomas Smith Tait (dismantled despite widespread protest in 1939) which was drawn and photographed from all angles for postcards.   38q

November 19th.   With the Second World War only a few weeks old G & T send this card of their volunteer ambulance unit (complete with shining new helmets) from London to Mr Greaves in Warrington to wish him a happy birthday. Their message ends, *Nothing exciting here yet*. Indeed there would not be for a few months yet until the blitz put an end to all thoughts of a 'phoney war'. Then these women in their practical slacks with two male volunteers in front of a pessimistically huge ambulance (a converted removal van?) would need all the spirit and humour they so patently possess.   39a

August 18th.   George details his slow recovery to Mr & Mrs Keen in Crowborough, Sussex, *Just a relic, which you should remember*. A bus advertising Ivor Novello's lead role in The Rat dates this card to 1924 as does the early colour film Wanderer of the Wasteland. The war was at least an alibi for postcard sellers to get rid of old stock.   39b

July 5th.   Guy writes to Henry F Hall in Amsterdam NY from the Automat, *These are our favourite eating places. Nearly all the cafeterias and restaurants are closed for the 4th so in order to get a good meal we had to eat here.* Those down on their luck could mix the two free ingredients, ketchup and water, to make 'vagrant's soup'.   39c

The Cenotaph and Whitehall, London.

OUR MODERN ARMY: "THE COLONEL SENDS THIS WITH HIS COMPLIMENTS AND HOPES THE NIGHT AIR WILL HAVE NO ILL EFFECT UPON YOUR HEALTH!"

September 4th (the day after war was declared). Anne in London to Minehead, *Dear Trinity. What terrible <u>news today</u>. If J is called up shall be coming down, but not for a little while I hope. He is doing duty at the clearing station. What a hustle Mollie had... will keep in touch with you if still alive.* Did Lutyens (now President of the RA) guess that his cenotaph would serve yet another war? A depressingly apt choice of card. 39d

August 30th. From Mr Collins in Enfield to his son in Guildford. *Dear John, Be a good boy & look after Mummie. I hope to see you both soon. Lots of love & xs from Daddy.* The simplest messages sometimes tell the longest tales. The wry humour of Reg Carter's cartoon about improved conditions for servicemen would not deflect the fears and uncertainties these few lines must have provoked. 39e

"We had Harricot beans for dinner to-day!"

August 29th. Phyllis in Lancing to Mrs Tapper in Choumert Rd, Peckham, *Many thanks for letters. Hope you all got on allright in your gas masks. Worthing is deserted everybody has rushed home. We are all anxiously awaiting the news, lets hope it will be good.* Everyone by now had been issued with gas masks and schools had gas mask drills. McGill's post Sunday lunch scene beautifully catches their grotesque aspect. 39f

March 21st. Lewis & Springer, motor dealer of Auburn NY sends news of the new Oldsmobile 70 with its Observation-Type Body by Fisher to the Rev Jerome Holubowicz in NY city. This is the car I imagine Philip Marlow driving, though his Olds was an earlier model: yet 1939 is the year Chandler published The Big Sleep, the greatest of detective stories, which gives my imaginings some authenticity. 39g

December 20th. We are back again after twenty one years to Somewhere in France. Arthur (or the RAF censor who has stamped the card) has obliterated the name of the place and the tell-tale location of the publisher. He writes to Mrs French in Birmingham *Just a card to let you know that everything is well. This is a photo of the vineyards of France. I have received a parcel from Ward End exservicemen club. Bye Bye.* 39h

December 29th. Kath West's father sends the first of many cards to his evacuee daughter now in Harrogate, *We hope you got back safely - on time and not too cold. I wish I could have come to Kings X but perhaps it was as well. We used the bath first time... it stood the strain splendidly. Trust you had a welcome that kept your mind off home. Lots of love. Dad xxx.* The music-hall song 'We're going to hang out the washing on the Siegfried Line' mocked Germany's French-border defences. 39i

"The State as such will not have any official religion, but will make a concordat with the Catholic Church as to the respective functions of each, thereby respecting our traditions and the religious sentiment of the immense majority of the Spanish people"—General Franco.

BING CROSBY   PARAMOUNT PICTURES.

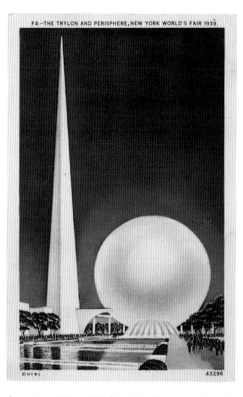

F4:—THE TRYLON AND PERISPHERE, NEW YORK WORLD'S FAIR 1939.

©NYWF   43296

February 13th.   EG in London to Col E Ryan in Tillingbourne *Thanks for yours of 11th. Yes. I am tackling the letter of which you enclosed cutting: will discuss possibility of another meeting in Dorking with C'tee tomorrow.* What committee in Dorking involving British officers sent memos on Why I Support Franco cards? Britain soon recognised Franco's government (to opposition cries of Heil Chamberlain!).   39j

November 22nd.   Beryl Atkinson's parents in London write to her c/o Mrs Outlaw in Berkhamstead where she seems to be an evacuee, *Shall have to write to you again dear, to tell you about the week-end... I hope you have been out in this lovely weather. It must have been perfect in the country.* Bing Crosby crooned his way through the thirties and forties. He and Bob Hope were just starting the first Road film.   39k

September 19th.   Bill G in Brooklyn writes from the NY World's Fair to Mr & Mrs Groves at the Douro Wine Shop in Duddlesborough, Yorks, *Dear Babs and Cliff, If things were as carefree in Europe as over here tonight I guess everything would be OK.* The World's Fair though not ideally timed was a great success. These two architectural sculptures with futuristic names were by Harrison and Fouilhoux.   39l

The Lake.

The Rose Walk.

TRENTHAM GARDENS

Trentham Hall.

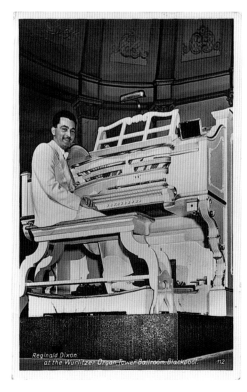

Reginald Dixon
at the Wurlitzer Organ Tower Ballroom, Blackpool.   112

September 3rd.   A in Stoke-on-Trent to Miss Drage in Paddock Wood on the opening day of the war, *I don't know whether you are still at Rustlington, but I hope things will be all right there... now that we know that it is war. There will probably be a lot of noise from gunfire but shouldn't be much else near Tonbridge. I shall try and get home one weekend when we see how trains and things generally are going.*   39m

November 17th.   Mother in Worcester to Miss Strother in Wolverhampton... *no news yet. Alf is OK and Dad and also the rest of us. Do you know this. Cheeriho. love from us all.* The first World War seems to survive in the military bearing of this AA patrolman. The Automobile Association appears to have provided better cut uniforms than the army. Gone are the days when such as he saluted from a motorbike each AA member.   39n

July 3rd.   From Lily in Blackpool to Enid in Eccleston, *Here again, quite a jolly lot we are, Mr & Mrs Smith are here... also Mr & Mrs Garside... have all gone about together... we all went Thursday in the Tower to see Norman & Reginald Dixon. Norman has still got the same crooner only a girl as well as a man.* Reginald Dixon played the illuminated cinema organs that rose up from the pit between pictures.   39o

> **"I** haven't got electric light— have you a set that will run off the gas meter?"**

August 18th.   From M in Hitchin to Miss Iris Cozins in Bournemouth, *Only 1 more day then I shall be seeing you. hope it will be a nice drive and not so much about...* To one who was educated by gaslight until 1948 the lady's confusion is not surprising (conversion to electricity was halted by the war). Behind her hand is a great bakelite masterpiece, the Ecko radio (to be found now only in museums, see 84o).   39p

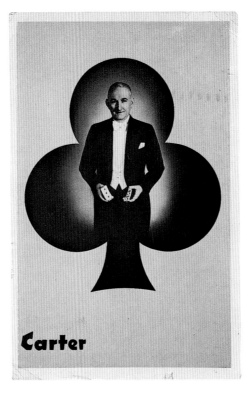

Carter

April 19th.   Carter's card is arresting and effective and he seems at the moment to be in demand addressing this to the stage door of the Coventry Hippodrome, *As I will not be coming on to Coventry with the show 'Wonder Rocket' I would esteem it a favour if you would forward any mail to me this week to the Empire Nottingham. Thanking you in —— anticisipation.* Was Coventry's loss Nottingham's gain?   39q

39a. Publisher unknown

39b. C F Castle. Lesco series

39c. Horn & Hardart Lumitone Photoprint NY

39d. Publisher unknown British Production Throughout

39e. Humoresque No 4779

39f. New Donald McGill comics No 856

39g. Oldsmobile

39h. Publishers name obliterated by censor. Field Post Office 26A RAF censor NC111

39i. Tuck Give 'em Socks postcard No 3064

39j. Spanish Press Services. Marshall & Co, Nottingham

39k. Paramount Pictures 47/Art Photo Co

39l. Manhattan postcard Publishing Co 43296

39m. Nuview series HSB

39n. Publisher unknown

39o. Tower Ballroom, Blackpool

39p. HB 4d (Hutson Bros). Artist unknown.

39q. Gebrüder Garloff, Magdeburg

39r. George Wenzel Studio, Milwaukee

39s. Metro Goldwyn Mayer Pictures No 14

39t. Detail of The Caves, Flamborough No 7. Publisher unknown

Dell Kuri

October 9th.   From Helen in Milwaukee to Edward J Wellmuth in Chicago, *Saw this girl jump off air-plane. Will see you soon.* Dell Kuri, like Carter, seems to have her own card showing her in action. It is hard to imagine anyone even in the thirties jumping from an aeroplane with so little protection, no helmet, no windcheater jacket. Surely these fashion sandals are the last footwear one would choose for parachuting. Nonetheless a very stylish image.   39r

CLARK GABLE   METRO·GOLDWYN·MAYER PICTURES

October 23rd.   Once again to Beryl the evacuee from her mother who is trying hard to get her the right film-star photos (though it seems Beryl is fussy). *I hope Mrs Outlaw had my letter... I shall be writing to tell you about the weekend. I havn't been able to get any turned round the other way yet but will try.* Clark Gable is already king of Hollywood. This year saw the release of one of the century's great blockbusters Gone With The Wind.   39s

August 28th.   May in Bridlington to the disastrously named Mrs Kraut in Chesterfield, *Here I am at Brid. and feeling a little fed up. I went on the Princes Parade this morning and imagine my horror when I saw a strange drummer. I asked Lionel John's where Eddie was this morning, and he said 'in the Army my dear girl' he's been called up as he is a reservist. L.J. was very chatty and told me quite a lot about Eddie, he thinks an awful lot about him, he took him to the Army Headquarters in Hull and tried to get him back, but he had to stay. Love May.* A sad tale well told, whose threads unravel so that we know quite a lot about May and Eddie and their as yet undeveloped relationship and of the band, and of the superior status of Lionel Johns (bandmaster?). We know little however about Mrs Kraut, and whether Mr Kraut was interned, or if they changed their names.   39t

September 20th.   Special indulgence must have been given to Valentine's the publisher for their use of full-colour printing on quality stock to make this patriotic card in their Helpful Thoughts series. The famous speech was made on June 4th only three weeks after Churchill assumed command following Chamberlain's resignation. Annie in Southall writes to Mrs White in Reigate, *The skirt arrived Sat. O.K. Many Thanks indeed it fits fine & will be so warm. H.M.V. won't release me yet but the Civil Defence are appealing against it as they want me. I shall know sometime next week. Essential work, packing. Isn't this a nice card?*   40a

November 13th.   Kath's dad once more to his daughter in Harrogate written in all too apparent haste, *Many thanks for your letter - We are still well and nothing to worry about. Hope to write you a letter one day but 9 - 5 takes up all day. Lots of love xxx.* Here in 1939, Oliver Hardy (absenting himself from Stan. Laurel) stars with Harry Langdon in Elephants Never Forget (called Zenobia in the US).   40b

Day & month unclear.   To Eleanor Mitchell in Los Angeles with a mimeographed message, *Well! Once again I am in New York working harder than ever to bring you back the buy you have been looking for. Ben Cohen, Your Furrier. 223 West 9th St. LA.* The writing looks trustworthy, the message is keen, yet with the hint of desperation that always taints a salesman's sincerity. Who now in LA buys furs?   40c

HAWKER "HURRICANE"

THE NEW STREAMLINER "400" — CHICAGO AND NORTH WESTERN LINE

TAPROOM In The TAVERN·LUNCH COUNTER·LOUNGE CAR Of The NEW "400"—Insert, POPULAR LUNCH COUNTER

October 4th.   WS in Blackburn to May Smith in Dereham, Norfolk, *Received P/O today. Have been off work again with a bad foot. Engine part dropped on it. But am all right now. Just off to see Robert Donat the film star in person in a play. The cake is all gone?!* It is the height of the Blitz when Spitfires and Hurricanes (the most successful combat fighter of the war) are in the throes of the Battle of Britain.   40d

September 18th.   MC in St Louis to Bill James in Miami, Oklahoma, *Hello Kid on our way to see Fro & Corky, almost glad we don't have bus passes any more - so we can go on the choo choo train: Emilie rather eat on the train than any thing on earth - going down town shopping for a grey sports hat - hard to find.* England never caught up with this chic railway practicality and now never would.   40e

HAVANA. CUBAN TYPICAL RUMBA.

The main medical and surgical block of the new Hospital for Sick Children, Great Ormond Street, which has just been completed to replace the old buildings, first opened in 1852

March 14th.   Paul in Havana to Jackson Cross in Brooklyn, *Jack - does this remind you of your sensational capture by the Heights Casino Rumba Championship - How about the setting. Been here visiting for a week - very interesting.* Before the Castro era Havana was a fun lover's paradise. Paul mentions Rumbas & Casinos and only needs a couple more words, prostitution and drugs, to complete the picture.   40f

February 26th.   E MacDonald of the Hospital's Appeals Dept. writes to Miss Marian Tandy in Sheffield, *Thank you so much for the cards & tin foil. We shall look forward to your next parcel.* Stanley Hall's new hospital block was completed in 1938 and incorporated the latest views on the maximum of light and fresh air: yet the complex is now under review again and may itself be replaced before long.   40g

ANNETTE · EMILIE · CECILE · YVONNE · MARIE
The Dionne Quintuplets at Callander, Ontario, Canada.-30

August 8th.   Nancy writes to Mrs Ruth Hanks in Richmond, Va, *Here we are way up here in Northern Canada. We are waiting to see these little people now, could hear them singing but they won't be on exhibition for a couple of hours.* Quintland as their theme park came to be called had regular public hours of play and feeding, like a zoo. Here some music pretends to be going on for the benefit of postcard variety (Cecile is playing a triangle with a triangle).   40h

September 1st.   Mabel in Crewkerne to Elsie Dourden in Milford-on-Sea, *P. Order received safely, sorry it was not right for you glad Edie looks better hope you are all well.* This British Legion card shows the factory in Richmond where Haig Fund poppies continue to be made. Virtually everybody bought one on Armistice Day. Even though the practise has waned somewhat in London thirty million poppies (not counting wreaths etc.) were produced in 1999.   40i

LESLIE HOWARD

GRUB'S GOING UP!

COMFORTABLE WINTER ATTIRE FOR MIAMI BEACH.   43260

November 17th.   Boys wanted cards of planes and trains while girls preferred film stars. Publishers of both did well out of parents writing to their evacuated offspring. Beryl Atkinsons gets a picture of Leslie Howard, archetypal screen Englishman of Hungarian origin (killed when enemy fire brought down his plane in 1943) *...be seeing you on Sunday. I will bring some stamps with me, you won't need any before then.*   40j

April 30th.   From Scotty in Lewes to Mrs Courage in nearby Burgess Hill, *This is just a P.C. (before I have to pay 2d for the post) to thank you for... Sunday - for the Rhubarb etc - which was lovely. I have some biscuits for William (seeing he wouldn't let me pay for it) ...I have got my new teeth - feel no end of a swell.* With the postal rate doubling, food was not the only thing that was going up.   40k

November 12th.   Mr Dolan, signing himself Johnnie Jerk, writes to Hal Springfield in Fairfield, Conn., *This is the way we run around down here, so natural don't you think? Down with my sister at pres.* The rules and codes of dress shift and change. Grown women can be almost naked now at Miami Beach but these minors might be covered up. Health, decency, fashion, custom, anarchy and law fight it out on the sand.   40l

"ATTACHED TO THE AIR FORCE"

"FOR THE TENTH TIME, WRONG NUMBER!"

August 13th.   Olive in Morecambe to Miss Illingworth in Leeds, *Am here for the week. Weather been perfect up to now. This place is overcrowded with Air Force chaps, so we are having a right good time.* The Women's Auxiliary Air Force was given full military status in 1941 but I doubt if their uniforms ever included gold high heeled shoes. According to his hat the sailor is from HMS Impudent.   40m

November 16th.   M North to Miss Iris Preece in Gt. Malvern, *The sentries do not stand out on guard outside this building in wartime. They used to look very splendid in the uniforms. Now it is Khaki and they are not cavalrymen. Hope you had a happy holiday.* It was no time for decorative soldiery or fancy ceremonies London now presented a drab sight of sandbags and lampless winter gloom, even in Whitehall.   40n

September 11th.   Doris in Morecambe to the Pooles in Stoke-on-Trent, *Having a rest & a few nights sleep here this week. Been terrible at home, will let you know later. The children are better for the change or else Dorothy is very nervy. Neither get panicky but afraid to go out. Six & seven warnings a day, then continual from 8.30 to next morning. What a life!!* A comic card that is a short story in its own right.   40o

U.S.S. NEW-YORK

June 19th.   From Henry in Norfolk, Virginia, to Zana Shipley in Kingsport Tennessee, *Hi Zana, How's everything O.K. I hope. I am O.K. and making it very easy waiting on my ship to return don't know exactly when but here's hoping soon, say what's come over William I have wrote him five times and have not heard from him yet, Hope you got your motor fixed soon it looks like I will have to get Hitler after all. Well you can get my address from mother.* This is Henry's ship and, like all ships, has its story. In the case of USS New York, a vessel with nine lives, it is a special tale. As a film biopic, with ship as heroine, it would begin with a Griffith-like sequence in the Brooklyn Naval Yard of 1911 and end with a scene tailor-made for Spielberg during the atomic bomb tests in Bikini Atoll in 1946. Even then there would be an epilogue in which, returning for a last time to Pearl Harbour in 1948, she is sunk as a target ship in full scale battle manoeuvres. The USS New York was flagship at Vera Cruz in the Mexico Crisis of 1914, and entered World War I at Scapa Flow in 1917, pursued by U boats. Present at the surrender of the German fleet in the Firth of Forth she then escorted President Wilson on his way to the Versailles conference. Between wars she was a training ship and in 1937 took Admiral Rodman the President's representative to the Coronation of George VI and participated in the famous Naval Review. In 1941, probably with Henry on board, she joined the Neutral Patrol escorting troops to Iceland and guarding convoys to Scotland against U boats. As a warship she entered the invasion of North Africa in 1942 and stood by at Casablanca before returning to America as a training ship. She departed again for Pearl Harbour in 1945 to join in the preinvasion bombardment at Iwo Jima. After some repairs she supported the assault on Okinawa where she was grazed by a kamikaze plane. At the war's end she returned with veterans to the West Coast and sailed thence to Bikini where she survived both the surface blast and the underwater explosion of the atomic tests. Even one like myself not usually stirred by accounts of naval warfare cannot fail to see in the mind's eye this Homeric tale unfold with its amazing variety of locations, incidents and personnel. No wonder Henry was impatient to greet his ship again.   40p

F73-NEW YORK ZOOLOGICAL SOCIETY EXHIBIT BUILDING, NEW YORK WORLD'S FAIR

45008

W.F.15—TRANSPORTATION BUILDING, ROCKET PORT, NEW YORK WORLD'S FAIR 1939

August 24th.   Paul to Miss Jean Hoseason in Swamyshott, Mass. *Don't suppose I should write to you so often but just tell you (if you at home) that we have seen the Fair. We spent 7 hrs there yesterday then went to the show until 3 this morning. We* cannot learn why Paul should not write to Jean. The World's Fair in its second year still provided these fascinatingly stylised cards. The round object is Beebe's Bathysphere massively enlarged as part of Harold Sterner's pavilion design.   40q

August 2nd.   To Mrs Trudaker in Port Arthur, Texas. Browns & Levy use the World's Fair cards to tell their customers about new stock, in mimeographed handwriting *What a fair! While in NY I bought new Fall and Winter styles for Men and Women and I'm happy to say the styles are better and prices are lower ... etc.* One can't help thinking as one looks through these eye catching and visionary cards that many of the displays were more like art installations, with more style than content.   40r

GERMAN "MESSERSCHMITT" ME.110

ALROPLANE PHOTOGRAPH
COPYRIGHT

38A-75

May 14th. Mr New sends a very topical card to his wife in Woking, *Dearest Topsy, Here is a picture of the plane in which Rudolf Hess flew to Glasgow. I have planted ever so many seeds in the allotment and must now wait to see them grow. I hope that the play will be successful tomorrow evening and that there will be a large and appreciative audience. D.I.D.L.Y.E.S.M.* [Darling I do love you ever so much ?] *B.C.* [big cuddle ?] *etc.* Hess parachuted from his Messerschmidt and was found by a local ploughman who offered him a cup of tea. Hitler's deputy claimed to be ready to negotiate peace terms of his own accord. He was merely detained and at the Nuremberg trials of 1946 was sentenced to life imprisonment. He died in Spandau gaol in 1987 aged 93.   41a

PICCADILLY CIRCUS. LONDON. W.1.

S.19454.

November 5th. Mrs Armstrong receives a child's scribble in Lynton, N Devon on the back of this view datable to 1932 by the almost completed Guinness Clock (lacking now only the word Time). A poster advertises Noel Coward's revue Cavalcade at Drury Lane which had opened in 1931.   41b

September 27th. Neat printed handwriting shows that these Fibonaccian spirals belong to Beekman Tower on 49th St where Ruth writes to Miss Coffin in Allston Mich, *Have changed my way of living. All furniture is at college now and I am living here.* Beekman Tower was built in 1928 in full Art Deco style and is now a hotel.   41c

THE SKATING RINK, EMPRESS HALL, BUTLINS HOLIDAY CAMP, SKEGNESS H.1508

I CAN'T GET ALONG WITHOUT YOU.

September 7th.   Gilbert writes to his Aunt, Rachel Davies in Glanamman nr. Ammanford in S Wales to tell her that he is in Skegness, *The buildings that you see in the photograph are the places where we get our meals. They are called 'houses' with several hundreds in each house so you can imagine the noise.* Butlin's first venture had now turned into quite another kind of camp as Gilbert describes (see note).   41d

February 10th.   To Miss D M Ottaway in Petham, *my darling. Have just arrived Kings X. Hope you are OK. Love Henry.* The practise of using toddlers in adult situations, so common in war cartoons, deserves a thesis in its own right. Brian White adds to the list with his Nipper series. This pedal car (with regulation masked lamps) laughs at the Motor Spirit Ration Book, and Pool Petrol (generic wartime brand).   41e

"WELLINGTON" BOMBERS.

Fulmar Petrel.

September 11th.   Auntie Silv in Norwich to Master M J Drew in Wendover *my dearest Michael, Here's hoping your new school has come up to your expectations. Fancy this is the only card I could find that I didn't see marked on the list. The shops are getting thorough wash-outs.* Michael got a good picture of Wellington bombers. The roar of such a formation was deafeningly marvellous.   41f

December 11th.   F stationed in the Shetlands writes to his wife Mrs Geidt in Swanmore... *only a postcard to-night... as I've still to prepare my talk for to-morrow. How sad the news is about Prince of Wales and Repulse* [sunk by the Japanese] *on other fronts or rather in Europe & Africa things seem definitely better, but how one longs to get a really good smack at those Japs. all love.*   41g

No. 338   U. S. ARMY MOTOR CONVOY   Photo by U. S. Army Signal Corps.

August 26th.   Dad sends his regular card from London to Kath in Harrogate, *Many thanks for your letter. Aunt Una, Ethel & Colin called yesterday - the child was wearing the blue romper suit. Hope you got the oranges and cigs yesterday. We are all looking forward to Saturday. Thought you might like a picture of peaches - at 2s,6p each they are quite cheap.* In today's money over £2. Presumably the cigs weren't for Kath herself: oranges would have been a rare treat.   41h

December 15th.   Henry Cairnes at Ayer camp writing to his parents, *Its swell up here. Food good. Fellows fine. Hope to see you soon. Best of luck.* Hitler and Mussolini had declared war on the US on the 11th December four days after the US fleet was virtually destroyed at Pearl Harbour. Henry may have been one of those rapidly enlisted in the following week. The sight and sound of these American trucks was to become familiar all over Europe.   41i

September 30th.   To Miss P Ashton in Oxted, *...arrived at about 7.30... There was a battle on just round grace's and we had a job to get along for soldiers and tanks. Mr H had already had his shop window broken... have just met paul going to tea with Ken. love from w.* Kettering looks quieter in this view from circa 1939 where a few people are sizing up the stills and wondering whether to see Sonja Henie, the ice dancer, in My Lucky Star at the Odeon cinema.   41j

April 23rd.   Dad to Kath, who is in what sounds like a transit point between billets at POSB No 5 The Hutments, St George's Road Harrogate, *Hope you are well, we have nothing to grumble about. Am getting on with the cellar. Hope to have it finished by the weekend. We are looking forward to Saturday - I shall be at Kings Cross. The damage last week was awful and travelling is very difficult.* On 16th April alone 500 planes dropped 100,000 bombs on London.   41k

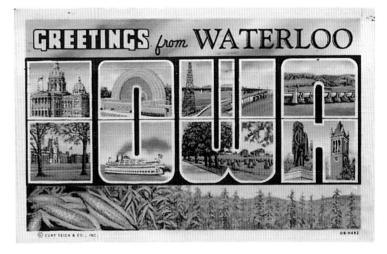

July 14th.   June & Ulto to Kay & Ed Schilling in Chicago, *Here's an example of what we are seeing. We're not sorry we came. America is a beautiful place to live in.* Mount Rushmore had just been opened to the public (after its creator's death on March 3rd). It is still a work in progress to be finished by Gutzon Borglum's son, Lincoln. June & Ulto must have been among the first visitors (see 31a).   41l

June 25th.   Valera Vickey to what seems to be a newish penfriend in Joplin, Montana, *Dear Friend, Liked the card real well. No I don't belong to the Legion Aux. Thought once of joining tho never did. I never made peach preserve. I've a real good recipe for pear jam tho - with dates and nuts - if you'd care for everyone likes it. Hardly know pears in it tho...* Curt Teich & Co at their best with this fine design.   41m

August 22nd.   PP to J Lewis May in London, *Cher Allié, You are right, the cost of stamps is alarming. So I save a halfpenny. My wife is like yours. We shall have to leave this hotel and find something cheaper. I should like to return to Nevern Sq but my wife won't hear of it. It will be a wrench to sell my books so carefully collected and many signed by their authors. I have to get my baccy matches & tobacco from Harrods.*   41n

August 1st.   Percy to Fred Elkins in Ascot *Many happy Returns... am at a large mansion on the banks of the River Exe near Lymstone, a lovely spot. It is the Regimental Training School and is very strict which unfortunately doesn't give us much chance for exploring the neighbourhood... the house is said to have belonged to Sir Francis Drake.* Brian White makes bold use of the blackout and both children dutifully carry their gas-mask boxes.   41o

PRESIDENT ROOSEVELT SIGNS THE LEASE-AND-LEND BILL
MARCH 11TH, 1941

Portrait by Cecil Beaton

"WE WILL FINISH THE JOB"
"We shall not fail or falter; we shall not weaken
or tire. Neither the sudden shock of battle,
nor the long-drawn trials of vigilance and
exertion will wear us down.
GIVE US THE TOOLS AND WE WILL FINISH THE JOB."
Mr Churchill's reply to Mr Roosevelt.

1941 MESSAGES·NOTES·PARTICULARS

41a. Valentine's/The Aeroplane 38A-7B

41b. Bridge House Real Photo Series S19454

41c. Manhattan Art Press, NY

41d. Valentine's H1508, The messages continues:-
There are 5,000 of us here. we have had our uniforms and serious training will begin on Monday. we have not much time to spare because of the amount of lectures and drills that have to be taken each day. The bugle calls us at 5.50am. cup of cocoa at 6.10am with marching and drilling in between. A young man from Kingsbury is staying in the same chalet as me and we are both doing wireless mechanics co-ordinating with Radio location. I have met one Welshman, Nantlais Williams' nephew from Aberdare.

41e. Valentine's Nipper Series 361 Artist: HBW (Brian White)

41f. Valentine's 38A-45A

41g. J O Rattan. Lerwick

41h. Ed J Burrows & Co, London Artist: Prof E Oyger

41i. W R Thompson. Richmond VA. No 338 Photo: Army Signals Corps

41j. Valentine's H1865

41k. Judges Ltd. L.659

41l. Publisher unknown

41m. Curt Teich, Chicago OB H492

41n. Sweetman & Son, Tunbridge Wells Solochrome Series 6322

41o. Valentine's Nipper Series 218. Artist: Brian White

41p. Tuck. Photo: Harris & Ewing

41q. Tuck. Photo: Cecil Beaton

41r. New Donald McGill Comics No 1111

41s. New Donald McGill Comics No 1108

41t. E H Wilkinson & Co, Toronto.

Hand cancelled 1941 by PO. Winnie & Bob Eldridge write to their parents *Bit windy yesterday ...went to Mr Lynetts village yesterday to see what it was like. Very nice little place. Bought this card in Aylesbury. Thought you would like photo of your boy friend. Love from us both.* Roosevelt offers military equipment on special terms to Britain comparing it (when talking on US radio) to lending a neighbour a hose to put out a fire. America was of course already active in giving escort to British fighting ships (see 40p) despite home opposition to such a non neutral role. 41p

August 16th. Dad to Kath, now in Harrogate, *Weather to-day is very wet but we must not grumble. Today is Elsie's big day - at 9.30 she starts at Southwark Billeting Office - I hope she will be happy. That unexploded bomb did not go off thank goodness. It is a large and powerful one from the accounts of wardens. It was lovely having you home - if only the War would end. Lots of love xxx.* If anyone was master of the soundbite it was Churchill, who planted memorable quotes with unerring aim at key points in his rhetoric. Cecil Beaton's photograph catches the mood. 41q

"Peace with very little on 'er!"

"There's two chaps I'd like to give a kick in the pants. Hitler an' that ruddy Quarter bloke!"
"Why, what's Hitler done?"

"COME, THEN, LET US TO OUR TASK."

January 20th. Trooper Don Jenkin writes to his mother in Penzance from Bovington Camp not giving her any news, *I received your letter OK, there is nothing wrong with me only that I have been so busy. will write a long letter soon. All my love.* McGill plays laboriously with the phrase Peace With Honour. 41r

February 23rd. Trooper Don Jenkin once more to his mother with no news to tell her but thanking her for her letter. One wonders whether he ever wrote the long letter he promised and hopes that his mother shared his taste for Donald McGill from whose 1939/40 pre-economy series these come. 41s

September 14th. From Tiny in Victoria, Canada, to William F Brewer in Los Angeles. *Dearest Bill. This Winston Churchill is really a marvellous man. Pictures of him are seen everywhere in Victoria & Vancouver. Also his head is framed in Neon a number of places. And Roosevelt is extremely popular here - in fact a lot of people here wish he was head of the Canadian Government. All the lamp posts have photos of Roosevelt or Churchill on them.* 41t

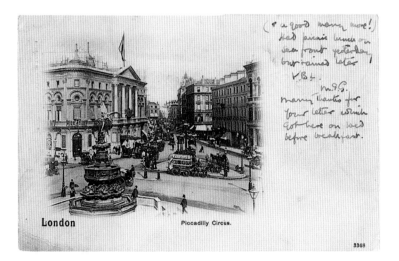

42

July 11th.   Private W E Sinstead serving with the Canadian army somewhere in Europe returns the card that accompanies a gift package of cigarettes to the donor, whose name and address is already inscribed (as above). He adds a more than usually expansive thankyou, *Dear Friend, Received your cigarettes and you will never realise how much us boys over here appreciate a good old cigarette from Canada. also the same as yourself my home is in Toronto just a few blocks east of dunlops, so thanking you again I'll sign off.* The whole operation was organised by the Overseas League. B95131 Pte Sinstead, W E No 1 Cdn. A.S.C.R.U. sounds as cheerful as the soldier illustrated. In the top right hand corner is the V for Victory with its famous morse code signature in the rhythm of Beethoven's Fifth Symphony.   42a

May 21st.   VBL to Miss Joan Gibbons in Holton le Moor, *I have given the word for the wash stands to be sold...* A time warp: the card is not merely pre-war (as is common) but pre Boer War, a fact that goes unmentioned by VBL. The 19thC view was printed in Hamburg on which Britain was now dropping bombs.   42b

June 9th.   American linen cards (as they were called even when they had no linen-style finish) are often so mannered that they make the world look as if it were made of marshmallow or fondant icing. Jon says *Hullo again* to Bert in Gloversville, N.Y., *Hellish hot but a cool breeze. N.Y. is very changed by the war.*   42c

V for Victory

THE SCOTTISH REST HOUSE FOR SERVICEMEN, 20 WATERLOO PLACE, EDINBURGH
THE CANTEEN

January 1st.   John writes from Hickory, NC, to Charles Martin in Fort Stanton, New Mexico, *Hello! How're you doing? It was very kind and Thoughtful of you to remember my Natal Anniversary. No one else remembers it, too near Christmas. Have you seen any V cards. I had several but they got away.* Churchill's V sign turned the will to win into a simple gesture.   42d

July 1st.   Ted at the end of a break at this Rest House sends a card to Miss Taylor in Brighton, *Dear Joan, Lovely weather. I am just getting ready to go back shortly. Look after yourself* (he ends with a V sign made of kisses). Were there flowers on the tables every day or just when the photographer came? Was water the only drink available?   42e

THE THREE BIGGEST SHIPS IN THE WORLD, WAR REFUGEES IN NEW YORK   (12)
QUEEN ELIZABETH (at right)   QUEEN MARY (center)   NORMANDIE (at left)
Gross Tonnage: 85,000   Gross Tonnage: 81,000   Gross Tonnage: 83,000

August 25th.   Marie Neuffler to Miss Maynice Kaetter in Reading, Ohio, *Greetings from New York and a lot of dark streets due to the nightly dim outs.* The Queen Mary now rests permanently at Long Beach, saved from the humiliating end of the Elizabeth which was fitted off Hong Kong as Seawise University. Before it was ready to open as such, howeves, a fire turned it into useless scrap.   42f

September 8th.   Bett in Bradford Pa., to Mrs Smith in Tioga Pa. *Dear Pearl, we are having a good time... Freda is getting rid of her boarder he came home drunk last night and made a mess all over her so you can hear her read it off. I guess louis is going to work to-morrow to Dressers. Saw a big parade Labor Day.* Many a Slip is the title of this comic from the slice-of-life school (like Bett's tale above).   42g

"SHEPPARDS HOTEL", GREAT ZIMBABWE RUINS.

WORLD'S LARGEST STORE, N. Y. . . . where 137,000 buy each day for cash in Macy's (Street floor).

June 6th.   Reedby in Fort Victoria writes to The Family in Dovercourt Bay, Essex, *This is part of the hotel where we are staying. We are surrounded by mountains. The flowers are wonderful, every colour you can think of.* Somehow the couple with the car exemplify the privileged life of whites in Southern and Eastern Africa. Their guide book to the nearby ruins would calculatedly tell them that these were built by Persians or Greeks or anyone but the indigenous black civilisation of the past.   42h

June 26th.   Leslie R Hastings to Hubert T Matthews in North Finchley, *Am celebrating my recent graduation as a commercial 'Air Navigator' right here in the Big City. I thought the view would interest you. Note the similarity of the interior to Harrod's man's shop. Expect to be back with you very soon.* One guesses that Leslie Hastings will be finding himself on very different aircraft before long. Macy's itself looks rather dimmed out though the view dates from 1939.   42i

October 12th. To Mrs Fred Doull in Portland, Maine, *Hello Vera. The base is near the farm. It's beautiful here... I've had all kinds of southern cooking. I like it very much. The plants and flowers are especially nice. Saw a chain gang working on the road today. Love, June xxx.* Army life, the southern cooking, the smells and sights of the south (including the chain gang) are a world away from Maine. 42j

June 1st. Mrs Edna Aberdeen to Mr Dixon in Knapton, *I know you will like to see our train, it wasn't drawn by this engine, one of the same type, Woodcock. The weather is rather too warm for much exertion.* The A4 Pacifics designed by Nigel Gresley were the most beautiful of English steam locos. It was yet another engine of this class, Mallard, that gained in 1938 (and holds) the steam speed record of 126mph. 42k

April 10th. Kath's dad to her in Harrogate, *Elsie will not be able to meet you so I will be at Kings X straight from office. E sits for her shorthand speed on Tues. and must leave her office early for that. She cannot leave early 2 nights.* Mr West does not mention (though he surely knew) that the Queen's Hall, where Henry Wood started his Proms and Thomas Beecham his orchestra, had been bombed some months before. 42l

September 28th. Ted in Dorking to Mrs Brazier & Family in Winslow, *Have got back here after my holiday at home which I enjoyed very much. It was nice to see all of them again. It's lovely here now, begins to look like autumn. Best of luck P.S. will let you know about the camp in due course.* The King sounds suspiciously Churchillian in his message. The ploughman's England will be lost either way. 42m

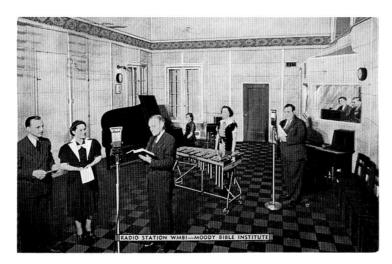

July 19th. June in Chicago to Miss Mary Carr in King George, Virginia, *having a wonderful time... have been so busy. Had two examinations today. Am taking Bible Doctrine and Children's work.* One of the more stable evangelical groups The Moody Bible Institute has had a long history. In broadcasting it was a pioneer with a radio station set up in 1926. This has now developed into a nationwide radio/TV network fed by satellite. 42n

April 8th. AMV to Mrs S Goldsmith in Lee-on-Solent, *Dear, we have had news of our darling he is a P.O.W. will write in a day or so. I am so overcome with the news what a relief it is to us all. I know how please you will be to hear. I should have written before only I know you will understand how I felt I just couldn't write.* This particular Bristol Bombay (already regarded as a noisy and antiquated type) crashed before the war even began. 42o

173.Z. ROYAL REGIMENT OF ARTILLERY MEMORIAL, LONDON. BEAGLES
ONE OF THE IMPRESSIVE BRONZE FIGURES FORMING PART OF THE MEMORIAL
ERECTED AT HYDE PARK CORNER.

June 24th.   Ralph sends a card from the Hotel Essex in Philadelphia to Kathryn Sheehan in Winona, Minnesota, *Dear Kathryn, Eve arrived day before yesterday. It's nice to have her here, even for whatever time I may have her here. I must admit Kathryn you are right about War. Have no idea where I'll be sent. Will just have to wait and see. Wish we were with you all.* This largely monosyllabic reflection captures the sudden uncertainties of war, as if Ralph had mused on his mortality for the first time. Sometimes in simple words you can hear somebody deepen.   42p

March 23rd.   Kath's dad again to her in Harrogate (temporarily c/o Mrs Fee), *Dear Kath, it is a week since I wrote but I have had a busy week and had run out of P.C's managed to get a few on Saturday, but mum wrote yesterday. You are helping the War Effort by your 10 shillings a week but some of it will be banked for after the war. Look after yourself...* Cards of memorials to the fallen are not the most cheerful to have found but at least Jagger, in his Hyde Park masterpiece, made the impedimenta of combat into poetry and proved that art is a matter of seeing and transforming.   42q

"SCAMP." WIRE-HAIRED TERRIER

January 6th.   Mr West (father of Kath) writes to his mother in Merrow, near Guildford, Surrey. *My dear Mother, received yours and Aunt's letters safely. The P.O. came through O.K. I had no intentions of your doing a thing like that, nevertheless your kind deed will not be imposed upon. I thank you very much and I want you to understand that I am steadily improving. I'm on the old place alright to-day and I am thankful. The news seems fairly good. 'Russia' is still forging ahead. Hitler certainly made a mistake in that direction. The 'Japs' are a nuisance but I feel sure that 'America' can hold them. Love Jack xx.* As well as finding one or two cards for Kath each week Jack West has to find it seems the same number for his mother though she appears to prefer dogs. On top of a nine-to-five office job he has regular Home Guard duties with responsibilities for others. The pressure and anxieties must have been hard to deal with. His wife is a slightly shadowy figure and Elsie, presumably the older daughter, also works.   42r

January 9th.   From Mr West again, in Hammersmith to his mother c/o Mrs Fagan. *My dear mother, I am back again on duty and my word isn't it cold. Thank goodness it is dry because I am stuck on the 'Station-Gate'. I am also on a very short property patrol (both sides of Church Street) so I will be able to call in and see my lady of the gloves. The first 2 hours of gate is over and I have seen my lady. I have arranged to call in at 9p.m. to hear the news. She is feeling a trifle sorry for herself because her husband who is now a soldier is leaving this country for some unknown destination. Very unpleasant (especially with two little kiddies) but there are thousands more in the same boat. Another doggie card. I have very few more left now. Keep living for 'der Tag'. Love Jack xx.* These two random snapshots of Jack West's routine have their own flavour as well as being characteristic of the period. One would love to hear more of his Lady of the Gloves with whom he shares the national ritual of the 9 o'clock news.   42s

May 8th.   Horace sends his mother from Westover this specially printed card which, placed in her window, will show she has a son on active service.   42t

043

November 20th.   Private Edna Hart writes to her friends Mr & Mrs Simmons in Newcastle, Indiana, from the base in Key West, *I have been in the army since July - and I love it. I have been in a typing and administration school. I am now in casual det. waiting for orders from Washington D.C. I think of you quite often.* In 1943 the Auxiliary was dropped from the Women's Auxiliary Army Corps and WAACS became WACS and could hold full army ranks. Private Edna is obviously as proud of her professional military status as are these girls sitting on Hitler in a crisply drawn cartoon by an anonymous artist.   43a

December 23rd.   Margaret to TMW Napier in Buckland Monachorum, Devon, *To wish you a very Happy Xmas & to say that Richard & Diana's present for you hasn't come yet - but it is coming.* This must be the saddest of all views of Piccadilly Circus (see 44a). The war has cut deep into so many of these lives.   43b

September 15th.   Alex Zogheib, off to Canada, writes to his son of the same name at the Biltmore Hotel, St Louis, before he goes off to Canada. This card was purchased by me for 50c at another hotel, the New Yorker (marked on this bird's eye view as No 6) at the New York Metropolitan Postcard Club's annual Fair.   43c

October 6th.   Lieut. Williamson in the CAPC officers mess at Craig Y Don gets a card signed *Guess Who??? Just my Luck,* from Southport, Lancs. Northern fortitude has its exemplar here. Other spectators have left or fled for cover but one stays on for the rain to stop, the sun to dry the ground and the white clad figures to resume play. Churchill would have been proud of such stoicism.   43d

February 23rd.   Private Ingenbrandt in Fort Dix NJ to his family in Deal/NJ, *Hello folks, arrived here Saturday afternoon. Don't know when I will be shipped out. Love. Wallace.* Lower ranks are creatures of the war machine's whim and are forever telling their loved ones how little they know of what is going on or where they are bound for or when. This atmospheric scene has the look of a film still.   43e

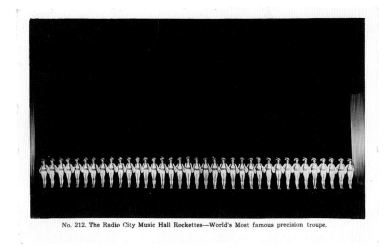

December 11th.   Evelyn to Everett Giles in Bath, Maine, *This is a grand old place & it seems I like it more each time I'm here. There is always something different in N.Y.* At the Radio City Music Hall in December there was always in fact something the same, for the Rockettes, here as uniform as the teeth of an ivory comb, danced as they still do in the annual Christmas Spectacular.   43f

November 29th.   Private Andy Lukas at Fort Jackson, S Carolina, writes to his mother in Perth Amboy, NJ, *Dear Mom, How are you hope you are feeling better. I'm okay and doing all right. Did you have a good Thanksgiving dinner I did but sure wished I was home. I'll try to get home for Christmas I hope I can.* I presume that by now there is more sophisticated looking equipment for sound detection.   43g

September 15th.   Mr Joseph Manga, Black Diamond S.S.Co in New York receives a card from somewhere in France, *Bertha, Here's one that the censor might not pass. I'm over here at one of the places we been to before. And I won't know whether we'll stay here, go some place else or go home. It's just a blank. So. Good-bye. Bro. Wiff.* The caption reads 'Tommies joyfully saluting the French coast on crossing the Channel'. The censor passed it.   43h

June 10th.   Brian in Skegness to Pete Wrigley in Handforth. *Having a super time here, plenty of girls and bags of good weather. How's work going down. OK? Went dancing last night. They've got Ivy Benson's Band here with 20 in it. Proper Sivvy. That's all.* The woman in Tempest's cartoon knows that men are in short supply (even when they're about they are in the Home Guard). Ivy Benson benefited from the shortage and her all-woman band was a favourite on radio and in the halls.   43i

September 17th.   To Mr & Mrs Poole in Stoke-on-Trent, *Blackpool calling. We are here and a great many more. I have never seen so many. There isn't a comic card to be had in the town. We have got a good place here, plenty of food. We two.* Dinah's boiler-suited child with barrage balloon was not their idea of comic. Hard to imagine Blackpool without its saucy cards.   43j

November 29th.   Staff Sergeant Tom Langdon from Fort Bragg NC. to Mrs Vernon Rand in North Bend, Nebraska, *You certainly must have your hands full keeping up with all those in the service. I for one want you to know that we appreciate it... Mother spoke very highly of the work you are doing.* We'll Meet Again is the refrain of a wartime song (sung by Vera Lynn).   43k

September 16th.   Margaret in Sparta, Wis. to the Spears in Cleveland, Ohio. *Dear Folks. Andy met me at the station and it sure was good to see him and hold him in my arms, if only Sunday would never come. The weather is nice but cold. I go out to the camp every day, but have to wait 4 to 5 hrs. to see him but I am only too glad to wait.*   43l

May 22nd.   Trummie in the US Navy to H Trumbonio Reading, PA, *Hiya Harold, just listening to a fine band organised in our Brk. Everything is O.K. How's the gals coming along. So long.* A characteristically cheap Mutoscope card with only two colours (and those out of register). These were dispensed from machines in the thirties and forties, the latter ones like this having (added?) postcard backs. This is as near as America gets to the comic double entendre.   43m

January 12th.   Kath's dad to her in Harrogate. *Many thanks for your letter arrived yesterday... found a shop with a lot more postcards so have a supply for some weeks to come. Look after yourself. Lots of love xxx.* Mr West chooses a view that would in 1943 be pointing towards a pile of rubble and sandbags. The Victorian high altar was destroyed in earlier raids but St Paul's as a whole stood firm. Judges Ltd make a masterly card full of decanted light from above.   43n

July 5th.   Geoffrey Eastman, presumably Somewhere in France, finds a French card to express his mood and sends it to his wife in Finchley N3, *This is how I feel! Do you? Never mind, eh? It has got to finish one day - our efforts will bring that day nearer if we try hard enough. Keep smiling - keep that dear chin up. Fondest love your Geoffrey.* In France too the child was used to express an otherwise too real adult situation as in this caption, 'Why must I always sleep alone'.   43o

Hillman, Michigan.

May 7th.   Geo. Beaty writes from Saginaw Bay, Alaska to Jim Smith in Salem, Oregon. *May 5 - arrived in Petersburg this morning. Be in Saginaw Bay tomorrow afternoon. Had a very good trip up. Weather is nice here. I sent my jewel from Kitchikan because someone was cleaning up on some of the passengers. Everything is O.K. See you in Oct.* Geo is on active service and there is a Joseph Conrad ring to the message. The card itself has that American directness that the English tend to read as crudity. In fact Japanese comic cards share the same brutal style. The card in any case, published in Albuquerque, New Mexico has travelled the entire length of the United States and halfway back again to Oregon.   43p

November 18th.   To Maurice Cole, Professional Bldg., Ferndale, Michigan. *How are things with you. This fellow wants to join The Vets, your Pal.* Neither this card nor its message traffics in subtlety as Hitler goes down the lavatory pan shouting to Mussolini for help. The strenuous pun on Führer is seen on other cartoons and there are many examples of Hitler with various lavatory associations (see 44g). Perhaps this was produced locally in Hillman, Michigan or elsewhere and distributed so that each place could have its own. It is certainly a home grown looking affair but what is particularly interesting is that the toilet itself is photographed complete with straggly string for a chain with the cartoon and lettering added.   43q

March 11th.   Kath's dad to her in Harrogate, *For your new Album I have several cards of this series. Thought they would be interesting. hope you are well, we went to Pride & Prejudice on Saturday. Had a good time but it was amateur. Weather very warm. Wings for Victory week is like a holiday at Trafalgar Square. Looking forward to your leave. Lots of love xxxx.* Wings for Victory was a National Savings campaign and evidently there was a bit of flair behind it. By now every postcard whether comic or grave carries on the reverse some stirring quotation from Churchill or the King or General Montgomery. This series has 'This is a time for everyone to stand together and hold firm' alternating with 'Let us strive without failing in faith or duty' (both from Churchill).   43r

April 28th.   Similarly to 8 Pannal Ash Crescent, Harrogate. *Dear Kath, This completes the series of the Ruins, only 12 have been issued. Hope you are well. We have had nothing to worry about but still have an alert now and again. E had a lovely time at the dance. I hope you got back all right and journey not too bad. It was good having you home again and it is not very far to Whitsun. Lots of love xxxxxx Dad.* Twelve such cards would not have raised Kath's spirits very much (and there is another series in the offing). With hindsight and even in memory bombsites had their own beauty and became grown over with grass and willow-herb with amazing speed. Present day children's adventure playgrounds are a tame imitation of what a mature bombsite was to the wartime child.   43s

PICCADILLY CIRCUS, GIRLS AND BOYS ON LEAVE

November 13th. Who is the anonymous master photographer who one day in the middle of the war shot from a low angle the three images of Piccadilly Circus, 44b (below), 43b and this most eloquent study of all? Cartier Bresson could not have done better. They form a triptych of mood, atmosphere, character and situation through which we can feel rather than merely observe how life was on that day of intermittent sunshine. The Circus itself given in softer focus acts as a scenic backdrop to vivid human lives. David Oxford in his book on Piccadilly Circus cards illustrates two of them with cogent captions. Of this one he writes 'Here are some very welcome visitors, their proudly-worn USAAF uniforms contrasting with the British Squaddy's baggy serge.' He makes no mention of the sad sailor and has dealt elsewhere with the covered base of Eros and its admonishing slogans (Less shopping, More shipping etc.), the lampless lampstandards and striped bollards and pavement edges (to guide motorists in the blackout) and the boarded up windows. Card sent to Miss C. Heuthood in Brigg, Lincs, *Dear Carol, love from grandpa.* 44a

Seal of the City of New York

THE BEAUTY of this early morning aspect of New York's skyline impresses immigrants and seasoned tourists alike—this is America!

LANDMARKS OF NEW YORK CITY

September 18th. Aunt Millie writes to her niece Dana Jean Daly in Troy, NY promising to buy her something since she is about to go shopping. 44c

Unposted (see above). The G.I.'s English girl makes a brave stab at summer fashion as do the other women civilians. The American car has hooded lights. 44b

PICCADILLY CIRCUS AT A BUSY POINT

GENERAL SIR B. L. MONTGOMERY, K.C.B., D.S.O.
"MONTY"
Promoted to FIELD-MARSHAL, September 1st, 1944

September 16th. Kath's dad to her in Harrogate. *Hope you are still well we are wondering. Had an alert at 6.00am this morning and have heard two mysterious bangs this morning one at 7.30 and another at 8.30 but don't know where. Still must not worry. Lots of love xxxx.* The mysterious bangs may well have been the first silent V2 rockets which started arriving in mid September and were the war's final home scare. 44d

Undated. Monica receives this cheery card from Christiane, *I am sending you a postcard which we find in France, since the Liberation. It is very common to see many Friendship Post Cards. We can buy many handkerchiefs on which there are allied flags. We put English American and French flags on anything. But if you will come to France you could appreciate the Friendship between English and French xxxxx.* 44e

June 9th. Ronald Elveritt in Stepney has sent to Hollywood for a photo of Humphrey Bogart and receives this card in reply with printed autograph and text telling him that 'funds for larger photographs now go for the purchase of War Bonds and Stamps'. He is pleased enough with this photo of his hero taken around the time of Casablanca (and in oddly suburban looking domesticity) to pin it up on his wall. 44f

"I'M GOING TO WIPE THEM OUT"

July 26th. Eleanor in Wildwood to Miss Taylor #9 Machine, National Biscuit Co. Philadelphia, *Dear Floss. working hard aren't you. Well I am taking it easy and enjoying every minute of it. Boy do they have the male here.* We have seen Hitler in conjunction with the lavatory pan: he is now joined by Mussolini and Tojo. Hitler and Mussolini will be dead within a year, one by suicide and one by mob execution. Tojo will fail in a suicide attempt, be tried and hanged. 44g

December 12th. Enid on Active Service to Eric & Rosalind Priestman in London NW3, *Just arrived from Brussels before we move on to gaie Paris. We are quite bewildered by the full shops here - all clothes off the ration - oranges tangerines etc. sold in the streets. It seems a land of plenty. It makes you realise how poor Germany is, where you can hardly buy a piece of paper. Thanks very much for irons. So cheerio.* Belgium had been liberated on Sept. 9th 1944. 44h

UNE CIGARETTE POUR PAPA, S.V.P.?
EEN SIGARET VOOR PAPA, A.U.B.?
CIGARETTE FOR DADDY, PLEASE?

November 29th. Cpl Max Church to his father in Detroit *Still in Belgium. Dear Dad, I spent a very nice day in Verviers today... I bought an electric iron Now I'm going to press uniforms to get back what I paid for it. It sure seemed good to get out and walk down the street like a civilian, even though I was just a civilian in uniform.* This is no.50 of the 365 cards sent back by Max Church to his father and brother from various parts of Europe (serving as a medical auxiliary). 44i

Bay Tree Farm, Stisted

No. 1622   Seabee Commando Landing Practice, Camp Peary, Va.   (Off. U. S. Navy Photo)

March 24th.   Pte Max Church (before he becomes Cpl Church and starts his regular series of cards home) to his father in Detroit. *This picture is very typical of the holmes over here. I hope to have many pictures... if you can get me some of #127 Verichrome I would like it as its almost impossible to get here...* Max is first sent to England before going to France, Holland, Belgium and Germany.   44j

September 11th.   Voils L Beck writes to his parents in Salisbury NC from Camp Peary in Virginia *Had another inspection & passed O.K. This is long handle weather at nite. Still sleeping under two blankets. Sue is fine.* The Seabees were the naval auxiliary force and their training was notoriously tough. Once again the image seems to echo or pre-echo the aesthetic formalism of the cinema.   44k

THE ROYAL FAMILY

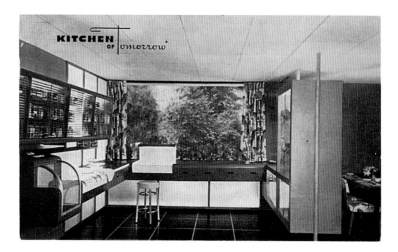

June 8th.   Audrey in Maida Hill to Beryl in Portsmouth, *I am enjoying myself. I can't write much because we are just going to see Ivor Novello's The Dancing Years. I'm sure you'll enjoy the picture on the front. See you then, Cheerio!* The Royal family (with now two members in uniform) poses seemingly on a lawn in front of a hazy pastoral backdrop. Daughters copy their mother's crossed ankles.   44l

August 15th.   Arlyne Suse in Waterloo, Iowa, tries out this modern free postcard on Mrs Ruth Parr in Oxford, Mass, *Maybe you don't collect these kind but I thought it would be different. Thanks for your note. Guess I'm here to stay.* With the great craze long past the postcard hobby is a quiet backwater of collecting and this card, advertising the virtues of glass in your kitchen, would not yet have acquired a nostalgic glow.   44m

October 17th.   Jerry in Bedbank NY to Miss Joanna Norton in Maryville, Tenn. *Hello cissy! Monday Ray & I felt like hiding from M.P.'s yesterday we got out on someone else's pass. We got back allright from New York though. Just 2 M.P.'s checked it!* The Military Policeman in such stories stand as the masters in school stories, both mocked and feared. Most of the wartime American cartoons are done by servicemen themselves (see 44r & s). The English tradition of professional comic postcard artists hardly exists in the USA.   44n

September 12th.   Stevie in Washington DC to Miss Edith Berg in Mariella, Ohio *How's this for a crazy card... Mrs Tite is back. Mary came in yesterday. Brought her parents back to live with her. Cramp her style? she says not. I miss your kid. Hurry back. Bought a new dress Sat. See you soon.* Both sexes in Britain would find this luminous pin-up arousing: men excited for obvious reasons (including the promiscuous caption), women because frills on underwear were still banned and such stockings were a dream away.   44o

THE HOME FRONT

July 14th. To Lucille Hall in Cambridge from Mummy in London *How are you darling? So glad to hear your voice on the phone the other night. Did you receive the goloshes & comics I sent. Tell Nana to kiss you for me. Will come down to see you when my cold's better. Lots of love xxx.* A chirpy Dinah card for an evacuee daughter. 44p

"LONDON UNDER FIRE"
CORNER OF DUKE STREET, ST. JAMES. 86878

September 29th. Dad once more to Kath *Hope you are doing well - nothing is doing and weather rotten. I have a cold but not bad. Are you coming home this weekend and when? Lots of love.* Another series of war damage scenes, this with fine portrait of a truck in the Piccadilly area. 44q

1944 MESSAGES·NOTES·PARTICULARS

44a. Photochrom Ltd. Photographer unknown

44b. Photochrom Ltd. Photographer unknown

44c. Designed & produced by Henry C Bairnam. E4330

44d. Tuck/Associated Press. Artist: Leclerc

44e. SP. Printed in France

44f. Publisher unknown. Printed reply card

44g. MWM. Aurora, Mo. AC114

44h. Editions Ario, Brussels

44i. Publisher unknown, Belgium. Artist unknown

44j. Publisher unknown

44k. Seabees publication, Camp Pearly, Va. 1622

44l. Photocrom Ltd

44m. Libbey Owens Ford Glass Co. Toledo, Ohio

44n. Curt Teich, Army Comics 1B - H4. Artist unknown

44o. Curt Teich, Modern Girl Comics C - 60. Artist unknown

44p. Tuck. Artist: Dinah

44q. Photocrom Ltd. London Under Fire 86878

44r. Graycraft Card Co, Danville Va. 307. Artist: Dave Breger

44s. Greycraft Card Co/King Features 319. Artist as above

PRIVATE BREGER
By Sgt. Dave Breger 307

"I had my mother knit this sweater just for you, Sarge!"

April 6th. Cpl Chappeloinck in Greenville Camp to Mrs Prover in Kettery, Maine, *Hiya Ila, Just got in will leave in a few minutes... swell trip and a lot of fun but the ground is still sweet enough for me. I never thought I'd get around like this but it came up all of a sudden. Leo.* The bug eyed private is drawn by Dave Breger who invented G.I.Joe in his syndicated cartoons, after which the term G.I. for American servicemen stuck. Private Breger like his cartoon self was conscripted in 1941 but was promoted to Staff Sergeant in 1942. 44r

PRIVATE BREGER
By Sgt. Dave Breger 319

"It's too quiet for him around here, so he's trying to stir up action!"

June 5th. Pte Kuckman in Springfield Camp, Mass to his daughters in Brooklyn. *How do you like these cards? I think they are pretty funny. They show conditions in the army pretty well because they were drawn by a soldier. Daddy loves you very much & I hope you are being good girls. Give Mama a big kiss for me xx Daddy.* Breger was serving in Britain when he drew this series. After a period in civilian life he served once more in Korea, drawing more cartoons. He died in a car accident in 1970. 44s

"WHAT A WAR!"
By Gilbert Wilkinson
With Acknowledgments to the "Daily Herald"

"I must say, it's not every day we get a Commando in the chair!"

November 19th. Master Walter Fraser in Edinburgh gets a card from his brother George *Tell mum it is nice here was you at the sea yesterday Sunday.* As well as the inimitable Grimes (see 45q) Tuck also reprinted the fine Daily Herald cartoons of Gilbert Wilkinson including this rare piece of anti-heroism. 44t

August 8th.   Although Victory in Europe was celebrated in mid May it was not until the capitulation of Japan in mid August (VJ day) that the war was truly over. Both events are reflected in this card picked up by Max Church in a defeated Germany, where he is serving, and sent three days after the nuclear devastation of Hiroshima, *Dear Dad, I guess that bomb is quite a thing. It sets everyone to thinking. I had a fellow ask me what I thought about it and we had quite a talk, I mean about the second coming of Christ.* The atom bomb provided an answer to a current problem but asked questions about the future of war big enough to haunt the rest of the century. Max is a cheerful soul but as a devout Seventh Day Adventist has a focus for reflection. This card (his 302nd) shows a landing strip in the Afrika campaign as seen by official German war artist, Schnürpel.   45a

August 13th. L Trinder to Mrs Hain in Pershore, *Am returning on Friday 17th as my ticket is up on the 18th. Will you please get me some bread & some milk. What splendid news !!! I mean VJ day. Love to you all.* A bright pre-war painting suits the return of peace and matches Mr Trinder's mood. How many London schoolchildren of the time (unlike myself) still have the VE day silver spoon and VJ day mug?   45b

February 3rd.   Dot from Brooklyn to her mother Mrs Humphries in Mayward, Illinois, *so glad to get your letter today, You should do what you want to do about things and not let Alan tell you what to do. I never kept Jenny home when the other kids went. Jimmy's boss came but isn't one you can push as to when he will come home. you are super to do this for me. loads of love.*   45c

March 3rd. **Dad** to Kath on a Swiss card scraped up from somewhere *...we had an alert at 3am today - heard a Doodle some distance off. The workmen are coming in on Monday to do the first repairs... Look after yourself.* This may have been the last strike on England of the war. The Germans abandoned their rocket base on the 7th March. Doodle is a variant of doodlebug the nickname for V1 & V2 rockets. 45d

July 20th. Dad to Kath *Hope you are still well. Am quite busy with Bath Room, hope to make it look better in a few days. Many thanks for the tools you suggested I should get. By the time I take my pension I shall have a good selection.* Here the Royal Family & Churchill greet a seething crowd (including the Phillips family) gathered outside Buckingham Palace on VE (Victory in Europe) Day. 45e

September 13th. Skegness rushes out its own Victory card complete with its well-known symbol of frolicking sailor and motto (Skegness Is So Bracing). ME buys one and sends it to Elsie Taylor in Leicester, *Weather nice... there are a big lot of people here and a big lot of Busses come here each day. I hope you have got all ready for Jill going and that nobby nutter is good boy.* 45f

February 7th. Corporal Stephen R Quinn in Paterson Field, Colorado to his kid brother Tim in Rochester NY. *Have been sick with flu... but hope to leave for Air Cadets School the first of March. Love. Ray.* The tin hatted soldier, Snuffy has migrated here from a comic strip. Ray Quinn plays the gag on himself. One of a group of cards that revive the Write Away tradition of forty years earlier. 45g

March 14th. SQM Charles Long in San Pedro, Cal, to his sister Ruth in Portland, Ore., *have not received the letter you said you had written. If you know any more about why Lona is coming to California let me know. I was surprised you cautioned me so on the phone.* Pastor is the last word you'd think to pin on this card's flamboyant insert. Aimee Semple McPherson died in 1944. Despite a juicy scandal in 1926 her showbiz-style evangelism converted (and made) millions. 45h

February 21st. Bill Hubbard, a POW in Stalag XVIII (Austria), writes to Lil & Frank Hockney, *So it goes into another year & perhaps we may meet sometime in this one. Shall be only too pleased to push up to the counter for a pint at the local pub. Feeling very fit & no complaints worth a mention. No news from Ted for a long while now... tell Jean to withold the wedding until my return... keep smiling.* These drab cards must have been the most welcome of all. 45i

Philadelphia   Main Concourse, 30th Street Station, Pennsylvania Railroad

January 2nd. From Major Knowlden, Merion Cricket Club, Haverford, PA to his parents in Weymouth, Dorset. *Now this really is a railroad station. Maybe it compares with Sandsfoot Castle Halt - or maybe it doesn't. love Dick.* What was a major <u>doing</u> playing cricket in Pennsylvania in 1945? What kind of sight did he and the team in white make, tumbling out of a train here amongst servicemen and women?   45j

May 7th. Max's 209th card home, *Well dad, on the very card designed to glorify the German war machine I tell of the total defeat of it. Tomorrow will be VE day but to-day they actually signed the armistice. if I ever had any doubt of this war (& I did at one time) It's gone now. After seeing the things they lowered themselves to, down beyond just ordinary warfare.*   45k

No Matter How "Tough The Goin'" — The Jeeps Can "Take It"

WHERE WAS SANDY?

WHEN? *LAST SUNDAY*
PLACE? *SUNDAY SCHOOL*

He was sleeping behind the kitchen stove at home, and we did not miss him. But WE <u>DID</u> MISS YOU. Please try to be present next Sunday.

Mrs Larson

March 25th. Pvte Augustus Smike at Camp Campbell, Kentucky to Mrs Ross White in Detroit, *How are you today. I'm on guard again tonite. So I guess I must be a good one. you can see from the reverse side our going gets tough sometimes. Your friend Gus.* The Jeep designed by Karl Pabst in 1940 for Willys took its name from GP (General Purpose): one of the resilient triumphs of military vehicle design.   45l

October 25th. To Master Larry Blust in Calva, Illinois, Mrs Larson writes *Dear Larry - Are you sick. I missed you from S.S. [Sunday School]. Try & come. We have some new things for you to play with at the sand table. So Larry try and come your teacher needs you to.* What would be the terrifying follow up from the SS after another absence? A visit from Mrs Larson? There could be no escape.   45m

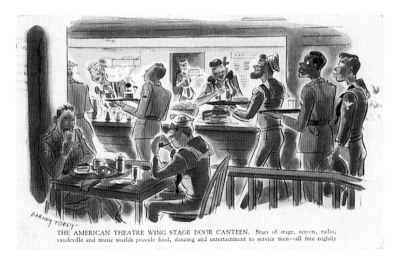

THE AMERICAN THEATRE WING STAGE DOOR CANTEEN. Stars of stage, screen, radio, vaudeville and music worlds provide food, dancing and entertainment to service men—all free nightly

AN ITMA WISECRACK — *Illustrated by Bert Thomas*

PROF. *Bumpo* PHRENOLOGIST

"Nothing at all—Nothing at all!"

July 25th. Master Bruce Armstead gets a card from his serviceman father, *Hello son, I am here in NY. Be a good boy now. will write later.* This canteen supported by the performing arts gives, as it says on the reverse, 'welcome to all men in the uniformed services of the UN without distinction of rank, race, colour or creed'. The black G.I. is evidence of that and it is the first image of an integrated black we have seen. In parts of the US virtual apartheid had twenty years left to run.   45n

August 23rd. Molly in Swindon to Betty Cripps in Didcot, *I have been going out a lot. I went to see a big bonfire Sat. night fireworks, buns, tea, music, it was very good. Sunday night... to the Town Gardens and listened to the band. All the goldfish have gone but there are still some pidgeons. Monday I went to pics with the lodger Al (25)... going to the picture club with Patrick.* Molly's Victory festivities are described on a card featuring a gag from ITMA, the war's most popular radio show.   45o

"Your face is familiar."
"Don't you remember me? I'm your little evacuee son."

July 12th.   Cassie Hobson in Nottingham gets a card from her parents in Huntingdon, *We are having a good time & we slept well. Valerie has hardly left the scooter... Mother is getting two rations here - so you go down & get yours at the Co-op on your book. Fond love.* The wartime sequence of Grimes cartoons in The Star were perceptively wry (and finely drawn) as in this dilemma of the returned evacuee.   45p

November 16th.   Nellie in Chesterfield to Mrs Jubb in Worksop, *Jean & I will meet you in town... I have been to the Doctor's with Jean nothing to worry about.* Grace Moore (killed in an air crash in 1947) brought operatic class and glamour to the cinema. Her autobiography, You're Only Human Once, appeared in 1944. Nellie & Jean faced a decade of post-war rationing: outfits such as this were wishful thinking. 45q

Max Church stuck to his word and wrote a card a day for a year. Thereafter he seems to have written only letters. The whole sequence was kept together, plus a card from 1947 which forms a strange coda to the story (see 47r).
Card No 365, also from Arolsen (to his brother) reads...
A year today, back in Holland I started writing my card-a-day. Since nothing is happening & I'm no longer in imediate danger I think this would be the best time to stop. I shall write letters to make up for it. I got a letter from Dad which I enjoyed. He said he heard I was coming home, I don't know where he got his information but I wish they would tell me.

WISHFUL THINKING!
TRYING ON HER DEMOB DRESS.

DE GAULLE

September 14th.   Ada in Selkirk to Sgt. Lowis serving with BAOR, Germany. *Am nearing the end of my leave - worse luck - but hope by Xmas to be a free woman once more. How is the 'demob' situation for you? Ted & Barbara are just marking time impatiently now. Cheerio.* Soon after this the demob suit for men (made of cloth that soon got shiny) was seen everywhere with standard hat and accessories. Women could get cloth and be more cunning and inventive.   45r

May 20th.   Max Church *Still in Germany* (Arolsen) writes home (his 222nd card). *Whit Sunday or some such thing. The civilians are all dressed up & parading up & down the street. Ray just got back from the concentration camp. He got some swell pictures of the dead corded up like wood & the furnaces, gas chambers etc.* The camp referred to is Buchenwald near the US Weimar HQ. Ray & Max use their hospital unit's x-ray room to develop their photographs.   45s

August 11th.   On this rather drab card with its timid drawing Trev, at Bigbury-on-Sea Youth Hostel, writes to his family in Birmingham. *Dear All. Still OK but lacking in cash owing to unforseen train journey. Could you please send £2 registered post to YHA Crowcombe to arrive 14/8/45? We've been on the sea in a rowing boat & I had to row most of the way as the others can't. Good news re Japan & atomic bomb, what? Love. Trev.*   45t

RESURRECTION

Wishing you a happy Easter. A+G.

April 18th.   The wartime slogan 'make do and mend' applied equally to the postcard. Miss Hall in Whittington Rd, Worcester, would no doubt have appreciated the double appropriateness of this Easter greeting improvised by A & G from a standard postal card and a cut out picture. John Piper, an official war artist seconded to cover war damage, became the poet of ruins. Here the rays of sunshine emblematically give life to spring flowers in the bombed out Coventry Cathedral.   46a

RAINBOW CORNER. off PICCADILLY CIRCUS. LONDON

January 7th.   Doreen to Mrs Jessie Brown, Shallow Water, Texas. *Dear Mrs Brown. This is the club I used to go to once a month. They used to hold meetings for wives of G.I.'s. It is right in the middle of all the London Theatres etc. & was well used by lots of Americans. Marvin has been there. Looking forward to meeting you soon.* Doreen has married Marvin and now writes to her far off new mother-in-law.   46b

A BRITISH BATTLESHIP IN NEW YORK HARBOUR   *From the original painting by Norman Wilkinson, P.R.I.*
Reproduced by permission of " The Navy."

October 9th.   Master John Whippley at Woodleigh School, Yorks. receives an English artist's impression of New York, *Hope the parcel arrived alright. I took your pen to Boots yesterday. They are going to send it away for a new nib. It will be about a fortnight. If I go to London tomorrow I will let you know. love Mummie x.* The card carries uplifting words from the King, 'Help to make the world a better place... etc.'   46c

German Cemetery at St Brelades, Jersey.

Gorleston Holiday Camp

September 4th.   Dick in Jersey to Monsieur F Fenner, Charpentier, c/o Messers Hull in Paddock Wood, Kent, *Cher Frank, These are beyond your aid but all here say they are the best ones. Lovely Island.* The German occupation of the Channel Islands bit deep into the national psyche. The card has its mysteries. Was it doctored by removing swastikas from the nearer crosses? What happened to these grave-markers?   46d

July 26th.   Aunt Hilda in Great Yarmouth to Hilda Hodgkins in Croxley Green. *Just a PC to let you have an idea of the camp... It's lovely, although the staff problems are wicked. There's about a third of pre-war.. They do us very well. The fee for a week is £6.10.0. though I get a reduced rate.* Gorleston camp looks as if ready and impatient for its first consignment of post-war holidaymakers.   46e

"Getting plenty of Ozone down here, old man?"
"Well, there's lot of it about, but I've got the missis with me!"

THE TRAPP FAMILY SINGERS AND THEIR CONDUCTOR, FATHER FRANZ WASNER.

July 5th.   From Lily & Bob in Brighton to Hetty Habens in Gosport, *Having a grand time and lovely weather. Are both keeping very fit.* Ozone has now retreated to an upper layer but in 1946 it had mythic health giving properties and was to be found, like this ill printed economy McGill card, at the seaside. On the back is a savings jingle, 'The war is won, your £.s.d./ has helped to bring us victory etc.'   46f

September 5th.   M Vinley in Highland Fall NY to the Rev Mother, Convent of the S.H., Fenharn, *...We spent over two months with the Baroness von Trapp in Vermont, had lots of lovely music... They intend to go to England for a concert tour sometime. To Father Monteith I sent a booklet of the family.* Bedirndled in Vermont and without Julie Andrews these are the authentic von Trapps of The Sound of Music.   46g

W-138—View of one of the Processing Areas, Oak Ridge, Tenn. "City of the Atomic Bomb"

February 11th.   Norton Longley Ltd send this promotional card for the new Hillman to Callender Cables in Uxbridge. The printing and artwork are part of the card and not added by hand. The figure peering over the roof is Chad who began to spring up everywhere (Wot, no tomatoes? Wot, no houses? etc) commenting on various shortages and joining such legendary graffiti heroes as Kilroy. His question is superfluous: there was a waiting list for any post-war car (we had to wait over a year for ours).   46h

April 25th.   To Esther Smith in Chicago, *Thank-you very much for the pretty Easter card... and for the birthday card last month. Best regards to all. Dick.* Oak Ridge has now toned down its name to America's Secret City. It was invented in 1942 as a major part of the Manhattan Project where the uranium was processed and enriched for both atomic bombs. It now has a population of 27,000 and is still a centre for research. It is open to the public. Even Russians are welcome.   46i

December 10th.   From Crystal City Texas to Robert Rice in Edgewater NJ, *Your nomad relatives are still abroad. We are completely spoiled by our travel and the hospitable entertainment encountered. Popeye salutes you. Much love Ellie & Frank.* The statue was erected in Popeye Park ' to the Spinach Industry of the Winter Garden District of Texas'. Science now tells us that Popeye was right about spinach.   46j

July 31st.   To Mavis Brooke in Romford from Mary in Scarborough, *I am on the spa writing this listening to the band. We have not been to see HMS Birmingham yet as one has to wait so long. Have you been all round London yet... see this picture I hope it didn't happen to you.* Useless Eustace in the Daily Mirror was a long running series of miniature epiphanies of the Little Man's struggle.   46k

September 15th.   Ann Nelson in Duffield gets a birthday card from Janet & Maureen whose uplifting thought printed on the back is 'There's always a silver lining'. By late 1946 it seemed to many that there wasn't. The liberties of peace were no longer novel and other restrictions, especially rationing, had become if anything more severe. 'Make do and mend' had been around too long.   46l

August 3rd.   Dick in Derby to Mrs Chapman in Loxley *We are having a nice time. Getting a good rest. Had a trip to Stanley yesterday.* Disney and cricket make their only appearance together. The score is nought for no wicket, Donald is at the crease and Goofy is the keeper. Mickey Mouse at slip must fancy his chances of a catch since the opening batsman's surname might be matched by his score.   46m

June 16th.   Mr Bechert at the Gramercy Pk Hotel, NY gets a message from his tailor in Minneapolis, *Dear Friend, I have to day sent your suit. hope you have it at this time. Please hang up suit and the wrinkels will come out hope you will like it. Sincerely JP Elliason.* Presidential is the name of the London shrunk suitings and presidential the style of the card and, one hopes, the quality of Mr Bechert's suit.   46n

December 24th.   From Whitstable to Miss Castle in Tankerton, Lady Cripps' secretary F Rumpole writes, *wishing you every happiness, peace and love and to convey thanks from Lady Cripps.* Cecil Beaton catches the fine qualities of Isobel Cripps; idealism, strength and good humour, plus her advanced style as Socialist Woman. Wife of Stafford Cripps, austerity's champion, she was president of the Aid to China Fund.   46o

ALL MY OWN WORK BY GRIMES   With acknowledgements To "THE STAR"

"See that you're polite to our waitresses—we can get plenty of customers."

Autobahn Germany - The Windmill

46a. Home made card on postal card. Artist: John Piper

46b. Tuck. Artist unknown

46c. Salmon & Co. No 4936. Artist: Norman Wilkinson

46d. Publisher unknown, Jersey

46e. Gorleston Holiday Camp

46f. D Constance Ltd. New Donald McGill Comic.

> Keep saving for a rainy day
>
> The war is won, your £.s.d
> Has helped to bring us victory,
> But saving still will pave the way
> To that new world, for which we pray

46g. The Collotype Co. Elizabeth NJ

46h. Publisher unknown

46i. Standard News Agency, Knoxville, Tenn. Photo: J E Westcott

46j. Sam M Sleicher. Uvalde, Texas No 29374

46k. Tuck/Daily Mirror. Artist: Jack Greenan

46l. Regent Publishing Co. No 7013 Artist: Kit Forres

46m. Valentine's. Walt Disney No 4041

46n. Curt Teich for Presidential Suitings

46o. United Aid to China Fund, London

46p. Tuck. Artist: Grimes

46q. Photo Sparuth, Belgium

46r. G R Rogers, Denmark Hill, Camberwell

46s. Publisher unknown/NAAFI

April 23rd.   To Mrs Robbins in Cricklewood from Winchester, *Although I got my usual bus I must have missed the tube as I had to wait until 6.30. when I got in I found a woman & little girl with a black cat. Eventually they got out & left the cat & another passenger said he thought it had got in the train at Stanmore. I wanted to tell the guard it was on the train & ask him to see that it went back to Stanmore but I couldn't get up to him in time so I hope the poor thing got back all right. Fondest love. Ladybird.* Grimes was described as drawing with amazing swiftness once he had formed his idea. The characterisation here of waitress, manager and customer is superb and one can catch the speed of the charcoal over the paper in the chair and the flower and the background figures. Cartoons of wartime austerity had a long afterlife: ironically the original of this now hangs in The Ivy restaurant, the hub of London's café society.   46p

May 31st.   Alan, serving in Germany, to his aunties Misses M & M Ellis in Pudsy, *Since last time I wrote I have been right up North of Germany on an armed escort for top secret equipment. Been to Hamburg... Like travelling from Leeds right down to Devon. Was in a Land Rover and lovely weather. It has been a great experience... we stayed at different camps. There was myself and a very good F/O who forgot all about is rank. This is a place we stopped at on the Auto Bahn. We travelled over 250 miles up the same road and it is 500 miles long. One way traffic either side... England would have to wait another fifteen years before it had a proper motorway.* The Autobahn was one of Hitler's better legacies as was this Volkswagen parked outside the YMCA, the people's car, whose first model Hitler saw come fresh from the works in 1936 while its designer Herr Porsche looked on. Such pre-war versions are now highly sought after classics.   46q

RUSKIN PARK

NAAFI / Montgomery Club BRUSSELS

May 28th.   Dad to Kath in Harrogate, *Glad to learn from your letter that you are well & will be home for Whitsun. I shall be at SE for 3 weeks from next Monday. Ruskin Pk is where I played Bowls, Lots of love xxxxx Dad.* This is the last card I have of the series: presumably Kath stays in Harrogate to see out the school year. The intimation of some messages is that their house had been badly damaged. Ruskin Park is in Camberwell. Each year since 1973 I have taken two photographs of it as part of a work called 20 sites n years. The first from near the second bench from the left, and the second a view of the bowling green itself, still active and unchanged, where Mr West played over fifty years ago.   46r

September 1st.   WVS Forshaw to her colleagues left behind at WVS Uniform Sales Dept, London. *Just a picture of where I am working at present. After travelling right into Germany from Calais and 18 hour train journey we stayed there 4 days & then got our postings. As mine turned out to be Brussels for the present I had to come nearly all the way back again! with another girl who has been posted to Toulon we travelled all night and reached Brussels this morning. It seems very pleasant & apparently (so they tell me) one can walk into the shops & buy practically anything so I am going to look for some silk stockings. Just to make mouths water there is fruit in abundance including oranges & bananas & all the bread is white. Daphne.*   46s

47

April 6th.   *We're having lunch here*, writes Connie to the Crawfords in St Petersburg (Florida), *had a long ride yesterday in the rain most of the time. Spent the night in Knoxville. Peach trees in Georgia were in full bloom.* Perhaps Connie had fried chicken for lunch, unaware as she licked her fingers that she was in at the birth of an empire at 'Colonel' Sanders first restaurant. Kentucky Fried Chicken (KFC as it is now known to avoid the taboo word Fried) was to spread its branches as far as Peckham and St Petersburg (Russia).   47a

May 10th.   *My dear sweet Line*, write Glad (& Jean) to Mrs Bollmann in Bergen, Norway. *Just a little line to you from our second 'patria'. We are enjoying the trip. But the English are not having a very good time as yet. But they're cheery all the same...* There were still very few new postcards available, hence we return to a view in the mid-thirties and Maurice Chevalier.   47b

Somewhat brisk words from Bayonne, NJ to Mrs Evadne Michelinie in Fort Spring, West Virginia, on this dramatically glamourised card for which photography provides only the humble starting point. *Dear Member:- Please reply to my letter of a month ago. I hope you are well as this leaves me. Want to receive a nice letter telling all about yourself and the 4 club. Frances Watson - member 2434.*   47c

HOTEL SHERATON
Lexington Ave. at 37th St., N.Y.C.

September 5th.   Alma, Joan and Peter in Easton Portland write to Mrs Graham whose house in Granbrook is intriguingly named Barracks. They are *having a nice time will write soon.* Chad is peering over his wall again, this time to complain about the absence of the saucy Daily Mirror cartoon strip, Jane, which fed so many male fantasies.   47d

April 26th.   Bettie writes to Carmine at an obliterated address somewhere in New York but evidently not where the action is, *Did you get the stamp "Big Boy". This is Midtown New York.* The see-through skirts and cocktail trays of these Sheraton waitresses spell late 40's sophistication. Big Boy was the code name of the Hiroshima bomb but that's surely not what is meant. 47e

August 21st.   Mrs Matthews in Blackpool to her son and daughter in law holidaying in the Isle of Man, *We have arrived here once again. Weather is perfect, walked into Ron & Doreen this afternoon.* A pre-war cartoon by the look of the car, proving that road rage, though named in the nineties, existed sixty years before. Like most rage it had its start in the home. 47f

Didn't I tell you a Helicopter was the best investment for our Gratuities?

September 12th.   Sent by Mr Lumanos in Cuba to Mr Trygve Lie the first Secretary General of the recently inaugurated United Nations in New York. This printed petition card begins *Spain is a sea of blood* and goes on to insist that the UN sever all relations with a regime whose extreme Fascism is here illustrated by a picture of Franco shaking hands with Hitler. America vetoed Spain's entry into the UN in 1948.   47g

July 29th.   From Great Yarmouth an anonymous card to the General Office of the Cambridge Borough Surveyors Dept, *I hope the young ones will take notice of the old ones failures.* The picture side is easier to follow and includes a miniature secondary scene at street level to show another mode of spending service gratuities. The helicopter is still a novelty and had only been in general production for three years.   47h

May 5th.   Marietta in San Francisco to Mrs O'Keefe in Seattle, *Dearest Violet. Have been shopping and saw this young man, so thought you might like him. Met Uncle Carl after shopping tour and we went to see 'Nora Prentiss'. We liked it very much.* This young man was by now the world's leading pop vocalist but had yet to reveal his gifts as a screen actor. Nora Prentiss is a film about a singer who ruins a doctor's life.   47i

"But surely, Darling, you're not going to bed in that thing on our Honeymoon?"
"Well, Dearest, Mother told me that if I was' sensible girl I should take precautions!"

August 7th.   From Southend to Mr R Reeves at the Wood Green Empire (Stage Door) in North London, *Grand weather fine time got to shift back now tide coming in Stand By cheerio Sid.* Sounds like one old trouper playing Southend greeting another playing the Empire. McGill's gas mask jokes were no longer topical but this one remained relevant since it dealt with the taboo subject of contraception.   47j

May 27th.   Aunt Margaret who writes to Anthea Dulley in Guisborough is still On Active Service. *I am staying in Brussels again and this picture shows where I went yesterday by bus... I have strawberries and ice cream every day. I will try to send Mummy some nylon stockings.* These horses graze where their frightened forefathers reared and strained in battle, at Waterloo.   47k

July 23rd.   Mum & Joyce send a card to Art Wills in Boscombe from Butlins at Clacton-on-Sea. *We are enjoying ourselves, you can hire combination bicycles, so Joyce and I went for a long ride on one it was lovely. Hope you are alright and having enough to eat.* Butlins rapidly expanded its empire of camps after the war. Mum & Joyce, once they had handed in their ration books, would not eat too badly.   47l

December 3rd.   Clang Ltd. send out to Potter Radio Co. in Kansas City, Miss. their Christmas greetings on a card featuring such seasonal items as spanners, wing-nuts and bakelite plugs. One suspects that Potters will reciprocate with robins and holly rather than valves and aerials. Nonetheless there is a sense of cheer about these dadaist items and at least the bicycle bell could be considered festive.   47m

October 26th.   Lenny in Minneapolis writes to Mr Louis Bachman in Le Sueur, Minnesota, *Thanks for letter. Rec. the papers O.K. & many thanks I read them from cover to cover. Nothing new to report at this time.* The fictitious archetype of the roadside Greasy Spoon (when and where did the term originate?) is a nicely cooked photo made (by Sox) from a picture of a derelict store somewhere near Nowheresville.   47n

October 14th.   Clarence in Ogden to Mrs Young in the Bronx, *This place is a sight to behold. Lights from one end of the town to the other card games dice gambling machines are rampant. Stopping in this hotel tonight.* The El Trovatore Autel was on Route 66. Autel is a non surviving variant of motel and although Clarence had witnessed in these early days a revelation of vice and lights, Las Vegas could have replied, 'You ain't seen nothing yet'.   47o

THE FREEDOM TRAIN

1947 MESSAGES·NOTES·PARTICULARS

47a. Colorpicture, Cambridge, Mass. 14895

47b. Postokim Cards

47c. Manhattan Postcard Co/Fotoseal 43

47d. Publisher unknown. Artist unknown. No 110

47e. Hotel Sheraton NYC

47f. Inter Art Comique Series No 7776. Artist: Mike

47g. Publisher unknown, Spain. (Cuba?)

47h. Publisher unknown. Artist unknown

47i. Photo: W G Gray, Los Angeles

47j. D Constance Ltd. Artist: McGill. 1105

47k. R.C.B, Belgium. Photo: Jean Wellens

47l. Valentine's Phototype H 3852

47m. Clang Ltd. 10M/2164B/1047D

47n. L L Cook Co, Milwaukee. Photo: Sox

47o. Curt Teich/Sal Sayeu Hotel

47p. Publisher unknown

47q. Photocrom Co ltd. 85657

47r. Card Crafters/Curt Teich, Springfield, Mass.

November 17th.   Ruthie in Syracuse NY, to Priscilla Clarke in Marlborough, Mass. *Dear Butch. Be sure to save this card for me! The letter paper is absolutely lovely; hope I get a chance to use it soon, too!! Thanks a lot. I'm dying to see you in your scout uniform - I'll bet you look really sharp. The Colgate game was wonderful - I've never been so excited in my whole life!* The Freedom Train in red white & blue livery started out on a two year journey in September 1947 stopping in all 48 states. In a manner paradoxically reminiscent of the Soviet Agitprop trains of the early twenties it was a travelling exhibition of democratic propaganda and patriotic memorabilia. The show included unique items that citizens in remote places would not normally get a chance to see, including a 1493 letter of Columbus, Washington's own copy of the Constitution, the Gettysburg Address etc. Long queues formed wherever it stopped and many waited four or five hours to get to see the show. The millionth visitor was a girl in Oklahoma who travelled sixty miles in a blizzard to view the exhibited wonders.   47p

PRESTATYN HOLIDAY CAMP, THE SWIM POOL   85657

October 19th.   This luridly humdrum card of the Shriner's Hospital for crippled children in Springfield, Mass. was sent by Max Church from Berrien Springs in Michigan to his father now in West Fork, Arkansas. It stands alone, outside the series Max wrote in the war, and was sent two years after the last of them. At that point Max, unsure of his military fate was hoping to study French culture at college in Paris. Perhaps it marks a parting of the ways between father and son for reasons that can be inferred from the message. *Dear Dad, I received your fine card Fri. You must be there and well established by now. Let me know as soon as you have occasion to write, how you like it there. Tell me how Grandma is. When you write next time would you include Pierre Braun's name, it will make him feel that my parents have accepted him as he's accepted me. All is going very well with us and Pierre likes it very much. He is starting to speak a little English now. Send some pictures of the new place as soon as possible. Well must close now. love. Max.* Remembering that this is 1947 the situation sounds sticky indeed. A small mystery is why Max chose this particular card of a place 700 or so miles from where he is living.   47r

August 18th.   Betty & her sister write to their parents in Gloucester from the Holiday Camp, *Dear Mum & Dad. Arrived at 2.30 after quite nice train journey! Got our little chalet, very sweet and had a look round the camp, it is a very nice place! at 6.30 we had dinner, very nice rabbit, greens, potatoes & baked apples. In the evening we went to the marvellous ball-room & had a good time. Guess what, this morning we went horse-riding on the sands Betty looked so funny! Breakfast was porridge, bacon, fried bread & tomatoes so we don't feel hungry at all. Went swimming too. We are now going sun-bathing.* (*love, Betty* is added in another hand). This card was produced in 1946 and carries the same savings jingle as 46f. Messages of the immediate post-war year often go into great detail about meals as if people had to pinch themselves to know that the recently unobtainable bacon, tomatoes etc. were really there. Fashions for holiday wear were improvised rather than stylish and men had no equivalent to the casual style of women. Army surplus trousers dyed anything but khaki and a tweed sports jacket would be a typical outfit until the ghastly blue blazers with brass buttons arrived.   47q

48

"Henry! you might have known a second-hand Jeep would stop at every Blonde!"

September 8th.   Everything in Britain was still in short supply except for army surplus goods. With new cars a luxury the Jeep lived up to its name (GP - General Purpose Vehicle) in civilian life and was subject to many makeshift conversions. Here however it appears in its authentic Willys styling as first manufactured in 1940 (see 44e & 45l). A different kind of memory of the American serviceman's friendly invasion is the subject of the joke. Mike in Brighton writes to Simon in Sheffield with a money grievance, *Please give me more details about this 5 shillings for Aileen as her present has already cost me 20 shillings. Sorry I shan't see you before you go. Food good. Hunting not bad. Letter following. Mike.*   48a

September 8th.   Des Wallace at the Transvaal Goldmines gets this 1939 view from Marjorie Brain in Streatham, *We have left the farm. Ron is off to the Far East. I am staying in London until Christmas when I hope to get a passage. London is looking fine.* Captain Fury, a Hal Roach film, is showing at the Pavilion and the Lyric Theatre is featuring Of Mice and Men.   48b

August 27th.   Ruth, Joe and Joan in Allentown Pa. to Mrs Joseph Lynn in Mamaroneck NY, *Dear Sis, Please do not look out for us over Labor Day, because we got the dickens for not spending a few days up home. So please come when you can...* City of Light was the title given to this diorama (the world's largest, it says) which was the Edison display at the New York World's Fair and, unlike most exhibits, was preserved thereafter.   48c

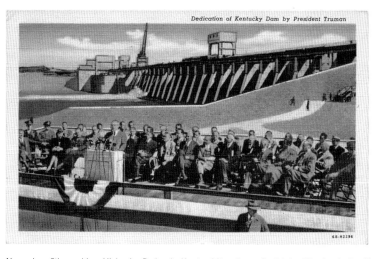

June 18th.   Carmine & Bob in Vitznau to the Josephs in Weybridge, *This is heaven in spite of the streaming rain today... have given up the fight and now follow behind my shameless tummy. We are polishing up our dancing nightly against the evening at the Oaklands Park Hotel.* Here with Swiss hills, lake and chestnut leaves is the apotheosis of the bench.   48d

November 5th.   Lina Hicks in Paducah Ky. to Miss Anna Sgalai in Cleveland, *I will exchange 50 oc cards at the time as quick as I go down town and get more. a pal.* Truman defeated a surprised Dewey in the 1948 election. The Kentucky Dam created a Lake with 2400 miles of shoreline. Only blue or brown suits were apparently allowed at the ceremony.   48e

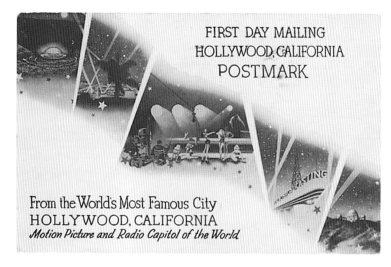

July 28th.   No message from J Roase to Miss Pike in Lowestoft. The radio station is in a familiar but then still novel style. The Bauhaus-derived modernist vocabulary is still the staple of urban structures today. Hilversum was also up to date in music. The young, rejecting the cosiness of the BBC Light Programme, turned to the Dutch station, or to Radio Luxembourg, for news of the Top Twenty.   48f

September 14th.   To Norman Farquhar in San Francisco from Hollywood *I hope I'll always be your favourite star. Love Anna Marie. Come and see me sometime!* Anna Marie, or whoever has the nice writing that has penned the promising message, has missed or preempted the First Day mailing date since the card only carries a Los Angeles postmark.   48g

October 22nd.   Stuart to John Stubbings in Goring-by-Sea, *Well here we are at last being sick all over the place, were just on the Bay of Biscay - up she goes etc. over the side - ah - that's better. We visit Madeira tomorrow evening!! It is a very good ship - plenty of everything cigs are 1/3 for 25 etc... RAF cadet pilots on board going to S.R. for training. the food is pretty good although I have not had a lot of it yet for obvious reasons - We had a film show yesterday - not bad but I made an exit in the middle.*   48h

December 13th.   From the improbably named Lulu Belcher to Jon Whatson in Glasgow, *Off to New York again! There is a hat on 5th Avenue that I* must *have, according to Molly so I have called them to say I am on my way. Robin wanted to fly but I said No - last time the vibration upset all my fillings and I spent a fortune on the dentist... back in time for your Xmas party - with a bit of luck (I shall* have *to* fly *back).*   48i

THE SUN LOUNGE, THE DEVON COAST COUNTRY CLUB

August 30th. Mary & Omer in Paignton to Mrs English in Sydney, Glos, *We are having a lovely time here. Everything grand.* Indeed it looks it in this marvellous study with its configuration of levels, intervals, planes and grids through which one can sense the summer breeze drift in as outside elides into an interior complete with progressive tubular furniture. 48j

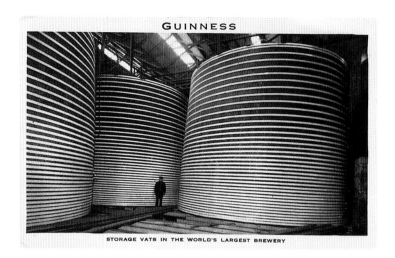

GUINNESS

STORAGE VATS IN THE WORLD'S LARGEST BREWERY

June 26th. Len sends this fine card to N A Morin in New Milton, Hants. *Just going to have a look round this place. How would you like to have three this size.* Once again (see 20l) Guinness in Dublin offer a set suitable for a science fiction movie or an installation that would be welcome in any major modern art museum from Bankside to Bilbao. 48k

"The Meeting Place of the World"
Jack Dempsey's Broadway Restaurant

June 14th. Willie seems to want Miss Susie Staley in Nashville, Tennessee, to imagine him sitting in the bar of Jack Dempsey's famous restaurant thinking only of her, *Have a drink here with me wouldn't that be fine girl tonite.* Dempsey (the Manassa Mauler) who first won the heavyweight title in 1919 retired in 1928. Unlike most boxers he did not fritter his purses away. Last orders were in 1974. 48l

RUTH   GERARD   RICHARD   QUIZMASTER JOE KELLY
CLAUDE   HARVE
Quiz Kids
SPONSORED BY ALKA-SELTZER
MARGARET   BLUE NETWORK · SUNDAY EVENING   JOEL

February 22nd. Kate in Winetta, Illinois to Miss Frankie Jones in La Porte, Indiana *Believe it or not Mark got yet another letter from Mrs O. today. They are wild over the men's suits and shirts - priceless in Holland but we send nothing of value to him or the women - so don't let this stop you - They got 5 boxes in as many days.* The Blue Network sounds like pornographic radio. The Quiz Kids were horribly popular. 48m

BIRTH OF A BABY   BIRTH OF A BABY

"The Broadway" Eccles

August 26th. Anne in Newcastle to Mrs Campbell in Wellington Northland, *I got home at 6.30 I rang them up at Leeds. I not made Saturday nights sleep up yet. No scullery done. got wool quarter oz for Joyce.* In the year of the Kinsey Report a documentary feature that does not sound too startling but is billed as For Adults Only at the Broadway Cinema. The film was banned altogether in many American states but not in Eccles (for those least desperate to know how babies were made). 48n

GREETINGS FROM ANN ARBOR Michigan
"Where Commerce *and* Education Meet"

September 8th. Jenny to Gene Huff in Packville, Missouri, *Hi Bass, we enrolled and is my program ever a mess but I don't mind too much so I guess it's ok.* The Gruss Aus tradition of the beginning of the century carries on in such brilliant conflations of image and information as this where photographic scenes combine with artwork of various kinds and inventive lettering. Unifying these disparate factors, each overlapping the other, is a feat of graphic intelligence. 48o

"Fifty thousand people at this football match, and a bird 'as to fly over me!'"

BOUQUET
CARRIED BY
PrincessElizabeth
AT HER WEDDING
NOVEMBER 20th 1947.

48a. H.B. (Harvey Barton Ltd) 6055. Artist: Comicus. Slogan PM Save Your Waste Paper For Salvage.

48b. Excel Series No 248

48c. Consolidated Edison

48d. Wehrliverlag Kilchberg

48e. Wilson's Paducah/Curt Teich 6B H 2296

48f. Herma

48g. Hollywood Chambers of Commerce

48h. Royal Mail

48i. Royal Mail

48j. Publisher unknown. PM slogan Blood Donors Are Still Urgently Needed

48k. Guinness & Sons, Dublin. GA11

48l. Jack Dempsey Restaurant

48m. Blue Network

48n. Publisher unknown

48o. Stofflet News Co. Ann Arbor/Kropp & Co. 2896N

48p. W Barton No 408. Artist: Mike

48q. Westminster Abbey

48r. Tuck/Pathe Pictorial. PM Slogan: Lend a Hand on the Land

48s. RA series. Artist unknown

January 22nd.   Eileen in Forest Gate to Miss L Hudson in East Ham, *Dear Lefty, How are you getting on these days in this cruel world... I brought a little pack of cards so we can play over the flats. Have you started eating over the flats yet. O.K.* In America 'over the flats' would translate as 'at the tenements'. Perhaps fifty thousand people and not one of them without a hat or cloth cap. Whatever happened to hats?   48p

March 3rd.   Miss Curtis in Bromyard gets a card from her mother, *Don't you think this card is rather interesting? The bouquet is photographed lying on the Unknown Soldier's tomb where the Princess laid it. You can see the lettering. I bought it in Westminster Abbey.* Over fifty years later the marriage still holds though all has crumbled around it. (The Queen would describe the anniversary year as her annus horribilis).48q

DAVE AND DUSTY The popular Pathé Pictorial stars featured every week in *The People*

"Stop looking at 'Superman'," says Dusty, "I want to get on to 'The mystery of the meat safe'."

GREAT EXPECTATIONS

Hand in Hand
DEWEY ~ CREIGHTON

VOTE STRAIGHT REPUBLICAN
THIS SIDE OF CARD IS FOR ADDRESS
Your voting place is ....
711 N. Penn St.
(ARMORY)
VOTE EARLY
Mr. & Mrs. Louis Fletcher
39 E. 9th St.
Indianapolis
Ind.

March 28th.   Carol Freeman in Croydon to Jane Cox in Cuckfield, *I hope you are well... How is bunney. I have still got one scab and three marks. have you got any marks yet. How is Maky-donald, when did you go outside.* Two schoolgirls comparing innoculation notes? Perhaps like me they saw Dave & Dusty at Saturday morning Pictures. Dave is wisely reading Superman. Better than watching Dave & Dusty any day.   48r

September 15th.   Dorothy & Bert write to Miss Cath Stafford *Having a lovely honeymoon. Weather nice but windy. Afraid jokes are few & far between here but I thought this might amuse you. Hope you have your chin up as regards work, you poor sucker. Ah! Ah!* Did Dorothy & Bert's marriage stay the course or were the Great Expectations of this strangeley horrific card brought to smaller account than Queen Elizabeth's. 48s

October 27th.   In a fine hand (how did he or she keep it up?) The Fletchers are invited to vote Straight Republican and help Dewey coast home to certain victory. A famous photograph shows Truman holding up the already printed front page of the Chicago Daily Tribune with its headline Dewey Defeats Truman. Dr Gallup and his pollsters were also made to look foolish by Truman's two million majority vote and control of both houses.   48t

May 4th.   Alone among the great artists of the twentieth century Picasso had a substantial postcard output, especially in respect of the communist-inspired Peace Movement he so actively supported. This image of a dove was chosen by Louis Aragon. Significantly Picasso named his daughter (born 19th April 1949) Paloma. Tom writes to Stella Draycott in Sheffield (which Picasso was to visit in the same cause in 1950), *Thanks for the note. Best Wishes for Peace in 1949. Looks a little more likely now. Will write.*   49a

August 10th.   *A grand holiday* writes Reg to Mrs Richards in Llandrindod Wells *but all good things come to a full stop.* For almost ten years through war and its no less stringent aftermath the Circus had been dark. Now on Sunday April 3rd crowds greet the return of the lights. It was not a full stop to mark the end of austerity but certainly a significant comma.   49b

December. 8th.   From Jessie Pringle to Sarah Orkin in Aberdeen, Scotland. *John is down here on business so I came along... a wonderful time as long as I stuck to the museums, But I'm a bit out of my depth in the stores. Saw an exhibition of Van Gogh then later visited The Museum of Modern Art. If he was insane so are the others - only they didn't kill themselves. Maybe I'm as confused now as my tenses seem to be!* 49c

Greyhounds Taking a Hurdle at a Florida Track

March 15th.   From Fort Lauderdale to Miss Leslie Harrison in Scarsdale NY, *How is Tippie getting on... I hope she is feeling better now & not ruining the rugs any more... I miss you, honey Love. Mommy.* Did Mrs Harrison really have a night at the dogs or did this vision of the Hounds of Hell just appeal to her. The complete colour makeover of American cards often breeds startling images.   49d

U. S. Military Cemetery, Margraten, (Holland)

July 3rd.   From Vaals in Holland, Peter writes to Miss Vivienne Jennings in Brighton, *We are on our way by car to Liege this is the Dutch - German - Belgian frontier.* A frontier no more, scarcely a border now. The embattled history of the region can only be adduced from its war graves. Cameras click and whirr as a high ranking US officer positions a wreath.   49e

"Look the other way Henry, we're passing one of those horrible nudist camps!"

September 10th.   Mr & Mrs Vicker & Bernice in Great Yarmouth to Miss Audrey Regment in Norwich, *Having a lovely time weather super.* Naturism and Nudist Camps were a gold mine for the comic card artist. McGill gives the subject a strange twist. On the back a new savings jingle ' We saved to win the war / Our efforts must not cease / By saving more & more / We'll surely win the peace'.   49f

UNION-CASTLE LINE TO SOUTH AND EAST AFRICA.

THE UNION-CASTLE ROYAL MAIL STEAMER "PRETORIA CASTLE."   28,705 TONS.

January 8th.   Mrs B at the Bay of Biscay to Miss Jane Pullin in Exeter *You would love this life - plenty of everything, and a shop where nothing needs coupons. Tom's greatest thrill was when he bought a bar of chocolate 'just like that'.* They are sailing to a land of plenty in South Africa where Apartheid is now (since 1948) the rule of law rather than merely a pattern of behaviour.   49g

848—Residence of Judy Garland, Bel Air, California

April 19th.   Kay in Long Beach sends her granny one by one the popular series of homes of the stars, glamorous dwellings of her idols and only to be glimpsed by her up driveways or behind high fences. *Dear Granny - Sure a lot of money represented here in Hollywood. Bet they have a real fireplace here. Wish I could go inside of some of these homes.* While Kay writes, Judy Garland (née Frances Gumm) is busily filming A Star Is Born.   49h

Home of Bud Abbott, Encino, California
Home of Lou Costello, North Hollywood

April 19th.   *Dear Grannie. This pool is where Costello's son was drowned. He has built a home for orphans now. Has a radio show on the air Sat. morn. and does a lot of good.* Kay knows the stories of all the stars and retells them to Granny at the rate of one or two a day. Abbott and Costello incorporated virtually all known vaudeville double-act routines into their films between 1940 and 1953 when Abbott (ten years older than his partner) retired.   49i

Harrods of 1849 — A Centenary Souvenir

Ann in Chelsea to Mrs Davies in Liverpool *Have decided to buy swim suit in France as I've been told they are much cheaper there. Have not been able to get my size here! Have been looking around shops most of today.* One of her stops was evidently at Harrods where she picked up this free card decorously celebrating the famous store's centenary. 49j

October 11th. From Sadh Mathuradas Lachminarain in Mitzapur to Metal Supplies Ltd. in London WC2, *Festival of Lamps. We extend our felicitations on Diwali (our New Year) Oct 21st.* Gandhi is pictured here as a light of love. With the assassination of the Mahatma the previous year that light had been extinguished, the last perhaps that represented a union of spirituality with a sense of political reality. 49k

June 22nd. Mrs Gill in Blaydon gets a card from Eliza in Edinburgh *I am writing this at the Forth Bridge. Bert is going to take the car over the Ferry.* The Edinburgh Festival started in 1947 and put the city on the world's cultural map. The Floral Clock was appropriately adapted in 1948 and concertgoers learned that at half past Grieg they should be making their way to the Usher Hall. 49l

August 17th. Fern in Spotted Horse, Wyoming to Mrs Fred Buchanan in Tulsa *Dear Mildred, staying alright in rapid city S.D. The hail is all over the ground it looks rather like snow.* Ted Hustead's Cowboy Orchestra still creaks into action every half hour at the Wall Drug Store though the drug store itself now occupies a large slice of the town (see 91d). 49m

May 31st. E Flint in Morecambe to Mr & Mrs Ward in Leicester. *Am having a grand time. The weather has been super... am going in a Veleta Competition Thursday evening. Have got a partner, a lady's husband who sit at our table and according to the talent here its in the bag. I have been coaching my partner in little points so that he will be ok. I think. Will let you know results.* Everyone is having a good time at this camp except the man in the foreground who looks as if he's on death row. 49n

January 4th. Henry in Boston to his wife Mrs Starr, *Darling - Really it was the best flight yet. Due to lack of 'equipment' (planes) they put me on at 1 after cancelling the 12 - but the Lord gave me wonderful joy in soul-winning while waiting; one of the folks just hungry and ready.* Sounds like a rapid conversion but it's put Henry in the buoyant mood that characterises this excellent promotional picture produced by American Airlines. 49o

231

14. Le Mont Blanc (4810 m)

September 17th.   Des writes from St Cergue in Switzerland to Ian Heelas in Thirlestone, Devon *Have just finished on a grand week here at an International Conference of the World Union of Peace Movements. My Swiss francs being very short I only got £3 'transit francs' I stayed with the Pasteur of the Village... I hopped over to France & visited Chamonix - a marvellous spot could not buy Swiss mint because of shortage of Frs.* English currency restrictions limited travel. Des (like Tom in 19a) works, in the shadow of the atomic bomb, for peace to have a voice.   49p

November 19th.   From Costermansville in the Belgian Congo AE Ritschard writes to Mr & Mrs Stokes, Boiler Inspector, Tanganyika Railways, Dar es Salaam *Nearly 3 months since we left DeS... we tried to see you on the line, but in vain. We miss DeS, our friends, our old car, and our swimming. Ritch.* This dignified study of a Sankuru chief decked out with the force of powerful animals comes from the remarkable series Vanishing Africa (L'Afrique qui Disparait).   49q

"Pop over for a quiet evening Reggie—I think there's something worth seeing on the television!"

July 12th.   The Staggs in Margate to Pam in Reading, *The food is so good we seem to be eating all day long. We are on the pier listening to Ivy Benson's band.* The old gag about the radio works better with this early TV set which could offer ample seating above its flickering blue picture. On such a set in a schoolfriend's prefab I first saw television (the 1949 Cup Final).   49r

August 25th.   Irving Spector (Society's Funster) Dead Pan Comedy Violin announces his dates for Pittsburgh shows to the Nunemaker Agency in Reading, Pa., his self description being a rubber stamp on the back of this excellent publicity photocard. He is typical of that last generation of true vaudevillians TV is about to make use of or swallow altogether.   49s

852—Home of Eddie "Rochester" Anderson, Los Angeles, California
NBC Comedian and Screen Star

April 19th.   *Dear Granny* writes Kay for the second time that day (see 49i), *Mary went to L.A. again today. Mummy sitting here looking out of the window. Vera wants me to give her a permanent tomorrow. Will take most of the day.* She does not speak of the house whose most unusual aspect is that it is the property of a black star though bought of course at a price; that of being a stereotype comic servant in a film career lasting from the thirties to the mid sixties. He was best known as Rochester, stooge to Jack Benny in a popular TV series. This did not endear him finally to black Americans involved in the struggle against the attitudes he was endorsing and he himself finally turned his back on such roles. By 1949 there had been little change in the patronising use of blacks in films with the exception of celebrity musicians like Louis Armstrong. Casablanca in 1942 was an early break in the mould where 'Sam' (Dooley Wilson) is treated as an equal. Eddie Anderson died in 1977 by which time the world was a very different place.   49t

Kon - Tiki ekspedisjonen

2/8

Month/Day unclear.   J writes from Norway to Miss Guthrie in Merstham, *saw the Kon-tiki on Thurs. most interesting to see the actual raft. Yes - we will both know the two men will work alright & that all will go well with the P - erection. How very difficult it is to keep a constant RA but how one benefits when one does have it. Doesn't my new pen write nicely? Thankyou my dear... and for the X words.* Kon Tiki was the publishing sensation of the year and Thor Heyerdahl became a hero overnight with his tale of courage in the service of knowledge. The 101 day voyage from Peru to Polynesia made in 1947 gave credibility to radical theories of prehistoric migrations.   50a

February 6th.   Will & Flo to Mrs Fox in Dover, *Have been having good times at the Hall & campaign at Putney. Monday is the last night. Will has been wearing his hat proper posh. Thought you would like this photo of the lights, we have seen them, so has Mary.* The Guinness clock shows it to be one hour later than the scene in 49b. The crowd begins to disperse.   50b

October 22nd.   Nellie & Walter to Mrs Agnes Waddington in Bradford, *Have arrived here after all. Weather very nice. We saw some of the lights last night and weather permitting will see the remainder tonight.* Two mentions of the weather tells us that we are in England. As part of the famous Blackpool illuminations this year the Statue of Liberty meets a truncated Chrysler building in a New York panorama.   50c

July 2nd.   Mr Jeffries at T.E.D./BSA Tools Ltd. Birmingham gets a card from Pembroke, *Dear Geoff & all. The weather is super except for a storm that spoiled the paint. Have finished the van in two shades of green. Looks posh. It's very quiet here after the racket at the BSA... The car came down very well. It's waterproof. It poured all the way down. All the best. Ron.*   50d

August 11th.   Miss Betty Johnson in Epsom gets a card from Mum & Dad who seem to be in a cosy sort of camp, *We had a lovely day Sunday and its very nice today. The camp quite good. food good. I hope Butch is behaving himself.* The people in the bar look like characters in a Terence Rattigan play. The poster advertises a reunion dance with Victor Sylvester's Orchestra, the leading strict tempo dance band of the day.   50e

October 11th.   To Annie & Julia Reavey in London SW9, *This: Palace Theatre, Preston/Next Empire, Dewsbury. Just got time to wish you (Both of you) many happy returns. We had rehearsals & already put some new stunts on. I think by Saturday we'll be ready for more, as we are playing the drums. Cheerio Love from us 3 little ones.* The circus family of dwarfs plays the halls in winter with no lack of pride.   50f

September 16th.   Bessie in Hamilton, Bermuda to Mr & Mrs Graw in Ashley Park NJ. *I haven't seen a lumber yard here yet. This picture tell an actual story & the homes are all beautiful & well built, whether they are large or small.* Sounds as if there is some mutual interest in lumber but Bessie is content to share this card of a Bermudan cutting the local soft stone which hardens when exposed to air.   50g

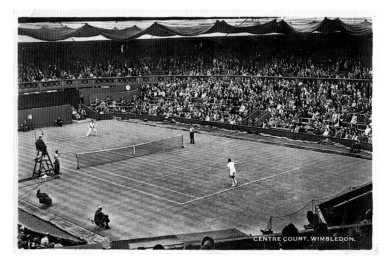

October 3rd.   To Mr Otto Maer, Bayshore NJ., *1lb cans pitted cherries 41 cts Boiling beef 31, Sugar cured bacon 35 Eggs 45 doz Home made sausage 49lb Weiners 49lb Country lard 11 Mason City prices. about 50 stores 2000 population. Trees enormous measured biggest Elm 14ft circumference. Most all streets paved sewers in. Haveing a hard time Eating Banquets.* A selective report on the Iowa city founded a century before and, as the cartoon suggests, still associated with Freemasonry.   50h

September 7th.   Rose to the Browns in Caldy, Cheshire. *I'm staying with Phil's at present, going to 'The Jordans' country next week & then to Nora's.* Wimbledon is seen in its years of sartorial schism. The fact that one of the men here is in long and one in short trousers is nothing to the excitement caused by glimpses of the frilly knickers of Gorgeous Gussie Moran (and other fashions by Teddy Tinling). This still amateur event would soon be turned by television into mass entertainment.   50i

March 23rd.   F to TM in Bloomfield NJ., *Hi! Spent Frid here at St Martinville went into this very interesting old church which has the grave of 'Evangeline' in the little cemetery at the back...* Here among the lakes and bayous of Louisiana it is a shock to find a surrealist reconstruction of the grotto at Lourdes which seems to throb and bulge out of the wall. Religion and Science Fiction have much in common.   50j

June 29th.   Martha to Andy Valbert in Bensenville, Illinois, *4th night we're in a cabin at Sheridan Wy. 200 miles from Yellowstone. We spent two and a half days in S.Dakota, many things to see... my eyes are bad tho. Harold doing all the driving.* Gutzon Borglum's model differs in many ways from the finished Mt.Rushmore. Such grey and ghostly giants in a room make a disturbing image.   50k

January 14th.   Margy to Mrs Tilley in Westbury-on-Trym showing where she lives *...hope your cold is improving dear. We are going to a show to-night at the Winter Gardens... Have you made any more mincemeat?* Location is everything. The massive Dolphin Square block was the biggest in Europe when built in 1937. In Chelsea it is select & exclusive. Anywhere else it might be a broken-windowed slum.   50l

June 23rd.   James Blow at Caltech gets a card from Pasadena with a mimeographed message, *Had a wonderful time at Sun Valley on location Duchess of Idaho*, signed by l Esther Williams the glamorous aquatic actress, seen here with leading man Van Johnson. Any minute now she will be swimming balletically in that pool to prove Joe Pasternak's pithy summing up of her career, 'Wet she was a star'.   50m

November 2nd.   From Joplin, Mo. to Mrs Wm. Ehle in Albany NY., *Just sent this card to show you the beautiful road we have been going over. We stayed outside of Rolla last night. you just can't describe these places. Mother & Dad.* Route 66 has become a legend and a cult as The Mother Road, now subsumed under other numbers (Interstate 55, 44 & 40 etc.) but still followed by nostalgic drivers and bikers from Chicago to Los Angeles. Its fame spreads in proportion to its disappearance.   50n

August 20th.   From Hanna to several people at the Rohr-Rdg clinic in Chicago, *Had our best dinner here. Their popovers are truly elegant. Saw 'Cocktail Party' & 'Member of the Wedding'. Trying to get into U.N. but our contact has gone to San Francisco to cover the Korean War.* The last thing you imagine that people were seeing in the theatre during the Korean War would be TS Eliot's new play The Cocktail Party (first produced in London the year before).   50o

September 5th.   Iris to Cath Stafford in Coventry, *Have been to shows here. Sunday Albert Modley at the North Pier and Ann Ziegler & Webster Booth in Saturday. And last night Norman Evans. Have been on a circular tour to Bleasdale.* All these are well known names from the halls and from radio, especially Ann Ziegler & Webster Booth, the love-song duettists, who later retired to live in South Africa.   50p

July 20th.   Elba, Jim & Curtis from Wenatchee to Ira van Doran in Westernville NY., *We saw this dam a.m. also a smelter in Idaho refining lead zinc silver & gold also a grain elevator at Spokane. Aunt Gertie waiting for us at Grandma Higby's ranch.* What did the shepherd do with his sheep before the Grand Coulee Dam was built? The harmony of epochs is here complete whatever is the case.   50q

General Douglas MacArthur

July 1st.   Flo in Ambrosden to Gladys in Hastings, *Pleasant journey down here. Met a Sgt.Major at Paddington & after tea & biscuits we travelled down together & met some Banbury people. Love to all at 172.* McGill with an elegant snatch of dialogue between two storks shows his skill at dealing with taboo subjects (pre-marital sex and menstruation) in a censor-proof fashion (witty in itself). Smoking chimneys would soon be taboo as well.   50r

September 25th.   Ethel in Smithburgh to Daisy Crawford in Los Angeles, *I collect only view cards & my collection is progressing very nicely. I have over 5300 cards now.* At seventy years of age a general might be expected to be growing orchids or writing his memoirs but MacArthur had just been appointed Supreme Commander in the Korean War. Truman had doubts when early victories led the autocratic General to think of attacking China itself.   50s

October 7th.   Elaine & Henry in Beverley Hills to Edna & Zach Levin in Long Beach NY, *Spent all day with Selma - what a woman! She misses you so much. Passed through Long Beach and the whole place is peppered with oil wells and highly industrialised - what a difference. Ate in this famous place but saw no celebrities. Hope all is well.* One guesses that by 1950 the Brown Derby on Wilshire Blvd. was entirely populated by the Elaines and Henrys of the world hoping to see the screen stars who long ago had moved en masse to this or that venue as fashion dictated. Its heyday was in another era and it features on many cards though this is the only one that I have seen that shows The London Shop whose olde worlde lettering constitutes a warning in itself. The Brown Derby is a fine name for a restaurant but the shape of a rimless bowler is more reminiscent of an observatory and fails to satisfy.   50t

951

August 13th.   Peggy writes to Ian Morris & Betty Trowbridge in London W4, from the Eastern Sector of Berlin. *Arrived safely in Berlin on Thursday despite everything. Plenty to do in Berlin. Situation here is highly encouraging. We were warmly welcomed by the German people. We are not starving.* This trio, politically immaculate in gender and ethnicity, come from a Sovexport film. Peggy is attending the IIIrd World Festival of Youth & Students for Peace. She has fallen completely (and understandably) for the party line as announced in the card's title, the special issue stamp, and even the slogan postmark, 'Youth. Unite in the Struggle for Peace against the Danger of a New War'. Ten years on, to the day, from the posting of this card the Berlin wall will be newly in place.   51a

September 17th.   Jimmie to J P Winterbourne in Cheltenham, *This is just to remind you of London ! I bought it in Woolworths in the Strand. Dad quite cheery & sends his love.* The Tricksters (with 'New Star, Deborah Kerr') and So Well Remembered (Dymytryk's film with Trevor Howard & John Mills) date the view to 1947, yet Flaherty's masterpiece, Nanook Of The North, at the Pavilion was made in 1921.   51b

February 3rd.   Bob writes to his Auntie, Mrs Wilbur Jones in Jamestown NY, on a card that tells one on the reverse that it was 'purchased atop the Empire State Building', *I am having a great time. Right now I am 1050ft above the city. My roommate is taking me all over.* This particular view and the way it is framed assert the island character of Manhattan.   51c

March 9th.   Nicholas Barton at Westminster School gets a card from home, *Donning clean clothes on a Friday/Makes the schoolboy trim and tidy/Washing makes the growing lad/Popular with Mum & Dad. (old proverb). P.S. Clever of them to photograph the exhibition before it exists*. The publishing of the model of the Festival of Britain caused great excitement though many still thought it an extravagance.   51d

December 4th.   Marie to Dora Torday in Bournemouth, *Just to ask you not to come tomorrow as the cat has been seriously ill. I thought we would lose her but Mr Turner pulled her through... have to feed her every two hours. Has Peter got an answer yet?* The King already looking frail makes one of his last public appearances on the typically rainy opening day.   51e

September 30th.   Win to Mrs Sutton in Sutton Coldfield, *Had a lovely day at South Bank yesterday but do my legs ache today. The exhibition is a wonderful achievement & when we left the crowds were pouring in for the Gala. We go to Battersea Gardens tomorrow, staying for lights and fireworks.* By September the consensus was that the Festival had successfully lifted some of the post war gloom.   51f

August 30th.   HBC to S C Preston, Building Surveyor's Dept., Town Hall, Bournemouth. *Have just condemned the Skylon as a dangerous structure & have enclosed it with chestnut fencing! Saw Denis Compton on Saturday - he holds his bat correctly!* Despite his admiration for the great cricketer HBC seems a bit of a killjoy, but Philip Powell's beautiful symbol of the Festival was not fenced in for long.   51g

July 25th.   Dad to Nicholas Barton again. *What about one of these for Mummy's birthday? (what are they anyway?). Maybe she'd prefer something smaller and I think I've seen the very thing, a chromium bracelet thing for her new watch. It costs 14/6 a bit more than you can afford but I'll give you the extra.* This was better than most of the sculpture on view. Such pavilions with their confident titles covered an area which had previously been derelict after wartime bombs.   51h

August 21st.   Elsie & Terry to the Johnstones in Swansea *This festival is a wonderful effort. So surprised to meet Jenny here.* A wonderful effort exactly sums up people's feelings after the initial scepticism; very much a phrase of the time. Leslie Martin's Royal Festival Hall is the only survivor of the South Bank extravaganza and is still one of London's finest post-war buildings, as well as its best concert hall. It was only recently restored to reveal the original internal dynamics of the structure.   51i

February 15th.   Sully to Mrs John Dupont in Marion, Illinois. *Dear Friend, not one of the eating places in this town had food like the chicken we had at your house way back when. In fact not any of the food impressed me - I'd hate to live in this town in summer it must be terrible.* Despite the lovely colour and the car and figures of their promotional card Corey's evidently failed to please.   51j

August 12th.   Margaret to James Hoggan in Dunfermline, *It poured all day yesterday, but we managed to get around all the same. I bought material for a frock - called 'Lovat' colour. bluegreygreen - and a hat to match & we visited this exhibition. I'm wondering what's happening about limekilns!* Holmes, here seated in a realistic reconstruction of his fictitious study, would have liked that last sentence.   51k

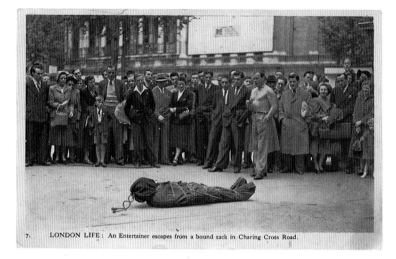

July 31st.   Charley in Cricklewood to Raymond Dutty in Emsworth, *Thank you for collecting my pictures... so glad you have managed to do some selling. Au revoir till Sunday. What do you make of this picture?!!* If Raymond had spent any time around Leicester Square he would surely have seen this man struggle out of his sack and chains. He would have also seen the three camp men do their Egyptian dance.   51l

May 4th.   Margaret to Mr & Mrs Ira Baldwin in McKenzie, Alabama. *Hello, we made it this far. will be in Kansas City tonight. will write.* Not exactly General MacArthur's finest hour, since the card is sent only three weeks after he has been fired by President Truman from his post as Supreme Commander. Truman accuses him of meddling in politics. MacArthur says Truman is blind to reality.   51m

June 20th.   Jamey to Mrs Williams in Stradbally, Eire, *So far we are having a hectic time. This is really a marvellous place. picked up with a young engaged couple The girl sleeps with Stella & the lad with me. C of I too we were lucky.* Butlin's spreads its empire to Southern Ireland and this Church of Ireland quartet recall the now distant proprieties of good God fearing folk of yesteryear. Mrs Williams would no doubt have been reassured by such an arrangement.   51n

May 12th.   Mum to Master Chris Acutt in Natal, *This is the hotel we are staying at in Tokyo... Principal cars used in Japan are V.8. Chev & Dodge.* Frank Lloyd Wright's masterpiece designed to withstand earthquake and fire was finished in 1922 and soon put to the test in the Kanto quake of 1923. It stood intact while virtually all around was reduced to rubble. Progress did what God could not: it was demolished in 1967 to make way for a high-rise replacement.   51o

m.v. 'EMPIRE WINDRUSH' 14,651 tons

November 30th.   Christine to Mrs Dandy in Driffield, *The Red Sea! We are on our way home once more! We are due at S'hampton on Dec 14th - We've got some great news - we're going to have an infant! Next June I hope.* The Empire Windrush looks ordinary enough, the sort of ship a child might draw. It did though, like Chesterton's donkey, have a special day when it made history. It was in fact a German ship launched as the Monte Rosa in Hamburg in 1930. The war saw it performing routine duties, sustaining minor accidents, acting as a troop ship and ending as a hospital ship before surrendering to the British in August 1945. Passed to the Ministry of Transport it was renamed in 1947 after refitting as a troop ship. On 21st June its niche in the story of Britain was secured when it docked at Tilbury with the first migrants from the Caribbean, many of them Jamaican ex-servicemen and their friends who had come along almost for the ride and expected to return in a few months. They found work easily but accommodation was harder to come by. These pioneers found a baffling mixture of warmth, curiosity and prejudice. Wanting to be ordinary they found themselves exotic in a virtually all white country. The comic cards below illustrate the music-hall myths they had to combat with their own reality. It now seems scarcely credible that I, a South Londoner who shopped every Saturday with his parents in Brixton, did not see a black person until 1946 when I was nine (an American GI).   51p

51a. Deutscherfilmverlag Berlin/Sovexport

51b. Publisher unknown 601

51c. Publisher unknown No 56

51d. R Tilbrook
Hugh Casson (later President of the Royal Academy) who died in 1999 was the overall guiding spirit of the Festival's design.

51e. Tuck. FB10
The figure behind the Queen is Herbert Morrison, the new Home Secretary. The Festival was called by its detractors Morrison's Folly. The current Jeremiads about the Millenium Dome are couched in exactly the same terms. The King seems to be recovering from major surgery but only has a few months to live. The Queen (now Queen Mother) is still with us and seems set to become a centenarian (see 99t).

51f. Valentine's/Official V.202

51g. Jarrold & Sons, Norwich/Official

51h. Tuck/Official FB14

51i. Jarrold & Sons/Official

51j. Colourpicture, Boston K1853

51k. Publisher unknown

51l. Charles Skilton, London. London Life No 7

51m. MWM, Aurora Mo. No 3346

51n. Publisher unknown (Butlin's)

51o. Imperial Hotel. Tokyo

51p. Publisher unknown

51q. Publisher unknown. No 47. Artist: Bob Wilkin
We shall hear more from Fred & Jean from various seaside resorts until 1977.

51r. Leslie Lester Ltd., Sussex. Artist: H Lime

"CHIEF, I'VE GOT YOU SOMETHING NICE FOR BREAKFAST!"
"O.K. I'M HAVING BREAKFAST IN BED THIS MORNING!"

"Yaas, honeychile, if youse a good girl ah'll let youse hold ma stick o' liquorice"

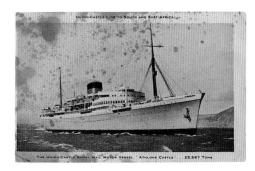

August 1st.   Fred & Jean from Brighton to Mr & Mrs Bird in Sunbury-on-Thames, *we went wrestling & mum got very excited & put earhole grip on me she is going to do the same to you Look out Ernie & Gert.* Cartoons have a small repertoire of exotic situations: cavemen are always white and cannibals (who customarily have missionaries for supper) black.   51q

July 26th.   DWK in Weston-Super-Mare to Mr H Smith, Works Manager, Fulon Works, Doyle, *Having very nice holiday.* Though the cannibals in 51q speak Standard English this couple talk in a music hall patois, a sort of black Mummerset which no one had ever really spoken. Blacks were legendarily held to have greater sexual prowess than whites.   51r

May 10th.   A week after the Festival opens the Athlone Castle, yet another vessel of the Union Castle Line (see 48h, 49g), heads for the golden promise of an easeful life for whites in South Africa. Pixie on board writes to Mrs Weston in Lea Bridge Rd. in London's East End *Dearest Carol, I left England with a heavy heart, it may be in a dreadful mess but it's still hard to leave. We sail at 4pm. Do take care of yourself and try not to worry as much as you do. We have just finished a very good lunch. xxx.*   51s

B.O.A.C. Comet Jetliner

November 27th.   *Just coming into London 6.5am, we left Rome at 3.30am. O boy! we have been flying at 38,000 feet.* Norman Hoyte conveys the excitement of flying on the world's first passenger jet, which must have made his friend at Westminster School, Nicholas Barton, green with envy. Comet I made the first scheduled flight from Johannesburg via Rome in May of 1952 and it had soon slashed the time of other long haul flights. Coincidentally it was at Rome airport (a month before the card was sent) that the first of many accidents occurred which led to the grounding of the Comet in 1954. Norman seems happily oblivious of this.   52a

October 10th.   *Dear All,* writes Les to the Cowles in Birkenhead, *By now you will have heard about my phone call. Well I'm all right & I go on nights at 6pm tonight. I've signed on & we sail at 3pm on Sat. You dare mention that to Edie. I'll try to write.* A poster for Danny Kaye in On the Riviera (1951) is going up and post-war cars are seen including a gleaming Standard Vanguard.   52b

October 20th.   Edna May to her Aunt, Mrs Elizabeth Rust (and Ella) in New Martinsville, Virginia, *I am having a much better time here than I anticipated. The girls here at school are wealthy & all college graduates but one so we are doing everything we can to make it a happy course all thru.* A pleasantly populated view with the new UN building rising up behind.   52c

November 10th.   Nell in Kensington to Mrs Gorman in Crawley, *could you make it Thursday as Lady H is coming tomorrow & we are having people in & I might not get much time to spare & another thing the shops are open until 7 o'clock on Thursdays.* Strange for a couple married five years to resort to photomontage for a portrait of themselves: though it does allow the monarch to seem as tall as the Duke.   52d

October 28th.   Gertie in Middelkerke, Belgium to Mrs Druce in Epsom, *I am very well & enjoying myself very much. I am having lunch at Niepost - & an English wireless is going on. I am having coffee to try to hang on to hear Cambridgeshire result.* We do not know whether Gertie heard what horse won but this fine animal (named after Raphael?) looks a likely winner of any race.   52e

November 7th.   George D Heltzell, a conscientious Rotarian from Clinton, Mo., uses his local club's card to report from Vancouver that he has duly attended their branch for the weekly meeting. He had it endorsed by the secretary, W G Randall. Despite its worthy but dull image the Rotary Club devised through this scheme a brilliant socially unifying idea which served business and the community.   52f

September 8th.   Mrs Al Orenholt in Goshen, Indiana receives this card offering a free trial of the Famous Whirlpool Automatic Washer from the local dealer Pierre W Cripe (one disadvantage of not showing the backs of cards is that it seems one is making up all the names). The lady in the home with its fifties furnishings and fittings 'experiences the thrill of workless washdays'.   52g

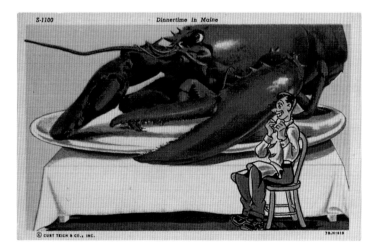

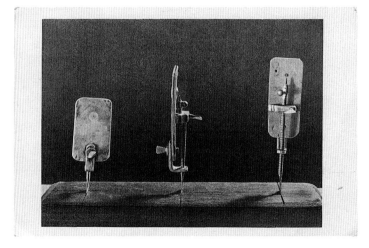

July 22nd.   Syd in China, Maine to Mr & Mrs Bailey in Meadville, Pa. *I've won bouts with clams and mussels now I'm going to take on this fellow.* Exaggeration is America's speciality in comic cards (men catching giant fish, huge apples occupying a whole truck, people riding horse-size rabbits etc.). Most of them are photographic tricks. Here the Maine lobster is a photograph visiting a graphic world including the miniature diner.   52h

July 10th.   These three table-top sculptures are seventeenth century Dutch scientific instruments. AWK writes from Delft to AHT Robb-Smith in Oxford *These are a great improvement on yours, so much more portable! The Museum of the History of Science is full of good things and so are the restaurants.* Both message and caption confirm that these are microscopes though it is difficult to work out how (The lens is in fact the pinhole by the end of the screw).   52i

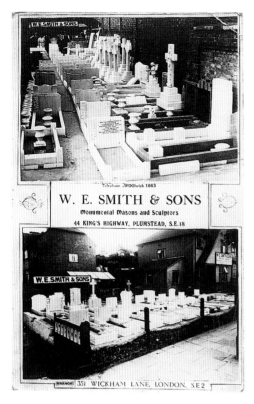

KNIT 'HEAD'–LINES

by

SCHUESSLER

July 30th. Mr Horrex in Bexleyheath receives a card from Smith & Sons, *We have pleasure in stating that we have completed the work to the memorial. Thanking you for your favour.* The staff of Smiths are gathered in the gloomy shadow of their sign at the top left, surveying their cheerless products which reflect industry rather than imagination. Their stock is good. The dead will not take them by surprise. 52j

May 20th. Schuessler's travelling salesman Mr Wichman is about to descend on Sterling, Illinois. He sends a card ahead from Chicago to the Girls & Women's Dept. of Wyne Denver Store saying that he will be calling this week with 'Knitted Headwear featuring fur trim mouton as well as many new novelty stylings'. The beret (bottom left) is almost stylish but the crochet cap with tassels (top left) is a real fright. 52k

March 22nd. Louise & Bill to Mr & Mrs Martin in Dunedin, Florida, *Hello Dearhearts: Miss you. & pussy. Have nice large 2 double size bed cabin in Lake Wales. Lots of mosquitoes!!* Lake Wales also boasts Prather's Laundry who produced this card of the local uncanny attraction. On this (one hopes not too busy) stretch of road your stopped car will appear to roll backwards uphill. Even the sky is spooky. 52l

October 10th. To Nicholas Barton at Westminster School, *Hope you had a good interview at the Middlesex. We've had a gay week. Yesterday Mum & I called on Ustinov. P at Wyndham's Theatre after his matinée. V.friendly & nice but a bit vague with 4 plays on his hands. Tonight... a film première & tomorrow night is the office dinner & dance. A mad whirl in fact. Next stop Wales. Get your pocket money from Preedey. love from Dad.* 52m

September 11th. Davey in Folkestone to Mr & Mrs Yoxon in Sutton Coldfield, *Dear Ron & Peggy. Having a good time in spite of rain & cold weather but it has not prevented us lads from getting about... not looking forward to Week End.* The nation is about to enter its fiftieth year of sending cards by the indefatigable Donald McGill who aged 77 was soon to face a new wave of persecution from the prudes. 52n

September 19th. M in Brixton writes to Miss Billing in Seaford, *V & I made a visit to these gardens yesterday & very much enjoyed our tea on the terrace. It is really a wonderful sight - I wish you had been with us to enjoy it.* The acre and a half of Derry & Toms roof garden was, even when the once rather snooty store became the fun-loving but short-lived Biba in the seventies, a fine place for tea. 52o

THE THIRD PROGRAMME?

VIOLINIST: "My boy friend's got an electric organ"

FRIEND: "Gee, that must be useful in the dark"

521   OPEN AIR ART EXHIBITION, HEATH STREET, HAMPSTEAD.

51.- CATEDRAL, MEXICO D.F.

52a. B.O.A.C.

52b. Lansdown Productions, London LP 487

52c. Alfred Mainzer NY (CT)

52d. Publisher unknown. Photos: Dorothy Wilding/Baron No 715

52e. Antony, Ostende

52f. Rotary Club, Kansas City

52g. Clarisse, Hanau NY FT2REV.A

52h. Curt Teich 7B H161

52i. Leiden, Rijksmuseum

52j. W E Smith, London

52k. Groganized, Daneville, Ill.

52l. Curt Teich L.W.12

52m. Charles Skilton. 536

52n. D Constance Ltd. 885. Artist: Donald McGill

52o. D.F&S for Derry & Toms

52p. Philmar Ltd. No 41 M1/975-7 Artist: T Gilson

52q. Leslie Lester, Hurstpierpoint 192 Artist: H Lime

52r. Charles Skilton Ltd. No 521

52s Dessentis, Mexico, 57

July 17th.   Norman in Porthcawl to Leslie Thomas in Carmarthen, *Having a lovely time here... Mummy has just reminded me that I shall have to practice all day on Sunday Hm. Shall see you on Monday as usual.* Perhaps Norman eventually got to play on the Third Programme the 'highbrow' station of BBC radio which had made a tentative start in 1946 (renamed Radio 3 in 1967). These diminutive intellectuals adopt the characteristic attitudes for serious listening to the concerts, talks and commissioned plays that made up the bulk of what was offered by this miraculously surviving network.   52p

July 20th.   Lil, Ken & Pat in Ramsgate to Mrs F Wood in Harpenden *Having a lovely time. Wonderful weather & digs. We are all nice & brown.* This simple and perfectly observed couple of music students by H Lime (which I always have taken to be a pseudonym since many comic artists used other names for their more risqué productions) are accompanied by one of the best organ jokes. Other copies of the same drawing (differently numbered) have alternative dialogues, much less pithy. Is it too early for H Lime itself to be a gag based on Harry Lime in Carol Reed's film of 1949, The Third Man?   52q

August 10th.   Edna and Ted (can one date postcards merely by the names of couples?) write to Mrs Allen in Brighton, *Dear Gran & Liz. This is just round the corner from where we are staying & is only open on Sunday mornings & then 5 minutes walk & we are out on the Heath & we saw a lot of men fishing in a pond... The weather was lovely we only had one shower.* Precious little else even in Hampstead would be open on a Sunday in the early fifties when the Lord's Day Observance Society still held sway. Such open air shows can make a cheery sight and pass the time amiably without any risk of encountering art in any serious form. Virtually everything is a pastiche of something else and by this time there would be tasteful versions of once unacceptable genres in the form of pastiche cubism and kitsch abstraction. It was on such railings (at the Embankment) that I first showed some of my own paintings in 1953. None sold.   52r

February 21st.   Kay in Mexico City to Mrs Raymond Carter in Winchester, Mass, *Hi, Enjoyed your note at Christmas as usual. judge & I are on a 17 day jaunt to Mexico - left the children with Mother. Saw Diego Rivera at work on a mural today. Leave Mex. City tomorrow to spend several days at an Hacienda & then a Spa in the mountains. Write us - Judge has a story in April "American Legend" Mag & I posed for one of the pictures. Love, Kay.* Rivera would have been working on his sequence of huge paintings in the Civic Hall (behind the tree on the extreme right). They form a panorama of Mexican history in Marxist terms. The three main threads of Mexico's colourful story are present in this vast and spectacular square. To the immediate right of the cathedral lie the formidable ruins of the Aztec Templo Mayor. The dying Gods of Marxism, and the dead Gods of the Ancestors are still overshadowed by the Christian's God who may yet join them.   52s

NOW SHE IS QUEEN INDEED

CHT 18   THE CORONATION PROCESSION OF HER MAJESTY QUEEN ELIZABETH,   A TUCK CARD
JUNE 2ND, 1953

June 10th.   Postcard publishers still could move fast on the great occasions as Raphael Tuck & Sons prove here capturing and captioning the essence of the Coronation atmosphere as a break in the clouds allows the gold of the fairy tale coach to gleam. Minnie must have written her card some days before posting it to Miss Poland in Sefton Park, Liverpool, *Having a fine time, saw all the Royal Family yesterday. I was right in the front.*   53a

EROS FLOODLIT, LONDON.   2Z1418

June 15th.   Still in the spindly style that characterised Festival of Britain designs the decoration of Eros celebrates the Coronation. Florrie writes to Miss Q Pearce in Rice Lane, Liverpool. *Dear Queenie, I am enjoying my visit to London very much have been <u>up</u> and <u>down</u> the escalatirs & am still alive (but only just). Have managed to crowd in a lot of sightseeing... easier to get about here than I expected.*   53b

May 18th   From the standard Governor's Island viewpoint, whose tree continues to perform its steadfast service to photography, Harry writes briefly to Tom Ching his friend who works at the distinguished Harley-Davidson Motor Co. in distant Wisconsin. *Spending a few days down here. A great place for crowds.*   53c

THE STONEHENGE MEMORIAL
Near the Maryhill Museum of Fine Arts, Maryhill, Wn.

U. S. NAVAL SHIP GENERAL H. B. FREEMAN   BOERSIG

June 1st.   Margaret to John Bachelor in Stockport, *We saw this from the car but didn't leave time to stop. Wind was blowing terrifically and we had only just come from school picnic.* As was the real Stonehenge in 1953 this replica (erected as a war memorial in 1929) is free and explorable. It has the advantage of being complete though the guide mentions a snag, summed up in the phrase Beware Rattlesnakes. 53d

July 27th.   Mr & Mrs Whiteside get a card from their son On Active Service, *I am feeling very well. I am in Korea now waiting to be assigned to my unit. There is no use writing me for a week or so as I won't get your letters for some time since we move from one place to another every few days.* He writes on the day of armistice and reflects the usual serviceman's confusion about where he is going and when.   53e

SNR 10   THE CORONATION NAVAL REVIEW AT SPITHEAD   A TUCK CARD
THE QUEEN WITH THE DUKE OF EDINBURGH
ON THE ROYAL YACHT "SURPRISE"

HENRY NEVER GOES OUT SATURDAY NIGHT NOW THAT THEY DEMONSTRATE THE SOAP THAT DOES EVERYTHING!

June 18th.   Charles & Jeanne to Miss Cruise at the Soura Starkes School of Dancing in Bath. *Thought you would like a line from Southsea, where we are sitting on the Pier watching the shipping in the Solent. Saw Cyril Fletcher's "Magpies" on Tuesday & going to the change of programme tonight.* This looks like a set for a modern dress production of HMS Pinafore with the chorus just about to break into a hornpipe.   53f

July 12th.   *Hello Pop,* writes Julie Warnecke in Flushing NY to her father in S.R.S. Home, Cotterkill NY, *Are you still having your naps you sure will have lots of time for your baseball on television. Any more nice widowers arrived?* The character seems more intent on soap than opera but, if he is watching in colour, is well ahead of the game since colour TV in its earliest phase was still a plaything for the very rich.   53g

"HAVE JUST ARRIVED!"

August 10th.   Gordon in Scarborough to Mrs Robertson in Leeds. *Hope Alan will take license in envelope to Tax Office for Refund... England seem to be going OK in the Test Matches.* England were indeed doing well and regained the Ashes after 20 years on August 19th. Out of his space-ship comes Dan Dare the Pilot of the Future as featured in the wonderful Eagle comic which delighted boys through the fifties. It was started by Rev. Marcus Morris as a British antidote to the violence of American comics. 53h

July 23rd.   Anne in New York to Edie Guiver in Wembley Hill, Middlesex. *This is the greatest convention ever. There were 132,811 yesterday and 4,640 immersed. It is very hot up to 96°. I am on Staten Island again & it takes 2 hours to get to the stadium. There are 2 new releases & we are hearing some wonderful things. wish you were here.* This is Kingdom Hall, the broadcasting centre for Jehovah's Witnesses in Brooklyn Bethel. Anne has presumably come from England to be there.   53i

Square Dance String Band, Fontana Village, N. C.

TERMINAL STATION AND SUBWAY, BIRMINGHAM, ALA.—A52

July 14th.   Bev in Fontana Dam NC, to Col H H Green at the Air Defence Command, Colorado Springs, *Hey Herby, Didn't know that you and Cy Farnham played in the same band. Leaving Aug 1st for Korea - 51st Ftr, Wing. Come on over for a weekend.* Aug 1st is a wise time to go to Korea, four days after the war's end. Square dancing had its vogue at this time in England, a staple of Community Centre evenings.   53j

February 3rd.   Jim Lass writes to his Dad in Elmhurst, Illinois, *Boy it sure is sunny and hot down here. I am now on route to Columbus. Birmingham is a pretty big <u>dump</u>. From what I have seen of the south, I know why they lost the war. Everything is starting to turn green. I bought 12 postcards in Birmingham.* Does that mean he told 12 people that Birmingham, Alabama, was a pretty big dump?   53k

S.18049.   STRAND PALACE HOTEL.   FOYER — VIEW OF BUREAU & ENTRANCE TO WINTER GARDEN.

March 13th.   Edgar & Ethel to Ben & Winn Pitt in Small Heath, *Just a line from the 'digs'. This is everything you said and more. We don't know how we shall get back to normal again. Talk about the lap of luxury... just going down to breakfast in Le Ravier (9.30 am)...* Perhaps the finest Art Deco interior in London this foyer was casually jettisoned in the sixties. The Victoria & Albert Museum was very glad to acquire it.   53l

May 28th.   Lewis Motor Company in Lebanon, NH entice Mr Woods of Bridgewater Vermont with a picture of the elegant new Oldsmobile while informing him of the work in hand, *I didn't forget you Glen the seat covers just came this a.m. If you will come down Sat June 6th about 8 or 9 am we will put them on Royal.* One can sense in the styling of this car that fins are not far off.   53m

Berlin. Am Brandenburger Tor

August 27th.   F in Bad Godesberg to John Ollgar in Columbo, Georgia, *Business is improving here all the time. our business making great strides.* The German economic miracle had a huge American input. This is the Coca Cola bottling plant in Rheingau, an expensive modern building showing itself off to advantage in this well photographed and finely produced night scene. I never did understand how a sticky drink came to rule the world: could it ever now lose momentum?   53n

October 15th.   Gene to Mrs Barry in Memphis, Tenn. *Dearest Mama, we arrived this morning & took a tour of West Berlin. This afternoon we hired a guide & private car & took a tour of the Russian sector. Went through one of the new apts. for workers on Stalin Allee. All so interesting.* It was workers on the Stalin Allee project who started the uprising in June which was duly crushed by Russian tanks. Tens of thousands of hungry and disaffected East Berliners fled to the West during the year.   53o

HER MAJESTY THE QUEEN.   727

LEATHER AND FUR FOR A NEW PAIR OF CHAPS

SKINNING A WEST TEXAS JACK RABBIT · LEPUS TEXIANUS

53a. Tuck CHT18. PM Long Live The Queen

53b. C Richter for Bridant

53c. Mike Roberts, Berkeley

53d. Maryhill Museum of Fine Arts

53e. Department of the US Navy. Photo: Boersig

53f. Tuck SNR10

53g. Tichnor Bros. 79514

53h. Valentine's 5098 Dan Dare Series

53i. Watchtower, Brooklyn. 46889

53j. Standard Souvenirs & Novelties, Knoxville 84763

53k. Ehlers News Co./Kropp & Co. A52. 11038

53l. Bridge House S18049

53m. Oldsmobile

53n. Max Göllner (publ. & photo)

53o. Rud. Praeht. Berlin 6

53p. Publisher unknown 727

53q. McCormick Co., Amarillo Texas. 28628

53r. Seymour Press 19718

53s. Kodak Ltd

June 13th.   Hilda in Brighton to Miss B E Lee in Blackheath, *We had a marvellous view of everything on Tuesday & did not get too wet. Were able to catch the 6.25 back to B'ton... saw lots of our E. African friends.* Like most British festivities the coronation took place in the rain. This became the standard crowned image of the Queen though it was taken a year earlier at the State Opening of Parliament.   53p

August 9th.   Little Jackie in Amarillo, Texas to Lottie Jackman in Houston, *Left Dallas in a rain storm now heading for Dumas or closer to Colorado. Plenty Hot.* This is the classic type of exaggeration card (see 52h) and is expertly montaged. Indeed the coolness and clarity of the image together with the human look of the hanging rabbit reminds one of paintings of the Flaying of Marsyas.   53q

THE GUINNESS FESTIVAL CLOCK
FESTIVAL PLEASURE GARDENS. LONDON · 19718

Labor Day Weekend

...grand time for making movies!

Take along your camera — and plenty of Kodachrome movie film!

See your Kodak dealer — today.

August 3rd.   Margaret battling with a recalcitrant biro of the period to Miss Jean Bain in Glasgow, *We are here tonight. For myself it is the first time. Reminds me of the 1911 Exhibition at Kelvingrove & also of the Tivoli in Copenhagen to celebrate the coronation I attended the Caledonian Ball at Grosvenor House.* Although the South Bank 1951 exhibition was demolished the Festival Gardens in Battersea retained its funfair, tree walks, fountains etc. of which there are still surviving traces.   53r

August 22nd.   Mr Mack Earle receives this promotional card from Kodak in Rochester, NY. For those who dreaded seeing friends' family snaps worse was in store. They would soon be showing home movies of their holidays, children's parties etc., which having no form would seem to have no end. One such camera however would be bought by a Mr Zapruder in Dallas.   53s

August 19th.   Detail of a rather dull Roumanian card sent from there by Kit to Max Gordon in London, *Should we write to Le Corbusier saying we are coming? I rather feel we should. That is assuming we still go - I feel rather cut off here since no mail has come thro' in 15 days, so anything may have happened. All sorts of architectural meetings have at last taken place, culminating in a fine party with an E. German architect professor who is rebuilding the Stalin Allee* [see 53o] *in the most atrocious style. Hope to be back. However - watch Reuter.* A message from deep behind the Iron Curtain (a term Churchill seems to have borrowed from Goebbels).   53t

"The biggest new entertainment event of the year." - LIFE

October 17th   Les and Margaret in Detroit have seen Cinerama and use the free promotional card to tell Mr & Mrs Pinions in St Leonards on Sea that it was *very real*. Cinerama despite the occasional wobble at the join of its three images had the same shock effect on its audiences as pioneer films fifty years before of trains coming into stations etc. Ever wider screens formed the cinema's Goliath-like challenge to the David of TV which was now a feature of almost every American home.   54a

September 4th   From King's Cross Station to Miss Jennifer H in Hawkhurst, Kent, *Jen: I am waiting for the train to come in & as you were asleep when I left this is to say goodnight & love to...* (rest not decipherable). Frank Sinatra is the star of Suddenly, in this same year, a thriller underwhelmingly described by Halliwell as a 'moderately effective minor suspenser'.   54b

June 30th   The United Nations Building quickly became the new star of New York views. Va to Mrs Anthony in New Bedford, Mass., *We are having a wonderful time here. Saw Carol Harvey in 'Pajama Game'. She is excellent. The weather not too warm. Went to Radio City this a.m. see a play tonight. Not a dull moment.* Simon Callow's 1999 London revival of the Pajama Game was designed by Frank Stella.   54c

September 21st.   Harry & May in Douglas I.O.M tell Jack Holt and all at Smiths Potato Crisps Factory in Stockport, Cheshire that they are enjoying themselves *weather not too bad, everything else just the job.* A pocket radio in 1954 would still be quite a bulky affair: it was not until 1958 that the first transistor made true pocket radios possible and affordable.   54d

September 23rd.   Arthur writes shakily to Mrs Partridge in Liverpool to say he *doesn't know which day,* but we don't find out for what. Kidderminster looks deserted. This is understandable, for at the Central Cinema they are showing A Streetcar Named Desire with Vivien Leigh at her most neurotic and Marlon Brando at his most erotic. Made in 1951 it would not have reached Kidderminster until '52 or '53.   54e

September 8th.   To Glenn Hill, The Sundial W.T.S.P., St Petersburg, Florida, *We're home. Arrived Labor Day. Travelled over 15,000 miles. Visited friends & Relations in Penna. before heading South. Please play 'Stars & Stripes Forever", The Myers.* The Corn Palace in Mitchell is redecorated all over with corn cobs each year. A resemblance in 1953 to the Kremlin is pointedly offset by at least 18 US flags.   54f

April 5th.   Maureen & Roy to Auntie & Harry in Portsmouth, *We're almost settled in our new flat now and I'm just getting used to my surroundings. The building of the p.card is the NAAFI shop where I do all my shopping. They sell everything from pins & needles to groceries... The coach and cars belong to the Army.* Not every NAAFI store for the British Occupation troops was as palatial as this.   54g

August 19th.   *A few days here is very nice* writes Margaret to the Fletchers in Parkstone, *listening to good music.* They certainly would have heard music of quality since Dartington, as well as being the birthplace of W H Mallock, was the country's leading summer school. In its idyllic setting major composers & performers have taught and made music. Stravinsky, Boulanger, Berio, Tippett and Birtwistle etc. have formed a tradition which continues to thrive.   54h

September 21st.   Ian in Cambridge to Charles Horrocks in Brassington, *Tomorrow we have a recognition exam so we will have many types to recognise including this Canberra... Life on a squadron is still just great. Just the job for you in a few years time. Be a good lad. See you soon.* The Canberra had a long history from the prototype in 1949. It captured the altitude record in 1953, '54 & '57 & served in various campaigns (lastly in 1982, on the Argentinian side, in the Falklands War).   54i

October 5th.   Sue & Goldie to the Hareys in St Louis, *Med & Mae have been showing us the town. Lou & Med heard Billy Graham last night. Mae & I are going tonight.* By 1954 Billy Graham's Radio Show had 15 million listeners, almost as many souls as were duped by that flamboyant crook, Huey P Long (assassinated 1935). The film of All The Kings Men, an archetypal tale of power and corruption, retold his story.   54j

November 17th.   R in Verdun to Mrs Kerrion in Great Yarmouth, *Here on office business. This was the bloodiest world war I battle area. a million men died here see you next week x.* Itself like a buried cross the Ossuary and lighthouse at Douamont is a bleak reminder of the Great War whose shadow still evidently reaches beyond World War II in this rather glum message.   54k

June 28th.   Betty to Kathryn Salter in White City Estate, *Having a lovely time here & so would you if you were here. They've just elected the beauty queen of the week, but they would never get me in entering... arrived here 8 o clock it was 10 hours travelling and was we tired.* Pontin's soon became the main rival to Butlin's and, judging by the girl in à la mode rolled up jeans, attracted younger campers.   54l

March 27th.   Helen in Havana to Mrs Boyd Page in Fairbury, Nebraska, *Wish you could have enjoyed this place with us last nite. We flew over here yesterday, going back today. It's a wonderful city.* Night spots like this 'Crystal Arches Room designed by Max Borges' attracted American pleasure seekers; but not for long. Though Fidel Castro was arrested in July 1953 it is not the last that will be heard of him.   54m

October 5th.   Dick to AE at the British Schools in Rome, *To wish you bon voyage back to this grey & misty land... & to these ponds & children which are your motifs propre. Your last splendid letter was read aloud to Pat S, Francis, Phillipa, Mary & Gillian. Everyone looks forward to you & your paintings.* If the photo was taken just before 1950 I might be one of the boys pictured here though I see no sign of my boat which invariably listed heavily. Later I got to know this band of distinguished artists.   54n

May 23rd.   Kirk in Barcelona to Miss Colleen Pretty in Norfolk, *Hi Fatso. Well we finally made it to Spain. All four of us are still operating on a shoe-string budget., but with our good looks 'no sweat'... tomorrow we plan on seeing the Bullfight. We would have liked to go to Madrid.* There were still financial restrictions on foreign travel but the British soon found that sun, food, sea and experience were to be had cheaply in Spain which here announces the beginning of popular tourism with a flourish.   54o

August 16th. Elsie to the Elsons in Halifax, *We are at Windsor today... lovely weather. Cheerio.* Churchill by now had been awarded every honour the nation can bestow and has also won the Nobel prize for literature (which he could hardly have imagined when he published his first novel in 1900). After a stroke in 1953 his activities had become more limited and he was to resign as premier in 1955 aged 80. This is nearly the last we shall see of him in these pages.   54p

June 15th. Tommy to Mrs Fais in Martinsville NJ, *Hi - Tho't you'd enjoy this before & after... May go from Livingstone to Yellowstone - Got your map handy?* It would now be inconceivable to suggest turning a National Park mountain into a sculpture: all sorts of eco-lobbyists and environmental activists would be there at the first clunk of a chisel. Perhaps the world has begun to suffer (as Gutzon Borglum did not) from a failure of nerve.   54q

54a. Shorecolour Co. NY for Cinerama

54b. A V Fry Co. Ltd. London. F.134

54c. Alfred Mainzer K3791

54d. Bamforth Comic Series. No 685. Artist: Tempest

54e. Valentine's K.3173

54f. Dan Grigg Enterprises. S Dakota. Photo: Rodney Prather

54g. BAOR. Photo: F Thomas

54h. Publisher unknown

54i. Publisher unknown

54j. New Orleans News Co. E C Knopp. 19655

54k. Verdun Editions. No 455

54l. Tuck SDH 39

54m. Publisher unknown, Havana. SK5850

54n. F Frith & Co, Reigate. CHM 8

54o. Clavi Postales, Barcelona

54p. Tuck

54q. Rise Studio No 843

54r. BEA

54s. Tuck. Photo: Lisa. 129K

August 12th. *Good flight and extremely comfortable. The aircraft was a real treat, had a chicken lunch* (M in Holland to Mr S in London). June 7th. *Very good flight - in a Viscount - quite smooth. Lovely scenery* (V in Lugano to Miss P in Fleet). August 28th. *Arrived here after breakfast in plane. Sir Arthur is very well* (J to Mr C in London). Three satisfied customers send the same card. A Viscount would be the first plane to depart from Heathrow Airport in 1955.   54r

August 1st. Chris in Barnet to Miss B Tingley in Lower Kingswood, Surrey. *Dear Babs, As you probably know I am at camp at present. It is super fun. I am longing for you when does your holiday end?* Who is the Duke of Cornwall? Just as Churchill in a long career earned so many honours so Prince Charles (for it is he) starts life with a fair bouquet of titles to choose from. Here is a face unclouded by the anxiety, tragedy and sheer bewilderment that have visited him since.   54s

August 14th. Detail of a card of Station Road, Edgware (Frith EDG25) sent by Cynthia to Miss Isobel Wardrop in Filby, Norfolk. Cards of the fifties are difficult to date since styles of dress for most people did not change very radically. The presence of a zebra-crossing (introduced in 1950) already somewhat worn would make 1952 a good guess. The message is resolutely mid-fifties, *well arrived and having a wonderful time. There are some real 'Bohemin Coffee Bars' here, much to my delight. This afternoon we are going to see some boys coussins of Janets & Pats, which will be good fun.* It is difficult to convey the excitement caused by the advent of coffee bars and the learning of words like Espresso and Cappuccino. Soho coffee bars saw the beginning of English pop music with Tommy Steele singing in the 2 I's.   54t

Viking Rocket In Flight - White Sands Proving Ground, N.M. 6-T-176

May 21st. Eugene writes from Las Cruces, N Mex. to Skip Hager in Bellevue, Ohio, *I work on rockets similar to this one...This is the same type that goes to the moon and various places.* This is bold talk. The Viking project (started in 1946) produced the first successful US liquid rocket. Viking 12 attained an altitude of 144 miles in February 1955 leaving the moon still a long way off. But Eugene is prescient; and young (as one imagines him) Skip Hager, who has the perfect name for an astronaut, is set to dream. 55a

July 13th. The scene is the high summer of 1954. A 3-dimensional film plays at the London Pavilion, The Phantom of the rue Morgue, which has to be watched through funny glasses. Outside the Criterion an Evening News van advertises 'Cricket latest'. Katie pencils a card to Miss Otley in Selby, Yorks. 55b

March 27th. *Darling Sally, I'm writing this looking out over the big lake in Central Park, and Susie Cooke is drawing beside me (she is just six). You ought to meet her some time. Love to you and Mummy from Daddy and* [child's writing] *Susie.* Sent to England (Cambridge). 55c

August 14th. To Mrs B Lawrence in Birmingham, *Had a good run up here... weather has been just the job & very hot. Mr & Mrs Clayton who came up with me on their tandem thoroughly enjoyed the Rally. With love, Ron.* Scenes of such robust bonhomie and spartan cheer remind me why I resigned from the Tooting Bec branch of the Cyclist's Touring Club in 1955.   55d

December 2nd. Grannie in Budleigh Salterton to Andrew Rossiter in Radlett, *Thank you so much for the funny clown. I have the card on the mantlepiece to look at. Lots of love.* Andrew is probably an admirer of Thomas the Tank Engine and will appreciate this picture of James the Red Engine, his friend in the moralistic but popular children's books by Rev. W Audry (who died in 1997).   55e

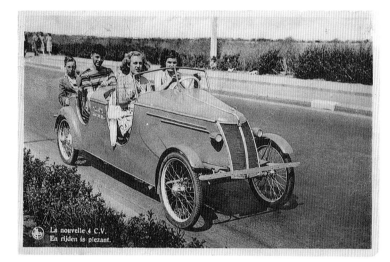

April 17th. To Mr & Mrs Tipton in Coventry from their son in Blankenberge, *Dear Mummy & Daddy. I hope you are fit and I am having a good time. The only things I don't like is the boy I sleep with and the room. with love from Barry.* The new 4CV, pleasant to ride, says the caption to this amiable picture of a seaside pedal car (luckily Blankenberge is very flat).   55f

December 14th. Gordon & June to Mr & Mrs Master in Newport. *Dear Mam, Dad & Kath. The £5-12-6 Billiard Table includes three balls only the snooker balls are £2 extra. Will get the billiard table with the three balls hope that will be alright if not let me know by Fri.* Earl's Court is looking the worse for wear. Going to the Motor Show was an annual October ritual with my father in this windswept place.   55g

July 29th. From J Lindsay at the Triumphant Kingdom Assembly of Jehovah's Witnesses to Mrs Morgan in Roehampton, *hope you got this alright. I'm foggy as to correct address. Tio Docon was reminding me of your 23,000 here today.* Here is Twickenham the home of Rugby Union (now a concrete nightmare). Wembley Stadium, home of football, had been packed with 18,000 (including me) the year before for Billy Graham's Campaign. God was the goal in each case.   55h

September 30th. MSM to the staff of Messrs Carlton, Solicitors, Dundee, *This is where I heard Mr Dulles speak. There are headphones at every seat & when foreigners speak all you do is turn the knob to the English translation. Will have to go back to the U.N with this card as with the UN stamps it must be posted in the UN building. Going to Washington on Monday... Then my dollars will be finished.* The General Assembly murals are by Leger who died a month after this card was sent. 55i

Life in a Trailer Park in Florida.

NAISH ESTATE HOLIDAY CAMP, NEW MILTON

February 17th.   Clara at Daytona Beach to Edna Maphis in Brookville, Ohio, *Dear Sister! ...we are in a nice trailer court. This is a picture of what these trailer-courts look like. Chester & a friend came in with 7 fish this afternoon, fishing not too good... We are having a nice trip & love our trailer.* Random colouring of flowers, awnings, dresses, trailers (and even fish) help to give the picture a sense of joie de vivre.   55j

July 27th.   T C Johns to Stourbridge *Dear Mum & Dad... weather is not very nice (rain) but it is clearing up. I hope you've tucked Ted up as I am lonely without him... I've marked the caravan right next to the lah-pom! [?].* Section D of the Naish estate does not have the flair & gaiety of Daytona Beach. Even the presence of a double bike fails to relieve the refugee camp look.   55k

12025

"The boy's very quiet--what's he been up to?"
"Oh--he's been playing with his organ most of the day"

July 25th.   From Great Yarmouth to Master Buckley, Stamp Shop, c/o Harrison Fisher, Sheffield, *Dear John. Having a good time. Hope they are not refering to you on the front of this card. Get on with that whitewashing & windowcleaning. Jim.* An organ joke by an anonymous artist. The couple seem American-influenced and the interior architecture of the house needs some explaining.   55l

August 27th.   *Hi people,* writes Lyle from Reno to the Kralls in Lebanon Pa., *Can't believe my eyes. Really fabulous. Saw Jane Froman at the Riverside Hotel. J.P. Morgan & Anna Maria Alberghetti are also in town. From the gambling city.* Note that Lyle hasn't actually <u>seen</u> the latter couple. The gambling looks desultory and suburban but the lady with the handbag is posing for all she is worth.   55m

WILBERFORCE STREET, FREETOWN, SIERRA LEONE

August 7th.   David & Clare in Fort William to Mummy & Ivy in Hove, *...dull, cloudy & freezing... it is thoroughly unphotographic (I did not say we enjoyed the trip to Trosachs only that it could have been worse) ...this morning we got a boat & went round the bay... I thought it would give some nice photographic angles - but the sun went in after 10 mins... Don't approve of coloured cards but all black & white are shocking. Must close - is raining - unphotographically.* Hard to beat this view.   55n

August 15th.   Ron to Miss A Marshall in Worthing, *Just beginning to settle into my life with the African people and I can say that I get along with them extremely well, but nevertheless there are a lot of things I miss about dear old England, especially fish & chips in a piece of newspaper.* A glimpse of pre-independence Freetown. Forty years on, this same view would show raped women, mutilated men and young boys waving machine guns in a bloody scene of dereliction.   55o

August 22nd. To Max Gordon in London NW3, *This is probably how it looked the day you saw it - bleak and grey. We had the most superb weather all the time we were there and squandered vast amounts of film... there can be few less inspiring companions to see it with than M.Burrell, whose pathological concern for his nice new car makes travel a slightly ritualistic business. I've scratched it already, needless to say. At the moment I am at Nancy... one of the most exciting French towns I've been in... St. Dié was a disappointment.* Sometimes architecture bypasses the imposing and achieves the sublime as here in le Corbusier's Chapelle de Notre Dame du Haut at Ronchamp. It was started in 1950 and finished in this year. Many progressive architects at the time thought le Corbusier had betrayed Modernism: he had in fact sent signals to the future. 55p

June 22nd. To Mrs Poole in Ipswich. *Dearest. Could not get fixed up at Lewes so came on hear. It is now only 5.30 & I have a nice place, but not without trying several places. Another hot day - my face is __raw__ - even with Valderma. Went to Bodiam Castle this morning. I am not much interested in places like Eastbourne but could not help myself...*

September 23rd. To Miss Wardell in Bounds Green ...*This is a very nice Guest House with white cloths and table napkins everything perfect and food good. We go out to a concert at the same place as last week & another outing on Wed. Rainy day yesterday. We are sitting at the bandstand at the moment & the sea is splashing up on us. Tell us the name of Jack's tobacco when you write. Mum & Dad.*

9th May. From HB at Pulborough Manse to Miss Doris Pettengell in Hitchin. *So regret I have not yet returned the most interesting report of the Forum that you so kindly sent me. All being well, I will send everything before this week is out. We were attending the Provincial Summer School for Ministers & their wives last week at Eastbourne. Tomorrow I have a County Executive Committee meeting at Brighton then return for Youth Fellowship.*

Three characteristic messages on very similar Norman cards of the Carpet Gardens Eastbourne. 55s

134L.   Photograph by Cecil Beaton

HER ROYAL HIGHNESS PRINCESS MARGARET

January 11th. From Hughie in London SW1 to Miss Pitt in SW5, *I have heard from Thursby - he is catching the 2-59 from Diss and hopes to call on you after tea on Sunday.* The old-fashioned decorum of the message matches this portrait by Cecil Beaton of Princess Margaret as a pretty young woman in a pretty dress. By the end of the year she would be a tragic figure forced to renounce the love of her life (her father's own trusted Equerry Group Capt. Peter Townsend whose only blemish was that he had been divorced) under pressure from family and the daft protocols of state. 55q

MARGOT FONTEYN   Homage to the Queen
Sadler's Wells Ballet

April 18th. Jill in London to Mr & Mrs Symonds in Oxted, *Tuesday... really did go off with a bang. I am amazed to see Fonteyn wearing coloured nail varnish.* Fonteyn (born Peggy Hookham) made her debut in 1937 and was made a Dame in 1956. She was still playing leading roles in the new Royal Ballet in 1959 the year she got mixed up in a failed coup in Cuba seemingly organised by her husband Sgr. Arias. 55r

June 8th.   In 1956 Grace Kelly appeared in High Society as a snooty rich girl choosing between suitors whereas in private life she had been playing in a documentary version of The Prince and the Showgirl. She never acted on screen again (though in 1962 there were rumours that she would star in Hitchcock's Marnie). She was to die in a motor accident in 1982. This style of card (called a Maximum) is prized by philatelists and was perhaps bought at a stamp shop. Phil uses it to write to Jane Runnells in Concord, NH., *Guess where I am now. Leave almost over.* It has the disadvantage of showing us twice the second rate portrait of the new Princess whose beauty was luckily perpetuated in Hitchcock's masterpiece, Rear Window. The Prince is made to look rather stodgy. A romantic event celebrated by a crude piece of stamp and postcard design.   56a

August 14th.   Ron sends an atmospheric night scene taken as usual after rain, (Ray Milland in Close to my Heart dates it to 1952) to Mr B Goode in Micheldean, Glos, *Arrived here yesterday as you will see over amongst the lights. Weather very much on the blustery side.*   56b

May 7th.   Alan Graham writes from the Hotel Gladstone to Giovanni Patrini in Parma, *I miss Paris and Italy a lot. Everyone here is very nice and very boring.* A Governor's Island view from the traditional spot. Such linen-type views are beginning to be phased out as too old hat for the Metropolis.   56c

November 24th.   Three days after Britain handed over to the UN in the wake of the Suez debacle. L A C Cook in El Adem, Libya writes to BBC Family Favourites, *I have now sent five cards to your programme for a record, perhaps my sixth will be the one. Would you please be so kind to play I'll Be Home sung by Pat Boone for my fiancée Elizabeth with the message 'I'll always love you Liz you are ever in my thoughts'.* 56d

August 23rd.   John Ball in Cosham to his wife in Gillingham, *Sorry to hear that TV is still away. If it's not back why don't you get on a bus & go & sort them out. Tell them to return the set & then get Gentry & Bailey to collect. Today it's fine so far but it didn't 'arf rain in the night. xxx.* Sweater-girls in films and magazines made shapely breasts obligatory. Falsies were the answer: this bridegroom is not the first to be surprised. 56e

April 30th.   Maude and Luis in Greenwood, SC, send this Laff-o-Gram card to Mrs Marshall in Sidney, Ohio, *This is the diet I have been on all along the road... Hit the high spots in Miami went to see The Vagabonds some night.* Nixon has just announced that he will seek renomination as Vice President and the young Kennedy will seek (and fail to gain) the same position for the Democrats. Eisenhower/Nixon will win. 56f

November 2nd.   To Ian Heelas in Kingsbridge, S Devon, from St Ann's Bay, Jamaica, *This is the Jamaican Walls* [i.e. ice cream merchant]. *Last night guests dressed as pirates (not us) & there was an attack from a boat at sea. Much firing of crackers & rockets followed by pirate feast of cock soup, hot dogs etc.* Man on Spot is a great name for this drink seller with his cool outfit and giant kazoo. 56g

December 11th.   R Lot at the Winter Olympics to R J Skilling in Grange-over-Sands, *It's wonderful here and although the British Team aren't winning they are putting up a good show. Thought you would be interested to know that the structure in the picture is made with Dexion Slotted Angle. In case you'd like to know more about this I'll send you some Data when the Games are over.* Anyone who has got in a tangle putting up Dexion shelves would be pretty impressed. 56h

March 2nd.   A Bent to Avril Loveless in Ferndown, *Auntie & I are spending the day here. There are lots of wonderful and interesting things to see, we have just eaten some of Weston's Hot X Buns baked here while we wait. Cakes being decorated. 2 lovely little Baby Calves with their mother advertising Jersey milk.* The clash of decor (functional stalls compete with medieval knights and fairy-tale castle) reflects an indecisive time in British design when Traditional jousted with Contemporary. 56i

COL. H. LLEWELLYN ON "FOXHUNTER."

June 20th. Auntie Joan in Eastbourne to Master John Ganbey at St Andrew's School. *Darling, how quickly the weeks pass... we are expecting Miss Palmer my old nursery governess to come & stay with us here in a few days... It will soon be half-term...* Show jumping, which handily took up hours of daytime television, grew from an upper class sport to mass entertainment with Col. Harry Llewellyn as its hero: for a time everyone knew about faults and clear rounds.   56j

October 8th. A greeting to Clara Fuga in Milan on this Camden Graphics card of a 1950 photo of Marilyn Monroe. She had spent her honeymoon in England with new husband Arthur Miller whose View From The Bridge was playing in London. She was still here when this card was sent and filming The Prince and the Showgirl with Laurence Olivier. Miller, granted every man's dream, found that like a character in a fairy tale the dream was a nightmare in disguise. Olivier fared no better in that the dream co-star became an incubus. He claimed that saying an airport goodbye to Marilyn in November was one of his happiest moments.   56k

AVRO VULCAN

April 3rd. Master Anthony Hughes in hospital in Thornton Heath gets an exciting card from an aunt in Bracknell, *I have several post-marks for you and I suppose we shall have a cub coming round to help us for a shilling as it is cub week.* Bob-a-Job week when cubs and scouts would knock on doors to ask for tasks was a feature of less nervous times. A single Avro Vulcan (this is the 1952 prototype) made the first British air attack in the Falklands war of 1982.   56l

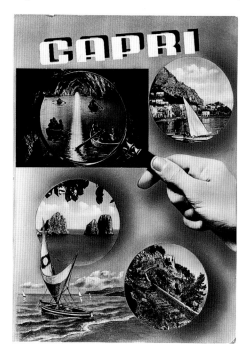

June 4th. From Maude & Henry to Mrs Brackwell in Hove, *Dear Mum. A very happy birthday wish to you from the Isle of Capri. We had a wonderful trip today then we went around a volcano then we visited the ruins of Pompaii it cant be described... and we saw Serento Naples - Mt Versiuvius - and all so very lovely with flowers & oranges & lemons walnuts it is all gorgeous.* Maude cannot spell the names but conveys the thrill of abroad to Henry's mother. Perhaps she also chose the excellent card with its stylish combination of photomontage and artwork.   56m

October 20th. An invitation from Ruth Thomas at 10930 W. 72nd St, La Grange, Illinois to her neighbour Mrs Fry at 10940. These plastic females show their plastic goods to lure her to the Tupperware Party. Earl Silas Tupper's household wares were withdrawn from stores in 1954 as part of Brownie Wise's sales strategy. While you have been reading this two Tupperware parties have started somewhere in the world.   56n

September 6th. A Benstead in Hunstanton to the Cators in Wisbech, *Dear Friends. sorry to be rather late with card will tell you all about things when I see you which I hope will be Sunday.* Television sets had become somewhat less monolithic but a passing van could throw the tuning out leaving a screenful of cuneiform writing, or a Fairisle jumper pattern.   56o

S.19896. THE NEW COCKTAIL BAR – THE "CHEZ-CUP", REGENT PALACE HOTEL, PICCADILLY, W.1.

56a. S.A.M.D.R. Monaco

56b. Lansdowne Publ. Co. LP842

56c. Acacia Card Company 62289

56d. Ediz. Ris. Folo. Aula, Tripoli

56e. Bamforth Comic Series. 1307 Artist: Taylor

56f. Laff-o-Gram. Baxtone, Texas. 19-D

56g. Mardon & Son, Bristol. Photo: L van McLure

56h. Rollprint Ltd.

56i. Daily Mail. 122/56

56j. Valentine's. RP 72. Show Jumping Series

56k. Camden Graphics PC 194. Photo: Frank Powolsky. Kobal Collection Ltd.

56l. Tuck. Flight A3

56m. Ediz. Vincenzo Carcavello, Naples

56n. Tupperware THP244

56o. E Marks, Comicard, London 225. Artist: Dudley

56p. Bridge House S19896

56q. Tuck. CVY40

56r. Orient Line.

September 19th. Dave to Mrs Jessie Blount in Ilkeston, *we are all having a good time and find things quite a change from home. The place on the other side is good for all drinks but cheap ones ! Love from all.* As was seen in 36j the Regent Palace Hotel was noted for its progressive interior decor. The bold wall stripes date from the pre war period but the newly revamped floor is here accompanied by benches and chairs with the most strikingly advanced upholstery. It seems to prefigure (if that is the right word for an abstract concept) what came to be called Op-art in the sixties, pioneered in Britain by Bridget Riley who at the time of this photograph had just left the Royal College of Art. What art-historical sleuth will one day discover that Dame Bridget was occasionally to be seen in 1956 in the Chez-Cup Cocktail Bar ? Artists would rightly argue that any source, buried only to resurface in another form, is legitimate. The appalling pun that forms the name of this bar would not now be admissible and it is hard to imagine that anyone ever said it out loud. 56p

CVY 40 BROADGATE, COVENTRY A TUCK CARD

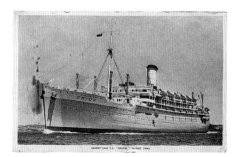

October 26th. Patricia Brown on board the SS Orion passing Gibraltar writes to Mr Cox, Ships Chandler, in Torquay, *Here as promised is the card of the ship - but owing to the Suez upset the Orion not the Strathmore.* It is the week leading up to the Suez war and perhaps the Strathmore has been commandeered as a troopship or ordered to stand by. 56r

September 8th. Mrs Eyles in Elland near Halifax receives a card from Coventry, *Dear Vi, I hope to see you Saturday & if convenient you can stop Saturday night if you like I hope Annie going on alright between 2 or 3 at the coach station so with love Mother.* The almost total destruction of Coventry in the IInd World War (see 46a) meant that what was in effect a new city had to be built from the ruins. Nothing in this view of one of the principal squares predates the war. The presence of a statue of Lady Godiva (here accidentally seen directly below the name of her husband Leofric which decorates the wall of the leading hotel that is called after him) is the only object which bears witness to the city's history. All else is generic modernism, perfectly decent but lacking in character and particularity and leavened only by an unvisitable island of urban greenery. This serves to control traffic (here represented by a stubby British Railways van and another delivering Procea bread which I remember as consisting mostly of air). Such was to be the look of most post war building though in 1956 work had just been started on Basil Spence's new Coventry Cathedral (completed 1962 see 63l) which would put the city on the map of progress instead of the scroll of tragedy. 56q

A message on the back of a card showing Field Marshal Montgomery in characteristic pose and outfit. Perce in Willesden writes to Andrew Minnion in Woodhouse near Sheffield on July 29th. *Many thanks for your letter - but you err greatly in thinking that HM Civil Servants have a weeks holiday at A.B.H. the Saturday referred to was the 4th. Apologies for use of a misleading term. If you could transfer arrangements or suggest alternate ones please do so. Photo overleaf one from I.W.M [Imperial War Museum] - very good - huge numbers of photos weapons, medals - in fact a militarists Mecca. What are your views on Lt. Col. Nasser? Send a Gunboat? I suppose it feels strange to have left KES [King Edward's] one becomes attached to a school. PS. A pleasant task would be the identification of Montgomeries ribbons.*

HOLMBURY ST. MARY YOUTH HOSTEL. SURREY　　　　C.O.I. Photograph

October 15th.　*What about getting that bike out!* exhorts Peggy writing to Ethel Clover in Rayleigh, Essex, a call to which so many (including, as noted,　the present writer) in this generation responded. *I was the only one here last night! No rising bell, watch stopped, came down at 9 o'clock! CHA provided packed lunch free of charge yesterday - thought you'd better know if you are contacting them. All the best.* The YHA and other organisations like the CHA (Countryside Holidays Association) made it possible for youth to travel cheaply about the UK especially during the immediate post war years before their horizons of travel widened so dramatically. The robust Peggy, our mid-October tourer, makes all-weather cycling sound somehow patriotic. The group seen here look a little more relaxed.　　　　　　　　　　　　　　　　　57a

September.　Bill & Mercia tell the Rhodes family in Blyth, Northumberland, *Went to Radio & Television Exhibition in Earls Court... & went to Wembley Stadium last night to the dog racing & won 27/-.* View in 1956. Fortes Popular Restaurant below the Coca Cola sign is one of the early ventures of a huge empire to come.　　　　57b

April 19th.　*Today we went through the fastest ship in the world the SS United States;* Richard Zweig signs himself *your pupil* as he writes to Mrs Carlston in Bayport, Minnesota, sending an aerial view from roughly the same position as that of 07c. 50 years have passed: much changed but not all lost.　　　　57c

March 18th.   Lily in the Bahamas writes to Mrs Burnett in West Worthing, *Have been riding round on cycle this a.m. but not dressed as overleaf - had to come back & reinforce fastening on white skirt - twas nice to ride on left hand side of road again.* Peggy (57a) would scorn these sybaritic cyclists as in mid March she battled uphill towards a distant hostel in the rain and wind.   57d

August 23rd.   Micheline F to Mr & Mrs Orkin in Aberdeen, *For five days I have again been Shoshanna's and Reuven's guest. The country, the house, the climate, the clothes were different but we felt for a few days that Aberdeen was not far away. Anyway I will never forget the life in a Kibbutz or Jerusalem.* The early pioneering idealism of the Kibbutz still inspired young jews in every country.   57e

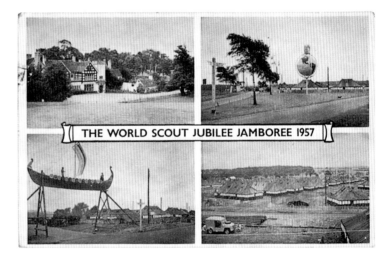

October 28th.   Peter in LA to Ed Hight of the Del Norte Co., Smith River. *Just going to our first meeting and what a crowd. Our hotel is one and a half blocks from main business meeting. We ate breakfast at the picture on the card at Fresno. No effects of smog yet.* Smog, especially in London was a silent killer of the fifties. Fed on films I drove my imaginary Pontiac here, to Fresno ('the Raisin Center of the World').   57f

August 3rd.   Bryan from this vast campsite near Sutton Coldfield writes to the Hansons in Durham, *I've been terribly busy. We've had 12 fires to date and some other incidents... That's me in the front kneeling in front of the jeep.* The jamboree celebrated fifty years of scouting and Baden-Powell's centenary. Fires were not a problem the following week when torrential rain fell. But what were the other incidents?   57g

August 7th.   Ella in Stratford, Ontario to Miss Clara Sohn in Jackson Michigan, *Staid all night at Stratford. Saw Hamlet - very good - even though Christopher Plummer played with a walking cast on one foot. On our way now to the Thousand Islands.* Tom Patterson founded the theatre in 1953. In 1957 it had just moved out of a tent but the show I would most like to have seen was the inaugural Richard III directed by Tyrone Guthrie when Alec Guiness played Richard.   57h

December 28th.   *Your Aunt Lizzie in far-away California* sends a card of the Pasadena New Year Roses Parade to Willa Clause in Akron, Ohio, *Haveing the time of my life never will forget it. We are going tonight to see Lawrence Welk in person. Jerry has a list to go a mile long she sure treats me like a queen I will hate to come home she is spoiling me waiting on me I will never forget this Xmas as long as I live Chas is so nice to me. He is a dandy. They just keep me on the go.*   57i

June 27th.   Nellie in Salisbury to Miss Musto B.A. at the North Riding Training College in Scarborough, *This does not convey the idea of the size of this building - but proves I went there.* Many cards of the time testify to the large number of people who simply went to visit the new Heathrow Airport to have a cup of tea and watch the planes. It now seems an almost perverse idea of a day out.   57j

May 28th.   Maude to Mrs B in Hove from Nüremberg, *...the city has been very badly damaged with air raids but the Germans are rebuilding it all as it was. The beds are really odd - no sheets or blankets only a huge thin eiderdown in an enormous damask cover you have to roll yourself up in them and then your feet stick out - it is a scream.* British tourists in their first encounter with a duvet, then unknown in the UK.   57k

April 3rd.   R H & J in Istanbul to the Malletts in Sheringham, *What a joy to receive youre wire at L.A.P. We're completely sold on this way of travel its super. Istanbul in half and hour! John is enjoying every minute. When will you come out on a visit. We'll have a kangaroo steak ready!* This early joy in long distance flying and proud relishing of in-flight meals is now unrecapturable by all but small children.   57l

March 21st.   The Paddys aboard ship to Miss M Hamilton in Glasgow, *Left Dakar, cruising to Santa Cruz. Good bye to all of Black Africa a fascinating continent and education. Cool now & out of the tropics.* This Senegalese card (apart from the oddly blue coloured thatch) captures the village atmosphere well as another goat is sacrificed. The camera is noticed but the moment seems real.   57m

Month/day unknown.   Peter by Forces Air Mail to Miss Everett in Elstree. *We went here today from Kure. Apart from the parts intentionally left you would not know it had been bombed.* Original photos of the scene of devastation show this single fragmentary building rising from a completely flattened city. Ironically it now must stand for all that fell. Kure was the advance base for British forces in the Korean war and closed down a few years later.   57n

April 18th.   Simon to Miss Rymer in Fitzroy House, London W1. *The neighbours brought me a big bone for my tea - I hope you are having the same. P.S. This plane just flew over the garden!* The Vickers Valiant was the first of the RAF's V bombers. It dropped the first atomic bomb from a British aircraft (over South Australia) in 1956 and, a month after this card was sent, dropped the UK's first hydrogen bomb in the waters near Christmas Island.   57o

Meiringen, Reichenbachfälle

"Oh Aunty! What a funny
place to keep the hairbrush"

August 11th.   To Teddy Slight in West Wickham, *Went round town & saw lots of performers from fête in very grand costumes... just made tour of choc factory at Broc... plenty of samples en route now in meadows outside where we have had a picnic lunch.* A finely composed old fashioned view of the Reichenbach Falls, scene of Sherlock Holmes' fictional (and as it turned out fictitious) death at the hands of Moriarty. 57p

June 26th.   D Underwood in Blackpool to Miss Vosper in Plymouth, *Hope this suits, gosh some of them I wouldn't dare post. Having a grand look around, the hotel is lovely & a nice crowd of people here...* A good gag with a built in alibi (the brush hanging on the wall) in case of trouble with the local Watch Committee. School of Donald McGill though the artist remains anonymous.   57q

57t. Leoni's, London. Artist: Peggy Crick.
The blurb on the reverse of the card quotes Hugh Maynton... 'everybody who is anybody in the theatrical and artistic worlds may be seen there'.

TOWER OF LEGENDS, (SINGING TOWER), SIOUX CITY, IOWA

August 20th.   Bess Gowdy to Laura Lawrence in Wethersfield, Conn., *enjoying the home state and seeing my old friends. Speaking of old friends how's Jerry.* This grimacing totem is in fact a 50ft high loudspeaker used to broadcast funeral services in the Memorial Park Cemetery. It has fallen into disuse 'because of volume of business'. What mysteries America will leave for future archaeologists!   57r

August 5th.   J to Miss N Morphet in Kirkby Lonsdale, *went as far as Berwick, Seahouses yesterday couldn't get in anywhere... Do you think you could pad the points of the scissors & slip them into a thick envelope so that Mollie could have them Sat... I'll give you the postage later.* Donald Murray takes a fine photograph, but we are not convinced of its spontaneity. Perhaps the face at the car window is Mrs Murray.   57s

March 19th.   Babe to Mr & Mrs Black in Park Avenue, New York. *Had lunch here today with nice man Bob Lloyd I met on the boat. Wonderful ravioli & chianti! Mrs Cook is having lunch with me at Berkely tomorrow. Had dinner with Winifred last night & will have lunch Monday with Barbara. All is fine. Everybody is complaining of the cold but the crocuses in Hyde Park are in bloom.* Quo Vadis, established in 1926, was the premier Italian restaurant. Others (see 62h) would follow in its wake in a street where Mozart, aged 7, gave a concert, and Johnson, Goldsmith and Garrick (the latter to visit his mistress) paid regular calls. Karl Marx lived for five years, in part of the building shown here. Dean Street has never lost its flavour. Throughout the fifties and sixties Muriel Belcher's Colony Club was where Francis Bacon held court. Today the Groucho Club continues to keep it firmly on the media map.   57t

S. S. Giovanni XXIII

December 14th.   Douglas W in the Vatican to Mrs Roper in Hurstpierpoint, Sussex, *The New Pope is very fat and of strong stock so that he should have a good many years at the helm...* Pope John XXIII, a progressive with leftist connections, was 81 when elected and would unfortunately have less than five years at the helm. It has not been an entirely lucky century for Popes and the tendency will continue. This Pope's predecessor Pius XII reigned for almost twenty years and considerably outstayed his welcome.   58a

August 28th.   Cliff Lord writes to his mother in Morecambe, *Hello Mum. Had a day in London yesterday, a beautiful day, walked miles round the Radio Exhibition at Earls Court. A storm started this morning at 7.30 it is now 11.30, hasn't stopped yet. Be seeing you.* At the Radio Show he would have had his first sight of the newly introduced Stereo/Hi-fi systems. The card shows rush hour in 1956.   58b

April 24th.   Evan writes to Modot Davies in New Rochelle, NY., *Nice suite 8th floor good old Astor now divorced from Sheraton. Rain doesn't dampen our ardour.* The Downtown skyline in here enlivened by SS Ile de France. In postcard terms both this and the Piccadilly Circus view are described by US card collectors as 'Chromes' (succeeding Linens in the US) and by English hobbyists as 'Moderns'.   58c

October 24th.   Paul in St Louis writes to Vaughan in Saco, Maine, *I have been in St Louis two days attending an Atomic Energy Commission meeting. Marge & Peter were in good health when I left Ohio... Peter is now a Junior High School Football Player!* The Mobile Exhibition originated from Oak Ridge (see 46i) to combat public mistrust of Nuclear Energy and publicise its nicer side; but atoms had a bad name.   58d

October 11th.   Mr Blair to Mr Brownlie in Bearsden, *This is it! The great day is past & London is fogbound... In for 5 classes - 5 tickets, 2nd for Tortie & White. Goldie was no.699!!! Everybody was very kind.* Mr Blair had entered his cats for a show and was evidently not mixed up in the advertised exhibition in which Nuclear energy comes a poor fourth after Engineering, Marine & Welding.   58e

July 4th.   From the Bristol Show to Mrs Rogers in Bournemouth. *Hello Pat. I took my party (29) out to Royal Agricultural Show. I was received at Overseas Pavilion by the Earl of Denbigh, a nice chap who was very helpful to me. I enjoyed the Parade of prize Bulls & cows very much (see over). At Harry Hebditch Martock stand I had talk with Michael Helyar. Tons of Love. Your loving Husband Tommy xxxxx.*   58f

No month or day.   An enigmatic unposted card addressed to Miss R Quinn in Keighley, Yorks, correctly stamped but with no message. Had its intended sender been let down by Lourdes? Had she failed to meet a miraculous cure and not lived to write the message or post the card? By what intercession did it find its way to the antique shop in far Cromarty where I was destined to buy it?   58g

September 10th.   From Nellie in Kirkby Lonsdale to Rosemary Caton in Kendal *...hope you will all have a nice holiday. Cardiff is very busy this week with the Empire Games. I am sure you would enjoy seeing some of the swimming and etc but perhaps you have seen some of them on the TV.* For Britain the game of empire was all over: Prince Philip's opening of the Empire Games must have seemed one of its last rites. Cardiff produces a card singularly lacking in sporting reference.   58h

November 14th.   To Mrs Sloane in St Petersburg Florida, a Thankyou card from Clinton School, Tennessee, for her donation towards Friendship Bricks to Combat Bombs of Hate. Clinton was forced to desegregate its schools in 1956 (as a result of the Supreme Court ruling). 600 National Guardsmen were called out to prevent violence to the first twelve black students admitted. In June 1957 Bobby Cain became the first black student to graduate from a newly integrated school. In 1958 three bomb blasts ripped the High School building apart.   58i

S.20594　THE RENDEZVOUS. REGENT PALACE HOTEL. PICCADILLY CIRCUS. W.I.

"IS THIS WEMBLEY?"
"NO IT'S THURSDAY!"
"SO AM I—LET'S HAVE A DRINK!"

A 'BAMFORTH' COMIC

December 15th.　Don to the Misses Atkins in Eastbourne, *Just arrived here today. Had a very quiet time in Thorney; studied quite a bit, not much to be done anyway. Will tell you about our two evenings here when back...* The Regent Palace Hotel pulls it off again (see 56p) with the latest in decor including crazy paving up the wall (a feature of many a coffee bar) matching the crazy paving carpet.　58j

August 28th.　Mum & Dad write to Mr & Mrs Mayoh in East Dulwich, *Dear Ethel Ted & Dennis, We saw Bebe Daniels, Ben Lyon, Derick Bond & Eileen Asky yesterday in a fashion show & they were the judges... awful thunderstorm on & cannot get out...* Did Taylor borrow this fine triple pun from a music hall sketch? If he didn't there's many a double-act would have been happy to use it.　58k

We have Something for the Boys in "LES GIRLS"!

December 22nd.　B in Tucumcari, NM, to Miss Peggy Watson in Withersfield, Conn. *Well, they struck & here we are... trip so far has been unbelievable - we'll considering writing a book about it - we have the whole train speechless... we always wanted to do this sometime anyway.* Route Sixty-Sixers no doubt. How can you go wrong at a place that is both on the Rock Island Line and the fabled highway?　58l

March 19th.　Walter Webster in N Vernon, Indiana, is advised by the Park Theatre to come and see Les Girls (rhymes, it tells him, with Play-Girls). Accompanying Gene Kelly here are lined up Mitzi Gaynor, Kay Kendall and Tania Elg. Not by the look of it a film for feminists but with music by Cole Porter it couldn't have been entirely bad. The sort of movie that now turns up on late night TV.　58m

July 18th.　Victor to Dorothy Brett in Sheffield, *Am now in Acora... you are putting East Africa on your envelopes but Ghana is <u>West</u> Africa... How would you like to live in one of these houses! Parkins should note other houses have cracks in too but these are home built.* Ghana has just celebrated its first full year of Independence and the special stamps show Dr Nkruma its first President.　58n

May 15th.　In a version of Esperanto V Sansky writes to Ewald Meyer in Sächs *I'm sending you another card complete with the new 40 Kopek stamp celebrating the 6th International Student & Youth Festival. Greetings.* The card itself of course celebrates the world's first man made satellite (Oct 3rd) and the space journey of the dog Laika (Nov 4th). Sputnik I was still in orbit at the beginning of 1958.　58o

ROBERT HELPMANN. "The Rakes Progress. (Act I)   PHOTO ANTHONY COPYRIGHT

March 28th.   Thelma in Richmond to H Dixon in London SW1, *Dear Dicky, ...just finished the Epstein autobiography I thought it was very interesting.* Epstein's Let There Be Sculpture is indeed a good read though his career was by no means over. In 1958 he would have been working on his Coventry Cathedral bronze (see 60h). Helpmann was Margot Fonteyn's partner (see 55r) in her sensational debut.   58p

July 15th.   Sylvia in Bonn to Pamela, Lady G in London W8, *Have I sent you this one already? You can have lunch in the topmost ball!! You should pop over & stay with Basil, as it is all worth seeing.* The Brussels International Expo like all such shows sought a memorable motif. The Atomium mirrored the excitement of the atomic age. Only the monuments of the New York World's Fair of 1939 compete with its capture of a moment's essence. Over 100m high it formed a dialogue between small and large that stays emblematically in the memory.   58q

"I want my guinea back"

JU-JITSU LESSONS DAILY
LADIES DEFENCE COURSE 21/-

11980

July 14th.   Ray in Margate to Derek Jordan in North Cheam, *I am now back among the peasants at Butlins. No more continental touring for me. I can just about afford a week here. Hope your mum does not think the card too fruity. All the best.* Women's self-defence classes were becoming popular. Professions still priced their services in guineas. I remember being paid in guineas as late as 1964.   58r

July 9th.   Jim to Dr Such in Kincardine, Ontario, from the Odessa Hotel, Moscow, *Yes... you certainly see much - their subway 120 feet deep, escalator takes 4 mins. There are many museums which in many cases were churches.* The statue of the great poet Mayakowsky has always baffled me. Had he not commited suicide in 1930 surely he would have ended up in the Gulag rather than outside the Pekin Hotel.   58s

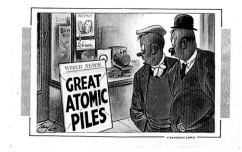

"BLIMEY! I'LL BET THEM AIN'T HALF PAINFUL, BERT!"

WORLD NEWS GREAT ATOMIC PILES

August 14th.   Fred & Jean (again) in Ryde on the Isle of Wight send a topical example of broad bottomed humour to Mrs E J Cook in Sunbury-on-Thames. *Dear Mum, It is very beautiful here & I like it very much better than I thought I would at first. it looks pretty dodgey when you first get here but when you look around it is surprising. The camp is right against the beach just a few steps to walk down & you are there. I had a big spider in my bed last night. Love.* The image of atomic energy in Britain never truly recovered from the Windscale accident of 1957. Somehow the idea of radiation leaking from nuclear power stations combined with memories of Hiroshima's tragic victims, was more sinister than the thought of pit disasters or oil slicks.   58t

Blick auf die österreichisch-ungarische Grenze

August 1st.   An unequivocal symbol of the Cold War where, on the borders of Austria and Hungary, old worlds collide. Jim seems to be ironically comparing his former relationship with Jess M (to whom it is addressed in NY) to his present freedom in Vienna attending the World Student Festival. He adapts the caption on the back (Greetings from Austria, free country on the frontier of slavery) to read, *from Jim a free man. On the frontier of slavery once with Mallsky but, Deo Gratias, finally free. Te Deum. Frieden und Freundschaft.* With the Hungarian uprising of 1956 fading to mere memory freedom had been put off again for another thirty years.   59a

November 17th.   A night view from this same year with Tunnel of Love playing at the Apollo Theatre. Judith writes to her colleague Angela at the Pen Corner at Jarrold's in Norwich *...saw Margaret at the weekend... she delivered my Sheaffer dem. apparatus. Thanks for sending them. The lights are just as bright.*   59b

June 29th.   Sent by Eva & Charles from the United Nations Building (postmarked World Refugee Year) to AJ Webber in Sacramento, Cal., *Hi! Webbie, Here we are in U.N. listening to a debate on Uganda & Tanganyika & Urundi. Having fun in N.Y. City. The UN seems to have done a pretty smart trade in cards and stamps.*   59c

December 15th.   Mother etc. in Mogadishu to the Bargnesis in Ivoryton Conn., *Dear ones, Just to wish you the best in holiday greetings and a healthy and prosperous New Year.* On the eve of statehood, as Italian & British Somaliland become Somalia, a card reflects the mood. Before the century's end Mogadishu will be a synonym for famine, anarchy, riot and blood feud; and UN impotence in Africa.   59d

May 31st.   JP Visser Esq. in W8 receives a mimeographed message from bandleader Edmundo Ros telling him of the club's new daytime Dance Studio. Middle class sophistication as things start looking up in Britain has some of the gaiety (without the sinister overtones) of Berlin in 1930. The card even seems to recapitulate the style (see 30p) as these decorous revellers dine and dance to Latin American rhythms.   59e

July 5th.   Mike in Johannesburg to Les Girls, English Speaking Union, Cambridge, *Having such a wonderful time. Give my regards to those that return from the long vacation.* Ndbele women paint their huts brightly now with house paints. The beaded aprons reflect traditional colours. But this is a show village to reassure tourists that all is well under Apartheid. The card was still popular thirty years later.   59f

Date unclear.   Tim in Damascus to his parents in Birkenhead. *Mother would love this place with its teeming humanity and terrific market... Col. Nasser is due to give a speech here this evening and the town is filled with troops... bought some Turkish delight, the real stuff but think you will like Mr Fry's variety better.* The United Arab Republic is a short lived affair and Syria will break the union with Egypt in 1961. 59g

Date unclear (August?)   Johnny to Mary Mercer in Speke. *We still got 8 days hollyday's to go . I'm glad to say I'm feeling fein again. The food is sometimes to rich. We still got a lot of parties to go too.* The term elder statesman fits Dr Adenaur perfectly. He has seen much since the moment in 1926 when, as Mayor of Cologne, he delivered a speech of thanksgiving for the departure of British troops at the end of their occupation after the first World War.   59h

September 10th.   Jennifer to Miss Maber in Pendine, *we are at Butlin's Clacton, as you said there is plenty to do And the redcoats are smashing We got one nice house captain his name is Ricky.* Any DJ (to use a term just coming into use) would envy this state-of-the-art console. It is coming up to 3.15. Some entertainment or event is just about to be announced with a short tune played upon a miniature vibraphone (used to alert campers to a Knobbly Knees Competition by the pool etc).   59i

" It's not so expensive when you think what the pound is worth to-day! "

LAURENCE OLIVIER

August 3rd.   Fred & Jean in Gt. Yarmouth to Marie B in Sunbury ...*lovely weather no storms here. We went to see Double Your Money last night & it is a fiddle.* The economy was improving and restrictions easing with bank-rate dropping bit by bit. Premier Harold Macmillan could famously say 'You've never had it so good', a slogan that saw him through the 1959 election. Either wife or card is a little out of date.   59j

October 20th.   Peggy to Mr & Mrs Hodges in Le High Acres, Florida ...*we are at Carries visiting. Going to Lushing tomorrow to fish. Hope you are getting fixed up & no more intrusions. They are picking oranges and G fruit here.* This is the Titan Inter-continental Ballistic Missile being tested. Its more peaceful use as a booster came when Titan II put the first Americans into orbit in 1965.   59k

September 1st.   M Dareff sends a Russian card of Olivier from Bulgaria to Mr Collard in Dorset. *Good Day Dear Friend. I am pleased to correspond with you in Esperanto, English or Deutsch.* He carries on in Esperanto to invite a reply. A terse note. *Ne akceptas inviton* indicates that he got no response. This is the young Olivier as Hamlet, a far cry from his current Archie Rice make-up in Osborne's The Entertainer.   59l

Seaside Heights, N. J.

May 25th.   D to Hugh Pitts in London SW7, *They are only allowed to sell these p.c.s in Monte Carlo nowadays - where we have been today. I could only find 2 there! I will give you the others and the cuff links for your birthday. Simply ghastly weather since we arrived - non stop buckets of rain & grey skies & sea. Have got soaked every day - most disappointing.* Princess Grace still glows with the glow of stardom. The Prince still looks like a used car salesman. Before her tragic end she will get mixed up in strange cults. 59m

May 28th.   Olvera Sign Co. send this rather amateurish looking card to Candelas Guitan in Los Angeles to tell him to *sign up to Plexiglas* as these shops have done. They are indeed signs of the times and perspex (as it is called in the UK) would soon dominate the High Street, putting the signmaker, unable to compete with photo-reproduced motifs and letters, out of business. Fortunately not all perspex signage is as ugly as this.   59n

July 24th.   Two aunts in Seaside Park NJ., send this to Pat Burke in San Leandro, Cal. *Hi Pat, Boy sitting on dock almost resembles you. We have nothing to do but sit around and look at rain... first time I seen so much.* For these all American boys the sun is high and the catch is good. The image lies somewhere between Tuke and Norman Rockwell. I have never figured out why there are so few Rockwell postcards.   59o

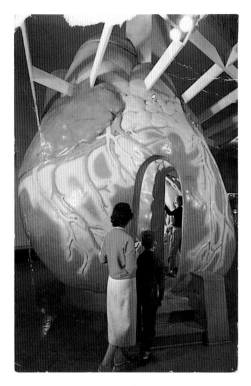

October 20th.　Bart to A C W Kazimirski at Milton Abbey School in Dorset, *Hi, Chicago's fine. Our school starts at 8.15 and ends at three. I then have three hours of swimming. Today we went to this museum. It's great. Funny. we didn't see the heart but we did see a captured German sub.* This gruesome exhibit ('it actually throbs' says the blurb) is redeemed in the card by the colour of the lady's sweater.　59p

December 1st.　Michael in the Hague to his family in Wanstead. *I hope all proceeds well with Uncle Joe... I bought your picture on Saturday last & it was posted today... the view of Delft is certainly very good indeed. Work proceeds well but at a pretty intensive pace. Its eggs, eggs, eggs for meals! Has Michael taken up tempera painting?* At the Keukenhoff Flower Show people look solemnly at tulips as if at their funeral.　59q

"BLIMEY BERT, I SHOULD THINK THAT IT'S **42** AT LEAST!"

BRA 32

A 'BAMFORTH' COMIC

BONNEVILLE CONVERTIBLE

November 10th.　Ray Kalagher of George Pontiac Ltd. of Worcester Mass., tells Mr Moulton that he also has a large selection of used cars. The special feature of this new Pontiac is its <u>width</u> according to the blurb.　59s

September 21st.　Miss Caroline Blackston gets a card from George, *Lovely. Let's meet next week. I am in Ilfracombe playing in Look Back In Anger & Plainliff In A Pretty Hat (Cliff in Look Back). Shall we go to a theatre & have a meal.* John Osborne's Look Back In Anger shocked (or excited) London in 1956 and gave birth to the Angry Young Men. A decent interval has elapsed and Ilfracombe is braced for Jimmy Porter's tirades. The scooter, still a novelty, was the transport equivalent of the duffel-coat.　59r

February 19th.　Erwin Clear of Ralph Brown Buick Inc. in Monticello, Indiana gets to Mr Row in Brookston earlier in the year but also mentions *For a bargain on a good Late Model Used Car call or see me for a demonstration.* This is described overleaf as Le Sabre, the Thriftiest Buick. It looks like the thirstiest Buick, yet at the end of the fifties these finny monsters were what roamed the USA, much to the amazement of any visiting Briton who pictured rather bashfully his Morris Oxford or Ford Anglia at home.　59t

July 17th.　Gwen in Hamburg to Mr & Mrs Duggins in Clacton. *Thank you for your letter. There are Many Poor. 1 Albert & Maria but they Have a budgerigar, a fridge & a wine cellar. 2 Ken & Barbara, they have a puppy, fridge, washing machine, radiogram. 3 Mollie & Frank, a car, a T.V., a Siamese cat. 4 myself, a car & foreign travels, Quite Amusing!. Marie is my little Mother, Very kind is & Always was, A Gentleman. Much Love.* A message hard to get to the bottom of, though intriguing. The image is a detail of a Hamburg view whose totality is no more or less interesting than this fragment. Contrary to popular ideas of the boring postcard it is the busy ones that are dullest.　59u

November 11th.   Miss Jay B at the Royal Deaf School in Exeter gets this card from Nailsworth, *Did you get your sweets yesterday. I saw this card in Boots shop. I thought you'd like it. Hope you are well and happy. We love you very much. Mummy & Daddy xxx.* The publisher (probably in 1959) hasn't quite got the name right yet, calling this young celebrity Cliff Richards. He represents and is idolised by a new and hitherto hidden constituency, youth. He is the home-grown version of more unattainable American models as only half-knowingly he leads the third revolt of the century. Workers are empowered, women long emancipated: now, the teenagers want their own domain and, given their ever growing purchasing power, start to gain it. Apart from standard adolescent rejection of parental values there is no ideology, yet their cadres are formed in the now ubiquitous coffee bars of the land. How many of those rebels without a cause, today like Cliff Richard himself turning sixty, followed him all the way and listened to the saccharin Christian of 1999 singing them into the Millenium with banality's ultimate double whammy, the Lord's Prayer swung to the tune of Auld Lang Syne?   60a

September 26th.   Keith from London Airport to The Staff at Stourbridge Public Library, *Working till 8pm every night. Last Saturday I went to Whitehall Theatre to see Simple Spyman and next Tuesday am going to Mermaid to see Brecht's Galileo. Hope Mary & Judy have a good time in the big wicked city.* Circa 1954. It, The Terror from Outer Space was a 3-D film with the X certificate devised in 1951.   60b

November 23rd.   From Margaret to the Brierleys in Stockport, Cheshire. *Dear Aunt Maggie, Uncle Eddy, I find America quite fascinating with many modern sky-scraping buildings but so Victorian decorations. They are a very kind and generous people but, oh, so sentimental.* Well, that's America dealt with, and this is an unusual view from the East Side showing the new Air Terminal.   60c

August 6th.   Mary in Benidorm to Mr GFM in Kingston on Thames, *Darling, This is typical and only 3 mins from the Hotel, only 1 road made up. No one speaks English using the Books like mad. Beach beautiful and everywhere very very quiet Very few people.* Hard to imagine that Mary is describing Benidorm which within a few years will be a mass of huge white hotels with discos, fish & chips and Watney's Red Barrel everywhere. Franco's Spain welcomed uninquisitive visitors.   60d

September 27th.   Cissie in Blackpool to Mr E F in Ringwood, *...The sun is glorious but of course a bit nippy. Crowds here my word there is some mony spent here. Tell Lou not to use the iron as the plug wants replacing.* Adam Faith one of the pioneer British pop singers is now a successful businessman and rather wooden actor. To his credit he cancelled in 1965 all his South African concerts when told he could not perform to multi-racial audiences.   60e

August 1st.   Ivy & Cecil in Feltham to Ruth & Bob in Lower Stanwick, *sorry the weather is disappointing. Today has been simply dreadful. Cecil & I are just making our way over to see chummie. He seems to be alright.* Princess Margaret seemingly recovered from thwarted love smilingly enters on a doomed marriage with photographer Anthony Armstrong-Jones, who became Lord Snowdon. They finally separated in 1976 and set a trend for royal couples.   60f

August 24th.   Bert and Doris in Chichester to Ron & Cherry T, in Guildford, *Weather good. Doris has started on the lager & lime and doing alright. Hope you arrived home alright, we just had time to have one at the Black Horse again.* This fine cartoon only dimly initialled JK (?) is a neat reminder of the GI's of twenty years before. Why extra-terrestrials came to be little green men (and have stayed so) no one can say.   60g

October 5th.   Vera to Mrs P in Gosport. *My dear Sue, one more year going by, have not been able to meet, we will one day, hasn't it been a terrible summer. I am busier than ever, poor mother is so blind now, its sad, 87, & Rick is an inverlid now, memory gone. Peg is a terrible worrier these days but keep smiling, helps a lot. The Cathedrle is huge, all in scofling inside and out.* Epstein's rhetoric dramatises a wall.   60h

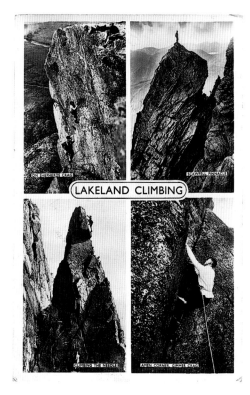

August 4th.   Sid in Ambleside to Mrs W L in Alverstoke, *we could not go on the farm where we went last year but have found another near Keswick everything going alright.* Perhaps Sid has returned to tackle one of these vertiginous climbs. Rather him than me on Scawfell Pinnacle or Gimmer Crag. I must admit to being rather impressed by the lunatic who has very nearly got to the top of the Needle.   60i

June 14th.   Hodkins in Minneapolis to Mr & Mrs O in Richmond Hill, NY, *All awaiting arrival of Vans. Busy, busy, busy, busy, love.* America will become one day the place to study one of the great architectural periods of history. By no means Saarinen's most important building, the Milwaukee War Memorial/Art Center has an immediacy that excites the viewer as it extrudes the inside of a block to form an interior space.   60j

November 3rd.   Heeltee in Summit NJ to Susan W in Long Meadow, Mass. *Grannie said you were getting to be a big girl and looked very stylish in your new dress.* It is only a week to the Presidential election and the US will have a narrow escape from an early Nixon presidency (there is quite enough to come). This well crafted family group oozes decent sincerity and eager virtue.   60k

Porch   The Paper House   Pigeon Cove , Mass.

August 2nd.   Grace Kellogg writes to her parents in Springfield, Mass., *Well, we had Swedish pancakes for breakfast & Ipswich clams for dinner. We saw this paper house - all the furniture is made of newspapers; so are the walls. It is now 5.15pm. I'll go mail this - post office is practically across the street.* Though all places in America may seem to look the same, each harbours some monument to eccentricity.   60l

March 1st.   Vesta & Jesse & Family to friends in Pacoima, California. *These cards bring back good memories. We would sure like to see each of you.* A promotional card for Kaiser Aluminium from Tomorrow Land. The beautiful metal construction would look better without the crude overprinting of their name. The spaceman's fancy dress looks terribly out of date but the archly posed children seem impressed.   60m

May 27th.   Pan, a service wife in Singapore, to Bideford. *Dear Daddy, I bought this card to show you one of the places we often go which is the Cold Storage on the left... interested to hear about the wedding - can we have some pitchers... we're going to see Ben Hur on Fri & to the Ocean Park Hotel for a Chinese Reunion.* Ben Hur is more up to date than the announced visit of Elizabeth Taylor and her husband. (Mike Todd died in 1958).   60n

August 27th.   Mollie & Eddie to Mr & Mrs Batham in Sheffield, *We are both having a grand time and the weather is really good. Every caravan here seems to have either a dog or a kiddie and sometimes both. Mollie has been dashing around in her shorts today and yesterday I was looking for a pair of shorts.* The mythical sixties just didn't happen to most people and life continued drably. On holiday most trippers paraded in awful outfits through surly resorts. Austerity was over but its habits lingered on.   60o

August 24th.   Kay in Oberammergau to Mrs Q in Keighley, *I have just had the biggest thrill, I have actually spoken to Mary & had her autograph, all without asking. I bought a set of Passion cards opposite the theatre, the old said something about Mary & disappeared inside with the packet he came out with Mary's picture autographed and took me inside to meet her. She is charming. I was speechless.* For Kay, Mary was Mary and that was that.   60p

August 24th.   This is the card that Mary, in the Passion Play enacted entirely by the inhabitants of Oberammergau, signed for Kay. On the same day N writes to Miss Higgs in Pulborough, Sussex, *The Play is quite magnificent. our rooms are so near that we are able to come here for mid-day break. We eat at a hotel which is owned by the 'Christus' & 'Mary' is the daughter of the house & serves in the little shop on the ground floor.*   60q

August 14th.   Fred & Jean in Ryde to Mrs B in Sunbury-on-Thames, *Dear Marie Just to let you know we are getting along fine. We have two cooked 3 coursed meals each day as well as breakfast & tea is served in the gardens each day. No tea in bed though, have to go to the snack bar & get it yourself but you can take it back to the chalet with you. I can't get away from cricket there is a match this afternoon.* The Goon Show's humour enters the postcard.   60r

August 18th.   Fred & Jean in Ryde to Mrs MB in Sunbury, *Spent our £5 worth of vouchers this morning. I have a new handbag one to match my shoes that Ernie got me & to match my Gert's shopping bag. Freda has some shorts & I have a bathing suit white with blue spots.* Fred and Jean, as can be seen, sample all the holiday camps in turn. In 1959 (see 59j) they were in Great Yarmouth. Their preference is for McGill's inuendos and double entendres.   60s

July 27th.   Maya in Split, Yugoslavia to Miss Dulley in Highgate, London. *Dear Anthea and I better make it to Gerry too. Have got this far after only 9 days hitching. we are therefore well ahead of schedule but as money is very short we shall have to give up the idea of Athens. The Italians were too forward for modest little me so we are going home via Vienna . Suppose you are both working hard but remember Be Good. Hope you have a very happy and prosperous vac. Love. Maya xxx. P.S. We are propogating the C.N.D. cause throughout Europe but regret Greece will not be included. BAN THE BOMB.* A perfect vignette of the early 60's students life. Two girls with little money hitchiking around the continent, dodging predatory Italian youths and spreading the message of the Campaign for Nuclear Disarmament (led by Bertrand Russell) which was effectively born with the Aldermaston March of 1958. The CND emblem is drawn on the back of this card. It appeared everywhere and is still seen.   60t

August 6th. A warm face from the Cold War. The handsome Yuri Gagarin became the first man in space on April 12th. Suddenly the West realised that Russia was taking the risks and making the running: the race to the moon was on. The cosmonaut became a world celebrity and a powerful public relations weapon, as this postcard image (complete with dove of peace) proves. By the time Gary Saint in London receives this card from Roy in Russia *wishing you all the best*, Gagarin has been to England and received an ecstatic welcome. But there was no thaw. Within a week the Berlin wall would be built, the Cold War's most concrete and visible emblem. 61a

January 1st. Barnaby describes his New Year festivities in two episodes to Miss Rosemary W. in Warminster ...*writing this from Mussetti's; Soho; where we have just had an excellent steak supper at 10pm. liquor sales have risen alarmingly since I have been in London... hope to finish up in Trafalgar Square. 1/1/61 Happy New Year! We managed... in time. How about The Ten Commandments at the Regal Wed or Thur?* 61b

May 13th. Marguerete to Mr & Mrs Gray in Ludington, Michigan, *Hi! you can have New York says Demmy. We have had a nice trip so far. Busy place & dirty. Hope our pictures are good.* The standard bunched-up end-on view of the Lower Manhattan skyline has from any distance an almost planned look as if each building were part of a single architectural project. 61c

July 8th.   Pat & Jack to Mr & Mrs Baker in Cape Girardeau, Missouri, *Hi there, we haven't seen Jack Kennedy yet. I wonder if he will ask us out for supper. We have been seeing so much that I think I will need glasses when I get home.* The new president has other things on his mind as the arms race gains critical momentum and the apparent easing of tension with the USSR over Berlin proves to be illusory.   61d

September 29th.   From CBS to Lou Kennedy in New York. The card shows Marvin Kalb, the reporter of The Moscow Scene on CBS Radio's Dimension program. His message is a reminder to listen in *to a story I reported... recently: the use of identical uniforms for all elementary schoolers in Moscow & throughout all Russia.* These Christian domes ironically remained the cue-sign of Soviet Union reporting.   61e

July 27th.   Mum & Dad to Gordon Bradly in Winchester, *They all wanted to know where you were and hope to see you next year.* According to the caption 'These little men have been collecting for charity since 1934'. Garden gnomes are still with us, and breeding. The taste for them is as mysterious as their origins. Could they be the only true pagan survival?   61f

May 17th.   M J Parker of the May Company in Cleveland sends this to Mr Paul Kreiss in Cleveland Ohio. Though he may not resemble these clean-shaven identikit eligible American males he may well wish to step into the Wash 'n Wear era with them. If so suits such as these will cost him $39.95 and he'll need no other, for 'to refresh this suit just pop it in the washer... and it will drip dry ready for the next day'.   61g

May 15th.   Dappy from le Touquet to Lady S in Worcester, *On my way back. Arrive Lydd about 12.55. I am longing to see you again. My much love.* In their heyday Silver City served the carriage trade, even squeezing Lady Docker's gold-plated Daimler between the jaws of this Bristol freighter. Cheap drive-on channel ferries spelled their end in 1962. This superbly organised photographic card by Artaud is promotional perfection both for the service and the desirable Triumph TR2.   61h

June 7th.   Louis & Kev to Nan, Bob & Boys in Chatham. *Here we are... painting the town (more or less). Last evening stood outside the Palace to see Kennedy's arrive and after waiting an hour got killed in the rush. Kev saw her ear-ring. I saw the flag on the car, ah well can't be always lucky... back to grind on Thur.* The Festival Hall, no longer a novelty, is now the heart of London's musical life. Kennedy was staying overnight in London on his way back from meeting Kruschev in Vienna.   61i

July 28th.   *Spent the day shrimping,* writes Christine to the Revd S in Enfield, *Found a man's canvas shoes & socks & a rock pool with a number of crabs (obviously his catch) but no man & the tide was coming in so bagged his crabs & took his shoes to a rock out of the sea's way. Mystery!!* The card looks as if it has been doing service to Nairn's caravanners since the thirties and (rightly) continues to please.   61j

July 4th.   Maurine in Metairie, La. to Mr & Mrs JJP in Austin, Texas, *Dear Ones - We are just going like mad and loving every minute of the trip of course I'd sorta like to hear from my little family.* Maurine it seems has been graciously dining in Holloway House at the Lakeside Shopping Centre where she picked up this free card. I hope the cake tasted a bit more natural than it looks.   61k

June 24th.   Fred & Jean in Sunbury are the recipients this time of a topical card from Bob Clinton in Hove, *Have you seen the Zebra Kid from USA he is a charlie 22 stone with his hat on It was a good laugh & as strong as an ox. He sat on the ref in the corner then the other chap picked up the ref & rammed in the fellows mid rif (guts) with his hat on. The Zebra was CCCC, That's what Gert said she did like it. WMGYF.*   61l

August 17th.   To the Taggarts in Springfield, Illinois, *Got in Tues Eve. Tom got a visitors pass & I'm in his apt. Real nice fold-up kitchen. I got him some dishes, silver, towels today - bowls, cups, pan. He is on all-night duty tonight. This is far from any place. He looks great - started a football team today... have yet to see Club. We stayed up late last nite talking & looking thru pictures! Slept this aft. I was more tense than I realised.* 61m

December 28th.   Nancy & Byron to Elmer Nelson in Los Angeles, *What a fantastic city. Today we took in the Guggenheim... Tonight Byron is taking me to see My Fair Lady for my birthday.* Building began on Frank Lloyd Wright's Museum as My Fair Lady opened on Broadway in 1956 and was finished in 1959 long before it closed. Such an imaginative container for art would not be conceived until Gehry's Guggenheim in Bilbao forty years later.   61n

July 29th.   Philip to RJSC in Whetstone, *Saw Cav & Pag here last night with Giulietta Simionata among others - simply electrifying. I suppose one ought to have seen Aida, but they managed to make a grand spectacle... the third possibility was funnily enough La Fanciulla del W.* Verona was the pioneer in rehabilitating Roman ruins for modern spectacles. Here in progress is the Aida that Philip missed.   61o

July 24th.   Margaret in East Germany writes from Dresden to the Radleys in Elstree. *Arrived here safely to a most warm welcome... We are having excellent meals, & tho there are shortages the food situation has been terribly exaggerated in our press. The destruction here was Terrible... little or nothing has been done in the way of rebuilding.* A pre-war view on a post-war card captioned Schlosskirche: Destroyed by Anglo-American Bombers 1945. This is truth with a twist.   61p

August 9th.   A writes to Todd Gladstone at the Camp Young Judea, Amherst NH from Oak Ridge (See 46i). *The atomic plant is great. I got for pieces of gold-plated cobalt free. The government pays $1.30 a piece. Met a wonderful girl here, and unfortunately I will have to leave tomorrow. To bad... Regards to Rhoda.* We see the Loading Face for graphite rods, the visible part of a reactor. Its use in pencils and Nuclear Power Stations gives graphite the versatility award.   61q

MISS C. C. TRUMAN.

July 13th.   Judy in Bristol to AC in Chelmsford ...*glad to hear that you are keen on tennis. I am too... an uncle sent me 2 seats for the finals at Wimbledon. I went up on Sat. with a friend. Our seats were v.near the television cameras and we had a wonderful view of the match between Christine Truman and Angela Mortimer. It was a tremendous tussle.* Wimbledon was still an amateur event as the card, which scores all possible portrait faults, confirms.   61r

February 7th.   The Fisher Research laboratory in Palo Alto send news of their latest metal detector to Edward Chaves in Silver City NM. Marianne, pictured here, writes *Sorry can't come myself but will be glad to send details of the best locator ever built!* Much to the annoyance of serious archaeologists lots of people (most not looking at all like Marianne) would be treasure troving for ancient artefacts with such a device from now on.   61s

October 14th.   'Blimp' at the Brighton Conservative Party Conference writes to the Tusas in Pimlico. *Having a lovely conference. All members look so well fed, & this plus sunshine and Dr Brighton reassures us that we have never had it so good. My address on behalf of the Attic dwellers Assn. went down like a bomb. Happily no fall-out. I think everything is going to be alright. Mac [Harold MacMillan] waved to me as he drove past. Is this a good sign? Even the p.c. humour is good old Tory traditional. Can't walk the prom for old age p's protesting - in fact had to push several into the gutter. Am in the Blue.* References and half-quotations abound in this tongue-in-cheek conference report.   61t

"The comic postcards down here are positively disgusting! I *must* send you one!!"

September 10th. Fred & Jean in their quest for the perfect holiday camp are at Weymouth and have not struck lucky. They write to Mrs C in Sunbury, *Dear Mum. Weather lovely today. A lot of new arrivals coming to the concentration camp today. Don't know what they are in for.* Donald McGill (born 1875) died a month after this postcard was sent; his new designs for the coming year were already completed. So prolific was he that George Orwell in his famous essay assumed (much to the artist's annoyance) that McGill, like Disney, was a studio enterprise of many hands. The artist's amplitude of spirit never yielded to the petty censorship that threatened both his work and people's liberty to enjoy it. He died in SE London where he had lived and worked. This card, as vigorous as ever, was probably designed in his eighties. It makes a good epitaph since it features a modest homage to the allure of his own unique craft.   62a

November 5th.   SS to M A K G Wild in Weiner Neustadt Military Camp, *London calling Günther Wild! I still cannot believe I have met Peter Armstrong your friend. Hearing him talk brought you much nearer to me - but still not near enough. I am saving all my money to come to Austria next year.* A fine Dixon card datable to c.1958 from Drango, a film starring Jeff Chandler, at the Pavilion.   62b

September 23rd.   Susie writes home to Wethersfield, Connecticut. *Dear Mom-a-loom, Hi there! I am really crammed with work. I need to know the balance of my checking account. Was it $200 or $300... And please send the stuff I need plus a couple of big white shirts for art classes... Things are really poppin' around here & I'm really keeping busy. I miss all of you loads. Honest!*   62c

HOVERCRAFT V.A-3
THE WORLD'S FIRST HOVERCRAFT PASSENGER SERVICE, RHYL-WALLASEY 1962.
CRUISING SPEED 60 M.P.H.   WEIGHT CAPACITY 2 TONS.
CARRYING CAPACITY 24 PASSENGERS AND 1 TRAFFIC OFFICER.

September 5th.   Auntie Joyce in Colwyn Bay to Master C Clarke in Rugby. *I expect you are getting ready for the new term, back to study. Haven't been on this yet, only seen it, but hoping.* Christopher Cockerell's totally innovative Hovercraft started life as a tiny prototype made from two cocoa tins in 1955. Eleven years later massive commercial Hovercraft were crossing the Channel. Cockerell died in 1999.   62d

August 1st.   Hilary Salter to her parents in Northampton. *Thanks for all the money you sent... Give my love to the dog because I am missing him. Going into East Grinstead and we are going to have a midnight feast tonight.* The wonderful colours chosen by Frith & Co to represent the English scene belong to no world except that of the postcard and are matched by their stunning compositions.   62e

June 6th.   Ray and Jane in Minehead to Mum & Dad, *After a wet start we are now enjoying a sunny time at Butlin's... really excellent especially food and entertainment. Hope you enjoy the cream we've sent.* The Somerset Hunt move across Exmoor, a species as imperilled as the fox they chase. In 1999 there was the usual outcry and the Hunts prepared to abandon the elitist Pink (was it all about class after all?).   62f

December 12th.   To Paul Merrill in Brookfield NY, *We have got as far as Scranton. Thanks for the message relayed from Mary from Dot (I don't know anything to do about it). We are well despite the cold. Our trip to Factoryville was successful and pleasant. Cordially, Bob.* Is it coincidence that these also are in Hunting Pink, albeit a democratic lumberjack version.   62g

May 10th.   Sinuccia sends greetings to her family in Milan from one of the ever increasing rash of new restaurants in London catering from the late fifties onwards to a world made more sophisticated by continental travel. By way of research I had lunch here on 31st December 1999. Now called Zilli it has moved slightly upmarket and is surrounded by competitors (both old: see 57t) and new.   62h

March 4th.   Jane to the Smyths in Bangor, Northern Ireland, *Dear Uncle Jimmy & Auntie Eileen, I'm in Berlin with the school and having great fun. We saw the wall & looked over it. Tomorrow we're going to the Eastern Sector.* Here at the once vibrant Potsdamer Platz the wall is its own self-sufficient metaphor and needs no gloss.   62i

August 30th.   Geoff to Mr & Mrs P in Palmer's Green, *Excuse bad writing, but the coach is jogging about like anything. We're almost at the end of our stay in Russia - it has been really exciting.* So eccentric is the colouring of the card that at first one imagines the people to be part of the artwork as it progresses from low to high relief (as a metaphor of its title, Glory To The Soviet People, Fighter For Peace!).   62j

March 27th.   J from Berlin's new Opera House writes loftily to Mr & Mrs T in London SW1. *Lucky to catch Schönberg's Moses und Aaron. Apart from that & the wall one thinks a lot about Niebuhr, Ranke, Mommsen, Schlegel, Bismarck & Hitler. One worries a lot too. I would like to live here really, it touches all the sensitive spots. One occasionally recalls Spengler too!! Lots of Love...*   62k

July 19th.   From Aberdeen to Olive in Gosport. *Miss Smith & I came here 2 weeks ago but the weather is most unkind. However we feast on lovely strawberries every day. with dear love. Annie.* For collectors of royal postcards (and there are many) this is one of the most obscure. 'The Queen is on her way to Balmoral with Prince Philip driving', the caption informs us.   62l

July 26th.   P in Thetford to Mrs GBG in Hickling. *Afraid we shall not be able to come on Saturday as we are definitely going to the Goss's... we enjoyed the day Sunday.* Thirty years have not done much for British motor sales techniques (see 33q). The picnic has moved into the showroom but flask and hamper seem the same. The man's shirt is advanced for the time but who wants a custard-coloured car?   62m

September 27th.   Mildred in Popham Beach, Maine writes to Doris Lane in Ipswich, Mass. *This is where we get the cards. It is wonderful down here now. See you when I get back if you are back too.* The small postcard publisher survives into the sixties. WH Ballard specialises in the Maine Coast and perhaps offers this card free to Taylor's Stores for stocking his wares. Taylor's have so spruced up their store and stripped all surfaces of clutter that it has an abandoned Third World look.   62n

June 11th.   Rosa to Sarah in Aberdeen. *Dear Sarah, Hope you had a lovely time at the wedding etc. I had hell here. I have patience and I am intelligent enough to avoid quarrels. It is a shock and at the same time heartbreak, to experience a derailed mind. I had to shorten my stay and S fetched me home. Weather was glorious and helped to overcome the difficulties to share a room... please make it clear to L's relatives that I have nothing to do with her spending her money...*   62o

April 13th.   To Dr & Mrs Casson in Chipping Sodbury *Having a gorgeous time. Weather is perfect. Already Major is having a great influence on the unconverted. Trust the late rain is not having a bad effect on you. Yours in Him. Cherry.* Ian Thomas devoted his life to evangelism at the age of fifteen and now lives in Colorado the head of the world wide Torchbearer operation which he started in England, at Carnforth, after distinguished service in World War II.   62p

August 28th.   Mabel & Taylor in Rotterdam send a birthday greetings card to three of the Sears family in Milford, Conn., *I suppose you... are getting ready for a winter of work. Your trip in the new trailer sounds fabulous... We are sailing on August 30th on the Rotterdam for NY.* From the LSO under George Weldon playing Grieg to a used tube of lanolin handcream this is a time capsule of taste in the form of worldly, cultural and natural goods.   62q

February 20th.   To Miss Smith in River Edge NJ, *This is the place. We are working alone. Not too difficult Friday worked 12.01am to 3.00pm - Sat 6am - 5pm, Sunday in at 8am. We are very isolated here no stores no nothing. no days off. Nuts. Dad (Big Day).* Posted on the day this rocket launched Col. Glenn, America's first astronaut, into orbit. Both the NASA Atlas-Mercury vehicle and its launching paraphernalia make a technoarchitectural ensemble of powerful grace.   62r

July 11th.   Marguerite writes to Sister Marie at the Immaculate Heart Convent, Hollywood. *Greetings from the Fair. Two of us visited up here in Seattle. Went up in the Space Needle. Lovely view at Sunset. Now on train to Vancouver.* The Space Needle looks rather sketchy compared with the realities of Cape Canaveral. This was to have been the site of Seattle's Millennium celebrations but threats of Algerian terrorist attacks forced the city to cancel festivities. 62s

September 18th.   Harold to Len Malun in Tetcham, Surrey, *I recollect that you reminded me of how we had been disappointed in the restoration of Caernarvon. On seeing it again I find it almost grotesque and Ethel who had never seen it before regarded it as entirely absurd - but, of course, she was comparing it with Conway, a perfect ruin, perfectly preserved. We also entirely approve of Beaumaris. While here in Conway we have seen the annual 'honey', or autumn fair, which reminded me of Baldock Fair - do you remember that ? Ethel loves hearing the cheapjacks as they raked in the pounds.* The Heritage question looms large and can end in a failure of nerve when all is preservation. The public love Caernarvon Castle, and its kitsch aspect will be well matched in 1969 with the designer history cooked up for the investiture of the Prince of Wales (see 69a).   62t

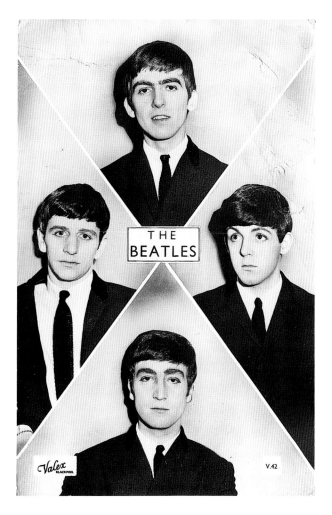

November 27th.   In the year of that first LP, She Loves You, and Please Please Me, Joan writes from Bromley to Miss PM Bridge in Allan, Stirlingshire, *Have you got this one. I saw it and thought you might like it! Have you got any of their records? Lots of love.* This (before the trademark collarless jacket) is possibly the Liverpool band's postcard debut and was published in Blackpool. 63a

August 12th.   Cissie writes to Alf and John in Barrow-in-Furness ...*We are going to a historic house some-where - are going to the bridge to find which is best.* A postscript says they *went to Luton Hoo. It was grand. Country lovely.* A No 12 bus heads for Croydon as ever via Peckham and the bottom of my road. The car at the left, in briefly fashionable two-tone, is a Nash Metropolitan. 63b

November 2nd.   Jo says *Hi! Hope you are feeling better* to Mr & Mrs O'Shee in Hallidaysburg, PA. The New York Airways Helicopter links the city to the airports a service that was discontinued in 1977 (after an grotesque accident in which five people were killed at the Pan Am building's heliport). For obvious reasons this odd shaped craft was nicknamed The Flying Banana. 63c

March 31st.   Philip C's parents send a card from the Forte's service area at Newport Pagnell, *We are having a cup of coffee on our way back along the motorway. We are going to dinner with AW in Northampton on our way home...* This first full stretch of motorway, with no speed restrictions, was often driven for its own sake. The service station became for a while a fashionable rendezvous popular with trendy youth.   63d

June 6th.   John, June & Robert to Mr & Mrs Virgo in Thundersley, *Dear Mum & Dad. Arrived safly the caravan was a picture the man who owns them had even put flowers in the van & it was so lovly and clean The caravan on the front is ours with this magnificent view of the sea as we sit at the table.* The idea of printing the card in blue to capture the sea and sky is a misjudgement: the final effect is rather arctic.   63e

April 24th.   To Ann in Cambridge from her husband in Kyrenia, *I have been asked to stay behind here for 2 days to draft the report for UNESCO. This is dependant upon getting a flight (which is difficult)... I shall fly to Tel Aviv or Istanbul Sunday... get to London on Monday. No letter from you at all. Are you sending Air Mail??* This is not Europe. The lull in the conflict between Greek & Turk will not last.   63f

July 13th.   Edwin in Shinnecock Hills NY to Mr & Mrs Justa in Thonotosassa, Florida, *Dear Folks, out to L.I. for only the 3rd week-end so far this year... Thanks for the article you sent. Going up town to shop.* The Big Duck acted as a store originally and now stands in retirement at Flanders, Long Island as a reminder of the fame of Long Island Duckling, and to give pleasure to tourists.   63g

July 18th.   Maggie to Mrs Taylor in Bristol *...we are staying quite nr here. Dolly took Peter sight seen in London but I have not been anywhere...* The Chiswick Flyover now reminds one of drab journeys from Heathrow on the, then unbuilt, M4. The overhead trolleybus powerlines would soon be redundant. Such advances in roadbuilding created new areas of urban wasteland, desolate places where no shop or human amenity could survive. A single half-hidden tree does little to cheer the spot.   63h

March (?) 12th.   Alan in Adrar in the Central Sahara to the Solomans in Broadstairs, *Out of war now, escorted by troops across two closed frontiers and leave eventually at Oudja - closed two hours later. Crossed desert for two days by way of Gt. Erg the actual sand dunes up to 200 ft high - what a sight at sunset. dates palms and camels galore plus 5 helicopters. getting along with French Foreign Legion & getting super photos.* Newly independent Algeria was in strife and would still be so in 2000.   63i

KENYA'S UHURU

12th December, 1963

A personal message from the Hon. J. Kenyatta, M.N.A., Prime Minister of Kenya.

I send the good wishes of the people of Kenya to the people of all countries of the world on the joyous occasion of our long-awaited Independence on 12th December, 1963.

Jomo Kenyatta

December 12th.   David in Mombassa sends the official greetings card to Miss Sassa in London WC2 ending with the Swahili injunction *Harambee!* (Hold together). Kenya is the 34th African nation to achieve independence in the years of the Wind of Change, with the traditional scenario of jailed rebel leader released to become revered head of state.   63j

July 24th.   Granny writes to Hugh Kennedy in Yattendon, *I went with Mrs Hampson on Wed. to hear an opera called 'Elegy For Young Lovers'. This is the opera house. The country round it and the gardens are lovely.* Glyndebourne is not all Mozart and champagne picnics. Henze's 1961 opera with a WH Auden/Kallman libretto was receiving its British première in a continuing tradition of performing new works.   63k

April 19th.   *I am at the Hist. Assocn. AGM at Coventry Training College,* writes Agnes Strong to Mrs Day in Newcastle, *and so is Mr Fowler. I miss Mr Simmonds! We were at an organ recital at the cathedral last night & I can assure you the cathedral is much more strange inside than out!* It had been an active place of worship for a year, but was still controversial since people knew what cathedrals ought to look like.   63l

August 20th.   Jim in Wichita Falls to Miss Phoebe Williamson in Darien, Conn., *Hi Sis! How was 4H fair. I did this same thing in that picture it was hard but I made it. Write and tell me about the fair.* Jim takes modest pride in his training and achievements in tense though relatively peaceful days. By the time he is ready for combat there will be a war waiting for him in Vietnam.   63m

August 16th.   Johnny Tirch and children to Mr & Mrs Bryant in Southsea, Hants, *Dear Mum and Sylvia, Just a few lines to let you know that we arrived at Bebington last night after spending the day at Blackpool. Love from us all.* So typical is this estate of low-rise developments it could be the set for a soap opera and could be anywhere in Britain. Cards of such areas were already scarce and now hardly exist at all.   63n

October 6th.   Mary in Gerona to Mr & Mrs H in London N11, *We went to see a bullfight and it is the first and last time I will go to one. In two hours there were six bulls killed - and gruesomely. however I am trying to forget this. When I get back will tell you more about the grand holiday - the beautiful mountains, blue & green sea - rocks - flamingo dancing - swimming and souvenir hunting.*   63o

P2014.   ABORIGINAL GIRL.

July 2nd.   To J & AT in London SW1. *Greetings and love as the sun sinks behind what may well be the MacDonnel Range though I wouldn't swear to it, in Alice Springs, where streets are wide and dusty, the aborigines wear high heeled boots and I have not yet seen a policeman.* This locally produced card tells a different story from the unflattering images of aborigines as mere ethnic curiosities earlier in the century (see 06e). Perception and intent are everything and the rise in status of the indigenous people of so many parts of the world can be measured via the changing nature of their portrayal. Here the aboriginal girl is almost idealised.   63p

September 6th.   Guido Allen receives this card with greetings from Donona in Loreto. Though the Beatles may have emerged in this year as the new princes of rock and roll the King had been securely on his throne since the middle of the previous decade as unassailably the greatest popular singer/performer of the century. Even in the long decline through a series of ever more vacuous films and perilous stage appearances until his death in 1977 there would be glimpses and echoes of the complete magic that made him the most exciting of all stars to watch and hear. His cult continues to the extent that in Britain there are pilgrimages to the only spot in the country where he once set foot. This was for two hours at the end of his National Service, on March 2nd 1960, at Prestwick airport where he greeted fans and phoned Priscilla his 16 year old bride-to-be.   63q

President Kennedy's Summer Home on Cape Cod

August 13th.   From Mason in Dennis Park to the Blachers in Riverside, California, *Dear Granny & Grampy. We will be at Cape Cod until Saturday. This is Dad's first week-long vacation from work. I know he's enjoying it, but he'll be glad to get back to the office. I feel the same way about my weather station. I hope to see you at my Bar Mitzvah.* It had been a long time since America could boast a good-looking and stylish President with a glamorous wife. The natural choice of this card for Mason to send from East Coast to West is almost emphasised by his not mentioning the Kennedys at all. At the time the card was written Jackie was recovering from the shock of a baby son dying only thirty six hours after his birth (on August 8th in Washington while the Nuclear Test Ban Treaty was being signed in Moscow). The Picture shows Irving Avenue in Hyannisport, part of the Kennedy compound.   63r

July 12th.   Lynn in Boston, Massachusetts to Mr Katz in Kensington, Maryland. *Dear Marc. we just spent a week at Cape Cod, which was very nice, if you like fog & rain & clouds. Because of the lousy weather we really went sightseeing. We went to Provincetown (an art colony) and we all saw the hippies there. Now we are visiting relatives in Boston which is really a beautiful city. Yesterday my uncle took us out on his boat on the Charles River. It was great. Have fun at camp. Love.* Though the word 'hippy' seems to have been born in the fifties it did not acquire all its cultural baggage of meaning until the mid sixties. Here it would probably signify no more than arty with a hint of easy-going life style. The card shows 83 Beals Street, Brookling, Mass., where Kennedy was born in 1917. It was on the 22nd of November in 1963 that he was assassinated in Dallas.   63s

August 8th.   The Unisphere which dominated the 1964-65 New York World's Fair can still be seen on the way from Kennedy airport to Manhattan. Both as symbol (Peace Through Understanding) and artefact it is rather trite compared with the Brussels Atomium of 1958. The sight of a globe tends to act as a reminder of how little Peace and Understanding there is, has been, and promises to be. Lorraine an early visitor sends the often repeated message to David D in North Weymouth, Mass. *The World's Fair is beautiful but my feet are killing me! It's worth it though.*   64a

July 3rd.   The Butlers in Walsall get a card from E saying, *TV business. Farewell Party.* The Bovril sign, bold pioneer in 1910 of the Circus illuminations, has disappeared to make way for Players Cigarettes. Of the same vintage but more durable is Charlie Chaplin, still in the limelight at the Pavilion (in a compilation movie). Did anyone ever prefer the trivialised version of the Guinness clock?   64b

May 5th.   Rita to the Kellys in Hull, Yorks. *We met a Mr Donoghue at the Pioneer Communion Breakfast and he took us down to the coloured quarter of New York and then down Broadway into Jack Dempsey's Restaurant... guess what I met Jack Dempsey and he autographed my photo. The meal was out of this world... 25 dollars. So work that out!*   64c

December 2nd.   JTP writes to Solomon L Gluck in Croton-on-Hudson NY, *Hi Pal, Enjoyed your visit to my upstairs den very much,* and leaves it at that. LBJ, the 36th President looks a little sheepish about occupying this space on the standard card of the White House (see 61d) though he has just legitimised his presidency with a landslide victory at the polls. Who decided to paint in a new flag to replace the limp Stars & Stripes on the Kennedy version of this card? (see 61d).   64d

July 26th.   Janet Hearn in Nottingham gets a card from Leslie, *Are these your favourites. They were in Blackpool Friday and there was a riot. Hope you are well.* Indeed there was a riot at the Winter Gardens with fans smashing chandeliers and a Steinway grand, seventy policemen called in and fifty people taken to hospital. Suddenly the Beatles seemed loveable. Cut the card in half and the three on the right still strut their stuff in the 21st century.   64e

July 3rd.   Theresa in Atlantic City to Miss Englested in Medford, Mass *Thanks for card from Maine. Hope to stop into Fair on our way to Boston to spend Fourth with Bob & Family.* This is the national finals of the Miss America competition, more lavishly regal than royalty itself. The caption would hardly please Canadians since it talks of '54 contestants representing 50 states including Canada'.   64f

August 30th.   Ruth & Henry to the Farnsworths in Upper Mountclair NJ., *This is a new building just opened last fall by the Queen it covers all commonwealth nations with exhibitions of their own specialities of landscapes etc.* Despite its worthiness as an idea the Institute has never become central to London life mainly because the notion of Commonwealth is of little interest to the British themselves.   64g

October 11th.   Mrs Wallden writes to Mrs Evelyn Chatham in San Diego, Cal., *Dear Mrs Chatham, Rec'd aprons today and I'm very satisfied. You do lovely work. Am giving one as a birthday gift and keeping lavender one. Best of luck to you.* Judging by the queue this ferris wheel disguised as a giant tyre advertisement was a popular attraction at the New York World's Fair. The Manhattan skyline from one of its best angles was visible once you got to the top.   64h

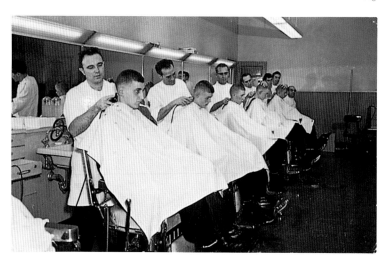

March 28th.   Danny at Waukegan (The US Naval Training Center) to Miss Rose Penella, Croton-on-Hudson, NY., *Hi, having a great time. Ha. ha. Boy it is rough. This is what we look like in hair cuts. How is Croton. This card is for you Mabali, your mother etc. See you soon.* This barber shop claims to have cut 450,000 heads of hair in a year. The scene is familiar from the many films based on a recruit's life but most of all from Elvis Presley's much publicised quiff removal in 1958.   64i

"WHY DON'T YOU GET UP AND DO **THE SHAKE**, MISS ? "

YEAH!
YEAH!
YEAH!

A 'BAMFORTH' COMIC

OWD2.   THE PARADE. OAKWOOD.   Copyright
Frith Ltd

September 3rd. Fred & Jean are in Jersey and select the latest saucy card to send to Mrs Crook in Sunbury, *Dear Mum, we are all fine. Everything is very expensive here. Costs more than at home. Camp lousy but food ok. Love.* The routine window cleaner/girl-in-bath gag is modernised by a transistor radio and an all too identifiable song coming out of it. The shake never quite existed as a dance.   64j

November 6th.   BMM in Southgate N14 to Mrs Becher in Worthing. *Having a thoroughly lazy time here - still knitting tho' shall be glad to see the end of it. This is our shopping centre - it is just around the corner - most convenient. Awfully cold these days.* Still just around the corner from almost anywhere were the Co-op, the Westminster Bank, the little newsagent & sweet shop, etc. Not for long.   64k

March 14th.   D in Milan to Mrs Miller in Cheltenham *Had a big thrill attending la Scala to hear Mefistofele by Boito... Marvellous singing, staging & sets and all the women in the audience wearing diamonds and mink - it was some show!* This famous tinted photo of orchestra (under Victor de Sabata) and audience is still the standard card available at the opera house.   64l

September 4th.   *Arrived here today*, writes Tibbie from South Queensferry to the Rutherfords in Newcastle, *& Helen was waiting for me. Have a nice place to stay. Cannot get seats for the tattoo. Tomorrow will be a big day here.* Tibbie sends this pleasantly ruminative view (complete with ugly commemorative stamp) of the latest engineering marvel, before crossing towards Edinburgh on its opening day.   64m

BUTLIN'S BOGNOR REGIS
A Carousel Pig and Whistle Bar

the N.A.A.F.I., Aldershot   ALD 24

July 26th.   Dora & Ern to Miss D Griffith in Birmingham, *Dear Dot. Hope everything is OK & blackie behaving himself. We arrived ok after a very long journey. I don't know if you will get this card on account of the postal strike.* Fashion can be flaunted at the inevitable Pig & Whistle (see 37n) but here it is the boys' turn with drainpipe trousers and one sporting a Beatle jacket. Perhaps these youths have been selected from the crowd to counteract Butlin's slightly dowdy image.   64n

March 1st.   To Jean Metcalf, Family Favourites, BBC, *Would you please play 'I'm the lonely one' by Cliff Richards for C/Sgt Edney & Sgt. Whittaker of 1st Bn. Para. Regt. with love from all at home. Julie & Marlene (wives) stationed in BFPO 53.* The husbands are serving in Cyprus according to the code number and may well not be able to listen to Cliff Richard in any case since British troops will be heavily involved in the fighting between Greeks & Turks before the week is out.   64o

June 10th.   Helen to Mrs RW in Cambridge. *Thought this would remind you of the lighter side of your subject! Hope the exams went o.k. There have been several juju's walking along the roads in the last few days looking very fantastic. One did a kind of war dance pointing his knife at our car... got into Lagos at 7.30. The wonderful masks in museums are in reality incomplete without their accoutrements as this fine Dan masquerader demonstrates.*   64p

June 15th.   This is Johnny the wire-walking lion with Stephano Repetto his Italian trainer at Thousand Oaks, Cal., Sent to Diana B in Fairburg, In., *Dear Di. This Jungleland is a fabulous place. The baby zoo is even better than San Diego. Aunt Pegi was sitting on a bench & a little kid bit her fanny. She's still laughing because a baby donkey nipped me in the derrier & I jumped. Love. Nannie.* An alarming story when read through English eyes.   64q

July 1st.   Amy's Beauty Salon in Danvers, Mass., contact Mrs Carlson in Middleton, *Dear Patron, Peeking into our files this morning we discovered that it is just about time for your next permanent wave. You see we're not guessing: that date is right here on our records. And so is all the other invaluable data concerning your particular hair. We've a special coiffure in mind you're sure to love.* I only hope Mrs C didn't get talked into a Smarty or a Dandy-Do.   64r

March 16th.   To Mr & Mrs Groom in Crudersport, Penna., *We ate our breakfast here on way home from Dallas. Could look out in JE hotel room on building where Oswald was and see the place where K was shot. We saw crowds waiting around courthouse also... went to Cattlemans Steak House boy never saw or had anything like that.* Jack Ruby was on trial for the murder of Oswald, Kennedy's assassin. Oswald's death before trial left plenty of room for speculation.   64s

September 7th.   From J/T May in RAF Akrotiri to his parents in Shoreham. *Dear Mum & Dad, I got here safely last Sunday morning at 4am after flying six hours from Stanstead in Essex. At the moment things aren't too good at all I'm afraid, no danger to anyone, its that there many evacuation plans ready to go in operation at a moments notice to get all wives and families out if necessary. Love Derek.* The innocent looking map shows as yet no dividing line between a Turkish and a Greek Cyprus (which is how the island keeps a tense peace at the beginning of this century). Derek is based in the South near Limassol now part of Greek Cyprus. The UN forces had officially taken over from British troops at the end of March, but there was no end to the fighting until the seventies when the island finally split into two.   64t

July 18th. Winston Churchill, who made the first of many appearances (08n) in these pages almost sixty years before, died on January 24th. Connie sends this card to Miss White in Ramsgate and affixes a commemorative stamp issued a few days earlier and based on the well known photograph by Karsh (to which the portrait that forms the centrepiece of this card bears a suspicious resemblance). A more exciting card could have been made to celebrate the great man's colourful life but I dare say Frith had all these images in stock. Connie's message concerns itself with the weather, *sun peeped out twice on Sat & went straight back but twas fine...*   65a

August 16th. This is a view of Piccadilly Circus from only the year before when The Beatles' debut film 'A Hard Day's Night' was playing at the Pavilion. John writes to his Grandma, Mrs Sheridan in Grimsby, Lincs, *Arrived in London wether hot ran into thick fog at Caister. Just had tea.* A handsome 3d stamp on the back reminds one that it is the centenary of the Salvation Army.   65b

November 11th. Rosemary writes to Miss MCR in Muswell Hill, London, *It was not much fun when we had the blackout for 11 hours the other evening. Some people were stuck in elevators for hours....and the Empire State Building is very high. We were quite safe & sound & Richard clinked down 20 flights of stairs & walked 6 1/2 miles home.* 'Howdy' seems a strange greeting from New York.   65c

April 12th.   Sandy to Mrs Mary Lischko in St Louis, Mo. *Hi beautiful! Boy - you should be here - this trip is just wonderful, Washington is so neat & right now we're on a bus to Mt Vernon.* The very simplicity of the Kennedy grave (also the grave of two Kennedy children) makes it a place of calm pilgrimage. The everlasting flame was lit during the President's burial service.   65d

February 25th.   Howard in Melbourne, Fla., to Mrs Spencer in Penn Yan, NY, *We were up to Cape Kennedy Sunday where they are preparing for the moon shot it is a big place.* This was the unmanned lunar photographic mission of July 28th. One of President Johnson's first directives was the renaming of Cape Canaveral, an appropriate gesture given Kennedy's enthusiasm for the space program.   65e

August 28th.   R to JBE in Richmond, *Well, we arrived 7 o/c Friday, were equipped with Butlin badges & this am it was wakey wakey at 6.30am for physical jerks on the lawn!!... full of entertainment here, Dancing, Bingo, Hurrah sessions & sing-songs. Never a dull moment.* Few more dismal scenes exist on cards than this which you could easily believe was issued by a rival camp.   65f

June 24th.   Pamela in Tarascon to the Misses Jennings in London W8. *I send you my good wishes on a most uncultured postcard as Antoine, Mark & I have just got back from the 24 heures du Mans. whew - what a heat dust and noise!* The characteristic start of the famous le Mans race well captured. In 1965 the trophy was won by Ferraris (Rindt and Gregory, USA).   65g

September 2nd.   Robin in Wimbledon to Sub. Lt JGT on HMS Excellent. *What is the matter with me? The time is 0100 and I'm smoking & listening to the radio - with buzzes. Thought the car looked quite handy for the shopping and laundrette but still prefer the Alpine for longer jaunts - or maybe its just the driver? keep busy... and please don't have a crew-cut. Thankyou for a blissful few days at Hove.* Ferraris of this vintage are classics among classics. This was Phil Hill's 1962 Le Mans winner.   65h

August 18th.   Gertrude & Lincoln R send Mr JH of the Control Corporation in Minneapolis this card of the new Los Angeles County Museum complete with period sculpture (by Norbert Kricke), *went thru this museum yesterday. Wasn't that something with those riots here? Think I should move on to a safer place - maybe Vietnam.* The Watts riots were still going on: a heat wave, and an ill judged arrest of a black, led to mayhem and ended with 34 dead and hundreds injured.   65i

August 20th. Pat, Tom & Nigel to Mother & Connie in Pinner, *Very sorry to hear about Mr Burton. We are very comfortable but Nigel is extremely trying and unfortunately most disobedient.* Sounds like Nigel didn't have much of a hand in writing the message. Frith's limited and somewhat apocalyptic palette creates a post-nuclear caravan site overlooking a grey, poisoned sea.   65j

June 25th. E to the Cooks in Poole, *...today its brighter and warmer. D Wilcox kept Birdie for about 10 days & the Austins have him now. Have you used the Errand Boy? I've had a wonderful rest: just go for a run in car.* Frith again in peak sixties form on the road to the end of the world. Such cards put reality in question as postcards in general show how many versions of so called naturalism can coexist.   65k

July 13th. Christine in Albertson NY has been to the World's Fair in its second year and sends this card of the Tower of Light to Kathy Donahue in Burlington, Vermont. *Hows Pops? The Fair is beautiful. see you soon.* The merry figure on the roof is Reddy Kilowatt a trademark character equivalent to Britain's Mr Therm. He no doubt entered the same oblivion. The public do not take such creatures to their heart.   65l

September 27th. *Hows this!* writes Anne in Birmingham to Mr & Mrs Road in Caithness, *Night Life of Brum!! I've never seen it look like this. Everyone pleased with the photographs. I have threatened to blackmail AWS.* Birmingham's red and grimy heart had been ripped out to make way for a City Centre dream that itself is now being replaced. This is the Smallbrook Ringway; urban life sacrificed to the car.   65m

September 11th. E Hackendom in Claymont, Del., receives (as did many fans of the musical entertainer) a mimeographed card, *Our first show in color will come to you from our Mobile Home Estates near Escondido... a fun-filled show featuring many of our musical family. Colorfully yours. Lawrence Welk.* Colour TV introduced in 1953 had only just entered most US homes. This is Lawrence Welk in person (see 57l).   65n

November 28th. Carol to Alma Eilers in Edwardsville, Illinois, *Surprise! I'm really enjoying seeing Berlin. we tried to walk over to East Berlin today but couldn't as we worked for the government.* They would have gone into another world, ill-lit, unkempt and impoverished. The winking lights of West Berlin were a calculated (and daily increasing) reminder to the East of what they had forfeited.   65o

September 8th.   Louise to Mrs W in Great Missenden, *Thanks (due to you then) for the money panic is over for the moment. I seem to have evaded debtors prison, Interpol & all... Please tell Chabot that I have at last bought him 2lb of boiled sweets & will send them as soon as I can lay hands on a suitable box. If you come to Paris you must see Vivian (female-american writer) and even Philippe if we are still in communication at that stage.*   65p

March 3rd.   Desmond to Mrs Prosser in Gosport, Hants. *...am now comfortably settle in. I've been for a walk this aft & am now at a Salon de Thé amid fashionable babble!* These evocations of the Paris Quais are the work of Albert Monier whose postcards (published and distributed by him since 1935) had defined them for Parisian and tourist alike, before the car finally took over. Albert Monier, still active until late in the century, died in 1998.   65q

September 16th.   Fred & Jean (now plus Ann) in Clacton write, this time to the Crooks in Staines, *Dear Mum, Dad & Marie, Weather not too bad. Ann has been very poorly but brighter now. This camp should be shut down. I have never been anywhere so dirty before.* Not a typical choice of card for Fred and Jean but very up to date both in gesture and fashion and the litany of names of groups in favour; the Beatles, the Rolling Stones, Freddie and the Dreamers.   65r

August 6th.   Sarah in Pwllheli sends to Miss Sarah Gregory in Whitchurch a Taylor card which completes the litany, including some names that are beginning to need footnotes, together with Cilla Black (who has changed into a generalised TV personality) and, of course, the perennial Cliff Richard. The pony tail for adult girls is a fifties fashion and for adult males belongs to the end of the century. Sarah tells her namesake *Lots of things to do. all day.*   65s

September 12th.   Another amazing Butlin's Lounge and Marie writes to Mat with a view from the other side, *I am very sorry that I haven't written before this. We just don't seem to have the time to sit down & write letters etc. We work from 9am - 6pm as shop assistants in a large store - one of the best jobs on the camp, largely because it is not nearly so exhausting as most. It's certainly very entertaining and amusing! We do overtime most evenings to increase our wage packets and have managed to save quite a lot. We get one day off a week - and the shops are open on Sundays too which I consider unnecessary but still that's the case... I am looking forward to seeing you next term and will tell you more then.* One suspects Mat will hear some good stories of Marie's holiday job.   65t

Your Personal Invitation to
Beeline Fashions Inc.
First in Fashion Through Home Style Shows.
(3-piece Knit Suit as advertised in VOGUE).

September 29th.   While the rash and the youthful wore mini-skirts or veered towards hippiedom, the mature and the recently young aspired to quite a different look. Carol Shaw invites Florence Metzger in Topeka, Kans. to her Beeline home fashion show. *It will be a lot of fun seeing and perhaps modeling the latest fashions* [printed caption on back]. Florence will know from this picture how to have her hair styled ready for 7.30 on Oct 4th & how to deport herself. Perhaps Crimplene, only introduced the year before, will be on the menu too.   66a

August 1st.   Elsie & Irene to Mrs Pledger in Consett. *The weather is bad. But we saw the Queen, Annie & Andrew.* With Eros boarded up the crowds watch the Election results (in October 1964). At more or less half-time Labour have 179 seats. The Tories 119 and the Liberals 2. Harold Wilson is well on the way to Downing Street. Meanwhile next door Iris Murdoch's A Severed Head is playing.   66b

April 6th.   *We've had 2 such hectic and exciting days here we are both just ready to drop into bed,* write Paul & Joanna to the Rev'd. A in Watford, Herts, *We must have seen every inch of New York - Manhattan anyway - The expense of everything is shattering. We leave for Washington tomorrow - reports say the blossom is out. It's all unbelievably exciting.*   66c

November 8th.   To Miss Buckley in Hove, *You'll let us know what train you can catch from Liverpool St on Saturday, won't you? Phone & reverse the charges. Longing to see you. Wish I was going where this train is.* The Cornish Riviera had set out every day at 10.30am since 1906 and is here hauled by an impressive diesel engine. The age of steam had all but vanished.   66d

February 27th.   Fred Bason, well known chirpy diarist of the time, writes from hospital to Mrs Bishop in Reading. *Darling Rosie, They will <u>not</u> let me out. Tuesday. I am getting better. Had electric treatment & it helps. I am not sad or miserable & I am doing what I am told... Everyone had visitors on Sat <u>except</u> me... visit Tuesday if you can afford it and it fits well. I can't yet speak but face is going back alright.*   66e

July 17th.   A card posted in North Vietnam reaches Len Morris (via East Berlin) in Ealing. *Best wishes from Hanoi* writes TE amongst many stamps and cancellations. One wonders what he is doing there a month after the first US bombs (but not the last) hit the city. The card's English caption describes this rooftop gun-crew as *A Student's Self Defence Group of the Polytechnical College.*   66f

August 1st.   Pat & Brian to the Williams family in Addlestone. *Trevor & Jeremy having a grand time... we went to Land's End on Thursday. St.Ives is full of beatnicks. hope to get upriver next week.* St Ives had long been an artists' colony and I suppose hippies would be nearer the mark, though another 20 years on the peninsular will rename them New Age. John Hinde studios make their usual vivid world.   66g

July 12th.   To Mrs B in Gloucester from Jeanne at the Rank Organisation Forton Service Area near Lancaster, *...we are almost at end of the M6 but it will be slow & by the time we are pitched the post may have gone. Nora has booked our site. God Bless.* Service areas were getting to look like airports. Forton, built in 1965 in the progressive mode, aimed high but T P Bennet's tower was not the right strategy. It was closed in 1989 and now serves as offices for Granada.   66h

August 27th.   Grace, Stephanie & Peter, at the Jehovah's Witness gathering in Richmond, to the Whites in County Down. *We are all enjoying the Assembly to the full!* What Has God's Kingdom Been Doing Since 1914?, asks the poster (what indeed?). Tomorrow will bring the answer: meanwhile there are chilly frolics to be had in togas and sandals participating in an all too English pageant on a Biblical theme; daft but not depressing.   66i

copyright— N.A.S.A.   Gemini two-man spacecraft shown in comparison to the Mercury capsule.   S.3

July 7th.   Stephen in Midhurst gets a card from London, *A Valerie has just given me your plastic shoe which Rowena took away she was wearing someone else's shoes this evening. Did you win with your match box? I expect you had a good time. love. Dad.* Opaque materials for a short story accompany a card in which the Mercury capsule is made to look fit only for an orbiting anchorite.   66j

February 14th.   Vera in Sydney to JP in London, *Are you a stamp addict? Here is a first day issue of our decimal currency stamp. Australia changes to this today. What fun!* As outer space is explored it will create a new term 'inner space' and give higher value to those at the nether end of the technological spectrum, such as this man who knows how to be still at Ayers Rock.   66k

The Old Lake, Thorndon Park.

Gardens and Clock Tower, Croydon   FRITH CYN.124

July 18th.   MMS to Mrs Prosser in Ryde IOW, *Very many thanks for your kind thought. this view is of a peaceful spot near Ingrave & is on Lord Petre's estate. My 'eye' report at end of Sept.* This is also one of the most peaceful postcards ever produced. Even the little group in mid-distance are only murmuring one suspects, leaving the card's heroine to gaze and ruminate.   66l

September 22nd.   Mrs Folland in Cosham gets a nicely wry card from Mal, *Dear Mum. One box, one bag & one son on way. box & bag first. Would you mind washing the clothes in bag. Son will wash himself. See you Sat.* Mal makes a poem of a prosaic request and Frith makes a poem of Croydon even (which will in a month create history as the first place in Britain with a postcode).   66m

"TANNOCHBRAE"

August 6th.   Nana & Grandad in Margate find a good card to send to Master Timothy Kitson and enter into the spirit of the picture. *Now our trip is over, and Parker has brought us home to Lady Penelope's Stately Home xxx.* Perhaps Timothy already has other cards from this 1965 series. Christine Glanville, puppeteer and designer for TV's Thunderbirds died in 1999. The puppet/actuality mix is called by its creators Supermarionation.   66n

July 30th.   Amy to Phyllis Newey in York, *we have turned Southwards for home just seeking B & B we have been very lucky up to now. The weather is beautiful, just caught the odd shower now and again.* Reality is subsumed into soap opera as the card calls this village by its Television name (as the site of Dr Finlay's Casebook). In the lesser reality it is Callander which gave its name to a Canadian village that also sprang to fame (see 36i).   66o

HOVERTRAM AND TOWER, BLACKPOOL ILLUMINATIONS.   ET.2258

August 18th.   To John Axford in Bournemouth. *We are staying here for a few hours. The lights are lovely. The car did 100 on the motorway.* That speed would now have them in a police station for a few hours with no glimpse of Blackpool's adventurous hovertram no 735. It was built in 1963 and is still brought out as novelty transport at illumination time, though now advertising Nat West rather than Shell. The graphic beam of the tower light adds energy to the image.   66p

June 9th.   From Rose, posted inside the Post Office Tower to Nana in Cheltenham, *We've just been up the tower & looked over London. Took an hour's wait. Going to the Mermaid Theatre tonight.* This is London's new landmark (opened in 1965 and still collecting queues) seen here rising above the ever characterful Charlotte Street. I doubt if Rose was tempted to eat at the inordinately expensive (and short-lived) revolving restaurant at the top.   66q

SO FAR, SO GOOD—
NOW LET'S TASTE
YOUR COOKING!

JUST MARRIED

February 1st.   Alice in Waikiki Bay, Honolulu to her friends at Northern Prazone Gas in Minneapolis *Hi, having a wonderful time. I have a little sunburn right now which I'll probably add to this afternoon.* Top class photo-trickery makes as if to garland the Ilikai Hotel in a decorative manner anticipating by a couple of decades the wildest interventions of Christo or the kitsch excesses of Jeff Koons.   66r

July 19th.   Olwen, Eric & David in Christchurch, Hants to Mrs Foster in Cowley *Dear Rose & Bill. Having a nice time. Rose pull the TV aerial out if it should thunder. Shall be glad to have the boys back down on Friday.* A cynical hardness enters the comic card as a new generation takes over, coupled with a meaner kind of image. With the last issues of Donald McGill there had passed a geniality from the earth.   66s

March 7th.   Pat on board HMS Circassia of the Anchor Line to the Rev. P at 1, Residency Rd., Bangalore. *The old ship chugging along on her last voyage with tremendous send off at the port - fully dressed ship police & naval guards, hundreds of people on the quayside dancing and singing - quite an experience but rather sad. Ship very full; accomodation lousy; good food; company friendly weather perfect so far! Hope you got 2 letters and Mice & Men from Bombay plus Rs 1000 draft.* The handsome ship is shown with the Gateway to India in the background. For all the romance of last voyages, ends of epochs, shipboard affairs and images of fine living on the high seas one must remember that, for anyone but the rich, long ocean voyages represented weeks of cramped boredom.   66t

February 13th.   David in Sydney to Mr & Mrs K in Horsham, *I'm hearing of lots of things you're doing for Sylvia whilst I'm here... weather is glorious. I just can't see enough of the beaches.* At this point in the construction the architect of the Opera House Jørn Utzon had resigned and closed his practice in Sydney, never to return to see the finished building. It was completed by Australian architects (with many modifications to Utzon's design) in 1973. Sixteen years in the making it wildly exceeded its budget. In 1998 to celebrate its quarter century attempts were made to bring the 80 year old Utzon to see it. He would not come although he did offer to advise those currently trying to bring it nearer his conception (It has never been fully satisfactory as an opera house even though widely acclaimed as a structure). It has of course become Australia's great ikon of modernity.   67a

August 30th.   In this view from 1968 the Union Jack in the top left hand corner warns the country that If Exports Go Up Britain Goes Down. For months the defective lights made it read, even more mournfully, If Exports Go Up Britain Go Do... Geronimo plays at the Pavilion. The Smiths get word in Lincoln from Lucy, *Ena's flat is lovely.*   67b

September 15th.   Robert writes to the Hall family in Aylesbury, Bucks, *just found work the other day for an advertising agency in Madison Ave. Have taken the pics in will be ready in about 1 week. New York seems very filthy to me. Miss London. Please write.* Looking across Welfare Island gives a pastoral illusion.   67c

November 20th.   Tony in the RAF at Abu Dhabi to J & JC in Saltburn, ...*one of the aircraft had to be hosed down just after lunch... its skin temperature was 124°F. This place is much better than Aden. They don't shoot at us!* British troops left Aden (S.Yemen) in November after 128 years of rule. What is it about the three Arabs by the Palace that called for a photo taken by a spy hidden in the shrubbery?   67d

November 18th.   The end of a competitive exchange of Dantesque postcards between myself and Adrian Henri. This vision of Hell Station with its notice saying HELL: GODS EXPEDITION (Goods Despatch) was his last trump card, *OK Phillips, give up - you'll never beat this one. love from Norway which is in deep snow. A.*   67e

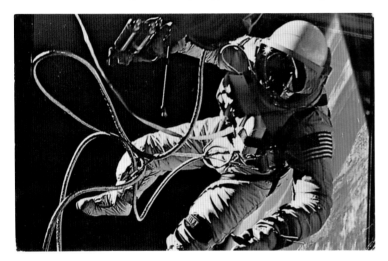

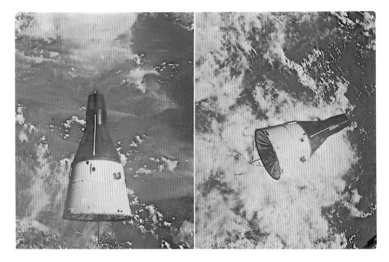

February 8th.   Deltrand in Daytona Beach to Mrs Alfred in Eastport NY, *We toured Cape Kennedy yesterday by bus. We rode 60 miles & saw all the launchpads & that big!! building. Some snow you had, eh!* This is Edward White of Gemini 4 the first American orbiting spacewalker. This and 67g are among the first postcards which cannot be said to have a proper way up.   67f

December 24th.   Leslie & Ruth to the Fischers in Chicago *What an exciting place this is... 2 1/2 hour tour of the Space Center. We have a lovely apartment: in Daytona Beach for 4 days. Just wish the children would stop serving mushroom soup for breakfast & wanting to cook!* These are Gemini 6 and 7 which made a rendezvous after 13 days in space.   67g

February 23rd.   Roger to the Shillakers in New Milton ...*here I am in the most fascinating city in Europe. Its like any other modern city but there's no denying that the "wall" adds to the excitement. Seen "wall", checkpoint Charlie...* The card testifies to what a deadeningly prosaic object the Berlin Wall was with its no man's land and tank traps and its use of the extant street facades plus a reinforcing of concrete. Not here and not yet, on the Western side, the bright graffiti of its final state.   67h

September 3rd.   Esther in Mayfair to Mrs G in Atlanta, Ga., ... *ate dinner at this club and won 50 - something for me to do - saw a wonderful show, That Girl In My Soup - haven't missed uncle.* The mob had moved in on London's gambling world. George Raft whose Mafia film persona merged with his life was, in 1968, barred from Britain (by Roy Jenkins) leaving the Colony Club to gamble on without his name. The owner of numberplate NM 777 still prefers to remain anonymous.   67i

May 12th. Norah & Tom to Ann in Cheltenham, ...*have been to Lewis's and booked in for the 18th May.* The Roman Catholic Cathedral of Liverpool was opened on the 14th May and had already been dubbed The Mersey Funnel. It also bears a strange resemblance to the Mercury Space Capsule (see 66j). Designed by Frank Gibberd it incorporates the crypt of the original Lutyens project abandoned in 1940.　　　67j

July 11th. Greta to her mother in Southampton, *We have just had a nice meal here on the M6... just leaving for the last 60 miles or so. It's been a beautiful day.* Forte's Keele (1963) was one of the bridge type service stations which excited visitors in the early days when, as here, motorists were welcomed by uniformed stewardesses (though probably not by the time this card was sent).　　　67k

August 15th. Fred in Birmingham to Beth in Castle Bromwich, *So sorry I could not make it last Friday, but it was raining heavily on the morning and I had left my mac at the caravan. Please let me know when to come to your house again.* The Alec Issigonis Mini was the emblematic smart car of the sixties, the first truly classless car (which by 1967 however was available in various de luxe and souped up versions) and an exact contemporary of the motorway.　　　67l

Precise date unclear. Mark & Lana at the Club Méditerranée in Portiragnes to Miss Jackson in London E18, *We spend a good deal of time on the beach watching muscular and tanned French disporting under the sizzling sun... we live in tents (and there are 900 of us, mostly French) which works surprisingly well even for born non-campers like us.* Club Med becomes the Butlins of the newly sophisticated who know their way around.　　　67m

June 26th. Susan in Montreal to Mr & Mrs Leach in Oakworth, Yorks, *Dear Nana & Grandad, Hi! The weather is really grand, but is Expo ever crowded! We tried to get into the British Pavilion, but the line-up was the longest in the entire place. But everything is really worth seeing.* The caption calls the British Pavilion 'an exciting group of buildings, reflecting the maturity, the strength, and the aspirations of the British Nation', whatever that may mean.　　　67n

August 27th. J in Stockholm to friends in Bristol talks of the great switch from driving on the left to on the right. *Arrived Friday evening & started work & haven't stopped since. Have filmed blind people being taught about roads. Have done ...road signs being changed. The actual changeover is on Sat & Sunday & we look like being up all night. We have special police permission to drive during the no traffic period. Everything is very expensive.*　　　67o

"SO DOES MINE"

June 19th.   Mary in St Louis, *Donna said hello. They have a cute duplex, and are getting settled down. We drove down to see the Arch on the front of this card last night...* Mary was right to see this beautiful aluminium clad structure by night when its faceted surface glitters and shimmers and makes an eerie noise like a deep shivering moan. Eero Saarinen its architect did not live to see it completed in 1964. 67p

July 7th.   Fred & Jean in Weston-Super-Mare to Dad in Sunbury, *Weather better now. Fred is out of the snooker again. He lost it when the other fellow got a foul shot in, but he wouldn't argue about it. See you soon.* Very good joke but Davo is no match for the Bamforth artists: I think this is what pop music would call a cover version of an earlier comic with a more bashful looking couple.   67q

August 9th.   Lorna in Leningrad to Mr & Mrs M in London W5, *Your tent is giving marvellous service!!... yesterday went to the summer palace by hydrofoil along the Neva.* Here is Lenin in a specially relevant place in St. Petersburg/Petrograd/Leningrad, the Finland Station, at which he arrived in a sealed train sixty years before, and to which he summoned his supporters in the city where he would assume power in the October revolution.   67r

July 31st.   Audrey & Bernard send routine seaside greetings from Broadstairs and trust that Aunt Edith in Cropwell Bishop is both unshockable and will get a joke involving computers (not quite yet in the general domain of experience). Taylor's sketchy machine is of a size that at the time would not have the power of a present-day laptop. Mini computers had just come into production the size of a family fridge.   67s

October 6th.   D & V in Manchester to Mr & Mrs Armstrong in RAF Northwood, *Dear Mum & Dad many thanks for your letter... and especially for the parcel - all sorts of things that will be very useful. Hope you are well - we are! Term (i.e. lectures) starts again to-morrow. On Friday night we went to see Half Way Up The Street by Peter Ustinov which was having a trial run in M/C before going to London. We found it very funny... and the theme - the reaction of a retired general on meeting his 'hippy' children - should appeal to you two... Thanks again for the parcel.* 67t

November 1st. Mary Toms in Willamette, Illinois to Mrs Snyder in Shawnee Mission, Kansas *Mid Anchell EN 26462 promised to do my names for me after Nov 5th sorry let you down. love M.* The campaign message tells the voting public to 'Vote like your whole world depended on it. Remember Polls don't vote, People do!' Things are hotting up for the November 5th election. This card published by United Citizens for Nixon/Agnew plugs the family man aspect of the candidate and happens to include Julie Nixon's boyfriend who bears the useful name of David Eisenhower. This is perhaps the only political campaign (except perhaps for that of Paderewski in Poland, see 01n) to have used a contender's prowess at the piano as a recommending factor. Nixon won and embarked on a presidency that was to end in shame and humiliation.   68a

April 25th. Cindy & Chris on a shopping spree to Julie D in Bardney, Lincs. *Having fantastic time but our feet are killing. Gorgous males around! I have bought shoes & bag. Cindy has got jacket, shoes, bag, jumper - super. See you Monday - Erk.* The showing of Cinerama's Grand Prix, a tedious motor-racing film, dates the view to the year before.   68b

July 20th. Audrey in big capitals, carefully spaced, writes heroically to Charlotte D in Albany, NY. *Hi Charlotte, was glad to hear from you but I was unable to bring my braille writer here. will type you letter soon unless I manage to make it to Albany, then I will call you to make arrangements.* The city, so often described in messages as dirty, looks outwardly clean in crisp light.   68c

July 25th.   GH to the Millers in Meopham. *Thought of you when I saw Lively Lady.*
Have you seen her? It seems incredible to sail the seven seas in this dainty little craft.
I am full of admiration for any sailor let alone a lone one. The boat had been on show
in London. Alec Rose had been knighted for his round the world exploit a few weeks
before GH sent the card.   68d

June 4th.   Ann to the Westlands in Ipswich. *Dear Nannie and grandpa. Today we went down to*
the beach and paddled, daddy didn't go in because he said it was too cold but
I didn't think so. Evidently Daddy was not made of the same stuff as Henry Blogg
whose amazing record of selfless devotion to saving lives is commemorated here with
a dignified monument.   68e

May 24th.   BH in Indian Head, Saskatchewan, sends birthday greetings to TP in
London, *why go to Milan when you can see it bolder and brighter at Pete's Café in Rocheport,*
Mo? & eat one of those burgers just like they have on the table. The name
of the artist who made this version with Charles Goslin is Pete E Christus, who may be
the proprietor. Every drive or jaunt in the US yields some such wonder.   68f

August 5th.   Harry writes to Frank R in Egham, *As you did not see the memorial I*
thought you would like this card. Tom looks great for his 81. Also seen Wilkie... the
Bush wire had gone round that I was in town. Jackie Kennedy came for the
dedication of this memorial in 1965. In 1968 she married the shipping tycoon and
playboy Aristotle Onassis.   68g

October 3rd.   Steve in Athens, Georgia to Mr & Mrs W in Doereen, Georgia, *Thought*
you would all appreciate this post-card. It tore me up when I saw it & just had to buy
it to send to his fans! Cute eh? Maddox drove blacks from his restaurant in 1964 and
shut up shop rather than desegregate it. Elected Governor with the support of the Ku
Klux Klan he fought integration in vain yet served a second term as Lieut. Governor
under his replacement Jimmy Carter.   68h

December 18th.   Richard in Montreal to RWW in the Estate Dept of British Railways,
The expo site is extremely interesting and many of the pavilions are still in position,
except for the Russian one, which has been removed. We landed about an hour after
the hijacked plane which you no doubt heard about. Buckminster Fuller's geodesic
dome had all the futuristic dynamism that the NY Fair's globe had lacked. It went up in flames in
1976, but the principle had been proved.   68i

BUTLIN'S CLACTON
The Viennese Ballroom

Anchorage
ALASKA

CLUB
25

September 5th.   Brenda to Miss Snell in Salisbury, *The weather is terrible. The wind and sea is pounding in on the beach at the moment. Gale force winds. Everything here is superb though: food, shows, so it does not matter much about the weather.* Future anthropologists will puzzle over these images and the meaning of the rituals. The card's title, Viennese Ballroom, will not help much.   68j

March 28th.   Glenn Weiss is serving in Alaska and writes to the Mantles in O'Fallon, Illinois. *A couple of guys and me have taken a couple of good long walks half hunting and half sightseeing. I am still working in the auto shop. I've got KP [kit parade] tomorrow on my day off I'm not too happy about that. Almost all the snow has melted.* Glenn makes Alaska sound almost a pleasant posting.   68k

February 21st.   Gerald in Grenoble to Mr & Mrs H in Basingstoke. *I had a wonderful two weeks of action. This photo shows the opening ceremony. I saw a little of it from the outside.* The Winter Olympics was remarkable for the performances of the Frenchman Killy who took three gold medals. The blue stairs are a masterstroke, giving the event a sense of exotic ritual.   68l

September 30th.   Anon, in Kuwait Yacht Club, to Paul etc. in Kensington. *Thursday, not that it makes any difference. Nice job that they make of the super paste up... Its hot (120°) Its sandy like in yer underpants. its not easy with thick Rabs getting in yer way. Its tiring. Things going wrong. No drink. No women so you might say in many ways I'm a touch clitfaced xx.*   68m

WVN.I.   WOLVERHAMPTON. DUDLEY STREET

FYLINGDALES MOOR

October 23rd.   Mike Horowitz, in Wolverhampton to read his poem about the Wolverhampton Wanderers (their once great football team), writes to JR & LP, *Wolverhampton is foggy. & I wish I was in Notting Hill/& my true love in my arms/& mushrooms in our grill/& politicians all transferred to Midland Dairy Farms/Leaving the city free for us to make such music as we can.* The card is too cheerful to capture the mood of Wolverhampton as I remember it. The sixties did not pass that way.   68n

August 5th.   May in Whitby to Mrs H in Patrick Brompton, Yorks. *Having a good time. Jean & Sara are paddling. L & F are shopping. The boarding house is very good - huge breakfasts. Plenty of bingo here.* These famous golf-balls were officially Radomes built in 1964 to provide a 4 minute warning of nuclear attack. A disgruntled employee once spread rumours of their detecting battleship-sized UFO's. They were replaced in 1992 by a less exciting looking system.   68o

WHICH BALLOON WOULD YOU LIKE
LITTLE NODDY?

Michael Horowitz was and is the editor of New Departures. This card was used as the basis of an etching, Dudley Street. At the end of the century Wolves, although not in the Premier League, were holding their own in the First Division.

May 5th.   Ann in Keswick to Elizabeth in St Mary Cray. *It's raining! we are going to a museum & on a boat trip. have you been to church. I am going tonight. we have a nice caravan its cream & blue all for now.* Enid Blyton, creator of Noddy and other staples of childhood reading, died in November 1968 twenty years before political correctness would consider her world sexist and racist and Noddy, with his gollies etc. would be banned from many libraries.   68p

March 30th.   From Gail in NJ to Sgt William S in Charleston, *Hi Billy, I think this one is going to be a doozy. There is (No more. Gail just ran off with the garage man). Guess what? she came back with a fireman! Boy these small towns He gets to know everything.* The splash bag is described as 'wonderfully gay and unbelievably useful... an original creation by National Handicrafts of Des Moines'. The whole still-life is a poem in pink and lime.   68q

WEST LONDON AIR TERMINAL

October 30th.   Dirck in Philip, SD, to Mr & Mrs Schields in Pike County. *Boys want to know what is our Man for next President, one & all are for V of Richard Nixon the man with experience with D Eisenhower. he will be the best.* This motel looks ripe for Norman Bates when he has served his term. I can see that vacancy sign winking now.   68r

March 17th.   To Mr & Mrs M in Derby, *Dear Mummy & Daddy. Arrived safe, lovley hotle. We ar now at the picture. on our way to Palma. Love Chris & sister.* In 1963 the West London Air Terminal was built in the Cromwell Road where passengers could check in with their baggage and then be whisked off to Heathrow by coach to join their plane. The full nightmare of late 20th century travel had not yet quite arrived, though the Package Tour world was growing with ominous speed, spelling doom for such arrangements.   68s

September 12th.   Fred & Jean (& Ann) are in Clacton this year and write to Mr & Mrs Crook in Stanwell, *Dear Mum & Dad, Give us Pontin's every time. But we are enjoying the change. No sleep no food no sun. Even Ann woke up before 5 o'clock this morning, see you soon.* The words 'I've got a Tiger in my Tank' were part of a massive publicity campaign for Esso petrol with posters and car stickers all over the place. It was fun, but since people stopped at whatever garage was nearest or cheapest and the fuel sold by the various companies was identical one wonders what effect it could have had.   68t

969

July 5th.   Sally Thomas at Cape Kennedy to Jane Ferguson in Sutton Coldfield, Warks., *We are all on vacation in Florida and have seen the rocket that will take the man to the moon.* The cards celebrating the lunar adventure were, with appropriate stamps, prepared in advance using photographs of earlier Apollo missions. This, despite the announcement in the then futuristic, now nostalgic, typeface, depicts Apollo 9 which carried out the first tests in space of a lunar module (here sketchily portrayed top right). After a series of man on the moon cards (see 70l) the postcard representations of space exploration started to dwindle, as indeed did public and government interest. However in human terms and as an aspect of the Cold War, this was the big one.   69a

September 21st.   Michael to Mr Egerton in Thomaston, Maine, on a 1963 view, *Have thoroughly enjoyed the English way of life for the past two weeks. Doris has a lovley home you would enjoy her lovley garden.* Strange how Americans have homes whereas the British have houses or flats. In England only the stately and the invalid can be found in homes.   69b

August 17th.   Caroline, Elaine & Helen to David H in Hipperholme, Yorks., *Having a super time. The boat is lovely. When we got on the weather was fine but since it has not been as nice. Yesterday it was quite ruff. This morning arrived and saw the moon men going through new york.* Manhattan offers inexhaustible opportunities to any photographer with an eye for a splash of red on a foreground barge.   69c

August 7th.   Fay & Ed in Bangor to Dr O'Relf in St Louis, Illinois, *Greetings from Wales! We are kept busy meeting everybody from Lord Harlech, Jackie K's ex-beau, to Lord Anglesey. Although the people are friendly and the land is wildly beautiful, we prefer Germany. We spent last weekend in Dublin Ireland and I found some nice clothes there.* See 69t for the full regalia this ordinary-looking chap had to wear.   69d

July 26th.   Gillian in Caernarvon for the Investiture of the Prince of Wales to Miss JH in Wallasey. *When Charles & I get married the lady in white will be known as Auntie Lizzie to you. Apart from all the people the castle would be very nice.* The castle (see 62t) looks more kitsch than ever with its Astroturf and banners and the heraldic plumes on the plastic awning which resemble a giant teddy bear.   69e

January 23rd.   Dad on the road to his wife, Mrs Zakutynski, in Moss Trailer Park, Bradento, Florida, *It is 2am and have a half stop in Florence, South Carolina. Keep Fluffy away from the flowers & plants near the trailer as Dick put Fertilizer on them and it may be harmful to him. The big bush at the back corner is OK. Bus is very good, had some sleep already.* This is what happened to the charabanc.   69f

June 14th.   S & D to Mr & Mrs W in Streatham Hill, *We are on the overnight train to Toulouse - sharing a compartment with four other rather garlicy-smelling Frenchmen! Thank you for your card and letter (whoops!) Love.* This was a small price to pay for the latest Car-Sleeper Express seen here setting off in an immaculately posed photograph (you can always spot a model by the angle of her knees).   69g

Virgin Rock, Ballybunion, Co. Kerry, Ireland.

Severn Bridge from Picnic Hill, Top Rank Motorport.

August 24th.   Felicity to Mrs Arkell in Shaftesbury, *...Mixed weather. good for fishing at present! Michael has caught seven salmon... We were sad about the riots - but we have just driven through Derry, Belfast etc & one sees little except broken windows in odd streets.* Felicity evidently did not go down the right streets. The scale of the Protestant/Catholic riots caused British troops to be flown in 'for a limited period' (which turned out to be thirty years).   69h

August 3rd.   Robert, Mary & Liz to the Dixons in Morpeth, *Just about to go over the bridge we are getting some petrol for the second time. it is half past one. There is some blue sky now but it has poured nearly all the way & has been foggy. We also went through some floods & through a farm to avoid them.* The wonderful new Severn Bridge was still an adventure. Motorway service stations made postcard sending an easy pleasure and provided some telling images of the times.   69i

September 25th.   A request from the Doveys to Family Favourites on the BBC for Cpl Keith D & his wife Beryl *for their 3rd Wedding Anniversary. They are stationed at RAF Seletar Singapore. Hope the record we've chosen fits in for they do a lot of sailing out there. It is 'Messing About On The River'.* Worcester's lovely cricket ground during play. The batsman awaits a ball from a fast bowler (judging from the position of the wicketkeeper).   69j

September 14th.   Jean in Beirut to the Bucknalls in Shoreham, Sussex ...*you would all appreciate the life, scenery & potential here. The war murmurs are heard off stage & I am even more pro-Arab than before. Philip drove us and a client from Turkey to this truly fabulous grotto yesterday.* Not for long would the murmurs of war be off stage. For the next thirty years Beirut would be the focus of regional antagonisms and would end up in ruins.   69k

June 13th.   Ethel in Cirencester to Mrs A in Wetherley, Yorks. *Enjoying the lovely weather... not too hot & the country is so green. I* think *I saw the Concorde fly over us today.* It is quite possible that she did since the UK-made Concorde 002 started its trial flights in April. There was in fact no likelihood of anyone mistaking its shape and the blistering sound it produced.   69l

September 4th.   Anthony sends a card of the New York Stock Exchange to Misses N & JM, *Having a wonderful time. Fascinating watching the buying and selling on the floor here. Trading suspended while I was here - computer failed - Loud cheers on the floor.* Despite such hiccups the financial world was changing, with the Chemical Bank in New York introducing, in 1969, the automatic teller.   69m

September 25th.   T to BH in Indian Head, Saskatchewan, *This is the one I meant with some bits left over from the Festival of Britain (pools, pavement, fountains etc.) and a wonderful benchful of people.* Much of the layout of the Festival Gardens in Battersea remains as it was in 1951 thought the tree walk has gone and the strange tent called the Dance Pavilion. Some memory of mine was fixed here and is frozen beyond explanation in sunlight and silence in the foreground group and the flowers.   69n

July 21st.   Posted at Jodrell Bank by Vic, Flo & Colin with the simple message, *Awaiting a moon landing.* An event now just over a week away. This is the Mark 2 radio telescope, even more powerful (and elegant) than its predecessor. The form is familiar in principle since, in twenty years time, the streets of the world will have become festooned with little toy simulacra of this mighty dish for the reception of satellite TV.   69o

69a. A Dixon-Louis production. L6/8607/T. Photo: NASA

69b. Publisher unknown. PT 1064

69c. Acacia Card Co. No 64

69d. Dixon. Wales 7726

69e. Ministry of Public Buildings & Works. IC11

69f. Dexter Press. DT 1485.C

69g. SNCF 1968 No 39

69h. John Hinde. Photo: John Hinde
John Hinde only rarely appears as the photographer of the cards he produced. His early work in the 40's showed him as a restrained perfectionist in colour photography. But in his postcard production he learned to 'turn up' the colour of the images taken by Ludwig and others to brilliant effect in a world haunted by red cars and ladies with vivid dresses. He sold his business in 1972 when sales had reached the fifty million mark. He died in 1997.

69i. Valentine. ET 5293R

69j. Salmon

69k. Jack P Dadian. Beirut/Kruger

69l. Salmon 2651c

69m. NY Stock Exchange 17.48.7

69n. Publisher unknown PT 8015
This is the principal source for Benches. See TP Works & Texts.

69o. Dixon. SP. 1347

69p. Ministry of Public Buildings & Works. I.C.44. Photo: Norman Parkinson

69q. CMS (Nigeria) Bookshops, Lagos

69r. Zoological Society of London. PT 7812. Photo: M Lyster

69s. Publisher unknown

69t. Ranscombe Photographics 10M. N1505

September 26th.   A cryptic message from EP in Kensington to Mr Keatey in Brooklyn, *So far no action. Everything else is AOK.* One almost feels sorry for the young Charles in the mad regalia of the investiture, whose symbolic staff and sword he grips as if his knuckles would break. He is trying hard to look like someone in history. Norman Parkinson, a royal regular, was responsible for the high camp of the photograph. The fatal design mismatch is the old style ermine cape over a modern military uniform making neither look distinguished or convincing.   69p

June 26th.   Caroline in Kano, Nigeria to Miss Fulford at St Francis School, Bexhill, *Arrived here safely and I am having a lovely time. The weather is beautiful... as it is the wet season. I'm afraid this card is one of the best I could find, because of the war we are short of quite a few things. Please send my love to all the school.* Caroline is very lucky to be in Kano far from the fighting in the Biafran war whose pictures of starving children provoked such outrage in Britain (but no stop to supplying arms). This Muslim drummer may be from the same area.   69q

April 14th.   J in London to Mr & Mrs S M in Whitchurch. On the back of this card of Guy the Gorilla, J sums up the animal's expression with the title of a sixties book of popular psychology (by Eric Berne) 'The Games People Play!'. Guy came to the London Zoo in 1947 and was an instant favourite, though mothers, trying to avoid explanations, sometimes ushered their young away in his more priapic moments. He died in an operating theatre in 1978.   69r

March 3rd.   Linda Sharp in Irving, Texas, sends an invitation to her neighbour Jean Askew for Sunday March 9th at 2pm. She is showing Overture to Springtime described as a Concerto of Spring Savings including these night-dresses called respectively Nocturn Gown and Rhapsody, and each available at $15.98 (an interesting variant on the traditional $15.99). Black and pink was a combination very much of the time as was the Dead Body make-up.   69s

October 17th.   John in Belfast to Mr & Mrs J T in Hampstead, *This really is a beautiful city as you can see and the barbed wire, petrol bombs, troops & strange opening hours add to its many attractions - wish you were here - I need you! love. P.S. But aren't the P & P's super!* Perhaps Ethel (69h) might have noticed a difference two months on when British troops were ordered to shoot at snipers and teargas was being used in the Shankhill Road.   69t

BAC/SUD-AVIATION CONCORDE.

The maiden flight of Concorde prototype 002. The Concorde supersonic airliner is expected to enter service in 1973 and will carry up to 144 passengers at speeds of around 1400 mph.

September 10th.   D in Aldershot to Hugh Matthews in Penkridge, Staffs. *Just think - next time you'll be old enough to come!* Concorde, which still looks the most advanced aircraft in the everyday sky (and has just flown over Peckham as I am writing) was over thirty years old at the Millennium. Despite the caption it did not enter service until January 1976. This is 002 the first UK-built model which, two months after this card was posted, first attained its designated cruising speed of Mach 2. The contrast between Concorde and ordinary flights from London to New York has increased as Jumbo Jets (also a product of 1970) have become slower   70a

May 13th.   Cecilia to Mrs Kestell-Cornish in Barnstaple, *It is a raging hot day... saw the Royal Academy... walked to Victoria via 'Buck House' explored Swan & Edgar - Tried to get a copy of the Christian Year at Foyles but no luck. am now exhausted...* If that was her eccentric route I'm not surprised. A half built Centre Point in the distance dates the view to 1966.   70b

August 2nd.   Tony writes to Dorothy in Hanover, Mass., *Hello Silly Granny, I'm having a wonderful time here - Next summer Mr Kafazas wants me to work for him $2.00 an hour. Start at $1.50. I'll talk to you on the phone when I get home. Goodbye for now.* The exposure makes a second river of headlights dramatising and giving distance to the view.   70c

July 12th.   Lemore, Gord & Jack to the Holdings in St Thomas, Ontario, *We left Wales yesterday and are now in Scotland. Our choir did very well - won <u>third</u> prize in the International Competition (19 choirs). Bulgaria and Iowa (USA) placed 1st and 2nd. We sang on the stage pictured upper right of this card.* They must have been good to gain even 3rd prize in this highly competitive festival.   70d

October 23rd.   RM in Kwangchon to Janet in London SE5, *Expect you're holding the fort womanfully. Hope you've not already had nine of the same card from the Delegation. Chief overall impression since last visit is that people are even more relaxed, confident and lively. Thanks to Chairman Mao and the Cultural Revolution.* This is the Yangtse Bridge at Nanking.   70e

February 6th.   To Jean Laune in Poole, *Arrived safely. Very nice house. Got a lovely little dog (Rex) bred Collie. Sharing with a girl from Skipton, Yorks. called Linda Burton. She's 18 1/2 very nice (right Yorkshire). How's Kaiser. Letter on way to mum Love Virginia. PS. Getting on OK with course so far.* A student arrives in London. Naturally she heads straight for Carnaby Street (see 71a).   70f

August 11th.   Auntie Madge (as Aunties have been observed to do) finds a good card to send to Trevor in Cuffley, *...weather perfect & not too hot even in Madrid today there is a breeze. Toured the city by coach this evening & thought of you as we passed the Real Madrid ground so here is the picture.* Real Madrid were at their peak and were Spanish champions yet again in 1970.   70g

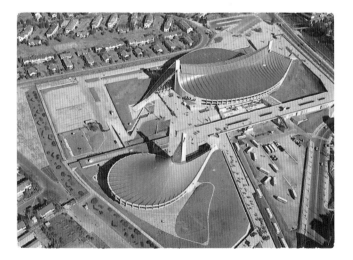

December 29th.   Bobby in Tokyo to Alex S in Aberdeen, *Tell Hector & all the staff I'm asking for them of course don't forget Angelo. he's quite a loner isn't he, you don't know where he's going to turn up.* The stadium complex for the 1964 Olympics is Kenzo Tange's masterpiece (he built the Hiroshima Peace Centre in 1949) and demonstrates how in architecture engineering can be the liberator of poetry.   70h

June 15th.   Colin to Jan in Hanwell *...waiting to go to Novi Sad 5am... arguing the toss with an immigration bloke at Subotica Station who insisted I must have a visa for Yugoslavia - I insisted that since 69 English visa's were not necessary. Language problems certainly a barrier... Palic we stayed in for 3 days during installation of the computer.* Palic and Subotica were both bombed by NATO in 1999.   70i

July 12th.   H to Mrs Pucheninz in Saltdean. *Dear Auntie Lal, arrived yesterday on the start of my 15 days holiday of the USSR.* Holidays behind the iron curtain were easy to arrange if you followed prescribed paths, like visiting the Soviet Exhibition of Economic Achievement. Its fronting statue by Vera Mukhina is that featured on top of the Soviet Pavilion in the Paris Expo of 1937 (see 37p).   70j

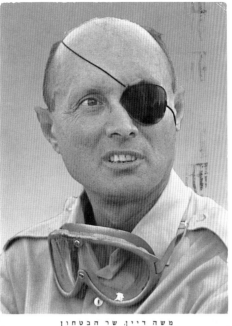

משה דיין, שר הבטחון
MOSHE DAYAN, MINISTER OF DEFENCE

August 11th.   Norm in Jerusalem to Dad & Mary in Wilmslow, *Hi!... we're having a good time. Sun, swimming, food etc. both understand why you haven't written which reminds me - I hope the move goes well love Adale & me.* Moshe Dayan the flamboyant General and Politician (and amateur archaeologist) was the man many wanted to lead Israel instead of Golda Meir who was elected in 1969. He died in 1987 after making Israel a military force that the Arab world took on at its peril.   70k

June 24th.   To Julie Fox in Los Gatos, Cal. *Good morning. This is a postcard from Nasa in Houston. Velly interesting! We went on a tour there. It was really neat. we saw the food the Astronauts eat. Yuck. It looks terrible. Tomorrow we're going to Florida and Disney World! Yeh! luv, Barbara.* This is Buzz Aldrin with Armstrong reflected in his visor. The culminating moment of the labours (and lives) of so many.   70l

Palm-fringed Beach—Palmenstrand—Plage et Palmiers   Photo : E. Ludwig, John Hinde Studios

January 4th.   Anon in Mombassa to Lawrence J in Maldon, Essex, *Christmas dinners 1. at Kimpurs 2. my cousins in London. 3. Egyptian turkey & pud in aeroplane. 4. Ugandan in Nairobi. 5. Kenyan in train to coast... now off we truck in camping car v. apprehensive, full of fears of dark East Africa to see wild life & hopefully not nourish it or be knifed for our goodies.* John Hinde via E Ludwig provides a reassuring and literally palm-fringed idyll; a generic card, cleverly mentioning no country.   70m

May 30th.   *Enjoying it all... our hotel in Latin Quarter - good position for viewing riots, brick-throwing, baton charges & tear gas! We've got mixed up with a private viewing of a new exhibition at Versailles with the whole of the Corps Diplomatique & cream of Paris society. I went up the Eiffell Tower v.expensive (8frs = 12/-) but A preferred to go down sewers.* Student unrest was always near the surface. Monier makes a super-cliché out of a cliché and the terrible inheritors of Monmartre's artistic glory.   70n

Severn Bridge from Top Rank Motorport Restaurant.   LT-5295R

May 5th.   Anne from Teignmouth to Miss EF in Sidmouth *Sunday TV service came from Gawsworth rather disappointing the scenery from the Village, R Richards read the lesson - is Wednesday the 13th to soon to come to you or will Misty be rather touchy still? Let me know. I will bring sheets & food. No more news about play school. hope you have some good scrabble.* Everything in the card looks new, the bridge, the Motorport Restaurant and what seems to be the new manager and his new assistant posing stiffly. 70o

A CENTURY OF
BRITISH POSTCARDS
1870·1970

70a. Photo Precision Ltd

70b. Harvey Barton L23

70c. Nester's Map & Guide Co. K30

70d. Salmon

70e. Foreign Languages Press, Peking

70f. Kardorama

70g. La Artistica Espanola, Madrid

70h. Japan, Travel Bureau Inc, Japan

70i. ZGP, Ljubljana, R1676

70j. Planeta, Moscow.
The title of the sculpture is Worker and Collective Farmer. Their respective hammer and sickle unite to form the Soviet emblem.

70k. Palphot, Herzlia 8671

70l. G P Slide Co., Houston. 310121/Nasa

70m. John Hinde. Photo: E Ludwig

70n. Albert Monier 10823

70o. Valentine ET 5295R

70p. Published by the Postcard Association of Great Britain to celebrate the centenary of the postcard.

70q. Frith Z.3.
Despite Boycott's 157 in the second innings the Rest of the World won by 4 wickets, thanks to a century by Kanhai.

70r. Publisher unknown, Portugal (detail).

August 3rd.   Olive in Reigate to Miss R in Redhill, *Noddy - Thought you'd like this, it's interesting, I've lived in 5 reigns, so I spose you have to... This heat is too much for me. Do you like it? I feel like a rag.* Had 1970 really been the centenary of the British Picture Postcard it would have put the title of this book in question. Various forms of what the specialist collector now calls Postal Cards were issued after 1870 but the picture postcard as it appears in the early years of the century was only legalised in Britain in 1894. Since this was in the reign of Queen Victoria the centenary card has got the general idea right. Unfortunately, for all the efforts of the Postcard Association who published it, the effect of the image is rather drab and its sequence reads rather like an indictment of British portraiture than a celebration of the rich visual treasury that the postcard has provided for (now) over a hundred years.   70p

Z.3 OVAL CRICKET GROUND

August 14th.   Christopher & Michael to the Rev. A in Salisbury hospital, *Dear Grandpa, we both thoroughly enjoyed our day in spite of the slowness of England's batting. Saw many players notably P.B.H. May and J.C.Laker and Peter West !!!...* It's ten past five in the afternoon in high summer. What better place to be than at the Oval with a Test Match in progress. But 1970 was no ordinary year, for the scheduled visit of the South African team was cancelled as part of the banning of the Republic from world sport. South Africa would not be seen again at the Oval for a generation. A series was arranged with a Rest of the World XI. The Rev. A's grandsons saw the likes of Sobers, Kanhai and (no doubt the slow scoring culprit) Geoffrey Boycott. Had they looked up to the Members' Pavilion balcony shown here they would also have seen the present writer.   70q

October 2nd.   Victor in Matosinhos, Portugal, to Mr & Mrs B in Bridlington. *Security measures in all airports following the skyjacking has resulted in long delays. Everyone is screened and sometimes searched. I am now waiting for a plane back to Lisbon which is already 1 hour late. It is very hot here just now, hotter than usual.* Three highjacked airliners captured by the Palestine Liberation Front were blown up in Jordan in mid September. Over three hundred passengers were taken hostage. All except 56 were released. These were kept hostage until September 30th when Western governments capitulated and agreed to release the terrorist Leila Khaled.   70r

October 24th.   The fact that Carnaby Street has been the subject of postcards for over a year or so (see 70f) means that it is no longer a secret gathering place for the in crowd but has become an institution and is evolving into a tourist trap. Its denizens are now there to be photographed (just as punks would later become the posing Masaai of Piccadilly). The sharp styles of the sixties have had their metropolitan day. John Stephen's shop can still be seen on the left. It was he, coming from the gay underworld of the original Vince's in the fifties, that started a trend (followed by other boutiques and then the whole fashion world). Even in the pedestrianised precinct of the new century the spirit survives in some small degree. But there is already a whiff of English Heritage about the area.   71a

August 10th.   Aileen and John write to the Rutherfords in Edinburgh, *We've been round a fair bit of London... just walking round... boy you should see it there's a whole street quite a big one and all the people stay in it are Chinnese. They call this bit Chinna Town.* The new paved area and Tom Jones (with Albert Finney) showing at the Pavilion date this view to 1963.   71b

November 7th.   NY's premier postcard club (which now meets at the New Yorker Hotel) here celebrates its jubilee with nostalgic views of the Flat Iron Building, the already demolished Singer Building and of course the Statue of Liberty. Postcards that were brand new when it started in 1946 are now, in a new century, almost as evocative and sought after.   71c

September 30th.   Lena to Roberta W in Union City NJ, *you have been so sweet to 'cheer' me want you to know I have improved some can walk to bathroom sit up in rocker but shakes in right arm hard for me to write.* Jimmie Rodgers the Singing Brakeman is honoured here in Meridian, MS., by the line he worked on. He died in 1933 during a recording session in New York.   71d

August 4th.   Peggy & Carl in Kitty Hawk NC to Mr & Mrs E in Paignton, Devon, *we didn't make it to Florida... Today we visited this memorial to the Wright Bros. and going down to Cape Hatteras tomorrow.* To the left in the mid-distance is Kill Devil Hill and the Wright memorial where man first properly flew (see 08a). What was new at the beginning of this book is already matter for monuments and Visitors Centres. 71e

BERWICK CHURCH, THE ANNUNCIATION (VANESSA BELL). *Sussex*

September 27th.   Richard in Bedford to SWW in Retford. *Best wishes for your year at Wye College... I have just started teaching history in Bedford, and fought a bye-election (as Environment Candidate) for the Town Council (got 515 votes, nearly 20% of total - quite encouraging).* The party changed its name from Ecology to Environment to Green but, like Vanessa Bell, never rose to be a true contender.   71f

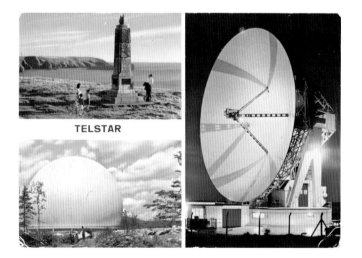

TELSTAR

July 8th.   Richard in Penzance to his parents in Bristol, *We haven't been here but I thought the picture would interest Dad. Incidentally, Marconi may have been a great chap but our portable radio won't give a whisper! We are eating Cornish pasties in the car on the beach.* The Marconi Memorial is linked with the Bell Telstar Station in Maine and the Goonhilly Dish Aerial that received the first TV pictures via satellite in 1962, sixty one years after Marconi's first transmission.   71h

February 1st.   Nancy in Accra to JT in Essex, *...we have had a very quiet revolution here, no bang bangs thank goodness, and everybody is waiting to see what happens next. This place is not nearly so animated as it used to be and many of our old friends are gone.* Ghana, though there have been many coups, has never gone in for the full revolutionary bloodbath.   71g

Bonhomie House. Opening by Elsie and Doris Waters.

October 24th.   GH in Southampton to Miss H in Maidenhead, *It's a lovely place. got everything & I can get my Beer. That's the boss on the left: his wife says I'm like her Mother.* One guesses that GH is a resident at Bonhomie House. Everyone in the audience is certainly old enough to remember Elsie and Doris Waters who, as Gert & Daisy, were entertainment stalwarts of the wartime radio music hall in shows like Workers Playtime.   71i

The Fortes Excelsior Motor Lodge, nr. Pontefract, Yorkshire. 5672XR

April 18th.   RM in Stockwell to TP in London, *Under separate cover you should receive the contact-prints of Tuesday's photo-session... also you will find a lovely shot by E Ludwig of the Oval, Cliftonville.* The sender of the card is gripped by what are often called boring postcards but which are in fact quite the opposite in their visionary distillation, as here, of life's absolutes.   71j

June 1st.   JT at Osborn-Smiths Wax Museum, Brading, IOW to Camberwell, *Ideal for the kiddies. Jasper was tickled pink by 'The Assassination' though it wasn't really Janice's cup of tea. Enoch [Powell] is speaking at the fête here next week so the Island isn't as conservative as people like to make out.* This bedroom scene is only one of the intimations present in 71j.   71k

December 18th.   Eva & Wallace in San Luis Obispo, Cal. to Mr & Mrs S in Santa Cruz, *Dear Blanche & Roberta & H ...we had dinner at the Madonna Inn coffee shop. We sure enjoyed our visit with you folks.* This is Room 137 at the Inn, The Cave Man Room, still available in 2000 (with bigger TV) at $185 per night.   71l

March 23rd.   Daddy in Djakarta, to S & FT in London NW3, *Thankyou very much for the apples, sweets, pencil and the message. yes, I am having a nice time. The weather is hot 80°... There are many soldiers around wearing pretty berets, but I haven't seen many weapons.* The bull in this cremation rite looks strangely Minoan.   71m

December 12th.   RM in Stockwell to TP. *This is an attempt to get in one more card before Christmas. It was on current sale in Amsterdam in July.* RM as may be gathered is a true postcard connoisseur, i.e. one that believes that the so called Golden Age of the postcard did not end in 1920 but continues to this day, as is proved by this remarkable confection of style, technique and social history. Realism takes on a different meaning here where all is narrative of a mood.   71n

January 25th.   Charles at Scott Base in the Ross Dependency to HP at the Central Electricity Generating Board, London, *Arrived at McMurdo 00.23 hrs this morning after US Coast Guard Ice Breaker had cut a channel for us. Everyone at base most cooperative and have given us lectures. Just about to go on shore.* By 1971 no place was safe from the postcard. Alan Bibby's Barne Glacier photo, however, justifies all, though on the spot sales must have been somewhat infrequent.   71o

1971 MESSAGES·NOTES·PARTICULARS

71a. Kardorama KLV81

71b. John Hinde. Photo: Franz Lazi. 2L65

71c. Dukane Press NY

71d. Crocker Mirro-Krome. DS701. Photo: H A Lowman

71e. Elizabeth City News Co. 79452. Photo: P Bayne

71f. Publisher unknown

71g. Ewad Pictures, Accra.

71h. John Hinde 2DC275

71i. Harvey Barton

71j. Charles Skilton & Fry Ltd. 5672XR

71k. Dixon-Lotus. L6/SP.2596

71l. Mike Roberts/Madonna Inn SC12483

71m. Indonesia Indah. 181/66

71n. Publisher unknown

71o. Kiwi/AH & AW Reid. SR573

71p. Wilh-Müller. Aslar. No 745

71q. Frith CGR72

71r. Jaboul Pub. Co. Evanston

71s. Bamforth Comic Series No 2259. Artist: Taylor.

July 5th.   Since this is my favourite card I posted it to several people once I had discovered it in Braunfels; in this instance to my children. *Here are some german people listening to some german people playing music. Can you find three ladies wearing the same dress?* I made no mention of the various dwarves and giants present, or the fact that the same people were here twice but not at the same precise instant in their lives, nor the fact that although they wore the same clothes these had changed colour. Nor did I ask how many moments might have been involved since two different groups are haunted by their cloned selves, nor invite them to speculate on this disruption of the space/time continuum or to search for Schrödinger's cat which no doubt lurked once or twice (unobserved) in the undergrowth. I conclude that it is the front group that is being watched by themselves as they both listen to the conductorless orchestra. What never ceases to amaze is the exertion and ingenuity involved in the making by hand of what, at least at first glance, is such a humdrum image.   71p

Chicago's Picasso

July 27th.   To Mr & Mrs W in Enfield, *Dear Vicar, Thankyou very much for assisting in the loading of our lorry. The camp is running very successfully so far. The Guides ask me to say they are enjoying themselves. yours sincerely, Captain.* As indeed they seem to be doing under the light of Frith's own leaden and particular sun.   71q

April 15th.   To Ruby Rice in Rindge, NH, *I Ruby, I got your note thanx right now I don't need anything. sincerely with respect.* Picasso, approached by Chicago in 1963, surprisingly agreed to make them a sculpture, finishing the model within two years. Refusing a fee he said it was his gift to the city. It was completed in 1967.   71r

October 22nd.   Rog in Melton Mowbray to Melvin B in Farnborough, *Gay Boy, Thanks a lot for all the letters. Show this card to others. Have got a lot of work to do unfortunately. Having a gay time though. Last night took one of the secretaries to Leicester for a night out. Her name is Penny (very nice!! say no more). Ended up being very expensive. Have just got back from taking her out this afternoon. I shall have to watch it as seeing too much of her will affect my work!! Hope you have got your oats off your college girls by now Melvin. All my mates up here were shocked (I think not) with the literature. After seeing that letter one of my mates became a gay boy. To shock him into his senses I stuck a label on his door saying 'I am a Gay Boy All gay young men come in!!' Since then he has recovered. Good job too. Don't do anything I wouldn't do. Rog The Dodge.* This could, word for word, be a script for Eric Idle in Monty Python's 'Say No More' sketch (indeed it even includes that phrase in readiness).   71s

Lest we forget . . .   *Kardorama Ltd.*

December 16th.   The title of this fine card, despite its solemn echo of the Remembrance Day obsequies it depicts, has acquired an ironic ring. Only Edward Heath, the then Prime Minister, remains in politics (right). Harold Wilson (centre) resigned in 1976. This was the year when revelations about the life of Jeremy Thorpe (left) amazed the nation and started his decline into terminal disgrace. Thorpe's head, the only one entirely surrounded by black, is an especially impenetrable mask. Collectors of modern British postcards rightly regard this little masterpiece as a classic.   72a

Piccadilly Circus, London   *Kardorama Ltd.*

August 24th.   Someone (name illegible) writes to Mrs Cobb in Bournemouth just before setting off for Salisbury, Rhodesia. The view on the card dates from 1968. Centre Point in the distance is now complete (and empty). At the Pavilion the James Bond series is still starring Sean Connery in Goldfinger, which, since it was made in 1964, proves again how unreliable dating by films can be.   72b

April 21st.   The caption on the back states 'The beauty of night reflections upon the East River blends into an unforgettable scene seldom to behold'. In less rhapsodic but more idiomatic English Mr Prakash writes to his friends the Kents in Isleworth, *Sorry I couldn't see you before leaving London a few weeks ago. I shall be in touch soon after I am back again.*   72c

Red-Eyed Tree Frog, San Diego Zoo

Home Of The Late Senator Robert F. Kennedy

August 14th.   Steve in LA to Deborah in Dallas, *I spent the weekend w. Ellen F in Disneyland... I've lost the apt. & the car since Brien came back unexpectedly. Been working at the Beverley Hills office which is infinitely better than downtown. Take care.* With the help of David Attenborough, people had been discovering that the real animal world was more vividly colourful and varied than any fictional one.   72d

August 4th.   Mary & Joe in Rockland ME. to Mr & Mrs F in Ruckford, Ill., *Hi... weather is hot. 95º. Took a ferry to Nantucket today. We saw all the Kennedy Homes.* With Robert Kennedy assassinated five years after his brother and Edward Kennedy in the murky shadow of the death by drowning of Mary Jo Kopechne, a visit to the Kennedy Compound must have had its morbid aspect.   72e

Three Generations of Eskimos

June 15th.   Auntie Barbie in Guernsey to Joanna in Amherst *...Tell Mummy we had some of the eggs to eat last night. Have you seen Basil Brush on television? He must be a good driver, I like his yellow car!* Basil Brush, using that license given to clowns and puppets, was an outspoken character who became an immediate hit with adults as well as children (as well as a big earner).   72f

August 7th.   Daryl in Anchorage to Mike T in Seattle, *Don't bother with the old couple to manage my apts... until the fall surge is over. $15 a week for Todd is a bit too cheap - offer him 404 for $25 or 101 for $15. That way nobody can be called wishy washy.* Certainly Daryl could not. The youngest of these Eskimos will no doubt expect to be referred to as an Inuit when he (or she) grows up.   72g

March 15th.   Eric to Mrs H in Liverpool. *Have just returned from over the wall via the famous check point. Quite an experience but I don't think I'll repeat it. The difference is unreal it really is two worlds even the atmosphere seemed different... we do not realise how lucky we are. Have just had large scotch to celebrate return to the normal.* This is the classic view of Checkpoint Charlie which in 2000 is a shop (where you can buy fragments of the wall) and a museum.   72h

July 23rd.   From Connie to Mr & Mrs L in Bangor, Co. Down, *As you can see I have been to East Berlin... I passed all these places and even more, I have quite a lot of photos... even got one of the Easterners doing the Goose step.* Leninplatz with the Stalin Allee was a showplace of Eastern promise. Now cosily if clumsily renamed Platz der Wiedervereinten Nationen (Reunified Peoples Square: English does not accomodate such names easily) it has a few more cars.   72i

January 17th.   Brian in Palm Springs to Mr & Mrs W in Los Angeles, *How about this - not very much, but it's home to them! Happy New Year.* This half-mile-square oasis in the desert was made by the then current US ambassador to Britain ('69 - '74) who, as a patron of the arts, helped promote modern American painting in London. This is also where President Nixon played golf on his West Coast visits.   72j

February 7th.   George in Capetown to Mr & Mrs T in Essex, *Remember the happy days we spent at this spot last year. Hotel very good.* A typical South African beach view of the time. What one never sees on postcards are the little notices saying Slegs Vir Blankes (Afrikaans for 'Whites Only'). Black nannies, however, were allowed to accompany their small white charges.   72k

February 29th.   Ruth in Stroud, Glos., sends her father a card of St Catherine's College, Oxford, *this is ruth 1. leo pushed me in the bog 2. I blew a candle out and candle wax went all over my face 3. I fell over and heart my hand when mumy had just said don't run. wasent that silly.* Aarne Jakobsen's severe looking design soon mellowed when his garden plans reached maturity.   72l

September 4th.   Dulce in Amsterdam to Richard B in Shepherds Bush, *These are beautiful lands. All are just going back to London.* After the John Lennon/Yoko Ono 'bed-in' of 1969, Amsterdam became the hippy capital of Europe. Here it is kaftan and bead-selling time in the Leidse Bosjes market where long hair is obligatory and there is no doubt a strange aroma in the air.   72m

August 20th.   Babs to Tessa & David in Poole. *Having a lovely time, so much to do, seen two variety shows, wrestling etc... everything for the children, Janes riding in the Donkey Derby.* Butlin's have their usual menu of entertainment but make efforts to compete with Mediterranean sea and sun. They have introduced South Seas exoticism and engaged the services of John Hinde Studios to wake up their postcard image. 72n

August 26th.   JV to JT in Horndon, Essex, *Best Regards from Munich. It's very nice here - everything very well prepared.* Indeed every effort was made to create a buoyant mood to contrast with Hitler's 1936 Olympiad. But no one was prepared for storming of the Israeli compound by Black September Arab terrorists on Sept 5th. A bungled later attempt to rescue the hostages ended in the death of all nine.   72o

"How d'yer get it through the wall, Alf."

April 6th.   H in New York to Mrs SW in London E10, *Picture of our hotel - very comfortable. Find New York interesting - if a little tiring.* The card of the Sheraton-Russell in its precise choreography of people and light out-Hitchcocks Hitchcock. All is both spatial (the row of figures parallel to the picture surface) and linear (the arrangement of shadows, the grid of horizontals and verticals) perfection.   72p

September 7th.   Fred & Jean in Jersey to Mrs E Crook in Sunbury, *Dear Ernie, High winds still blowing, but at least its dry now. Dissapointed with camp. Lost my snooker in Semi-Final today but am in final for Darts. Cheerio for now.* This nocturne by Trow proved one of the most successful of the post McGill cards. I'm not sure whether Fred ever won any of the many contests he went in for.   72q

"YES, MADAM, THESE ARE ESPECIALLY GROWN WITH THE LADIES IN MIND— THE APPEALING PRICKLY CACTI AND THE EVER-WELCOME RED-HOT POKER!"

December 7th.   Charlotte to Julie in New York City, *Best regards from the Apollo 17 moon shot at Cape Kennedy.* Charlotte seems to be there for the lift off of the last and longest Moon shot involving a 3 day stay on the Moon surface with the Lunar Roving Vehicle. On the giant transporter is Apollo 14 which made the third Moon landing. Mirrored in water (one of the oldest visual tropes) the craft has a double grace. 72r

October 9th.   A in Durban to JT in London NW3, *I find this an interesting comment on S.African censorship - all the press with possible exception of R.Daily Mail are of News of the World content & this sort of card is sold freely... but they massacre films. Hope to be home before long from an utterly impossible post. One can't 'advise' unless they've reached a certain level & my lot haven't even started.*   72s

August 9th.   R in London to Mr & Mrs K in St Louis, Mo., *Hi Ozark headed friends. Missouri has its own beauty but London is a rare sight. Today in Piccadilly Circus the police were hosing off the square while the hippies stood aside until completion - so they could take over again. I never saw so many kids HTC looks like St Stephen Kindergarten by comparison. Have fun at Tantara.* The hippies hung out peacefully for a few years round Eros as did the punks later on. Groups yet unimagined will do the same, one hopes. Here, on yet another ethnographic card, the Queen riding side-saddle, sets off from Buckingham Palace for the Trooping of the Colour. The chap in the outrageous hat is Prince Philip.   72t

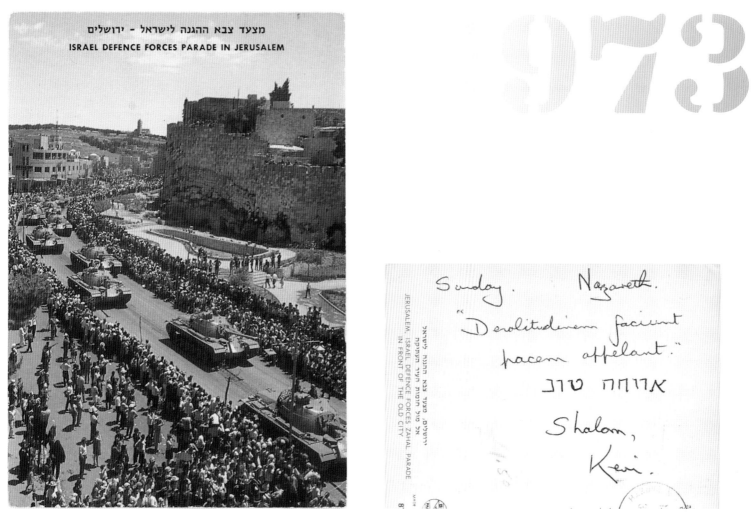

מצעד צבא ההגנה לישראל - ירושלים
ISRAEL DEFENCE FORCES PARADE IN JERUSALEM

April 21st.   In all three languages the words Kevin writes from the Holy Land to St John's in Guildford seem weighted or ironic. Even the day and the place seem meant to communicate his baffled rage to his fellow seminarists. It is the year of the Yom Kippur War which will flare up in October. The message in order reads, *Sunday, Nazareth. When they have created a wasteland they call it Peace. Cheers. Shalom.* The Latin quotation (from the Agricola of Tacitus) is apt for the many killing fields of this war-strewn century.   73a

November 7th.   To Miss SL in Takapuna, New Zealand, *Dear Shirl. This is a picture of picadilly where we are close to at this time. We have seen a little of London & hope to see more.* E Ludwig and John Hinde Studios are at their rich and colourful best in this nocturne. Peter Sellers and Elke Sommer in A Shot In The Dark dates the view to circa 1965. The couple in the foreground have more charm than reality.   73b

September 10th.   Paul to Sharon N in Sterling Heights, Mich. *Hi! Well I'm done with the Mich. Nat'l Guard, but now I'm here for a seminar... would you believe that Fri I leave for a 3yr European tour?* Once again the fallibility of dating by film is demonstrated (The Bible & Lord Jim appeared in 1966 & 1964 respectively. Peter O'Toole features in both epics).   73c

Cliff Railway linking Lynmouth and Lynton, Devon.   Photo: E. Nagele, John Hinde Studios.

April 9th.   RM honours the death of the century's finest artist (on April 8th) by improvising in the time honoured way a postcard from his own photograph; in this case a photo of a photo, taken in the art school at Repton in 1961. Though it appears in this book at least six stages removed from the original image Picasso's legendary gaze survives. The cubist angles and forms of easels and still life objects on shelves both in and above the photo make the artist inhabit a world and an aesthetic that he himself brought into being.   73d

August 24th.   T & H to KD in Catford, *Wowee zowee what a holiday! Like, er, man we've Nortoned it all along the South coast, cut across to Cornwall, hit St. Ives, zapped 'em in Newquay, found the perfect wave, changed down, flew straight at 8 grand revs, couldn't stop & we're here. Tomorrow it's - Ye Gods - Porlock Hill, downward backwards, to Frome for a night's kip before the Final Blast. Yeah! Tim & Hilary (Born to be Wild). PS. Back on Sat - like where's the action?* Easy Rider had a lot to answer for, though Newquay and Frome somehow don't sound like Vegas or Fresno.   73e

July 2nd.   Margaret to Mrs S in Exeter, *What a way to advertise a place! Well, I suppose there wasn't anything else! It was cold & wet even now in summer. Daphne, myself, Vic (owner of the car) who is Japanese Canadian & Phil, 20 year old from a Shropshire farm - doing the same sort of thing as me. We should be in Calgary tomorrow. The Queen is following my route!* A perfect cast assembled round Bardon's Esso station at White River for another Road Movie, this time on Highway 17.   73f

January 9th.   Jonathan Williams in Roswell, New Mexico, to TP in London, *It is the 60th Birthday of the personage on the other side. No collection should be without him, obviously...* This frightening likeness of Nixon is in the Denver Wax Museum. In January all looks set for Nixon as he is sworn in for a second term with blame for Watergate safely apportioned and the case closed. But the newshounds sniff on.   73g

June 12th.   Angela in Houston to Mrs S in Chesterfield, *Tony is busy at work in the building overleaf. I have been confined to the hotel & adjacent shop most of the time because we have had the most incredible 12 inches of rain or more since yesterday and its still coming... floods all over the place but this afternoon that exciting real life drama The Watergate hearings are on the Tele.* Nixon, bluffing it out at the moment, will before the month is out have the road to impeachment staring him in the face.   73h

October 26th.   From Rancho Palos Verdes, Cal., to Mrs S in Newquay, *Have arrived safely into the sun... so nice to feel warm after so much rain in Vancouver.* Frank Lloyd Wright's Wayfarer's Chapel like a glass prow in an evergreen forest (not yet fully grown) is designed to unite religion and nature in a Swedenborgian fashion, like a spiritual spaceship. The horizon dividing the circle emphasises the unity.   73i

September 29th. Marjorie in Famagusta, Cyprus to Mr & Mrs D in Tonbridge, *Weather scorching. Our hotel is right on the beach. We saw the old monks in the picture. They paint ikons ages 75 & 83!* Within a year that peaceful beach will be divided by barbed wire. After Turkish tanks invade Famagusta, its modern sector of high hotels & apartments will become a ghost town for the rest of the century. 73j

January 27th. Ivy in California to Miss W in Exeter. *Many many thanks for the letter which I read when in the sunshine above the clouds. Wendy & Norma gave Mary a birthday party. you would have been interested to see how they arranged everything.* Did Ivy really have this amount of leg room on Pan Am's 747? Integration takes a symbolic step forward with the incorporation of blacks into images of high life. 73k

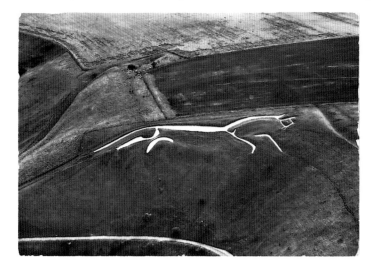

June 19th. Jeanette & Brian to Mr & Mrs D in Catford, *Just a small card mainly to ask you if you could dispose of some sausages that we forgot about. They are in the cupboard under the sink in a dish... I fear they will rot away if they aren't removed.* The White Horse of Uffington is the finest (and oldest?) of Britain's hill carvings. Picasso had helped reveal how magnificently drawn it was. 73l

July 10th. Margaret sends a perfectly composed picture of Connemara ponies to VB in Bristol, *Weather lovely, trade not so. People nice (despite VAT <u>awful</u>!). There's a wonderful chemist/grocerie in Liskeard where they sell herbs ground & loose.* VAT was introduced in 1973 to replace purchase tax. Another victory for the better off or better organised. 73m

February 11th. An elegiac mood haunts this quiet card by Frith where an even narrower palette than usual is employed to lend silence and mystery to a black and white photo. The spell is broken by its being addressed to The-Lead-Kindly Light Mission to Distressed Poofs c/o Sri Mahdavi Clarke in East Dulwich with a desultory message from Jill & Benny, *Dear People. Don't know what to say really.* (in another hand) *me neither. with love.* 73n

March 22nd. KW to Mrs G in Potton, Beds., *Greetings from Shanghai. It's like being on another planet here quite unbelievable. We are like walking exhibits being stared at all the time but we don't mind as everyone is excited to see us and so kind.* The People's Square, Shanghai's version of the now notorious Tiananmen Square, is surrounded by Maoist banners and slogans while the Chairman himself benignly surveys the huge parade ground. 73o

PLACE 'COMPOSER' OVER ANY PICTURE POSTCARD SO THAT BOTTOM AND RIGHT HAND EDGES ALIGN THEN EXAMINE THE CHANCE COMPOSITION DEFINED BY THE RECTANGULAR HOLE

December 11th.   Richard Hamilton in Hornsey sends a morning greeting to TP in Camberwell. Another of the small band of artists who like Dieter Rot found seventies inspiration in the postcard. Here as a homage to John Cage, pioneer of musical indeterminacy, RH makes a device called Composer which provides invariably intriguing chance compositions. Here it is laid over one of RH's own cards. When chance is thus invoked there are no failures although some of the revealed images might be ahead of their time.   73p

OFFICER: "By gad, man! Haven't you got a better tool than that?"

COOK: "Yes, sor, but I keeps it for making holes in doughnuts"

September 7th.   Fred & Jean (with Ann & now Trudy) in Chichester to the Crooks in Stanwell, *We are fine. it is much colder here today, it is the first time we have had to wear trousers. Ann went horseriding & loved it. The camp is not nearly so good this week but it is still a nice rest.* An old style card from the hand of the enigmatic H Lime reaches an extremity in the world of unsavoury jokes.   73q

H.R.H. The Princess Anne, London.   *Colour Photo by Giulio Di Marco.*

October 29th.   RM in Stockwell to TP in Camberwell, *Welcome back to England at the start of the month in which Pss Anne becomes 'a Phillips'.* The card printed in Italy, shows a cheerily colourful Princess moving surrealistically through a black & white London. Unfortunately she is yet another Royal trundling towards a blighted marriage. RM goes on to describe, all too vividly, the sort of fair in which most of the cards in this book have been bought (see note).   73r

YOU HAVE BEEN CHOSEN TO CARRY THE BOMBS!

STRIKE NOW!

UP THE REBELS!

DOWN WITH IT ALL

August 26th.   Dave in Blackwood to Tim E in Worcester Park, *We have had a camping holiday in Pembroke when it should have been Glamorgan (only 200 miles out!) and are now back at my auntie's house in Monmouth.* Fashion in bombs and bearded rebels do not change much in the cartoon world from the anarchists at the beginning of the century to the terrorists and urban guerrillas at its end. A beard and roll neck sweater combined was certain trouble.   73s

1973 MESSAGES·NOTES·PARTICULARS

73a. Palphot: Herzlia. No 8743

73b. John Hinde. Photo: E Ludwig 3L 64

73c. Manhattan PC. Pub. Co. 20644-C

73d. Privately published

73e. John Hinde. 2DC 444. Photo: E Nägele

73f. Ailard Photography, Thunder Bay. Ont.

73g. G R Dickson, Denver, Col.

73h. Astrocard Co. Houston, Texas. AC - 105

73i. Mittock & Sons, N.Hollywood, Col.

73j. Takis Mouretos, Nicosia 157

73k. Pan Am

73l. Ministry of Public Building & Works. 1.

73m. John Hinde 2/1018. Photo: J Willis

73n. Frith. DKG112

73o. Official Card, Shanghai, China

73p.   Richard   Hamilton/Studio   Marconi,   Milan   plus   Richard Hamilton München/Bordeaux Friedensengel. 1971. Edition Tangente Heidelberg.

By way of further illustration here is the Richard Hamilton Composer making its excerpt from 73a. This is the only intentional example of aleatory art in these pages.

73q. Constance 141. Artist: H Lime

73r.   RM continues, *I went to the annual postcard bazaar in a church hall in NW8., an astonishing experience, hundreds of friendly maniacs wedged immovably between groaning stalls, half of which were selling old 78 r.p.m. records - one addict told me that unplayable 78's of Bill Haley's Rock Around The Clock cost £60!! At no time was I not in very considerable discomfort. There were queues 100's long; desperate cries volleyed back & forth over the stalls - 'Ships?', 'Actresses?', 'Dorset?', 'Military?', etc, as in Happy Families. I don't think I could stand it ever again, though I did get some really exquisite cards.*

Intercolour Vision Photo Ltd. Photo: Giulio di Marco L/DM 337

73s. Publisher unknown, Artist unknown. 100064

74

August 11th.   The postcard is continually being enriched from new sources. The best bargains from the seventies were propaganda cards from China, mostly of scenes from Chinese Ballet. These were available at Left Wing bookshops and the small emporia in Chinatown in both London and in California, where Brian Eno selected this episode from The Red Detachment of Women to send to TP in Camberwell, *Hope you are all well. This is a Chinatown special - one of a collection from San Francisco.* The caption describes how 'Party representative Hung Chang-Ching teaches the fighters that the revolution is... a matter of emancipating all mankind. Her class consciousness raised, Wu Ching-hua follows the company commander in energetically practising marksmanship and grenade throwing'. No more nor less whacky as a story line than Les Sylphides and it certainly looks more exciting. Most Western ballets that I have seen would have benefited from the odd grenade.   74a

Piccadilly Circus, London.   *Kardorama Ltd.*

June 12th.   Stella to Mrs EC in Southampton, *London gets worse. People do the best they can I suppose but you pay the earth for precious little in every way. Still I love just walking around...* Antonioni's Blow Up at the Pavilion dates the view to circa 1967; it took an Italian to capture the essential mood and real disjointed look of London in the sixties. Doctor Zhivago is also on release. This is the card used in Dieter Rot's famous Piccadilly Series.   74b

May 3rd.   Marjorie to Mrs J Pachero in Storrs, Cal., *Ate at Mama Leoni's last nite. The food was delicious and soooo much... but it will be great to get back to CA.* Yamasaki's World Trade Center is the new star of the New York skyline. It was completed in 1973 which may account for the absence of detail and lack of superstructure on the two towers.   74c

January 27th. Sarah in Brisbane writes to Mrs Crow in Cambridge, *I have just returned from Sydney where I had been staying with a friend from Kenya. Today I move into a flat... and Wednesday start work out at the University where I have been very fortunate in getting a job.* The fireworks celebrated the opening (three months before) of the already famous building. Top right shows how dull the competition is. 74d

August 5th. Us in Oshkosh, Wisconsin to Mr Notting in Chattanooga, *Dear Daddy, this has been a busy week. Not much time to get my reading done I brought along - too much going on. Gene got a big trophy!* A scene of great actuality and little pretension, just like the hair-raising contraptions to be seen there, from microlites to pedal-powered planes. A forum for women was 1974's innovation. 74e

July 25th. George & Wilma in Honolulu to Mr & Mrs M in St Louis, *Aloha!! Everything is so beautiful. Wish we could stay a couple of weeks longer.* This extraordinary structure is the USS Arizona Memorial designed by Alfred Preis to match the battleship that lies submerged below (together with the bodies of the 1177 crewmen who perished when it was sunk in Pearl Harbour in 1943). 74f

June 2nd. M in Yugoslavia to Miss MM in Birmingham, *Visited this village this morning and saw a display of dancing just as shown on card.* You bet. The thousand villagers of Cilipi condemned themselves to an eternity of folklore as tourists, following in the wake of anthropologists, flocked there. With the help of UNESCO (who perhaps supplied the microphones) they recovered from Serb attacks in 1991 and '95. 74g

September 20th. David Rudkin in A Nikolaos in Crete to T & JP in London, *They have them in Crete too. It was as much as even I could find the face to do, to buy this.* This Greek card has no caption and does not seem to want to advertise anything. It would seem to be merely a picture of life in Greece for a contented young family lounging around in thermal undies on a sofa; a study in texture. Perhaps the English book on the table, The Strategy Of Perception, provides a clue. 74h

May 3rd. Paul Bitmead of Moss Motors in Walford writes by hand to Mr Rowe in Bushey what must be the all too familiar message *Thinking of changing your 1303 beetle? I think you will after you've driven the new VW Polo. Call me now on Watford 27371.* An enterprising rainy advert makes the tinny new vehicle gleam but Mr Rowe should stick to what he's got, one of the century's classics (even when made in Brazil). The Polo is a Beetle for squares. 74i

July 24th.   Catherine in Naperville to Mrs Sharples in Little Lever. Lancs., *Hi Grandma, Did you have a good flight back to Manchester? We have had some pretty bad storms here and many floods...* When Mrs Sharples visited her granddaughter she would not have seen the Sears Tower completed. This card itself is only a graphic prediction of what the Skidmore, Owens & Merrill giant would look like (minus its crowning antennae). Chicago, the birthplace of the skyscraper, had the world's tallest building for only two years (until the Kuala Lumpur towers of 1976).   74j

July 14th.   Connie who has been in Berlin some time (see 72l) with British Forces sends another card of the wall to Master SL in Bangor, Co. Down, *Here's another card for your collection. You will see me in 3 weeks. What is Paddy like now he has had his coat cut?* Before and after cards are always interesting especially as here when someone gets the place and angle right. Connie would be amazed to return to the same spot at the very end of the century and see the next transformation as the Potsdamer Platz evolves into one of the architectural showcases of the world.   74k

July 7th. Dorothy in Ballater to Mrs Parry in Llandudno, *Dear Auntie Winifred. Today we have come to Balmoral Castle. I am writing this in the grounds so that I can post it in the box by the side of the castle. It is a lovely house we wish we could see inside it.* Lichfield's photo shows the Queen in happy mood. She could be any woman in her garden (though few could boast a water feature quite on this scale) with her dogs. Her love of this breed is so well known that Michael Leonard's fine picture of her with a dog in the National Portrait Gallery has been nicknamed Corgi & Bess.   74l

May 5th.   RM in London to TP in Braamfontein, S Africa, *Overleaf you see the sort of ceremonial that has started to occur in London since you left. The guards' training for this feat is long & arduous...* One of the glories of the postcard craft is its retention of innocence. It seems to remain oblivious to the kinds of delight it gives rise to, or the mysterious depths it unwittingly plumbs. Artists are rarely so daring. RM's reaction is not one of mockery but of wonder.   74m

July 26th.   Robert, returned from Granada, writes to Julian T in Hammersmith, *now hard at work on new book. I was also visited by the Guardian man. R still in Spain.* The caption gives Our Lady's Anguish as the translation of Nuestra Sra de las Angustias (usually Our Lady of the Sorrows). One would rather describe the Virgin here as serene, if not somewhat smug, as she shows the guardsman apprentice a thing or two about levitation.   74n

August 7th.   Ernest in Copenhagen sends this card with its ponderously worded promotional message to the Nicholsons in Knockholt, *Hi, just finished a delicious Danish luncheon... Some beautiful models passed among us in the famous Danish Mink-furs... and the charming tables are set with Danish Handicraft in modern design...* Someone should have told them that people who say Hi at the start of a message don't have 'luncheon'. Chair by Arne Jakobsen (see 72g).   74o

November 4th.   JT in Falmouth to JP in London, *I had to come down here again this week so I'm afraid we'll have to postpone our evening. I'm tied up here in fact till 11th December.* This card is no 3 in a series from The People's Physical Culture Publishing House in Peking and is entitled The Mass Callisthenics Song in Praise of the Revolution. As well as scenes from ballets such as The Red Detachment Of Women (or Modern Revolutionary Dance Dramas as the cards' own text calls them) other sets of propaganda cards like this were available at incredibly low prices, especially in Collett's Left Wing Bookshop in the Charing Cross Road which groaned under the complete works of Marx, Lenin and Mao. Although published (with captions in English and French) in the late sixties they mainly surfaced in London in the seventies and were eagerly purchased, by the faithful and politically agnostic alike. One imagines the dazzling card above to be the merest segment of an infinity of boys in brown dungarees and girls in blue. There is an illuminating paradox at the heart of totalitarian culture, earlier met with in Nazi Germany (see 38a), where people en masse can be treated as units of abstraction whereas individual artists may not express themselves by means of the abstract. But Callisthenics may be classed as a craft (which has never had any ideological trouble with the abstract). What is most bewildering in China's case is that Socialist Realism is obliged to borrow Western modes to exist at all, as in their ballets where Western style music and dance steps are the appropriated means to express Maoist aspirations. This went for painting too, even for architecture. Virtually everything intrinsically Chinese was, for the Party, polluted with the country's aristocratic past. This card thus represents a rare instance of authenticity in Maoist culture.   74p

גולדה מאיר ראש הממשלה
PRIME MINISTER GOLDA MEIR

December 9th.   From Galilee to Mr & Mrs M in Hawick, Scotland. *Having a really enjoyable time up here on the Lebanese border. Kibbutz Bar-Am is half a mile from the border... the people are great. Volunteers, Army and Israeli Youths (among the volunteers there are 10 guys and 11 girls - Not bad?). The situation was a bit tense for a while. Everyone was preparing for war. There were bombs falling two weeks ago, and the flares were lit all along the Golan Heights. On my travels I've heard different views from both Arab and Jew... in Haifa an Arab showed me his house and his uncles house, they had been blown to ruble, (he did not hold it against the Jews). Acre has been the highlight of my travels with the subteranian crusaders tunnels... I'm working in an apple-packing factory here. I'll write again. Shalom, John.* Golda Meir, here coopted by means of John's intervention to be an unlikely supporter of the Scottish National Party, was reelected in January only to resign in April. After Kissinger mediated a truce between Israel and Syria things had been somewhat quieter though John's visit to Acre might have told him how long a history there was of religious and territorial antagonisms. Golda Meir who was already suffering from Leukaemia died in 1978 aged 80.   74q

September 11th.   Fred & Jean in Jersey to Marie in Sunbury (Fred & Jean is the usual signature of their cards whichever's mother & father are being addressed. Most are written by Jean), *Hope you had a good time at the wedding. There will be no wig or eyelashes for you to try. They are much more expensive than they are here. Be seeing you soon to tell you all my moans.* The breathalyser quickly became a new theme for the seaside postcard after its introduction in the sixties. Here it is in one of its early forms.   74r

75

March 1st.   Edwin in Arizona to KR in Sonoca Cal., *Hi Ken. We were here the other day. Some place. Weather good but no rain. Its in the 70's days.* London Bridge was indeed falling down when it was bought by Robert McCulloch for Lake Havasu City (which he founded in 1964). The bridge was rebuilt there stone by stone. Water had been channelled to run beneath it by the time it was dedicated in 1971. Much to its surprise London Bridge passed its 150th birthday under a strange sun partnered, as it had never been, by 'an authentically designed English village with real British Pub Restaurant'. T S Eliot (who died as dismantling started) once celebrated its air of gloom which even in this cheerful landscape it has somehow managed to retain. Who but an American would buy the world's largest antique?   75a

September ?st.   Mathias writes to his family in Ludwigshafen. *Greetings. The weather is rainy, the hotel squalid but cheerful, the town worth seeing, the traffic a catastrophe, the driving on the left maddening, the prices amazing etc. The College is a waste of time - planning totally confused and the surroundings dismal. Only the food is good here.* What's more the Guinness Clock had disappeared (in 1973).   75b

December 1st.   To Mr & Mrs F & Darlene in Stealton PA, *Dear Alice & All. Arrived home OK. Got to Jersey City at 7.30. In the house about 9 not bad got home to late the cat died of heart trouble just fell off of the chair dead... well so long, good luck to all of you. Uncle Frank.* An aerial view that shows the twin towers to good effect. A sober view appropriate to the sad end of the nameless cat.   75c

Assassination Site President John F. Kennedy

July 13th. Lona, Joe & JJ to Mr & Mrs F in Molalla, Oregon. *Lots to see - no house yet, live in Motel with kitchen. Like it here only hot! Joe does really well driving in Dallas. I'm lost! prices are close to Oregon's. Lots of work.* Conspiracy theories were rife but this postcard and its successors take the official line that Oswald was the lone assassin on that infamous Friday in November. 75d

August 2nd. To Mr & Mrs Maurice A in Farningdale NY, *Hi, first postcard I saw of the tube. We're riding it all over. Our hotel's fine, quaint & old-fashioned looking on the outside. The weather's beautiful. love Holly.* She seems to be having a better time than Mathias (see 75a). The tube saw little change. Capstan cigarettes (without health warning), Benedict Peas and Start-Rite Shoes indicate the early sixties. 75e

July 6th. Pop in Betws-Y-Coed to Hazel R in Lingfield. *The weather has been very warm so far. We have had a grand tour today from Cardiff to Betsy-Coed. I think the mountains are better than Scotland.* Another mad ethnographic card from Wales with, I suspect, some cheating. First, second and third girl from left are surely the same person and the last of the row seems to be a giantess. 75f

September 15th. Clivvy & T-Shoes write on a Singapore Airlines card to Mrs D in Cranbrook, *we shall be here till March 76. Sufficient work to keep me going. We both enjoy Indonesia... countryside just like low-country Ceylon with lovely views.* No doe-eyed beauty like this ever woke me from uncomfortable slumber on a plane. I would count myself lucky to see even a raddled version of 75p. 75g

May 12th. Pete in Peihai Park (the card shows Chiung Hua Islet) to Liz S in London, *China is everything I had hoped it would be. It seems to be working. People are placid & full of purpose. The whole society seems very healthy on a superficial impression & on the basic discussions with English teachers here. It is not perfect but nonetheless achieved a lot especially in relationships between people & attitudes.* This does not include the 20 million peasants who had died in The Great Leap Forward. 75h

September 12th. Eunice to Mrs LM in Indianapolis, *Went to see stadium today. What a sight. Took a brewery tour and they served us all the beer we wanted. Beer is bad enough, but at 9am. The food is something else and no speed limit on the big highway - they pass you like you're standing still when you're doing 90mph.* Munich's trademark towers now have to compete with Behnisch and Otto's stadium complex which pioneered the now much imitated tent roof system. 75i

LONDON · Fortes Scratchwood Service Area, M1 Motorway   ET5726

BUTLIN'S FILEY—A Corner of the Beachcomber Bar   Photo : E. Nägele, John Hinde Studios.

June 28th.   M & D to DP in Chichester. *We have just stopped here for our evening meal en route... Lovely sunshine this afternoon - very tempted to use your Polaroids! We will be back in Bognor on Wednesday.* Though British collectors still concentrate on earlier or regional postcards two subject areas have gained a following, Motorways and Holiday Camps. This hymn to pea green plastic, and 75k explain why.   75j

September 15th.   Doll & Ernie send this anthropological feast of a card to Rose & Ray in Bilborough, *Having a lovely time. Very nice here. Sandras kiddies love it here, its a kids paradise everything you would wish for. It would suit you and Ray as well. We went in this bar last night for a drink its lovely.* The scene manages to be exotic beyond the hopes of any tropical clime it aims to invoke.   75k

November 11th.   Chris D in Ontario to Cokey Monkey D in Palm Bay, Flo. *Dear Mom, my room is a miss, I mean mess, better clean it up. Bye.* The card shows the Lunar Module and the Lunar Rover with Astronaut Young or Duke perched behind it in what was to be the penultimate Moon landing in the Apollo program, which by this year was being wound up.   75l

July 14th.   Martha to Jean R in Dallas, Oregon, *we finally made it to New York. What a mad house. What prices. Horrible traffic - no place to park. postcards are no longer cheap, almost everywhere they are fifteen cents.* This card (which cost me fifty cents second hand) shows 'China designed for the White house during the Johnson Administration'. The photo is of Ladybird presumably using it.   75m

2.1 THE LIGHT DIET ROOM, ENTON HALL, WITLEY   C. G. FUTCHER

May 21st.   TT to Mr & Mrs T in London NW3. *Something of a euphemism to call hot water a light diet. I call it no diet. Puritanically am convinced hell is good for one. Love to all.* Hell was a Health Farm, places of punishment for refugees from the good life. Here plump executives could thin down in preparation for the next round of the three hour lunches that were then indulged in. On the wall is a still-life. As so often it depicts food, but that is not all (see note).   75n

September 16th.   Ken to John & Vivien M in London, *Arrived safely. The Grand Hotel is! 500 Bedrooms. Just managing to find my way around.* The card seems to be the official greetings card: it is difficult to believe it was not the product of an opposing group. How could a party choose to advertise itself by means of a bare ruin in a deserted place? Especially when its own leader Jeremy Thorpe was about to be as exposed, and as irretrievably wrecked, as the castle on this card.   75o

LONDON

FLY *Canadian Pacific*

June 18th. Bob in Santa Maria, Spain, to Mrs D in West Vancouver, *Just going to sleep. Did not manage to get off in Montreal with Mrs L. She was 1st Class and feeling no pain... Glad that you have Mary and all with you at the start of this long separation.* Either London or Canadian Pacific mysteriously identifies itself with a woman in twinset and pearls holding a bunch of daffodils that are starting to wilt in the glare of the camera lights. 75p

The Post Office Tower by Night, London. *Colour Photo by Giulio Di Marco.*

June 3rd. Mandy writes to Jackie R in Leighton Buzzard. *The hotel is very nice and very posh. I'm working in the restaurant at the moment, which is a candlelit place where everybody who is anybody goes for dinner. The people here are friendly and I've got a very nice room to myself.* This must be one of the phone-boxes saved from BT's purge in the eighties; a classic K6 box by Giles Gilbert Scott. It thrives in the shadow of its towering new master. 75q

August 25th. RM in Durham to TP in Camberwell on a card entitled Year Around Fun At The Pomegranate Inn In Aspen (Colorado). *Here is a card which Marina Vaizey acquired in Aspen & gave me at a dinner party... to give to you... While, on the way up here we were picnicing in nature silence beneath Henry Moore's King & Queen on a Dumfriesshire hillside, fighter jets on a NATO exercise suddenly screamed terrifyingly over... actually for a second touching (visually) the bronze 'crowns'.* Any resemblance to the then 29 year old Bill Clinton is accidental. 75r

Expressway Complex, Detroit, Michigan *Photo Jae Clark H.B.S.S.*

July 10th. Julie to Gaye C in Newport IOW *...we had sweetcorn for dinner with ice-cream and raspberries. There was 34 different ice-creams to choose from. We went into Detroit yesterday. but it scared me, lots of horrible people. Be good and look after my bedroom and Sandy. see you.* Not only in the USA had inner-city life become perilous. Better perhaps to be gliding from Expressway to Interstate on America's incomparable road system, the fluid geometry of whose junctions is celebrated as the New Pastoral in so many bird's eye view cards. 75s

1975 MESSAGES·NOTES·PARTICULARS

75a. Petley Studios, Phoenix. Photo: J V McLaughlin

75b. Golden Shield 12. Printed in Spain

75c. Manhattan postcard Co. Photo: Jim Doane

75d. A.W.Distributors (CT) C3

75e. Photographic Greeting Co/London Transport 112

75f. Colourmaster PT 28461

75g. Singapore Airlines. Accompanied with, as caption, a quotation from Byron,
There be none of beauty's daughters
With a magic like thee.

75h. Peking Post Office

75i. Publisher unknown. US Army cancel over stamp commemorating International Women's Year.

75j. Charles Skilton. ET 5726

75k. John Hinde. 3F64 Photo: E Nägele

75l. Nasa Tours Ltd. 129975

75m. James Tetirick. Photo: Bob Cunningham

75n. C G Futcher. Z.1.

75o. Carillon Press. Loughborough. PM advertises Dunlop Masters Golf/Ganton.

What looks like a conventional still-life on the wall of the Light-Diet Room with its normal quota of fruit, knife, bowls and bottle (albeit of milk) turns out under magnification to include a unique ingredient, a weighing machine. It seems that Enton Hall Health Farm has a policy of reminding its luckless clientele of privation's duties wherever they are, even if they seek solace in art. One cannot be certain but what seems to be being weighed, and must be contemplated by those who have been found wanting, is flour, the source of so many forbidden foods.

75p. Canadian Pacific

75q. Photo: Giulio Di Marco

75r. R.C.Bishop. Colorado. 907. Photo: R.C.Bishop

The heads of Moore's statues were later removed by vandals, or scrap metal thieves.

75s. Hiawatha Cards, Detroit 54814.B

76

25 ABRIL...LIBERDADE!

April 28th.   Joe in Lisbon to Jane in the Hospital for Women, Soho Square, *In 3 days I have already talked to so many people I suffer from sensory overload... it all seems more complex this time. The threat of fascism so real and the left so fragmented. Went to 3 political rallies last night. Ended up at the communist rally at midnight... still more than 10,000 people there.* Clearly the CP has strong worker support. Amazing to see old ladies in black waving communist flags. The Iberian peninsular had been in political aspic since the thirties. Portugal seemed particularly slow in facing the world's realities: having been the first to arrive in Africa they were the last to leave. Here street celebrations greet the new constitution. Joe, if he stays, will see the country steer a safe course between the troubling extremes.   76a

April 21st.   Peter writes to his aunt in Vienna wishing her a happy Easter, *lovely weather and wonderful shopping opportunities.* According to the card's colourist a lot of people are wearing blue in 1975, the year of this image. At the Pavilion, Report To The Commisioner (disguised by its English title Operation Undercover) is showing.   76b

November 23rd.   Patricia and Pip describe their trip to Sybil in Rowhedge, *Just a line from little ol' New York - fabulous more than ever! Food & atmosphere delicious... Had a really happy dinner last night with some old working friends of mine who live in a magnificent house in Westchester. Shopped today with great success.*   76c

CANADA 1976

1930   DE LA WARR PAVILION, BEXHILL ON SEA.

August 11th.   To Robert G in Athor Mass., from Brockville. *Today we toured the Ontario side of the International Power Plant at Cornwall. Hug Doug & Sue for me. love Jane.* Politics cast its shadow over Montreal's Olympics, boycotted by African athletes (because New Zealand continued to play rugby with South Africa). Nadia Comaneci, a 14 year old product of Rumania's brutal training of gymnastic infants, won all her events and scored the first perfect marks in Olympic history.   76d

August 31st.   Marion & Ivie to Mrs S in Crawley Down, *The flat is lovely & we can lie in bed & watch the sea.* Women hold on to their hats in windy Bexhill, unlikely site of Britain's first welded steel-framed building, a masterpiece by the visionary Erich Mendelsohn completed in 1935. Postcard fairs are usually held in dingy, all too civic spaces. Bexhill's is the exception and this card was bought in the light, airy and spacious Pavilion it illustrates.   76e

MARKET PLACE HATFIELD HERTS.   C 2675X

August 10th.   Kathleen to Miss McC in Bangor, N. Ireland, *This is not a town, but seems to be a village stretched out to meet the next, and the one beyond that. We are enjoying the rough and the smooth of four vigorous youngsters.* A Judges card that faces up to modern life with a crane signalling more to come. The photographer has requested an art display of rolled rugs and a lamppost is called George.   76f

July 15th.   Grandma and Grandad in Hassocks send this no doubt well chosen card to Master Niel A in Elgin. *I hear you have been camping out. I guess you enjoyed camping very much and you certainly would enjoy the air display.* Toytown started life on Children's Hour in the forties (When Radio 4 was The Home Service) but by the time it reached television as a puppet show I had somewhat outgrown it.   76g

BUTLIN'S FILEY—*The Viennese Ballroom.*   Photo : E. Nägele, John Hinde Studios.

Christian Greetings from Filey Holiday Crusade

June 1st.   Marc & Fan to Mr & Mrs C in Send, *Dear Mum & Dad... very wet journey here and it is rather cold with rain... we only need woollies and wellies! Chalet not bad... rather too much walking involved everywhere. I can't get Peter away from the snooker and the kids fight over who is going to play him, but it's queues all the time. The camp is a long way from everywhere... we're off to the chairlift before it rains.* Judicious tinting brings some cheer however to the Viennese Ballroom.   76h

September 21st.   Mary, Ernie & David to Mr & Mrs P in Barnard Castle, *Having a good time on our Filey Holiday... weather fine and sunny. We are enjoying great Ministry, and music from different Artists.* After the summer camps have gone the Viennese Ballroom is transformed with a crusading theme. Evangelism Today produce this card without the services of John Hinde and all looks drab. The ceiling decorations have turned to seaweed and the dress code seems to be brown.   76i

September 29th. Rita to Alan in Paddington, *Weather not too bad, had a lot of rain but never mind if one waited for the weather we would stop in all the while digs good very nice food who could ask for more I won't want to come home.* A chirpy cartoon (she is holding a leaflet on Abbeys & Ancient Monuments) with cartoon figures against a photo background of tea and ice cream stalls on the beach and the famous tower.   76j

October 18th. S to Mr & Mrs D in Guildford, *Super flight over, weather baking hot - burnt me boobs! hired 4 mopeds - only crashed once so far - Hotel very sweet - unusual food - Italian fellas def. after IT! not getting it either. Off to super deserted beach tomorrow to expose our all.* With haughty disregard for light direction the publisher inserts his favourite sunset into the distorted scene.   76k

June 28th. On the generic Holiday Inn card Don, Linda & Tracy write to their parents Mr & Mrs S in Shownee, Oklahoma. *Pueblo, Colorado. Having a great time may not come home. Everything is going OK. No trouble.* A stereotypical message on a card that served the hotel chain throughout the US. The presence centre stage of a balding senior citizen as well as the usual cast is a bold and shrewd move.   76l

November 14th. R & H to Trevor D in London, *I am sharing the wonderful room 408 in the angle and we are enjoying the luxury of it. Service is fine, prices are frightening.* Dannat's sensitive Inter Continental Hotel in Rijadh is the start of its Western architectural adventure. The Gulf States had Europe literally over a barrel when it came to oil, but British architects siphoned off some of OPEC's surplus. 76m

April 7th. Nigel in Madrid to Matthew G in Muswell Hill, *I gather we now have Mr Callaghan for PM and I've just read about Mr Silly Billy's budget. There'll be a fuss about that I bet. I hope the pound doesn't go down too much and that all is well in Muswell Hill.* Madrid's famous fountain shares the honours with an elegant traffic light. The pound continued to fall and England had to go cap in hand to the IMF.   76n

June 13th. Nigel in Rotorua N.Z. to Mrs D in Margate, *Mutton on the hoof, went here after seeing the geysers.* In view of the immense difficulty of assembling this choir of sheep it seems more than discourteous that no one has turned up to see or hear them. The caption calls this the Famous Expo Ram Display, Central Feature of New Zealand's National Agricultural Centre. The stag's head adds a discordant note.   76o

September 21st.   R & D to Arthur in Carnforth, Lancs., *Enjoying our holiday with friends whose house is almost next door to the house of the great philosopher René Descartes. We return 27th we hope if there are no strikes.* They make it sound as if they could just drop in on René Descartes if they had any existential problems. The French, having respect for such figures, renamed his home village, Haye de Touraine, which is now known simply as Descartes.   76p

October 6th.   Maria in Falkenberg to K H in Winchester, *My dear little Kat... was so glad to see you here in Sweden, you must come back for me soon.* The card shows the wedding of King Carl Gustav XVI and Queen Silvia (formerly Silvia Sommerlath, whom the King met at the Munich Olympics of 1972 where she was hostess/interpreter). The King has an excellent motto: For Sweden, with the times. Like all weddings this is attended by many women in strange hats.   76q

Fog Over the Golden Gate

July 13th.   Kevin in Salen, Argyll, to Mr J G in Chelmsford, *We are having glorious weather and have been swimming in a jellyfish-clear bay. Mark has caught a small sea trout and I have been doing some canoeing...* The osprey, long absent from British shores, made a tentative reappearance in Scotland in the fifties. The suppression of DDT and early protection of nesting sites (after initial depredations by egg thieves) made it possible for this magnificent bird to thrive and be introduced south of the border.   76r

August 24th.   To Elmer S in St Jacob, Illinois, *Dear Dad. Netherlands beautiful flowers all over. Fields of wheat just getting ready for harvest. Pepsi is only 75c a bottle - Coffee $1.00 a cup. Vern says send money quick he's run out of funds. Holland people so friendly different than English who are more formal... Lots of milk cattle. Vern and Honey.* If they hang out with this hippy crowd around Amsterdam's phallic National Monument they will know the price of other things. Cannabis, legalised in 1976, was freely available.   76s

May 18th.   Colin to Jeff L in Edinburgh. *Thanks for your beautiful letter, I am in the process of explaining to you what is happening. At the moment I am in San Francisco with a huge bus load of people from M.L.C. So far it's been a total riot, everything is amazing and everyone very wonderful. Since we've been here (The Joan Baez Non-Violent Center) we've been threatened with a bust for staying together, discovered this building is shot at a lot, sneaked on by neighbours and generally had a fantastic time in S.F. Look after yourself.* The haze of pollution adds enchantment to the view of the Golden Gate Bridge in sun and fog. Somewhere beneath this shroud Colin and his friends enact their archetypal scenes of seventies Californian life. Perhaps they discuss it all over a latte at the Caffe Trieste (see 87l).   76t

77

September 30th.   Big science is in every sense exemplified by the Fermi Accelerator in Batavia, Illinois, in which particles of indescribable minuteness are urged to unimaginable speeds at its four mile circumference. This cyclotron is the descendent of Cockroft's linear atom-smasher of the thirties but is itself only another staging post towards the frontiers of the sub-atomic mysteries. The paradox seems to be that the smaller the particle you investigate the larger the device you need. E writes from Batavia to JT in London, *Is this the same card as I sent before? Building at bottom left is 15 storeys high & one of the best I have ever seen. I am fit & in strict training so prepare for titanic squash.*

77a

Eros, Symbol of Love, Piccadilly Circus, London.   *Kardorama Ltd.*

Lower Manhattan   *New York City*

August 13th.   A 1972 card shows Michael Caine in Pulp. The advertised bargain (one way?) flights to Australia at £99 heralds the world of the bucket shop. Harry to Michael B in New York, *This is the Times Square of London - that's Eros on the pole. Get the message! The flight was superb... Why the stewardess changed outfits three times en flight I shall never know.*

77b

November 2nd.   Inge writes to Fred at Movielab in NY, *Apologies for my sudden departure. It seems there are still problems. I hope sincerely they will be sorted out and I will be back. If not, thankyou very much for your help and work so far. If at all possible please have the London prints sent to M.Ophuls after checking with Paramount.*

77c

July 5th.   From Weymouth to WS in Parkstone, Dorset, *Dear Dad, Hope you are well. We are going to Bristol Zoo on Tuesday. We are going to have a picnic lunch & fish & chips, on our way back. How's the ginger lemonade going? See you Saturday. Love Doll xx.* This seems to have been the nearest to a ceremonial Jubilee card (albeit printed in Spain) though the Jubilee was the last Royal event wholeheartedly celebrated in the century.   77d

September 1st.   NS in N'Djamena, Chad, to Mrs H in Casterton, Cumbria. *I hope that you are both well and that the water shortage is not too bad. I have received my 'O' level results. 2 A's, 4 B's, 2 C's (Maths & French). Ironical that I should go to a French speaking country after my O level.* He is also far from where this scene purports to be. John Hinde likes to give good value. Since cloning is not yet a possibility these must be the same lion repeated. Which one (if either) is actually there?   77e

February 16th.   V serving in Brussels sends this card of the Headquarters of OTAN, otherwise known as NATO, to Ronald M in Shambrook, Beds., *J is due to arrive back at Ouse Manor on Wednesday. I arrive late on Friday night. We leave 29th but that morning Finnegans are coming to see what needs doing to the outbuildings, garages etc.* Nato headquarters seems to be manned by a staff of one.   77f

August 28th.   Angie in Solingen to Mick R in Blyth, *So far I'm having a very nice time. The family I am staying with are all very nice to me, the mother is the best every time I see her she gives me a handshake, kiss and cuddle. The boys up here are all very sexy so I have to try to watch my step (Ha Ha).* Buildings that look like universities tend from now on to be supermarkets.   77g

September 13th.   Julie & Go to Mrs W in Ryde, IOW, *Plenty to do all the time!! Flatlet quite nice and well equipped. Carol won 2nd prize in the Tarzan & Jane contest and she's entering the Space Hopper competition today. Swimming lessons evenings and a show last night.* Girls in mini dresses with hair dyed silver and piled high should be datable to the fashion historian. John Hinde improves on past views of Butlin's lounges but nostalgically includes a comatose woman and a suicidal adolescent.   77h

July 28th.   Joe to Mr & Mrs N in Ilminster, *Down here to see Eric & Kath. Eric not broken up yet so amused myself for a few hours. 'Ecological Smallholding' turns out to be 2 steps up from a slum and populated with crazy intellectuals who cannot run their own lives let alone a self sufficient farm. Nothing wrong with the concept - just everything wrong about the way they go about it.* Sounds like the beginning of the end of a commune. Enough to make a sail turn yellow.   77i

September 14th.   V & G from Death Valley to Trevor D in London, *Not quite your sort of place - or ours - but fascinating to visit & a necessary corrective after a visit to Taliesin West & Paolo Solieri's nonsense. Have been driving through amazing landscape - quite breathtaking!* A city made of signage has its own organic energy (see47o) though it would provide a culture shock to pilgrims coming from the Frank Lloyd Wright shrine at Taliesin West.   77j

June 7th.   To Mr & Mrs H in Poole, Dorset, from Port of Spain. *Just a quick note from TT airport. Have really had a super time here. Hope SA is as good! Even blue birds here. Am on 2nd peel now. Even my ears. Take care. love Deb.* Perhaps it is for Deb to take care if her skin has peeled off, but refreshment is at hand from Kathy Girl's (In God We Trust In Man We Burst) snowcone stall, at least until the global corporations make her (and Make Hit cigarettes) pay the price of progress.   77k

September 2nd.   BG in Memphis to H & LS in Syracuse, NY., on a card entitled Big Smashup on Regent Street. *Howdy folks, still looking for work, doing mental R & R in meantime... if only I didn't have guilt feelings. Only goes to show still, have to break social shackles, get down to exercises. Paint, run, scream, cry, love, do...* The car is also confused. It used to be so dramatic to crash (see 06m) and now it's banal. 77l

May 23rd.   *Dad in Monte Carlo to T & TB in Chelmsford. Smashing weather and hotel life gose on all the time hear. We are staying in Italy but I don't understand them.* Here is a Ferrari at the Tobacco Turn of the Monaco Grand Prix with behind it another car in the same now universal Formula 1 style, bearing no resemblance to anything on the everyday road (unlike Ferrari's Le Mans winner in the sixties, see 65h).   77m

July 11th.   Mum & Dad in John O'Groats to Mr & Mrs P in London, *I have learned that Loch Ness is 27 miles long - we drove by the side of it. We have had sunshine all day each day. I thought T might be interested in the artistic lines of the photograph.* Though beautiful in the abstract I have never been able to make anything out of the top right image, certainly not the amazing creature in the artist's impression (bottom left) of Nessie the loch's legendary monster.   77n

January 25th.   Geoffrey S in Washington writes to EHFD Division (after one or two crossings out) Room S4116, Dept. of the Environment, London SW1, five days after the inauguration of President Carter. *See, I even forgot the latest name of the Division! Very much the new Administration this week. Hard to get to talk to DOT people because they're all on tenterhooks.* Given his political background (see 68h) Carter was a liberal. As presidents' wives go Rosalyn Carter looks rather natural.   77o

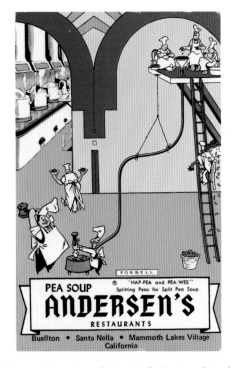

February 8th.   Anne & Larry in California to Beba & Max H in Glenside, Pa., *We're really enjoying ourselves. 10 days in Los Angeles and now on our way to San Francisco.* Andersen's (as their Heath Robinson type illustration shows) are a bit on the cutesy side. They are still California-based and cultists have organised a 24hr rally course that visits all their four restaurants to eat pea soup. There must be something else on the menu.   77p

May 31st.   Clare in Norfolk to Kaye S in Sevenoaks, *Sorry I haven't written for ages but among other things I've been swotting for exams etc. At the moment we are on holiday in Stalham. Its quite boring cos theres nothing to do and the weather's not particularly fantastic either. I've just put this false tanning lotion on and it's gone all stripey! Well, write back soon, see ya.* Another cover version of an old joke.   77q

July 8th.   To Fred & Jean in Sunbury from Vi, Pete, Stephen & Paul in Clwyd. *Having a smashing time. Had quite a bit of sunshine. Lots of things to do for us and the boys. The chalet is very nice and the evening entertainment is great. Sorry if this is late but haven't had much time. Been traveling and looking at the views they are very pretty. See you soon.* This is the last we hear of Fred & Jean (Bird) who have been camping in these pages since 1951. This card is to, rather than from them, which perhaps indicates that with children now grown up their days at Butlin's and Pontin's were over. From the pile of over a hundred cards that I bought in a postcard auction in Croydon under the heading 'comic cards, seaside type, mostly vulgar, all postally used', the first was sent for twopence (under 1p) and this last cost almost nine times as much to post. Ironically their friends seem to have had a good time and good weather in their holiday camp in contrast to the largely disappointing experiences of Fred & Jean themselves.   77t

September 9th.   Anne in Hammamet, Tunisia, to Mr Turner's office at Smith Bros, Whitehaven. *Well I actually arrived all in one piece... Well, there are your wonderful camels on the front of the postcard. I'm afraid they have missed off the stones but I'm sure they will be lying nearby.* Half way between a giraffe and a pyramid, camels make good cards with their philosophical expressions. Evidently David, Joan, Marian, Gordon & Stephen in Mr Turner's office had requested them; but that leaves the mystery of the stones.   77r

September 14th.   Catherine at Waterloo Station to Miss B in Slough, *I am waiting here for John who is taking me for lunch. Last night at Covent Garden lovely. Another late night tonight. I'll be dead but it will be worth it. London is a treat, but I'm glad we live in the country!* The Georgian elegance of the Burlington Arcade in Piccadilly makes shopping a delight on a rainy day when you need a cashmere wrap or handmade chocolates or a gold-plated pen (if words like bank manager don't scare you).   77s

78

May 7th.   J at the Gare Montparnasse to TP in London, ...*do the French promote their mayors to glory while still in office (would the Booths be jealous?) or can you think of the real interpretation of this depiction in the sky?* The reference to the Salvation Army's founders is apt (their monument near Ruskin Park gives the date of their deaths in the Army's traditional form, Promoted to Glory) since evidently salvation for Paris is here distinctly on the cards. Unidentified Flying Objects had of course been seen by the late seventies over every capital but Identifiable Floating Politicians is another and distinctly immodest story. There are as yet no reports of Mayor Giuliani hovering over Manhattan nor Livingstone over London.   78a

July 20th.   Kay to Shirla McD in Mt View, California, *This is one beautiful city. Took a tour... on one of the red busses pictured. Found a nifty pub straight away. The city care for the tourist - writes on the street look left - or look right... I shouldn't get hit by a cab & will be back all too soon.* A view circa 1966 with an ominous single cloud to balance the composition.   78b

September 6th.   Math to the G family in Muswell Hill, *I didn't mean to - I only gave it a little push... Has Hugo got a suit? Has Paul got his equipment? ...C's flat is superb xxx.* Michael Langenstein's nicely collaged Statue of Liberty doing the crawl past the New York skyline is typically iconoclastic, i.e. imagery for an age when there were to be no more sacred cows.   78c

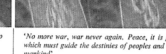

'In this age which boasts of its atomic power, it no longer makes sense to maintain that war is a fit instrument with which to repair the violation of justice.' **Pope John XXIII**, *Pacem in Terris*, **1963.**

'No more war, war never again. Peace, it is peace which must guide the destinies of peoples and of all mankind'.

Pope Paul VI to the United Nations, 1965.

April 25th.   Marguerite at Daytona Beach to Gertrude & Anne S in Escondido, *Received your card from Salvang. I have a slide that I took like it. Today at Cypress Gardens where we saw a water show like this.* The Human Pyramid One Dozen Strong described by the caption are smiling, no doubt through gritted teeth, as once again they give a small pleasure with disproportionate effort in their horrid though patriotic outfits.
78d

September 3rd.   RM to TP in London, *Here is a topical card written in Durham ...scenes up here of empty cartridge cases & distant bangs among the heather, aggressive riding instructresses who snap that there is no such word as 'can't', & a skating rink of indescribable squalor.* RM's card is more topical than he knows in a year when three Popes reigned. Paul VI died in August: John Paul, crowned the day this card was posted, died a month later: John Paul II was elected in October.
78e

Date unclear.   KW in Notre Dame de Gravenchon to Master L in Isleworth (Angleterre, as he adds with 'dig the French' in brackets). *We had a rough channel crossing. This photograph is a picture of the village near our house.* This is the Place de la Republique in Gravenchon where two petrol stations stare at each other across the road at a spot whose dullness sorely tests the tinter's art.
78f

May 30th.   V to Mr & Mrs JT in Hampstead. *No wonder its called the Florence of the North. How about the Stevenage of the South. Still there are other things. Marvellous museums & the music excellent.* One of the more architecturally optimistic cards from East Germany (see 72i). The postmark glumly recommends The Army Museum of the DDR, which is not one guesses on V's list.
78g

April 12th.   John B to Carlos G in Barcelona, *Greetings! The meetings are outstanding. We have a big God! Friday to Barcelona. Hasta luego!.* Gradually the Berlin Wall acquired its signs and shrines and floral tributes to many who lost their lives trying to defect. The inscription reads '13,000 wives separated from their husbands! How much longer?' The crosses and wreaths are in honour of Peter Techter who, climbing the wall in 1962, was shot down by border guards and left to bleed to death.
78h

October 9th.   Jane in Amsterdam to Miss R in Witham, *Ray dear... we saw this house on a canal trip. Best of all has been a RIJSTAFEL meal at a real Polynesian restaurant - 25 dishes - an experience. That was our wedding anniversary celebration. We are bang in the middle of Amsterdam - can see all the world from our bedroom window.* Anne Frank's room became a haunting place of pilgrimage for the countless readers of her diary including new generations for whom the war was not even a memory.
78i

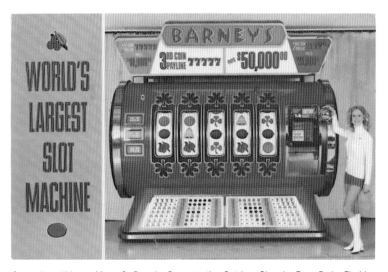

June 28th.   Auntie Trix in York to Mr B in Fishponds ...*back to Durham to pick up David's things. It is dull today but warm... attended the B Gillian Society boy's party here at the university.* Aarup's elegant slimline bridge frames one of Britain's most secret architectural treasures built by an architectural co-operative in the sixties. From its windows Durham Cathedral can be splendidly seen. Currently it is the Students' Union & no doubt where the party was held.   78j

September 15th.   Mom & Ron in Reno to the Butcher Clan in Fern Park, Florida, *Some machine! Put a dollar in it. Spent 3 days @ Tahoe gambling & had a ball! Won lots of jackpots but of course we fed it all right back... Back @ Reno now. Sure am homesick & miss you guys something awful.* Barney's Casino claim this to be The 8th Wonder of the World. It certainly allows the visually challenged to lose their money on equal terms.   78k

October 20th.   D in Stevenage to Miss H in Welling, *Returned from Lincoln yesterday. Rose being O.P.D. 3 times a week. No admissions due to "industrial action" - but may get into a small local hosp. My hands are very painful, otherwise O.K.* Throughout the seventies car shapes tended to merge with each other into a general rectangle. It became increasingly difficult, until the mid nineties, to tell one from another.   78l

Date/month unclear.   Tante Jo in the Dutch Antilles sends hearty congratulations to Rotterdam. Though sent from Aruba and captioned 'Romantic Tropical Rhythm of the Netherlands Antilles' one suspects that this American Dexter Press card depicting a West Indies band called Viceroy serves a large area. The cool steel ensemble is nicely portrayed with lettering of just the right rhythmic bounce.   78m

Vickie in Taunton to All the trogs c/o JW, The Stables, Charlcombe, *To all on the intercity 125 (that I know). They're a funny lot out here! mind you they were a funny lot back there! Julia Thank you so much for writing I will write to you personally soon. God bless...* These characters (Lady Rosemary, Constable Knapweed, Lord Basil, Belladonna etc.) are from The Herbs which first arrived on BBCTV in the late sixties. The hero is called Parsley. What better symbol of the age than a green lion?   78n

May 15th.   Kath in Rome to Miss B in Chandlers Ford, ...*seen most of the things we wanted and were not too badly hampered by local events (death of Moro). We did not go down here* [the Appian Way] *but went to Ostia Antica which looked similar.* Aldo Moro was kidnapped by the Red Brigade in March who held him hostage. After much talk of ransom and deals the ex prime minister was finally found dead on May 9th squashed into the boot of a small Renault.   78o

FIND THE LADY !

July 25th.   Pam, Ben, Stella & Leslie in Clacton to Alan P in Enfield, *Having a smashing time, weather OK. and once we got in Chalet OK. Went to the fairground with the kids today and left our guts on one of the roundabouts. Hope you solve the puzzle before you read this side Ha Ha.* Arnold Taylor, emboldened by recent absence of censorship, revives one of the oldest forms of pictorial puns (see 11n) with a sure and simple, if somewhat repulsive touch.   78p

July 5th.   Grandma & Grandpa in Llangollen to Mr & Mrs C in Reading, *Having a lovely time... our digs are fine & we have the key of the door. A Reading girls choir has been singing this morning and they are also on tonight. John Lill is the great artist. Lots of colourful costumes & plenty of music. Crowds of people too.* They are at the International Musical Eisteddfod and have found a local choir to support. These 'Dancers from Northern Ireland' are unaware that in a dozen years time, thanks to Michael Flatley, Irish dancing will have become very big business.   78r

Part of the office

A Students bedroom

March 7th.   RM in Stockwell to TP in Camberwell ...*I am hoping that the blood tests and x rays of which I'll have the results from Raymond this afternoon will turn out to have been unnecessary... have been thrilled to read that book about the actual life of the Monet/Hoschedé family. of course one always wants to know more...* As indeed one wants to know more about the people on this card and the tenant of the empty room at the Harrogate Equestrian Centre.   78q

PAS DE CHAPEAU...
CE N'EST PAS UNE FILLE SÉRIEUSE.

August 29th.   Anon to SB in Cheltenham, *I thought this card was too good to be true - it sent me wild with delight! Well done I.T. 'onze wickets Botham' and GB 'sept wickets' England. Tour team to be announced in about a week. Nous voici en Chartres, much inferior to Tours in terms of town. I got a double bed! Any takers?* In one test match the twenty-two year old all-rounder Ian Botham beat Pakistan almost single handed. The caption of this card is probably best translated 'No hat... not a respectable girl at all'. Saucy French cards are big on buttocks (see 79g).   78s

September 9th. (though stamped by H.M. Prison Pentonville's Censor's Office September 18th). Eddie in Pentonville to JLD in Brixton Prison, *Dear Geordie, Thank you for your letter. I'll write in a few days if I'm still here. I get pay next Saturday and will send you two or three pounds. Best if I get further credit from the co-op I'll square up with you completely. If I move from here and you'd like to keep in touch with your Uxbridge acquaintants you could write to your former fellow guest Mr M.* The stamp has been removed on receipt at Brixton Prison (in case of hidden messages) as a security routine. A stock multiview (which includes the card featured in 72t) with Concorde inset in its British Airways livery. Concorde began its New York service as late as 1977, the same year in which the prototype 01 entered the Imperial War Museum's display at Duxford.   78t

79

August 13th.   Catherine in Birmingham, Alabama, to Nuns in Sacramento, *...on the lake for a day, to a movie and miniature golf - Kath & I went to Mass on Sunday and then the Muppet Movie (I like the TV show better but...). I'm having a "good" time.* Star Wars (and The Empire Strikes Back which followed it in 1980) created a new mythology which still continues with sequels and prequels. The best bits are like Wagner in space. The Muppet Movie (featuring among the puppets one of the last sad appearances of Orson Welles) also had a sequel but not the same staying power.   79a

Piccadilly Circus with Eros, Symbol of Love, London. Kardorama Ltd.

May 4th.   Sue B to TP in London, *Back in Plymouth after three days in London 'doing' the galleries... I'm a foundation student at Plymouth Art School, kids all settled (Baby Ben is now 15), Rod doing well. We're always broke of course but so is everyone else. In your catalogue I read that away in 1974 your mother was still alive... we've both thought of her fondly often (big deal!).* The view is from the same publisher and by the same photographer, perhaps taken on the same sunny day in 1972 as 77b.   79b

August 22nd.   John to Mark B in Stockwell, *As you can see N York was built on a different scale to bonnie old London. Everything is far cheaper ('Gas' at 30p an US Gallon) including tapes and cinema's both of which I intend to make use of. I'm afraid I've been eating and eating without taking any exercise - like most Americans. See you in Eton or London.* King Kong strikes back with new buildings to maul, showing that a good myth has lasting strength (he was also the hero of a Harrison Birtwistle opera in the nineties).   79c

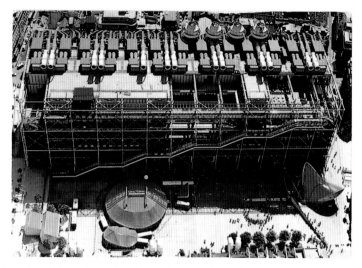

August 2nd. Vicki & Josh to the T family in London. *As you see on the front we are in Paris... It looks like New World Intestines.* The Piano/Rogers Beaubourg Centre redefined architectural possibilities with brilliant invention. Some of the 'intestines' are possibly ornamental but the concept is revolutionary and this is its first and most extreme example.

79d

September 13th. Jackie, Ruth, Sheila & Liz to Sylvia S in Manchester, *We're having a great time... 4 of us in a 2 man tent. No cooker & miles from the shops! We're sitting outside this amazing place at the moment, on a park bench drinking a bottle of wine as it gets dark. You should have come you fool!* The young gravitated quickly towards the most exciting space in Paris.

79e

February 19th. Alan in Los Angeles to Jean B at Arch Motors, Huntingdon. *Visited Disneyland & film studios. Everything larger than life here, including the meals. Prices quite reasonable though.* Frankenstein's Monster, and the Incredible Hulk are ready, thanks to the Universal Studios make up artists, to do their walkabouts on the Lot and to bring a little pleasant terror to visiting children.

79f

October 29th. T in Arles to JP in London, *A purple heron just flew by. Some French postcards are incomprehensible. I simply can't get to the bottom of this one.* This is entitled Promenade sous bois, Effets des Eaux (Woodland Walk: Waterworks) and involved four people on location plus a photographer. Like local wines some humour does not travel.

79g

August 20th. S sends this from Charles de Gaulle airport in Paris to Richard E at the BBC TV Centre in the White City with a three word message, *About the re-shoot...* Presumably he bought the card in Memphis where Elvis Presley's home had become since his death in 1977 one of America's great shrines. The gates (by a local artist) with their lurching perspective and nonsense music were one of the few artworks the singer commissioned. Elvis loved them.

79h

July 2nd. E & S to Hawkes in Stratford on Avon. *Bula Bula. Here we are booking into our lovely Hotel!! If you ask me the native is being a trifle too friendly!!* This card carries such an inexhaustible load of ethnographic complexity that a full commentary would amount to a doctoral thesis. Even disregarding the holidaywear fashion and the corresponding adaptation of Fiji costume, the crude version of a Kava bowl with mock tapa cloth speak their modern story (as does the matching luggage).

79i

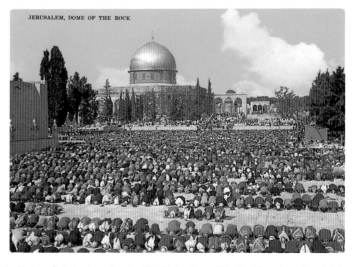

February 28th.   John in Rio de Janeiro to Pamela G in London, *Tonight is carnival night. We shall all go mad to the rhythm of the samba. Rio's wonderful beaches are smothered with dark lissom bodies. My miserable body has gone red.* He would be wise to avoid Copacabana Beach for a while. In the foreground of this nightmare view a pair of what look like identical twins attempt to get an identical tan.   79j

July 23rd.   Pete in Jerusalem to Nita M in Herne Hill, *Greetings from Israel! I leave tomorrow so will post this in Thailand... have packed into 6 days as much as possible. It has been wonderful the Lord has guided and helped me so far. Little miracles all along the way. God bless and guide you.* These Moslems praying at the Dome of the Rock during Ramadam do not have the same Lord, but have a share in Jerusalem.   79k

February 17th.   Coza in Sydney to Mr & Mrs JB in Sevenoaks, *...managing to see a lot of family and friends, and myself having had a lot of useful meetings. Hope that everything has been going well for you and that news from Ireland is good.* E Ludwig feeds Claude and the long tradition of European landscape painting into his fine sundowner shot of the Glen Helen Gorge.   79l

January 31st.   David in Orlando to Auntie Grace in Dursley, Glos., *Everyone is so helpful & easy to get on with... Spent the first night at the Hilton Hotel but am now living with an employee of Sea World.* David sounds like a fast worker. The Miami Seaquarium became Sea World with Hugo and Lolita, the killer whales, as its stars. It is claimed that these magnificent beasts enjoy such stunts.   79m

September 10th.   Mum & Dad & Philip & Mark & Heather to Portsmouth, *Dear Robert & Susan, Just a line to say, haveing a nice time. Weather good.* This minimal seaside message appears on one of the first six comic cards by Besley. These were produced by J Arthur Dixon in this year. Rupert Besley lives a mile away from his publisher and his morbid view of the alleged pleasures of the British holiday has made him the most popular postcard cartoonist of the century's final decades.   79n

July 14th.   Sharon to Auntie Kit in Birmingham, *...a card while I'm up here in downtown Manchester! and also because there's a baby Laker plane on the front. At the moment we're having a really good time. had a really long & busy flight yesterday to Crete... off to Barcelona.* Sharon seems to be a hostess with Freddie Laker's airline which in 1977 launched Sky Train, the first cut-price scheduled transatlantic service. The big Airlines, with Mrs Thatcher's help, had destroyed Laker by 1982.   79o

MARION MARKHAM
279-9321

April 5th.   Marion Markham in New York sends her publicity card to Beverly Anderson on Broadway, *I am currently in rehearsal for an off Broadway musical 'Not Tonight Benvenuto!'. It should be previewing on April 28th at the Carter Theatre. Please come.* The number given here is (wisely) an answering service but no longer serves Ms Markham. Not Tonight Benvenuto sounds like a comedy musical on the life of Benvenuto Cellini. It has a doomed ring to it.   79p

March 4th.   Jean in Perranporth to Mrs OLJ at the Maldon Bookshop, *Georgie & I are having a second honeymoon and 'getting away from it all'. Imagine how cross we were when a photographer popped out of a hole in the cliff and insisted on an 'informal' snap. Publicity follows us everywhere!* In Jean's world every phrase is somehow in inverted commas. The arch here, almost as vaginal as that in 26f, has a Dali-like surrealistic look with echoes of the Expulsion.   79q

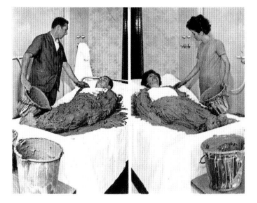

Date unclear.   Mrs K in New York gets a Mother's Day card from her daughter Monroe with love & kisses. The caption says it is Yet Another Kenzicard Made in Kenziland by Kenzoids. It seems to be based on a hasty snap of Rudolf Nureyev who had just featured in a fantasy biopic of Rudolph Valentino (see 24q) in which Nureyev, playing the silent screen hero, dances with his own idol from the past, Nijinsky. In a Ken Russell film anything can happen.   79r

July 26th.   From Lourdes to Mr & Mrs R in Derby... *lots of pilgrims here. We came with the Nottingham Diocese. Mrs Costello is here. She is in our hotel. I gave her the Mass Card. There is another lady with her from Derby St Magdalen.* This is one of the ribbed-type 3D cards, then still a novelty. It is significant (although there are examples from NASA etc.) that they are mostly of religious subjects. A welcome reappearance of Our Lady of Lourdes.   79s

June 16th.   Mary in Abano Terme, writing to Mr & Mrs J in Pont St, London SW1, sounds both caring and cross though her dyslexic spelling and baroque handwriting are hard to decipher, *Egain her, how are you, we did miss you in Cannes? wy? Hope you are both all rigth. Please write some time.* Another Dantesque trial for health seekers, here seen being punished at an Italian spa. The buckets of slimy mud are still poised so we must assume the job is not yet complete.   79t

July 17th. Wolfgang, writing to Vera Leitner in Vienna has a stab at English, *The loviest greetings from London* before collapsing back into German *Auf baldiges Wiedersehen* [see you again soon]. The London Pavilion in 1977 was cleared of its advertising and looks again as it did at the beginning of the century (see 00b). The three yellow stripes on the pavement mean Don't Even Think of Parking Here. 80b

December 23rd. A QSL Ham Radio Card from N2 BJO NY to Radio 2D7BW. *tNX vry Much Jerry hope to catchu agn. I'm only surrounded 3 sides by water Hi. which is only a quarter mile away try agn especially for patience on the net. thankyou. Marlon N2BJO Bkln.* By now the standard contact card for hams is the picture postcard, customised, or, as here, adapted with a stuck on element, though the old style QSL card (see 28i) is still in use. The words 'on the net' oddly prefigure what will bring about the quick obsolescence of this mode of contact. 80c

November ?th. Sally to Ann & John in London NW3, *I must have known deep down that if I waited long enough before thanking you for a smashing evening I'd find exactly the right card on which to do it. I could find only three of these - do you suppose the rest have been bought up and destroyed? It just shows what they mean by image-making - gives me heart!* Sally sacrifices a once pinned-up treasure for her friends. The card reproduces a photo of a much earlier Margaret Hilda Thatcher than the lady who has now been Prime Minister for well over a year. She will put her stamp on the whole decade and beyond as, for better for worse (and in her case both), a doctrinaire leader of the nation. 80a

March 24th.   Tessa to Sarah, F & Vicki in London, *All the rivers are frozen over and it is -6°c most of the day and colder at night. The Russians really do wear furry hats and people keep asking us to swap chewing gum for their badges.* E & C add *...we have not yet staged anti-nuclear marches!* This view of the Kremlin shows one of the century's most beautiful buildings, the tomb of Lenin (and Stalin until 1961), a Constructivist masterpiece both inside and out.   80d

February 17th.   Mr B, in Lake Placid NY for the Winter Olympics, writes to his class at the Gemini Elementary School in Melbourne Beach, Florida, *Dear residents of RM21, ...saw Eric Heiden win his <u>2nd</u> gold medal in the 5000 metre speed skating & also the luge races. My how fast they go on those luges!!... Wish you all could see this beautiful area. Hope u r all being good.* The field events in Moscow were boycotted by the US & W Germany as a protest against the Russian invasion of Afghanistan.   80e

BUTLIN'S CLACTON—*The Blinking Owl Bar*   Photo: E. Nägele, John Hinde Studios.

June 17th.   Frank & Della to JM in Camberwell, *as you see we are having a well earned holiday. But Oh for a monkey-pole as without one I am completely helpless in bed. To make matters worse I fell out of my chair on Good Friday... I'll leave you to guess what a mess we are in but still smiling.* This was written in the week that Billy (by then Sir Billy) Butlin died (on June 12th).   80f

September 25th.   H & PB to Miss EB in Bishopsthorne *...fine sunny weather. Mt St Helens hasn't erupted again as yet as anticipated, but enough damage has been done when you see the square miles of sheer & permanent devastation.* Dormant since 1857 Mt. St Helens suddenly erupted on May 18th. Apart from the huge environmental damage 60 people lost their lives.   80g

August 3rd.   Master Martin W in Chesterfield gets a card from Uncle John in Bedford, *I bought this card yesterday in London, and then forgot to send it to you - typical uncle John. Well we've finished school at last. We <u>work</u> at our school.* Then follow some schoolmasterly questions about the armbands of these policemen, who are beginning to look positively Gilbertian in their dress uniform.   80h

July 30th.   Doreen in Orkney to Leoni R in Bexleyheath, *It was as you say, good to meet again and we mustn't let another 22 years pass! Enjoying ourselves - weather sunny...* Though almost fifty years old such causeways (built by Italian prisoners of war and called Churchill Barriers) look quite new and might easily be mistaken for a typical early eighties art installation.   80i

July 9th.   Mary B in Kill Bay NY, to Our Lady of Mt. Carmel Church Choir, *Hallo gang & Fr. Nicalodi. Having a great time - miss you all,* after which she starts to list all the choir but gives up on Frank, the eleventh. The Adironda Hot Air Balloon Festival is one of many such events held in the US; this one takes place according to the caption 'in Glen Falls NY during the Flaming Leaves Season'.   80j

September 17th.   Mike & Lizi in Perth to Lt Col GY at Imphal Barracks, York, *so glad 15 Sept went well, both at RDU 19 and at the ports/airport, still rueing the 20lb Tay fish that turned out to be a pike and the salmon that snapped my new line. Golf at Carnoustie excellent. The scots still know how to empty a tourists pocket.* Here is the new Tay Road Bridge with strange minimal sculpture.   80k

May 24th.   Jill, Alan & Claire to Mr & Mrs A in Brighton. *Dear All. Weather is very hot & humid. Thunderstorms every evening so far. The sea however is delightful for swimming. This afternoon we are going on a tour of Miami now that the riots are over & the curfew has been lifted.* The National guard was called in to quell race riots in which five people were killed. Miami was changing fast. The Mariel boatlift from Cuba had started a month before: soon half of Havana would seem to be there.   80l

September 8th.   V & G in Morecambe to Elsie & Albert C in Acomb, *Had a lovely run here through all the villages after leaving Skipton it was lovely & warm. The lights are far nicer this year was a display of fireworks last night. Margaret thought IRA had arrived.* The lights of the cars look as exciting as the decorations in this view. Perhaps these were the illuminations of the previous year, now according to V & G much improved upon.   80m

June 6th.   AR in Aberdeen to LH in Twnberry, *All goes well here but sad to read in today's Times of death in Spain of Alfonso de Zulueta who was a pal from Chelsea Swimming baths where he swam in his spectacles.* Occasional group kilt-wearing is one of the oddities of this not overly Scottish family. The young Princes may have forgotten their kilts and must hide behind the parapet.   80n

March 23rd.   J in London EC1 to VG in Gravely, Herts, *Reggie and Val and Roy all offer heartfelt thanks - you make such a nice change from Shakespeare (well, Shakespeare commentators) and big encyclopaedias.* Another glimpse of the flyover (see 63h), plus the Odeon and an unidentifiable street, make up an eccentric card published in this year.   80o

80a. Ian Wallace Collection/Clouded Tiger/Paul Harley

80b. Continental Cards 581

80c. Alfred Mainzer Inc.

80e. Dean Color. Glen Falls NY. 60042D

80f. John Hinde 3C28. Photo: E Nägele

80g. Anderson's Scenic Postcards. Oregon. (Andre) B10168

80h. Young's, London. LD25

80i. Photo Precision Ltd.

80j. Dean Color, Glen Falls NY. Photo: W Grishkot

80k. Hail Caledonia Card/Whiteholme, Dundee 1714

80l. Koppel Color Cards. FNC 5992

80m. Photo Precision Ltd. PLX 18676

80n. Whiteholme, Hail Caledonia 253. Photo: Patrick Lichfield

80o. Birch et Birch 1980. IU03

80p. Ceylon Pictorials

80q. E Møller Jensen, Dragør

80r. American Discount BV.ASD

80s. Americards NYC #6.1980

80t. Aber Studios, Aberystwyth

August 13th.   G in Colombo to Miss R in Oxford, *Just coming to the end of the Commonwealth Education Conference. No better than any other conference but lots of very interesting people to meet... no sea bathing but while the final report is invented, am sitting on the shore and getting covered with spray.* G's world weariness as a conferee is contrasted with the spring and poise of a Sri Lankan drummer who might be modelling for a miniature.   80p

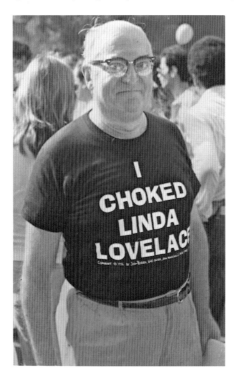

April 5th.   RM to TP in Camberwell ...*Friday 18th. The Collinses are coming then too. Cecil is yet again the subject of one of these absurd age-dismissal crises, this time at the ILEA's City Lit where the Principal, dept Head, students etc. all want him to stay.* The nonsensical nature of Cecil Collins' dilemma is clear, which is more than can be said for this amazing Danish site described in the caption merely as Stejleraekkerne (fishing rows).   80q

Peter in Amsterdam sends a typical scene from the Red Light District of Europe's most liberal city to The Lads at Spottiswode Ltd in Colchester Essex, *Having a good time and doing plenty window shopping. Weather very warm. nice crack!* Somehow every English postcard writer, no matter what the message, has (like the writer of haiku) to get in some mention of the weather. Whatever liberties prevail in Colchester, were Pete even now to walk the streets of London's Soho he would be met with euphemism and evasion and none of the frank attitudes to sex exemplified by this prostitute in her strangely padded showroom with its beckoning door, that leads to suggested pleasure.   80r

August 10th.   Pierre in New York to Robert, Karrie & Lydia in London SW6. *Insanity incarnate, fabulous time - living in the village surrounded by all gays of the world - no half measures here. See you soon.* The card is entitled Grandpa. Linda Lovelace is the best known of all porn movie performers as a consequence of Deep Throat (1972) in which she plays a woman who achieves true sexual fulfilment only when she discovers her clitoris is in her throat. After her years of immersion in drugs and sexual adventure she became a strident opponent of pornography. Perhaps the fin de siecle starts here.   80s

Mrs W''s son James writes to her in Stoke on Trent from Colwyn Bay, *We went to 'The Centre for Alternet Energy' there were one or two scientists there (like me and Dad) but all the rest were hipies. Then we went to a slate mine by the way the picture is this way up [arrow] PS I have got to write others now. Byee.* The grey abstraction of this card makes James instruct his mother which way up to view it, though once one spots the figures all is plain. This is the slate mine of which he speaks. Presumably James is also refering to the Centre for Alternative Technology and confuses 'hipies' with their more earnest successors in this Community of Self Sufficiency (as it described itself when founded in Machynlleth in 1975).   80t

April 3rd.   Ronald Reagan became the fortieth President of the United States on January 20th of this year. His wife Nancy accompanies him on this standard card of the time as indeed she became a constant part of the Presidential image. The Wagners, passing through Washington *(sunny gorgeous days. Cherry blossoms are in full bloom now)* on their way to Philadelphia, buy this card and send it to their relatives in Crestwood, Mo.   81a

PICCADILLY CIRCUS, LONDON

July 30th.   Grace writes to Gussie L in Plympton, *having a nice change, Wasn't the wedding marvellous ? Street parties here yesterday. Kept up until midnight!.* Piaf is advertised at the Piccadilly Theatre on this view of a sunlit day in 1980, posted by Grace on the day after the wedding of Charles and Diana.   81b

March 27th.   Mrs Judith P in Brooklyn sends a card to Gerbers in Freemont, Michigan, *I saw your ad for Gerber free bowls in Family Circle's magazine. I would like the 3 bowls, the 50c coupon & the 12 recipes from Gerber.* She uses one ad to reply to another. It all sounds too good to be true. I hope there wasn't a catch.   81c

June 30th.   Hortensia Ramy in Houston Texas, signs a petitioning card produced by the Save The Whale Campaign, addressed to the International Whaling Commission in Brighton. The text runs ...'Commercial Whaling is a dying industry and no longer serves a useful purpose. Please support a moratorium on commercial whaling". Greenpeace, founded in 1971, gave coherence to a slow crescendo of concern for the environment throughout the last quarter of the century.   81d

November 5th.   Andy in Liverpool to Natasha S in Crouch End, *Good seeing the pair of you*. The riots in Toxteth, Liverpool, in July came fast on the heels of the Brixton riots in the spring. Though the South London violence was the result (according to Lord Scarman's healing report) of 'racial disadvantage' explosively expressed, Toxteth was more an outburst of general disaffection in a slum area. The card is poorly made though the hurried Samizdat look may even be deliberate. Why a puppy?   81e

August 8th.   Tony & Kate to the G family in Wokingham, *Having a good time in Paris. Weather varies from pleasant to V.hot. Brigitte has moved across the hall... her address is the same.* The raffish fantasy of the Moulin Rouge has not survived a kind of Disneyfication. The Battle For The Planet Of The Apes is the fifth of a series that began in 1968. The Moulin Rouge itself similarly has the look of a remake.   81f

July 27th.   Lu & Tom in London SE1 to John & Maggie P in Manchester, *Thanks for a wonderful night... The Fair was nearly as exhausting as this week in Berlin.* The title of the card (one might guess that it comes from San Francisco) is TV Trim-Down. It takes a little working out and even when understood still leaves a question or two. Perfectly of its time in every way.   81g

The Carrier Dome

October 19th.   Ernest in Syracuse NY., to Mr & Mrs Smith in Skipton, Yorks, *we shall probably be home before you get this. Yesterday my nephew took me to a ball game. The noise was terrific. Excuse writing, had my thumb trapped in a car door & spent 4 days in hospital!!* The covered in Carrier Dome of Syracuse University looks ideal for all-weather cricket, though I doubt if this has occurred to them as a possible use. This is the Gipper's real game (Reagan won a Varsity E for football).   81h

January 2nd.   Jeanette in Nairobi to Joy B in Chandlers Ford. *Wonderful weather now. Hope you aren't having too bad weather & that you had a happy Xmas? Our New Year has been slightly marred by the tragedy at the Norfolk Hotel which no doubt you heard about on the news. Best wishes for 1981.* The bomb that destroyed the proud and colonial Norfolk and killed 15 people seems to have been planted by an anti-Israeli group (the hotel's owner was a prominent Jew). This is Kenyatta Avenue.   81i

August 4th.   *Thanks for your birthday wishes to me in June,* Writes Charles in Bournemouth to Gp. Capt. O in SE London, *I arrd. at the ripe old age of 89. "screws" are a bit loose & a little more unsteady on my feet... I am waiting to have gas heating installed. a £500 job but I think it will be worth it.* If they are old comrades it must be from the First World War. This couple needs no introduction however in the week of their engagement.

81j

July 31st.   Margaret & Geoff in Blackpool to Bess H in Birkenhead. *Writing this whilst watching wedding on TV. There is a party in the road later which we hope to join in, Geoff a bit better. all having a good time though a little cool at times, See you Monday.* The engagement photo doth boldly furnish forth the wedding card. Charles and Diana are of similar height: he must be standing on a step. A Modern Saga begins.

81k

January 19th.   Jasia R in Notting Hill to TP in Camberwell, *I've just had a letter from Leon & E asking me to remind you that you met him at Kitaj's opening & agreed to participate in the Medellin Bienal.* This archetypal picture of an intellectual (Stefan Themerson) is sent by another mentioning a third, met at a show of a fourth. All except the recipient (who as a result, will find himself in Colombia) are emigrés. A characteristic fragment of London's artistic life.

81l

September 30th.   Roy A in Eire to Terence & Victoria in Gravely, Herts., *Having come to Kerry via Cork we have seen a very <u>mondaine</u> side of Irish life all the same - we discovered for instance a gay bar in Skibereen.* Ireland was one of the first destinations of this ever travelling Pope. He made many appearances in his patent Popemobile and urged Irish Catholics to seek peace. 'On my knees I beg you to turn away from violence' was his message in Drogheda.

81m

Swanboats in the Public Garden   Boston, Massachusetts

July 14th.   Marjorie in Boston to Margaret H-J in London, *How wonderful for 'you-all' that you are to enjoy the Royal Wedding this month! Charles is a <u>favourite</u> of mine Lady Diana is lovely too. Within 1 yr's span I have attended the weddings of 1 nephew. 2 nieces. Adorable young people! One in California, 2 in Maine.* The swan boats betray their years of neck repairs and frequent repainting.

81n

C'EST LA LOI

Sans cette ceinture obligatoire, ce serait plus facile !

August 4th.   Jimmy & Sally to Mr & Mrs S in Tunbridge Wells. *Well here we are in Royan which, though not unlike Clacton, cost two hundred times as much to get here... Environs quite beautiful and explored in Renault 5... Foreign plates allow us to hoot & gesticulate at English tourists.* The caption reads, 'Things would be easier if we didn't have to wear safety belts'. In England this only became obligatory in 1983.

81o

September 24th.   Paul from the Kennedy Space Center to Mr & Mrs N in Southampton, Hants., *This is America calling. Hello there y'all. yup we's having a great time. Went to see the lil old rockets and space ships but missed the shuttle. We gotton our selfs a Thunderbird. Have a nice day - Ya hear.* Paul has seen too many episodes of Dallas back home. This is the first space shuttle (i.e. with returnable vehicle). A major breakthrough in April of this year.   81p

December 6th.   Desmond in Stuttgart to J & AT in Hampstead, *I'm having a very good trip and have seen a lot of interesting things. It's very snowy here... very cold but luckily german central heating is efficient. I hope you're keeping Tessa in order, difficult tho' that may be.* It's easy to forget how fustianly dull cards in museums used to be. Here is a miniature wasp trapped in amber 40 million years ago. Beauty inspires wonder and even the wild speculations of Jurassic Park.   81q

March 23rd.   Coralie in Sacramento to Alma & Herbert A in St Petersburg, Fla., *Hi - I really appreciate you remembering me by sending your unique cards. how nice of you.* She uses appropriately the latest Coral-Lee card to return the favour. 'A candid shot of Reagan at his Santa Barbara ranch'. The new President looks convincing as an outdoor man in this the US equivalent of a cap, tweeds and gun.   81r

January 20th.   SM to Shirley M in Morrison, Ill., *From Reagan country on the date of his inauguration.* No sooner does a President get elected than his home town brings out a card to show from what Log Cabin he started his journey to the White House. Here a local amateur artist sketches Reagan from the photo of 81a and adds the requisite biographical sites of birth place, school, and church (plus a mention of Mom).   81s

July 28th.   Julie & Kalie in London to Mrs G in Ripon, *We are in London today, showing Nathalie the sights. It is very busy but a terrific atmosphere. We were lucky to see H.R.H. and Lady Diana (in real life) at HMS Mercury on Saturday.*

August 3rd.   To E.D. in Fraserburgh, Aberdeenshire. *Dear Gran. having a lovely time come in sweating each night. Went to the fireworks but couldn't get moved bye. Your most loving grandson Roy P.S. Baught a camra Roy.*

Two messages appearing on this often sent card (based on the same photo as 81k).   81t

May 12th.   The Campaign for Nuclear Disarmament finds its poet in Peter Kennard whose incorporation of Cruise Missiles into Constable's idyllic landscape aims to stretch tired imaginations. He takes his cue from the official statement that such weapons are small enough to be transported round country lanes. 160 of these additions to English rural life were due for delivery in 1983. Mark writes to Paul at St. David's UC, Lampeter, *Sorry I never got around to writing... I'm alive, happy and well and retaking my exams in Bangor. I have two part-time jobs which keep me financially secure (despite my big overdraft). They are boardmarking in a betting shop (one of my all time musts) and barman in a pub. Yours momentarily, Mark. P.S. Great postcard what?*   82a

PICCADILLY CIRCUS, LONDON

Sunset Over New York City

August 8th.   Knut and Trod are on a cycling tour of England and send this from Oxford. *Caught the train into London... the trip has been trouble free with many valuable experiences. The weather has been changeable but even if rain drums on the roof as I write we are pleased considering it is England.* The conductorless buses (the view is in 1980) are still a novelty.   82b

June 27th.   Derrick & Eleanor McR in London SW4, *Not quite the same thing as London. Busy & lively round the clock ie shops restaurants etc. with the notorious muggings it's not too bad - though I haven't left yet... Local food pretty terrible. Worth a visit but a bit to modern & hectic for my taste. All seems quiet enough as the sun goes down over Manhattan.*   82c

June 28th. Gwen in Benidorm to Mr & Mrs M in Chelmsford, *Plenty of night life. We went to Cabaret & dance at the hotel. I got asked up (& said no) 5 times !!! They must have been short-sighted! Perhaps they knew my cash is sewn in my you know whats!* Gwen is evidently not concentrating on the early stages of the World Cup (won in the end by Italy). This was the year the penalty shoot out was introduced.   82d

April 16th. Het in Stratford on Avon to HAL in Kingston-on-Thames ...*Most of our roads are up with massive jams & our water is off all day for work on the mains so we're doing our best to make the tourists welcome.* Air France produce a beautiful card with cloud map over Roissy airport. Despite its renaming as Aeroport Charles de Gaulle many stick to the old version.   82e

July 16th. Gerald to Mr & Mrs Coulter can't resist starting his message with *Howdy!* He continues, *Dallas really is a fantastic place. Though I haven't started work yet it is plentiful.* Everyone in England knew of Dallas from the TV soap opera (broadcast in 91 countries) whose characters were as awful as they were rich. The city was never shown so poetically as in this shot at sunrise.   82f

November 12th. Diana in New York to HP in Raleigh, N Carolina, *A very strange performance artist is performing Sat. & Sun. afternoon. I hope you'll be able to go with me one of those days.* Being very strange was the essence of Performance Art, then very much in vogue. These small performers look to be in Brazil but are in fact in the Junior Dancing Championships, Bargoed, Wales.   82g

PEGWELL BAY · The Viking Ship and Hovercraft   ET5715

Precise date unclear. Andrew in St Agnes, Isles of Scilly to J & JT in London. Not as one would immediately suspect a work by a contemporary land artist but, according to the caption 'built by a bored lighthouse keeper in the 18th century'. *Terrific camp site right on the beach. Can't see why the lighthouse keeper got bored, but that's the 18th Century. It's gorgeous anyway.*   82h

June 16th. Annie in Southampton to Mr & Mrs F in Burridge, *Dear Auntie & Uncle. I am having a lovely time. When I was on the sisal trail I was blindfolded and my friend Keri Hinton was guiding me along and she was trying to push me in.* This is the dream card for collectors in the transport category with a fine conjunction of red car (parked) hovercraft (speeding) and Viking Boat (stuck).   82i

362

Big Surf in Hawaii   Color by Dan Merkel

September 11th.   Shitzer in Honolulu to Matt G in Sussex University, *High!!!* *(absolutely) Are you still a goat or have you changed to a boring man?! Well, whatever you are now I would love to hear from you. By the way I'm still as gorgeous as ever!!* A magnificent wave and no ordinary holiday surfer. This is Pat Conroy the surfing champion at Honolulu Bay.   82j

December 12th.   Tim in Kyoto to Liz W in Solihull. *Everything in Japan is very modern, organised and efficient - there are modern electronics and computers everywhere. Seichi is very well but his new wife is pregnant!* These two Maiko dancers at the Golden Pavilion are devotedly picturesque but perhaps conceal radios or computers up their sleeves.   82l

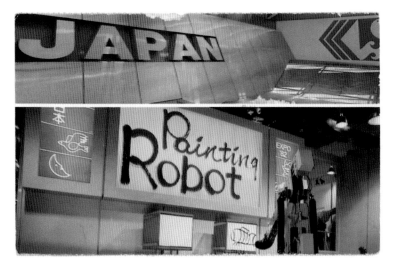

May 10th.   Mary & Dick from Chattanooga to Mr & Mrs B in Ventuare, NJ, *large crowds, l-o-n-g lines. China the most popular. The wait in line was 2 to 3 hrs. We gave up.* Mary & Dick are early visitors to Expo 82 in Knoxville. Though they gave up on the Chinese Pavilion (where people were perhaps queuing to see the Terracotta Warriors), they got to Japan's display, here confusingly illustrated. The Painting Robot seems only able to draw.   82n

April 2nd.   Tim in the pictured Pension Schwalbenthal, Abterode, to JP in Eisenach, East Germany. His last two words have a coded feel, *here on top of the mountain we are experiencing a blitz Schneesturm. Drive carefully.* The symmetry of tables and chairs is so perfect in this amazing card one might (wrongly) think of mirror images. The landscape, however, is palpably inserted.   82k

Elgar Statue and High Street, Worcester   W.3817

August 19th.   Trudy & James in Hereford to Gretta L in Halstead, Essex, *From a very nice place overlooking Worcester on the Malvern Hills we send you best regards.* They are very much in Elgar country and send a card of the Elgar statue unveiled the year before by Prince Charles. Elgar (see 04k) was a more poetic figure than this bluff headmaster. Malvern itself, even more belatedly, is also to have a monument.   82m

April 26th.   From Mexico to JL at the Royal College of Art. *Flew... to Frisco where I coincidenced Bruce & Pam. I'm just going back, because Latin America could get very crazy quite soon, Guatemala is very heavy, don't know what happened in Falklands. Much music and incredible revolution art... got into some sun. If the world doesn't go bananas in the next few days... love & peace Charlie.* Here in Teotihuacan news of the ongoing Falklands war must have been more rumour than fact.   82o

82a. Campaign for Nuclear Disarmament/Leeds postcards. Photomontage by Peter Kennard.
Kennard dates the work as 1983 but I have seen one of these cards posted in 1981.

82b. Photo Precision Ltd. PLX9981

82c. Manhattan Postcard Co. C178

82d. Promotrade Artes Grafices, Barcelona

82e. Editions Nugeron H146

82f. Texas postcard Co. D 134. Photo: Sherman George

82g. Welsh Arts Council. Photo: David Hurn

82h. Dowrick Designs. Photo: Robin Lenman

82i. Elgate Postcards

82j. W W Distributors, Honolulu

82k. Thorsden Verlag, Hamburg

82l. Nippon Beautycolour, Japan

82m. T W Dennis 12

82n. Knoxville Energy Expo.

82o. Anmex Asociados, Mexico

82p. Florida Natural Colour Inc. FNC 3014. Photo: Ted Lagerberg

82q. Turislika Stamp, Belgrade 4206

82r. Cosy WJ14, Austria

82s. Le Roye Publications. 621

82t. Chez Solange Restaurant.

March 12th.   Catherine in Rochester III., to Lou S in Los Angeles, *Thanks for the info on Ordinary Miracles. It didn't I promise, vanish into the piles of things about my office. It's just that there are many more books than writers...* Jack Ruby assassinates Lee Harvey Oswald, forever, in the Chamber of Horrors at Josephine Tussaud's London Wax Museum, St Petersburg Beach, Florida. The detective looks glumly on, his right hand in any case incapable of action. Oswald is coloured as if already dead.   82p

May 10th.   Nellie & Alf in Podaora, to Mr & Mrs T in Godmanchester, *It's windy, but warm, very rugged but interesting. Thanks for the phone calls.* The formal symmetry of the image matches the mood of Tito's Shrine in Spornan - Park, Belgrade. He died in 1980. At his funeral world leaders united in praise of his unification of Yugoslavia. By the end of the century his ghost will look upon a shattered dream. Belgrade itself, now the HQ of warlord Slobodan Milosevic, was bombed by Nato forces in 1999. It had long been a no go area for tourists who would not now find such a well groomed mausoleum.   82q

JOHN McENROE

January 2nd.   Eva in Sirnitz, Austria to Mr GMH in Hullbridge, Essex, *Hi honey! I am having a reasonable good time. As you can see on this postcard you miss quiet a lot? When are you coming? I know I kept asking the same question but I want you to know that I miss you very, very, very much. hope I see you soon.* Eva offers this exuberant vision of topless skiing bimbos to lure GMH to the slopes of Sirnitz, with more than a hint of Après-Ski delight.   82r

Verity in Peterborough to Esther A in Boscombe. *Went to Wimbledon yesterday. Had a lovely day and saw McEnroe playing twice, once doubles & once singles & he won both. Enjoying my week off now all my exams are over!* John McEnroe, wild-haired, loud mouthed and irascible and one of the greatest players of the century is here seen concentrating in perfect balance and readiness. In 1982 he was beaten in the Wimbledon final by Connors.   82s

July 29th.   John, at the friendly and very French Chez Solange Restaurant which always seems to have been in Cranbourn Street, to Mrs M in Crew Green, Shrewsbury, *Ma Darling, we ate here last night after the reception at No.10. I asked Mrs T. where the picture of the first P.M. to live there hung & she said many S.Y.Socialists* [Shropshire Young Socialists] *supported her. We ate at this place with Sarah L. who booked us into the Ebury Court hotel. Beautifully decorated but noisy traffic... Tons of love.* Even Mrs Thatcher might have been surprised at her stronghold of support among the alleged Young Socialists of the West Country. But that is what happens when you win a war. The whole evening sounds very Pooterish. 82t

February 13th. All is peaceful now at Jubilee Villas, an unremarkable terrace were it not in Port Stanley, where only a few months earlier the Argentinean troops surrendered (after almost a thousand lives had been lost in the Falklands War). Ray, from British Military HQ writes to Jim in Alvaston, Derby, *arrived eventually on 12 Feb after leaving Scotland on 29 Jan. Ten day cruise from Ascension Island, 7 days sun then 3 days of heavy swell. Life here is quite hectic 6 1/2 days working week no union here weather has been quite beautiful with blue skies but strong wind.*

83a

October 13th. Michael to Mr & Mrs W in Gosforth, *Yesterday went up to town to see Poltergeist at the Empire Leicester Square. Fantastic. Bye for now. P.S. Please could you put any post for me in the in tray on the desk in the office.* This view from around 1960 shows The Final Countdown (starring Kirk Douglas) at the still newly sparkling London Pavilion.

83b

July 21st. Brenda & Tony to Mrs O'T in Portsmouth, *Many thanks for having Simon. This was the view we saw as we cruised into NY on the New Amsterdam. Simon would love it here just for the cars.* Simon would have to hurry. By then, on the roads of the US, only the last generation of truly American-style cars were in use (though stretch limos, still unknown in Britain, would be a novelty).

83c

July 26th.   Mo in Auckland NZ to Sue W in Notting Hill Gate, *...I have bought the place - just signing up mortgage documents... it is a rather ordinary house but has a nice view. Mortgages are scary things though and the interest rates are frightening.* The witty change of address card features Chateau de Balleroy, a balloon built for publisher/playboy Malcolm Forbes: the heaviest looking of all floating objects.   83d

July ?th.   Florie in Hants. to Mrs McK in Skipton, *Came here to the Shakespeare Theatre Co. We had good seats & it is air conditioned so so cool & nice, Sat outside near the fountains at the Interval... From the post card it looks modern & ugly but its really quite nice when you get used to it.* Although not much loved by Londoners its excellent program has made the Barbican a cultural magnet.   83e

February 2nd.   Anthea in London to TP, *I found this card in Brighton and thought I'd post it from the appropriate place! Fraid it isn't the sunniest of cards... hope you enjoyed the break in Africa (and managed to avoid the mass exodus from Lagos).* [a reference to the expulsion from Nigeria of all foreign unskilled workers]. Here the postcard (in a series called Real Britain) starts to parody its former self.   83f

February 27th.   Dave & Glenis somewhere in the United Arab Emirates to Hazel & Stan C in Burton-on-Trent, *We are in a villa on the edge of the dessert. Sand from every window!! I've already met a Duchess, been round a Sheik's garden & visited a very primitive maternity home run by a group of Christian women... the goods are unbelievably expensive.* This is a boat race watched by men.   83g

Black Creek Pioneer Village, Toronto, Ontario, Canada.

October 19th.   Raymond & Claire in Toronto to Minnie O in Lomond Grove, Camberwell, *Went to the Pioneer Village yesterday, really good, had lunch in the old halfway House, some of the buildings were on their original sites, no electricity or water etc. made you appreciate all our mod-cons. Take care.* Though these uncannily clean reconstructions can be fun as R & C have found, they prove that the past (like early scenes and events in his book) is another and unvisitable country.   83h

August 13th.   Ian in Poole to RF in Tadworth, *Money situation back in red! You must go to Motor Museum. Sorry I couldn't get a pic of the Lagonda. Did Hilary pass the cycling test?* Henry Segrave (see 27d) battled it out with Malcolm Campbell for the land speed record which he took in 1929 at 231mph. The rocket-like sleekness of his Golden Arrow, one of the star attractions of the Beaulieu Museum, makes it look far from old-fashioned either in 1983, or even 2000.   83i

May 12th.   Ninian in London SW1 to TE in SW9, *Mias - many thanks for your note. How are you in this gloomy chilly spring. Keep in touch.* The magic light of an English summer afternoon gives a honeyed glow and luminous shadow to the court and to the girl transforming a buttock joke into a poem: what was the story behind this photo which has been reproduced by the million? The photographer is not credited by Athena the card's publisher.   83j

May 19th.   John in Paddington to VG in Graveley, Herts., *I don't quite know what this one proves - but just to say how very much I enjoyed your article in last week's Sunday Times.* John Sturrock (it is probably he that is writing) takes a photograph at the Confederation of British Industries and captures four industrialists expressing confident solidarity. At the shop-floor level things are very different as Mrs Thatcher, continuing her war with Trade Unionism, targets the miners.   83k

August 25th.   G in Cambridge to Sue & Edward in Notting Hill, *I'm not too pannified to enjoy the heat - have passed driving test (at last) - bookshop 'iffy' but we're still smiling (incipient hysteria) - love to come to P.V. leaving wombats with babysitter.* Chix Pix Studios produce 'Is This Reality?' their new anti-nuclear card. Not quite the graphic punch that the eighties have come to require in protest postcards. October's CND rally in Hyde Park was the largest for two decades.   83l

June 11th.   Tom in Spain to the Electrical Dept. of Calverton Colliery, Notts., *Buenos Nockers Senors. Weather not food ok. beach is straight outside hotel plenty of topless bathers what a sight for saw eyes see you later as I'm on the run.* Tom's witty pun probably went down well in the canteen and the card looks to have been pinned up for some while in the office. What happened to such frolics in the long miners' strike, the closure of Calverton Colliery in 1993, its brief independence,   and its final end in 1999?   83m

June 13th.   MS to Bob C in Princetown, Ma., *Dearest Bobby - baby you are my only friend that I have... written to this year - which shows you how much I miss you dollface! Much of the same shit has happened - my political group got closed down by orders from above without my knowledge (how leftist); Jeanette left without even uttering goodbye. Shula & I are in a heavy-duty girlfight: but I feel great.* Evita was still running in London in 1983 though Crying for Argentina was not much on the national agenda.   83n

September 12th.   Mum to Simon G in London NW1, *Hope you had a nice time in Paris and that you don't hate the place any more. Missed you after you'd gone but the weather is better & I can't even remember London. Hope all is well at 32. Don't want to know if it isn't. T sends love to his Bridge Partner xxx.* George Lucas has the magic touch. After the success of Star Wars comes another blockbuster, Raiders of The Lost Ark, also with sequel possibilities. Spielberg has it too, and so does Harrison Ford.   83o

83a. A R Charles, Stanley, Falkland Islands No. 14 (1982)

83b. Fisa. Printed in Spain.

83c. Nester's Map & Guide Corp. No. 137239

83d. Acme Cards. MW13. Photo: Mike Wells

83e. Robert Wheal postcards. Photo: Chris Morris

83f. Real Britain Ltd. Sunday in Hyde Park. Photo: Lliam Blake No.5

83g. International General Stores, Dubai. IGS/C27

83h. Royal Speciality Sales, Toronto

83i. Pitlain Pictorial Postcards/Topical Press

83j. Athena 9120.

83k. Expression printers, London. Photo: John Sturrock.

83l. Chic Pix Studios, London. R37

83m. Publisher unknown, Spain.

83n. Card Ee-Yak Arrest Co. NY, by Sari.

83o. Nugeron Editions E70.

83p. Virago, Collector's Cards No. 9

83q. Foto Flaneu. Panama. FF8010.

83r. Elgate Postcards. Printed in Ireland.

83s. Seghers Club, Zaragoza.

83t. India Tourism Development Corporation Ltd. Vakils NR 037.

October 26th.   Pete to his parents in Polegate, *spent 3/4 days with our PTL team - a good bunch of young men & excellent leadership. Much literature given and many NT's* [New Testaments] *sold (they value it more if they pay a few rupees!)... No time for shopping or sightseeing! I think this trip will be much more ministry this time... in Bombay to speak to O.M.* [Overseas Mission] *team & a big convention for Christian business people in a 'posh' part of the city.* Pete possibly sat next to someone on the plane who was going there to <u>seek</u> enlightenment. No postcard book is complete without the world's most beautiful building.   83t

C in London WC2, to VG in London NW1 (or NW1 9BL as Londoners were starting to get used to writing). *What a <u>very</u> late note this is. Just to say one million congratulations for Vita. I can quite see you have a <u>V</u> interesting time with R.* The splendidly named Virago Press gave new voice to forgotten women authors in handsome editions. This series of postcards of their rediscoveries takes its aesthetic cue from cigarette cards, a schoolboy collecting craze of the thirties and forties.   83p

October 5th.   Florence in Aruba in the Dutch Antilles to Fr. Aloysius in Barnstaple, *Mailed a card without stamps sorry. The Vincentians take care of the spiritual needs of these delightful & colourful people. The trip is fabulous.* The San Blas Islands women make these intricate appliqué shirt fronts that became much collected in the eighties. The certainty possessed by missionaries in remote places of the spiritual needs of others is always frightening.   83q

The Italian Gardens, Holywell Retreat, Eastbourne.   ET.5206

May 25th.   RM in Stockwell to TP in Vicarage Grove SE5, *Note the sculpture which is the focus of attention overleaf... how can I best find the current address of Charles Howard? It is wanted by the daughter of Wadsworth whose ptg. in the de la Warr Pavilion Howard actually executed... let me know if Peter Greenaway's Dr/s Contract drgs. are going to be exhibited anywhere in London.* The sculpture on the lawn must forever remain an enigma. Could the man be wearing a shirt <u>quite</u> as blue as that?   83r

June 20th.   Ray in Malaga to Mr & Mrs Hill in Burlesdon, Hants. *I'm just out of sight behind the piano! Haven't sampled many activities yet, concentrating on the tan... slight lack of male talent but there's a big new intake tomorrow. here's hoping.* Not quite the decorous music & movement of the Bourneville Trust (see 34d) but the beat is no doubt stronger here at the Seghers Club which claims to combine music, dance and sport with 'nature philosophy'.   83s

June 9th.   Orwell's 1984 made this year an approaching cloud in the sky of the latter half of the century. It brought no new apocalypse but many places in the world matched his glum prophecies, and certain of his terms came into all too valid currency (e.g. Newspeak) whereas Big Brother had long been a familiar figure to millions. For the ordinary Westerner the kind of value confusion and informational overkill that this card wryly celebrates offered its own anxieties. From S in London EC1 to VG in NW1 asking for a review of the new D M Thomas novel.   84a

June 19th.   E writes to S.W. in Venice, *If you stand here for twenty minutes you either get propositioned or arrested.* This of course is the same view as 83b, produced by the same publisher and likewise printed in Spain. However, for no apparent reason and with no significant benefit to the image some people have changed their clothes and red has come more into fashion (see note).   84b

November 29th. JL to her parents in Aberdeenshire. *Quite an incredible place. Talk about tall buildings! ...Statue of Liberty's enwrapped in scaffolding. Tons of galleries too many to see. Had thanksgiving dinner with J's godparents. Everythings unbelievably expensive - but mostly because of the $ rates. Hope the floods have subsided at home... By February 1985 the pound equalled the dollar.*   84c

May 22nd. D & E in Stockwell to MCK in Stockport. *Found this card at NT bookshop - called in for a drink and got 1/2 price stand-by tickets for St Joan (Frances de la Tour) - very good. Alas 'A' level set book so half audience 17 year olds (nearly all girls) who didn't want to clap - but did at the end. GBH is a long way from GBS but not too remote from Joan's rebellion.* In this Real London picture of contrasting and simultaneous cultures these Punk 'Soldiers of Destruction' are, even if posed, the real thing.   84d

September 5th.   Kate in Liverpool to Helen O in Warrington, *Vinny - glad to hear about 'right-on' house. I'm hoping to get up to Edinburgh on Sunday 30th - is that convenient? Don't know the defo date yet...* The old emblems plus tokenism in the crowd are brought out by the National Campaign Against The Police Bill (legislation which gave the police frightening powers to put down strikes). Arthur Scargill, the miners' leader, became a folk hero as the High Court ruled a pit strike in Maltby unlawful.   84e

June 3rd.   Frannie to Mr & Mrs T in Exeter. *I'm still here in Cebu! I have changed yachts once more!! 120' steel rust bucket schooner SOL. Getting expenses & pay $50 wk. ...2 wk dive trip with 6 wealthy divers from US. Only four on board. Helping in galley with a great gal Judy. May go o/land to Manila.* She would be well advised not to linger in Manila where protest was building up against President Marcos and his shoe-collecting wife. This Jeepney with its mixture of languages is the popular form of transport.   84f

July 30th.   Heather to Mr & Mrs A in Edinburgh, *This city or sprawling mess is full of Olympic madness. Today's the big day. The car parks near the main area cost £30 per day! The organisers want people to use buses but Americans especially in this city of motorways aren't used to them. The sky is swarming with choppers - security, traffic control + private I suppose. must be the fastest way to get around!* Politics, predictably, undermined the Olympic ideal once again as the Soviet bloc withdrew to remind the US of 1980. Drugs also began to play their part. 84g

December 26th.   L in Casablanca to RP in Highbury, *At present sitting in a café sipping* [Arabic script copied from a bottle] *or coca cola as it is more generally known. It is Christmas Eve... waiting for a train to take me to meet the others and go on to a Christmas soirée laid on for us by the mafia. However 'soirée' implies that we can only eat, drink & be merry after some music, so as far as the concert prog goes, we're going to have to play it again, Ruth.* Such cards are common in North Africa. It is difficult for the outsider to decipher the aspirations they reflect and what part is played by American socks, an empty bookshelf or a photo of a tree.   84h

June 13th.   Hal N Ottaway in Wichita to Marilyn N in Northford, *Our club's show postcards are not back from the printer yet... glad that you liked the design so much! I think it is one of our best yet!* Postcard collecting is by now a big, organised hobby with magazines, fairs etc. The Wichita club hosts one of the best gatherings and their fair is invariably advertised via a card commissioned from Rick Geary, the leading specialist US postcard artist, who has here designed Hal Ottaway's wants card.   84i

November 27th.   Colin in Port Stanley to Mr & Mrs B in Bath, *We are all settled in our duties down here in Fl. The weather is bright but very windy - 4 seasons in one day! We are kept busy at work... No excuse for getting lazy here as the sporting facilities are excellent. Quite a lot of Jolly Jack Tars around - on or off their boats, so Mr B you would feel quite at home!* The islanders would remember their 150th Anniversary which started with a triumphant visit of Mrs Thatcher.   84j

April 9th.   R in Berlin to SS in New Cross. *Traumatic journey - plane struck 2X by lightening as we took off! Safe of course. Visit to E. Berlin tomorrow and lots of evening trips... very exhausting but interesting.* The menacing red sky looks real as well as symbolic in this nocturne of the wall. If this were a film I should be waiting for something to happen involving that sinister car. This is as usual the Western side with the Eastern plunged in darkness.   84k

August 16th.   Roz in Gloucestershire to JL in Brixton. *Thanks for letting us stay & taking us to the groovy wine bar (get him yet?). The house in Clapham was no good, so I'm still looking...* The derelict small shop became an all too common sight in the London suburbs, complete with graffiti (sometimes, as here, quite sensible), boarded-up windows and peeling signs. Some got turned into the fashion of the time, i.e. groovy wine bars.   84l

October 23rd.   Mum & Dad in London to Mr & Mrs P in Mevagissey, *Eventually got to Central Hall. We have a clinic at the end of each meeting today 3 people got healed. It was all very quietly done and leisurely. Today is raining... so had to find a quiet spot outside chapel to eat but when we came in lots of people were eating inside in spite of notices saying do not take food inside.* Sales of yellow jumpers must have plummeted after this photo of Charles & Diana with Prince William.   84m

August 27th.   Austin in Adelaide to Prof.P in Lancaster, *...given about 36 lectures... plus the odd broadcast. I'm enjoying myself hugely and my reception has been threatening to make my head swell along with my waistline. Next stop is Brisbane for a big conference at which fellow-lecturers include Keith Thomas (with whom I dined in Wellington).* More fun than function in the foreground but Australian light lends enchantment to the Festival Theatre.   84n

May 16th.   F & J in Forest Hill to J & AT in London NW3, *Many thanks for a smashing supper and for all your understanding and good cheer. Caught the Rattler with aplomb and felt much better.* Wells Coates' wonderful Ecko radio design of 1935 showed, with an elegant arrangement of circles, that the world of bakelite and plastic had a poetic potential all its own. How quickly it made its way from a shelf in a comic (see 39p) to the Geffrye museum.   84o

84a. Hold the Mustard Productions 1980 at Alcatraz in Scenic Oakland. Califusa. 94609. g.HM-26

84b. Fisa. Printed in Spain. No 12

84c. Manhattan postcard Co.

84d. Real London No 24. Photo: Neill Manner

84e. Leeds Postcards for Nat. Union of Mineworkers. Artist: Paul Morton

84f. National Book Store, Manila. TRP

84g. Drawing Board Greetings Cards. Olympic Official, Los Angeles 40PZ0031

84h. Imprimerie Moderne, Casablanca

84i. Rick Geary. (Limited edn. for Hal N Ottaway) 220/400

84j. Falkland Islands post Office No 7 (of 11)

84k. Schikkus, Berlin.
PM announcement for Nostalgia 84 Antiques Fair.

84l. Deviant Productions. Photo: Jill Posner

84m. Thomas A Benacci Ltd. London. Photo: Tim Graham. LO51

84n. National, Australia

84o. Geffrye Museum, London

84p. W.F.L.O.E. Glangors. Designer: Ian Campbell

84q. Bamforth (with quotation from St John)

84r. Messaggero di S. Antonio - Padova.

84s. Schöning & Co/Gebrüder Schmidt

Details from 83b and 84b respectively (actual size) showing changes made to the colour between the two printings. This might help to dispel the impression that such cards are 'realistic' by demonstrating what random and capricious colours have been used. We have no way of deciding in, say, the case of the man whom we see next to the lamp post's top, whether he was wearing a deep yellow or a bright red or (equally possible) a white shirt. Thus a postcard is no evidence of anything having been as it is shown to be.

May 21st.   Shirley & Malcolm in Aberystwyth to Jean & David V in Chesterfield, *The Tunleys are coming your way! Is there a chance we could see you and possibly stay the night 20th July. Our boat for Holland (and a cycling tour) leaves Sheerness about 11 o clock on Sunday 21st. We promise to be good and leave all CND banners and Red Flag songs in Bow Street... we would bring sleeping bags and only need floor space.* Despite the brave effort the days of such banners are numbered.   84p

September 26th.   KL writes form Skegness, *The 2 J's. having a good time good fun, friends and fellowship. Food is good - we do it ourselves. See you. love & prayers.* His Place (which fits awkwardly above the shop windows out of a mistaken desire for symmetry) is a Christian cafe which has hijacked a favourite seaside postcard motif and caption. Chicken salad is 48p which sounds very reasonable and the inside does not look too threatening.   84q

June 22nd.   Sue in Venice to Het & Will H in Stratford on Avon. *This card marks the falling out of the 'Suore Comissare' on the Giudecca. I've been staying 4 nights with nuns, but now I'm not as keen on them as I was (told to go to my room at 10.15 last night - hard for a woman of 33!). Can you pass this card on to E.* Studies of study and reflection as devotees file past the bones of St Anthony of Padua.   84r

August 1st.   Dad & Mother in Travemünde to Debbie & Kevin in Little Rock, Arkansas. *We are in Germany & stayed the night on this beach. We have stayed in old castles till we got here. This was a new modern skyscraper. That is Communist East Germany in the background.* What would Martians make of these strange devices? What do these Americans think as they look out over part of the Communist bloc?   84s

July 19th.   Frances S in Sheffield sends to VG in London NW5 one of the cards of the century, but writes, *Apologies for this grim card - my usual supply of more decorous p/c's from Brit. Mus. & elsewhere is used up.* Mrs Thatcher had been in power for ten years and seemed like a permanent fixture. This remarkable photo with its echoes of Orwell's 1984 had gained sharper pertinence since the Falklands 'Campaign' (as it was still officially referred to). Sheila Gray's inspired framing of the word 'war' from the banner slogan 'Forward Together' of the 1980 Conservative Party Conference is a masterstroke.   85a

August 24th.   Sue to Mr & Mrs W in Eastbourne, *writing a stone's throw from Eros . There's a constant hum of traffic and plenty of tourists milling around. Working in an office with two other girl consultants in an Executive Secretarial Agency (Christian) - very friendly and pleasant, relaxed atmosphere.* View circa 1980 with a more varied crowd 'hanging out' around the fountain.   85b

August 6th.   Karen & Kelly to Aunt Marge & uncle Fran in Clarence NY., *The big [drawing of an apple] is as wonderful as ever! Saw the South St. Seaport Sunday (a new complex down by the old Fulton Fish Market). Have tickets for 'Cats' ($45 each!) for Wed. Classes great!* Apart from the mis-spent $90 on a vapid musical, New York seems kind to Karen & Kelly.   85c

April 16th. Sherilyn to Leo V in Brixton, *So hows goldfingers, these days going by. Am whittling away the hours myself clicking the camera over graffity and generally strolling wild. Went to see Al Jarreau in concert which was wonderful... Well, my dear shall slip this through the yellow slot so that it reaches you before I come knocking on your door.* More and more ambitious graffiti appeared on the wall. 'Hand over the key, Erich!' this says to Mr Honneker. A trompe l'oeil hole in the wall reveals another wall beyond. 85d

April 19th. Aubrey in NY to Tim & Jim, University Way, Seattle, *Hey Guys! So there I sit in this broiling 85° on a bronze statue of a nude woman! She has huge breasts. Over to my left is a small Asian eating a brown paper bag. And in front of me is a huge assemblage of Columbia jocks - ooh they are doing frat stuff. There is a very large Miller truck parked about 20ft from me. Aubrey is an excellent camera.* This sinister card is frighteningly entitled First Date. Unfortunately the unwitting children have perfect expressions. 85e

September 10th. Peter to JL in Herne Hill, *I got interrupted by Jehovah's Witnesses at the moment I started this card. What does that mean I wonder? Otherwise I have been maniacally busy over the summer - writing - all I could manage was 4 days off at a conference in Provence - not much of a rest really.* The ad at the top left is very much in the mating/dating genre which by 1985 had made its way from fringe magazines (and the New York Review of Books) to even the snootiest newspaper. 85f

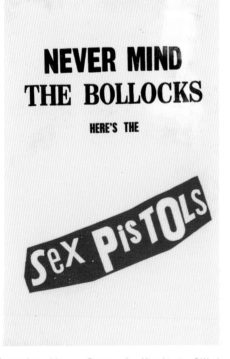

September 4th. Duncan in Utrecht to DW in Bournemouth, *...having a great time here! I wondered if they might censor it on the way. Unfortunately I didn't get the job so I'll be back in about a weeks time. P.S. I just found out I got the job in Lyons. I'm going for it!* Never Mind The Bollocks is the only authentic Sex Pistols album (designed as here by Jamie Reid). Sid Vicious died in terminal squalor in 1979. The group lived on in various guises (including P.I.L.). Their manager Malcolm McLaren at the end of the century was standing for Mayor of London. 85g

June 8th. Jen to Miss S in Birmingham, *Hi Dibble, ...so far I've bought 40 postcards of 17thC art to put on my wall next year. I'm looking very attractive, bouncing around Paris in my stripey shorts and running shoes with about 5 text books & a camera, not looking at all like an American tourist. Arf! Arf! I'll be in 'Haimates' at 11am Saturday... be in Brum until 20th June for knickers buying.* I don't quite share Jen's taste for Bernard Nugeron (son of the famous postcard publisher) but she gives a vivid cameo of a Midlands girl in Paris. 85h

February 16th. T in Abidjan to LP in London SE5, *Hello from the Cote d'Ivoire from me and the man with gold to spare. you ought to see him smile! He's not a big chief but he's a v. big cheese. When his wife shows up at the Gold Festival she can hardly lift her arms. The President is building a more than full size replica of St Peter's Rome in the capital (his village) for the Pope to bless. I'm helping to fund it by staying at the insanely expensive Ivoire Hotel.* The foundations of the world's largest church (completed 1990) were blessed by the Pope on 10th August 1985. 85i

December 2nd.   Inez in Minneapolis to Megs K in Bogota NY, *Had a nice flight staying in a lovely suite. Took a cruise on the Miss. R. with supper, banjo music and lots of Barbershop singing.* Ravel's Scarbo is hardly a piece you can whistle as you pass by, but it makes an imposing wall for those who park their car by Schmitt's Music Center. It's still there (restored by popular demand) at 88 South Tenth St.   85j

September 30th.   Kevin to John T in London, *Many thanks for the interview which we only cut by five or six minutes - HP had been told by a Holland Park waiter on Sunday that it had given him hope. alles beste.* Peter Kennard's montage (see 82a) advertises the Royal Shakespeare Co's production of War Plays by Edward Bond at the Barbican and makes all too concrete poetry.   85k

Margaret in Dover to VG in London NW5, *Many thanks for encouraging letter and p.c. With support like this I shall weather the campaign intact! Hope you and T and puppy (whose name I forget) are flourishing.* The Women's Press issue this cartoon by Sarah Webb as Feminism enters a new self questioning phase (much to the relief of scared men in the eighties). The outfit is perfectly caught (see 11l).   85l

Month & Day unclear.   Pat in Egypt to her mother in Huntingdon, *Tuesday, Spent the day in Alexandria, what a place! Egypt is certainly different. We're to be up at 5.15am tomorrow!! Sailing at the moment.* Precision flying meets precision photography as the Red Arrows make a geometry that unites five thousand years of technology and beauty. The pyramids serenely play their part.   85m

August 8th.   Simon in Cluny to W in Finchley, *I did a total of 585 miles of which 500 were from Calaise to Taize. It is realy good here meeting with people from all walks of life and nations. The morning Bible study is very good - led by one of the brothers. The discussion groups are getting good as people open up more.* Quiet days in Cluny among the ghosts of its great medieval Christian past.   85n

THE YOUTH HOSTEL, LITTON CHENEY, DORSET

April 27th.   Bob & Sheila in Dorchester post this to Mr J in Cheltenham, *This hostel is one of the early pre-war ones, it used to be a cheese factory! Warden cooks some of the best meals in the YHA which is just as well as the country is very hard for cycling and one needs feeding. One can't imagine Peggy (of 57a) feeling so feeble in the Dorset hills.* The structure seems as timeless now as a thatched cottage.   85o

September 18th. J, Y & S in S Devon to Andrew & Caroline in Eastleigh, Hants. *The weather, would you believe, is pretty good. We actually saw some sun today!! However the company is excellent so who cares if it rains. We trust you found some food in the house, we must have taken nearly everything with us.* The comic card lives on and the jokes (albeit single entendre now) endure unchanged. Taylor can still draw this boy's back with one sure line. 85p

September 17th. John F in Woodchester to TP in Peckham, *I just had a letter form Marvin to say he would like to see us for dinner. 27th or 28th. Which would suit you. 27th best for us but doesn't really matter, Cheers.* This is a Chix Pix True Life Drama card which borrows the technique of the photo-cartoon book, the literary equivalent of soap opera. They are concocted of all the situation clichés. This card reflects the new ones as economically indicated by the man at the sink and the mention of the women's group (men's groups were also starting up). 85q

January 5th. Alison & Henry to TP in Peckham sending New Year's greetings on a well chosen example of Glen Baxter's transcendental versions of schoolboy humour. These subvert a familiar style of illustration and captioning to anarchic or esoteric ends. This improbable meeting brings a character drawn (literally) from one world to face another, for which encounter he is (literally) ill-equipped. The cartoon dates from 1980 when Baxter was a secret cult. By 1985 he had gained nationwide popularity. 85r

14th (month unclear). Ann in Kathmandu to Tim C in Seattle. *Is this not picturesque? Hope you are okay and all. I've been focusing on my womb but it hasn't done much for me... In another attempt to work out my life I headed for the mountains twice but I think the exercise only helped my body, not my mind, despite what Jane Fonda says about it. I'm heading for Japan, Are you still thinking of taking a boat there?... I really want to talk to you because, well whatever. The East seems determined to keep its secret.* 85s

November 14th. Steven in Santa Rosa, Cal. to RP in Camberwell. *I am playing the Elgar in this town, the home of Charles M. Schulz, no less - ha!!! Are you gainfully employed. Are you madly in love as usual? I'm trying to learn a piece by Ginastra that's worth so much less than the paper it's printed on. See you soon.* The card is entitled Mrs Orbison and Alice Harding, Sidney, Ohio, 1910 and comes from Stars and Garters produced by the Gotham Book Mart under the direction of America's most fastidious postcard connoisseur, Andreas Brown. 85t

August 5th.   Sarah in London to her Granny in Pewsey, *I saw this card yesterday & thought of you! I went out last night and got in at 5.00am so I'm half dead today... a club in Leicester Square - dancing away all the food I ate with you! Been invited to a wedding... first church wedding I've been to. Trouble is I haven't got anything to wear that's weddingy. Typical.* By 1985 when this picture was taken by Sally & Richard Greenhill punk had reached its peacock phase, an outsider style of innocent flamboyance far from the late seventies anarchy of the Sex Pistols' 'God Save The Queen'. Perfect in hairstyle and accoutrements this dandy passes by a rueful graffiti message which reflects on 1983 when the country endorsed with its vote Mrs Thatcher's campaign in the Falklands.   86a

PICCADILLY CIRCUS
LONDON

August 8th.   M & J write to Auntie Jane in Saltdown-by-Sea on the back of an up to date view which incorporates novel colour effects involving blue buses etc., *May mosey on down to S.Coast... let me know what it is you're anxious about on pensions!* In the distance behind the double-decker tourist bus a notice for Andrew Lloyd Webber's Starlight Express lures the unwary towards a dismal evening.   86b

September 8th.   Michell writes to Caroline in Brighouse, West Yorks, describing the standard things she has seen and done before her departure en route for Canada.These have to include of course a visit to the Statue of Liberty which celebrates its 100th birthday this year and here shows the green benefit of a century of patination. The buildings, however, look, at sunset, as if newly cast in bronze.   86c

August 14th.   H in Sudbury to Jane McA in Old Newton, *Thankyou for a splendid evening. Feed the cats next time - corpses must be thought of as a hint!* Ronald Reagan and Nancy appear in one of their many postcard transformations. Perhaps Nixon's disgrace had broken the spell of presidential reverence. Reaganomics (coined in 1980) turned out to be a concept that gathered complexity. Cutting taxes did not seem to square with the billions of dollars to be spent on projects like Star Wars.   86d

October 3rd.   Annette in Cambridge to Mrs P in Louth, *Dear Mum. Do hope you are able to get out into the garden in this lovely autumn weather. Alan & I are off to London on our Metal Exchange week & have to host two dinners on Sun. & Mon. Staying at Curzon Hotel.* The Order of the Yellow Pullover passes to Prince Andrew and Fergie shows the obligatory ring. Another Royal couple set off on the now familiar route to a shaky marriage. Above them, on the curtain behind, a shadowy Queen looks pessimistic.   86e

September 21st.   To Tim C in Seattle from Greg in Los Angeles. *Doing a lot of walking read about 300 paces a atlas shrugged on way out I am looking at gazongas of skinny Philipino girl huge anti Larouche campaign. 'No 64' staying at Barrington it is cool hopefully Lupes. you should send some OTDEs down for Paul to distribute. hopefully I will find Trish and stay w her a night. She is very near Haight.* This intermittently coherent message is on a card entitled New York's Finest. OTDE may be the beginning of an enterprise (Off The Deep End).   86f

CLINT EASTWOOD

January 4th.   Peter in San Nuys, California, to Mrs T in Callington, Cornwall, *Dear Auntie Joan. Having a great time in good old U.S.A... bought a truck in Canada & drove across U.S.A. to L A, camping along the way. We've been caught in two snow storms...* I don't think this is an official card for Clint Eastwood's campaign to become mayor of Carmel. Yet with his wonderfully distressed clothing and hat, (and indeed face) he looks as if he'd take no nonsense. Noone was surprised when he gained a landslide victory in April.   86g

September 15th.   Geraldine in Paris to Jennifer T in Wentworth, *Yves St Laurent exhibition is absolutely WILD: I had no idea that he is so original, and 30 years of his work on 5 floors was terrific... also seen Paul Poiret's exotica...* Helmut Newton saturates the greenery to highlight this dramatic redhead and captures the angular mood of the early eighties. The dog works hard to balance the composition. One of those dresses, so fine on an anorexic model, which would make any other woman look like an old lamp-shade.   86h

December 26th.   John in NY to VG in London NW1 with *all good wishes for 1987.* This 'Composite Male Movie-Star' made by Nancy Burston in 1984 combines the faces of Jimmy Stewart, Gary Cooper, Cary Grant, Clark Gable and Humphrey Bogart (with some assistance from the GPO). The result has a slight Montage of Frankenstein look and I cannot really detect Bogart. Overall I think Archibald Leach, the boy from Bristol who died a month before this was sent, wins out: i.e. the incomparable Cary Grant.   86i

August 9th.   Graham & Nakki in the Vendee, to David P in Wandsworth, *Here I am sunning myself in France. No ugly bikini marks pour moi. Il est tres beaux here and je l'aime it very much. Even better news is that I able to collect le cheque a 'l'Edge de Fear' sur mon return qui je expectez will make you tres heureux.* Edge of Fear was a TV serial starring Bob Peck. Full (if not full frontal) nudity (female) was now readily acceptable if the context was a beach.   86j

February 5th.   Mr D in London writes to Mrs D in Lancaster with a dextrous mixture of gush and diplomacy. *I shook her hand! I spoke to her! however you are still no 1 in my heart my beloved! so breathe again. Thank you for your letter card - bless you. All my love S.* As well as having passed the disastrous yellow jumper to Andrew, Charles in this Snowdon photo seem <u>almost</u> to be affecting a trendy designer stubble. Happy Families is still the name of the game.   86k

June 7th.   Jeremy to Mr & Mrs S in Buckland, Oxon. *...performing in tents to audiences of varying sizes... columns of water pouring over one's head in mid-song. So much for show-biz! This church... still stands albeit without most of its spire. The wall, on the other hand is more or less forgotten by most West Berliners. One told me that when they think about it at all it is with affection, for it helps create the curious cultural madness of which the city is so proud.* Berlin in 1939 revisited.   86l

February (?) 8th.   Anabelle in Slough ? (PM difficult to decipher) to J & J in London SE15. *Thankyou so much for the great watch (it ticks louder than the other one!) and also for the delicious supper. That was a super cake, the only birthday cake I had!!!* Chic Pix produced this card in 1985. The real scare came in 1986 itself with the disaster at the Chernobyl reactor. Dangerous radiation levels were reported far into Scandinavia and a cloud of radioactive dust was said to be on its way to Britain.   86m

October 18th.   RM in Ireland to JL in Herne Hill, *our containers arrived from Uganda - very exciting - yet to see how the stuff has travelled!... Come and bring your man to stay soon.* The title of the card is Rape. At first a novelty in Britain bright yellow fields of oil seed rape soon spread to destroy the possibility of atmospheric landscape painting altogether. Minimalism and nostalgia compete in this card and the next.   86n

June 21st.   KVW in Southend-on-Sea to Mr & Mrs N in Durban, South Africa, *P.S. to my last letter. What type of video do you have V.H.S. or Beta?* The war between the two video systems was already all but over: it was won by the less satisfactory VHS, though a few stubbornly kept on with Beta for a while. The Women's Institute sponsored whole series of cards from photographer members like Mrs Popplewell.   86o

86a. Acme Cards. SRG31. Photo: Sally & Richard Greenhill 1985

86b. Dixon. Photo: CRH PLO295/5

86c. City Merchandise. CM92.15. Photo: Alan Schein

86d. American Postcard Co. 337. Photo: Alfred Gescheidt

86e. Post Office Picture Card Series PHQ95a7/86
Stamp design: Jeffery Matthews. Photo: Gene Nocon

86f. Sights, Ontario. Photo: Alan Schein/Fotopage

86g. Compania Mansona AP, Tijuana

86h. Editions du Desastre. Photo: Helmut Newton

86i. Fotofolio. Photo: Nancy Burston

86j. Editions Cely N.5882

86k. Thomas & Benacci. Photo: Snowdon

86l. Schikkus/Schoning u. Schmidt

86m. Chic pix R97

86n. John Hinde Ltd. 96 Photo: John Kennedy

Old style landscape painting uses the aerial perspective of colour which gets bluer and dimmer over distance. As train travellers know, a field of rape comes out and hits you in the eye.

86o. East Suffolk Women's Institute. Photo: Mrs B Popplewell

86p. NASA/Smith Card Co.

86q. Nucorvue Productions, Mellowne

86r. Illinois Distr. Co. B8721

86s. Columbia Publ. Co. Photo: David Rubinoff

86t. Arthur Waite Publicity

Fiona to Paul in Brighton. *How are you these days? Still scrounging off the state? Good. In case you're fascinated I got elected Chair Events here... at least that means you will see the back of likes of Mud & The Rubettes - Calling Up Ball! and the front of the likes of Primal Scream if nothing else. This year I've seen Julian Cope, Ted Hawkins, & Primal Scream who were bloody lovely. Sadly they didn't play Velocity Girl - they say they can't!? I have booked the overleaf for the Xmas ball & we're having Jeffrey Archer as compère and a sexy stripper. What a night.* The Indie group Primal Scream are as far away from the Heidelburgers as one can imagine and are still with us (their latest being entitled Kill All Hippies). 86t

November 12th.   A & G to Mr & Mrs S in Elstree, *visited the center - most interesting. Thousands of tree swallows descend on this place yearly.* The caption states that the photo was taken by remotely operated 35mm camera between September 1982 and May 1983 which seems like a long exposure. This was not a happy year at Cape Kennedy with the catastrophic explosion of Challenger in January. The first 'citizen in space' (Christea McAuliffe) was on board watched by her family.   86p

March 15th.   Julia in Preston, Australia to EG in London. *Thought you needed a more intellectual card than Graham... I am enjoying actual post grad reading and being away from the telephone. There have been no reported disasters so I am hoping all is well.* March in Australia should have been perfect for viewing Halley's comet but there as everywhere it was, at least this time round, only a disappointingly faint blob and not at all like this picture (or 10q).   86q

Fine Arts of Chicago

February 3rd.   LP to TP in Peckham. *This is the first decent p.card I've seen in this city. I found it in a Latino record shop that was playing a Latin version of All Shook Up. The store manager was singing along too until he realised I didn't speak Spanish.* Chicago celebrates again its Picasso (see 71r) plus the huge Calder Stabile. The moon is a fragment of a Chagall mosaic. The two men by the end of the Calder look suspiciously like Gilbert & George which would have been quite a coup, though by then the artists were not giving live performances.   86r

April 29th.   To Ricardo Ramirez. Prison Booking 821.9.866. L.A. *Hi Richard. How is things these dark days with you. Hope real, real fine. Don't worry... you will win. Did you get your tooth fixed. Hope so. Do you get excercise? Did you get your glasses Hope so... tell your lawyers to keep putting pressure on the Judge. you must be treated good. Jesus is the answer. your friend & sister in Jesus. Emilia.* Another fan letter for the Night Stalker, a serial killer who ended up with nineteen death sentences and still awaits his fate in San Quentin's death row.   86s

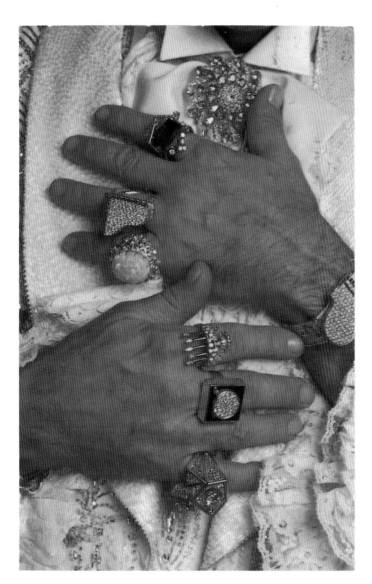

August ?th.   Anon in Boston sends sequinned greetings and a found poem, *Lulu La Bamba/They let visions/dance like sugarplums in their heads,* to L in London NW2. There are no prizes for guessing to whom these hands belong. Liberace died in February 1987 and Coral-Lee's card tribute is perfect for the flamboyant showman who would waggle one of these rings at a young member of the audience and say, 'See what you get if you practice...' Even his swimming pool was shaped like a piano. Although it was denied to the end he almost certainly died as a result of Aids, the great new taboo plague of the eighties which by 1987 in the UK was claiming a life a day. Since such an admission was virtually synonymous with coming out as a homosexual, denial in these early years was commonplace. Rock Hudson was the first celebrity to admit to being an Aids victim before he died in 1985.   87a

Date unclear.   Joseph to Grandma, *I am writing to you from the big Entrance hall to the house of commans/lords. Today mum and I went to get some A.D.S. stuff from the London office... we walked across the bridge where Grandad proposed to you and had a picnic in St James Park (we saw Buckingham Palace!). Then we went on a No 19 Bus and saw the Water Stones bookshop and Hamleys.*   87b

May 22nd.   Ray & Anita to Mr & Mrs T in Bradford. *Weather in the 80's - no air. Done all the usual things and been in Central park and watched a Martin Luther King Parade... there's some very queer people about (down & out etc.) Seen all the glamorous shops.* Under a wonderful moon the tapered tower of the Citicorp building shows to good effect.   87c

July 20th.   E in Upton NY at the Brookhaven Natural Laboratory to the T family in NW3, *Recognise me after being zapped by an electron beam? Great combination of intellectual stimulation + sun, sea; all spiced with marvellous Ollie North for President goings-on.* This is the Cockroft Walton preaccelerator. Col. Oliver North was spilling too many beans about US arms profits from sales to Iran funding the Nicaraguan Contras. Reagan was in danger of impeachment.   87d

April 18th.   John T in Pyongyang to TP in Peckham, *Greetings from the People's Democratic Republic of Korea! Unfortunately we will miss the Great Leader's birthday celebrations on Wednesday due to inconvenient flight schedules but have still benefited greatly from our visit.* JT is in North Korea for the April Spring Friendship Art Festival. He has played before the Great Leader (Kim Il Sung). While S. Korea is in chaos, in N. Korea all is sweetness and light.   87e

October 8th.   April in San Jose to Tim C in Seattle, *Rosie is a wannabe 'deadhead' now! Did you know that OTDE is reviewed in 'Anomalous Thoughts' Vol 1 #3? What are you going to do for Halloween? I can't decide. I hope sweet & Swishy comes soon. I'm going to become a rocker/slut/feminist. I just got an issue of BITCH.* Jim Bakker with his natural and homespun wife Tammy. Another corrupt televangelist he will soon be in prison for fraud (and divorced).   87f

Month/day unclear.   Joanie & Nim to Rene & Penny H in London SE26, *Hotel best we've ever stopped at. I feel like Joan Collins I'm trying to find a toy boy right now!! There's loads of 'circuit girls' here and they are a real laugh. Four of which are from West London! The weather is glorious so nice and brown - not all over. Keeping me boobs covered up!! I just stick 2 plasters over them - corn size!! The disco's and bars are fab - anyway must dash - got to file & polish my nails ready for the kill tonight...* The more serious collector would file this under postcards featuring postcards.   87g

May 20th.   Ali to Mum & Dad in Crawley, Sussex. *I'm writing this on the Inter City back to Sheffield just to let you know I got the train okay, thanks Mum... The bottles of drink which you gave to me are very good if you drink them via the mouth, but a jolt on the train has just made me shower... never mind, the lady opposite got a share too. Election Special Delivery.* Mrs Thatcher will soon enter her third term of office much to cartoonists' relief. This picture of her with the Hungarian Deputy PM must surely have been a template for Spitting Image's caricature puppet.   87h

July 14th.   Francoise to Mr & Mrs S in Brightwell-cum-Sotwell, *Fete Nationale! Thought you might like this amusing card. All going well & weather ideas for lots of photography. Godfrey has been doing a lot of work.* It's unlikely that Francoise and Godfrey will find a more touching motif than this or capture it as well as Phillipe Gautrand. The painter seems to be doing a good job but has had to add from another source the bowing arm. Bach (as ever ahead of his time) thus possesses a modern bow and adopts a standard 20th century grip.   87i

Venice, California

September 23rd.   Martin & Zoe in Cavalair-sur-Mer to Kris & Chris in Peterborough, *Cher dudes. Sound place this South of France. The race was good... journey, weather & food good too. Looking forward to the ride home but not looking forward to P/Boro.* The multiplicity of logos leaves only the wheels alone. Cigarette adverts would soon be banned from all sport (except motor racing).   87j

October 14th.   Martha R in Marina del Rey to Little Buddy in Paisley, Scotland, *Hi!... This is a picture of two kids skateboarding - a very popular activity for young boys out here...* The boys are Morgan Weisser and Eric Shaw who skateboarded for Dogtown. The skateboard, born in the sixties, took another ten years to get to England (where it rarely reached these heights). Dogtown is still a top team.   87k

August 27th.   Red to Paul T in Brighton, *Here I am sipping my café latte and pigging on a chocolate amaretto slice and not eyeing up any attractive waiters, and feeling quite sad about leaving this city of loonies, hookers, smackheads, cockroaches and falafels. Do you know the way to San José?* - let's hope Mr Greyhound does. The name of the Caffé Trieste raises a sigh among those San Franciscans who remember evenings when hair was long, espresso young, and Ferlinghetti dropped by.   87l

May 27th.   Tessa in Port Winston/Arromanches to Nixie & Charles in Worthing, *Hotel excellent... comfortable coach... Things are very dear in France. No foreign cars only French surprised me. Not too many people on ferry so that was nice.* In wartime such seaside towns became invasion beachheads. After a lapse of years they became resorts again, now with added tourist interest. Trim cemetery lawns replaced the mud of battlefields.   87m

October 18th.   Dorothy in Crowborough (whose High Street is pictured here) to Miss DW in Pinner, *Just to wish you good luck for Sat. The countryside is devastation all round and we go thro' it all each day to Tunbridge Wells - very depressing I find & everyone working so hard to mend lines and make trees safe etc. Sorry to moan.* Two days before Dorothy's card this area was in the path of England's unforecasted Hurricane. Winds gusted at 110mph and weathermen hung their heads in shame.   87n

October 1st.   D in Peking to Mr & Mrs T in Poole, *Have had a very busy and successful 3 days in Peking. The signal from the Hong Kong transmitter is very loud & clear* [i.e. of BBC World Service]. *Annie has done a little sight-seeing - but mainly it has been official receptions.* On January 1st 1987 thousands of students marched in Tiananmen Square; one of the preludes to the great demonstration of 1989 which left this square littered with corpses and gave it a grim name in history.   87o

1987 MESSAGES·NOTES·PARTICULARS

87a. Coral Lee, California

87b. Thomas Benacci

87c. Manhattan Postcard Co. D.0127 Photo: Bart Barlow

87d. Dexter Press

87e. PRK Pyongang. The Revolutionary Martyrs Cemetery

87f. McGraw Color Graphics. 981092

87g. Dominiguez. Madrid. Fisa. No 15

87h. Art Unlimited, Amsterdam. Photo: Attila Manek

87i. Editions Marion valentine. Photo: Phillips Gartrand

87j. Rothmans

87k. Venice Postcard Co., California. Photo: Jeffrey Stanton

87l. Pop-Cult Postcards, San Francisco

87m. Editions Normandes LeGoubey, Caen

87n. Toyco, Crowborough. VN18

87o. TTP, China

87p. Bamforth Comic Series No 983. Artist: Fitzpatrick

87q. AMM, London

87r. Gebr. Spanjersberg, Schoten

87s. Publisher unknown

87t. Edition Hansjörg Mayer Stuttgart, Dieter Rot collected Works Vol. 36 No 12. The work is made up of chocolate and acrylic paint applied to photographic print on canvas.

May 20th. HJM & Mimi reply to the same invitation as 87p & 87q. *Yes, thankyou we will stay for lunch we moved our Poland visit to be back for this memorable game.* They chose one of Dieter Rot's amazing variations on a postcard of Piccadilly Circus (see 88b opposite). This one is entitled Giant Double Piccadilly: it is one of a series of 96 finished in 1973. Dieter Rot also attended the party (see 87p and q) and thus saw his first and last cricket match.   87t

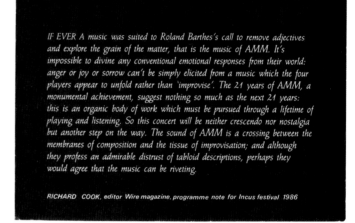

May 22nd. A reply to an invitation to a cricket match at the Oval (Artist versus Critics) to celebrate this writer's 50th birthday. The late Brian Johnstone, most cheerful of commentators on radio's Test Match Special sends his favourite cricket cartoon, *Many Thanks for kind invitation to your match. Alas I cannot come but wish you a very happy day & half century.* BJ kept his schoolboy humour intact to the end.   87p

May 22nd. A more severe looking reply to the same invitation comes from AMM who, alone among improvisation groups that I have heard, sometimes broke free of music's gravitational field, *Yes, we will be coming. Eddie [Prevost] will also be there for lunch and able to play if needed. Rohan [da Saram] too. Keith [Rowe]. John Tilbury* was also there and, in spirit, Cornelius Cardew.   87q

August 4th. Simon to Anyone at 141, Leighton Rd, London NW5. *Dutch architecture is stunning. No good postcards though. 'Coffee Shops' which openly sell cannabis are done up like 50's US bars - rich image makers must have had a great time deciding 'how to market this produktje'. Amsterdam is very clearly self-consciously 'arty' - but actually most of it really seems to be good.* The aesthetic of the card is uncertain but has an appropriately easygoing flavour.   87r

February 22nd. Barbara & Peter in Sheffield to Pam N in Keightly, *Thought you would appreciate this card. We really enjoyed the show. Tommy Steele - makes me sick!!! he doesn't look any older!!! how does he do it. We had a lovely day - it was worth being broke!!* It is rumoured that at one theatre Steele was so unpopular with the staff that men working high in the flies would save their urine up to mix it with the simulated shower for the title song.   87s

384

Vietnam War Memorial

WASHINGTON D.C.

December 6th.   John O to his family in Brighton, '*More than two months since your note about the Catholaity Bazaar was posted - it has followed us to Washington where we suddenly find ourselves assigned for 2 years. The metropolitan area enjoys the highest average US income - $36,000 per household - and also the highest murder rate, nearly one a day... a surprising density of homeless begging folk and destitute families. St.Mary's prospers by British relativities, but would probably rank as a needy area in those of America. Does Ruth enjoy Manchester? Andrew thrives at Surrey. Maya Lin designed this wall of names while still a student. She was only twenty three when it was dedicated in 1982. The Vietnam Women's Memorial stands nearby.*   88a

March 25th.   Ron C to Toowong Bus Depot, Brisbane, *Thought this card seemed appropriate. All is pretty but very crowded Went close to getting a job 'On The Buses' but the thought of a holiday seemed better. Keep those buses rolling! Going to Scotland for a change of comparison...* A Hard Day's Night takes us back to 1964 (see 65b). This is the card used by Dieter Rot for his variations (see 87t).   88b

March 24th.   To 'David' c/o Ms Williams (the first use of Ms in this book comes not surprisingly from the USA) in Luton. *Honourable Binky. We have officially named you to the Binkhood of New york. love Binky's Boys.* The story of 'David' and his attempt to get into the Gunness Book of Records has yet to be told (see 88j). Who or what are Binky's Boys?.   88c

September 9th.   Merjorie & John MR in Oxford, *we are just returning from 2 weeks in Argentina & Brazil... International Congress of Agricultural Economists. The Argentines have not forgotten the Maldives. Still signs at select points claiming that they are theirs!* `This is Niemeyer's cathedral in Brasilia, the ailing capital, declared a World Heritage Site in 1987 by UNESCO; a blow from which it may never recover. 88d

April 14th.   Clem in Nelson NZ to Miss B in Blandford, Dorset, *Hi mum, Lovely to speak to you last weekend. I'm working very hard and was top picker last fortnight! - unsure about winter work here - maybe some pruning but haven't spoken to the top man... finish picking end of April. We'll hopefully get down to the section then for some maintenance...* Performance Art in all its solipsistic solemnity comes to N.Z.   88e

April 11th.   Anne tries out her French on Mrs C in Hertford but falls at the first hurdle. *Bonjours! Je suis en gai Paris. J'ai vu la Mona Lisa... Je suis allée sur La Seine... Hier je suis allée au Musée d'Orsay autrefois La Gare d'Orsay.* Scenes of the Gare d'Orsay in 1981, and in 1986 when the transformation into a museum was complete. Orson Welles filmed Kafka's The Trial here in the station's earlier more dilapidated state.   88f

March 23rd.   Eva in Reykjavik responds to the David appeal, *Here's a picture of our president. She doesn't live far from Reykjavik where I live. We don't have a woman as Prime Minister yet as you do.* Any one who can answer 'Who was Iceland's President in 1988?', (and pronounce the answer) will do well at a pub's quiz night. Even the English on this tongue-twister card is quite hard to say after a drink or two.   88g

October 24th.   Tim in Medugorje, Yugoslavia to LS in Battersea. *No road to Damascus moment yet in this adventure playground for the devout. A fat Filipino lady waddling towards the mountain in high heel shoes... reminds us that Christ carried the cross on the first ascent. The discomfort of high heel shoes must be seen in its true perspective. My cynicism lies uneasily in a place where others are having the time of their lives. A spy in the house of love.* Religious tourism found a new shrine after an appearance of the Virgin Mary in 1981 to the usual spooky little girls.   88h

April 8th.   S in Mexico to PW & CP in York. *Few visitors, despite the spectacular monuments at Palenque... for this is where the Jan 1st peasant revolt began. Strange to think that just over the hill the rainforest serves two latter day functions 1. A Biosphere reserve 2. an exercise ground for (Zapatista) revolutionaries... who want to put the clock back to the traditional and small scale. All v.ecological but suffused here with romanticism, & that rarely succeeds, tho' disillusion with Mexican new liberation (Washington calls the tune) seems nationwide. Sweltering ly, S.*   88i

MADONNA

March 10th.   Another 'David' card, this time from York to Luton, *My name is Emma, my Grandma is Mrs S Walker. I gave her your address. I hope you get a lot of postcards and get in to the ginise book of records. If you do then I shall read about you...* Madonna is not yet like Michael Jackson (worth 600 times his weight in gold). In any case she is more substantial (if less talented). The cringeing caption to this card says 'The damsel... has a dog called Hank and once made the extraordinary claim 'I am a nice little ducky!".   88j

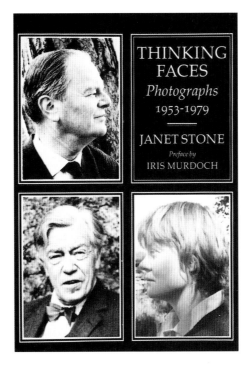

October 10th.   C to VG in London NW5, *of course I understand, reading and writing about them is almost as good, though not quite. But you have a great number of other very important things to do, that I know.* There doesn't seem to be anything special about these photos and one could say that by snapping the celebrated and the brilliant one has so to speak a head start. Neither Kenneth Clark nor C.Day Lewis looks to have the spirituality of the young Iris Murdoch; but then they didn't.   88k

June 6th.   Sarah P, 17, from Chelmsford, goes in for a BBC Radio 1 competition. The phrase used in such programmes, Answers on a Postcard Please, hints at a main use of the modern card. Sarah's answers include The Girl Is Mine. The prize is tickets for Jackson's Wembley concert. The singer's face is made of little that he started out with, and one dreads to think with what he will end up. He and Madonna compete for Eyebrows of the Year. Frankenstein would have made a tidy living in the late 20th century.   88l

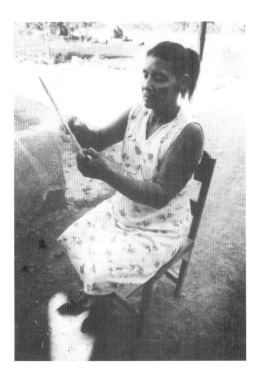

November 12th.   Liz from the office of Bristol Link with Nicaragua to AMP in Nottingham, *Greetings to... everyone in the Women's Group - hope you're still meeting! Not much Spanish teaching around but I'm working for BLINC - we have a Week for Nicaragua planned for the new year. Did you celebrate the result of the plebiscite? Nov 8th doesn't look too hopeful for Nicaragua does it? Concarino y Solidaridad.* America was obsessed with Nicaragua through the eighties. Others were obsessed with their obsession.   88m

March 14th.   T in Adelaide to A, N, M, A & C in London. *Things went well in Miami & are going ok here at the Festival. Just been listening to a Lesbian couple talking about the proprietorial rights of Aborigines - to the use of dots in painting! No dots for whities! They seem to run the Aboriginal painting racket and, judging from the prices, makes a huge profit. (i.e. No cash for Abbos!). I keep on being in the wrong place for cricket (big Botham match would be in Perth!). Nice people. Terrible food.*   88n

March 21st.   K & C & K in New Zealand to SW in Ladbroke Grove, London, *Kate has just pulled all the tissues out of a box and is now eating (must rescue them & her). Later... The weather is just wonderful (after the cyclone). Does Cosima have teeth? N.Z. is a great place for baby/childhood.* The picture is called Californian Car Wash and is by Sally & Richard Greenhill (how do two people take a photo?). Being published in Gloucester and sold in NZ gives depth to a wonderfully random moment.   88o

February 2nd.   Claire in New York to PMG in Brighton, *Hey Bro! What's happening? Thought I'd treat you to a bit of the local lingo. Having a swell time here. Is there life before 1pm? Not for me there isn't. Start work in a clothes shop on Broadway tomorrow. Early start 11am. Havn't managed to locate your hat yet. Said hallo to Quentin Crisp in a bar. Stay cool, my man.* Is the milk for the boy or the picture? Leonardo da Vinci who would approve of the scene (as would Quentin Crisp) lurks among the pile of books.   88p

August 22nd.   PW in York to BH in London, *My last postcard will have been delayed by the York postal strike so hope you enjoyed the Oval Test... managed to locate a few reels of 35mm film - but I've yet to go through it, and with care, as some of it is good old blow-you-up Nitrate stock...* This, in the Muybridge tradition by German Ulrich Kohls, simultaneously shows all the phases of a hurdle race. Lane Six leads all the way despite the efforts of a man at the start to nobble her. The crowd presumable are only shot once.   88q

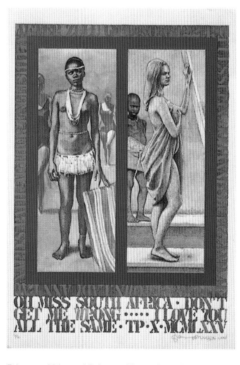

December 22nd.   Nick T in Capetown to TP in London, *You said you liked getting postcards from strange places or was it just strange postcards. Anyway, here's one. Doesn't she look relaxed? Nothing's really changed out here. Not that we could notice anyway.* The last sentence is puzzling but the outward status quo in S.Africa was forcefully maintained (four anti-apartheid demonstrators were tried for treason in November). A well-chosen image that I had in fact already used (see next card).   88r

February 28th.   LP buys this card at the Australian National Gallery, Canberra, and sends it to his father with a spoof message, *Having examined your early work here, I have decided to do my thesis on your wonderful book A Honeymist... Phil Lispoke.* The painting was made in 1975 using four cards as sources (inc. 88r). South Africa was represented in the Miss World contest that year by Miss South Africa (white) and Miss Africa South (black). The card of the Zulu girl dates from about 1920.   88s

February 3rd.   AC to P & C in York, *Just a PC to let you know that all things being equal you should see the downfall of capitalism by next Friday. Sceptical? Well its in my stars for this week. its Sunday already and I haven't a clue how I'm going to achieve it by next Friday - bit of a tall order really - any ideas?.* This cosmic egg with its self-devouring snake, which could come from any ancient culture or from the Opus Alchymicum, is by a new artist, the computer, and made up of the months of the year.   88t

89

October 8th.   Val in Dover to Mrs EC in Llangynhafol, Clwyd, *John & I are in Kent to see a friend of John's from his National Service days! We've been to see the Channel Tunnel exhibition which is really interesting. We popped into Whitstable on our way down.* This is the start of five years' tunnelling, a cinematic view of the machine that makes the hole for a yet larger machine to use. It is as if we are looking at a wall over 25 miles thick. Meanwhile above ground the battle rages as to the route the high speed trains will take (they were intended to pass fifty yards from where I write). Still they trundle through London sedately while at the other end they hurtle into Paris at full speed.   89a

June 7th.   *Have you ever seen this place,* writes April to Mr & Mrs P in North Myrtle Beach, SC, *The weather in Geneva & Paris was lovely. Here it is lousy, cold & rainy.* The Pavilion suddenly (and briefly) contains a museum of pop music. Along the facade appear, absurdly with Gary Glitter in the centre, effigies of Buddy Holly, Diana Ross etc. They will soon go, though the vague classical deities will remain.   89b

October 19th.   *Dear Grannie and Grandpa,* writes Danny to the Rev and Mrs W in Longniddry, *I am having a spectacular time in New York. We have been up the Empire State Building, walking, ice skating, shopping and went to Theatre to see Cats it was spectacular. Can't wait to see you and Bruce. Hope you are well and copeing with little Brucey.*   89c

June 6th.   Carrie in Ayr to Mr & Mrs M in Paisley, *Hi there! Having a great time. See when I phoned you I had a lump in my throat I was nearly crying I miss you lots and I love you but I am still enjoying myself. I can't wait to get home. It's not the same without you here say hi to Rona, Bamm Bamm the fish, the hamster and the snails. xxxxx.* Except for word-processing the computer was still a specialist engine.   89d

July 4th.   *Danish design exceeds even one's highest expectations doesn't it?* writes J to TD in London. *The sheer quality of detail is breathtaking. Today we went to an Utzon church and his Fredensborg housing. Sailing home Tues.* This is an earlier masterpiece, Klint's Grundtvig Church, in which it seems the organ's sound has swollen till the vast array of pipes envelopes the building.   89e

HANG GLIDING   C6515

Robin Hood Marathon, Nottingham.

August 2nd.   Anon in Barmouth to David B in Oswestry, *first three days were sunny and hot. On Monday I bought a surf board. on Tuesday we went to RAF Valley and saw Hawkes, Tornadoes and one phantom. We also went to Maes astro village which had a nature trail, Air shelter, RAF Museum... I have bought you a present.* Nature for David B's friend can't compete with manned flight. No cliff in Britain was now free of these often beautiful craft.   89f

October 7th.   Brian in Nottingham to Chris H in Nutfield Park, *Many Thanks for postcards for our charity auction at Lakeside in November.* The London Marathon was first run in 1983. Even heroism became democratised. Major cities everywhere started up their own Marathons. Nottingham's is named (as is everything else there) after Robin Hood and is here memorialised by the leading figure in British postcards, Brian Lund, in a campaign to revive the local-interest card.   89g

PARIS *la Pyramide du Louvre*

1789 - 1989 Bicentenaire de la Révolution

February 9th.   Daphne in Paris to JT in London, *What a fantastic tape and a brilliant birthday present... Have you seen the Pyramid yet? ...better in reality than in this photo - much better than everyone was expressing when the idea was first mooted.* IM Pei's delicate construction silenced all objections when it opened in 1988. Below ground all is not quite so happy. The Museum as Mall begins here.   89h

September 11th.   David & Mollie in Jerusalem to Mr RM in NY, *Very best wishes for good health & contentment in the New Year.* This is Hoshana Rabba prayer at the Western (Wailing) Wall. An ethnographic image of devotional intensity. The essence of religious ritual is that no one except the initiated could or should have a clue as to what is going on.   89i

Die Mauer am Checkpoint Charlie

July 24th.   Hazel in Lagro to Liz in Preston, *This is an amazing place - so much traffic, so many people & the smog is so thick the sun rarely gets through. It is very hot & sticky though so your dress is ideal - I can wash it at night & wear it next day! I'm sure you've heard about the earthquake - we are all safe but the schools have been closed for a few days.* Marcos (whose thugs assassinated Aquino in 1983) fled in a US helicopter with his wife, Imelda of the thousand shoes, when Aquino's widow took power. He died in November. 89j

June 15th.   To BP in Keighley, *I was there when he was!*, writes Rachel beside the caption of this card which reads 'Archbishop Tutu addressing the July 17th rally in Hyde Park attended by 150,000 people'. The ebullient Desmond Tutu was John the Baptist to the imprisoned Nelson Mandela. With Trevor Huddleston he led the Freedom March from Glasgow which culminated in this rally on the eve of Mandela's 70th birthday. The fearless and outspoken Archbishop was a perpetual thorn in the side of Apartheid rule.   89k

June 9th.   Ingo to Jonathan M in Stevenage, *Hi, I'm here in West Berlin for the German Church Day. It's much fun. of course we visited the Wall and East Berlin and guess who I met: Yes, Noreen my penfriend of GDR (but not by accident, we've planned it). We sleep in a school in the 'alternative' part of the city.* Neither Western Ingo nor Eastern Noreen could have imagined the amazing events of November when this seemingly permanent fixture was breached and its graffiti were hacked off for souvenirs.   89l

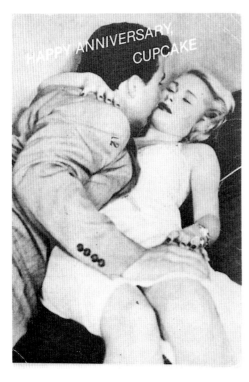

July 21st.   R in San Francisco to Paul in Brighton. *What a pair - 2 weeks not seeing eachother and we're having nervous breakdowns... our anniversary was probably one of the worst days of my life. As soon as I woke up I was crying I felt so down. I cheered up a little after I spoke to you on the phone. I felt so miserable again once I got to work. Travelling home was the worst...* (continued in notes).   89m

August 1st.   Oliver in Glasgow to SW in York, *Have just sat down for a sherry after a gruelling day of lying in the park watching the pretty patterns of clouds across the blue sky. Life I conclude drifts by and you can view it as clouds disturbing blue sky or glimpses of blue sky through clouds...* or you can stare at this staircase photographed by Jim Laragy and view it as a question mark surrounding a woman.   89n

April 3rd.   Joanne in Whitehaven enters the People's Moonwalker competition. Her answers are i. Bubbles ii. Frank Diles. Now the quiz could be What Were the Questions? This is an animal rights cartoon published by the British Union for the Abolition of Vivisection. Unlike more militant, bomb throwing, factions they have a sense of humour. Nor do they only support cuddly creatures. Even rats figure in their campaigns.   89o

89a. The Channel Tunnel Group Series 2 No 3

89b. Thomas Benacci Ltd. A125

89c. Alfred Maintzer 1675X

89d Bamforth That's Life Series H38

89e. Agenda, Copenhagen

89f. Judges Ltd.

89g. Reflections of a Bygone Age. 7. Photo: Tim Self

89h. Benoit Perrin publisher/photographer. 247

89i. Palphot, Israel 2107

89j. National Book Store, Manila PS 60111. Artist unknown.

89k. Publisher/photographer Kevin Ramsey

89l. Kunst und Bild. Photo: H-J Burmeister

89m. Galas Exoticards, San Diego PX - 203

The message continues... *I felt so frightened as when I got to train to Berkeley and come out of the station I couldn't find the bus stop and the area was deserted except for tramps & drunks. I managed to get a taxi home but once I got home I broke down - poor Nat thought I'd been attacked... I just felt very unstable the whole day - strange, eh! Well I watched Torch Song Trilogy on video last night that was very good... saw Steve Martin's new film - crap. Miss you.*

89n. Art Unlimited, Amsterdam. Photo: Jim Laragy

89o. British Union for the Abolition of Vivisection. Kittosi(?)

89p. A Doucer, Lourdes. Bernadette at Bartrés Keeping the Sheeps

89q. K Rune Förlag. Photo: Lennart Lindfors

89r. Nippon Beauty Colour Inc

89s. Publisher unknown, Hiroshima

89t. This card is printed by Battley Bros of Clapham, already an old established firm when I first met them in the early fifties. They printed my school magazine The Thorntonian, and hence my first mawkish attempts at poetry.

June 1st.　G to Moira T in Liss, *I got asked to do so many 'little' things by so many that together they amount to a major distraction - but I will love to be asked again - after the book! (But of course then I will not have the photo-copier!).* The card is from the UK Information Office. I voted Green. They got 15% of the votes and ended up (as a result of the mad British voting system) with no seats. This made the whole thing seem rather a waste of time.　89t

August 4th.　M in Lourdes to Sister Agnes, *You ask my permission to go to Lourdes with Mrs M. - yes you can go if it will not be too tiring for you. Remember what happened in Rome! It is very hot here as well as the famous 'Lourdes Bug' is rampant and many have been very ill indeed. Discuss it with Sister MC.* Or with Sister Bernadette (who is responsible for all this) pictured here amidst real sheep, unreal buildings and a collaged dog.　89p

October 6th.　Nanny & Grandpa in Sweden find what may be the right card for Rachel H, *We have been to see where Father Christmas lives. He was very busy collecting all his orders for next Christmas.* Though this looks like the storyboard for a Monty Python sketch it may have excited Rachel (if she was under six). Otherwise it would only have provoked a world weary sigh. Neither performer nor photographer shows the slightest trace of imagination.　89q

osaka

March 18th.　Andrew to Mr & Mrs T in Hampstead, *Hello from Japan - Bow, bow. (Here's my card). Osaka is v.industrial. Australia was fabulous. Gig tonight will be a fine experience followed by 2 in Tokyo. India is in melting pot 'cos of Rushdie etc. fingers crossed.* The fatwa against Salman Rushdie on St Valentine's Day proved ironically to be Iran's curse on Islam. Environmental pessimists think the whole surface of the world will eventually look like Osaka.　89r

July 19th.　Rachel to the O family in Brighton, *I have just left Hiroshima and am staying at Nagasaki youth Hostel. I visited both peace parks... such a mix of emotions run through you, and so many question - especially why?* As the fearful symmetry of this cenotaph at Hiroshima is to Rachel so was the Somme to another age. The Why is eternal and echoes through time. Only its location changes from generation to generation.　89s

90

"Berlin, nun freue Dich!"

January 5th.   BJM to Mr & Mrs H in Weymouth, *Well here I am, at the Wall, with everyone hammering away like mad with their pick-axes. I actually had to <u>buy</u> a piece for CM's church raffle... very cold here - definite thermal undies weather.* It is a fortnight since the Berlin Wall was breached at the Brandenburg Gate allowing Chancellor Kohl to step through and greet East German Prime Minister Modrow. The meaning of the wall had already collapsed on November 9th. This card, produced with old fashioned speed, marks the Grand Finale of its demise, the euphoric celebrations on New Years Eve. Those historians who favour the model of a Short Twentieth Century, beginning in 1914, make this night its defining end.   90a

November 29th.   Olive writes to the Almquists in Oslo, *Dear Dolores and Stig. We'll leave on the night train on Wed 19th but haven't booked it yet. Hope that suits you?* It is 1989, the year of the green litter bin, a brief campaign. One man studies a lamp-post and two others appear to be relieving themselves in the fountain as a tourist bus passes by. Straight ahead is Piccadilly itself, with Eros, at last, in true alignment.   90b

July 25th.   Sophie in West Jersey is having a wonderful time on visits to New York, she tells the Rev & Mrs E in Dane End, Herts. She brings the litany of sites of obligation up to date by visiting the Trump Tower, *We are hoping to go to Boston at the weekend to a baseball game and then I'm going to stay with Mary. Have been to a Modern Art Museum.*   90c

February 7th.   Annabelle in San Antonio to FP in London SW7. ... *in the middle of nowhere in 5000 acres... spend time riding around the hills. Everyone listens to country music... they eat an enormous amount of junky food and everyone has been divorced twice and is being sued by someone. Hope things are looking up.* Perhaps Dallas was near the mark after all. Horses always behave as if they are expecting to be photographed.   90d

October. 5th.   Annie in London to Mr & Mrs D in Geneva, *received the software safely - I decided to wait before buying a Mac. They are bringing out a new model which should be cheaper than the Mac PC is. Did you see IG got a KBE... LSE 'official' weekly bulletin quoted him as saying that while he was WF of UNDO he would arrange to be on another continent when Waldheim called a meeting.* Mike Wells' brilliantly spotted coupling of legs in SW London makes Annie ask *Is this a peace card?*   90e

April 11th.   L & E in Bradford to SW in York, *We are currently having a great break in the Dales. In a fit of madness we bought a fine stone trough. God knows how we will manhandle it out of the car. Overleaf must be one of the most eccentric scions of the aristocracy.* This is the Marquis of Bath with Marquis, the first of the lion cubs born on his Safari Park.   90f

August 23rd.   *I agonised over this card!* writes T in Lincoln to SW in York, *hope it raises a smile!! Had a good run back to Lincoln - 1 1/2 hrs. Best of luck with all your projects from the attic to the Derwent and back again...* Committed Cards borrow a 2nd world war picture of a 1st World War theme (What did you do in the War, Daddy) and adapt the title to match a current crisis.   90g

February 21st.   James in Gloucester to VE in London NW5, *Your club has let me in ! In future I am to be addressed as an Academician! Thanks & love.* For 'Women Axe Section 28' (which banned schools etc. promoting or endorsing homosexual relationships) Angela Martin provides a gentle cartoon based on The Green Cross Code (a junior road safety campaign). Section 28 remains a charged issue.   90h

May 7th.   Mike in NY to JW. in Camberwell, *Big Music should be out immediately - as soon as Declan gets supplies sent out!! Gerard Talbot is very helpful & lots of fun... getting a mortgage for my apt. here.* Post-modernism strikes deep in this installation/performance artwork by Sandy Skoglund, shown at the appropriately named Sharpe Gallery in New York.   90i

September 24th.   Laura in Stirling to SW in York, *Well, you have made it, the Daily Telegraph no less... I am in the cold North... long walks by the sea, long talks and listening to Country & Western music & Abbess Hildegard of Bingen (Gothic Voices) - you see I am unpredictable as ever!! Have survived at work, now hopefully with a new lot of committees - Women's and lesbian & Gay which hopefully will be more interesting.* In December 1989 the ever-exiled Dalai Lama received the Nobel Prize for Peace.   90j

November 29th.   Dave & Sue to Mr & Mrs C in Merseyside, *Arrived OK, Sue has cramp in her hands never out of her purse or writing cheques so I am writing this, very cold very crowded and expensive see you Friday.* This looks a bit like rentabobby meets rentapunk-or-two. To make it even more of a London scene they stand in front of the all but vanished telephone boxes. As so often the postcard depicts as typical that which is almost no longer there (which could also be said of policemen on the beat).   90k

October 25th.   *What an exciting time to be in this city,* writes Erika to Lou S in Sebastopol, California, *Many problems but incredibly dynamic. The wall is no more except parts of it which artists are using to paint on (both east & west). Visited my birthtown Neustrelitz in the northeast. Russian officers maintain their privilege there. Talk to you about the book soon.* A later report than 90a, this mentions the problems that had to be faced. There were traumas in the wake of those first heady moments of victorious euphoria.   90l

October 15th.   John in Walford to Trevor L at BBC Radio Cambs, *I am pleased that you put two editions in the fridge while you were away - so much better than handing over to a Rolling Stones fan!! 'Strike up the Band' was used by AFN. They took 'Music While You Work' from the BBC. We need more 30's & 40's music not less.* The perfection of tone here announces the work of Robert Mapplethorpe who died of AIDS in 1989. A Washington retrospective let loose the hounds of wrath. Government arts funding came into question.   90m

May 9th.   P in San Francisco to HP in Raleigh, NC, *Picked this up in Balt Museum... Baltimore surprised me most of all on my East Coast swing. It was totally action-packed. Desmond was the highlight. Fun to see your own country through a foreigner's eyes. He was aghast at the clunking air-conditioners & old fashioned phones & rude & ignorant cab-drivers. Reunion was an insightful experience. Previewed Universal Studios. Makes Epcote look like a Model T Ford.* This card is from a book of tear-off cards called Housewives in Hell.   90n

January 2nd.   Roy to T & V in Kentish Town, *I shall decode this card for you when next we meet - that was a lovely lunch in your memorable garden - sorry I had to run away early - it's a life of deadlines...* Roy will have a job decoding even the list of ingredients in this work by performance artist Bobby Baker entitled Drawing On A Mother's Experience. They include Cold Roast beef, skimmed milk, frozen fish pie, Guinness, Greek strained sheep's milk yoghurt, tinned blackcurrants, tomato chutney, sponge fingers etc.   90o

90a. Schikkus, Berlin. Silverfest am Brandenburger Tor.

90b. Thomas & Benacci A63. Photo: Brandalise

90c. Ogden Allied Leisure Services. (Alma) 1217

90d. Texas Postcard Co. T219

90e. Acme cards MW26. Photo: John Wells

90f. John Hinde. 2EAT5

90g. Committed Cards PC576

90h. Leeds postcards for Women Axe Section 28/The Pankhurst Centre. Artist: Angela Martin

90i. Sandy Skoglund/Fotofolio Z108. Neo-Auto: The Lost and Found. Photo: S Skoglund

90j. Das Color, Kathmandu. Photo: Alison Wright

90k. Whiteway Publications WPL 1984. Photo: Joe Cornish

90l. Kunst und Bild, Berlin.

90m. Fotofolio/Robert Mapplethorpe. RM12 Cedric 1977. photo: Robert Mapplethorpe

90n. American Postcard CO. 1243 from Housewives In Hell. Photo: Petrified Film Archives.

90o. Bobby Baker. Photo Andrew Whitlock.

90p. Art Unlimited, Amsterdam C 1025 Flowerpower No 20. Photo: Paul Huif

90q. Leeds Postcards/El Salvador Committee for Human Rights. Refugees of El Salvador - A Hope in Hell. Photo: Mike George

90r. Dragon Publishing Co, Llandeilo. Photo: Tegwyn Roberts

90s. Leo Cards, Eastbourne. Photo: Don Carr

90t. Beautiful Photographs, Leningrad 1988 (detail).

May 21st.   Hilary in Leningrad to Mr & Mrs TVW in Holloway, *Picture shows Pushkin's Bronze Horseman rearing up in dismay at first sight of western tourists. it is lilac time in the Kremlin & under Gorbachev they sometimes even sell ice cream on the streets. Moscow TV shows the Deputies fighting for their lives every day. The Supreme Soviet - like watching the French Revolution in action... meanwhile looking at pictures till our eyes pop out & our heads spin.*   90t

June 4th.   *Best of luck tomorrow with your show,* writes Vivian in Keswick to artist and rose-grower Tony E in London SW, *sorry I couldn't be there very much enjoyed photographing your garden.* If either Tony's roses or Vivian's photographs come out anything like this (in Paul Huif's picture entitled Flowerpower) they will be well satisfied.   90p

April 2nd.   Lucinda worthily to MO in Brighton, *Many thanks for offering us all the opportunity to consolidate our thoughts of the Vigil. I am encouraged that we all feel animated to continue working for social justice whether it be in the local community or the International arena.* In this case for El Salvador which squeezed a guerrilla bloodbath in between a major earthquake and Hurricane Mitch.   90q

August 8th.   Bobbie in Gwent to Mr & Mrs B in Brentford, *Hi, having a lovely time but not getting much sleep (about 2 hrs per night). P.S. I've got to walk 2 - 3 bloody miles to the pub every night. It's killing me.* A very druidic moment called in the caption Listening to the Adjudication. The ethnic robes (except for the vacated outfit on the left) reveal a fine array of Eisteddfod expressions.   90r

August 14th.   VJS & R to Becca G in Norwich, *We were at Worthing yesterday - All England Championship - the Greens have changes since this photo was taken. Saw both Norfolk teams lose! Bought one Fairing in Arundel. No C.R.'s in sight.* Bowlers replace themselves so that if you pass a green daily for forty years it seems as if the same people of the same age are playing an endless game.   90s

November 15th.   D in Paddington to Jane in Stowmarket, *Perhaps this is where I should be! Very relieved to talk to you instead. I'll write and you'll write and then have some lunch.* This is no ordinary couch. Of all couches it has symbolic preeminence being that belonging to Sigmund Freud and thus the avatar of all psychiatrists' couches in life and in film and in cartoons about shrinks. Freud's reputation rose with the dawn of the century (his scientific study of dreams was published in 1900) and he became one of the most influential figures in world thought. In more recent years, however, his reputation as a scientist has gone into steep decline as one by one his researches and theories have been discredited. Yet he changed forever the way we talk about the mind. Anna Freud, his daughter, now under a similar shadow, died in 1982 and the London house where the exiled Freud spent the last year of his life was turned into a museum.   91a

January 15th.   Katherine to the Boggs family in Welham Green, *Just wanted to say thankyou for the lovely weekend. Also thankyou for the boots. They're WICKED (Innit!). I'm REALLY looking forward to Switzerland SO much. I've practically told the whole college. Hope we don't get bombed at Heathrow!* The hippies seem to have gone but summer sunshine brings out the worst in shirts.   91b

November 9th.   Pat writes to Aunt Rube in Hindhead, *It's a long way to come to write a thank you note! We're here with some friends to run the New York Marathon - not me personally. Seeing all the sights. Thank you so much for the birthday cheque.* John Lantero takes the best yet of the classic bird's eye view panoramas on what seems (apart from the pollution layer) a perfect day.   91c

October 23rd.   FLR in Buzzards Bay MA, to GG in Bellingham W17, *Big Big News. Wall Drug may be coming to the East Coast - Wowie Zowie and all that enthusiastic kind of stuff. RU ready?* This is, according to the caption, 'Ted & Bill Huckstead toasting the travelling public with ice water, in camera's eye view of the World's Most Famous Drug Store'. The South Dakota store just grew and grew (see 49m).   91d

May 28th.   Tony in Hathersage to Mrs N in Carshalton, *Holidays can be quite a 'grind'. Caravan has all 'mod cons'. Countryside is superb with some great walks. Cheers.* It looks like yet another artwork on some improving sculpture trail but the punning message has already given the game away. These are gritstone mill wheels abandoned in the place they were made.   91e

May 15th.   P in San Francisco to HP in Raleigh, NC, *I'm going to have to employ you //y time as my agent in Raleigh. Things are heating up there & I'm receiving my usual full quota of neglect... SF only recently beginning to look appealing again. Fancy new sushi spot & flower shop 3 blocks away, neighbourhood ascending.* The card, untitled, is another in the series Housewives in Hell.   91f

July 25th.   Ruth & Dom in Runaway Bay to Fernando P in Kensington, *Latest news bulletin: Left IMP starting my own company called Fusion with the Virgin Account. Came back to Jamaica for a break. Missing you.* The card is simply entitled 'Hurricane Plane' though the plane of course is not a Hurricane. Plane blown there by a hurricane? From the airfield behind the wire? Answers on a postcard please.   91g

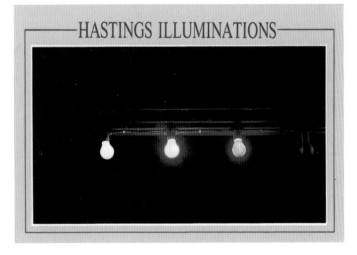

July 26th.   From Hastings to Mr & Mrs C in Tonbridge, *Thought you might like the lovely lights of Hastings!! having a nice time but the weather's iffy at the moment. Andrew's drunk, Joan's paraletic and I'm broke (normal conditions for us!) see you soon on the phone.* Even the seaside card now joins the trend and dabbles in ironic photography. Messages will be seen to gather exclamation marks by the year.   91h

May 20th.   D in Bucharest sends a card of its Centre for Creativity to VW in London, *I hate to think what sort of 'creativity' goes on in this building... Rum. of itself far more depressing than last year. Magyar/Rum. 'problem' seems to me even more like N.Ireland... a self indulged psychosis on both sides, explained tho not excused by real past grievances.* The Balkan turmoil seen in Freudian terms.   91i

July 19th.   Sarah & Rodney to Mr & Mrs W in Camberley, Surrey, *Yes, he's even reached Jersey! I just can't get away from him. Hotel is fantastic & the food terrific. Weather has been dry & cool. Have just been for a swim & now getting ready for dinner (tea!).* The Simpsons properly got under way in 1990 to give hope and laughter to other dysfunctional families. Bart may be an anagram of brat. Matt Groening their creator worked at a sewage treatment plant before making what many think is the funniest TV show. 91j

March 1st.   *Remember me?,* asks Steve in Orlando writing to WPC Ann R at Shoreham police Station, *I am working for British Airways at Gatwick now, so I get a generous discount on air travel... in a couple of weeks I am off to Spain to run the Barcelona Marathon. Take care of yourself.* If this character, seen presiding over Disneyland's Neuschwanstein, takes Bart's question personally he can confidently answer that he is M. Mouse and certainly the senior cartoon character around here.   91k

March 15th.   Alison in Berlin to her mother in Market Harborough, *All well here - apart from cash - I have an offer of a Teaching block in May. The museum [Haus am Checkpoint Charlie where the card was purchased] v.interesting - stuffed full of propaganda. my friends (Eastern) were amused!* Difficult to know what to make of this message considering the choice of card, which shows an East German soldier trying to let a child through. Needless to say the soldier; caught red handed by the camera, was dismissed.   91l

May 25th.   Tim in India to Jane in Old Newton, Suffolk, *What an action packed few days this has been! all very interesting and of course the death of Ghandi overhanging it all. I just managed to get to Simla before everything ground to a halt. Simla is an amazing place.* Rajiv Ghandi was publicly cremated on May 24th, having been assassinated by a suicide bomber three days before. He had led the country for the seven years since the assassination of his mother. The card shows the striking Kutab Minar in Delhi. 91m

December 28th.   Joz to JS in Grimsby, *I've finally got around to writing to you from our beloved Red China. how's the RAF? I'm writing from Beijing; a nuclear bomb shelter turned into a cheap hotel (na na na na Naaa, you can't get me!)... just spent Xmas with a guy who is famed for running the length of the Great Wall and retracing the Long March... The Terracotta Army still stands if you want to pass the message on to MI5. However they're still recovering from Maggie's visit.* Mrs Thatcher inspected these troops in 1982. The individuality of their terracotta faces does not remind one of Socialist Realism.   91n

June 11th.   Nellie & Jack write to Mr & Mrs S in Dewsbury, *Having a nice time weather mixed but we are making the best of it. Going out for the day to Cromer.* After almost a hundred years of comic cards a new threshold of taboo is crossed with a play (after so many tools and cockerels and sticks of rock) on the word 'penis'. The question remains: did the saucy postcard actually undermine rather than encourage sexual frankness?   91o

91a. Freud Museum, London

91b. E.T.W. Dennis (in this year approaching their centenary as a publisher of picture postcards).

91c. Manhattan Postcard Co

91d. Wall Drug Custom Print

91e. Peter Pedley Cards. PP52. Photo: Mike Williams

91f. American Postcard Co. Petrified Film Archives 1233. Photo:

91g. New Market Investment Co. S134, Jamaica

91h. Leo Cards, Eastbourne. HAST48

91i. Arta Grafica, Bucharest. Photo: M Andressaw

91j. Classico San Francisco. The Simpsons

June 6th.   R & M in Babenhaus to Miss K in Chelmsford, Essex. *Today warm & sunny. Relaxing after yesterday's trip to Hessenpark (see over). Tomorrow to the USA Base for the celebrations of the return of troops from the Gulf. both young people in good heart - trying to diet!* Operation Desert Storm was launched against Iran in January. This must be the first wave of combat troops to return. The rest came back to their bases in July.   91t

91k. Walt Disney's World. With kind permission

91l. Haus am Checkpoint Charlie no. 21

91m. Publisher unknown, Delhi

91n. HKMH 015

91o. Bamforth & Co. Comic Series 96

91p. Excursion Boats at Lake Geneva, Wisconsin. Wuttke Enterprises. Photo: Virgil Wattke

91q. Perrod/Hiawatha 2103

91r. Legoland, Denmark. LB122

91s. Bata Shoe Factory

91t. Verlag Schöning und Schmidt

November 25th.   *Shalom, God's peace to you in Kalamazoo,* writes Moishe K in San Francisco to the Eriksons in Piccadilly Rd. *I'm here at Delevon Wi., for our Jews for Jesus Ingathering. About 150 Jewish Believers are here on this retreat. I wanted to thank you for your donations of Nov 6 and 14. Thankyou for helping us to grow.* Jews for Jesus frankly takes the biscuit.   91p

July 14th.   M in Kalamazoo to HP in Raleigh NC., *I am visiting Roger B at his summer house, a sleek glass & steel structure set in an overgrown jungle of a marsh. New Buffalo is a hoot. Every other person has a Junktique store.* In brilliant sunshine New Buffalo demonstrates that Main Street USA is not yet dead. I have scoured the picture in vain for a Junktique store.   91q

August 7th.   Karen & Wayne in Billund, Denmark, *Smashing here. Journey not so smashing! Have a mind to walk back!! Everything is costing the earth but it is a once in a life time experience.* This is the original Legoland. It is hard to tell who or what is made of the little bricks. Mount Rushmore makes a last plastic appearance in these pages, constructed rather than carved. Le Goldmine is a linguistic mystery.   91r

May 4th (?).   Dasu in Djakarta to JT in Horndon, Essex. *Many thanks for the books, what a nice surprise! We listened to your talk on Pakistan - any chance to hear about our own country - when?* This is the Bata shoe factory, a harmonious and airy looking structure. It would be difficult to talk about Indonesia without mentioning its genocidal acts in East Timor, where half the population was killed by Suharto's forces.   91s

September 5th.   Prince Charles dutifully inspects some grand decoration he has been awarded by his host the Amir of Bahrain while Crown Prince Hamed looks on. Also present, but only just, is Princess Diana (she seems to have been edited in to the image by the Bahrain publisher or merely perhaps shunted closer to the central group). With hindsight we can see the signs of the disaffection and bodily malaise that we know to have been her lot. In December the couple separated. Willie, a US Naval Officer isn't having much of a time either. He writes to L.P. in Nottingham, *just finished 10 days training with the Royal Saudi Marines. They need some work....we ate field rations for the duration and I'm ready to exit the Gulf. Why don't they provide high rise hotel rooms for the marines???*   92a

August 6th.   Susan writing to AMB in Keighley, Yorks, tells of a tiring week of shows and shopping, *Matinee performance of Cats (super). Today... early aft. we took in Far & Away with current heart throb Tom Cruise. Super film thoroughly enjoyed it. Lucky enough to see a kingfisher in our 'orchard' on Sunday.* Relaxed youth has cut its hair & tidied up and there is not, as yet, a baseball cap in sight.   92b

October ?.   A classic view revisited (see 58c & 65c) and still one of the grandest. Barbara sends it to the Barvins in Marlborough Wilts, *Lovely to see the family again after all this time...Lindsay is a very grown up 18 months, and so good. Spending tomorrow sight-seeing in New York, theatre and dinner which should be very nice. Returning Thursday.*   92c

March 28th.   Paul & Fiona to VG in London. *Here is the US version of culture... great on the inside but not so wonderful on the out. Good things: the library, the manuscripts, the cost of eating out. Bad things, New Haven (everybody on the inside white, everybody on the outside black) New Haven, New Haven, the telly. On the outside the Beinecke Library looks to be solid marble yet the panels are wafer thin and light shines on the interior through the patterns of their veins.*   92d

June 4th.   Anon to D & TC in Islington, *Staying at EWA Women's University a very exclusive college for intelligent and well-to-do much sought after young & chaste Korean beauties. A country of great paradox and in chaos, ...rapid migration from countryside to city ie Seoul (pop 12 million) ...maybe see you in a week or two as I'm supposed to come over to see Manchester new airport plan.* This is S Korea's National Assembly building looking appropriately civic.   92e

May 10th.   Sandra in Livingstone, Zambia to A & SH, *Here's looking at you! We're having a brilliant time in Africa... we just had a five-day crusade & about 200 people gave their lives to Christ. I'd say about 90% of them were under the age of 15. Now we have a lot of work to do as far as follow up goes... The falls are amazing... been there half a dozen times. Well, I pray God is continually blessing you in Bradford.* 92f

October 30th.   *It's a GIRL!!* write jack & Sue from Gatwick to Pat & Andrew in Wareham, Dorset, *I can't believe it after all those boys. Aren't we so lucky. Kitty - 8lbs. We flew to Gatwick last night so the timing was perfect. Kitty was born at 3am & we're off to Devon to be the backup team.* Where did they find this perfect and appropriate card of a child in ultra smart trainers heading for a minilav?   92g

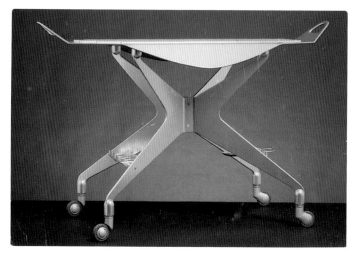

November 12th.   Luce in York to BM in Brighton, *Went in here yesterday, it's lovely! Am spending a week with my Grandma and having a lazy time. Hope you are all well. Mary gave me some news of you last time we spoke. My firm relocates early next year, too far for me to go so not quite sure what will happen then. Alan's fine though his health is much the same...* and so Luce carries on as if she were indeed chatting in Betty's excellent Tea Rooms in York which manage somehow to be both grand and homely, and whose cakes are second to none.   92h

January 8th.   Amanda & Jan to FP in London, *A million thanks for the lift home on new year's eve - without you we would have had to walk. Hope to see you soon at the Ivy.* Jeremy King and Chris Corbin of the enviably successful Caprice reopened the ailing Ivy restaurant in 1991 and commissioned leading artists to enliven its interior. Even the waiter's trolley was completely reconceived by Future Systems. The Ivy revived the tradition of café society for a new fin de siècle and remains without rival the hub of London's social energy.   92i

May 5th.   *You should try to see this one day,* write John & Geraldine in Spalding to Mum & Dad in Sidbury, *it's really worth it. We been really lucky with the weather not too cold & only a couple of showers.* This is part of the Spalding flower parade. Such things prove how near an already extant tradition are those works of art that seem so new and radical (like Jeff Koons' Flower Dog see 99m).   92j

February 11th.   Pearl in New Zealand to Miss W in Salisbury, *At Rotorua today. Went to this church. Window looks very impressive, only figure is engraved rest is real view of lake. Touring in Carol's car having great time, plenty of pictures.* In a Maori cloak Christ seems to float above the water into the church which is decorated in a neo-aboriginal style.   92k

October 14th.   Mum in Folkestone to Mr & Mrs W in Chelmsford, *We have been to look at the Tunnel this morning, the huge borer machine is up for sale for £1 million "one careful owner"! The puppy is lovely but has very sharp teeth so we have to take her for long walks to tire her out. The sea looks nice & calm today.* The tunnel is dug but is still two years away from inauguration.   92l

March 12th.   Nick writes a hurried note to his grandmother giving his new address, *I'll write soon when things have settled down.* The French often give things names which noone uses. This amazing structure is referred to as the arch of La Défense , one of the flurry of Grand Projets that make Paris look modern and confident as well as old and gracious. Spreckelsen, its architect, did not live to see it completed.   92m

October 29th.   Mrs W in Nottingham sends a competition entry to Film on Four Giveaway using one of a set of cards illustrating the Quaker Tapestry of Reconciliation. Its very homespun and amateur awkwardness, humanising a more often demonised subject, makes fresh associations. For most of us, who only think of hunger strikes, dirty campaigns, break outs (and the numbing cul de sacs of argument that end every negotiation over Ireland) it gives an alternative perspective.   92n

April 4th.   S to VG in London NW1, *Prague is a remarkable uncertain place poised for the free market, pushed in that direction by a ghastly sea of tourists and businessmen looking for profit and a fin de siècle fix. A fragile crossroads - the left in crisis everywhere. Nothing green except that boiled pork and dumplings seems like a fair exchange for the almost total lack of consumerism.* Strange how Eastern Europe brings out the essayist in everyone (and mirrors their own confusion).   92o

NEW YORK DOLLS

September 22nd.   Tony to J & JT in Camberwell, *here's a hello from the noise, the dirt, the heat, the maze, the streets, the heart of New York.* The ubiquitous Barbie Dolls, so often shopped for by pestered parents, themselves go shopping. Barbie was born (though not without progenitors) in 1959 with ponytail and a black and white striped swimsuit. If lifesize her statistics would be 39 - 23 - 33. She has more or less kept up with the times and 'Chelsie' in the Generation Girl series was equipped with a nose stud, though piercing was not pursued.   92p

August 15th.   G to The Technical Office, English National Opera at the Coliseum, *Further travels of G. I missed this one off the life plan. Something I have always meant to do. Now I am stranded on the Isle of Dogs... I will experience the Dockland Light Railway by way of escape. P.S. Broke down! Took bus instead - like a theme park, bizarre but recommended.* This is the Greenwich Foot Tunnel with lacklustre art additions by Kate Whiteford. G is exploring parts of the growing new Docklands to which this hundred year old tunnel built for dockworkers gives access.   92q

December 10th.   Robin M on the Sussex Coast enters the Batman Returns Giveaway Competition at the usual type of address. Such cards find their way back on to the market by way of Oxfam etc. Though lacking messages other than answers to quizzes they often as here represent, for competitive reasons, the cream of available postcards. This card advertises Your World published three days before by Harvill though the title of this haunting and haunted picture is not given nor its photographer credited.   92r

June 29th.   Peter in Costa del Silencio to One and All at the Duke of Yorks Theatre, London. *Busy doing nothing working the whole day through trying to find lots of things not to do busy going nowhere isn't it just a time we'd like to be unhappy but we never do have the time.* The message does nothing at all to clarify the hugely referential and allusive image but we are near the beginning of the Freecard era when such cryptic pictures begin to get produced in great numbers for the racks in bars and cinemas.   92s

March 4th.   M in Paris to LV in Camberwell. *Yo Leo! Spring arrived this weekend with cats howling, birds fucking and leaves 'coming out' of the winter closet. Met Ben Paterson in a bar last week - a 60 year old American artist who worked in the Fluxus movement, Jim Dine, Josef Beuys etc... been raving a lot lately, all nighters in Warehouses to get the cobwebs out of the system. They're into techno-pop a lot here but last Saturday was more funky with Adam X & Frankie Bones. A rare assortment of friends - Russians, some mushroom people & Roma who makes art for distributor machines. you put in 10F and get a piece of art etc. That, and Bernard's dinner parties, bourgeois. But they're all a bit mad, those French. All high metabolisms - must be the food... see you here some weekend. Take a shower before you come. I'm quite enjoying marinating in the bodily odours, mind.*   92t

November 29th (?).   David C whose only answer or statement seems to be, 'Liverpool University Bsc(Hons) Orthoptics', sends in his entry for the Penguin/Blackwell Student Competition. If the winner is the one supplying the best card he stands a good chance with this recycled illustration in the Glen Baxter mode. How many footnotes will be needed in 2093 to clarify such a litany of Correctness? No wonder Mr Major was preaching Back to Basics (which were not much different from his predecessor's Victorian Family Values). With such a list not only will the python rightly take fright but will sense that New Labour cannot be very far away.   93a

September 8th.   C & M to Lorin C in Cornell University Office, Mo., *Soaking up the Irish culture here in Britain after major early fuck-ups (nearly, no kidding, got deported) all is settled down & groovy here in London.* In this wide-angle view a rubbery bus bends round the Circus towards a leaning tower of illuminated signs. 93b

June ?th.   Auntie Kate to Mr & Mrs B in Guildford, *Well, we travelled on Concorde on Monday to New York. I can't describe it - the flight was wonderful on Thursday we go to Niagra Falls & on Friday we board QE2 on Docks.* Sounds as if Auntie Kate took a special offer of Concorde out and QE2 back at a bargain price.   93c

September 20th.   Harry in London W1 recommends a poetry reading (by Jonathan Williams and Tom Meyer at a venue called Workfortheeyetodo) to Richard L in NW6. *Should divert. By the way EONTA Vol 2 No 1 seems to be out.* The photo of Harborough Fish Bar makes an appropriate invitation in the Jonathan Williams manner of Found Poetry. An isolated phrase can gather weight (as if they sold gravity).   93d

July 25th.   Gill in Manchester to the Walters family in Camberwell, *Many thanks for classy photo frame... you'll be pleased to know I've <u>passed</u> my placement (& thus the course) leaving just (!) the MA to do.* Iris Murdoch's lovely idea seems here coupled with a design that, while appropriately joyous, lacks some of the more delicate aspects of the British flora she probably had in mind.   93e

January 29th.   Sent by Jordan in Wolverhampton to an address in Bosnia this card is returned with a Royal Mail sticker obliterating the original message. This states 'Due to the situation in the former Yugoslavia we are unable to find any route for mail to the state of Bosnia - Herzegovina. Please accept our apologies...' Any political map of the area rapidly becomes out of date. There is no mention of Kosovo though the Serbian tank is ominously pointed in that direction.   93f

July 15th.   Mimi & HJM in Laos (or Lao as the stamps and the people say) to TP in London SE, *Something for the postcard collection. Touching somehow I found.* Perhaps they refer to the youth and femininity of the uniformed operator or the slightly antiquated looking Morse Code transmitter (which nonetheless is supposed to indicate technical progress in the Peoples Democratic Republic). Her watch too appears nicely timeless.   93g

August 9th.   Nicholas in Oxford to VG in London NW5, *That was a terrific dinner. I felt a little appalled with myself that I didn't speak more to the Canadian lion [Robertson Davies?] - who seemed enchanting - but then again I suspect he was well spared the experience.* Great colour photos are rarer than those in black & white but this double recapitulation of Inca history by Paul Yule, made in Cusco, is eloquence itself.   93h

January 11th.   Rosane (?) in Atlanta to the Medical Secretaries Section of Oswestry Orthopaedic hospital. *Hi Ho! friends, how are you. having nice time in Disney World. Nice sunshine too. Happy New Year.* M Lavach, D Jeffrey Buck, B Scott and M Swatik are the models for this salty beefcake quartet. What does the handkerchief signify? The giants of postcard production, John Hinde and Curteich, join forces.   93i

November 18th.   David & Millie in Uzbekistan to Mr & Mrs V in South Witham, Lincs. *Superb medieval architecture; also more recent mud-houses and very recent concrete buildings... pretty peculiar food; erratic plumbing.* That's the mixture for those who will tread the Golden Road to Samarkand now that tourism revisits this fabled destination. Uzbekistan became independent of the Soviet Union in 1991 and had survived border disputes as well as earlier eruptions of ethnic violence.   93j

June 28th.   On this Oxfam card Isobel in Blackheath tells Dan & Hilary R of the next two meetings of LOCG, *13th July at 65 Granville Park and 25th August at 9A The Orchard both at 8pm. Help and cakes required for people's day of 17th July.* The militant feminist quotation comes from a speech at the final conference of the UN Decade for Women. The woodcut style of lettering and picture harks effectively back to the earliest chapbook and broadsheet forms of protest literature of the 18th and 19th centuries.   93k

February 25th.   Andrew Logan sends his own Illuminated Portrait of Alternative Miss World (a competition of his own devising) to Charles & Ken in London SE16, *Alas I will be in USA for the 'Importance' - Hope all goes well. See you soon.* Logan's jewelry full of startling mirror fragments and chunks of coloured glass make the glitterati gleam but his influence in the larger world of gender flexibility (and what was later known as Gay Pride) has been courageous and persuasive.   93l

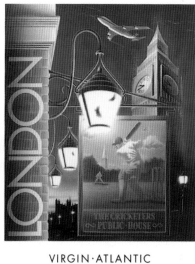

August 30th.   Dentist Barry H Steinberg of Yorktown Heights sends Leo L a reminder of his imminent dental appointment. He uses a Star Trek card based on Spock's famous phrase 'Beam me up, Scotty'. My own fears would not have been allayed by this gimmick. I would rather be teleported anywhere than to (the no doubt kindly) Dr Steinberg. Presumably these cards did the trick. Recent articles in Scientific American suggest that even though Teleportation was originally a mere sci-fi invention, it may at some level be technically feasible.   93m

August 28th.   Zoe in Graulhet, France to Alice K in Lewisham, *...thought you'd prefer this to another village picture. I'm missing you all and the venue... it's so hot here that we spend our whole time in rivers, lakes and waterfalls.* Robert Smith (described as a Heart-throb for the Discontented) and Betty Boop are a rich culture combination. She was the flapper cartoon-film heroine of the twenties based on 'boop a doop' singer Helen Kane. Smith's make-up seems to echo Betty's. His gothicky post punk band The Cure still thrives into the 21st century.   93n

John at 3.00am on the 6th March cannot restrain himself from writing to Bob & Kate, *Somewhere over the North Atlantic en route home from a US business trip. I've been listening to the classical music channel of the in-flight entertainment which includes ...the famous 'Cat Duet' long attributed (wrongly) to Rossini... delighted to hear the announcer say that modern musicologists now think it was by Robert Lucas Pearsall...* He carries on in this pedantic fashion on the back of this agreeable piece of new nostalgia, complete with cricketing image and echoing plane. 93o

93a. Recycled Images

93b. Kardorama. photo: Pictor International. SV55

93c. New Image post Card inc. Photo: Alan Schien

93d. Workfortheeyetodo. Photo: Pip Culbert.

(Harborough Fish Bar 1992)

93e. Pandora Press. Morrison Dailey/Kate Figes.

Series: Fitting Words from Famous Women.

93f. P Davies. Designed by Jean Phillipe Porcherot

93g. Lao P.D.R. A005

93h. Berwick Universal Pictures. Photo: Paul Yule

93i. John Hinde/Curteich 2FG201. Photo: Randall W Galling

93j. Uzbekistan. Photo: V Doroschnikogo

93k. Oxfam Development Postcard No 4

93l. Andrew Logan. photo: Robyn Beeche

93m. Paramount Pictures/Smart Practice

93n. The Cure C352

93o. Virgin Classic poster Series

93p. Bamforth. ET6588

93q. Viewpoint, Yorkshire

93r. Baxter's, Edinburgh

93s. Granada TV

93t. H.W.Theiss, Windhoek.

November ?th.   Jimmy in Windhoek, Namibia to Clem & Jan M in London E5. *This... is where the Herero fought their last battle against the Germans - then the Germans drove them into the desert. I bin there - and there ain't a <u>word</u> about such nastiness - though the restaurant is an old German police post, built looking out over the desert. So I'm in a fighting mood - about the suppression of <u>African</u> history & the <u>African</u> experience, and the continued dominance of Boer ethos. WHAT does this have to do with tourism you ask? Quite a lot.* Perhaps it is symptomatic that this card is captioned in only one language, German.   93t

June 6th.   Tricia & Alison & Minnie etc. from Bradford to Mrs DT in Southampton, *We are all enjoying our stay... our flat is very nice amid lovely scenery, horses, sheep and rabbits out side the window which is twice as long as at home.* Another piece of Britain sanctified by soap. Tannochbrae was the first (see 66o) but the shrines are spreading fast: this is the new heritage.   93p

September 16th.   Dot in Manchester to Mr & Mrs H in Somerton, Somerset. *Enjoying our holiday very much. We had a cup of tea in Ivy's cafe in Holmfirth.* You can count the bricks in this dogged painting of a pub made famous (and profitable) by the TV series The Last Of The Summer Wine. Is someone preparing a route map joining such sites. Holmfirth (home of Bamforth cards) is already a postcard mecca.   93q

June 21st.   Bunty & Vic in Aberdeen to Mrs A in Sheffield, *Had a nice bus run on Wed, up to Fochabers to see Baxters where they make all the soups.* This presumably is the shop attached to Baxter's where they sell all the soups. The style is Precinct Heritage Modernism a typical hybrid not exactly matching the title (Mrs Baxter's Victorian Kitchen) yet indulging the collusion of fantasy between producer and consumer. Security cameras are an up to date touch.   93r

April 6th.   Jackie, Ted & Colin in Worthing send greetings to Mr & Mrs F in Angmering, *Just a little postcard instead of Eastercard to remind you of our happy times together. See you soon.* Coronation Street is almost 35 years old (see 95i) but is slipping behind as a mirror of modern life. Eastenders had an openly gay character in 1986 and an Aids related death in 1992. In 1994 Brookside will feature a lesbian kiss. How is it that one knows at a glance that these aren't real people in a real pub.   93s

DAVID RAYNER
LONDON

MARK MEREDITH
LLANDAFF NORTH

RICHARD BARRACLOUGH
WAPPING

RICHARD ADAMS
RYE

MAN
GAY PRIDE

JUDITH KELHAM
NOTTINGHAM

December 2nd.   Amelia is applying for a Pingu Giveaway, and uses a card from London Cardguide (what Americans call a Rack Card and the English call a Free Card) which promotes World Aids Day. The Red Ribbon as illustrated top right has become a sign of support for Aids victims and Paris (as in 1993 when a giant condom sheathed the obelisk in the Place de la Concorde) is the focus for Aids support (with no cure in sight). Except for ever larger figures & some alleviation for those in the richer countries things had not changed very much by the millennium.   94a

October (?) 24th.   Ant, Nick & Chris to Aunty Glad in Merthyr Tydfil, *We are having a lovely time. We have been to the parks to play football. We also went to feed the horses and Uncle Dick has taken us for walks all around even to Pollys.* Atmospheric double exposure, beloved of TV advertisers, makes the postcard world move, in a blurry sort of way, with the times.   94b

June 21st.   'Spiderman' to the staff at Leigh College ...*already several interesting experiences which will wait until return (an item for the newsletter?). They have T shirts here and you can have printed whatever you want on them – so Gillian will you dare wear it!!* Did she dare? and how horrible, suggestive or propagandist was the image or text?   94c

February 11th.   *I hope this card qualifies,* writes Ollie (perhaps a reference rather than a name) in Charleston SC., to Jean C is Chestnut Ridge NY., *Had a good letter from Webb recently. Here's to a strong nat'l defense.* Haircuts are even shorter than in Elvis's day but these recruits are going through the same hoops in the Parris Island Camp, South Carolina.   94d

September 26th.   Gill in Maidenhead to C in Reading, *Thought this card would interest you. I've been looking at the Kent Shell Guide… I hope Tess finished her maths & prepared the cooking. Hurry on Friday. I'm using the Parker Pen.* Only the most dedicated Bloomsbury shriners make their way to the Woolfs' Sussex home in Rodwell. This is Virginia's bedroom. The tiles and the still-life tell their story.   94e

July 1st.   Cath in Marina del Rey, Cal., to Fernando P in London WC2, *I'll be in London the week-end of the 15th – so get your dancing clogs out!! Can't wait to catch up on all the gossip!!! I'm staying at Dangerous Janet's.* These cards of intimated dysfunction in apple-pie lives are America's best answer to the postcard cartoon and are invariably anonymous.   94f

June 15th.   Joyce in the Hague to Lee P in London E2 sends congratulations on the birth of a baby, aptly named June. It looks as if one baby plays all these notes. If the nappies are the notes this group of harmonies in C sounds pleasant. The picture implies a crescendo at the end starting in the bass which is difficult to bring off. But the ideal card for the occasion.   94g

January 5th.   Clive D to John W in London DE15, *I don't know whether you ever listened to the Tony Bird album – but I thought I'd let you know that he's playing at the Mean Fiddler on the 18th. Hope all is well with Unknown Public. If you don't come to Tony's gig we could meet for a chat sometime.* Perhaps at the sign of the Double Globe and Eggs. This computer sculpture by William Latham (made at IBM) is beyond any artist's capabilities but somehow remains marginal to art itself.   94h

June 21st.   Nick in the Balearic Isles to Phil W in Withenshawe, *This is about the most unusual card I've seen (got it on the plane coming over). Hope you can do these hidden images. if not it's a yacht and you'll have to take my word for it!!* Even on this scale the 3D yacht can be released (just) from its background. This is another marvel of computerised imaging and digital witchcraft. (See note for somewhat vague instructions).   94i

October 7th.   Ruth at Derby University to Mrs E in Ilkley, ...*nice picture & nice to hear from you. I understand it can be hard to sit down to writing, I have the same trouble! I have more space now I'm just sharing with one person & not 31. It's strange being a student again, I'm not sure whether I like the course or not, yet!* NALGO, the white collar union of Local Government commissioned a banner from Ken Sprague in 1980 and got good value even though Trade Unionism's glory days were over.   94j

December 15th.   Miss Davies of Darlington sends a request for a Classic Movie CD to the Radio Times. This is a fragment of the 60 ft long Durham Peace Mural designed by Barrie Ormsby and painted by fifty County Durham people. It is perhaps the only epic painting done in the UK in the Socialist Realist mode. Here the Jarrow Marchers turn into CND protesters and face the ecological threat of nuclear dumps in a continuous bannered crusade through time.   94k

September 13th.   Dorothy F to Mr TC in Market Weighton, *Just a line to check if you are alright. I sent some cards, a letter, & a request for a further supply of Chantry Classic Ships earlier this year probably around June, but have had no reply. I usually log my mail but don't seem to have a record of sending those cards.* Welcome to Shopping City says the notice. Well, the clouds are nice.   94l

August 1st.   Phil to Mrs H in Peterborough, *Tried to ring you but sorry didn't catch you in. Hope Janet filled you in! Weymouth Beach is lovely but parking is hopeless. Joanne has stayed with a friend but can't get rid of Matthew... Too hot for Tara – won't bring her again.* Colour printing begins to get to the point when its crispness equals that of earlier black and white photos.   94m

October 14th.   *Dear BBC,* writes Fengai Mbayo to Programme Guide, World Service, London from Oidu Town, Sierra Leone, *I am regular listener to most of your programmes particularly on Africa. I feel uneasy when I fail to listen to your broadcasts most times.* Sierra Leone, one of the poorest countries in a largely poor continent, spends millions on committing suicide.   94n

August 25th.   B.H (who may fail to remain anonymous) in Bergen to Ken & Charles in London, *My Scandinavian Audience. Actually they were SCREAMING with laughter last night! love Barry.* Even when not screaming Munch's characters are a glum bunch and BH's collaged balloon gives voice to their despair. What <u>do</u> people in Bergen make of Dame Edna?   94o

May 14th.   Elaine in Sydney to Gemma C in Eccleshill, Bradford, *Just a quicky to forewarn you of our (me & the aussie) imminent arrival in your hemisphere. Still trying to find a flight to get us there that doesn't involve a large debt, 12 stopovers in dodgy countries for refuelling & propellers... hope we can get to see you, so long as there's no laughing at the aussie!* The camera has been having a love affair with Sydney Opera House for twenty years and finds itself rewarded from almost any angle.   94p

August 11th.   Don in Torella, NSW., to Mrs Jenny A in Bromley, *So pleased to receive your card   carried across the world by your faithful bearer. Thomasin is delightful. Peter should find this card interesting.* David Messant the photographer turns from general views of the Opera House to details. Here is a fragment of the tile pattern that covers the huge shells and (as can be seen from 94p) echoes the pattern of the waves in Sydney Harbour. The alternating glazes of the tiles are what make it glow and sparkle in the sun.   94q

February 22nd.   Gill to pat in London, *The next planning meeting for the SPINA seminar at the Tavistock Clinic will be 7 March at the MEDACT office. Hope you can come.* This frightening looking queue outside St Thomas' hospital is meant to represent the waiting list for treatment which in 1993 reached a million for the first time. The Medical Campaign Against Weapons who produced the card thought it crazy that Tridents were plying the waves at a cost of a billion and a half each per year. They still are.   94r

December ?th. T in Amsterdam to Budge B in Shoreham with a studded tongue in cheek message, *Just some guys that we met. They've been showing us a pretty good time (what I can remember of it). See you soon!* Dario and Klaus, in Stefan Richter's series Hidden Exposures, are not lone curiosities. The boom in body tattooing was matched and overtaken by an epidemic of piercing most commonly, or rather visibly, on parts of the face (including one aristocratic tongue). Few men however can be as well hung as these.   94s

May 11th.   Janet to Margaret in Oxford, *I turned over a Christmas card from you just now & thought I'd send a few spring greetings from Devon. Perhaps next year will be the year I circumnavigate the UK and visit everyone! It's a thought.* No occasion is now left unheralded by an ill-designed stamp. This celebrates the official opening of the Channel Tunnel, briefly named the Chunnel (though that did not stick). The Queen went back and forth to inaugurate it with President Mitterand on May 6th. Janet was quick off the mark with her card though it does not bear the stamp in question.   94t

(THEY'RE EVERYWHERE)

September 4th.   Suddenly they <u>were</u> everywhere, in restaurants and bars, cinemas and theatres; racks of cards you could just help yourself to. London Card Guide, Go Cards (as here) and, in 1995, the British advent of Boomerang cards which started life in Holland and tend to provide the most inventive selection. Jeremiads about the death of the postcard (reports of which, as I hope this book proves, were greatly exaggerated) were rendered nonsensical. The nineties provided as rich a gathering of design, wit and relevance as any decade in the century. Though more have been collected than used (as was the case ninety years before) they proved immensely popular for entering radio and TV competitions as in this instance where Miss B in Manchester applies for a special offer to a drab Box no. address in Godalming.   95a

Date unclear.   Mummy & Daddy to Toby. *I am writing this in a taxi... to London for the day to do some shopping - work hard - good shooting - Lucy has got into the netball team & is playing her first away match today - Hugs is into everything - sorry about scrawl taxi wizzing around corners.* Paul McCartney's Wings advert dates this to 1979, otherwise the Year of The Yellow Bins.   95b

November 4th.   Harry to Betty K in London NW11, *...anxious to leave a town that to so many has magic appeal. To me it is like a big ant hill that has been kicked over except the ants have white, black and brown faces, and speak with either an Irish, Portu-Recian or Jewish accents. Some of the ants even wear fur-brimed hats and even have PIE-US... Would gladly exchange this treat for herring and byguls...*   95c

413

November 20th.   Dick in NY to J & JT in London SE15. *Thanksgiving this week, we will miss you. Let me know how you are. With no access to the web what can I do? internet. http//www.artsbsponyc.com.* The net begins to stretch, the web to spread: These are still early days but the exponential chain reaction is not far off. This is a seated performance artist, Jim Anderson at the Ronald Feldman Gallery.   95d

September 10th.   AM to TP in London on a card showing a new work of art from the Serpentine Gallery ...*I had intended to ring you this week to arrange a time to buy a picture. But in the event I have friends staying and quite a few things to organise...* Entitled The Maybe, Cornelia Parker's box contains the sleeping figure of actress Tilda Swinton. A naked woman would have had greater art-historical resonance, though this work caused a certain stir.   95e

where do you play yours?

February 10th.   Sally to Fiona H in Oxford, *I tried to get you on the phone, & missed. The group has now settled on 8.30pm on a Thursday, which doesn't suit everyone but is the best we can find. People just come when they can... P.S. I did like the woman with the snake!* Gameboy by Nintendo hit the compulsive mark that defines a craze i.e. full employment of the mind in a mindless occupation.   95f

August 7th.   HD to EG in London W10, *The dream ticket! Interviewing old men and surveying lavatories in Tower Hamlets! Perhaps it was a Grauniad misprint... should have read 'incompetence strategy'. No LA should be without one.* Here, far from Tower Hamlets, is the rebuilt Glyndebourne with a glimpse of the unchanged house through the new Michael Hopkins tented foyer and doorway.   95g

Coronation Street

February 19th.   Joan in Weatherfield on the Granada Studios Tour to Mr & Mrs L in Shoreham-by-Sea, *been sat in the snug at the Rover's* (see 93s) *We've also seen Fred's weather map.* This is the old Coronation Street card though of course not as old as it pretends to look in this nostalgia-style vignetted view. Most who watched the early episodes in the sixties, however (on their black & white screens) saw just this. A street with no parked cars can only be a fake.   95h

April 22nd.   Nicole & Simon to Mrs P in West Kirby. *Hello from Manchester! We're spending a weekend courtesy of Britannia hotels. We're staying in the Country house Hotel, Didsbury... lovely - We've even got a jacuzzi in our room! Today we were taken round Granada Studios.* Apart from a new lamp post or two, the closed arch, and (significantly) a burglar alarm on the Rover's Return little has changed in this 35th Anniversary card. And it's still quite easy to find a parking place.   95i

March 2nd. F & R to Mr & Mrs D in Mitford-on-Sea, *Had a tour of the Globe yesterday. Will be quite unique when finished - I won't buy a ticket if it's raining!! Keep well.* Here amidst the new is the newest , the reconstruction as a working theatre of Shakespeare's great Globe itself. Neither Sam Wanamaker, who had worked so hard to realise a dream, nor Theo Crosby who made it a practicality, lived to witness its opening (by Wanamaker's daughter Zoë) and its public success. 95j

March 23rd. Nicci at the Guardian (the paper referred to as the Grauniad in 95g, a Private Eye joke) to VG in London NW5. *I did enjoy talking to you on Monday (thankyou for the green tea)... the interview has been postponed until a week on Sunday - but you'll see it then.* Tim Page proves that, from the Baroque to Diego Rivera via Delacroix, artists did not exaggerate in their groupings of figures. Prince Sihanouk leaves Cambodia in 1983 in a UN helicopter, showering dust on his supporters. 95k

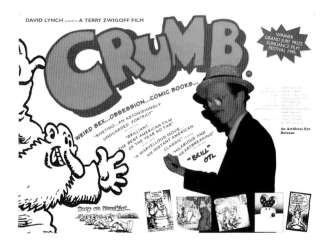

October 9th. Ben in North London to John W in EC1, *I've been out of touch because I've been moving house. Good news from the Prudential - imagine it's a real shot in the arm! Just listening to Borbetomagus versus Sonic Youth on Shock. Fine stuff. Beatnik fury lives on!* Some sort of existential fury also lies behind Crumb's obsessive drawings. The name David Lynch assures us we are in serious cinematic territory. 95l

No postmark, but it arrived safely from Luxor to the English National Opera Workshop in Stepney, *So far so good. We've seen a man knocked off his motor bike by a train. A dead donkey being eaten by wild ducks and I've got the shits. proberbly that's why they have big statues of people sitting on the toilet! PTO found a good slurp house. Pops.* By which he means the surprising anomaly of the King's Head. 95m

December 15th. S Webb in Worthing is hoping for a palm top computer as he/she sends this card to the Radio Times. A deft play on the toyshop name Toys 'R' Us reminds people (appropriately towards Christmas) of the danger of giving pets as presents. A Dog is For Life was the slogan. This is a Boomerang card , one of their first in Britain, produced for the National Canine Defence League. The vandals at the Post Office have made a symbolic blindfold with their cancellation. 95n

November 20th. The secretary of John W Pittman II, Deland, FL. sends an ominous note to Eldora M in Eucalyptus Drive, Orange City. *Dr Pittman found a suspicious spot on the x-ray. He would like you to come back soon to double check.* I can imagine few more unwelcome cards to receive, even if enlivened by Snoopy from Peanuts. Schulz, the creator of Charlie Brown died, aged 78, as this book was going to press. His last drawing was published on the day of his death. 95o

September 14th.   To The New Chairman, O.R. in Sissinghurst from H in the American History Museum, Washington, *Have seen this Bill and Trowell in the lift with Martin McGuinness - v.v. heart palpitating. Hope PC is correctly addressed?* The long preliminaries of the Northern Ireland Peace Process included valuable support from Clinton. The President was already embroiled in other legal preliminaries though the worst was yet to come.   95p

July 14th.   Hugh in Greece to Syd & Joyce in York, *I have also sent Ken one of these pictures but I thought you should have one as well in case he was too embarrassed to show it to you. Everything going well as usual.* This is evidently a montage of two events. Had it been achieved in one shot it would have been a miracle. As an image it definitively illuminates one aspect of sacred sites. Even the ribcage is echoed in the more distant hill.   95q

Caption: After what the Japanese did to the hotel room, the Pentax Espio Mini should come as no surprise.

May 4th.   Two days before the 50th Anniversary of VE Day Janet & John R enter a Radio Times Competition, correctly identifying Luneburg Heath as the site of surrender. The excellent Crown Copyright postcard shows an ex prisoner of war returning home from the Far East in October 1945. Home had become in his absence a prefab, but the welcome Hector receives has not suffered. Some prefabs, including a small group near where I write, still survive in London with traces of their proudly kept garden plots.   95r

July 3rd.   Mary P in Skegness to Mrs QLC in Hove, *Queenie Love! wish you were here*, spent the day at Butlin's on Sunday, *would not like to go for a week... rain forecast for today. Having good meals in the 'Coffee Shop' as all ways...* The man with the cap and clipboard comes from a line stretching back to Nosey Parker (see 21h). Smoking is his target now, as the cartoon wryly shows. Earlier taboos have fallen one by one round the ankles of the old proprieties, leaving the smoker as the last renegade to be rounded up. 95s

June 8th.   John in Bristol to VG in London NW5. *How I agree about Tony Blair's incessant glazed inanimate smiling! I had always thought people whose mouths are always open are unelectable. But what about Clinton? Just as bad!* This Japanese man at first glance seems to be on television but, rather, in terms of space, he is *in* a TV set. He is of course installed in a Capsule Hotel where the miniature rooms are stacked one above another like a chest of drawers. Needing neither bed nor chair the travelling Japanese businessman finds this cheap alternative bedroom quite acceptable.   95t

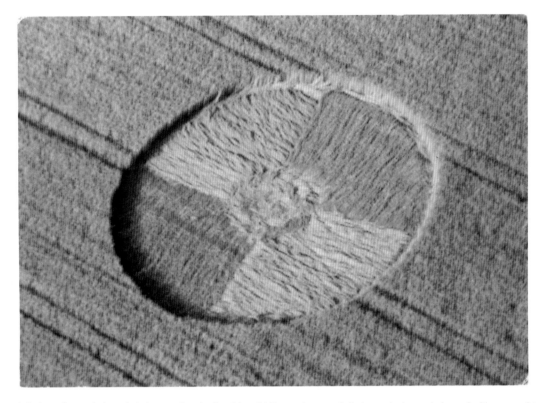

August 3rd.   Crop circles started appearing in the late eighties and were at first genuinely mysterious, inviting a variety of theories and explanations as to their origins. Was God (or Gaia, or Little Green Men) making some sign? Certainly, there were those who claimed the circles could not have been made by any human agency. Then someone with a stick and a piece of string demonstrated how simple it was. This did not deter believers. Yet more sophisticated crop markings were sighted. These were documented by the Centre for Crop Circle Studies who published this card in 1990 with the caption, 'This exquisite circle was the masterpiece of the Circlemakers in 1989. The exact quartering is related to leyline patterns'. Whether extraterrestrial messages, terrestrial art or mere sublunary hoaxes the results were often, as here, elegantly intriguing.   96a

May 17th.   Clare to Sarah B in Honiton. *I'm here and it's my Birthday!!! FORTY YEARS OLD TODAY! YIPEE!!!! (and I'm not pissed yet!)... off to the Tate now... Ruth goes back at 6pm. I've sussed out some great gigs - a choice of Delta Blues, Russian and Gypsy, and jive and swing jazz. All or some of it and a meal first - sounds great.* The pop idols have left the Pavilion, frightened perhaps by Clare's musical menu. 96b

October 19th.   Ralph to Alice W in London, *It's 1am Saturday night back at the YMCA on 23rd & 7th. Tonight went to see a top film called Happiness then went to a bar in Soho where World Series was on & lots of whooping & high fives took place... bought some trainers, jeans, comics, spending most of time in East & Greenwich Village, found ace organic veggie restaurant this evening...*   96c

June 17th.   A in Stockport to JW in Camberwell, *Thanks for the recent 'advance delivery'! I feel privileged to have a pre-season viewing - but I don't think it's very good at all! Most of the national press have had enhanced sports coverage for several years - I don't see a market niche myself!* Euro 96 took place in England. Germany won. Dixie Dean and Stanley Matthews remind one of England's former football glories. Gary Lineker makes up the trio.   96d

November 6th.   A in London SW7 to Charles O in SE1, *We haven't had Sutcliffe's book yet but if for some obscure reason you want it tell Faber... and I daresay they'll oblige. AN Wilson is getting sillier and sillier, & Booker are suing him under the impression he's <u>Angus</u> Wilson. not joking.* Only the woman in this trio is (laptop and all) a novelty in this age-old situation. Even in 1996 some men (like the one on the left) did not spot the threat until it was too late.   96e

June 23rd.   John in Dorset to Mr & Mrs P in Towcester, *Haven't quite made it to Florida, but am a couple of countries West of base, which inter alia has afforded opportunity to visit the Tank Museum. Also so far, 2 houses, 1 castle and gardens.* The tank on the left (in front of the generic Facilities Buildings) is the brother of that shown in 18g, while the Challenger is the 1988 model still in current use.   96f

May 29th.   Anthea to all at Opal Ltd., London W11, *This is the best sight here from the outside at night. Once you get indoors it's just fruit machines & shops! All really ghastly & crowded with very fat people!* The caption mentions an additional attraction to 'the great Sphinx of Giza' in the form of 'a water screen depicting Egyptian holographs'. And it's miles away from the King's Head Pub, (See 95m).   96g

December 20th.   The Edisons in St Louis, MO., to Lorin C at 7024 Cornell, *The Edisons are coming! We all look forward to seeing you on Sunday December 29th.* The card is captioned Molly Martian Wishing You Were Here. These classic flying saucers, fresh no doubt from tending corn circles, fly over and through Saarinen's arch. Somehow their shape already identifies them as artefacts of the fifties.   96h

March 11th.   Jane in the Ukraine to all at the Hampstead Theatre (spotted there by me, pinned up behind the bar). *Hi everyone. postcard choice is limited but isn't it great? We've been completely fed & vodka'd out! I feel I've been on holiday, not work.* A typical card of the Brezhnev era; militarism disguised as will for peace. The soldier scrawls Victory and is accompanied by the Order of Glory 1st Class.   96i

May 8th.   TGT to Revd. Patrick F in Hevingham, *Trust you are well... On a fact finding tour here as part of Dio Links with Luthrens in Germany & Berlin in particular. It's demanding but worthwhile, have seen some grim reminders of WWII. There has been so much change here since 89.* Christo's wrapping of the Reichstag in 1995 was the strangest, if most temporary, of those changes.   96j

March 2nd.   Mike in London E1 to VG in NW5, *This should have been sent sometime ago but I have been preoccupied before the spring comes with planting up our 'country park' in the shadow of Canary Wharf. how nice that you know K. He is an old friend and a fine man. I can see London's only skyscraper from where I write but this,* from Mudchute Park, must be the most hallucinatory view.   96k

November 27th.   Mrs H in Kent answers a tricky question in a Radio Times competition, *The Mona Lisa was painted by Leonardo da Vinci.* Here is quite a different artistic pairing. Jeff Koons portrays himself with his wife Cicciolina, Hungarian porn-star and Italian Green Party pioneer; a Rhapsody in Kitsch. Their long, publicity conscious union ended with dismal wrangling over the custody of their son. Cicciolina ('Cuddles') lost the battle in 1998 when an Italian court ruled her an unfit mother.   96l

November 2nd.   Bruce & Jen in Mid Wales (postmarks seem to have got more generalised since 1990) to Isla & Norman in Tunbridge Wells, *Sorry we can't meet up this year but your idea at Bury St Edmunds sounds attractive. you probably realised it was St Edmunds Day 20/11 !* The BSE scare led to most of Europe boycotting British beef , a dispute that was to last well into the new millennium. England's cows it seems were the maddest of all. Kierkegaard would have enjoyed this joke.   96m

March 29th.   To Ellie LS in Haslemere from London South (another vague new-style postmark). *This is the train that Granny & Grandpa are going on. It looks very exciting. Be good. Look after Lebbit, Rocka & Wupple. And try and help Mum Mum.* Indeed the Eurostar that plies the tunnel route does look exciting (as Trains of the Future used to look in my engine-spotting books of the forties).   96n

February 25th.   Willie, on board ship again (see 92a), is in the Adriatic Sea and writes to LP in Nottingham, *My mum forwarded your Hong Kong card. Does this ship look familiar? I'm on #4 VS #1 this time out and on the other side of the world. Things have been dull off Bosnia but we have had a few good ports. our next stop is Israel.* Maybe he had to scurry back to the Gulf in September when a new crisis threatened.   96o

ALL I WANT OUT OF
LiFE aRE WORLD PEace
aND THiN THiGHS...

...ACTUALLY, I DON'T CaRE
THaT MUCH aBOUT
WORLD Peace.

August 5th.   R in Portsmouth to DG in London W1, *Have spent most of my time explaining and apologising for Geoff's behaviour a few weeks ago. Bessie would like the name of your solicitors. Back in office for 13. Next course in Mexico!* Edward James also needed some explaining. To many he seemed to be frittering his wealth & talents away as patron of the surrealists and supporter of eccentric authors like Collam, or building (as here) a fantasy city in the depths of Mexico. Rich or poor, individual expression (as in the case of Simon Rodia, see 96s) is worth fighting for.   96p

August ?th. Laura in Leeds to Sean M in Valais, Switzerland, *...had an argument with Rory... I'd been out one afternoon and when I got back there was a massive bunch of flowers & we all assumed they were from Rory so I told my mother to have them and I did not want to see them. A few hours later I thought I'd read the card and found to my dismay they were from Henry. He's actually driving me mad. He's at my home 3 times a day and he's now even started going up to the Squinting Cat... can't get away from him. I'll never find a husband with him hanging off my arm...*   96q

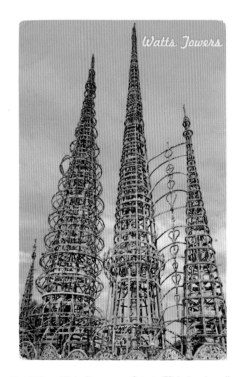

March 2nd.   Friends of the Earth send a card to Jill S in Petersfield (on 100% recycled paper of course) from their London HQ suggesting that members ring in toll-free to save even more paper. They invite her support for the current campaign to save precious bits of countryside from the threat of the Newbury By-Pass, one of their most hard fought campaigns. Although doomed to final failure the tree squatting and other tactics held up work, gained concessions and made the government conscious of a strong lobby against the blind escalation of road building. The internet was also coming into play as an even more efficient method of orchestrating protest.   96t

June 11th.   Alan in Brooklyn to Sol Gluck in Croton-on Hudson, NY, *Dear Sol, It took a nice Jewish boy to compose probably one of the most popular songs of Xmas. Hope to see you again soon.* Irving Berlin first appeared in those pages in the year the Titanic sank (see 12m) as the composer of Alexander's Ragtime Band. Here he is in the fifties with a couple of other moderately well known songs in an evocative photo by Arthur Rothstein.   96r

May 24th.   LB in Penngrove, Cal., to TP in London, *I've wanted to send you this card for some time. We first saw the Towers in 1963 soon after LA city failed in its attempt to demolish them & just before the Watts riots almost succeeded. A few years later we found Rodia's burial place in the town my father was born.* Only in 1996 did proper conservation work begin on the largest construction in the world made (between 1921 & 55) by one man on his own.   96s

Posted on September 15th this epic and ornamental text (see Notes for verso) from an American visitor gives an interesting perspective on the end of Princess Diana in the form of a diary chronicling the days from the news of her death to her funeral. Sales of this card alone boosted the trade in oversize shaped cards which had been in evidence only for a few years and now seem set to outlive their mere novelty.

Dear K J A & N. Woke today to unbelievable reports of Princess Diana dead! High speed chase at 120 mph in middle of night being pursued by flock of photographers. GRIM. The poor sons. As afternoon unfolded - TV reports of outpouring of sentiments reveal she was loved by the populus - I was no fan of hers but my feelings for two already damaged kids at such vulnerable ages so needlessly it seems. One eye witness said the bloody photographers were taking pictures and not even calling ambulance or helping the people in car. A sorry statement of man's concern for fellow man. Wonderful.

Monday 1st Sept. Zillions in London putting flowers at BUCK Castle, Kensington Palace & Harrods Dept. store. The last locale bizarre - Open. Business as usual. The driver apparently drunk. Wonderful! Another fine comment on mankind! By nite-fall intelligent persons commenting on Diana's Landmine concerns and possibility of assassination by the manufacturing countries, middle men, buyers, or the Palace itself. Parallels to JFK conspiracy being drawn. Didn't take very long to reach KGB, CIA, Communist plot. 'Communist' means any one available to blame stuff on - as usual.

Thursday 4th September.

The silence of the survivor is underlined with silence. His injuries & therefore his medical condition & ability to testify to events is probably being squashed so as to get beyond the funeral whose route has tripled in length to accommodate the expected crowds & their expectations to see something. Diana's Saintly appreciations are getting out of hand. Tons of fresh flowers wrapped in plastic are rotting hip deep at Kens Palace & Buck. Castle. Think of the money wasted that could have been applied to her charities! People! obscene waste. (Continued under Notes & Messages etc.)　　97a

LONDON　　Piccadilly Circus

November 7th.　T to FM in Oxford, *hello darling, aaaargh! I shall miss you. Big queues still for the Sensation show (Myra is back on the wall behind a plastic shield). I found the book you wanted at Waterstones...* The picture in the Royal Academy's controversial exhibition based on a photo of Myra Hindley had been attacked with ink and paint. This crisp sunshine view of the Circus dates probably from 1996.　97b

NEW YORK

July 12th.　Sarah to Mrs AS in Neasden, *Dear Auntie Minnie, having a lovely time but it's so hot. Mid 90's! Everything is so big here and the pace is so hectic. I've been running a few times in Central Park. There are many kosher restaurants - one near us is called Moishe Peking... Lower Manhattan looks as clean cut and sharp edged as its replica in Legoland.*　97c

May 2nd.   PW in York to AW in London, *John Major has just announced (on the World at One) that he will be going to the Oval (after seeing the Queen)... The Labour win has been described as a 'seismic shift' a 'tidal wave' and a 'landslide'. Did the earth move in Brockley? Hope to see the hanging quilt soon.* One of New Labour's earliest moves was a failed attempt to ban fox hunting, a strange priority. But May was honeymoon time. The term New Labour itself was an early sign of spin doctoring, a term that soon came into daily use.   97d

April 21st.   Tim in the Czech Republic to Lucy S in Pimlico, London, *This is how they feel about the election result too. At least twenty wasted years entitles them to an opinion. I've had a great time.* Perhaps the worst of the century's many monsters presides over his legacy, the putrefying corpses of a dream. I was taught at school about Uncle Joe, our kindly ally, and had friends who would hear no word against him. How many tens of millions of the dead lined his path to power cannot now be calculated. 97e

21st June.   Alice & Rick to L, B & A in London SW1, *Hello, This is the worst mud bath I've ever seen! At least it's not raining at the moment (Yes it is, says Rick). Hope your vegetables arrived without incident - you might see me sooner than you expected. Rick's really keen and he's disappointed reading this.* The psychedelia of Woodstock lives again in this Mad Cow and Magic Mushroom card with its rainbow rays. (Even the famous Bethel mud of 1969 has been cunningly recapitulated).   97f

November 20th.   Michael in Jamaica to Christine P in York, *Inadvertently arrived here on one of the greater days in the Island's history. Jamaica has qualified for the World Cup... streets alive with jubilation, flag-waving, car-horn tooting, chanting. The Prime Minister in a fit of pre-election generosity ordered a national holiday... which the leader of the opposition deemed illegal. Football is all.* Jamaica did not get very far, but neither did England. This man, Bob Marley, is Jamaica's greatest son. His museum in Kingston now has a No Smoking notice in its entranceway.   97g

July 7th.   Jonathan W in Dentdale to TP in Camberwell, *You need to materialize to see if Mike Harding can photograph you for our book, Corn Close, and make you look like a bloody Yorkshireman (see other side). We are safely back in the Remote Dale. It remains amazingly QUIET, and few places make you say that in 1997. What will RBK find to talk about in LA? Don't think I'll be watching Old Trafford this afternoon, somehow. Tour de France, yes?* Here are the uncannily similar David Hockney and Alan Bennett, both sons of Bradford.   97h

June 8th.   *Thanks for the hospitality, tabs, beers and shirt,* writes Tim in Bristol to L & MD in London SW1, *It was good to see you all so well. Still very embarrassed by my opulent new blue shirt, but it did at least prompt me to get something for Mo. Life here largely script marking but some offchance of a day or two in Glastonbury Chemical toilets. Will phone later in the week about London Globe dates.* Glen Baxter in his later coloured mode tackles love and domestic terrorism as enacted through table-tennis, the true sport of intellectuals.   97i

July 27th.   M & D send this magnificent card from North Haven Ct. via Siena to Jake T in London SE15, *You can see where I am spending much of my time at the moment. This masterpiece in cast gold alloy must be as near as dentistry gets to fine art and is the work of Richard V Tucker in association with Jensens. The abstraction of the shapes and their liquid continuity with the formal masses is perfection.*   97j

May 27th.   Jennie in Tonbridge to Mary F in Hammersmith, *I too will be sad not to see you on 12th or 18th - 19th is a live broadcast so perhaps you could tape it? Have been* <u>much</u> *occupied with twins! In London soon - reh. for house of Bernarda Alba at Man in the Moon, King's Rd.* Handel's Theodora gets a radical treatment at Glyndebourne. Peter Sellars directed with stunning sets by George Tsypin (made up of huge shapes like blown glass).   97l

June 4th.   J at the Women's Institute Conference in Glos. to Mr & Mrs P in Stoke-on-Trent, *So far not so good & a muddled meeting. Don't know where we are on the agenda or who are the 'Special Guests' coming to speak. So far Mrs Roche (?) MP, Minister for Welfare of the Industrial Base - whatever that means - spoke well but boringly about everyone becoming IT buffs. She was mercifully brief. Met my IFL friend Jean from Richmond for lunch.* Sounds like J might stalk off in emulation of this departing bird.   97n

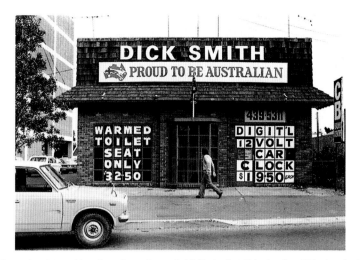

September 1st.   Mary from Town House Publicity to Ken T in London SE1, *A note to say how sad I am you are leaving C4. Not just sad professionally but no matter what happens it just won't be so much fun.* Dick Smith on Pacific Highway Sydney can teach Ken T & Mary a thing or two about publicity. If you can sell warmed toilet seats to leathery Australians you've got the right touch.   97k

August 20th.   Jean in Ipswich to Rusty W in Ingatestone, *Happy Landings! No doubt your whacked and emotionally drained but at least you have your own front door! You can shut the world out if you want. C got the specialist registrar job at St George's on the Renal Team. Such a relief.* One of the Globe's opening productions, Winter's Tale, directed by David Freeman with costumes and sets by the present writer. The mud comes from Dorset.   97m

August 27th.   Matti to Sue C in London N16, *Finally our training is over and we are ready to go to Bosnia. our camp is in Doboj, which is at the moment everything seems to be one fucking big mess... but I'll survive. Ok this card is a mess just because I can't thing clearly. sorry!! As you see the address is in Finland where our supply routes come.* The sign points to land-mines and misery whichever road you take, Tuzla the refugee centre, Gracanica, 5 miles from Pristina, the capital of Kosovo, and Zenica a human dumping ground. Turning back is probably just as bad.   97o

October 2nd. Paul in London to A K in Winchester, *Oh, how we miss her! hope everything's OK up/down there in sunny (but cold) W. and that when I come down your housemates will still talk to me!... my projects have gone a little skew whiff as usual and today I went to have a brain scan in the hope of getting some pictures of my brain to use in my project somehow. my head is hurting but I think it's because it was clamped down on a trolley for 3 hours!...* Same photo as 97a and also cut out. In the shaped version she loses half an earring and quite a lot of hair. 97p

1997 MESSAGES·NOTES·PARTICULARS

97a. cont... *Thursday Eve. City still totally engaged in building the world's largest compost pile. J B & I walked to Kensington Palace to see it. It was unbelievable! Thousands of people along the way all carrying bouquets. Old people on crutches, in wheel-chairs - families with babes in arms or carriages. 10.30 at night traffic stopped all around. People herded like cattle to the in gate - one way pedestrian traffic. The sea of flowers is up to your knees. Trees are candle-lit shrines - insence burning plus smell of rotting flowers is rather nauseating. When you think of atrocities of our lifetime and the way people conveniently ignore or forget their role as citizens of the world whether it be lowering the ZYCLON GAS pellets or supporting the tabloids who make money off Princess Diana photos - (in distress and let's hope it gets worse & worse - more and more obscene. The MILLIONS & MILLIONS OF pounds used up on flowers could have been given to her charities and done some good. This is at a point of MASS MOB mentality and feeding off itself. It's like a huge Fair. It's hard to imagine how the funeral can be anything but worse.*
Friday 6th September. Clicking on TV at intervals are dominated by processions - moving the coffin for tomorrow's procession. Coverage is unbearable. Crowds are expected to be from 2-8 million hot and heaving humans, and the flowers continue to accumulate and rot. Queens address to kingdom was more than possible but she did it - and sincerely for the sons.
Saturday 12th September.
Like all The Sheep in Kensington Gardens but in privacy of TV room - we too watched for hours the processions and the service at Westminster Abbey. Verdi Requiem with 32 voices + soloists for the Kyrie was fine except organ reduction was ghastly. The high point - of course being Elton John - a doughy pop singer - very odd looking singing an adaptation of a hit from which will be made further millions of pounds - it's a rock festival. I saw last nite people with black Diana visors - presumably if it's sunny & black Diana umbrellas if it rained but of course as they are interchangeable. It's all a bit much. The newspapers are putting out special editions with Diana supplements. Diana's brother seems a good chap, married someone more disturbed than Diana & had to commit her. Tragic & bizarre to say least - Love Susan xx
The verso with its stamp and cancellation like an eye seems itself a strange ghost of the picture side.
Shapes. WPL. London. Printed in UK. B.19.

97b. Fisa. Golden Shield.

97c. Alfred Mainzer. 1539. Printed in Thailnad.

97d. Boomerang/Ministry of Sound/League Against Cruel Sports.

97e. BB art, Czech Republic. Photo: I Beranek

97f. Moore and Moore. The caption also tells us:-
'This card is made from forest thinnings from Nordic forests where 2 to 5 saplings are planted for every tree felled. Woodchips from the mill are also used in the pulp. Bark and waste are used to fuel the mill. This card is biodegradable, recyclable and chlorine free. Forests generate oxygen and absorb carbon dioxide'.
Well, that's the card, what about the ink, stamp, ballpoint pen, and GPO franking?

97g. Bob Marley Music Inc. 2792. Photo: Adrian Boot

97h. 1853 Gallery. Photograph of David Hockney and Alan Bennett, 1994 by Jonathan Silver.

97i. Glen Baxter/Santoro Graphics. PB26

97j. Jensen Industries Inc. Richard V Tucker.

97k. Acme Cards. MW20. Photo: Mike Wells

97l. Glyndebourne Festival Opera. Photo: Mike Hoban.

97m. Shakespeare's Globe. Photo: R Kalina

97n. Judges Ltd. C11392

97o. SFOR. Photo: Martti Tikka

97p. Kardorama. Photo Rex Features. SV279

97q. Editions Guy, Paris.

September 2nd. Zoe in Paris to Peter I in York, *Dear Dad, maybe this could be the final image in the fairy tale picture book which tells the sad story of the Princess Diana. I was more shocked than I would have imagined may be because it happened in Paris, maybe because she was a familiar symbol of England for me - remember my kitsch collection of objects on the royal wedding and how I used to spend half my pocket money on Charles & Di keyrings at Jone's the newsagent? Have a good trip to Ireland...* This must have been written within 48 hours of the event. 97q

98

GUGGENHEIM BILBAO

May 13th.   Maria to KOS in London W8. *Dear V & K. As I am not certain that you received my e-mail, I would like to thank you once more for the lovely dinner.* As the century began with a great and confident museum building, The Grand Palais in Paris (see 00a), so it draws to an end with equal swagger and flair with Frank Gehry's magnificent titanium-clad dream in Bilbao. While London starts to make do with engineering in the form of a temporary tent, architecture is again something that happens somewhere else.   98a

April 30th.   T in London to Arabella and Flora CM in Oxford, *This is to test how the Post Office manages with weirdly shaped giant cards: if they can deal with this they can deal with anything but I expect it will arrive scrunched up with some sort of blemish in the middle.* T was wrong. It arrived in good condition: its just the square ordinary cards they can't seem to deal with. 98b

November 9th.   Mark T to RD in Sacramento, Cal., *Hello Bob! How are you? I finally got settled into N.Y. and school which is great. I am living in the Chelsea Hotel - perhaps you've heard of it. Is Mark being patronising or does Bob live on Mars?* Here is Goya's child-devouring Saturn standing in for King Kong and looking very much at home.   98c

November 24th.   Simonetta to MV in London SW1, *Haven't got to the show yet, so keep it up. Who should be the next Prime Minister, Gilbert or George? Sorry you missed the Guggenheim lecture that Tom Krens gave at the RA.* I doubt if either Gilbert or George were very pleased at this nonetheless skilful pastiche of their work. John Major & Tony Blair double for them to launch a compilation CD of '35 Great Social Comments' (inc. Manic Street Preachers, The Divine Comedy, Stripper Vicar, Blur and the Sex Pistols). 98d

April 15th.   Tina in what the postmark still calls 'London North' to J & JT (in London South). *We had such a lovely lunch and happy afternoon with you... I'll call soon and make some new dates with you.* The gap between shop interior and art installation is now so narrow that one does not know which is moving towards which. Paradoxically only the flowers tell you this is a clothes shop (or Collection as it is called in the caption to confuse even further). Calvin Klein in Paris is a long way from Men's Outfitting. 98e

April 10th.   Chris in York to TP in London, *Web site Directory is called 'U.K. Directory: the definitive guide to British sites on the Internet'. Issue 3 is £2.50 from newsagents. (I don't use mine much, - prefer to use on-line classified directories such as YAHOO if subject seeking or search engines like Alta Vista when looking for specifics. Can't be doing with typing U/R/L/S/).* Five years ago scarcely a soul would have understood a word of this. Black woman in space suit with book on bench in field would qualify for any new Iconologia. 98f

February 3rd.   Francesca in London South to Terry J in ditto, *You shouldn't have, but you did! Thank you so much for taking us all to the tapas bar last night, it was a real treat... a great evening (even if I'm suffering now). Come and have some supper when Ali gets back.* Freecards and movies go hand in hand: their racks are often to be found in cinemas. It would be good news for many that Tarantino's compelling, funny and gruesome Pulp Fiction was out on video. The ripped off rip-off of a pulp cover and steamy girl reading Pulp Fiction has the right wit and flavour. 98g

July 23rd.   To Lorin C in Santa Fe, *No, thank whatever I am not 'caught in the grips of despair'. To the contrary, an incautious optimism has gripped me in the form of TRUE LOVE (X true romance). Her name is Kate, a naughty Italian-Irish-Russian Catholic girl from Nyack... an old friend introduced us & life has not been the same since.* In an already established tradition of transformed ephemera (dating from Duchamp) this elegant Valentine was designed by Keith Bates for Boomerang. Many prints masquerade as art that are not half so elegantly conceived and made. 98h

April 14th.   June in Los Angeles to Mr & Mrs H in Cirencester, *We have 'done' Hollywood and Beverley Hills and I think the stars can have them! I'm not jealous!! Peter drove us up to his mountain ranch - it was glorious - we were greeted by wild turkey, quail and deer and lovely clumps of wild flowers on the hillsides. Went to Hearst Castle - Greek Goddesses abound in the gardens.* What with the homes of the stars and an echo of Citizen Kane it sounds like a cinematic time as here exemplified by the Chinese Theater that was Grauman's and is now Mann's (see 30k). 98i

August 17th.   *My Dear Jenny, I am feeling at home here but in a double-sided St Petersburg. On the one hand there is the pleasure of hearing my own dear Russian language & seeing familiar faces, but on the other there is the hardness of life here, the bitterness and discontent with what is going on. I've been here since 1st November and am flying back 'home' on the 16th. Please write me a few lines, your V.* But there was the added pleasure of no longer having to call the city Leningrad.   98j

May 14th.   BH in London to Mrs H in Indian Head, Canada, *We must be nearing the end of something when conceptual art comes to Madame Tussauds. They'll have to have another one to go with it now for dead Diana. But maybe EJ is waiting for the Queen Mother to keel over.* Elton John's Candle In The Wind was given new words to be recycled for Princess Diana's funeral. If this is a Tussaud's installation then it represents a big leap in imagination from what I have seen there.   98k

April 15th.   Melanie S in Swansea sends in to the Radio Times her entry for the Jersey Competition (whether she gets a Jersey or goes there is not disclosed) with a card produced by Action Space London Events. Roger Brooklyn's photograph shows that London in the nineties is not all Piccadilly Circus. This scene of inner city life could be replicated within half a mile of where I write and in a dozen other areas.   98l

February 2nd.   *Tunisian humour at its best?* ask J & M on their card to Brian E & all at Opal, *Let's hope not.* Even when the English is adjusted towards the idiomatic (He: Weren't you supposed to get back earlier than this? She: I've come straight from the hairdresser) the joke seems pretty opaque. The graphic presentation and trilingual text, however, outdoes most things available in London.   98m

December 5th.   Mitch in Oklahoma City to LB in Penngrove, Cal., *Here is the OKC bombing card. I photographed it in early May just prior to the final demolition. At this point all the bodies had been recovered except for three which remained buried in the rubble until the site was cleared.* The card's caption, Terror in the Heartland, is the response of OKC's postcard chronicler, Mitchell Oliphant to the 1995 bombing of a civic building in which 168 people were killed. Timothy McVeigh, a gulf war veteran, was sentenced to death in 1997 for the outrage.   98n

December 5th.   A in London South to Caroline W in Wimborne, Dorset. *Did you get the fax about the organic bakery in Boscombe? You should try to get a job there... you can see the Dome from Chris's flat... even better from the roof but a bit precarious. You can see the Cutty Sark and all the fireworks on Bonfire Night for free!* The basic building of the Dome was completed in June of this year. Although Tony Blair (here drawn unrecognisably) promised the greatest day out on Earth its proposed contents were still a mystery and people were (rightly) getting suspicious.   98o

98a. Kardorama. DC 69. Pauvel Libra

98b. Fantasy & Surreal Postcards

98c. Storming The Empire. Collage by Michael Langenstein.

98d. Sony Music/TV

98e. Calvin Klein Collection. Photo: Nicholas Bruant.

98f. Booksellers Association of GB.

98g. Boomerang.

98h. Boomerang, Designer: Keith Bates.

98i. Mitlock Publishers. 2USCA 1584.

98j. The Singer Building now   House of Books. Photo: V Melvinkov.

98k. Madame Tussaud's.

98l. Action Space London Events.

98m. SAT, Tunisia.

98n. Mitchell Oliphant OKC. Terror In The Heartland.

98o. Recycled Images.

98p. Peak Productions, Mammoth Lake, CA.

98q. Deadly Designs, Harare. DDP86.
Africa Journey. Gill Bond

98r. Risch-Lau, Salzburg SA14607.
PM advertises Esperanto Museum in Vienna.

98s. Feuerpfeil Verlag, Bayreuth.

98t. Makmai Studio Ltd. Photo: Pinit Srimuangkao

January 14th. William in Thailand to FP in London, *I've married a local Thai woman and I'm staying. Not true... however this place is absolutely beautiful (and cheap too). THis beach was the site of the maddest party I've ever been to there were thousands of drugged, Fluoro painted, club Freaks dancing from midnight until midday to celebrate the Full Moon (what better excuse!). I'm going to stay for a while (eternity)...*   98t

September 28th.   T & D in Reno to KOS in London W8, *This card is a substitute for a rendez-vous in Provence. D's doing research on her book at UCLA (plundered journals!) so I've joined her for our very own Road Movie (minus video-cam!).* One advantage of the postcard is that one can enjoy Mono Lake without the brine-flies that gave these tufa cathedrals their native name.   98p

September 19th.   L to CC in Suffolk, *So loving it here, Partly on move (eg to Vic Falls) partly on Elly & Weil's farm miles into the sticks outside the Wild West town of Bulawayo... I feel so at home.* The card has all the optimism with which Zimbabwe started its independent life as a nation almost twenty years before. Now Dr Mugabe urges the country towards strife, and the sad anarchy of so many African states.   98q

August 7th.   Rodney M in Salzburg for the Festival greets FM in Oxford, *Goodness, the whole ROH from C. Southgate down, past, present and (?) future seems to be here - what a waste of an air fare. As for the performances... words fail. Why Am I Here?* Each time the Royal Opera House reached what seemed its darkest hour a darker one loomed up; hence the question mark. Members of the orchestra even stood with buckets to collect funds outside the Albert Hall. Mozart hated Salzburg.   98r

August 31st.   Ailene & Douglas to CO & KT in London. *We greatly enjoyed the Agatha Christie talk - thanks for the drink ! Tristan Act 1 & 2 had weird production but our old team of D Baremboim and W. Meier triumphed in Act 3 with a Liebestod that really deserved its standing ovation...* A century on (see 02p) and the pilgrims could fill the opera house twice over. The cards are still severe. Busts of Richard and Cosima, by Hitler's favourite sculptor, Arno Brecker, do nothing to cheer things up.   98s

99

February 11th. (top). M & M to Jean L in Horsham, *Talk about dear 'Old Blighty' - They'd be amazed if they saw it now & where has the Romance of Piccadilly gone to - for all of our generation. This place was something special. Many thanks for Broadway PC that brought back memories too. You sounded fine on the telephone. Keep well.* This Routemaster bus is already heading for the nostalgia depot; last of a recognisable 50 year continuum. The brash signs will one day seem a quaint memory. A clock on top of the Foster's sign counts the days to 2000.

December 31st. TP in Piccadilly Circus sends copies of both these cards to David Oxford in Hampton, Middlesex. *As you can only see on the square one it was 870 days to the Millennium when both were taken - seemingly a nanosecond apart judging by the alignment of people/bus/cab/bicycle. This on New Year's Eve was the most recent card available! Nescafé took so long to put up their sign to replace Foster's that it defeated the purpose of the countdown clock!...* They are the same photo of course with the bus moved bodily over.   99b

March 1st. Lew B in Penngrove, Cal., to TP in Peckham, *A fin de millennium glimpse of Manhattan on a penultimate-year-of-the-century card.* The mystery at the century's end is why all these offices are needed, since most transactions can be made electronically. Filing takes up no space and business could as easily be done from a lap top on a beach in Bermuda as from one of these amazing monoliths.   99c

January 27th. P in Riversdale, South Africa to Miss MC in Salisbury, Wilts. *Hi - thought you would like this card - serious Heat-wave but I swim most of the time in my tidal estuary - & sleep out under the stars and just enjoy BEING instead of all the frenetic DOING 98 seemed to consist of - if you come across a GREAT Book, WISDOM of the AGES by Wayne Dyer. Read it - IT'S BRILLIANT.* This rather uncomfortable looking shaped card of Africa carries the face of Nelson Mandela, surely the unrivalled candidate for human being of the century. To find such a card on sale in South Africa would have seemed improbable even at the beginning of the decade. At the beginning of the century the idea that a black African might by its end be the world's most respected political figure would have seemed laughable. Born towards the end of the First World War Mandela's career followed that standard recipe of the century in which freedom fighter undergoes a lengthy period of imprisonment (in his case 27 years in the penitentiaries of a police-state) to emerge as populist leader and eventually to be revered as an elder statesman. Mandela retired as president in 1997, the embodiment of the world's most needed commodity, a spirit of reconciliation.   99a

April 13th.   Aunty A in York to Miss C in Edinburgh, *Darling Phil, This is obviously aimed at the Old Heroes generation but us too. We shall have to take to the hills & bear down on them in our chariots! lots of love.* Any referendum on acceptance of the Euro as our currency would show this to be a typical response. Kitchener in the famous recruiting gesture of World War I (see 14a) is still a potent nationalistic ikon.   99d

December 16th.   David & Marie F to T & FP in Oxford, *Not many people can boast a post card from Pinnaroo. Marie's sister-in-law did the mural on the Farm Museum wall 40º yesterday & the living is easy. The London freeze doesn't beckon. Saw 60 kangaroos in the bush - you're not allowed to shoot them now, so they're overpopulating.* A fork-lift truck is the other main attraction in Pinnaroo.   99e

April 26th.   'Dumbells' is the answer given by Rachel to the Holland & Barratt quiz at P.O. Box 144, Plymouth. As with many recent promotional cards it's difficult to guess what is being advertised and this one would be a quiz question in its own right. The answer is Selfridges, that once august Parthenon of Oxford Street. A new London Life series could be started with this, The Urinal (or The Transvestite).   99f

December 31st. (received Jan 10th).   LB in California sends TP the most recent card of the famous shop. Thus the promise made in 1900 (see 00p) is kept. *It is now a chic shoe store & design shop - apparently run by the young Japanese who were inside playing guitars & did not respond to my knock. The Women stylists in the barbers shop said they're never open.* The lettering is more Dickensian than in Dickens' day.   99g

February 10th.   T in London to Arabella CM in Oxford. *My friend Iris who died on Monday & who was ill with Alzheimer's found the Teletubbies one of the last things she enjoyed... but I've only glimpsed it once when you and F were watching it.* So what's this all about? George Orwell, credit cards, Toys 'R' Us, the devil and an impaled Ginger Spice are all involved in this apocalyptic vision based on a children's TV series that spawned its own shoal of purchasable merchandise.   99h

August 12th.   P in Devon to JD in London SW11, *Dear Dolly, Well, we watched from above the bay looking across Plymouth Sound. Nothing at all to see in the sky but the speed at which it got dark (and cold and windy) was extraordinary. The Dog went mad and Kitty howled!* This card is a fine example of the kind of merchandising here. The card's publisher wants it both ways, total eclipse and brightly lit people watching it. He was wise, though, to make the card well in advance.   99i

Monica Lewinski on Presidential Love

I don't need Viagra . . .
. . . I got me Cornish Pasty!!

May 27th.   Rick to A in Forest Hill, *Hello!! It's sunny. Unlike last 2 years (see front pic) it's really hot & the place is unrecognisable. It's great. Seen some bands - Marianne Faithful, Kula Shaker, watched film, eaten top food at Manic Organic, drank tea at Tiny Tea Tent. Off to get some lunch...* The Woodstock spirit was born in mud in 1969, and Glastonbury's Festival managed (in that respect at least) to be a true echo. But Rick seems quite happy in the sun.   99j

February 19th.   S in Saxton's River, VT, to BH in Indian Head, Sask., *Dear Bill, your presidential namesake is having a rough time but chances are he'll wriggle out of it. How juvenile it will all seem one day and what a waste of everyone's energy!* Monica Lewinski is now into designer handbags and the beginnings of (she thinks) a film career. Investigator Starr just overplayed his hand and ended up looking morally shabbier than the all-surviving President. 99k

August 11th.   Mrs D in Plymouth to Miss AW in London, *Our view of the eclipse was totally clouded over but the sudden darkness, flowers closing, birds nesting bit was very exciting. When it was dark all we could see were 1000's of camera flashes right along the coast. Do you think this man is on Prozac?* Exaggeration comes to British humour in this repellant card with a joke about Viagra the new resurrective elixir for men.   99l

Worried about the result of your last student union?

June 17th.   T in Bilbao to Flora CM in Oxford, *This is the biggest Floral animal in the world - about twice as big as our house! We saw it this weekend in Spain.* Jeff Koons again, that strange spirit of the age who makes monuments from trivia. This work involves a complete hydraulic system which feeds the living flowers that make its surface. The Puppy stands in front of Bilbao's Guggenheim Museum and has become, for locals the favourite thing to be photographed with. They vote for art with their smiles.   99m

October 20th.   S in Glasgow to AK in Winchester, *My hair is hardly any different. It didn't come out as red as I had wanted but now I've got a couple of highlights. There are 18 rooms but I don't know everyone here... the only interaction is when there is a phone call. What do you mean by friends Halloween Wedding? Are they gonna dress weirdly? Fri 30th a Rocky Horror Party. BJORN AGAIN on 4th Nov... I've got an extra part in a film called SEX, CHIPS & ROCK 'N' ROLL.* A muted pun announces Clearblue pregnancy test kits.   99n

June 5th.   Sue, Dave, George, Jess & Sam to Mrs T in Ingatestone, Essex. *What a holiday. Mickey Mouse, NASA, heat and bright lights. We're loving it all!!!* This is the space shuttle Atlantis connected to the Air Space Station. When Mir was launched by the Soviet Union in 1986 no one envisaged that it would outlast the USSR itself. Though ailing it is still, fifteen years later, the only object of its kind in space. The sort of station imagined in Kubrick's film 2001 (made in 1967) is now feasible but the will and the money are absent.   99o

August 11th.   *Had a great time at Patrick's*, writes Stan from Devon to Bee in Cricklade, *are now at Earth Centre Doncaster. It is wonderful here, the eclipse was o.k., we didn't need the projection cards we were given, But in a room they had a large screen T.V. and that was good. Have bought you a souvenir.* These giant ear trumpets are part of a Japanese sensory trail at the Doncaster Earth Centre. Perhaps those elephantine World War II listening devices (see 43g) were not so old-fashioned after all.   99p

November 2nd.   KRH in Hanborough has a last shot of the century at a competition. She wants a free dishwasher: let's hope it does not suffer from the millennium bug, the big nineties scare story. Planes were to drop from the sky, missiles inadvertently to be fired at ex enemies by the superpowers, and your fridge would implode at midnight on December 31st because computers did not understand 00. All those disasters were averted: chaos and anarchy were postponed.   99q

December 20th.   T to Arabella and Flora M in Oxford, *I first saw the lady in yellow over fifty years ago! I waved at her as I stood with my parents outside Buckingham Palace on VE day in 1945. She was on the balcony waving back. When I met her a few years ago I reminded her of it but she didn't remember me although I was waving a Union Jack at the time. But then she's very old and old people forget, so I wasn't upset, especially as there were a few thousand others waving at the same time.* Queen Elizabeth, the Queen Mother, from the balcony of the age has seen the whole of the century pass by. Her life has seemed exemplary through war and widowhood. Her grandson, looking bemused, might preside over the end of this amiable and strangely useful charade (that can only after all continue if the people wish it). Our revels now are ended.   99t

1999 MESSAGES·NOTES·PARTICULARS

99a. Shapiro SA 102, South Africa.

99b. Whiteway Publications WPL 1997. Photo: Pawel Libera

99c. Collector Card CTY 1006. Photo: James Blank

99d. This England Campaign

99e. Eastfocus. Pinnaroo

99f. London Cardguide

99g. Charles Skilton

99h. South Atlantic Souvenirs

99i. J Salmon Ltd. 2.99.00.65

99j. Moore & Moore PC152

99k. Micro Edition. Created by Gerry Bison

99l. Ashley Peters, classic Cornwall Cards No. 53

99m. Guggenheim Bilbao. Artist: Jeff Koons. Photo: Baharona Ede

99n. Clear Blue

99o. Aerographics B.2108. Photo: NASA

99p. Earth Centre, Doncaster

99q. Boomerang. Designer: Georgina Hinton

99r. Maxracks

99s. Alzheimer's Disease International

November 28th.   LB in San Francisco writes to TP in London, *When I saw this card I remembered the day Stalin died. Walking to school in 1953 & the newspapers in their racks headlined Stalin Dead! What a relief I felt - nothing more to fear. That day at school we began a new routine of air raid drills - preparation for nuclear attack.* The card of Lenin's statue with a rope around its neck is part of a capitalist advertising campaign and offers greater reassurance. Or at least that's how it seems.   99r

December 20th.   S in NY to BH in Saskatchewan, *Can't remember your names but have a good millennium, warmest greetings from, er, thingy.* The shutters of a merciless disease have come down for this man, to give him a third and last role. Neither the worst actor nor the worst President that America has known, his final bow is taken as a sufferer from Alzheimer's. Every complaint has its emblematic representative to show that disease is no respecter of privilege. Advances in research on Alzheimer's provide a gleam of hope at the century's end.   99s

BIBLIOGRAPHY

There is no book that deals with the whole range of postcards either as a genre, an art form or a sociological phenomenon. It begins to seem odd that a medium which attracted the attention of writers as influential as George Orwell and Roland Barthes remains without any academic forum. Despite the huge holdings of postcards in institutions like Smithsonian there is as yet little scholarship outside the world of postcard enthusiasts themselves.

The two comprehensive sources of information are both periodicals. For the British postcard in particular there can be no rival, either as a gathering of expertise or as a sustained act of editorial heroism, to Brian Lund's Picture Postcard Monthly and its attendant Annuals which, over the last twenty years, have provided the arena for debate and exchange of knowledge among enthusiasts. Without such a compendium of pioneering studies this work would have been an impossible chore

The other great frontiersman of postcard knowledge is the French *amateur* Gerard Neudin whose monumental series of eccentric catalogues produced over a similar period constitute a multi-faceted directory of postcard themes, publishers, artists and photographers. Also from France the magazine Cartes Postales et Collection (though tending to concentrate on French topography) has a very high standard of general articles.

Curiously enough, for all the interest in cards in the USA, no such magazine has come into existence there at any professional level. While Barr's Postcard News is a special national treasure and the Postcard Collector is useful for its listings of dealers, there is as yet distinct lack of nourishment for the serious American collector, who still awaits a Neudin or a Lund.

When academe eventually looks towards the postcard as a field of scholarship it will find the spadework has been done and much fruit is already ripe for picking. Meanwhile the collectors, dealers and aficionados have the terrain to themselves and provide scholars from amongst their ranks. There are excellent books on specialised branches of the study and postcard artists are beginning to be the subjects of learned *catalogues raisonnés*. Listings abound and are freely exchanged and augmented by the primary findings of fellow enthusiasts.

The kind of research undertaken by so many to enlarge the database of postcard studies and inaugurate the beginnings of a critical discussion is exactly what, in other fields, is undertaken by tenured professors in comfortable libraries.

Amongst the most valuable books for my own purposes have been those that deal with large topics such as the two World Wars and the history of the emancipation of women as reflected in the postcard (by Toni and Valmai Holt), and those on the Boer War and English Politics by Ian McDonald. Two regularly consulted handbooks have been Anthony Byatt's Picture Postcards and their Publishers and Nouhad Sakh's Guide to Artists' Signatures &. Monograms on Postcards.

There are fine books of, rather than on, postcards, most notable the amazing, obsessive and lyrical collection of Falling Water by Tadanori Yokoo, Richard Bonynge's Theatrical Postcards and the canonical album of photographic cards, Prairie Fires and Paper Moons (by Hal Morgan and Andreas Brown) which I found at New York's temple of deltiology The Gotham Book Mart. All three in their different ways have been inspirational to this enterprise.

My main library has been a pile of reference books with much recourse to The Chronicle (published by Longmans and reissued in the nick of time by Dorling Kindersley as The 20th Century Day by Day). The US equivalent, Our Times, published by Turner has been valuable for its American coverage. Stanley Gibbons' Stamp Catalogue has always been at my side as have Halliwell's two encyclopaedic directories of the cinema.

There can never be a definitive postcard catalogue. Unlike with the world of stamps the State (except in certain countries during wars and in the Iron Curtain years) has played little part in postcard production. Gradually however, in want of such a master catalogue, a useful set of study tools is being built up, such as the first hesitant steps in the area of topography made by the Chalford Archive Series (from which comes David Oxford's book on Piccadilly Circus). But new discoveries are made every day and this book itself contains many cards that have never before been published.

February 7th 1962. To Miss B in Bounds Green, *Dear Pauline, Having a nice time here in Basildon. As you can see by the photo the shops are all new. Hope you're enjoying work. How's Jean. Please write back. I've put the address at the top of the postcard. See you Monday, Love, Shirley.* Perhaps this is a card that has not been published, an excellent late example of a Real Photo card by Frith and sent very soon after issue by the look of the archetypal sixties development, whose crane indicates there is more to come. Since it celebrates the absolutley new it is the sort of card that will become more and more nostalgic.   Fig. 58

ACKNOWLEDGEMENTS

From the outset this task has received the special support, help and encouragement of Patrick Wildgust, indefatigable Autolycus of printed things whose generous searching and finding has been much appreciated. The main burden of the typing and collation has fallen on Alice Wood and the index has been compiled by Lucy Shortis who also provided much of the research. Both these have also given their commentary and critique as the work has progressed which has widened the scope of reference and saved me from many blunders. My wife, Fiona Maddocks, has acted as an unofficial but wary and experienced editor (and arbiter of style). Lewis Baer whose name will be familiar to American postcard collectors has been a hand across the ocean and has twice helped me through the jungle of the New York Postcard Fair. Special thanks also to Piero Grunstein and David Oxford.

The following list includes the many people who have kindly offered me cards to work from, ranging from those who provided (or surrendered) a single card to those who, with singular generosity and abandon, handed over all that they had ever received. It also includes those who have given me advice or information. Faulty memory on my part, and modesty on the part of some who anonymously slipped a card or two in an envelope and sent them to me, means this list is far from complete. I apologise to anyone whose name had been left out. To those who have found themselves unwittingly quoted and who have been surprised thus to enter the public domain, I offer my retrospective respect and thanks.

The list is long and reflects the huge amount of assistance I have received from:- A1 Waste Paper Co., Norman Ackroyd, David Alexander, Diana Armfield, Ann Ashworth, David Attenborough, Julia Auerbach, Janet Baer, Alan Berman, James Buchanan, Alan Bullock, Nils and Marina Burwitz, Simon Callow, David & Shirley Cargill, Tessa Carr, Arabella Cooper Maddocks, Flora Cooper Maddocks, Colin Crewe, Gillian Crowther, Lorin Cuoco, Katrine Davidsen, Jeremy Daniel, Trevor and Ann Dannatt, Maria de Botello, Ben Drury, David Edgar, Evelyn Eller, English National Opera, Brian Eno & The Opal Team, Richard Eyre, Tony Eyton, Mary Fedden, Jane Ferguson, Rosemary M Forrest, Simonetta Fraquelli, David & Marie Freeman, Judy Fraser, Edward Getton, Robin Gibson, Victoria Glendinning, David Gordon, Antony Gormley, Kellie Grube, Richard Hamilton, Tina Hardiment, Adrian Henri, Emma Hill, Barry Humphries, Bill Hurrell, Jeremy Isaacs, Stephen Isserlis, Charlotte L Johnson, Terry Jones, Alice King, Jeremy King, Michelle Konnie, Michael Kustow, Brian Lund, Tom Maddocks, William and Dorothy Maddocks, Jane McAusland, Martin McClellan, Ron McNeil, Candia McWilliam, Michael Mansur, Emmeline Max, Rodney Milne, Richard Minsky, Richard Morphet, Dodi Nash, Tarik O'Regan, Ann & Steve Parker, Huston Paschal, Fernando Peire, Helen Pelou, Terence Pepper, Jill Phillips, Leo Phillips, Ruth Phillips, John Pull, Barbara Rae, Liz Rideal, James Robinson, Mandy Rose, Norman Rosenthal, Ruth & Marvin Sackner, Colin Shortis, Howard Skempton, Martin Smith, Buzz Spector, Annie Stables, Carol Stetser, Sylvia Sumira, Ken Thompson & Charles Osborne, John Tilbury, Jeff and Jake Tilson, Nick Tite, Jenny Topper, John and Ann Tusa, Massimo Valsecchi, Leo Verryt, John Walters, Simon Warren, Rick Weller, Len Whittaker, Jonathan Williams, Mr & Mrs T L Williams, Sue Wilson, and special thanks to Narisa Chakra who has helped so much to steer this book to harbour and to Paisarn Piammattawat and Suparat Sudcharoen who, with the Thai printers, have been so uncomplaining about the ever-growing number of illustrations and emendations.

July 27th 1918. Master Jack Plynn at Lancing College gets a card from his mother in Brighton, *I hope you were not late the other eve: Daddy began fussing dreadfully about it, but I was able to say it was not my fault this time!!! What a nice boy that was we gave a lift in the car! Can't you chum up with him a bit & find out where he lives? If near, we might ask him over in the Hols. The vicar has gone off to Newquay with Monica but not Mrs Hill, as she did not want to leave the Depot. I believe he has only gone for the inside of a fortnight. We have been playing whist as usual this eve: with the de Vitré girls. I went with Katie to see Aunt Cathie this eve: I said I would bring you to see her. God bless you. Very much love. Mum.*

This card quoting the refrain of a popular song, bids you farewell with its perfect cameo of upper middle class family life at the close of the first World War.   Fig. 59

GENERAL INDEX

"Here's a fine example of Wren's work."
"Holy smoke! Them dames are a smart bunch."

April 9th 1945. Ladybird in Winchester to Miss Robbins in Cricklewood, *I found Alice's letter on my pillow. It contained a note bearing Easter Greetings & a little calendar, just like the one I bought. It had the badge on the front but is not as nice as the one they got last year from Selfridges. I've heard nothing about Church Parade and as 'C' Coy is overdue... I think it's pretty safe to hope 'a's OK for next week end.* Not only is the gag about the WRENS a good one but Grimes here captures the world speed record for drawing St Paul's cathedral... in about six minutes I would guess. Fig. 60

INDEX OF PUBLISHERS

September 4th 1906. W pencils a card from Tobacco Smoke Farm, near Leeds to Mrs LD in Bishop Auckland, *Dear Cousin, Thanks for ever welcome letter. We have slept here every night. Mr O'Hellowell and Miss Hellowell to the left. Mr Nathan and Miss Withell to the right. In the centre 'Yer Humble'. Can't find ink. Health good. Business same. If James will train down to my weight I will wrestle him for a quid. Ta ta.* I presume these are not the sleeping arrangements in this tiny tent.   Fig. 61

January 2nd 1917.   Mabel in Clapham to Mrs Davey in Hockwold, Norfolk. *Thanks for letter. I heard from George the same post glad he is going on alright I expect you will soon be having him home once more the children were taken by someone round the street the little girl had them out...* These three infants look warily at the man with the camera. Even the baby in the pram understands the perils of photography. The girl on the left is already a hundred years old.   Fig. 62

October 11th 1904.   Reg in Reading to Mrs Lambert in Alton, Hants, *Herewith is the first 'result'. I think its very good especially of you. Miss Watson must have moved a little; she's decidedly fuzzy. The Hindhead photos are A1 negatives: Shall try to print the picnic tonight should I get time. The plates take some time to dry in this damp weather...* Reg prints onto postcard stock, the latest thing, with a good outcome allowing for that silly Miss Watson.   Fig. 63

INDEX OF POSTCARD ARTISTS

November 6th 1992. Tina in London NW writes to the Rev. Richard M in Ilkley, Yorks. *Tom Phillips at the R.A. is excellent. Many Thanks for visiting Uncle T. Hope he didn't prove totally unresponsive... Hope all the 'piece-work' comes in O.K for Sat. I have lots of inspiration down here: Margaret St... & Liberty's. love Tina.* The picture is my portrait of Samuel Beckett done when he was in London in 1984. I have very occasionally come across my own cards at postcard fairs but this is the only time I have found myself mentioned, so to speak, in despatches. Luckily Tina enjoyed my retrospective exhibition at the Royal Academy. Would I have included this card if she had said the show was rotten? The card is issued by the National Portrait Gallery, but not at 5p which is what I paid for this one.   Fig. 64

April 18th 1922. Joan Johnston's mother in Brentwood writes to her in hospital nearby, *Isn't this a vulgar card? It is all I have got to-day. I thought you might laugh at the poor mother & all her babies. Ted & Dunks have gone to see the football match. Fond love from all. Mum.* An artist (whose style must by now be recognisable) draws a photographer's studio. It is published by Inter-Art.   Fig. 65

INDEX OF PHOTOGRAPHERS

August 10th 1909. Mrs Good in Somerston gets a card from Ned & Ted in Brighton, *Received Rube card glad you are both ripping and not dripping weather is simply glorious and backing winners is good up to now but don't shout as the week is not finished yet.* The fantasy car in the photographer's studio has a touch of the Rolls Royce about it. Fig. 66

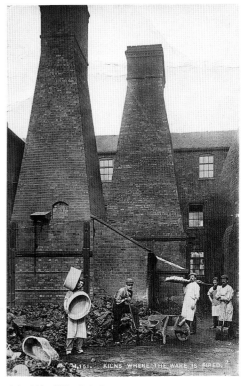

July 29th 1919. G in Burslem to Mr & Mrs Ratcliffe in Tamworth, *Dear B&W I am sorry you will not be home this week-end but still the rest is what W wants and I hope you will soon be home for good.* A beautiful Real Photo of a scene in the pottery town. Fig. 67